Praise for A Choice of Enemies

'A solid and comprehensive account of how, for better or worse, America became such a force in the affairs of the Middle East'
Literary Review

'Very substantial [and] impressive . . . succinct yet comprehensive . . . an excellent book, exceedingly well written'
Times Literary Supplement

'[A] major new history of America's engagement with the contemporary Middle East' *Washington Post*

'One of the most fascinating, comprehensive, clearly written and subtle accounts I have ever read on United States' engagement with the Middle East' *Jewish Chronicle*

'Provocative . . . a sweeping overview of the United States' responses to foreign policy crises in the Middle East over the past 30 years . . . impressive [and] tightly written' *Foreign Affairs*

Lawrence Freedman is Professor of War Studies & Vice Principal at King's College, London, and is one of Britain's most distinguished historians of contemporary military and political strategy. In 2009, *A Choice of Enemies* won the the Lionel Gelber Prize.

By Lawrence Freedman

Evolution of Nuclear Strategy
Kennedy's Wars
Official History of the Falklands Campaign
A Choice of Enemies

A
CHOICE OF ENEMIES

—— *America Confronts the Middle East* ——

Lawrence Freedman

PHOENIX

A PHOENIX PAPERBACK

First published in Great Britain in 2008
by Weidenfeld & Nicolson
This paperback edition published in 2009
by Phoenix,
an imprint of Orion Books Ltd,
Orion House, 5 Upper St Martin's Lane,
London WC2H 9EA

An Hachette UK company

1 3 5 7 9 10 8 6 4 2

Copyright © Lawrence Freedman 2008

The right of Lawrence Freedman to be identified as the
author of this work has been asserted by him in accordance
with the Copyright, Designs and Patents Act 1988.

A CIP catalogue record for this book
is available from the British Library.

ISBN 978-0-7538-2588-4

Printed and bound in Great Britain
by Clays Ltd, St Ives plc

The Orion Publishing Group's policy is to use papers
that are natural, renewable and recyclable products and
made from wood grown in sustainable forests. The logging
and manufacturing processes are expected to conform to
the environmental regulations of the country of origin.

www.orionbooks.co.uk

To Ruth, who asked the question.
I'm sorry the answer is so long.

Contents

Dramatis Personae

United States

Albright, Madeleine, Permanent Representative to the United Nations, 1993–1997; Secretary of State, 1997–2001

Allen, Richard, National Security Adviser, 1981–1982

Armitage, Richard, Assistant Secretary of Defense for International Security Policy, 1983–1989; Deputy Secretary of State, 2001–2005

Aspin, Les, Congressman, 1971–1993; Secretary of Defense, 1993–1994

Baker, James, President's Chief of Staff, 1981–1985; Secretary of the Treasury, 1985–1988; Secretary of State, 1989–1992

Berger, Sandy, Deputy National Security Adviser, 1993–1997; National Security Adviser, 1997–2001

Bolton, John, Undersecretary of State for Arms Control and International Security, 2001–2005; Permanent Representative to the United Nations, 2005–2006

Bremer, L. Paul, Director of Reconstruction and Humanitarian Assistance, Iraq, 2003; head of Coalition Provisional Authority, 2003–2004

Brown, Harold, Secretary of Defense, 1977–1981

Brzezinski, Zbigniew, National Security Adviser, 1977–1981

Bush, George H. W., Vice President, 1981–1989; President, 1989–1993

Bush, George W., President, 2001–

Carlucci, Frank, National Security Adviser, 1986–1987; Secretary of Defense, 1987–1989

Carter, Jimmy, President, 1977–1981

Casey, George W., Commanding General, Multi-National Force, Iraq, 2004–2007; Chief of Staff, U.S. Army, 2007–

Casey, William, Director of Central Intelligence, 1981–1987

Cheney, Richard, Secretary of Defense, 1989–1993; Vice President, 2001–

Christopher, Warren, Deputy Secretary of State, 1977–1981; Secretary of State, 1993–1997

Clark, William, Deputy Secretary of State, 1981–1982; National Security Adviser, 1982–1983; Secretary of the Interior, 1983–1985

Clarke, Richard, National Coordinator for Security, Infrastructure Protection, and Counter-Terrorism, 1998–2001

Clinton, William, President, 1993–2001

Cohen, William, Secretary of Defense, 1997–2001

Deutch, John, Director of Central Intelligence, 1995–1996

Djerejian, Edward, Ambassador to Syria, 1989–1991; Assistant Secretary of State for Near Eastern Affairs, 1991–1993; Ambassador to Israel, 1993–1994

Dobbins, James, special envoy Somalia, 1993; special envoy Haiti, 1994; National Security Council staff, 1996–1999; special envoy Kosovo, 1999; Assistant Secretary of State for Europe, 2000–2001; special envoy Afghanistan, 2001–2002

Downing, Wayne, General, National Director and Deputy National Security Adviser for Combating Terrorism, 2001–2002

Duelfer, Charles, leader, Iraq Survey Group, 2004–2005

Eisenhower, Dwight, President, 1953–1961

Ford, Gerald, President, 1974–1977

Franks, Tommy, Commander-in-Chief, United States Central Command, 2000–2003

Freeh, Louis, Director of the Federal Bureau of Investigation, 1993–2001

Frum, David, White House speechwriter, 2001–2002

Gates, Robert, National Security Council and CIA staff positions, 1966–1981; Deputy Director of Intelligence, CIA, 1982; Deputy Director of Central Intelligence, 1986–1989; Assistant to the President and Deputy National Security Adviser, 1989–1991; Director of Central Intelligence, 1991–1993; Secretary of Defense, 2006–

Garner, Jay, General, Director of Office of Reconstruction and Humanitarian Assistance, Iraq, 2003

Gerson, Michael, President's chief speechwriter, 2001–2006

Glaspie, April, Ambassador to Iraq, 1988–1990

Gonzales, Alberto, White House counsel, 2001–2005; Attorney General, 2005–2007

Gore, Al, Vice President, 1993–2001

Haass, Richard, Special Assistant to the President and Senior Director for Near East and South Asian Affairs, National Security Council, 1989–1993; Director of Policy Planning, Department of State, 2001–2003

Habib, Philip C., special envoy to the Middle East, 1981–1983

Hadley, Stephen, Deputy National Security Adviser, 2001–2005; National Security Adviser, 2005–

Haig, Alexander, Secretary of State, 1981–1982

Indyk, Martin, Special Assistant to the President and Senior Director for Near East and South Asian Affairs, National Security Council, 1993–1995; Ambassador to Israel, 1995–1997 and 2000–2001; Assistant Secretary of State for Near Eastern Affairs, 1997–2000

Jordan, Hamilton, White House Chief of Staff, 1979–1980

Kay, David, Director, Iraq Survey Group, 2003–2004

Kennedy, John F., President, 1961–1963

Kirkpatrick, Jeane, Ambassador to the United Nations, 1981–1985

Kissinger, Henry, National Security Adviser, 1969–1975; Secretary of State, 1973–1977

Lake, Tony, National Security Adviser, 1993–1997

Ledeen, Michael, Special Adviser to the Secretary of State, 1981–1982; consultant, National Security Council, Department of Defense, and Department of State, 1982–1986

McFarlane, Robert, special envoy to the Middle East, 1983; National Security Adviser, 1983–1985

Mitchell, George, Senate Majority Leader, 1989–1995; special envoy to Northern Ireland, 1995–1998; head of fact-finding mission into Arab-Israeli conflict, 2000–2001

Murphy, Richard, Assistant Secretary of State for Near Eastern and South Asian Affairs, 1983–1989

Muskie, Edmund, Secretary of State, 1980–1981

Nixon, Richard, President, 1969–1974

North, Oliver, National Security Council Staff, 1981–1986

Nunn, Sam, Senator, 1972–1997

O'Neill, Paul, Secretary of the Treasury, 2001–2002

Perle, Richard, Assistant Secretary of Defense for International Security Policy, 1981–1987; member of the Defense Policy Board, 1987–2004 (Chairman, 2001–2003)

Perry, William, Secretary of Defense, 1994–1997

Petraeus, David, Commanding General, Multi-National Force–Iraq, 2007–

Poindexter, John, Deputy National Security Adviser, 1983–1985; National Security Adviser, 1985–1986

Powell, Colin, National Security Adviser, 1987–1989; Chairman of the Joint Chiefs of Staff, 1989–1993; Secretary of State, 2001–2005

Reagan, Ronald, President, 1981–1989

Regan, Donald, Secretary of the Treasury, 1981–1985; White House Chief of Staff, 1985–1987

Rice, Condoleezza, National Security Adviser, 2001–2005; Secretary of State, 2005–

Ross, Dennis, Director of Policy Planning, Department of State, 1989–1992; Special Middle East Coordinator/Middle East Envoy, 1988–2000

Rove, Karl, Senior Adviser to the President, 2001–2007

Rumsfeld, Donald, Special Presidential Envoy to the Middle East, 1983–1984; Secretary of Defense, 2001–2006

Schwarzkopf, Norman, Commander-in-Chief, United States Central Command, 1988–1991

Scowcroft, Brent, National Security Adviser, 1974–1977 and 1989–1993

Shelton, Henry, Chairman of the Joint Chiefs of Staff, 1997–2001

Shinseki, Eric, Army Chief of Staff, 1999–2003

Shultz, George, Secretary of State, 1982–1989

Sullivan, William, Ambassador to Iran, 1977–1979
Tenet, George, Director of Central Intelligence, 1997–2004
Truman, Harry, President, 1945–1953
Turner, Stansfield, Director of Central Intelligence, 1977–1981
Vance, Cyrus, Secretary of State, 1977–1980
Vessey, General John, Chairman of the Joint Chiefs of Staff, 1982–1985
Weinberger, Caspar, Secretary of Defense, 1981–1987
Wilson, Charlie, Congressman, 1972–1996
Wilson, Joseph, Acting Ambassador to Iraq, 1990–1991
Wolfowitz, Paul, Undersecretary of Defense for Policy, 1989–1993; Deputy
    Secretary of Defense, 2001–2005
Woolsey, James, Director of Central Intelligence, 1993–1995

Afghanistan

Amin, Hafizullah, Masses Faction ("Khalq"), People's Democratic Party of
    Afghanistan (PDPA); President, 1979
Daoud Khan, Mohammed, Prime Minister, 1953–1963; President, 1973–1978
Hekmatyar, Gulbuddin, leader, mujahideen faction, 1980s; Prime Minister,
    1993–1994, 1996
Karmal, Babrak, Banner faction ("Parcham") of PDPA; President, 1979–1986
Karzai, Hamid, Chairman, Transitional Administration, 2001–2002; Interim
    President, 2002–2004; President, 2004–
Massoud, Ahmad Shah, mujahideen commander; Defense Minister, 1992–1996
Najibullah, Mohammad, Banner faction ("Parcham") of the PDPA; President,
    1986–1992
Omar, Mohammed ("Mullah Omar"), leader of the Taliban, 1994–; head of state,
    1996–2001
Rabbani, Burhanuddin, leader of mujahideen faction; President, 1992–1996
    (nominally until 2001)
Taraki, Noor Mohammed, Masses faction ("Khalq") of PDPA; Prime Minister and
    President, 1978–1979

Al Qaeda

Al-Muqrin, Abd al-Aziz, leader of al Qaeda in Saudi Arabia, 2003–2004 (Saudi)
Al-Zarqawi, Abu Musab, leader of al Qaeda in Iraq, 2004–2006 (Jordanian)
Al-Zawahiri, Ayman, founder of Egyptian Islamic Jihad, founder of al Qaeda
    (Egyptian)
Atta, Mohammed, leader of the 9/11 hijackers
Azzam, Abdullah, leader of Afghan Arabs, 1979–1989 (Palestinian)
Bin Laden, Osama, founder and leader of al Qaeda
Mohammed, Khaled Sheikh, planner of the 9/11 attacks (Kuwaiti)
Rahman, Omar Abdul ("Blind Sheikh"), leader of Gama'st al-Islamiya (the Islamic
    Group), in U.S. prison, 1995– (Egyptian)
Yousef, Ramzi, leader of the 1993 World Trade Center bombing (Kuwaiti)

Egypt

Kamel, Muhammad Ibrahim, Minister of Foreign Affairs, 1977–1978
Khalil, Mustafa, Prime Minister, 1978–1980; Minister of Foreign Affairs, 1979–1980
Mubarak, Hosni, President, 1981–
Nasser, Gamal Abdel, President, 1956–1970
Sadat, Anwar, President, 1970–1981

Iran

Ahmadinejad, Mahmoud, President, 2005–
Bakhtiar, Shapour, Prime Minister, 1979
Bani Sadr, Abolhasan, President, 1980–1981
Bazargan, Mehdi, Prime Minister, 1979
Ghorbanifar, Manucher, businessman
Khamenei, Ali (Ayatollah), President, 1981–1989; Supreme Leader, 1989–
Khatami, Mohammad, President, 1997–2005
Khomeini, Ruhollah (Ayatollah), Supreme Leader, 1979–1989
Larijani, Ali, politician, Secretary to Supreme National Security Council, 2005–2007
Mossadegh, Mohammed, Prime Minister, 1951–1953
Moussavi, Mir Hussein, Prime Minister, 1981–1989
Pahlavi, Mohammed Reza, Shah, 1941–1979
Rafsanjani, Akbar Hashemi, Speaker of Parliament, 1980–1989; President, 1989–1997

Iraq

Al-Bakr, Ahmed Hassan, President, 1968–1979
Al-Jafari, Ibrahim, Prime Minister, 2005–2006
Allawi, Ayad, leader of the Iraqi National Accord; Interim Prime Minister, 2004–2005
Al-Majid, Ali Hassan ("Chemical Ali"), Secretary General of the Northern Bureau of the Ba'ath Party, 1987–1989
Al-Maliki, Nuri, Prime Minister, 2006–
Al-Sadr, Moqtada, opposition politician and militia leader, 2003–
Al-Sistani, Ali, Grand Ayatollah, 1992–
Aziz, Tariq, Minister of Foreign Affairs, 1983–1991; Deputy Prime Minister, 1979–2003
Barzani, Masud, leader of the Kurdistan Democratic Party (KDP); President of Iraqi Kurdistan, 2005–
Chalabi, Ahmad, leader of the Iraqi National Congress; Deputy Prime Minister, 2005–2006
Hussein, Saddam, President, 1979–2003
Kamel, Hussein, head, Military Industrialization Commission, 1987–1995
Talabani, Jalal, leader of the Patriotic Union of Kurdistan (PUK); President, 2005–

Israel

Barak, Ehud, Prime Minister, 1999–2001

Begin, Menachem, Prime Minister, 1977–1982

Beilin, Yossi, government positions in Finance, Foreign, and Justice Ministries, 1988–2001

Ben-Ami, Shlomo, Minister of Public Security, 1999–2001; Minister of Foreign Affairs, 2000–2001

Dayan, Moshe, Minister of Defense, 1967–1974; Minister of Foreign Affairs, 1977–1980

Eshkol, Levi, Prime Minister, 1963–1969

Halutz, Dan, Chief of Staff, Israeli Defense Forces, 2005–2007

Kimche, David, Director General of the Ministry of Foreign Affairs, 1980–1987

Livni, Tzipi, Foreign Minister, 2005–

Netanyahu, Benjamin ("Bibi"), Prime Minister, 1996–1999; Minister of Foreign Affairs, 2002–2003

Olmert, Ehud, Prime Minister, 2006–

Peres, Shimon, Minister of Defense, 1974–1977; Minister of Foreign Affairs, 1986–1988 and 1992–1995; Prime Minister, 1984–1986 and 1995–1996

Peretz, Amir, Minister of Defense, 2006–2007

Rabin, Yitzhak, Chief of Staff of the Israeli Defense Forces, 1964–1968; Ambassador to the United States, 1968–1973; Minister of Defense, 1984–1990; Prime Minister, 1974–1977 and 1992–1995

Shamir, Yitzhak, Minister of Foreign Affairs, 1980–1986; Prime Minister, 1983–1984 and 1986–1992

Sharon, Ariel, Security Adviser to Prime Minister Yitzhak Rabin, 1975–1976; Minister of Defense, 1981–1983; Minister of Foreign Affairs, 1998–1999; Prime Minister, 2001–2006

Weizmann, Ezer, Minister of Defense, 1977–1980; President, 1993–2000

Jordan

Bin Al Hussein, Abdullah II, King, 1999–

Bin Talal, Hussein, King, 1952–1999

Kuwait

Al-Sabah, Jaber III al-Ahmad al-Jaber, Emir of Kuwait, 1977–2006

Lebanon

Al-Hariri, Rafiq, Prime Minister, 1992–1998, 2000–2004

Berri, Nabih, leader of Amal, 1980– ; Speaker of National Assembly, 1992–

Gemayel, Amin, President, 1982–1988

Gemayel, Bashir, leader of Phalange Party; President-Elect, 1982

Jumblatt, Walid, leader of Progressive Socialist Party (Druze), 1975–

Lahoud, Emile, President, 1998–2007
Musawi, Abbas, founder of Hezbollah; head of security apparatus, 1982–1991; leader, 1991–1992
Musawi, Hussein, founder of Islamic "Amal"
Nasrallah, Hassan, leader of Hezbollah, 1992–
Siniora, Fouad, Prime Minister, 2005–
Suleiman, Michel, Commander of Armed Forces, 1998–

Libya

Qadhafi, Mu'ammar, head of state of Libya, 1969–

Pakistan

Bhutto, Benazir, Prime Minister, 1988–1990 and 1993–1996
Bhutto, Zulfikar Ali, President, 1971–1973; Prime Minister, 1973–1977
Khan, Abdul Qadeer, head of Pakistani Nuclear Program, 1976–2004
Mehsud, Baitullah, warlord, Waziristan
Musharraf, Pervez, Army Chief of Staff, 1998–2007; Prime Minister, 1999–2001; President, 2001–
Rahman, Akhtar Abdur, Director General of Inter-Service Intelligence, 1980–1987; Chairman of the Joint Chiefs of Staff, 1987–1988
Sharif, Nawaz, Prime Minister, 1990–1993 and 1997–1999
Zia-ul-Haq, Mohammed, Army Chief of Staff, 1976–1988; Chief Martial Law Administrator, 1977–1988; President, 1978–1988

Palestine

Abbas, Abu, founder and leader of the Palestine Liberation Front (PLF)
Abbas, Mahmoud (Abu Mazen), Prime Minister, Palestinian National Authority (PNA), 2003; President, PNA, 2005–
Al-Rantissi, Abdel Aziz, cofounder of Hamas; leader, 2004
Arafat, Yasser, founder of Fatah; Chairman of the Executive Committee of the Palestine Liberation Organization (PLO), 1969–2004; President of the PNA, 1996–2004
Barghouti, Marwan, leader of al-Mustaqbal Party and head of Tanzim militia
Dahlan, Mohamed, leader of Fatah in Gaza, number of security posts in PNA, 1996–2007
Erekat, Saab, chief Palestinian negotiator, Camp David Summit, 2000
Habash, George, founder and leader of the Popular Front for the Liberation of Palestine (PFLP), 1967–2000
Haniyeh, Ismail, Prime Minister, PNA, 2006–2007; continued to be recognized in Gaza
Nidal, Abu, militant and founder of the Abu Nidal Organization (ANO)
Qurei, Ahmed (Abu Ala), Prime Minister, PNA, 2003–2006
Shiqaqi, Fathi, founder and leader of Islamic Jihad, 1975–1995
Yassin, Sheikh Ahmed Ismail, founder and leader of Hamas, 1987–2004

Russia/Soviet Union

Andropov, Yuri, head of the KGB, 1967–1982; General Secretary of the Communist
   Party of the Soviet Union, 1982–1984; Chairman of the Presidium of the
   Supreme Soviet, 1983–1984
Brezhnev, Leonid, Chairman of the Presidium of the Supreme Soviet, 1960–1964;
   General Secretary of the Communist Party of the Soviet Union, 1966–1982;
   President, 1977–1982
Gorbachev, Mikhail, General Secretary of the Communist Party of the Soviet
   Union, 1985–1991; President, 1990–1991
Gromyko, Andrei, Foreign Minister of the Soviet Union, 1957–1985; President,
   1985–1988
Putin, Vladimir, President of Russia, 1999–2008
Ustinov, Dmitri, Defense Minister of the Soviet Union, 1976–1984

Saudi Arabia

Al Saud, Abdullah bin Abdul Aziz, Crown Prince, 1995–2005; King, 2005–
Al Saud, Bandar bin Sultan Bin Abdul Aziz, Ambassador to Washington,
   1983–2005; Secretary-General of the National Security Council, 2005–
Al Saud, Fahd bin Abdul Aziz, King, 1982–2005
Al Saud, Khalid bin Abdul Aziz, King, 1975–1982
Al Saud, Turki al-Faisal, head of the Saudi Intelligence Services, 1977–2001

Somalia

Aidid, General Mohamed Farah, Somali warlord and President, 1995–1996

Sudan

Al-Bashir, General Omar Hasan, President, 1989–
Al-Turabi, Hasan, political leader, 1989–

Syria

Al-Assad, Bashar, President, 2000–
Al-Assad, Hafez, Prime Minister, 1970–1971; President, 1971–2000

United Kingdom

Blair, Tony, Prime Minister, 1997–2007
Parsons, Sir Anthony, Ambassador to Iran, 1974–1979; Ambassador to the United
   Nations, 1979–1982
Straw, Jack, Foreign Secretary, 2001–2006
Thatcher, Margaret, Prime Minister, 1979–1990

International

Annan, Kofi, Secretary-General of the United Nations, 1997–2006

Blix, Hans, Director General of the International Atomic Energy Agency (IAEA),
   1981–1997; Executive Chairman of the UN Monitoring, Verification and
   Inspections Commission (UNMOVIC), 2000–2003
Brahimi, Lakhdar, head of UN Assistance Mission, Afghanistan, 2001–2004;
   Special Adviser to Secretary General, 2004–
Butler, Richard, head of UN Special Commission on Iraq (UNSCOM), 1997–1999
Ekeus, Rolf, head of UNSCOM, 1991–1997
Elbaradei, Mohamed, Director General of the IAEA, 1997–
Pérez de Cuéllar, Javier, Secretary-General of the United Nations, 1982–1991
Picco, Giandomenico, Assistant Secretary-General of the United Nations for
   Political Affairs, 1973–1992
Waldheim, Kurt, Secretary-General of the United Nations, 1972–1982; President of
   Austria, 1986–1992

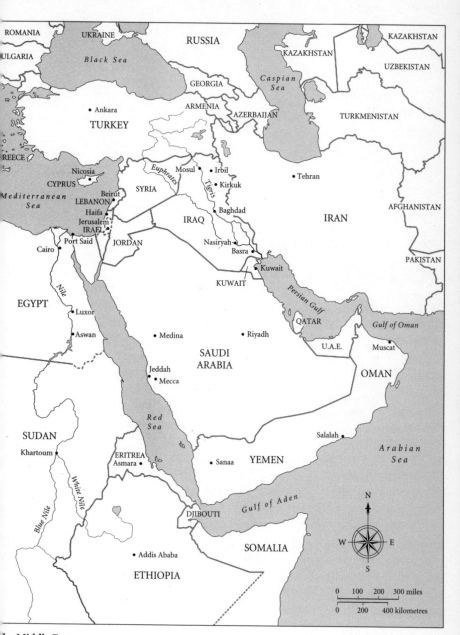

The Middle East

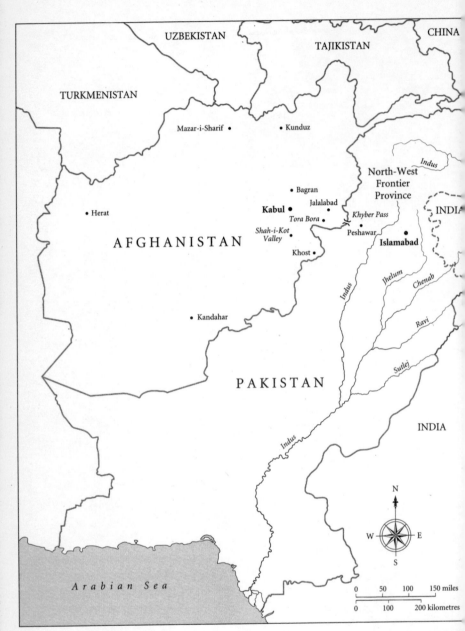

Afghanistan and Pakistan

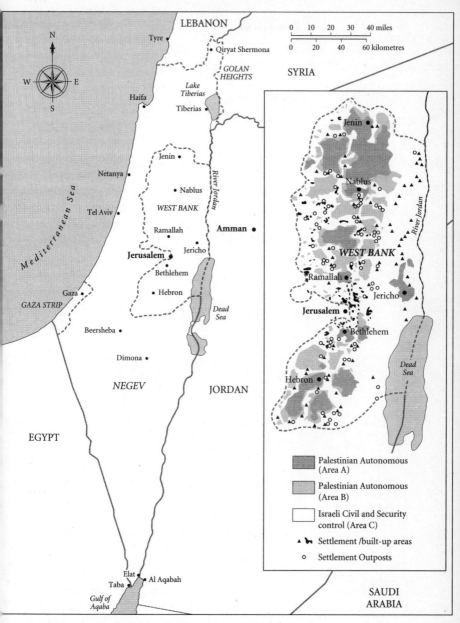

Israel and West Bank, adapted from *Foundation for Middle East Peace*

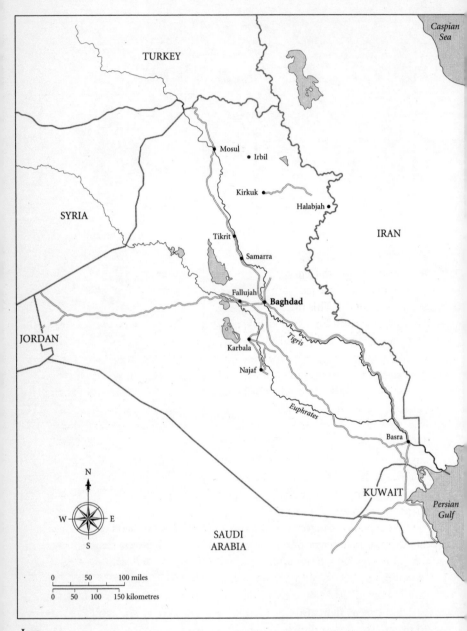

Iraq

Preface

"On balance," Michael Oren concludes at the end of his magisterial survey, *Power, Faith, and Fantasy,* "Americans historically brought far more beneficence than avarice to the Middle East and caused significantly less harm than good."[1] This might well be true for most of the 230 years Oren covers, but it would not be a consensus view for the twenty-first century. The United States has fought an unpopular war in Iraq, has continued without resolution an acrimonious dispute with Iran, has done little to resolve the Israeli-Palestinian dispute, and, having helpfully dislodged the Taliban from power in Afghanistan and denied al Qaeda its sanctuary, watched instability grip Afghanistan and extend into neighboring Pakistan. This was not the result of avarice, even though many believe that a determination to control oil supplies governs all American policy. Nor was it even for a want of beneficence, though the guiding principle was national security, often rather narrowly interpreted. With genuine conviction, commitments were made to work to improve the lives of ordinary people in the region.

Oren explains American relations with the Middle East through three themes: power, in terms of the pursuit of America's interests through a variety of means, including military; faith, in terms of the impact of religion in shaping attitudes and policies; and fantasy, less well defined but a romantic idea of the Middle East that draws Americans to it. The problems of recent times might also be understood in these terms, but with particular twists. The power dimension is self-evident but unavoidable. Until the 1970s, America's most substantial military engagements were in East Asia. Since then, they have been in the Middle East, including active support of allies fighting others. The critiques of recent U.S. policy often focus on the incompetent, careless use of this power in both the military and political spheres. The faith dimension has also become increasingly salient, not only because of the importance of the Holy Land for a country with a strong Christian tradition and a significant Jewish minority, but also because of talk of a clash of civilizations centered on a region where Islam can inspire militant ideologies as well as everyday religion. Some might say the fantasy dimension has become particularly pronounced, with the Middle East being used as the testing ground for a great experiment in democracy promotion and conflict resolution, in conjunction with the simplistic and arrogant views of America's historic mission that tend to be labeled as neoconservative.

Although the Bush administration has had a particularly jolting encounter with the region, previous administrations also struggled with the same set of problems in their earlier forms, and while they often adopted quite different approaches, the results were rarely satisfactory. To take one instance, few items in the standard repertoire of foreign policy options were not tried with Iraq, including complete disregard, a strained partnership, containment, and occupation, each without ever finding a winning formula. All administrations have at some point tried to get the Israelis to think about the long-term implications of their efforts to construct settlements in Palestine and all have been rebuffed. Terrorism makes grim appearances, leading presidents to promise an unrelenting campaign against it, only for it to return with depressing regularity.

Furthermore, the United States is not the first external power to struggle in this part of the world, and it will not be the last. It is hard to think of any power, regional or global, that has demonstrated a consistently sure touch. The region contains multiple sources of tension. The potential for rivalry and division appears to be ever present, within countries and religious faiths, and between notional partners. There are many potential sources of difference: Muslim, Christian, or Jew; Arab, Persian, Kurd, or Turk; Sunni or Shia; monarchy or republic; secular or Islamic; with or without substantial oil reserves; large or small in territory or population. This list is by no means exhaustive. These differences can at times be subdued and irrelevant, or dominant and antagonistic. Their interactions are complex. Old friends can fall out while strange alliances can emerge, born out of expediency and the proposition that "my enemy's enemy is my friend." Of course, shared attributes also produce common interests and durable alliances, but the Middle East has lacked the economic and political integration that has worked to encourage more cooperative relationships in other parts of the world. It is not surprising that the intricate politics of the region have defeated to varying degrees Britain, France, and the Soviet Union.

Edward Luttwak argues eloquently and almost uniquely for the irrelevance of the Middle East. It was once, he notes, "the world's most advanced region, but these days its biggest industries are extravagant consumption and the venting of resentment." He comments on its lack of productivity and economic accomplishment, warning against the "very odd belief that these ancient nations are highly malleable." The peoples of the region, he proposes, "should finally be allowed to have their own history—the one thing that middle east experts of all stripes seem determined to deny them."[2] Given its complex and frustrating nature, it would no doubt be a relief for Western policymakers to abandon the Middle East and expend their energies and resources on countries that are more productive, tractable, and grateful, but this is not possible, and when they try to ignore it they get drawn back in. The Middle East's importance to the global oil market, projected to grow to 45 percent of the world's oil production by 2030, its concentrations of extreme wealth and despairing urban youth, the culture of anti-Western militancy and its violent expressions, the turbulent states on the edge of Europe and astride the main trade routes, continue to demand attention.

The American ability to influence events has declined. Richard Haass, who served in the administrations of both the elder and younger Bush, has written of the end of "the American era in the Middle East." There may have been visions of a "new, Europe-like region," with peace, prosperity, and democracy, but instead there is more likely to be "a new Middle East that will cause great harm to itself, the United States, and the world." He attributes this decline largely to the decision to attack and occupy Iraq in 2003. The American era began in 1991 with a necessary war against Iraq. "It is one of history's ironies," Haass suggests, that "the second Iraq war, a war of choice, has precipitated its end."[3]

This book is about choices. The title *A Choice of Enemies* was initially meant to refer to another historical irony. I was struck by how the United States had managed to find itself in conflict at the same time with Iran, Iraq, and al Qaeda, all of which were antagonistic to each other. The more I looked back over the past three decades, the more appropriate the title seemed, but without any need for irony. Faced with the unfolding dramas of the Middle East and given its pivotal role in regional affairs, the United States has had to choose whom to oppose and whom to support, and then how, with what conditions, and to what degree, to oppose and to support. Such fateful commitments could depend on quite singular combinations of circumstances. My aim, therefore, is to provide a reasonably thorough account of how successive presidents, from Carter to the younger Bush, engaged with the Middle East. The subtitle reflects the fact that this engagement has, certainly recently, appeared rather confrontational. Of course not all American relationships with the region are confrontational and the aspiration is for complete harmony. There is a tension in the American approach, torn between the traditional instinct of a Great Power to protect the status quo from aggressive states and radical movements and an underlying dissatisfaction with the status quo. One reason is that those conflicts, particularly but not exclusively the Arab-Israeli, that appear to the United States as distractions from its top strategic priorities are extremely important to those in the region. It is also because supporting the status quo means backing states which do not embrace the values of liberty and freedom that Americans claim to cherish most. The sentiments expressed by President George W. Bush about wanting to see more democracy in the Middle East, and his distrust of the notion that autocracy equals stability, reflect a long-standing unease. In its political relations with the Middle East, the United States often appears to be in an argument with itself, as a status quo power that wishes to change the status quo. This tension has added drama, and sometimes poignancy, as American presidents have made their choices.

To explore these choices I know of no better approach than to consider the available evidence in an effort to sort out the sequence of events and the influences on decisions. The most challenging part of this book has been to explore the extent to which decisions on one conflict influence those on others. It is the interconnections between superficially distinctive strands of policy that make it important not to focus on, say, Iraq or Afghanistan in isolation without considering how they relate to each other and other conflicts under way at the same time. The origins of this book lie in a conversation with my daughter Ruth during the Lebanon War of the summer of 2006, when the straightforward answer she sought (she is, after all, a physicist) got lost in the complexities of what Hamas was up to in Gaza, the state of Israeli politics, the role of Syria, the rows over the Iranian nuclear program, and the fallout from the insurgency in Iraq.

As this is largely a political history, there is not much room for broader cultural, social, and economic factors, although I have tried to acknowledge their importance. There is now a substantial literature which explains American relations with the Middle East in terms of cultural differences and antipathies. These factors should be treated with caution when explaining the content of policy. Salem Yaqub suggests differences in "power and geopolitical circumstances" provide a better guide.[4] What I hope comes over in this study is the importance of the prevailing assumptions about the sources of power and how it can be exploited. A recurring theme is the failure to come to terms with the limits of power, and not just by Americans. Equally I do not follow the trend in the scholarly literature on international relations which attempts to put the subject on a proper scientific footing. This can have the unfortunate effect of squeezing out of the analysis everything that makes politics so fascinating, notably the interplay of chance, personality, and circumstance, which have been the ruination of many a good theory. Behind every individual decision there is a churning background of economic and technological change, geographical continuities, cultural predispositions, institutional biases, and practical considerations, all of which deserve careful study, but to the fore there are human beings, fallible and infuriatingly unpredictable, capable of being passive in the face of golden opportunities and bold on the basis of unsubstantiated hunches.

Some choices look worse in retrospect than they did in prospect, and part of the challenge of this book is to try to convey how issues presented themselves to the decisionmakers. Many of these decisions were controversial at the time, and others became so as their consequences became apparent. Political and not just historical points are made about Carter's responsibility for destabilizing the shah of Iran, or the supposed backing given to Osama bin Laden by the CIA during Reagan's time, or the elder Bush letting Saddam off the hook at the end of the 1991 Persian Gulf War, or Clinton's management of the 2000 Camp David summit, or exactly what persuaded the younger Bush to invade Iraq in 2003. I have tried to consider the evidence carefully in all these cases to provide the most credible account of events.

The other minefield for anybody entering this arena is the argument that U.S. Middle Eastern policy has been driven by the demands of the "Israel lobby" rather than any sensible appreciation of American interests. The most prominent set of claims comes from two leading academics, John Mearsheimer and Stephen Walt.[5] This argument has a number of layers. At one, relatively uncontroversial level, there is the proposition that Israel has a lot of noisy, influential supporters in the United States who demand U.S. backing for almost anything Israel chooses to do in the name of its own security. They can get very agitated by any perceived slight to Israel or sympathy for its enemies. The indictment, however, goes much further to blame the lobby for hijacking American foreign policy to direct it against Israel's regional enemies, notably Iraq in 2003 and more recently Iran. This leads on to the proposition that Israel and its lobby are responsible for the hostility directed toward the United States in the Middle East, up to and including the terrorist attacks of September 11, 2001.

The claims made about the influence of the Israel lobby (on occasion by the lobbyists themselves) are exaggerated and in many cases plain wrong. When it comes to decisions that are about Israel, no American president can ignore Israel's supporters because they do have political clout, but that will be only one of a number of considerations. They will be getting strong representations from other governments in the region who cannot be readily ignored. Other searches for the hidden forces shaping American policy have put great stress on oil companies, which have tended to find the association with Israel a nuisance. The "military-industrial complex" has been identified as another distorting factor in American foreign policy. While Israel is a significant customer for many American military products, this is dwarfed by the size of the Arab market. Some of the most spectacular congressional battles fought by the Israel lobby have been about arms sales to Arab countries. I do not address the issue of the Israel lobby in this book as a broad generalization but historically, in the context of what successive presidents felt they were trying to achieve and the situations to which they were responding. This results inevitably in a much more complex story.

This is a history of not only recent American foreign policy but also the contemporary Middle East, which I address with great diffidence. I am not a regional specialist and I therefore rely considerably on the work of those who are. Once one starts providing historical context, then it is often difficult to know when to stop, especially in a part of the world where routine references are made to events in the Old and New Testaments and the life and times of the Prophet Muhammad. Although many histories of the Middle East go back centuries, this one does not really get going until 1979. This is to keep the narrative manageable but also because that year saw the start of a new era in the region's politics, marked by the Egyptian-Israeli Peace Treaty, the Iranian revolution, and the Soviet invasion of Afghanistan. It was also the year Saddam Hussein became president of Iraq, pilgrims were attacked in the Grand Mosque of Mecca, and Pakistan proclaimed itself an Islamic state. This was, as David Lesch has put it, the "year that shaped the Modern Middle East."[6] The book ends in early 2008, with many pressing issues still unresolved. For reasons that should become apparent, the geographical scope has been kept vague. The Middle East considered here certainly moves into Southwest Asia. The boundaries in time are marked more clearly than those in space, for ease of organization according to presidential terms.

In many respects this is a depressing, at times tragic story; but I will not be arguing that the ending could have been a lot happier if only had the sensible policies I advocate been followed. This does not mean that my approach is not critical, for there have been some staggering misjudgments. At times policies have been decided without due care and attention, sometimes in panic and sometimes with a cavalier optimism. My main concern, however, is to understand how the choices presented themselves to presidents and why they chose the way they did.

1

CHOOSING ENEMIES

WHEN WAR COMES, choosing an enemy is normally the least of a government's problems. The choice tends to be obvious. Speaking after the "unprovoked and dastardly" Japanese attack on the American fleet at Pearl Harbor
on December 7, 1941, "a date which will live in infamy," President Franklin
D. Roosevelt saw no need to elaborate on the meaning of these events: "The
facts of yesterday speak for themselves. The people of the United States have
already formed their opinions and well understand the implications to the
very life and safety of our nation." The next "unprovoked and dastardly" attack against American territory, on September 11, 2001, was naturally compared to Pearl Harbor. Yet in this case the facts did not speak so clearly. Four
commercial aircraft had been hijacked. Two had been flown into the twin
towers of the World Trade Center in New York City, a third into the Pentagon in Washington, D.C., while a fourth, probably destined for the U.S.
Capitol Building, crashed in Pennsylvania. The immediate cost in lives was
higher: 3,021 (including nineteen hijackers) as against 2,382 in 1941. A measure of the traumatic impact, however, is that early estimates suggested that
some 10,000 might have died as the two towers collapsed into dust and rub-
ble. Moreover, the enemy had struck from within the United States, and a
link with foreign organizations or states could only be assumed. There was
no transparent sequence of events with which the attack might be linked: no
crisis, no failing negotiations, no ultimatums, no warnings. When the president spoke to Congress about the attacks on September 20, he realized that

he needed to address a number of questions that "Americans are asking." The first was, "Who attacked our country?"[1]

The apparent culprit was al Qaeda, a terrorist group led by Osama bin Laden, a dissident member of a wealthy Saudi family, who had issued his own declaration of war against the United States. Bin Laden had found sanctuary in Afghanistan, run by the Taliban, a sympathetic regime that was turning the country into an Islamist state. Multiple, spectacular attacks fitted in with the group's known aspirations and tactics. American targets had been attacked before—embassies in East Africa in 1998 and a warship, the USS *Cole*, off the coast of Yemen in 2000. The CIA had been warning that al Qaeda was planning something for 2001. Although an obscure Palestinian group tried to take credit, the Agency merely required a look at the passenger lists of the hijacked aircraft to confirm suspicions. The manifests contained the names of people the Agency had been investigating.[2]

The enemy did not own up. Bin Laden denied responsibility. At first he suggested, somewhat disingenuously, that the attacks seemed "to have been planned by people for personal reasons."[3] He repeated the denial on September 28. "As a Muslim," he said, "I try my best to avoid telling a lie. I had no knowledge of these attacks, nor do I consider the killing of innocent women, children and other human beings as an appreciable act." There were all sorts of people who could be responsible, he suggested, "from Russia to Israel and from India to Serbia." Perhaps it was "the American Jews, who have been annoyed with President Bush ever since the Florida elections and who want to avenge him." Maybe it was the "intelligence agencies in the U.S." They "require billions of dollars' worth of funds from Congress and the government every year" and so "needed an enemy."[4]

Bin Laden was not unique in suggesting that this might be a largely manufactured incident. This idea had, and still has, considerable currency around the world, especially in Muslim countries, and even has some credence in the United States. Allegations were soon circulating that the twin towers were felled as a result of a controlled demolition, or that the Pentagon was really struck by a cruise missile, or that there was a quiet exodus from the twin towers of people (Israelis/Jews) who had been alerted to the coming tragedy.[5] In the absence of definite proof that al Qaeda was responsible, more fanciful theories could gain ground.

So President George W. Bush's political task was more complicated than Roosevelt's, even though the military task in 1941 was bound to have been much greater. Bush had to name the enemy and explain the enmity, as well as set out a strategy for its defeat. He had to do this for a country that was angry, shocked, and fearful of further attacks from unknown sources. His method was a series of carefully scripted statements culminating in the address to Congress and the American people on September 20, 2001, supplemented on occasion by unscripted, sometimes casual, remarks. Much of the rest of his presidency was shaped by the strategy decided upon and described over those days.

On September 11, Bush knew that al Qaeda was probably responsible and was convinced that the country was at war, but he made neither thought explicit. In his very first comments he referred, somewhat awkwardly, to "those folks who committed this act," as if they might otherwise be friends.[6] That evening he was only slightly more authoritative as he spoke about the "evil, despicable acts of terror" that had ended thousands of lives that day, declaring that the United States would not be frightened into "chaos and retreat." According to Bob Woodward, his speechwriters wanted to include the phrasing "This is not just an act of terrorism. This is an act of war." Bush scrubbed it out, arguing that the need that evening was for reassurance. It was not until the next morning that he made this statement. Yet that night he did talk about "the war against terrorism" and also made one important statement of policy, after consultation only with Condoleezza Rice, his national security adviser, "We will make no distinction between the terrorists who committed these acts and those who harbor them." The word "harbor" was Bush's own, since he considered the original "tolerated" or "encouraged" too vague.[7]

In the context of al Qaeda operating out of Afghanistan with the connivance of the Taliban regime this was not unreasonable. Demands were already being formulated. The Taliban must surrender bin Laden and his close associates, close all terrorist camps, and comply with all UN Security Council resolutions. Soon, General Tommy Franks, the commanding general of Central Command (CENTCOM), was considering how to deal with the lack of plans for invading Afghanistan. The CIA began to develop proposals to engage al Qaeda by working with Afghan warlords opposed to the Taliban.[8]

In addition to the important tactical and diplomatic issues to be faced with regard to Afghanistan, the most difficult strategic question was whether the campaign could stop there or whether it would have to be extended into other countries. Some extension seemed unavoidable. George Tenet, director of central intelligence, pointed out that al Qaeda agents might be found in as many as sixty countries. "Let's pick them off one at a time," said Bush. But Secretary of Defense Donald Rumsfeld posed a larger question to the National Security Council (NSC) on September 12: "Do we focus on bin Laden or terrorism more broadly?" Secretary of State Colin Powell responded that the goal was "terrorism in its broadest sense, focusing first on the organization that acted yesterday."

There were no prior deliberations to consider the wisdom of taking on all terrorism. In the fraught and fevered hours after the 9/11 attacks, there was no time to think through the implications of that policy and subject it to any sort of critical analysis. Powell may just have been trying to postpone discussion of future campaigns until the United States had dealt with the matter at hand—al Qaeda and its Afghanistan base. There was at any rate a well established commitment to take on all forms of terrorism. This was not a new departure in American foreign policy. It had been present since the 1980s, when Ronald Reagan spoke regularly about the need to "stamp out the scourge of terrorism." There were regular references then to a war on terror, a phrase that could be interpreted either as a reference to a real war or a rhetorical device to mobilize the nation to address some great problem, akin to the way previous presidents had also declared wars on poverty, drugs, crime, and cancer. Unfortunately, as Grenville Byford observed, and as these earlier campaigns demonstrated, common nouns "never give up" and so cannot be defeated. These were wars against categories with contested meaning and disputed boundaries. It was better to wage wars against proper nouns, "for the good reason that proper nouns can surrender and promise not to do it again."[9] That is what Powell wanted to do. Al Qaeda posed an urgent and demanding challenge, giving focus to all the government's efforts. Powell had been garnering international support for whatever might have to be done next and was anxious not to put this fragile coalition at risk by extending the fight to places where American allies were less prepared to go.

The broader the definition of the task ahead, the wider the net, leading the United States into a range of conflicts with a variety of groups. Furthermore, as Cheney was keen to point out, one consequence of going after "terrorism," broadly defined, was "then we get at states." Rumsfeld was even prepared to skip the intermediate targets of the terrorists and go straight to their state supporters, because "it's easier to find them than it is to find bin Laden." To Rumsfeld, the notional leaders of these groups were less important than those pulling the strings. He warned against playing bin Laden up too much, arguing that even if he were eliminated, this would not solve the basic problem of terrorism.[10] At a Pentagon briefing on September 13, in response to a question about the broadness of the coming campaign, Deputy Secretary of Defense Paul Wolfowitz made the point publicly when he insisted that the task was "not just simply a matter of capturing people and holding them accountable, but removing the sanctuaries, removing the support systems, ending states who sponsor terrorism."[11]

What states did they have in mind? One potential candidate was Saudi Arabia. Not only was Osama bin Laden a child of one of the country's leading families, but fifteen of the nineteen hijackers were Saudi citizens. Although the Saudis expressed outrage and concern at the time of the attacks, and had already banished bin Laden, there was a long history of the kingdom appeasing Islamists at home by supporting mosques and madrassas (religious schools) abroad. The more Western-oriented members of the Saudi elite kept control of military and economic affairs but allowed the more zealous members of the religious establishment to control the ministries overseeing religion and education. The Saudis followed Wahhabism, an austere form of Islam, named after the eighteenth-century preacher Mohammed ibn Abdul Wahhab. The combination of oil wealth and a creed wary of modernity was toxic and led to a vast proselytizing enterprise, linked to groups of equal severity around the world. This effort was given added impetus in the 1980s, as a counter to the Shia revival prompted by Iran and the Soviet intervention in Afghanistan. This gave the teachings of radical Wahhabist imams an increasingly political edge. Wahhabism is a form of Salafism. The underlying thesis of Salafism is that Islam was perfect when first formed and that later innovations can only distort the original and true message. Though dogmatic, Salafism is by no means synonymous with militant violence. It is the case that many of those who have embarked on this path have tended to be Salafists.

There was a particularly important link between Saudi Wahhabism and Pakistan's Jamaat-e-Islami, a group that campaigned against corruption and secularism, in this case with the tacit backing of the country's military dictator, General Mohammed Zia-ul-Haq. It was out of the madrassas in Pakistan, many of which had been preparing militants for the war against the Soviet Union in Afghanistan, that the Taliban emerged. Thus it could be argued (as did a lawsuit) that the Saudis were culpable in creating the ideological climate that nurtured al Qaeda. Craig Unger has argued that George W. Bush was prepared to let the Saudis off the hook because of his family's close personal and financial links with Saudi Arabia. The major piece of evidence for this allegation was the fact that 142 Saudis, including twenty-four members of the bin Laden family, were allowed to leave the country in a private jet on September 14, without the FBI even screening them to see if terrorists were escaping. This latter point was rejected by the 9/11 Commission, which reported that the FBI's handling of the flight was thorough and appropriate and that the approval had come from Richard Clarke, then in charge of counterterrorism and later a fierce critic of the administration, and not from the president or vice president.[12]

A second possible terrorist sponsor was Pakistan itself. Prior to 9/11, the United States had faced considerable difficulty in persuading Pakistan to cooperate in its attempts to extract bin Laden from Afghanistan. Pakistan's Inter-Service Intelligence (ISI) agency had created the Taliban and kept it supplied since 1996.[13] Pakistan was thus one of the few countries in the world to have diplomatic relations with the Taliban regime. There were also regular reports that ISI, which tended to operate its own foreign policy, had its own connections with al Qaeda and may even have provided some of the funding for the attacks. Islamists were known to be high up in the government. President Pervez Musharraf had been responsible, prior to becoming chief of staff and then mounting a coup, for the unofficial campaign waged against India in Kashmir. Pakistan was already suspected of being lax when it came to controlling the spread of its nuclear technology, although just how lax was not appreciated. There were already disturbing signs that individual Pakistanis were helping al Qaeda pursue its interests in chemical and nuclear weapons. One member of a CIA panel set up in 2000 to review all the evidence on what Pakistan was up to concluded that "the US number one enemy was looking more and more like Pakistan."[14]

The 9/11 Commission reported that the Principals Committee on September 13, chaired by Rice, considered the possibility that the United States might still not be able to persuade the Pakistanis to turn against the Taliban, which they had helped create. The conclusion was that if Pakistan failed to help the United States, it would put itself at risk. Powell and his deputy, Richard Armitage, had already decided there was no time to mess around with Pakistan, and Musharraf had to be told to choose sides. That day, Armitage met with the Pakistani ambassador and the head of Pakistan's ISI, who was usefully in Washington at the time. According to the U.S. record, Armitage set down the steps required of Pakistan, which involved not only denying support to al Qaeda and the Taliban but also handing over intelligence information and allowing the United States to use Pakistan as a base for the coming military operations, which meant full access to its airspace and borders. According to Musharraf, the message was brutal, or as he put it, "very rude." He was told by his intelligence director that Armitage said, "Be prepared to be bombed. Be prepared to go back to the Stone Age."[15] Armitage denied making any military threats, though his admitted statement that Pakistan must decide if it was "with us or against us," when put in the context of the time, was not much less brutal.[16] Whatever Armitage said, the message was clear. The reply came back almost immediately from Musharraf accepting the U.S. demands, while noting how unpopular this would be with many Pakistanis. This made it easier for the Americans to then formulate the proposed ultimatum to the Taliban.[17]

Rumsfeld and Wolfowitz's candidate for military action was quite different, although it was a country with no known links to al Qaeda. To both men, Iraq was as important as Afghanistan, and probably more so. According to one report, barely five hours after the Pentagon building itself was struck, and having been told of al Qaeda's likely culpability, Rumsfeld asked to see plans for a strike against Iraq. A note kept by an official quotes the secretary of defense as saying he wanted "best info fast. Judge whether good enough hit S.H. [Saddam Hussein] at same time. Not only UBL [Osama bin Laden]." He was quoted as saying, "Go massive . . . Sweep it all up. Things related and not."[18] Wolfowitz already was of the view that there was a link between Saddam Hussein's Iraq and al Qaeda, and so he suspected that Iraq might well have been responsible for the 9/11 attacks, believing the planning and execution had been too sophisticated for a terrorist group and must have involved state sponsorship.

In this view Wolfowitz was influenced by Laurie Mylroie of the American Enterprise Institute, who published a book in 2000 pulling together circumstantial evidence connecting Iraq with the February 1993 bombing of the World Trade Center. The front cover of Mylroie's book contained an endorsement from Wolfowitz ("provocative and disturbing").[19] NSC staffer Richard Clarke reported that Wolfowitz used Mylroie's arguments (which Clarke described as "a theory that had been investigated for years and found to be untrue") as early as April 2001 when questioning the idea of terrorist groups operating independently of a sponsoring state.[20] Wolfowitz argued to the NSC that Iraq was not only a plausible culprit but also a much more manageable enemy. He was not alone in his concern that there was a risk of getting bogged down in the difficult terrain of Afghanistan, as the Russians had, or triggering such chaos that Pakistan next door might be destabilized. On September 15, as Tenet outlined CIA plans for getting at the Taliban and all were gathered around a large map of Afghanistan, Rice recalls, "Everybody looks at it and says, 'Oh, God, isn't that where great powers go to die?'"[21] This could have been an argument for caution, but it only led Wolfowitz to present Iraq as a more straightforward proposition, with a brittle and oppressive regime ready to break.[22]

There were a number of objections to such an approach. Nobody other than Wolfowitz suspected Iraq was responsible for the 9/11 attacks; campaigning on too many fronts at once risked a loss of focus; it would be wrong to use the war on terror to settle an old score; and ease of attack was not in itself a good reason to choose an enemy. Al Qaeda was expected to be the first priority, and there would be confusion at home and abroad if it was not. If al Qaeda was dealt with successfully, then Iraq, and other hostile states, would still be there for the next stage. For the moment, Bush was also wary of diversion. He took the view that the American people expected him to start with bin Laden. If that succeeded, "We've struck a huge blow and can move forward." In general, while accepting the more ambitious objective, he remained cautious about the next steps. Iraq was an issue that could wait. The terrorist threat was a "cancer" but should not be defined "too broadly for the average man to understand." This was not a war that would conclude with a "big bang" but one that would be fought with "many steps."[23] When Bush met British prime minister Tony Blair on September 20, the president commented that "Iraq was not the immediate problem." Acknowledging that some members of his administration took a different view, he pointed out that "he was the one responsible for making the decisions."[24] But he had not ruled Iraq out. At the time, the assumption was that Iraq would move into the frame if it could be shown to have links with al Qaeda.

★　　★　　★

Although his strategy was developing a sharp focus, in his public presentations Bush described a remarkably broad approach. Only in answer to a reporter's question on September 15 did he acknowledge that Osama bin Laden was the "prime suspect."[25] He was more concerned with communicating the idea that the country faced a new category of enemy that could not be quickly defeated. The enemy "hides in shadows, and has no regard for human life . . . preys on innocent and unsuspecting people, then runs for cover." He spoke of a conflict "without battlefields or beachheads, a conflict with opponents who believe they are invisible." Terrorism would not be defeated "in a single battle, but in a series of decisive actions against terrorist organizations and those who harbor and support them."

He also added another dimension to the problem, taking it beyond national security and into the eradication of evil, a matter of morality as much as strategy. This fitted in with both the awfulness of the attacks and the natural impulse in American politics to describe enemies as the embodiment of wickedness, this time not just an extreme and vicious political movement but as Satan himself. In the 1980s, Ronald Reagan had spoken of the Soviet Union as the "focus of evil in the modern world" and as the "evil empire." On September 12, 2001, Bush spoke of a "monumental struggle between good and evil." There was not going to be much scope for compromises and middle ways. Soon there were more references to barbarism, evil, and evil-doers, and an unscripted description of the war on terror as a "crusade."[26] In the West, "crusade" might suggest something positive, a struggle for a cause in which you really believe. For Arabs, the reference is to religious invasions launched by the West. Bush's "crusade" was soon translated into Arabic as the "war of the cross." The Bush administration immediately realized the metaphor was unfortunate and withdrew it from further use.

Bush's address to Congress on September 20, 2001, gave him the opportunity to sort out the various messages and describe the chosen strategy. His biographer described it as "the greatest speech of his presidency" because he knew exactly what he wanted to say. His sense of its importance was illustrated when he struck out a quote from Roosevelt, insisting, "I want to lead! I want to be the guy they quote!"[27] To the question "Who attacked our country?" he could now provide an answer: "A collection of loosely affiliated terrorist organizations known as al Qaeda." Bush described al Qaeda as being Mafia-like, but its goal was to impose its radical beliefs on people everywhere. Although it claimed to act on behalf of Islam, this was "a fringe form," a perversion of Islam's "peaceful teachings" and so "rejected by Muslim scholars and the vast majority of Muslim clerics." Its leader was a "person named Osama bin Laden." Crucially, it was "linked to many other organizations in different countries." There were therefore "thousands of these terrorists in more than 60 countries," who had been trained in the ways of terror at camps "in places like Afghanistan" before moving on "to plot evil and destruction."

Later in the speech, Bush explained that these people hated America for its freedoms, wanted to overthrow existing governments in many Muslim countries and drive Israel out of the Middle East, and were hostile to Christians and Jews. They were "the heirs of all the murderous ideologies of the 20th century. By sacrificing human life to serve their radical visions—by abandoning every value except the will to power—they follow in the path of fascism, and Nazism, and totalitarianism." This elevated al Qaeda into a special category of enemy, the very worst. Its members shared the ambition of these great enemies of the past to reshape the world according to their extreme beliefs. However, they lacked the ability to mobilize the power of a modern state. In terms of capacity, the Taliban regime in Afghanistan, with which al Qaeda was linked, was relatively puny, although undoubtedly deeply unpleasant. Because it sponsored, sheltered, and supplied terrorists, the Taliban was "committing murder." Bush demanded that the regime hand over to the United States the leaders of al Qaeda and close the camps. Ultimately, he said, they "will hand over the terrorists, or they will share in their fate."

"The enemy of America," Bush was anxious to state, "is not our many Muslim friends; it is not our many Arab friends. Our enemy is a radical network of terrorists, and every government that supports them." It was clear from Bush's earlier remarks that chasing al Qaeda out of Afghanistan would not deal with all those who had been trained in the camps, now dispersed around the world, and the like-minded groups linked to al Qaeda. Bush went further: "Our war on terror begins with al Qaeda, but it does not end there. It will not end until every terrorist group of global reach has been found, stopped and defeated." From this followed a warning to all nations: "Either you are with us, or you are with the terrorists. From this day forward, any nation that continues to harbor or support terrorism will be regarded by the United States as a hostile regime."[28] Left unclear was whether support was being demanded for a war just against al Qaeda or against terrorism everywhere, however defined and in any circumstances.

★　★　★

For the next couple of months the focus was on the war in Afghanistan to destroy al Qaeda and topple the Taliban. By the middle of November, it seemed that this campaign had reached an apparently successful conclusion. Attention now started to turn to "phase two" of the war against terror. One possibility was Somalia, which might have been used by al Qaeda as a base for the August 1998 bombings of the U.S. embassies in Kenya and Tanzania. There was some intelligence that al Qaeda had a base near the Kenyan border, although Somali officials said that it had been abandoned. In Yemen, there were suspected al Qaeda camps in the northern mountains. Both these options could be explored, but neither represented as serious a target as Iraq.

The earlier administration assumption was that the United States would act against Iraq only if evidence could be found demonstrating a firm link with September 11. A group in the Pentagon was trying to find compelling evidence and soon began to convince itself, if not others, that the search would bear fruit. There was, however, another approach, one that meant concentrating instead on what could be done in the future about Iraq if the various programs under way there for producing weapons of mass destruction were successful. Such weapons in terrorist hands were a dreadful prospect. How likely that was to happen was another matter, but the president was not going to take any chances. On November 26, 2001, he said that the war against terror would not stop with Afghanistan ("Afghanistan is still just the beginning") but would now take on states that had either acquired or were after such deadly capabilities. "So part of the war on terror is to deny . . . weapons to be used for means of terror getting in the hands of nations that will use them." Both North Korea and Iraq were mentioned, and it was required of both countries that they admit inspectors to assess the state of their programs. When asked what would happen if Iraq did not do this, Bush said Saddam Hussein would "find out."[29]

The annual State of the Union address, scheduled for the end of January 2002, was the setting for the president to evaluate the first months of his war on terror and set out his strategy for the next stage. His starting point was to express confidence in a victory in Afghanistan, where al Qaeda had its headquarters and where the 9/11 attacks had been planned. The United States had

> rallied a great coalition, captured, arrested, and rid the world of thousands of terrorists, destroyed Afghanistan's terrorist training camps, saved a people from starvation, and freed a country from brutal oppression. . . . The American flag flies again over our embassy in Kabul. Terrorists who once occupied Afghanistan now occupy cells at Guantanamo Bay. And terrorist leaders who urged followers to sacrifice their lives are running for their own.

Yet terrorist training camps still existed "in at least a dozen countries." Bush mentioned four examples of this "terrorist underworld"—Hamas, Hezbollah, Islamic Jihad, Jaish-i-Mohammed—operating in "remote jungles and deserts" and hiding "in the centers of large cities." The identification of Hamas and Hezbollah as part of the enemy network was not considered remarkable, yet their links to al Qaeda were tenuous, and their main significance was their role as popular and militant movements in Palestine and Lebanon, respectively. Islamic Jihad was another Palestinian group, whereas Jaish-i-Mohammed operated in India and Kashmir.

The most significant aspect of the president's speech lay in his determination to "prevent the terrorists and regimes who seek chemical, biological or nuclear weapons from threatening the United States and the world." He described the obnoxious nature of each of the regimes in turn: North Korea's citizens were starving; the Iranian people's hope for freedom was repressed; Iraq continued "to flaunt its hostility toward America and to support terror." These states, with their terrorist allies, constituted

> an axis of evil, arming to threaten the peace of the world. By seeking weapons of mass destruction, these regimes pose a grave and growing danger. They could provide these arms to terrorists, giving them the means to match their hatred. They could attack our allies or attempt to blackmail the United States. In any of these cases, the price of indifference would be catastrophic.

Faced with such threats, the president warned, "Time is not on our side. . . . I will not wait on events, while dangers gather. I will not stand by, as peril draws closer and closer. The United States of America will not permit the world's most dangerous regimes to threaten us with the world's most destructive weapons."[30]

Later, administration figures expressed surprise that the phrase had received so much attention compared with other parts of the speech, but given the context it was hardly surprising, especially as this was also the speech's most arresting phrase and the paragraph had received a lot of high-level attention. Where did this notion of the axis of evil come from? Bush's chief speechwriter, Michael Gerson, saw an opportunity to "mold and rally public opinion" and set out the president's new direction for foreign policy. David Frum, on Gerson's staff, was asked to produce language on the Iraq issue. Frum was eager for the United States to go after Iraq but realized that certain rationales would not wash. He could detail the tyranny of Saddam Hussein's regime, but if it was so bad, that left open the question of why the United States had not acted sooner. Reference to the attempted 1993 assassination of Bush's father, former president George H. W. Bush, risked making it look like a matter of Bush family *omertà*. Despite the best efforts of the Pentagon cell investigating the matter, there was as yet no strong proof of any connection with 9/11.

To get some inspiration, Frum looked at Roosevelt's "day that will live in infamy" speech with which this chapter opened. The aspect that intrigued him was the similarity of Roosevelt's strategic problem to Bush's. Just as the United States had been attacked by al Qaeda, with Iraq really being the greater threat, so in 1941 the United States had been attacked by Japan, though Germany was the greater threat. Because many in the country and Congress wanted to focus sharply on just Japan, Roosevelt added the sentence "I believe I interpret the will of the Congress and of the people when I assert that we will not only defend ourselves to the uttermost, but will make very certain that this form of treachery shall never endanger us again." Frum claimed, "For FDR, Pearl Harbor was not only an attack—it was a warning of future and worse attacks from another, even more dangerous source." He seems to be overinterpreting this sentence. It could be read simply as a promise to deal with the Japanese regime. At any rate, Roosevelt had no need to be cryptic when talking about Germany. In his fireside chat on December 9, 1941, he explained at length why the United States was effectively already at war with Nazi Germany: "We expect to eliminate the danger from Japan, but it would serve us ill if we accomplished that and found that the rest of the world was dominated by Hitler and Mussolini."[31] This was before Germany (and Italy) clarified the situation further two days later by declaring war on the United States. Frum made the tenuous connection between Roosevelt's challenge of dealing with enemies who could not be palpably deterred or contained and the recklessness of Saddam. Saddam had launched wars against two of his neighbors, Iran and Kuwait, and while fighting the United States had tried to start another war with Israel. This aggressiveness could soon resurface if he became able to get access to chemical or nuclear weapons, though more worryingly, this might be expressed through terrorist groups.

This was the "axis"—between "terror organizations and terror states"—Frum had in mind in his memo for Gerson. When challenged on the limits to the comparison of the self-defined Axis powers of World War II and Bush's somewhat contrived "axis of evil," Frum was prepared to defend the analogy, pointing to the fact that the original Axis powers disliked and distrusted each other and only had in common "resentment of the power of the West and contempt for democracy." However, this was not the point he was making in January 2002.[32] Although Frum has been credited, not least by himself, with the "axis of evil" phrase, his main contribution appears to be the word "axis." His original formulation referred to an "axis of hatred." Gerson, who had helped develop the distinctive Bush style that "fused biblical high-mindedness and the folksy," changed this to the "axis of evil," which made its members sound even more sinister.[33]

Rice considered the focus on links between weapons of mass destruction and international terrorism appropriate. The thought had been around during the drafting of the September 20 speech, but anxiety levels were already high enough then not to be raised higher by talking about even more nightmarish possibilities. Rice's concern was with singling out Iraq as the embodiment of the axis, which could be taken as a virtual—and premature—declaration of war. Rather than tone down the concept, she argued for expanding it. This expansion created a notion of axis that was not so much about links between dangerous states and terrorist networks, but more a combination of dangerous states, all of whom had an interest in weapons of mass destruction. Alternative members of the axis were suggested. The vice president's office suggested North Korea, which fitted the criteria, but also Syria, which might have been squeezed in, but the decision was not to try. Libya was proposed by undersecretary of state John Bolton, on the basis of its connection with both terrorism and WMD. He did not know, however, that secret talks were under way with Libya, and the British, who were closely involved, urged the Americans not to do anything to jeopardize them.[34]

Iran was soon put in but then was almost taken out. It was the most problematic country because its internal political structure had democratic elements. According to Rice this was not because of Iran's nuclear program, since the intelligence was not received until later in the year showing how advanced this was, but because of the terrorism link.[35] This included its link to the Lebanese group Hezbollah, and it had just been discovered ferrying arms to Palestinian groups. There is yet another reason why Bush wanted it kept in. Somehow he thought that by linking Iran with the other two, by describing the repression they faced, this would "inspire those who love freedom inside the country." He believed in a U.S. responsibility to promote freedom "that is as solemn as the responsibility is to protecting the American people, because the two go hand-in-hand."[36]

Whether this noble objective could be discerned within the terse sentences of the speech is doubtful. Yet the administration appears to have believed that it was sending an important, reassuring message to antiregime forces, and that this was a good, propitious time because Iran was on the verge of revolution. According to Frum, Michael Ledeen, whom he described as "a former NSC staffer who follows events in Iran closely" and who was then with the American Enterprise Institute, was claiming that "Iran was moving toward revolution" so that a "signal of support from the United States could hurry things up."[37] This reference to Ledeen is intriguing. Ledeen had a long and checkered past, with spells in government agencies and think tanks. We will meet him again later when we consider the Iran-Contra scandal of 1986, when he played a central and undistinguished role. He was well connected to the more militant parts of the U.S. government. According to one account, Ledeen was an adviser to Karl Rove, Bush's top political aide. They had met after the 2000 election. Ledeen claimed that he had been asked by Rove to send him his "good ideas" and that every month or six weeks, he would send over "something you should be thinking about."[38]

Ledeen had never lost his interest in Iran, but he had come to combine this with a despairing view of the reluctance of the U.S. national security bureaucracy to take the initiative in uprooting hostile regimes and a conviction that the country should find fear and violence ("creative destruction") more efficient than trying to set moral examples of restraint and conciliation. His basic philosophy, as outlined in a book he published in 2002, was to take on what he called the "terror masters," a term that reflected his view that the problem was bad states rather than unruly nonstate groups.

> While we will have to act against secret terrorist organizations and
> kamikaze fighters, our ultimate targets are tyrannical regimes. We will
> require different strategies in each case. We will need one method and
> set of tools to bring down Saddam Hussein, another strategy to break
> the Assad family dictatorship in Syria, a very different approach to end
> the religious tyranny in Iran, and yet another to deal with Saudi Arabia's

active support for fundamentalist Islam and the terror network. But the
mission is the same in each case: Bring down the terror masters.[39]

Ledeen was to the fore in arguing for an invasion of Iraq but in January
2002 was also stressing the need to "show our contempt for the leaders of Iran
by endorsing the cries of the Iranian people for freedom and democracy."[40]

According to the memoir of George Tenet, then the director of central intelligence, at the same time the "axis" speech was being drafted, he discovered Ledeen in Italy, with some Pentagon officials, talking about secret
contacts with Iranians opposed to the regime, and a $25 million program to
destabilize the regime. More annoying still, Stephen Hadley at the NSC and
Wolfowitz at the Pentagon knew about this, and Ledeen was claiming that
the Iranians would only deal with the Pentagon and not with the CIA.
Working with Powell, who was also furious about this private enterprise,
Tenet got these efforts stopped.[41] But by then Iran was well established as
part of the "axis of evil," put into the frame because of unwarranted optimism about the political benefits of an adverse mention of Iran in a presidential speech. Now that the Iranian regime had been described as evil, it
was hard to think of it as anything other than a potential enemy.

★   ★   ★

From the culprits of September 11 to the Taliban regime in Afghanistan had
been a short step, politically unavoidable and strategically sensible. From the
headquarters of al Qaeda to its associates and affiliates around the world had
a certain logic, and the implications in many cases would be no more than
giving support to particular governments that were already trying to cope
with their local threats. Deciding to eliminate the evil of terrorism was an altogether bigger leap, offering potentially endless and limitless conflict. To
then place Iraq, Iran, and North Korea within this global war on terrorism
was a bigger leap still, because while that gave otherwise ill-defined campaigns a sharper focus, it also risked turning them into actual confrontations
with named states.

There was no natural resting place on this journey, unless the government
was prepared to reverse course. There were no further terrorist spectaculars
along the lines of 9/11, but al Qaeda and its associates kept busy around the
world, not least in Iraq. The March 2003 invasion and occupation provided
both a rallying call for Islamist militants and an opportunity for regular and
serious violence, directed against coalition forces but also against rival communities and political factions. Afghanistan remained unsettled. Iran became even more of an irritant. By the time of his 2006 State of the Union

address, with matters not going entirely to plan, Bush acknowledged that the United States was now engaged in a "long war against a determined enemy." Yet the president showed no inclination to step back from his ambitious post-9/11 goals. If anything they had expanded: "We seek the end of tyranny in our world." Now the analysis showed that the "only way to defeat the terrorists is to defeat their dark vision of hatred and fear by offering the hopeful alternative of political freedom and peaceful change." He offered a simple dichotomy: "Dictatorships shelter terrorists, and feed resentment and radicalism, and seek weapons of mass destruction. Democracies replace resentment with hope, respect the rights of their citizens and their neighbors, and join the fight against terror."[42]

While Bush could point to increasing evidence of democratic practice in the region, at least in terms of the holding of elections, their results were often ambiguous and certainly could not be linked to any decline in the local incidence of terror or broader political stability. Elections in Iraq were followed by sectarian violence and continuing insurgency, in Lebanon by Syrian-backed attempts to destabilize the government and a war with Israel, and in Palestine by the election of a group associated with terror leading to a split between the West Bank and Gaza. The regional opponents of the United States were hardly subdued. At least Bush could say in January 2007 that the United States now had "a much clearer view of the nature of this enemy." He identified two distinct strands of threat, based on the Sunni-Shia divide. This reflects the split in the Muslim world that began almost immediately after Muhammad's death, over the question of succession, between those who took a pragmatic view of leadership (Sunni) and those who assigned a special status to Imam Ali, the Prophet's cousin and son-in-law (Shia). The divisions this caused remain deep, as evident in the violence between the two communities in Iraq. Bush found that at the extreme of both traditions was enmity toward the United States. On the one hand, there was "al Qaeda and its followers." They were "Sunni extremists, possessed by hatred and commanded by a harsh and narrow ideology. Take almost any principle of civilization, and their goal is the opposite. They preach with threats, instruct with bullets and bombs, and promise paradise for the murder of the innocent." They intend to "overthrow moderate governments, and establish safe havens from which to plan and carry out new attacks on our country." On the other hand, however, there was now "an escalating danger from Shi'ite extremists who are just as hostile to America, and are also determined to dominate the Middle East. Many are known to take direction from the regime in Iran, which is funding and arming terrorists like Hezbollah—a group second only to al Qaeda in the American lives it has taken." These were "different faces of the same totalitarian threat."[43]

*   *   *

How had the United States gotten itself in this position, entangled in the confusing and often violent geopolitics of the Middle East and beset by enemies on all sides? As far as the Bush administration was concerned, the events of 9/11 were so horrendous and the new threat so dire that allies and partners must understand that the United States was now entitled to do whatever was necessary for the sake of its security. But the administration had choices in terms of goals and methods. Was it going to focus on all extremist groups trading in political violence or just those culpable for the attacks? Should it seek to eliminate these groups or address those conflicts which gave them their sense of grievance and purpose? Was this an opportunity, while the country was in such a belligerent mood, to try to deal with a range of other foreign policy problems even if they were not directly related to the attacks? How much could be achieved through the sheer assertion of American power, and to what extent would it need willing allies? How far dare it follow a preference for the unilateral in the face of pleas to work with the rest of the international community and show some care and caution?

The approach to these questions reflected the sense that history had started afresh on 9/11. The fact that the United States had been hurt so badly was in itself a commentary on the failure of the old ways, while the situation was so unprecedented that the past provided little guidance on how to respond. Even those who worried that the administration risked leaving the United States isolated and feared, just when it was most in need of friends and good advice, were often also tempted by the thought there was a chance to start with a clean slate. As the United States prepared for a new struggle, there was a resurgence of the hope that often accompanies the end rather than the start of wars—that this was the moment for bold and imaginative policies that might push aside visceral hatreds and destructive practices. It is, however, always unwise to disregard history. History gave context and meaning to the various conflicts in which the United States was getting involved, and provided a framework with which to evaluate American options and judge the possibilities for success. This was also not the first time the United States had been the target of radical movements with a tendency to terrorism.

2

THE FIRST WAVE

MUCH OF THIS BOOK is about the U.S. response to what I call the "second radical wave" in the Middle East, which was led by Islamists and is normally considered to have begun with the 1979 Iranian revolution. The "first radical wave" was led by Arab nationalists. Its first hero was Gamal Abdel Nasser, who became Egypt's leader after the coup to overthrow King Farouk in 1952. Since many of the current crop of Arab leaders emerged out of the nationalist tradition, the influence of the first wave remains, although it lost its radical edge some time ago. The two waves were anticolonial and anti-Zionist, and both enjoyed their early political development in Egypt, all of which helps explain why they were also deadly rivals. As we shall see, within these two waves there were many different tendencies, which created more scope for rivalry and conflict. With both the first and second waves the United States sought to find points of contact and failed, although as the radical energy drained away from the first wave it was able to make some accommodations. This chapter concerns the rise and fall of the first wave.

* * *

After World War II the U.S. government showed great sympathy for anticolonial movements. It had fought its own war of independence, and saw in the nationalist movements a progressive force, likely to triumph against the feudal monarchies and puppet regimes that continued to serve the imperial cause in Asia and Africa. The Truman administration was of course aware that the Soviet Union could also claim to be the champion of progressive forces. Communism embraced the cause of the masses against the capitalism epitomized by the United States. The way to counter this was to find nationalist leaders who had populist appeal but also understood the superior merits of the American as against the Soviet system.

The ability of the United States to align itself with the nationalists was hampered by its alliance with antiprogressive forces, and in particular Britain and France, the first targets of the nationalists. In arguments that would be repeated in subsequent decades in different forms, the British and French took the "realist" stance, telling the Americans that they were being naïve and sentimental. Nationalists were not naturally democrats and were easily manipulated by the Communists. Better to stick with the local autocratic rulers, even if their claims to power rested on weak, and often quite recent, foundations. In response, Americans worried that attempts to retain what was in effect colonial control would aggravate anti-Western feeling. In addition, an automatic identity of interests did not always exist. American and British oil companies had long competed for access to oil reserves in the Middle East. Yet in the end, all three countries were allies in Europe, which was the front line of the cold war, and oil reserves and supply lines gave the Middle East a strategic significance that meant it was bound to become another front. It was the British who took the lead in resisting a Soviet drive into the Middle East, and they claimed to understand its tiresome complexities and distinctive culture better than anyone else. The Americans found themselves siding with the status quo.

The other source of difficulty was Israel. This was also at first an anticolonial, nationalist cause, which is why the Jewish state was also supported by the Soviet Union as an oasis of socialism. There were many in the State Department—as there were in the British Foreign Office—who thought that this was a big mistake. But the British who governed Palestine had promised the Jews their homeland in 1917, a claim that was much harder to resist in the aftermath of the Nazi Holocaust in Europe and was actively supported by American Jews. Initially Palestine was divided into a Jewish and an Arab state, but the borders were never likely to hold. As independence was declared in 1948, 650,000 Jews were fighting for their survival as well as for the expansion of the territory under their control. Encouraged to flee with the promise of a return with victorious Arab armies, or else hounded out by Jewish militias, 750,000 Arabs left their homes to become refugees, a status that became permanent as they were settled in camps across the new borders. There they were maintained as a rebuff to Israel and a source of agitation and militancy. The only other victor was Jordan, which took the portion of Palestine, including half of Jerusalem, that Israel failed to acquire. For the Arab people, Israel's survival was a deep humiliation and added to the unpopularity of their leaders. Arab governments could not make Israel disappear, but they insisted on a continuing state of war and refused any political or commercial contact. This was despite Western attempts to encourage them to do so and to focus instead on the common Soviet enemy.

∗   ∗   ∗

This was the background against which, in 1952, the dissolute King Farouk of Egypt was overthrown by the Committee of the Free Officers' Movement. Nasser was the dominant figure in the Committee, although the first president of the new republic was General Muhammad Naguib. The movement was vehemently opposed to the British control, but otherwise had no uniform ideology. It soon ran into trouble and quickly abandoned democratic politics. The two political organizations whose influence might have given ideological clarity to the new regime were suppressed. The Communist Party was outlawed and remained so even while friendly relations were being established with the Soviet Union. A more serious challenge came from the Muslim Brotherhood, which had been formed in Egypt in 1928. This was a genuine mass movement, founded on a belief in the supremacy of Islamic law and combined with a populist anti-colonialism. Many of the radical Islamic movements operating today are linked to the Brotherhood, and the books of its leading ideologists, such as Syed Qutb, remain influential. The Brotherhood had welcomed the 1952 officers' revolt in Egypt, but then wanted the new government to create an Islamic state. Nasser used an assassination attempt by a member of the Brotherhood to push Naguib aside during 1954.

Under President Harry S Truman some effort was made to work with Nasser, but this faltered under Dwight D. Eisenhower, although in the end it was Eisenhower who saved Nasser's regime. He was particularly irritated by Nasser's support for anti-colonialism and his embrace of the nonaligned movement. This anti-colonialism was reflected in Egyptian support for the rebellion in Algeria against France. The crunch point came when Nasser also decided that he needed to build up his forces to cope with Israel.

By the time he first came to power, and despite American (and Israeli) hopes, Nasser had concluded that a peace treaty with Israel was a step too far. Then tensions grew as a result of Israeli reprisal raids for guerrilla attacks launched from the Gaza Strip, then part of Egypt and where many of the refugees lived. Having been rebuffed by the Americans because of his insistence on nonalignment, Nasser negotiated an arms agreement with Czechoslovakia in September 1955, representing a breakthrough for the Soviet Union in its efforts to gain some presence in a Western-dominated region. The American response was to reduce economic assistance (particularly for the high-profile Aswan Dam project). This set the scene for the following year's Suez Crisis.

The nationalization of the Suez Canal, then still run by a Franco-British company, was seen both as economic theft and strategic threat, because of the canal's importance in transporting oil supplies. The anger in London and Paris was not matched elsewhere, and the Americans opposed the use of force to resolve the issue. Regardless, in November 1956, Britain and France attempted to reoccupy the canal zone, in collusion with Israel. After some fierce fighting, the Egyptian air force was destroyed and key ports along the canal were occupied, but the attack was universally condemned. Britain and France were compelled to agree to a cease-fire before they had reached their objectives, and then to withdraw. The most effective form of coercion was economic pressure from the United States. Israel, which had taken the Sinai, was also obliged to withdraw, but a UN peacekeeping force was placed on the Egyptian side of the border with Israel and on the Gulf of Aqaba to ensure the free passage of Israeli shipping. Nasser was the true victor of the crisis. By standing up to Western imperialism, he became a hero in the Arab world.

Eisenhower was furious with the British for the illegality and stupidity of their tactics, for distracting the international community when it should have been focusing on a simultaneous crisis—the Soviet suppression of the Hungarian Uprising—and for not consulting or even informing him. He hoped that by opposing the colluding powers he would gain some credit in the Arab world, but the Soviet opposition had been louder (even to the point—when it was safe to do so—of issuing a nuclear threat). As Eisenhower contemplated the situation after Suez, he realized that the British were now so discredited that the United States would have to assert itself more in the region, and that Nasser was so buoyed by his triumph that he was going to be even more disruptive as well as flirtatious with the Soviet Union. In January 1957, the "Eisenhower doctrine" was promulgated, promising to help nations protect their independence and integrity against "overt aggression by a nation controlled by international communism." The reference was clearly to Egypt.

It was also a reference to Syria. In 1954, a right-wing military regime had been overthrown by the combined efforts of the Arab Socialist Resurrection (Ba'ath) Party and Communist parties and dissident elements of the Syrian army. The link with Nasser, the access to the pipeline connecting Iraq's oil fields to Turkey, and the potential for Syria to further destabilize the region and provide another entry point for Soviet influence added to Western anxieties. A year after Suez, the British were hatching a plan to assassinate the ruling triumvirate in Syria in the context of wider disturbances (including stirring up the Muslim Brotherhood) in the hope of creating conditions that would give Iraq and Jordan a pretext for overthrowing the regime. The plan was abandoned when these countries refused to cooperate.[1]

★ ★ ★

Nasser was presenting himself at the head of an apparently irresistible movement. If there was an ideological impetus, it came from pan-Arabism, an idea that dated back to Ottoman times and stressed the unifying qualities of an Arab—as opposed to an Islamic—identity. In the name of Arab unity, Nasser urged Syria to join Egypt to form a new state. The United Arab Republic (UAR) was proclaimed in 1958, with Nasser as president and Cairo as the capital. It did not last. The Syrian elite could not easily reconcile themselves to a secondary role, the two countries were not contiguous, and they had different structures. The union collapsed in 1961 when there was yet another military coup in Syria, with members of the Ba'ath Party to the fore. Ba'athism was another example of the strength of narrow, nationalist impulses. Ba'ath ideology was set out in the 1940s by intellectuals who synthesized nationalist, socialist, and some fascist ideas. It was influential in Iraq as well as Syria. When in 1958 the Hashemite monarchy was overthrown in Iraq, as it tried to form a union with Jordan to compete with the formation of the UAR, Ba'athism might have been expected to provide a source of togetherness. It took a succession of military coups before the Ba'athists came to power in Iraq in 1963, but then, once again, apparent ideological compatibility failed to overcome national rivalries. By the end of the 1960s, the two Ba'ath parties sustained their own separate versions of the true faith in hostility to each other.

The evident divisions among those occupying the same ideological space undermined Nasser's cause. He retained immense popularity among the Arab masses, but this took him less far than he had hoped. Particularly damaging was his unsuccessful military campaign in Yemen in order to sustain a republican government that had overthrown the monarchy but was buckling in the face of a royalist counterattack. The royalists were backed by the Saudis, who saw Nasser's ideas as deeply subversive and un-Islamic. This war involved at its peak 75,000 Egyptian troops, and ruined what chance Nasser had of getting on good terms with the United States, which under President Kennedy had started to woo him again. This would have enabled him to reduce his dependence on Soviet support; instead, Yemen became a drain on resources and added to intra-Arab tensions. After the June 1967 war with Israel, Egypt had to accept defeat and withdraw its forces.

More than anything else, it was the June 1967 war with Israel that undermined Nasserism. Nasser had deliberately upped the ante in the preceding months but then could not cope with what he had unleashed. He first expelled the UN force from the Sinai and then imposed a blockade by closing the Straits of Tiran. Israel realized it could expect no help from a Vietnam-preoccupied United States. Reluctantly, Prime Minister Levi Eshkol accepted the arguments of the generals that the country dare not wait until it was attacked but must take the initiative. The subsequent campaign was conducted with startling efficiency. Within a week, Israel had pushed Egypt out of the Sinai Peninsula and Syrian forces away from the Golan Heights. Jordan lost all territory to the west of the Jordan River. Suddenly Israel was more than three times its previous size. Nasser's bombastic rhetoric of glorious victory was revealed to be without foundation. After the humiliation, Nasser offered to resign. Although he accepted popular calls to stay, the aura was gone. By 1970 he was dead.

✷   ✷   ✷

The 1967 war created a vacuum in radical Arab politics. The Israeli occupation of the West Bank and Gaza aggravated further the grievances of the Palestinians; and with their Arab supporters weakened they sought to gain control over their own struggle. When the Palestine Liberation Organization (PLO) was founded in 1964, it was closely tied to Nasser. It was given to exaggerated talk of battle, revolution, and liberation and not taken seriously. Its charter spoke of the illegality of Israel and denied the right of the Jews to be considered as "one people with an independent personality." Initially, the land over which it claimed sovereignty specifically excluded the West Bank and Gaza, for they were then spoken for by Jordan and Egypt. After the 1967 war, the question of whether they should confine themselves to liberating these occupied territories, accepting that the core Zionist entity would remain, was one that even the pragmatists found hard to address. The PLO was taken over by the Fatah group led by Yasser Arafat, who appeared to have a more practical approach to armed struggle and guerrilla warfare. Fatah, however, was not the only faction in the PLO. The second largest was George Habash's Popular Front for the Liberation of Palestine (PFLP), which was backed by Syria and embraced Marxism-Leninism, describing the Arab struggle as part of a wider anti-imperialist struggle. The first modern terrorist event is normally identified as the hijacking of an El Al flight from

Rome to Tel Aviv on July 22, 1968, by George Habash's PFLP. Most of the passengers were released at Algiers, but seven crew members and five Israeli passengers were held hostage for five weeks until the Israelis agreed to an exchange for Palestinian militants in Israeli prisons. Habash argued that the publicity from such events was far more valuable to the cause than the deaths of Israeli soldiers in battle. These bold acts did not stop the PFLP from suffering from factionalism. Another group, the Popular Democratic Front for the Liberation of Palestine (PDFLP) believed in more ideological struggle and not just military action, stressing in good Marxist fashion class rather than nationality.

The centrality of the Palestinian cause meant that it was impossible for any Arab leader to ignore. Most states, certainly the more radical of them, sought to influence the PLO's policies and behavior by developing ties with at least one of its factions. This encouraged the factions to outbid each other in their aggression. As a result, the PLO became not only self-important but also unruly, growing in militancy, and intolerant of those who urged moderation or contemplated any sort of deal with Israel. The ideology of armed struggle led to futile attacks on Israel and gradually became expressed in acts of international terrorism, often supported by extreme leftist groups in the West that adopted the Palestinian cause as their own, especially after the cause of the 1960s—Vietnam—lost its potency.

In the first instance, the most likely victim of this militancy seemed to be Jordan rather than Israel. King Hussein wanted to recover his lost territory. This required negotiations with Israel, but he did not dare move against the currents of Arab opinion. Although he did manage informal, secret talks, he could never risk a separate peace. The PLO added to his difficulties by using what remained of his territory to mount attacks against Israel, which resulted in the inevitable Israeli reprisals. By now, the Palestinians had become a significant section of Jordan's population. Arafat used the prestige gained by mounting attacks from Jordanian territory against Israel to bolster his leadership of the PLO. Within Jordan, the Palestinians began to set up a state within a state and to act with impunity when mounting raids against Israel, while refusing to accept any attempt by the government to assert authority. Tensions grew when Jordan accepted UN Resolution 242, which set peace for land as the basis for an Arab-Israeli settlement. Hussein was denounced by Palestinian groups who then began to plot his downfall. As if a series of attempts to assassinate him were not bad enough, the king's patience was also tried by a spectacular series of aircraft hijackings, concluding with a number of aircraft being gathered by hijackers at Dawson's Field, an old RAF base in Jordan. This was the final straw. On September 16, the king declared martial law and began to attack Palestinian headquarters and units. The fighting was vicious. A further complication arose when the Syrian-backed Palestine Liberation Army (PLA) intervened. Only when Israeli aircraft began to fly over the PLA's tanks, demonstrating their vulnerability, did it withdraw. The Americans prepared a full intervention to help Jordan if necessary. At the end of the month, Nasser brokered an agreement between the king and Arafat that allowed Palestinian fighters to operate so long as they stayed away from the cities. The strain, however, caused Nasser to have a fatal heart attack.

The immediate consequence was that the agreement was stillborn, so the king pressed on and within a month had reached another agreement with Arafat, this time securing the dismantling of Palestinian bases and asserting his control over his kingdom. With thousands dead on both sides, the Palestinians retired from Jordan. But they were bitter about what they called "Black September" and expanded their ambitions to acquire Jordan along with Israel for their new Palestinian state. Another consequence was that the Palestinians set up their bases in southern Lebanon, where the government was much weaker. The destabilization of Lebanon turned out to be more calamitous than that of Jordan. Syria was also destabilized. The defense minister, Hafez al-Assad, a Ba'ath activist who had been an opponent of the union with Egypt, came to power in a coup. Assad then effectively turned Syria into a one-party state. He was an Alawite, a minority sect close to Shi'ism that deifies Muhammad's son-in-law, Ali. Because this represented only 10 percent of the population, and went against the faith of the majority Sunni population, Assad was even more secular than the other radical regimes. A contrast at the time was Libya, the most recent state to overthrow a pro-Western monarchy in 1969. There, Colonel Mu'ammar Qadhafi, who mounted the coup, sought to create his own revolutionary creed through a mixture of Islam and socialism, which left the clerics deeply unimpressed but at least demonstrated the growing influence of religion on radical politics as Nasserism lost its allure. Assad could take no such risks. He therefore stressed Arabism, which came at the expense of Kurds, and suppressed the Muslim Brotherhood, which gained adherents as the Sunni population became increasingly disaffected.

★   ★   ★

The succession to Nasser also had far-reaching consequences. Vice President Anwar Sadat had been Nasser's associate in the agitation leading to the officers' revolt and he remained by his side thereafter. He never gave the impression of having distinctive views or ambitions of his own. When Nasser died,

Sadat was the natural replacement, at least until arrangements were made for a more permanent leader who was likely to be close to Moscow. Sadat was, of course, perfectly well aware of this possibility, and as he had no desire to accept an interim status, he was planning from the start to take Egypt on a different course. Even as Nasser was being buried, Sadat made known to the American delegation in Cairo for the funeral that he wanted to shift from the pro-Soviet orientation of the past fifteen years. The underlying calculation was straightforward. The connection with the Soviet bloc had brought only failure in war, economic stagnation, and an impasse on the dispute with Israel, which left Israel holding on to the Sinai Peninsula. The country could not move forward unless it escaped from the confrontation. The Soviet Union was not judged to have been a reliable ally. It did break relations with Israel as a gesture of solidarity with the Arabs, which had the effect of ensuring that it was of no use as a potential mediator. The Americans could play this role, offering serious economic support and helping the country avoid the socialist distortions introduced by Nasser.

Even though neither the Americans nor the Israelis appreciated the opportunity he was trying to give them, Sadat pursued his course. The pro-Soviet group found themselves out of government, and in 1972 Soviet advisers were abruptly told to leave Egypt. The Nixon administration had been skeptical, but the sudden prospect of removing such an important Third World state from Soviet influence appeared as a big prize and Sadat was actively courted. The predominant role of Warsaw Pact weaponry in the Egyptian armed forces meant that there was little choice but to patch things up in the buildup to the 1973 war, though in the aftermath Sadat once again discarded his former patrons. On October 6, 1973, Egypt launched a surprise attack against Israeli forces in the Sinai, ostensibly to reclaim the territory captured during the 1967 Six Day War but more to gain revived international engagement and create a new balance of power with Israel. Even though the military strike was only initially successful, and within two weeks had been completely reversed, it was a psychological victory. The Egyptians were pleased to dwell on the unexpected military achievements of the first days of the war rather than their eventual defeat, but they knew that the war had confirmed their limited ability to change the regional map by force of arms. Rarely mentioned at the time, but sufficiently often for it to be recognized as a factor, was Israel's nuclear capability. If Arab armies really looked like they were going to march on to Tel Aviv, then there could be a terrible retribution. Arab military options were running out, so diplomatic opportunities had to be taken more seriously. After the October war, with Secretary of State Henry Kissinger acting as intermediary, forms of tentative diplomatic engagement began. By September 1975, Egypt had signed two disengagement agreements with Israel and so recovered a portion of its territory, to be followed by a limited agreement involving Syria's Golan Heights that November. Syria, Libya, and Iraq continued to reject the possibility of recognition of Israel, and with their client Palestinian factions caused ructions within the PLO when Arafat began to hint that the best they might achieve would be a binational state. Yet the PLO was able to establish itself as heir to the West Bank, and despite Jordan's protests, this was recognized at the 1974 Rabat Arab summit.

★   ★   ★

The 1973 war triggered a major shift in the international oil market, giving tremendous leverage to the oil-rich powers of the Middle East. The shift was overdue. Until the 1970s, the price of oil had been both stable and cheap. It had hovered at around $3 a barrel since the late 1950s, though in real terms this meant a decline of about 20 percent. At the start of the decade, U.S. domestic oil production peaked. By 1973, production was already failing to meet the rise in consumption, so imports were growing. As the U.S. dollar (in which oil was priced) was also weaker, Third World oil producers were seeing their revenues go down. This added to their already substantial sense of resentment. Those for whom crude oil was their main source of income, and who had come together in 1960 as the Organization of Petroleum Exporting Countries (OPEC), were convinced that it was underpriced. With the decline in its own domestic production, U.S. influence over the oil price also declined. Demand reached the point where it was vulnerable to even relatively small changes in supply. OPEC now had its chance. Petro-politics was about to move to center stage.

The seven Arab members of the organization had a secret agreement to take joint action in the event of a new war with Israel. When this came in 1973, they imposed an embargo on those countries that supported Israel. Initially this was targeted at the United States and the Netherlands, although it was later extended. It was never going to be precise in its application. Any shortages affected the global price, which shot up from $3 to $12 per barrel. Iran, which continued to supply oil to Israel during the crisis, still raised its prices, judging with its fellow OPEC members that the oil companies would not be able to do much about it. The embargo ended in March 1974, but the economic consequences were still working themselves out, and the price did not fall.

The sudden rise of OPEC transformed international relations. Countries that had either been colonies or the next best thing seemed to have found a way to turn the tables on Western countries. The control of the Arab producers over such a vital energy source was one explanation for the speed with which the European Community adopted a relatively pro-Arab stance in November 1973. Compared with the 12 percent of oil the Americans took from the Middle East, the Europeans took 80 percent. The big Arab oil producers became important not only because of their influence over the price of oil but also because they were accumulating extraordinary wealth as they received revenues they could barely absorb. Only sales of advanced weaponry appeared to provide unlimited opportunities for recycling the petro-dollars. The mid-1970s turned into a boom period for arms manufacturers, feeding the oil producers' apparently insatiable appetite for modern weaponry. In general for Western states it was not so good. Stock markets collapsed and economies contracted. There was an unusual combination of inflation and recession.

It took time for American policymakers to come to terms with the rise of OPEC. There was a cursory consideration of whether the best response to a future embargo would be a military takeover. When asked about the possible use of military force at the start of 1975, Kissinger had replied that it would be inappropriate in a dispute over price, but not necessarily when there was some "actual strangulation of the industrialized world." This "strangulation" formula was used by other members of President Gerald Ford's administration, including the president, but the impracticalities arguing against such a step, especially given the possibilities for sabotage, were overwhelming. In the event, the trend was in the opposite direction. It seemed wiser to stay friendly with the two rising and vehemently anti-Communist oil powers, Iran and Saudi Arabia, in the hope that they would moderate OPEC's policies. In the short term this policy course, and the accompanying flows of arms, seemed only to be reinforcing existing balances and alignments rather than creating a wholly new strategic configuration.

*   *   *

Over the longer term, there was a more insidious effect. The Palestinian cause was still largely the preserve of radical groups with secular, pan-Arabist origins. Outside of the PLO, leftists were weak. Within individual states, Islam rather than socialism was starting to become the inspiration for radical movements. This was the start of the second radical wave, although at first the role seemed more reactionary than radical. The Muslim Brotherhood supported King Hussein in his battle against the PLO in 1970. Sadat purged Soviet supporters and released the Muslim Brotherhood leadership from prison to counter any continuing leftist influences. This worked, and the

Brothers were soon diverting support away from the leftists in the universities. But he could not control the direction of the debate, especially in the mosques, one of the few places where radical ideas might still be nurtured and propounded. The clerics claimed that the effects of this shift to religion were evident in the improved military performance of 1973 as compared to 1967. The battle cry under Nasser had been "Land! Sea! Air!" Under Sadat, it was "Allah Akhbar!"[2]

The full implications of this trend were obscured for a number of reasons. It was a transitional period. The hold of leftist and pan-Arabist ideals had not yet been broken, while the political implications of an Islamic critique of society had yet to be felt. Up to this point, the political role of Islam was largely judged in the West to be positive and essentially conservative in its effect. A region in which Islam was so strong was never going to be fertile ground for atheistic communism. This could be seen in the continuing tension between socialistic regimes and Islamic movements. But a transformation was occurring because of a changing social setting. Middle Eastern populations were, following dramatic population growth, younger (by 1975, 60 percent were under twenty-four). People had also moved from the villages to the cities, creating urban masses, economically disadvantaged and susceptible to the polemics of radical Islamists. Under the banner of Islam, one could now find social revolutionaries as well as conservative elites.

As Sadat removed the restraints imposed by Nasser (although not the formal ban), the Brotherhood soon flourished, opening new mosques, schools, and banks. While the senior members of the Brotherhood were prepared to play the political game with Sadat, those who had emerged from years in prison or clandestine organizations were more intolerant and took on new political forms, separate from the old guard. They certainly dealt with the leftists, initially chasing them out of the universities, but their determination to impose their religious values on the whole society made them an increasingly intimidating and antidemocratic presence. By 1974, they were turning their attention to Sadat himself. He tended to play down the significance of the virulent rhetoric of the young Islamists. It took until 1977 before the Egyptian president started to realize the potency of the force he had helped to unleash. The Islamists were never going to tolerate his interest in peace with Israel. By 1978, Sadat's experiment was concluded, but as he tried to rein in the Islamic movement, he found it could not be turned off as easily as it had been turned on.

The Saudis had provided the Brothers with a base after they had been expelled by Nasser, and they continued to nurture them as a weapon to be used against secular leftists. When Sadat started to court the Brothers, the Saudis provided enthusiastic support. In both countries there was a belief that there was a close fit between religious and political conservatism, and that young hotheads could be manipulated, for use against enemies, but controlled if they looked like they might go too far. Here the Saudis took the greatest risks, as they assumed that the best way to prevent the Islamists' causing trouble was to encourage them to direct their energies elsewhere. Wahhabism set such standards for religious observance that up to this point, it had lacked mass appeal beyond Saudi Arabia. It was generally considered to be too purist and sectarian for clerics who wished to stay close to the traditions of their local populations. Now it was gaining influence among the young Egyptian radicals, many of whom had spent time in Saudi Arabia. The Saudis also had the funds to proselytize on a grand scale, with the objective of breaking the hold of nationalists on public opinion, gaining friends by demonstrating charity and goodwill, and keeping their own clerical establishment content. This "Petro-Islam," to use Gilles Kepel's phrase, encouraged the notion of a wider community of Islam beyond the Arab world, with a shared concept of struggle.[3]

*   *   *

It was not only the oil and the Arab-Israeli dispute that were causing the Americans to pay more attention to the Middle East. Britain's traditional role as the leading great power in the region, undermined by Suez in 1956, was now at an end. Britain had been accused of being too pro-Israel during the 1967 war and then had suffered an ignominious retreat from Aden (now part of Yemen). In 1968, it gave up almost completely when it decided at a time of economic crisis to withdraw from its military role "East of Suez." By abruptly abandoning its role as protector of the small Gulf sheikhdoms and accepting diminished influence in Iran and Saudi Arabia, the British created a vacuum. The conservative monarchies now looked to the United States to help them deal with threats from both the Soviet Union and the radical states. As they were often also the custodians of the larger oil reserves, their anxieties were difficult to ignore, despite their autocratic nature and Saudi Arabia's hostility to Israel. If these "twin pillars" became strong enough, they could contain any Soviet adventurism without the previous levels of reliance on American support. Under the post-Vietnam "Nixon doctrine," the preference was always to boost local forces rather than commit those of the United States to deter local threats.

The main threat was still assumed to be the Soviet Union, working through radical, secular regimes such as Egypt, Syria, and Iraq. The reason to worry about any source of instability in the region was the probability

that it would be exploited by Moscow. Indeed, to some the very fact of instability was sign enough that Communist agents were at work. For Washington, this created a strong predilection in favor of the status quo. If the
established power structure was strong enough to resist Soviet influence,
that was a strong point in its favor, even if the relevant regimes were hardly
paragons of liberal democracy. If divisions opened up among American
clients, then the United States must work toward reconciliation, lest any division create opportunities for Moscow. Israel was always a particular difficulty. Because all Arab countries were hostile and refused to grant it any
legitimacy, this was a ready issue for the radicals to exploit. It was a natural
thought that if only the United States could resolve Israel's disputes with its
Arab neighbors, life would be a whole lot easier.

The basic objectives for American policy in the Middle East therefore were
to keep the oil producers sweet, reduce Soviet influence, and sort out the
Arab-Israeli conflict. By the mid-1970s, progress was apparently being made.
Iran, Saudi Arabia, and the other Gulf states appreciated the great attentive-
ness to their needs and wishes. The October 1973 war warned of the region's
continuing potential as a flash point in the cold war. Toward the end, as Israeli forces threatened the beleaguered Egyptian Third Army, the Soviet
Union appeared to be preparing its forces to mount a rescue. The United
States moved all its forces, including nuclear, to the highest level of alert—
DefCon (defense condition) Three. While both sides were probably bluffing
at a time when President Nixon was also beleaguered as a result of the Watergate scandal, this was still a reminder of how a proxy war might escalate to
disaster as the superpowers weighed in on behalf of their clients. The year
1973 was in fact the last time there was any such risk. Soviet relations with
most of its Middle Eastern clients were already uneasy and its position was in
long-term decline. After the war, it was Kissinger who negotiated the disengagement agreements between Israel and the two Arab belligerents, Egypt
and Syria. In addition to lowering the level of tension, this established the
United States as best placed to broker a large peace deal. That in itself was a
symptom of Soviet decline. The main reason for the decline was that the radical regimes that had caused the problems in the past were suffering their
own crises of legitimacy. The benefits of links with Moscow had become
questionable in terms of the limits of the Soviet economic model. Possibly
more important, the limits of Soviet military equipment when pitted against
Western equipment in the hands of the Israelis had also been revealed. After
Egypt abandoned the Soviet Union for the United States, Iraq hedged its bets
by developing a close relationship with France. Syria remained more loyal but
was wary about becoming too isolated.

The Arab states looked to the United States to broker a deal because they believed Israel was so dependent on American financial and economic assistance that it would have little choice but to accede to American wishes in pursuit of a settlement. Despite the supposed political clout of American Jews, until the 1960s relations between the United States and Israel had been cool. The Eisenhower administration found Israel a complicating factor in its relations with Arab states and was irritated by its belligerence. It resolutely refused to sell its arms on the grounds that Israel was capable of looking after itself without help. Should the United States start arming Israel, Washington then argued, it would just encourage the Soviet Union to reinforce its military relationship with the Arabs, resulting in an arms race or even worse, should a conflict lead the two superpowers to feel obliged to get involved. Better for Israel, the argument continued, if the aim was to secure a lasting peace with the Arabs, for the United States to be in a position to do the mediation. Better also for the United States, lest too close an association with Israel annoy powerful Arab states, jeopardize access to oil, and create opportunities for the Soviet Union.

The difficulty with this line of argument was that the more the frontline Arab states got from the Soviet bloc, the more Israel would be at risk if it had to make do with old equipment or what could be obtained from France and Britain. It also required some evidence that U.S. attempts to stay friends with the more radical Arab states, and in particular Egypt, could produce real breakthroughs in their political orientation and readiness to deal with the Israelis. Furthermore, the promise of arms sales also provided some potential leverage over Israeli policy. With the Kennedy administration, the arms policy began to be relaxed—first with air defense missiles and then tanks. When in 1967 France switched its favors from Israel to the Arabs, having concluded that this was the better side to back over the longer term, the United States had little choice but to become Israel's primary supplier. Deliveries of Phantom aircraft were the first manifestation of this. During the October 1973 war, when Israel was at its most beleaguered, rocked by the early Arab advances that were held back only with great effort, the United States stepped in with a massive airlift of vital military supplies. The Arabs saw this as demonstrating the huge potential American leverage over Israel, which they assumed could readily be translated into the sort of pressure that could extract major Israeli concessions in any negotiations. The Israelis had a similar fear. They had found their desperate dependence on American supplies in the middle of the 1973 war to be a source of both anxiety and political vulnerability. For this reason, after the war they accumulated huge military stocks for their reserves. High expectations that the United States would be able to put sufficient pressure on Israel to change course were thereafter usually frustrated.

Israel was prepared to be stubborn in defense of its security. The sweeping gains of 1967 had given it formidable bargaining chips, although they could only serve this purpose if there was a real willingness to bargain them away. After the experience of 1956, Israel was not going to return captured territory meekly without proper peace treaties with its Arab neighbors. Even though battered and humiliated, at first the Egyptian and Syrian governments refused to contemplate what they considered surrender terms and decided to preserve their dignity and prepare for the next round. In August 1967, Arab states gathered at Khartoum and promised to continue the struggle and insisted on the three "no's"—"no peace with Israel, no recognition of Israel, no negotiations with it, and insistence on the rights of the Palestinian people in their own country." Yet two months later, in November, the UN Security Council unanimously adopted Resolution 242. It called for the "withdrawal of Israeli armed forces from territories occupied in the recent conflict" and "a just settlement of the refugee problem," but also the "recognition of all established states by belligerent parties of each other and . . . the establishment of peace and secure and recognized boundaries for all parties." At the time, it was accepted only by Israel and Jordan. The resolution implied a trade of captured land for peace, but the peace on offer was ambiguous.

In the context of continuing hostility, the Israeli priority was to use the acquired land to improve their security so they would never feel so vulnerable again. That meant using the new borders for the first line of defense, keeping the Arabs on the other side of the Suez Canal and the Jordan River, and away from the high ground of Golan. Their security calculations were complicated by two factors. The first was that it was hard to look at all the captured land in functional terms. The West Bank in particular was not just any land but full of sites that recalled Bible stories and throbbed with religious meaning. The remaining western wall of the old temple was in East Jerusalem, from which Jews had been barred when it was under Jordanian control. Second, there was a demographic element. There was a tradition of using settlements to establish claims to contested land and guard borders. Although illegal under the Fourth Geneva Convention, it was considered tempting nonetheless. The movement that was eventually known as Gush Emunim reflected the conviction that it was a religious duty to settle the historic land of the Jewish people, even if this meant ignoring the law and rebuking the authorities. By February 1968, there were ten outposts with 800 people in the "administered territories." At the time of the May 1977 election,

when the advocates of settlement gained power, there were nearly eighty settlements with a population of 11,000, in addition to annexed East Jerusalem
where 40,000 now lived. Compared with the hopes of the settler movement,
these numbers were not large, but they did enough to blur the borders of the
state. In some cases the rationale was security, to thicken Israel's thin waist
or to help hold the Golan Heights. In other cases, claims were being established to land because of its religious significance, even if this started to en-
croach on Palestinian land.[4]

Although the Palestinians of the West Bank and Gaza had initially been
quiescent under the new regime, and indeed began to enjoy economic benefits through their association with Israel, this was not a stable situation and
over time was bound to become more unstable. The Israelis could not agree
on what to do with the Palestinians. There was no appetite for their incorporation into the Israeli state. At the time, Israel's Jewish population was just
under 2.4 million, and its Arab population was less than 400,000. The combined populations of the West Bank and Gaza added around another 1 million, still leaving Jews in the majority. Over time, however, the higher Arab
birthrate would tell. So if the Palestinians were granted the same rights as
the existing Arab population of Israel, then their numbers would come to
threaten the demographic balance within the state; if they were denied these
rights, then Israel would be putting itself in the position of the colonialist.
From the start there was a conundrum: Israel wanted the land and not the
people—or as Prime Minister Levi Eshkol put it, the dowry without the
wife. If the people could not be expelled, then they must be granted some
form of self-government.

The ideal was an agreement with Jordan. This would have suited King
Hussein, but he never dared go against the tide of Arab opinion. This was
why he had lost the territory in the first place. Despite Israeli messages not to
get involved, and unaware of the extent of the blow already delivered to the
Egyptian air force, he felt in June 1967 that if he did not join this great pan-
Arab enterprise he would be denounced forevermore. After a year, there was
a secret meeting. Jordan was now prepared to accept the prewar borders and
grant some rights in East Jerusalem, for the king a big concession, but Israel
now wanted to move on. It expected all of Jerusalem, where it offered the
Arabs rights, and wanted to hold strips of land of strategic importance.
There was no deal. Worse, in 1974 the Rabat summit pushed aside Jordan's
claim to the West Bank. Yasser Arafat's Palestine Liberation Organization,
with its faith in armed struggle and its commitment to eliminate the Jewish
state, appeared to be an impossible interlocutor.

The support given to the PLO in the United Nations, with Arafat treated as a head of state while Zionism was denounced as racism, and the appeasement of oil-rich Arabs by European governments, hardened Israeli attitudes. Israeli governments became torn between conflicting pressures and imperatives, and were as inclined to postpone fateful decisions as grasp them. Personal and political rivalries canceled each other out and added to the paralysis. By leaving unresolved the big questions of land and peace, of settlements and occupation, and by their inability to agree on firm boundaries for the state and preserve areas for future concessions, the Israeli government left the way open for popular movements to reshape the debate. The peace camp warned of the total lack of international support for the settlements and the developing Palestinian resentment. The voice of the peace camp tended to be less strident than that of the settlers, aware of their vulnerability to charges of playing fast and loose with national security. They lacked the activists who were prepared to set policy through their own efforts. On the other hand, the October war, while confirming Israeli military capabilities, demonstrated the dangers of complacency and the consequences of remaining on hostile terms with their neighbors. With 2,656 dead over nineteen days, it felt like a defeat. All this had softened up the region to expect diplomatic movement. Although plans were rife, all based on variations of the land-for-peace theme, the basic questions—what it would take to get the Israelis to hand back Sinai and the Golan Heights to Egypt and Syria, and how political rights of Palestinians were to be met—still lacked definitive answers.

By 1977, therefore, when Jimmy Carter came to power, the region was in a transitional state. The first radical wave was well past its peak. Its decline threatened the legitimacy of the secular, nationalist governments it had helped bring to power. The second radical wave was starting to gather pace, but it was as yet unclear whether this was a harmless, largely conservative and antileftist force or something that could develop into a destabilizing and disruptive force in its own right. The period was transitional in another sense for the United States. With Britain no longer a major regional player, Soviet influence declining, and oil an increasingly important consideration, the Americans were being drawn more into the politics of the Middle East. In particular, they were seen to be unusually well-placed to address the neuralgic issue of the Arab-Israeli conflict.

PART ONE

JIMMY CARTER

★ ★ ★

3

CAMP DAVID

Jimmy Carter reached the White House in the aftermath of the Watergate scandal, which had led Nixon to resign and demoralized the Republicans. Cynicism in foreign policy and dirty tricks in domestic politics could be presented as being of a piece. During the 1976 election campaign, Carter scored as an upright, decent, and religious man who would seek to do what was right as much as what was expedient. He gained the Democratic nomination by offering a way to transcend the arguments that split the country and the party. As a governor, he had yet to be corrupted by Washington politics. As a southerner, he could draw on one part of the party's traditional base, but as a progressive, he could do so without alienating the rest. Carter did not see it as his task to make America feel good about itself. His inclination was to confront harsh realities.

He inherited a country that had been buffeted by a series of economic and foreign policy crises. Vietnam still cast a long shadow. The country was cautious about further military adventures, especially if ground forces were likely to be involved over an extended period. The military certainly shared the view that in the future, it would be best to avoid interventions in messy Third World conflicts, with their unclear battle lines, an enemy able to move in and out of the local population to catch you by surprise and tempt you into atrocity, and where decisive victory was unobtainable. The military mission was to prepare for big wars against big enemies, most likely the

Soviet Union in Europe. Its doctrine, weapons procurement, and training were refocused accordingly.

While the military prepared for classical warfare, the civilians engaged in classical diplomacy. Henry Kissinger, the dominant figure in U.S. foreign policy during the Nixon-Ford years, was a student of the masters of nineteenth-century Great Power statecraft. He sought to arrange the exit from Vietnam, and then manage the consequences, through a series of deals with North Vietnam's allies, the Soviet Union and China, who also happened to be deeply hostile to each other. By drawing the two Communist giants into a complex web of relationships, taking advantage of both their mutual wariness and their search for ways to revive their struggling economies, Kissinger sought to encourage détente.

By the time he left office at the start of 1977, Kissinger's achievements, which had seemed dazzling a few years earlier, no longer seemed quite so impressive. One reason for this was that the Soviet Union did not appear to observe the constraints of détente as seriously as the United States. The suspicion grew that President Leonid Brezhnev had concluded that the "correlation of forces" had moved in the Soviet direction, so he was taking advantage of it by acquiring footholds in the Third World. In addition, any strategic choice that involved accommodating Soviet power apparently required ignoring constant ideological repression, abuses of human rights, and regular violations of treaty commitments. One consequence of this growing distrust, even disgust, was the rise of neoconservatism. Although more recently it has come to be associated with Republicans, its origins are in the security-minded wing of the Democrats and the reaction against the party's takeover by antiwar supporters of presidential candidate George McGovern in 1972. If there was an early neoconservative political leader, it was Democratic senator Henry Jackson, effectively supported by his congressional aide, Richard Perle, who demonstrated his potential influence by challenging the Strategic Arms Limitation Treaty of 1972, and then, with Representative Charles Vanik, making support of most favored nation status for the Soviet Union conditional on allowing Jews to emigrate. Until Ronald Reagan recruited some prominent neoconservatives into his administration, the debate between the neoconservatives and more mainstream liberals played out within the Democratic Party. The starting critique may have been of soft liberals, but the argument had been developed against the foreign policies of Richard Nixon and Gerald Ford. The Republican Party was associated with Kissinger's "realist" approach, taking a clear and unsentimental view of national interests rather than attempting to improve individual nations or make the world a better place.

Carter sought to unite his party by straddling its foreign policy divide, not so much by following a woolly middle way but by pursuing the more idealistic aspects of the two competing traditions. The liberals could applaud his suspicion of cold war rhetoric and his proposals to wean the American people away from their fixation with the Soviet Union, cut back on military expenditures, and control the arms race. In another respect, he was with the neoconservatives in his conviction that, however awkward for the geopoliticians, there had to be a moral core to American foreign policy, and that this should involve stressing human rights and democracy. A man of evident integrity, he aimed to recover the standing of the United States, with fewer deals with dubious regimes, forged in secret and cemented by arms sales.

His knowledge of foreign affairs was limited, but he could pride himself on being a quick learner, surrounded by an impressive foreign policy team. The collective impact of their experience was to qualify his idealistic urges but also to generate tension at the heart of policymaking, for individually they represented different political tendencies. His national security adviser—Zbigniew Brzezinski—seemed to follow in the Kissinger mold of hyperintelligent and hyperactive professor of foreign accent and hawkish disposition. By contrast, Cyrus Vance was a traditional secretary of state, with a long history of public service and a patrician bearing. These tensions, and in particular the competition between the distinctive approaches to foreign policy within the person of the president, were disconcerting for both friends and adversaries, although mainly for allies. Any authoritarian regime, whether Communist or anti-Communist, would be challenged by the promotion of human rights; but a president disinclined to use military force could prove to be more of a problem for allies, as they would be uncertain of the reliability of security guarantees.[1]

Acknowledging the work done by Nixon and Ford in easing tensions with the Soviet Union, establishing relations with China, and getting out of Vietnam, Carter soon focused on the Middle East.[2]

★   ★   ★

The Carter administration did have a blueprint for the peace process. This was found in a set of proposals in a Brookings Institution study of 1975 in which key figures in the new administration, including Brzezinski, had been members. It also provides a useful summary of the conventional wisdom of the time within the U.S. foreign policy community. The report stressed the danger of another war "with perilous and far-reaching consequences." This gave urgency to the situation that could not be met with more interim arrangements that left the basic elements of the dispute untouched. Hence, the group argued for a comprehensive settlement. This would be an integrated package, providing for security as all parties committed themselves to respecting the sovereignty and territorial integrity of the others and refrained from the use of force; a staged withdrawal to the boundaries of June 4, 1967, with few modifications but safeguarded by demilitarized zones; and the end of all hostile actions, including blockades, boycotts, and propaganda attacks against Israel to be replaced by the development of normal economic and political relations. With regard to the Palestinians, they should have self-determination so long as they accepted Israel's sovereignty and self-determination, although the report was agnostic as to whether this should be a separate Palestinian state or an autonomous unit within Jordan. No solutions were suggested with regard to Jerusalem, other than to insist on free movement within it and the potential political autonomy for national groups within the city. Because a settlement of this sort would not be reached if it had to rely only on those directly involved, "initiative, impetus, and inducement" might well have to come from outside. That essentially meant the United States.[3]

The conviction that this was the time for a comprehensive approach represented an important departure from the incremental, step-by-step approach adopted by Kissinger. Incrementalism assumed that taking the easier issues first would help the parties understand each other's perspectives and gain confidence as they realized that deals could be agreed to and made to work. They could gradually move on to more difficult issues, until one day they would realize that they were effectively "at peace." Success depended on gathering momentum, providing the impetus to move through a set of progressively more difficult issues. Otherwise the process would grind to a halt. The advantage of a comprehensive approach was that the trade-offs necessary for a final agreement could be arranged through one grand set of interconnected bargains. The problem here was the "all-or-nothing" quality. Should negotiations break down, there would be nothing to show for the effort, other than even higher levels of distrust and a discredited process. Just setting up such a conference could involve tedious negotiations over procedural matters, often as mundane as seating arrangements, which were seen to encapsulate wider issues of basic principle. The trick was to entice all the different interests and parties into a single room and then into signing a final document. One awkward customer could create an impasse, and the Middle East was not short of awkward customers. Excluding the awkward customers, however, would lose comprehensiveness. In practice it was best not to move to such a conference until a sufficient level of preparedness and support had been sorted out in advance.

The underlying formula of "land for peace" was deceptively simple. Israel held land to which it had no right but was denied a peace it deserved. Israel's reluctance to return some of the seized land for a mixture of security and ideological reasons was well-known, but the Arab reluctance to offer peace was less well understood. Recognizing the "Zionist entity" was a big step for countries that had always resented a Jewish state on Arab land. Hostility to Israel served as a rhetorical rallying point, helping to legitimize regimes, such as that in Syria, where Hafez al-Assad otherwise had little else to offer his people. There was then the problem of the refugees from 1948, determined to return to the territory from which they had fled, many still stuck in camps that were preserved as a symbol of Israel's perfidy. De facto recognition of Israel might be a pragmatic necessity for Arab regimes. It might even be possible to end the formal state of war. But de jure recognition—according Israel the full respect due a sovereign state, with diplomatic and commercial relations—appeared a step too far. Yet Israel could not contemplate any lesser form of peace, and until proper recognition was on offer would not relinquish the land that gave it leverage and additional security.

The engineer in Carter almost seemed to relish working out how the elements of the complex Middle Eastern scene could be brought together to form a functioning whole. He was prepared to learn as much as he could about the problem and by the end of his presidency could claim considerable mastery of its more arcane detail. He could draw upon numerous schemes and plans, including the Brookings report. His inclination was to work backward from what seemed to him to be a self-evidently sensible deal, which would serve everybody's true interests, rather than move tentatively forward from intransigent starting points. If the end point was in grasp, then the more unwilling elements would fall into line lest they lose out. He would involve the Soviet Union if that gave the radicals some comfort, while Saudi Arabia would be encouraged to use its newfound, oil-fueled political status to encourage the more recalcitrant Arab countries to accept compromise. A diplomatic push would come as no surprise: One was widely expected, and the underlying conditions seemed as promising as they had ever been. The United States was best placed to bring together the key players.

*　　*　　*

By October 1, 1977, Carter seemed ready to go. That day the United States and the Soviet Union issued a joint communiqué on the Middle East. The two superpowers, having convened the December 1973 Geneva conference, now wished it to be reconvened in the coming December. There was a need to achieve "as soon as possible, a just and lasting settlement of the Arab-Israeli conflict." The settlement should be "comprehensive, incorporating all parties concerned and all questions." It would lead to the "withdrawal of Israeli Armed Forces from territories occupied in the 1967 conflict," but this would be balanced by the "termination of the state of war and establishment of normal peaceful relations on the basis of mutual recognition of the principles of sovereignty, territorial integrity, and political independence."

The use of the adjective "normal" before "peaceful" was a new formulation. This gained less attention than another novelty, at least from the American side, in the call for the "resolution of the Palestinian question, insuring the legitimate rights of the Palestinian people." Here the previous formulations had spoken only of "legitimate interests." The communiqué went on to discuss the role that the two superpowers might play as guarantors of any agreement. These aims could only be achieved in the "framework of the Geneva Peace Conference." All parties should be involved, including "representatives of the Palestinian people."

One problem with this communiqué was that its origins were only partly connected with the Middle East. Cyrus Vance wanted to include the Soviet Union to show that there was still life left in détente and the two could work in partnership together. He recognized Brzezinski's concern that the Soviets might act as spoilers but took the view that this was more likely if they were excluded. Moscow's actual role in Washington's frantic, preparatory diplomacy prior to October had been marginal at most. If it had one in the future it would probably be to influence the response of the Syrians and the PLO. Another problem was that it was something of an act of desperation, a device to cut through the procedural knots that had been tightening over recent months as the Americans discussed with all relevant parties how to get the process under way. In the event, instead of providing the final push to a Geneva conference, the communiqué ensured that it never happened. Instead of providing the groundwork for a comprehensive settlement, it set in motion a bilateral deal between Egypt and Israel, and so set back for a decade any movement on the Palestine question. The reason for this was that the document had been put together with little thought as to its likely impact on the two key players in any peace process—Israel and Egypt.

*   *   *

The most enthusiastic regional promoter of a new peace effort was Anwar Sadat. Although Sadat was described as the "Hero of the Crossing" as a result of the opening salvo of the 1973 war, he did not enjoy, either in Egypt or the Arab world more generally, anything approaching Nasser's prestige and authority. Furthermore, in spite of economic reform, new Western investment, and substantial U.S. aid, Egypt's economy continued to decline, resulting in work strikes and riots over food shortages. Sadat feared that time was running out. His restlessness was reflected in a tendency to act in a bold and impetuous manner. He was given to grand gestures and impatience with detail. Vance described him as "strong on principles; weak on implementation."[4] His restlessness was also a product of a deeper political bind. He knew that a separate peace with Israel would be denounced by the rest of the Arab world, but he believed trying to reach an agreement that would satisfy the others could delay matters indefinitely. His relations with Assad of Syria were particularly poor. He assumed, with some justice, that Assad's main interest in the process was to prevent a separate Egypt-Israel deal rather than to achieve anything positive for Syria. Nor, having just broken with the Soviet Union, was he excited by the prospect of working with the Soviets again, especially as they were most likely to reinforce Syrian intransigence. His commitment to a Geneva conference was therefore not deep. He could see merit if it provided a form of cover for substantive agreements, well prepared in advance, but not as a negotiating forum in itself.

What he really wanted, and here he was not unique among Arab leaders, "was an American plan that the United States would impose on Israel."[5] He had great faith in America's ability to sort out Israel, and so his strategy was to get as close to Carter as possible. This was a clever move. Carter always placed great store in personal relationships. He sought friendship with foreign leaders, and if they appeared distant and cold, his attitude toward them was affected. He never achieved harmony with Israeli leaders. Another example was Syria's Assad. When he first met him in Geneva, Carter declared him a close friend after a few minutes' acquaintance, but this soon soured.

Sadat, meanwhile, played Carter masterfully. There was genuine warmth between the two men, reinforced by the coincidence of their views. When they first met in April 1977, Carter was excited by this "shining light" that had "burst on the Middle East scene." Here was someone both committed to peace and prepared to show flexibility.[6] For example, though Sadat's first response to the proposition that there would have to be full recognition of Israel was "not in my lifetime," when Carter insisted that nothing else would work, eventually Sadat conceded that this was something he must explore to get the Sinai returned. In a later interview, Carter became quite lyrical about Sadat:

> He put faith in me to protect Egypt's interests. No matter what I did, he felt that I would never lie to him. . . . It was kind of an immediate sharing of trust. And when someone puts implicit faith in you, you are just

not going to betray them. And I felt the same way about him. . . . Sadat
saw himself as the bold leader who would make history. And he saw me
as an eager ally.[7]

Other members of the administration were less sure. Brzezinski described
Sadat as warm and gracious, but added "even ingratiating," and noted his
occasional difficulty in distinguishing fact from fiction and his tendency to
become carried away by his own words.[8]

The contrast between Carter's relations with Sadat and those with Israeli
leaders was stark. This was largely because of what he was asking of them.
They were not enamored with a comprehensive approach, suspecting that it
would serve as a pretext for Arabs to avoid direct negotiations. The Israelis
would be constantly on the defensive at a conference, because the only thing
the other participants could agree on was what they should give up. They
preferred to deal with Arab states directly and individually. Yet with individual states Israelis believed in comprehensive deals. Once in direct negotiation with an Arab state there was no easy first step, and whatever was agreed
on with regard to territory, Israel had to have recognition in return. Otherwise there was no point.

The Israelis would have been happy to continue with Gerald Ford and
Henry Kissinger. Getting the American relationship right was an imperative
for any Israeli government. Faced with a new president and his bright ideas,
they were inclined to play along until the harsh, underlying realities of Middle Eastern politics asserted themselves. In this case, however, the Israelis
were up against a strong policy consensus in Washington, certainly shared
by Vance and Brzezinski, that they had to make the big compromises for
peace. They were used to the underdog position, a small brave democracy
facing the unrelenting hostility of much larger and more numerous Arab
autocracies. When it came to the Palestinian question, they were now taking
on the appearance of the oppressor, but resented the label. Carter was certainly influenced by this appearance. The parallels he saw with the situation
of blacks in the American South help explain the intensity with which he
embraced the Palestinian cause.

Carter's enthusiasm for the task led him to ignore the politics of the situation. It has become a commonplace observation that the U.S. ability to put
pressure on Israel is constrained by domestic politics, and in particular the
role of the Jewish community in electoral politics. Up to this time this had
been an important but not overwhelming factor. The Jewish vote was largely
tied to the Democrats, so when Republicans such as Nixon and Ford did
something deemed harmful to Israel, they were put under pressure but were

largely able to cope. Up to this time, the blockages to peace had been seen to come from the Arabs, not Israel, while the Palestinians had lost sympathy because of their associations with terrorism and their destabilization of first Jordan and then Lebanon. The land-for-peace formula had broad support in Israel as well as the United States, although the scope for contradictory interpretations of what this might mean for Israel's security was already evident. Initially, Carter took Israel's backers in the Democratic Party and Congress for granted and did not draw them in as supporters for the difficult times ahead. Hamilton Jordan, the White House chief of staff, later observed that the Jewish lobby was "something that was not part of our Georgia and Southern political experience and consequently not well understood."[9]

Carter was insensitive to the position of Israel's prime minister. Yitzhak Rabin had been chief of staff of the Israeli Defense Forces (IDF) at the time of the 1967 war, then served for a spell as ambassador to Washington, and was only elected to the Knesset, the Israeli Parliament, in 1973. A year later, with Israel still reeling from the October 1973 war, he became prime minister. As he showed during his later spell as prime minister in the 1990s, Rabin had important qualifications for peacemaking. He had demonstrated a tough-minded devotion to his country's security, yet was known to be ready to withdraw from the seized Arab territories. In 1977, he was, however, in political trouble at home, with an election scheduled for May. For the first time since the foundation of the state, the once dominant Labor Party was under threat, weighed down by the intelligence failures leading up to the October 1973 war, allegations of corruption, and infighting at the top. This had left Rabin almost immobilized, unlikely to move until he had a more secure government. The last thing he needed was a public quarrel with the United States over matters of fundamental strategic interest. Hoping that Carter's support might bolster his position, when he arrived in Washington in March, he discovered instead a president in a bold and determined mood, disregarding the Israeli political calendar.

Rabin's short political career had never depended much on charm and warm embraces. Carter found him an unsympathetic figure, reserved, introverted, and not given to expansive gestures. He had seen the Israeli prime minister as a "kind of peg on which I could hang my whole Mideast peace ambitions," yet Rabin turned out to be "absolutely and totally uninterested, very timid, very stubborn, and somewhat ill-at-ease. The fact was that he had no interest at all in talking about negotiations. It was just like talking to a dead fish."[10] As the discussion progressed, Rabin became even warier. Carter was dealing casually with issues that were fundamental to Israel's security, while suggesting penalties for not going along with his own cavalier interpretations of what was best. Rabin wanted to leave any shifts in Israeli policy until after the elections, especially if any private concessions were likely to be immediately leaked.

Rabin was first undercut on the question of arms sales. This was a topic on which Carter had strong views. He was appalled at weapons being traded for short-term commercial gain without any thought for the long-term damage they might do. His determination to dampen the trade hit Israel in two areas. The transfer of cluster bombs was refused, although this was an area where Rabin thought he had an agreement left over from the previous administration. In addition, Israel was refused permission to sell Kfir fighters to Ecuador, because they had American engines. All this indicated that Israel could expect no special privileges from the new administration.

Even more challenging was Carter's description of Israeli settlements in the West Bank as illegal and demands for changes in how the occupied territories were governed. Rabin was looking for an arrangement with Jordan. This was a long-standing objective of the Labor leadership, which had always seen King Hussein as the natural partner for peace. Although the West Bank had been Jordan's territory and the kingdom still declared an interest, since 1974 the Arab League had supported the PLO's claim. From both the American and Israeli perspectives, the king was the preferred interlocutor, but his freedom of maneuver was limited. Carter sensed that the PLO could not be so easily disregarded. He wondered aloud about drawing the organization into the negotiations, should it signal its seriousness by accepting UN Resolutions 242 and 338 and abandoning those elements of its charter that called for Israel's destruction. Resolution 338 was the cease-fire resolution for the October 1973 war. It concluded by asserting that "immediately and concurrently with the cease-fire, negotiations shall start between the parties concerned under appropriate auspices aimed at establishing a just and durable peace in the Middle East." It was unnerving for Rabin to be told that "it would be a blow to U.S. support for Israel if you refused to participate in the Geneva talks over the technicality of the PLO being in the negotiations."[11] After the summit, when Rabin suggested in public that Carter supported the idea of defensible borders, rather than simply those in place on June 4, 1967, the White House issued a clarification, which increased the sense of estrangement.

After a sobered Rabin returned to Israel, Carter continued to talk openly, but also loosely, about the 1967 borders and a homeland for the Palestinians. He responded to a question at a town hall meeting in Massachusetts by observing, "There has to be a homeland provided for the Palestinian refugees who have suffered for many, many years."[12] This remark apparently brought tears to Arafat's eyes and was welcomed by the Palestine National Council. To the Israelis, however, Carter was conceding the PLO's basic demand without getting anything in return or thinking through the political consequences—for Israel, Jordan, or the United States. At the same time, he was undoubtedly gaining in credibility in the Arab world.

It is unlikely that Labor would have won the election of May 17, 1977, if Carter had been more solicitous of Rabin's political needs in March. After all, Rabin felt obliged to resign as prime minister before the election, in April, as a result of a relatively minor scandal surrounding an illegal bank account held by his wife, Leah, during their time at the Israeli Embassy in Washington. Nonetheless, the next months would have been a lot easier for Carter if there had not been such a major shift in Israeli politics. Labor lost one-third of its votes, and so the right-wing Likud (Unity) Party became the largest in the Knesset and formed a government. The Americans were quite unprepared for this turn of events. They knew little of the new prime minister, Menachem Begin, and what they did know they didn't like.

Begin had been a Zionist militant since his youth in Poland. When the Nazis invaded, his family was slaughtered but he escaped, reaching Palestine via the Soviet Union. As World War II closed, he became a leader of the Irgun, a movement dedicated to liberating the country from British rule, if necessary by violent means. After independence he founded the right-wing Herut Party. Other than his membership in the national unity government at the time of the 1967 war, he was in constant opposition. He left the government in 1970 in protest at Israel's acceptance of Resolution 242, and then formed the Likud coalition. Begin was an unlikely politician. In a country that treasured informality, he always wore a jacket and tie. In a country where military men had a special status, he lacked military experience, although he was pleased to have a number of former generals in his government, as if their very presence demonstrated a determination to stay strong.

Begin was guided by his inner convictions and had little interest in international opinion, which he assumed to be hostile to Israel as a matter of course. He was more than just on the extreme end of a known spectrum, and therefore capable of being brought back to the center ground through inducements and threats. His whole philosophy was different from that of the Labor leaders who had governed Israel up to this point. For him, Israel's legitimacy derived from biblical times, and this meant that Israel had an "unchallengeable, eternal, historic right" to the West Bank, which he described as Judea and Samaria, as well as Gaza. Begin had no interest in a deal with Jordan and was not worried that the oft-stated view of his housing minister, Ariel Sharon, that the best way to deal with the West Bank Arabs was to ship them into Jordan, was ringing alarm bells in Amman. He did, however, see advantage in a deal with Egypt and realized that Sadat might be a willing partner.

It took time for the Americans to get the measure of Begin, to realize that he did not assert a tough position for bargaining purposes but rather because he meant it and that, despite his austere formal manner and his legalistic approach, he was also a tricky operator. If his statements were not contradicted directly, he would claim agreement: Positions never made explicit could not be assumed to be implicit. Only gradually did they appreciate that he truly believed in Judea and Samaria and was committed to more settlements whatever the impact on the negotiations. Carter later observed that Begin never gave him a pleasant surprise,[13] yet the president showed enormous patience, finding ways of appealing to Begin's sentimental side, through talking of family and sharing their knowledge of the Bible.

The initial response of the administration to the new Israeli government was to go into denial. Begin's views on the exclusion of the West Bank and the PLO from future talks were disregarded. There was a glimmer of light in the appointment of Moshe Dayan as foreign minister. Dayan had been the strongman of 1967 but had been caught out by the surprise Egyptian attack of 1973. Begin brought him into government to demonstrate some flexibility and continuity, though Dayan had limited success in getting the Americans to appreciate the new Israeli position. Although he was anxious to limit the damage caused by Begin's drive to build new settlements, which he thought was mistaken, when he tried to explain the position to Carter, he was told, "You are more stubborn than the Arabs, and you put obstacles on the path to peace."[14]

The developing dismay in Israel was soon reflected in the American Jewish community. No attempt had been made to consult with their leaders, many of whom were unconvinced by Likud's policies, to explain how Carter's initiatives might work to the benefit of Israel over the longer term. Brzezinski's memoir shows the development of the problem. After the first public utterances in March about the Palestinians, Jewish opinion in the United States began to be aroused. Brzezinski thought this unfortunate, because as yet there were "no Arab concessions to show for our efforts." It was helping create the "impression that the new Administration was tilting away from Israel." Then in addition to the arms sales issue, by late May, Carter was talking about "reparations for the Palestinians" without making it clear that this would only be in the context of a comprehensive settlement. Brzezinski felt this required action, perhaps using Vice President Walter Mondale to repair relations with the American Jewish community. Once these issues were

out in the open, they were harder to control. Thus, when Carter tried to redeem himself with an impassioned statement of his commitment to Israel,
the "word" in the Jewish community was that if "they press hard enough the
President will yield."[15]

Carter's political mistake lay not in his opposition to Israeli settlement activity in the territories. Any U.S. government would have taken the same position. Where he took an unnecessary risk, alienating the Israelis and their
supporters for little purpose, was in his futile pursuit of the PLO. This was
the main thing that unnerved Israelis and Jewish opinion in the United
States that might otherwise have supported Carter in a showdown with Begin on the settlements issue. His foreign policy team did not understand
how objectionable it appeared to many Americans, not only Jews, to even
hint at engaging with a group mainly known for bloodcurdling rhetoric and
aircraft hijackings. It should also have been apparent that none of the Arab
governments wanted the PLO to have an independent voice in any negotiations. They all claimed to be able to speak *for* the Palestinians. Nor would the
PLO disavow its charter without being sure this would mean the Palestinians
would get hold of the West Bank and Gaza, for this was their only bargaining
card. The Geneva conference did not even require the presence of the PLO,
as there was an agreed plan for a unified Arab delegation that would include
notable Palestinians, but not PLO members.

*   *   *

Nine months' activity since Carter's inauguration had demonstrated a desire
to make urgent progress on the Middle East and on all fronts at once. The
Americans held secret and open meetings with the various parties, reached
what they thought were tacit understandings, issued statements, drafted
treaty language, and described procedural fixes to get around whatever obstacles were being put in the way of the historic conference that would, once
and for all, deal with this exasperating dispute. Quandt described how the
Americans "seemed to feel the need to knock on almost every door in the
hope that one would be opened."[16] The activity was not always mutually reinforcing. Messages were implicit and explicit, deliberate and inadvertent,
and so the signals to the different parties became muddled, and the whole
effort risked grinding to a halt. The joint invitation to the conference, issued
with the Soviet Union on October 1, 1977, brought matters to a head.

The Israelis were infuriated by the joint statement's emphatic references to
Palestinian rights and representation, and also that such an important document had been negotiated with Moscow and not them. The more paranoid
saw the Great Powers preparing to impose a solution upon them. Belatedly,

Carter sensed the political danger. He asked to meet Moshe Dayan in New York on October 4. The discussions began with Carter and Vance putting pressure on Israel to accept not only the communiqué but also the procedures that had already been agreed on with Arab governments on how the Geneva conference should be conducted. Carter warned the Israelis of international isolation if they continued to resist. Dayan retaliated with a threat of his own—to mobilize Jewish opinion against the administration.

He was something of a celebrity after his role as Israeli defense minister during the 1967 war and knew how to play American politics skillfully. Quandt thought it a mistake for Carter to even talk politics with Dayan, because it immediately gave him an opening.[17] Brzezinski watched, appalled, as rather than warning Dayan not to challenge the president of the United States in such a way, Carter instead "leaned over backwards to be reassuring, accommodating, pleasant, and gave Dayan the impression that he was not dealing with someone who was very tough."[18] In effect, Dayan "blackmailed the President by saying that unless he had assurances that we would oppose an independent West Bank and that we would give them economic and military aid, he would have to indicate our unwillingness in his public statements here in the United States." The result was that Dayan and Vance were tasked to produce a new working paper that contained the Israeli concept of a conference, one which would almost immediately split up into a series of bilateral and disconnected encounters with individual Arab delegations, and a mechanism to ensure that Israel could object to attempts to get the PLO included or a Palestinian entity discussed. Even this caused some difficulties with Begin because this was the first time Israel had accepted the possibility of Palestinian representation. The more Dayan traveled in the United States and talked up the October 4 document, the more the political pressure on Carter eased and the prospect of a conference faded.

Sadat was unimpressed. He could live with the joint U.S.-Soviet statement, despite his dislike of the Russians, because the content was acceptable. What had now been agreed on with the Israelis suggested that Carter lacked the determination to impose his will on them. This Sadat assumed to be the precondition for an agreement. Since the other Arab states would insist on keeping the bilateral meetings connected, if only to stop Israel and Egypt from reaching a separate agreement, the prospect now was of protracted squabbling over procedures and agendas with no actual movement on substance. As it became evident that Geneva was not going to happen, Carter looked to Sadat to inject some new momentum. In a handwritten letter of October 27 to his friend, Carter acknowledged the impasse and urged Sadat to consider some "drastic action." Carter may have thought this would be directed toward Syria or the

PLO, but Sadat was planning something altogether different, and had been doing so for some weeks. The Egyptians and Israelis had been in touch since September. Neither was at all eager to engage with the Soviet Union, Syria, or the PLO. Without telling the Americans, emissaries discussed the possibility of direct talks should Sadat visit Begin in Israel.

So that he could not be talked out of his plans, Sadat did not bother sharing them. On November 9 before the Egyptian Parliament, with Yasser Arafat in the audience, he announced that not only was he ready to go to Geneva, but he "would go to the end of the world to spare an injury to one of our men, much more the death of one." He then slipped in his bold gesture: "Israel must be greatly surprised to hear me say that I am even ready to go to the Knesset and discuss with them." It took a while for it to sink in that he meant what he said. A common initial reaction was that this was rhetorical fluff. It was unlikely that Begin would respond and, if he actually did send an invitation, that Sadat would accept. But though many in Israel suspected a trick, this was not an offer they could refuse. The symbolism of an Egyptian president visiting the Israeli Parliament was too good to miss. Out went the invitation; back came the acceptance.

With their intense focus on getting to Geneva, the Carter administration was nonplussed by the sudden turn of events. Sadat's announcement demonstrated a lack of confidence in their plans. It might also lead to separate deals, neglect of the Palestinian issue, and alienation from the rest of the Arab world. The Israelis were unlikely to be inspired into a reciprocal gesture. This was not a government that compromised deeply held convictions in the enthusiasm of the moment. In the end, however, the administration could hardly object to two old adversaries getting together.

Nor, already under severe criticism for consorting with the enemy, was Sadat going to depart from mainstream Arab positions on the various requirements for peace. In his speech to the Knesset, he claimed to be speaking not only for Egypt but for the Arab nation and the Palestinian people. He offered a compelling vision of accepting Israel as a reality and living in peace, of "no more war"; but in return there had to be a complete withdrawal from all the occupied lands, an "Arab Jerusalem," and Palestinian self-determination. In his reply, Begin welcomed Sadat, expressed his own hopes for peace, but also said he wanted negotiations to proceed without preconditions as to where they might lead. He gave no hint of movement on any of the key issues.

The genuine emotion of the occasion encouraged unrealistic hopes that the two sides could each move sufficiently closer to find the basis for an agreement, even without American help. It soon became painfully apparent that while both sides wanted peace, this could not be on any terms, and their terms were still far apart. The Syrians and the PLO were furious with Sadat. They well understood that extracting the Egyptian threat would simplify Israel's military planning and leave it immeasurably strengthened in its dealings with the rest of the Arab world. The Israelis had the same understanding, so Begin pressed the case for a separate peace, but still refused to accept that this would require any major concessions on his part. The Israelis admired Sadat for going out on a limb, but feared that he was so far out on a limb that he might easily be cut off by those in Egypt, never mind the rest of the Arab world, hostile to his move.

Begin understood that the status quo was not tenable, but that did not mean he was going to follow standard Arab demands. He did not have a simple concept of territory, population, and government. This was reflected in his proposals for Palestinian autonomy without sovereignty, which involved holding firmly on to the West Bank and Gaza while accepting the need for forms of Palestinian self-government. This demonstrated some flexibility, but nothing that would impress an Arab audience. In addition, the same reasoning meant he could envisage returning land to Egypt without uprooting settlements.

In December, Sadat called a preparatory conference in Cairo, boycotted by all other Arabs, attended only by the Israelis and the Americans, with whom no progress was made. The next month there was an equally disastrous meeting in Jerusalem, at which an already miserable Egyptian foreign minister, Muhammad Ibrahim Kamel, was patronized and rebuked in equal measure by Begin. This was partly because Begin was coming under pressure from his own hard-liners, who distrusted all deals with Arabs and sought a harsher tone. Kamel's treatment brought discussions to an abrupt halt. All this added to Sadat's continuing and deep sense of frustration. He was being denounced as a traitor and an honorary Zionist, making humiliating homage to those who had caused the Arab nation such distress, and risked having nothing to show for the effort.

With the Geneva proposal now dead, Egyptian-Israeli talks offered the only area of possible movement, and even they were foundering. To get the talks back on course, the Americans got more engaged, but movement was still slow. The initial engagement of the Americans saw the differences narrow, but not sufficiently. Sadat was getting even more impatient, so much so that, to the alarm of his aides, he started to place Egyptian needs on a far higher plane than the Palestinians, let alone the Syrians. If he was going to be denounced whatever he did, then he was less inclined to sacrifice Egyptian interests for the sake of calls to stay solid with countries and leaders that he generally held in contempt. Carter also was starting to conclude that an Egyptian-Israeli agreement was all he could get in the first instance.

In February, Sadat visited Washington for the first step, where his charm and moderation gained him political ground. Begin's visit in March was delayed by a Palestinian attack on a bus that killed thirty-five Israelis. If the timing was intended to derail any peace process, it almost succeeded. Soon the Israelis launched Operation Litani into southern Lebanon. They were seeking out PLO bases, but by the time they arrived, most of the militants had escaped. Not for the last time, the civilian population suffered. The Israeli incursion caused about 1,000 casualties and many more refugees. Carter was furious. This "disproportionate" action led to U.S. support for a UN vote condemning Israel, combined with exasperation with Begin's stubborn disinterest in Palestinian rights and insistence on building illegal settlements. The Israeli government began to move deeper into its bunker, preparing to add the United States to its list of antagonists. In July, a meeting at a secluded castle in the United Kingdom helped move things back on track a little, at least in terms of officials getting to know each other, develop some trust, and open up the difficult areas for discussion. Relations between Begin and Sadat, however, remained poor. Carter therefore decided to move forward with an idea that had been germinating for some time. He sent a handwritten note to each man with an invitation to a summit at the president's retreat at Camp David, Maryland.

★　　★　　★

On September 5, 1978, Sadat and Begin arrived at Camp David with their delegations. Normally, the settings for great diplomatic efforts are public buildings, government offices, and the occasional hotel room. At Camp David, Carter hoped to keep the media at bay and offer a relaxed and secluded atmosphere for serious discussion. It did not turn out to be a relaxing affair. Compared to the warmth shown by Sadat, Begin was a constant source of exasperation. Despite the relaxed informality of the Americans, he always looked, observed Brzezinski, as if he were going to a funeral. He often implied that that was in fact what he was being asked to do. The asymmetry worked in another direction. As Avi Shlaim has observed, whereas on the Egyptian side, Sadat was flexible while his delegation was rigid, on the Israeli side, "Begin was obstinate, while his delegation was flexible and even indulgent." Dayan and defense minister Ezer Weizmann had their work cut out preventing Begin from closing all doors to an agreement. "There were times," wrote Dayan later, "when only by clenching teeth and fists could I stop myself from exploding."[19]

Sadat was hoping to turn his friendship with Carter into a joint plot to ambush Begin. In this he overestimated the extent to which any American president could appear to collude with an Arab state against Israel and underestimated the extent to which he wanted a deal more than Begin did. Begin came to Camp David reasonably confident in his position. He may have suspected some Egyptian-American concoction, but he was the one who held the territorial cards and he understood the limits of presidential pressure. He had a promise from Carter not to use Israel's economic and military dependence on the United States to force him into concessions he could not defend with good faith before the Knesset. He had been stubborn with Sadat and he was prepared to be stubborn with Carter. On the other hand, if the negotiations broke down, he did not want to take the blame and was nervous about the idea of competing for American influence with Sadat.

Carter's starting assumptions were that the truly bilateral aspects of a deal—the conditions under which Israel would withdraw from Sinai—would not be too difficult, for here some progress had been made, but the most challenging issues were connected with the wider peace, and in particular the Palestinian issue. When Kissinger had arranged disengagement agreements after the 1973 war, Egypt had done the first deal and then Syria had come along later. Carter hoped that with sufficient momentum, Jordan, and then Syria, could be drawn in with Saudi Arabia in support. This was always optimistic, even if Begin had been prepared to offer something substantial on the wider issues. More alarmingly for Carter, Begin was even reluctant to withdraw completely from the Sinai. Israel had been acquiring stakes in Sinai—settlements, airfields, and an oil facility—that he did not want to relinquish. Begin had allowed his officials to discuss these issues in negotiations but not to make concessions. As far as the West Bank was concerned, he could be persuaded not to pursue a claim to sovereignty, but he was not going to renounce the possibility.

Carter was advised that because of their mutual irritation, it might be wise to keep Begin and Sadat apart to start with. The president, however, preferred a more personal approach. It was not only animosity but tactics that caused this approach to fail abysmally. Sadat had worked out his opening gambit. This would begin with his maximum demands. Carter would then ask for concessions, having already been told that these would be forthcoming. Begin also intended to start with a hard stance but, unlike Sadat, without any hint of softening.[20] Sadat began with his maximum demands. Begin fumed quietly, and then suggested leaving his points till the next day, giving no chance for Egyptian concessions. The next day, he offered a point-by-point rebuttal, starting with the areas he found most objectionable—the suggestion of a separate Palestinian state and the redivision of Jerusalem. Sadat charged him with wanting land more than peace. The main result was to stoke further the personal antagonism between the two men. If Carter thought that in a few days he could move through an agenda in a businesslike manner, he now realized that this was going to be more difficult and take longer—assuming that the two men did not just walk out and return home.

Soon the process settled down into progressive responses to a series of American drafts, of which there were twenty-three in all. Sadat by and large conducted the negotiations on his own, with his advisers fretting in his rooms that he was giving away too much. Soon the larger issues, against which Sadat would eventually be judged by his Arab peers, became descriptions of a drawn-out process of indefinite duration, with other Arab governments coming in at various stages. Meanwhile, the issue of Israeli settlements in Sinai became the sticking point. Begin, furious with Brzezinski for likening the settlements to colonies (Brzezinski had replied that it is how they would be viewed in the Arab world), continued: "I want you to understand that my right eye will fall out, my right hand will fall off, before I sign a single scrap of paper permitting the dismantling of the Jewish settlements." Dayan later told Sadat, "Mr. President, if anybody has told you that Israel can leave the Sinai settlements they are deluding you."[21] This produced a crisis. After concluding that he was not even going to get a bilateral deal, Sadat prepared to go home. Carter, realizing that the situation was desperate, went to Sadat's cabin, where the suitcases were already packed, and asked if they could talk. An immediate departure, Carter warned, "would harm the relationship between Egypt and the United States." He would also be "violating his personal promise to me," thereby damaging "one of my most precious possessions—his friendship and our mutual trust."[22] He persuaded Sadat to allow him one more chance. The compromise was eventually found by Begin's agreeing to ask the Knesset to decide to take a step that went against his own convictions. This was acceptable to Sadat.

This agreement had been reached with an extraordinary commitment of energy and ideas from the American president. Each time they wanted to walk away, they had to calculate the costs of such a deliberate snub to the president. What, though, did they achieve? It was a collection of agreements rather than a treaty. It fudged difficult issues. But most important, it offered a complete Israeli withdrawal from the Sinai in return for normal relations. There was to be a "just, comprehensive and durable settlement" of the conflict through peace treaties. When it came to the West Bank and Gaza, the "legitimate rights of the Palestinian people" were acknowledged to be achieved through "full autonomy" after five years, which to Begin meant that this was the maximum they could expect. The mechanisms were left vague, from setting when the five years would begin to the absence of any commitment to full withdrawal, and also deciding how to replace a military government and civilian administration with a self-governing authority. Settlements and Jerusalem were not mentioned, and it would take little imagination to work out that not much was going to happen about refugees.

✴   ✴   ✴

Once he was committed to a negotiation, Sadat was in a weaker position. He never deviated from his conviction that he had to have the whole of the Sinai returned and the Israeli withdrawal had to be complete, but after that everything was detail, including the views of his fellow Arabs. He had reason to believe that he had achieved language on Palestinian autonomy on which others might build, but there was no one on the Arab side prepared to take the political risks he was taking, and Begin was soon wriggling away from whatever commitments he had made by exploiting the ambiguities of the language in which they had been couched. Sadat was mainly concerned that Begin allow him to claim with a modicum of credibility that this was not a separate peace but was linked in some way to the wider issues. With neither Begin nor Sadat making much of an attempt to persuade other Arabs that there was a lot in Camp David to interest them, it was left to the administration to point out the references to Palestinian rights, but it was hard to be persuasive when neither of the main protagonists was taking them at all seriously.

A further complication came from events in Iran, where the shah was deposed in January 1979. This was seen as a failure for Carter and added to his need for an offsetting success, but it also removed a key supporter of Camp David and a partner of both Egypt and Israel. It created a particular difficulty for Israel, because Iran had been its oil supplier. There was an oil well in the Sinai that Begin was reluctant to give up. Additionally, there was not much time left before Carter's decisions would have to be increasingly influenced by the demands of the coming year's election campaign. Brzezinski, who worried about these matters more than Vance, sent a note to Carter on January 23, 1979: "I am firmly convinced for the good of the Democratic Party we must avoid a situation where we continue agitating the most neuralgic problem with the American Jewish community (the West Bank, the Palestinians, the PLO) without a breakthrough to a solution." He was starting to conclude that the Israelis would like to see Carter defeated. As the election got closer, the president would find it even harder to convince Begin that he had any leverage over him.[23]

Most damaging was Begin's continuing attachment to settlements. At Camp David, Begin appeared to respond positively to Carter's call for a freeze on new settlements, but appearances had been deceptive. Carter considered this sabotage, observing that "there was never any equivocation when we left Camp David about the fact that there would be no settlements during the interim period, during which we would be negotiating the final peace agreement."[24] Begin was in trouble with his own right wing, so he got only two-thirds of his own coalition voting for the accords at the end of September. Facing opposition from some of his erstwhile closest friends, Begin started to row back. He combined the cabinet's support for the Camp David Accords in October with an announcement that the West Bank settlements would be expanded.

Against this background it proved to be extremely difficult to turn the accord into an Egyptian-Israeli Peace Treaty. Vance, who was not short of patience and staying power, described the negotiations as "appallingly tedious."[25] There were questions of timing, so that the more symbolic steps, such as exchange of ambassadors, would only be taken when there was confidence that everything else was on track, but also questions of principle. Sadat wanted to start Palestinian self-government in Gaza, where Egypt had an interest. Although the territory itself was of less interest to Begin than the West Bank, the security implications seemed more serious, because it was a finger sticking into Israeli territory. The Americans were also unconvinced because they wanted to keep the Palestinian issue together. The real problem was that Begin was becoming averse to any discussions on Palestinian self-government, even his own autonomy plans, because he feared that they would soon turn into discussions about Palestinian independence and sovereignty.

There was just not enough here on which to build anything else. King Hussein was cross that the issue of Jordanian sovereignty over the West Bank had been ignored and plans were being made for this territory without consulting him. A man who was a natural for the moderate camp was turned into a rejectionist. The balance of risks—which the king spent his life calculating and recalculating—argued against participation in a process that was offering him little and was soon bitterly opposed by everyone else in the Arab world. Carter later acknowledged that he should never have allowed Sadat to even suggest that he was speaking for King Hussein, but it betrayed a certain naïveté to even begin to think that he could. The king remained furious with Carter for putting him in such a difficult position. Just as Sadat's bold diplomacy showed what could be achieved, at least on a limited front, King Hussein's unavoidably more cautious diplomacy carried on through secret talks that never quite produced anything tangible and continued to leave the most explosive problem in limbo. The West Bank could not be annexed by Israel or returned to Jordan or handed over to a new Palestinian state.

In March, Carter decided to visit Egypt and Israel. Vance judged this to be a "breathtaking gamble and an act of political courage." Carter described it himself as an "act of desperation," against which he was strongly advised by those who felt he was setting himself up for a fall.[26] As expected, his visit to Egypt was rapturous and unproblematic. Israel was a different matter. Carter found the discussions with Begin impossible. There was no give and lots of demands. Yet when Carter spoke to the Knesset, he could also see that Begin was by no means the most extreme and was being hounded by his old colleagues from the right for the modest concessions already made. Frustrated and despondent, Carter decided that he might as well go home. It looked as if he had failed and that was how it started to be reported. Now at last Israeli ministers found their voice, as many took fright at the implications of both losing the chance of a treaty with Egypt and being blamed by a furious Carter. Weizmann went so far as to threaten to resign. Begin relented to the extent that he allowed others to make the concessions that he would not touch himself.

Quickly there was agreement on the schedule for Israeli withdrawal from the Sinai, a U.S. guarantee of a supply of oil, and a timetable for the exchange of Egyptian and Israeli ambassadors. When he stopped back at Cairo to pass on the good news to a relieved Sadat, Egypt's new foreign minister, Mustafa Khalil, asked for further revision. Carter now could take no more: "For the last 18 months, I, the president of the most powerful nation on earth, have acted the postman. I am not a proud man—I have done the best I could—but I cannot go back to try to change this language."[27] On March 26, 1979, the Egyptian-Israeli Peace Treaty was signed with a grand ceremony on the South Lawn of the White House.

One lesson that has been drawn from this episode is that peace deals are more likely when hard-liners are in government, both because they are forced to appreciate the realities of the situation and because they are unlikely to be effectively challenged from the right. Given the polarized nature of the Israeli debate, there is some truth in this observation, although it may be more accurate to say that with hard-liners in power, there is a chance for peacemaking but their predispositions mean that it is still rarely taken. Without Carter's efforts, there would have been no deal between Israel and Egypt at this time. Begin always gave the impression that he would rather have been doing something else and disliked being opposed by his usual political friends. The American role in brokering the first serious breakthrough in normalizing relations between Israel and its neighbors was crucial, but it implicated the United States in the major failure of Camp David. The strong impression was left that those involved cared little about the Palestinians and had no idea how to address their growing grievances.

4

REVOLUTION IN IRAN

CARTER'S PRESIDENCY was marked more than anything else by his failure to cope with the Iranian revolution. According to one view, he caused the revolution in the first place by insisting on pursuing a human rights campaign in complete disregard of the particular political conditions prevailing in Iran. According to another, the problem was the opposite. Having been convinced of the country's geopolitical importance and the goodwill of the shah, he jettisoned the principles on which he had been elected and put the United States on the wrong side of a popular revolution. Either way, his administration was caught out by the intensity and dynamism of the revolutionary process. The president and his senior aides only really truly appreciated the fragility of the shah's regime late in the day, which left them scrambling to prevent a foreign policy disaster. In the course of this scramble, all the underlying divisions within the administration were exposed, leading to a confused set of responses that in some way matched the shah's own confusion. Faced with a choice, possibly illusory, between encouraging a military crackdown and establishing productive links with the opposition, they achieved neither. Then, once the new regime was in place, any chance of developing proper relations was lost by a failure to appreciate the sensitivity of the American connection in Iranian politics. Out of this came the hostage crisis, which conveyed a humiliating sense of American weakness. The result was that rather than the United States controlling regime change in Iran, Iran was able to effect regime change in the United States.

The hostages returned to the United States on the day of Ronald Reagan's presidential inauguration.

In trying to evaluate the charge sheet, it is important to keep in mind that the root of the problem lay in the mismanagement of his country's affairs by the shah. He had bold ideas for how Iran could become a modern and powerful state, but these were lost in the corruption, decadence, waste, and repression that became hallmarks of his rule. He managed to unite almost all sections of Iranian society against him and then lost his nerve as he floundered in the face of protests and demonstrations. If he had identified a course to follow during 1978 and stuck to it, then the United States would have been obliged to back him, whether he went in the direction of opening up to the opposition, and even abdication, or military rule. It was always going to be difficult for the United States to set a course for the shah.

This was despite the common belief in Iran that it really was the Americans who ran the country. If there was one aspect of the Iranian revolution that the Carter administration constantly failed to grasp, it was the assumption, at times shared by the shah, of a constant conspiracy to control Iranian affairs. The motives imputed to American policymakers were not always completely off the mark, but the assessment of their ability to manipulate affairs was always exaggerated. Not only did the Americans have a limited grasp of the political forces at work in Iran, but they also had few means of influencing them.[1]

* * *

Mohammed Reza Shah Pahlavi was installed as monarch of Iran in 1941 after British and Russian forces deposed his father, who had refused to expel the Germans from his country. The young shah always struggled for legitimacy. In 1953, he lost power to Prime Minister Mohammed Mossadegh, leader of the nationalist National Front Party. He was reinstated after the British and Americans, concerned about Mossadegh's Communist leanings and nationalization of their oil interests, engineered a coup d'état. This was something about which the CIA thereafter remained rather proud, as a model of how these things should be done. The shah himself had left the country after Mossadegh refused to be dismissed. Army officers, backed by a mob, arrested Mossadegh and invited the shah back. He stayed in power, but these events undermined his legitimacy and authority and cast him in the role of an American puppet.[2]

The rapid rise in oil income from 1973 aggravated the shah's problems instead of easing them, as might have been expected. Revenues surged from $885 million in 1971 to $17.8 billion in 1975. He attempted to use them to grow and modernize Iran's economy, as part of his White Revolution, introducing new industries and reducing dependence upon oil, but the effort was too ambitious and the economy could not cope. At the same time, he became obsessed by military strength. The military budget rose from $1.4 billion in 1972 to $9.4 billion by 1977. Partly to balance the trade flows and partly to build up the shah as an agent of American regional policy, Washington made available to Iran almost any weaponry desired.[3] The distorted priorities, corruption, and growing inequalities fed social unrest. So did the increased numbers of foreigners in Iran. By 1978, there were several hundred thousand expatriates, of which 60,000, including 45,000 Americans, were connected with military programs. The cultural impact of the Western connections challenged the Islamic character of the society. Meanwhile, the middle classes, which might have been expected to provide some support for these trends, did not feel that their economic interests were supported and, after one-party rule was established in 1975, were unhappy with the increasingly authoritarian nature of the regime.

During the course of 1976, the shah began to worry where this was leading. Having been diagnosed with lymphoma, he was starting to worry about the legacy he would leave his son, the crown prince, and whether he could widen his political base and do something about the regular condemnation he received from international human rights groups. He was also concerned about a potential shift in American attitudes. During the Republican administrations of Richard Nixon and Gerald Ford, he had been looked after well, indeed rather indulged. Iran was a pillar of stability and a bulwark against communism at a tumultuous time in a turbulent region. The Americans avoided criticism of how the country was run and stayed clear of opposition forces. The shah's magnificence and wisdom were as likely to be praised by Western visitors as by local sycophants. He could point to any item in a military catalog and place an order, and he frequently did. This was made possible by the hike in oil prices, for which the Arab oil producers tended to attract the blame more than Iran. The shah's open preference for Republican administrations was therefore not surprising. As Jimmy Carter's campaign advanced during 1976, the reason for this became clear. Two of Carter's core foreign policy themes—denouncing unrestricted arms sales and disregard for human rights—seemed almost to be directed at him personally.

To the extent that Carter's human rights agenda helped destabilize Iran, as claimed after the revolution, it was mainly at this moment before the election, when Carter was already running a strong campaign, that it had an effect. The shah's anticipation of what might happen should Carter win was one, but only one, reason for some small liberalizing changes that began in

1976 and continued after Carter's victory. The press was given a bit more freedom; SAVAK (the feared National Security and Information Organization) a bit less. In terms of dealing with the new president's preoccupations, this seems to have worked. Carter was prepared to be convinced that Iran was moving in the right direction, that gentle persuasion was working and there was no need for a row with a country that was still evidently vital to U.S. strategic interests. When the new secretary of state, Cyrus Vance, raised the human rights issue in March 1977, it was in the spirit of encouraging a process already under way. Meanwhile, arms sales proceeded as before. At first Carter's new, more restrictive, arms trade policies seemed to apply to Iran. Yet soon the administration was arguing for seven airborne warning and control system (AWACS) aircraft to be sold to Iran. This led to a major—but successful—fight with liberals in the Senate. As late as September 1978, on the eve of his fall, the shah sent a shopping list for equipment worth $12 billion over four years, including fighter, maritime patrol, and tanker aircraft.[4]

Thus, despite the new president's close identification with tough, liberal policies, it took very little to persuade him that Iran was doing enough. To be fair, the shah's preemptive liberalization was more than a token. Grievances were being expressed more freely than before and political activity was gathering pace. Unfortunately for the shah, this did not produce gratitude and greater legitimacy. Instead of relaxing political control when economic and social conditions were improving, he was doing so when they were deteriorating, and there were substantial reserves of pent-up anger. The many promises he had made to his people had not been met, and the much proclaimed White Revolution was faltering. Attempts to cool an overheating economy were leading to increased unemployment. As the political system opened up, the number of grievances in play increased. Moreover, opposition leaders were emboldened because they assumed that this represented less of a genuine change of heart and more American orders. If so, then it would be more difficult for the shah to change his mind and reverse course once again.

Carter did not pay much attention to Iran for the first months of his presidency. In preparation for the shah's visit to the United States in November, Carter was advised that his task was "to establish a close personal relationship and to persuade him of your commitment to a continuation of the special relationship." Although there was no suggestion that his regime was in danger, the tensions surrounding it could not be ignored. Both pro- and anti-shah demonstrators made their way to Lafayette Park near the White House, and there were riotous scenes as they fought. Whiffs of the tear gas used to disperse them reached the two heads of state and their wives as they went through the ceremonial greetings. This emboldened the opposition even more. The administration's failure to stop the demonstrations appeared as an important sign of the limits to its readiness to protect the shah.

Such signs were inadvertent. In a private session with the shah (so as to avoid embarrassment), Carter did raise the human rights issue. He noted the vociferous complaints from the shah's Iranian opponents. Could anything be done either "by closer consultation with the dissident groups or by easing off some of the strict police policies?" Alas, no. The shah explained patiently how the Communists were a severe threat and it would be imprudent to relax. The complaints came from precisely the troublemakers who were out to undermine the country. Fortunately they represented only a small minority of the Iranian people.[5]

If the Iranian opposition thought Carter was being tough, they were soon disabused. The president and his wife, at the latter's apparent instigation, decided to pay the shah a visit at the close of 1977. At a sumptuous feast, Carter, reflecting his tendency to confuse diplomacy with friendship, went out of his way to praise his delighted host. With a touch of hyperbole, insensitive to the seething discontent already starting to grip Iran, the president warmed to his theme: "Iran, because of the great leadership of the Shah, is an island of stability in one of the more troubled areas of the world. This is a great tribute to you, Your Majesty, and to your leadership and to the respect and admiration and love which your people give to you . . ."

He concluded in a similar vein, as was so often the case, suggesting that relations between countries could benefit from warm relations between their leaders. "There is no leader with whom I have a deeper sense of personal gratitude and personal friendship."[6] This was a man he had just met for the second time, and with whom he spoke at most twice on the phone afterward.[7] Having first, albeit inadvertently, given the opposition some hope, the president had now come firmly down on the side of the shah. The timing was even more unfortunate, because the shah had just decided that liberalization had gone far enough and was becoming downright dangerous. As the clampdown came, with customary ferocity, the opposition had no choice but to trace this back to the United States.

*   *   *

In Iran, opposition to the shah was wide-ranging.[8] Among the more liberal opponents were the remnants of Mossadegh's National Front of the early 1950s, which had survived as a loose coalition of reformers and nationalists. They were often joined by jurists, writers, and academics who did not have a wider political program much beyond the need to respect the rule of law and allow basic freedoms. The other traditional focal point of opposition was the Communist Tudeh Party, but it had suffered as a prime target for official repression. Over the 1960s and 1970s, the opposition became more violent. Paramilitary groups initiated guerrilla campaigns. Among these were the mujahideen, who combined Shi'ism with an anticapitalist ideology and a strong nationwide organization, and the leftist Organization of the Iranian People's Fedayeen Guerrillas. They could each claim to be the nucleus of a revolutionary army while their confrontation with the security forces encouraged the regime in its repression. They were both also close to a variety of Palestinian groups, with whom they had often trained.

The living symbol of resistance was the Ayatollah Khomeini, an intense critic of the shah since the early 1960s. Now seventy-seven, he was residing in holiness and exile in the Iraqi city of Najaf, a center of Shia theology. His status as leading ayatollah came from his reputation as a religious leader of integrity and an uncompromising opponent of the shah. Scowling behind a long, thick beard, framed by a black robe and turban, Khomeini offered an uncompromising and unrelenting vision of an Iran free from malign foreign influences and the institution of the monarchy. This vision was articulated in sermons that were reproduced in pamphlets or captured on tapes that were distributed via the mosques and bazaars. The religious networks made it possible to organize and mobilize the masses, appealing to their deep attachment to Islam. Khomeini could take advantage of an extensive network of followers, including his students. His message had been honed over the years and drew on Western philosophy (which he had taught) in ways expected more from leftists than clerics. Khomeini created the broad themes of the revolution of unyielding antimonarchism and sympathy for the poor. This allowed him to keep the leftists on side during the course of the revolution, disregarding the anti-Communist aspects of Islamist philosophy and outmaneuvering the liberal secularists who were loath to abandon the monarchy. As is so often the case in revolutionary times, the old-style politicians, this time the National Front, believed that they would be the natural leaders once a democratic system was established. Already, the religious groups were wary that an open system would permit the return of Western, secular influences.

The shah was particularly incensed by the role taken by the Islamist movement. His response was crude and stunningly counterproductive. An attempt to smear Khomeini in early 1978 led to seminary students rioting in Qom. A number were killed by the police. This in turn triggered more protests in other cities. Over the following months, demonstrations and riots, often violent, became common occurrences. The mosques were at the center of these protests, with religious leaders increasingly prominent. They generalized the challenge away from the repressive nature of the regime toward the malign influence of the West. The cultural and economic symbols of such influence, from nightclubs to banks, became targets. The origins of the fire at the Rex Cinema in Abadan in August 1978, when more than 400 people died, may well have been militants, but there was an early popular readiness to blame the intelligence agency, SAVAK. The shah started to worry. To stem the tide of religious protest, a new government made a number of concessions toward Islamic concerns—for example, all casinos and gambling clubs were closed—but these measures were inadequate. The demonstrations became ever more radical. On the night of September 7, 1978, martial law was declared in twelve cities, including Tehran. The further repression was no more effective than the earlier concessions. On September 9, many people were killed when troops fired into a demonstration at Jaleh Square in Tehran. As the revolution passed through each new stage, the opposition was being radicalized and moderate elements marginalized.

The shah unwisely convinced Iraq to expel Khomeini from his base at Najaf. The Ayatollah ended up in Paris with unlimited access to the world's media. As the acknowledged spiritual leader of the revolution, he gained authority as events appeared to follow his will. Early in November 1978, the leader of the National Front, Karim Sanjabi, traveled to Paris to meet him. The two strands of the revolution were coming together under the demand for the shah to be deposed and formation of a new "democratic and Islamic" government. On this basis, the traditional liberal-nationalists and the Islamists could unite. The revolution's most formidable weapon became the strikes of public sector workers, with oil workers and customs officials to the fore. These were largely led by leftist groups (which later made it hard for Khomeini's emissaries to get them back to work). Their demands moved from being largely economic, which could be met at a short-term price, to becoming more political. By November, economic activity was effectively shut down. Fuel was in short supply, other raw materials could not enter the country, and little could be moved.

The shah brought in yet another new government, this time led by the army chief, who promised to abrogate all laws that did not conform to Islamic principles and to draft future laws "with the guidance of the great ayatollahs." The shah addressed the nation, acknowledging the people's "revolutionary message," promised to correct past mistakes, and urged a period of quiet and order so that the government could undertake the necessary reforms. A number of the old elite were arrested, while more than 1,000 political prisoners were released. Initially this appeared to have helped, but Khomeini demanded continued protests. The government by now had lost its nerve and did not clamp down on the strikers. By December, hundreds of thousands of Iranians were on the streets. The shah began to talk with members of the moderate opposition, leading to a new government under Shapour Bakhtiar of the National Front. His condition was that the shah should leave the country. Although he claimed he was only going on holiday, after he left on January 16, 1979, the shah never returned to Iran.

*   *   *

Until well into November 1978, senior members of the Carter administration assumed that the Iranian issue was how to support a loyal ally through a trying time. The CIA view in August was that Iran was not even in a "prerevolutionary situation" and Carter received intelligence in September 1978 predicting continuity. The next month, he referred to "a great stabilizing force in their part of the world." In November, the word "stability" could still be used in the same sentence as "shah." On December 12, 1978, Carter observed, "I fully expect the shah to maintain power in Iran, and for the present problems in Iran to be resolved . . . I think the predictions of doom and disaster that come from some sources have certainly not been realized at all. The shah has our support and he also has our confidence."[9]

By this time, though, just at the end of November, the Tehran Embassy had actually warned that the shah might fall. In Washington, this was hard to believe. The shah appeared so much of a fixture, so in command of his state, that Iran could barely be imagined without him. Ambassador William Sullivan was instructed to inform the shah that he was supported "without reservation," with full confidence in his judgment. If the shah were to seek American advice, it would be to take decisive action to restore order and then prudently promote liberalization. Even as it dawned on officials that perhaps an authentic revolution was under way, the official line was that the shah would come through. Nonetheless, with this dawning came the question of whether the United States should seek to cut its losses and establish a dialogue with the opposition or encourage the shah to face down his opponents, if necessary through a military crackdown.

This was exactly the sort of question the Carter administration was illsuited to address. It had been spending 1978 on the sort of tasks for which it was most geared—mending fences between old antagonists. In addition to the Camp David endeavor, a new strategic arms treaty with the Soviet Union was a big priority. Here again progress was being made, but as with Camp David, the main qualities required appeared to be patience and attention to detail. These attributions were less appropriate when faced with huge, disorderly, and dynamic upheavals. It did not help that the revolution was well advanced before the administration started to grasp its potential.

The government was poorly served by its intelligence agencies and the Tehran Embassy. At its peak, the embassy had 2,000 employees and 3,000 dependents, as well as another 2,000 Iranian nationals. Many were involved in the surveillance of the Soviet Union, a function that was due to become more important under the prospective SALT II Treaty. It was less effective in surveying Iranian politics. The shah took a dim view of any contacts with his opponents, leaving the United States overdependent upon SAVAK's interpretation of events. There were specialists in Iranian politics in and out of government in the United States. A number realized that this crisis was more severe than those that had gone before, but few recognized the depth and intensity of popular anger, the range of groups working against the shah, and the determination and organization of their militants. The key players—the National Front, the Tudeh Party, and the various other leftist and Islamist militants—were all known, but their combined impact was underestimated. As British ambassador Sir Anthony Parsons later observed, "Where we went wrong was that we did not anticipate that the various rivulets of opposition, each of which had a different reason for resenting the Shah's rule, would combine into a mighty stream of protest which would eventually sweep the Shah away."[10]

In particular, Khomeini was an unknown quality. He skillfully presented himself as an opponent of tyranny while being vague as to what he did support. As an aloof and forbidding figure, indifferent to the daily maneuverings of the political classes, he was assumed too easily to be something of a figurehead. Yet it was Khomeini who regularly squashed any hint of compromise when it came to the future of the monarchy. The National Front politicians, who felt that their moment had come at last, were impatient for power, and if Khomeini had not been so rigid, then potentially durable deals might have been struck. They were also fearful of a bloody confrontation with the army. As it was, thousands of lives were lost in clashes with police, SAVAK thugs, and military units. The numbers of casualties from late 1977 through January 1979 have been put as high as 12,000 killed and up to 50,000 injured.[11] Troops regularly fired on demonstrators, and anybody opposing the shah was likely to be beaten up or suffer violence in some form. Khomeini told the opposition to prepare for sacrifice, lest they be coerced into submission. He understood the danger of this escalating into virtual civil war, but he also understood the limits to the army's power and perhaps of the shah's famed self-confidence.

By contrast, the shah was unsure and uneasy throughout. When he was tough, the opposition was more angry than cowed. When conciliatory, the

impression was of weakness and vulnerability. Concessions were evidently
the result of pressure rather than a genuine change of heart. As early as May
1978, a faltering television interview helped to puncture the aura of invincibility the shah had created around himself. Even the embassy worried that
the shah was "losing his touch."[12] His advancing cancer, which he had sought
to keep a secret, was one reason for his ineffectuality. It sapped his strength
and left him dwelling on his mortality and legacy. He had been ill since 1974,
and though it is often supposed that the U.S. government must have known,
as a result of his regular consultations with physicians (they were French), at
the senior level this does not appear to be the case. Visitors were aware of a
loss of vigor and confidence, but it was only at the end of 1978 that his illness really started to show through. He was personally shrinking along with
his throne, ailing as well as politically confused. Retaining a sense of his position as the monarch of all Iranians, he knowingly refused to unleash a full-
blown civil war. So as Khomeini geared his supporters for the final struggle,
the shah recoiled from it.

There were senior army figures ready to order their forces onto the
streets, but the order never came. This was why Parsons suspected that it was
SAVAK agents and soldiers in civilian clothes who attacked his embassy and
the British Airways office on November 5, "to teach us a lesson because of
our opposition to military government, and, by the same token, to convince
the British that it was futile to continue to press the shah to strive for political solutions."[13] There was a prevalent view, to which the shah on occasion
gave credence, that the British were stirring up the discontent because they
had never forgiven the shah for making the United States his favorite Great
Power. The hapless army chief of staff, who suffered a minor heart attack after being made prime minister, told U.S. ambassador Sullivan: "The shah
will not permit me to use military force, and if I cannot use military force,
this country cannot survive. You'd better tell your government." In some respects, therefore, it was the shah who provided the greatest surprises during
1978. American analysts assumed that Iranian stability rested on the security
apparatus and that it would be deployed ruthlessly when necessary. As the
shah hesitated, the question became whether it was up to the United States
to urge the hard line.

The Americans were not prepared for the question and lacked the knowledge to provide a sensible answer. Faced with an inconsistent and vacillating
shah, the administration displayed similar tendencies. These played on and
exacerbated existing tensions within the administration. As the hawkish
Brzezinski argued with the dovish Vance, the president gave a little to each
without wholeheartedly embracing either. Brzezinski was described as

"never accepting defeat" as final or a policy as decided if it did not please him. "Like a rat terrier, he would shake himself off after a losing encounter and begin nipping at Vance's ankles," and then find means to "tell the world that he had won, or that only he, Zbigniew Brzezinski, hung tough on the national security game as a foreign-policy realist."[14] With Vance often absent from key meetings as he tried to sort out the Arab-Israeli dispute and relations with the Soviet Union, Brzezinski was in the end a more effective advocate. The price of the tension was that communications between the NSC staff and the State Department broke down, and outsiders were brought in to offer advice and to make visits to Tehran to form their own assessments. Some of the Iranian contacts, such as the former ambassador to Washington, Ardeshir Zahedi, added to the confusion as a separate source of communication but also because their personal political interests naturally affected their judgments. To add to the difficulty, there was declining confidence in the ambassador in Tehran, William Sullivan, because of his late warnings on the gravity of the situation, and then, as we shall see, his individual enterprise in seeking a way out.

Leaving aside the policy differences, there were limits as to what could be done in directing the shah. For example, when veteran diplomat George Ball addressed the issue for Carter in December 1978, he concluded that the shah was finished and some transfer of power was needed to a more legitimate authority. Carter took the view then that he could not tell another head of state what to do. Through this period, the shah had regular conversations with the American and British ambassadors, as well as with the range of visitors frequently sent to Tehran to form their own impressions of his mental state and tactical inclinations. The real issue was whom else to talk to: the military or the opposition. Neither was homogenous; both contained distinctive strands of opinion. As time passed, matters became more polarized, and the more extreme strands in both came to the fore. This reduced further the chances for a compromise solution, thereby making the choice of whom to contact a judgment on who was likely to end up in charge.

Brzezinski, as the strongest voice in Washington, favored "a firm military government under the Shah"; Sullivan, the man on the spot, thought the shah was finished and that the military was demoralized and split. Faced with this unhelpful advice, Brzezinski sought a more robust presence in Tehran. At the start of 1978, General Robert "Dutch" Huyser was dispatched to work directly with the Iranian military, many of whom were close acquaintances. It was widely assumed that his task was to repeat the trick of 1953 and organize a military coup, should the government fall. He described his role as acting on behalf of the U.S. government "to stabilize the Iranian military and to encourage the Iranian military to support their legal government," but this still required a government capable of calling on the military as well as a military capable of responding. Without them, there was little Huyser could do.

By now the Bakhtiar government was in place. Would-be military plotters made their way to the U.S. Embassy on the assumption that they could develop plans to keep the shah on the throne and clean up the country. Brzezinski was excited, but Vance wanted none of this. Sullivan was told to find out the shah's attitude. The shah queried whether "he was being advised to use the iron fist even if it meant widespread bloodshed and even if it might fail to restore law and order," as if he wanted the Americans to make the fateful choice between abdication and crackdown for him. It really would be easier for the shah if he was an American puppet and could assign the United States the blame. Sullivan's response was that he "doubted that he would ever get such instructions from Washington" that would allow the United States to take responsibility for the shah's actions: "He was the Shah and he had to take the decision as well as the responsibility."[15] There was little left for the shah but to leave. As he did so, he claimed, "The Americans have told me I have to leave."

*　*　*

Sullivan now thought contact with Khomeini was essential to avoid a disastrous confrontation with the armed forces, so he began to explore the terms for a meeting. At the same time, Washington decided to keep clear of Khomeini, as any conversations were unlikely to make much difference. Better to support Bakhtiar as he tried to defuse the revolution. When it was realized how far the ambassador had gone in his private enterprise, he was reined in, at the last minute, by an irritated Carter. The ambassador sent back an equally irritated response to Vance, suggesting that the president "had made [a] gross and irretrievable mistake by failing to send an emissary to Paris to see Khomeini." Even the Iranian military wanted this meeting, and the failure to arrange it could "permanently frustrate U.S. national interest in Iran." This missive turned out to be a poor career move.

Bakhtiar, having persuaded the shah to leave, was trying to calm the country by meeting key demands, lifting martial law and restrictions on the press, releasing remaining political prisoners, dissolving SAVAK, and scheduling free elections. The new course in foreign policy involved terminating oil supplies to Israel and South Africa, and a shift away from the United States, including canceling US$7 billion worth of arms orders. By recent standards this was a bold and fresh course, but for the revolutionary forces an insufficient break from the past. The new government still derived its authority from the old order. Bakhtiar tried to prevent Khomeini's return by closing airports, but was faced with mass demonstrations, more virulent than before. On February 1, 1979, the Ayatollah returned to Tehran, having refused all contact and negotiations with Bakhtiar. Three million Iranians gave him an enthusiastic welcome as he denounced the new government and urged more strikes and demonstrations. Bakhtiar's government now lacked authority and could not count on the loyalty of the armed forces. After mutinies and insurrection, senior military commanders announced on February 11 that the armed forces would observe neutrality in the confrontation between the government and the people. The next day, Bakhtiar went into hiding and the revolutionaries began to take control.

Khomeini's first prime minister was Mehdi Bazargan, another National Front politician and, in the context, surprisingly moderate. But as is the norm in revolutionary situations, power had been lost by the center and had passed instead to independent revolutionary committees and worker and student councils. Revolutionary justice was implemented as former generals, SAVAK agents, and political leaders were executed. The Kurds demanded autonomy, other regional movements claimed a greater share of oil revenue, and leftist groups pushed traditional socialist demands. Bazargan found himself sharing power with the new Revolutionary Council, also established by Khomeini in January. Soon the internal power struggle was well under way. Leftists and intellectuals began to worry about the authoritarianism of the clerical elite, though not all clerics were comfortable with the trend of events. In March, Khomeini put a single question in a referendum: "Do you want the monarchy to be replaced by an Islamic republic?" The almost unanimous answer was "yes," and the Islamic republic was proclaimed on April 1, 1979. In May, a new force, the Revolutionary Guards, was established. This was clearly intended as a counter, if necessary, to the regular army and also to any leftist forces. By June, the press, along with leftist political parties, was being curtailed, while at the same time banks, insurance companies, major industries, and certain categories of urban land were nationalized.

Khomeini had implied in exile, to the point where key followers believed him, that he would remain a largely spiritual leader and not engage in government. Now his taste for more direct involvement was getting stronger. The draft constitution of June 18, 1979, included a strong president but did not give clerics a prominent role in the new state structure. At this point Khomeini was prepared to accept this draft, but it was considered by the newly formed Assembly of Religious Experts, and this produced a new constitution that would give the leading role to the Shia clergy. This constitution was approved in a national referendum in early December 1979. By this time, Bazargan had resigned, following the seizure of the U.S. Embassy in November. He was not replaced until the scheduled elections for the new president in January 1980. Abolhasan Bani Sadr, an independent associated with Khomeini, was elected with 75 percent of the vote.

★   ★   ★

By any assessment, the collapse of the shah's regime was a devastating blow to American foreign policy and led to numerous recriminations (though not personnel changes) within the U.S. foreign policy establishment. The old problems remained in the NSC–State Department divisions on policy and a lack of any real idea about what was going on in Iran. Contacts with the new players in Tehran were few and far between, and there was little grasp of the internal power struggles that were soon under way. The diplomats and intelligence specialists sent to try to pick up the pieces of U.S.-Iranian relations lacked any expertise in the ideological wellsprings of the Islamic movement.

This was an unprecedented situation. Washington had plenty of experience in dealing with military coups and leftist bids for power, but here was something quite different. Because clerics were not generally known for their lust for power or their appetite for government, the comforting assumption was that their role would soon be circumscribed by proper politicians. U.S. officials had no contact with the clerics or the Revolutionary Council but dealt instead with the relatively moderate Bazargan government, which wished to stay on good terms with the United States to avoid isolation and to sustain the economy. Popular sentiment might still be anti-American, but the regime appeared to want to keep it in check. One critical episode came in February 1979 when there was a takeover of the U.S. Embassy in Tehran. Khomeini's men ousted the militants. Those involved were leftists. The Islamists would not allow them to steal their revolutionary thunder. This episode not only led to complacency the next time the embassy was threatened but also reinforced the presumption of the time, that when it came to the crunch, Islamists were more a menace to the Communists than to the West.

This presumption became the basis for what the administration hoped could be an opening to Iran, as the role of the Islamists became hard to ignore. Brzezinski's main concern was of a Soviet push into Asia and Africa, and he could see the possibilities of Iran joining with America's local allies in helping to counter this push. By September, there was little response. Attempts to manage the new relationship were hampered by the lack of access to the supreme power. Assistant Secretary Harold Saunders described the position to Vance: "We have no direct contact with the man who remains the strongest political leader in Iran. His hostility towards us is unlikely to abate significantly, although there have been fewer venomous statements against us recently. Clearly, a first meeting could be a bruising affair." The real problem was that to meet with Khomeini would be to signal "our definite acceptance of the revolution." This might ease the Ayatollah's suspicions but would cause dismay elsewhere. We "would appear to cave in to a man who hates us and who is strongly deprecated here and by Westernized Iranians. Thus, we would want to be careful not to appear to embrace Khomeini and the clerics at the expense of our secular friends."[16]

Any attempt to engage with Khomeini might well have been rebuffed, adding to the humiliation. Domestic politics, however, inhibited the Americans from even trying. The exile Iranian community in the United States (which had expanded rather rapidly) was already blaming Carter for the fall of the shah and making common cause with establishment figures who counted themselves among his admirers, notably Kissinger and David Rockefeller, and who believed that someone who had been described by six presidents as a "friend" should not be snubbed so casually. The growing strength of the Pahlavi lobby made it difficult to get closer to the new regime. A Senate resolution in May, sponsored by Jacob Javits, castigated the new regime for the persecution of Jews and Bahais. This was taken in Tehran as evidence of a developing American plot to reinstate the shah.

The sort of concessions demanded in Tehran, such as the extradition of those accused of past repression and the delivery of weapons and spare parts paid for but still withheld, would cause an outcry. Moreover, the viciousness of the new regime was leading to abuses that deserved condemnation, even if comparable abuses perpetrated by SAVAK had been ignored. Moderates were sought out and cultivated, but when this was against the backdrop of such an evident hope that the revolution would fail or consume itself, association with Americans was bound to be dangerous. Even when they failed to recruit potential sources, as with Bani Sadr, the eventual president, the fact that they had tried told against the target.

The issue that triggered the crisis was whether the shah should be allowed into the United States for medical treatment. Carter resisted such a step for nine months, aware of the potentially inflammatory consequences. When Rockefeller and Kissinger urged him to admit the shah, he had asked, "What will you do when they seize our embassy?"[17] But then as he later explained, "I was told that the Shah was desperately ill, at the point of death. I was told that New York was the only medical facility that was capable of possibly saving his life and reminded that the Iranian officials had promised to protect our people in Iran. When all the circumstances were described to me, I agreed."[18] In his time, he had been feted as a friend of the United States; to refuse him now seemed cynical and inhumane. On October 22, 1979, the shah and his empress arrived in New York. This led to huge pro-revolution and anti-American demonstrations in Tehran.

At the same time, Brzezinski went to a ceremony in Algiers to celebrate the twenty-fifth anniversary of the Algerian revolution, one of the old sort that had been led by leftists and nationalists and ended in dictatorship. Robert Gates, of the CIA, who was present, described the meeting as an "intelligence officer's dream come true," for all "the principal thugs in the world were present." He listed Assad, Qadhafi, and Arafat, as well as General Giap of Vietnam. The Iranian delegation asked for a meeting, which appeared friendly.[19] To the Iranian masses at this time, television pictures of Brzezinski shaking hands with Bazargan in Algiers were evidence of shameful collusion.[20]

*　　*　　*

The plot to seize the U.S. Embassy in Tehran on November 4, 1979, was hatched by some young Islamists who defined themselves solely by their commitment to Khomeini.[21] At least 300 militants (largely young and not wholly accurately described as "students") occupied the embassy compound. They took hostage sixty-six diplomats and marines. Kenneth Pollack has suggested that the regular reference to the shah's entry into the United States was something of an afterthought, for it made no difference that he left on December 15 or died in Egypt on July 27, 1980. Yet the fears of a repeat plot along 1953 lines and of further humiliation at American hands were factors.[22] The February 1979 episode, which had been quickly defused, had convinced the embassy that it would set the pattern for the future, despite the changing political context and the warnings about the inflammatory consequences of the shah being permitted to enter the United States. This time, Khomeini's people had taken the initiative, rather than leftists, and it was clearly a popular move. After the foreign minister had gained agreement from Khomeini that he could get the U.S. diplomats released, but before he acted, Ahmad Khomeini, his son, was invited to see how the students had carried out his father's call for an "attack" on the Americans. He was so overwhelmed by the enthusiasm he found that he persuaded his father to endorse the action.[23]

The students themselves were unsure what to make of their achievement. They claimed they had uncovered a "nest of spies," although with some exceptions the shredded documents they found, which they laboriously put together, represented the mundane business of an embassy rather than

fevered plotting against the revolution. Reflecting their sour view of U.S. society, they released thirteen women and African Americans to serve as a rallying call for the dispossessed of America. The demands appeared on
November 12: Return the shah and his assets to Tehran; end interference in
Iran's affairs; and apologize for past crimes against Iran. The Iranian negotiating style was calculated to infuriate the Americans. If the motive was to
undermine the moderate faction in Tehran, they soon succeeded. By November 6, they had Bazargan's scalp, demonstrating to Washington that
there was not going to be an easy resolution to this crisis. If the motive was
to infuriate the Americans, there was also success. The administration expressed fury, and in response the militants became national heroes, confirming the Americans in their belief that they were dealing with irrational
fanatics.

Carter had spent the previous months trying to address the lack of confidence in his presidency. He was being challenged for the Democratic nomination by Senator Edward Kennedy. The economy was in a wretched state,
not helped by another surge in oil prices, and he was aware (because
Brzezinski had told him) that an aura of weakness surrounded his foreign
policy. The mistreatment of America's representatives appalled the public
and led to a surge of national feeling. "I was glad the people cared," Chief of
Staff Hamilton Jordan later recalled, "but bothered that they cared so
much."[24] The intense public and media reaction made it harder for the administration to change the subject. The crisis was, as Mark Bowden noted, "a
ratings dream, a conundrum, a scandal, and a tearjerker, with no clear resolution in sight." The story could be stretched by television: "From an exotic
foreign capital to their own neighborhoods. America was riveted."[25] Six
weeks into the crisis, the wife of the chargé d'affaires in Tehran (who was living in the Foreign Ministry) reported that she had tied a yellow ribbon
around an oak tree in her yard, following the advice of a 1973 song, which
her husband would one day untie. Soon yellow ribbons were everywhere, including on the White House Christmas tree.

Against this backdrop, Carter made the fate of his hostages his personal
priority. At Jordan's suggestion, when the crisis first broke, he immediately
canceled a foreign trip, attended a prayer service, and met with the families.
Thereafter, he talked about their plight regularly, expressed anger and concern, and achieved a warm public response. But he could not get the
hostages back, and once again his ineffectuality became a more salient factor than his human decency. Soon began the inevitable procession of self-
proclaimed mediators who hoped to obtain some hostages by offering
denunciations of the shah and past American policies to Iran. We cannot be

sure of the alternative history. The crisis might have petered out, had Carter not raised it to the highest level from day one, and then blustered as he found it impossible to bring it to a resolution. Carter appreciated belatedly that it might have been best if he had said as little as possible and refrained from making regular statements.

The first effect of the embassy seizure was to undermine those with whom the United States might have hoped to negotiate a solution. It had been undertaken in the name, and then with the support, of a supreme leader who hated the United States. When it came to a choice between economic privation and the purity of the revolution, Khomeini inclined toward purity. Against other opponents, the president might have been able to use economic sanctions, and Iran appeared vulnerable. Oil production had plummeted to barely a quarter of its postrevolution peak, but Khomeini cared less about this than other leaders because of the corrupting influence of oil wealth on society. The United States ended all trade, except food and medicine, would not buy Iranian oil, and froze Iranian assets in U.S. banks, worth $12 billion.

The more the Iranians realized that the hostages were a real asset, the more the Americans were weakened. Three events led the administration to wonder whether they might be able to sort out a deal. First, after treatment, the shah moved from New York to Panama. This made no difference, although two intermediaries who were supposedly to ask Panama to return the shah actually wanted to establish contact on behalf of the Iraqi foreign minister with Hamilton Jordan, Carter's chief of staff. This did lead to a negotiation, which by March looked like it might yield a result. Second, the Soviet invasion of Afghanistan at the end of December, which both Iran and the United States condemned, created an opportunity for an anti-Soviet alliance. At the same time, despite the Islamic connection, there was also anxiety in Washington when cold war tensions were high that volatile states such as Iran might somehow be pushed into the Soviet camp. Third, at the end of January, Abolhasan Bani Sadr became president. He was known to have opposed the embassy seizure, and there was some hope that he might be strong enough to cut a deal. Unfortunately, the political turmoil in Iran continued unabated. The Islamists were strengthening their hold. In the run-up to the March elections to the Majlis (Parliament), the twelve-man Council of Guardians, charged with ensuring that all candidates were properly Islamic, in a move that became a regular technique, ruled out politicians with divergent political agendas. This ensured that the Islamic Revolutionary Party (IRP) was in a dominant position. Those who had supported the revolution but now found themselves being pushed into opposition once again stirred up unrest. This was particularly the case in the universities, which were shut down until they had been cleansed of un-Islamic elements. Inevitably, Bani Sadr was soon in conflict with the Majlis.

The United States enjoyed international support, as the Iranian hostage taking was blatantly illegal. On December 4, the UN passed a resolution calling for the immediate, and unconditional, release of the hostages. There was no shortage of people urging Tehran to do the decent thing and release the hostages, but there was little appetite for sanctions among America's allies. Only as the United States began to talk openly about some of the military options, such as mining harbors, did the Europeans move a small way toward sanctions. Diplomacy was getting nowhere. The Iranians' intermediaries would insist "that the United States made concessions up front to which the Iranians could then respond, with no guarantee that they would."[26] Meanwhile, covert options were limited because the CIA now lacked agents in Iran, and all the congressional investigations earlier in the decade had discredited "dirty tricks" as a means of addressing problems of foreign policy. A military operation either had to release the hostages (and the model in mind was bound to be the successful Israeli rescue of hostages at Entebbe airport in 1976) or else attack military or economic assets. They could grind the oil economy to a halt, perhaps even seize Kharg Island, with its major export terminal, but these required accepting a risk of retaliatory killings of the hostages as well as additional casualties, and even action against oil tankers. The fact that hostages had been taken meant that any tough action put them at risk, and Carter wished to avoid accepting that cost. An ultimatum backed by a threat of tough action against Iranian assets might shake the Iranian elite into action, but then again it might not, and the hostages could well be executed as the United States engaged in punitive action.

By April, U.S. patience was exhausted. Carter was getting no help on sanctions and no response to diplomacy. There had been a farcical attempt to get the hostages released in return for a UN-led commission into the crimes of the shah. By March, Jordan's secret negotiation with the Iranian foreign minister had led to a plan involving the transfer of the hostages to the Revolutionary Council, which would then arrange for their release in exchange for some token concessions. Khomeini would not go along, as the hard-liners denounced the concession. His slogan was not encouraging: "We fight against America until death."[27] Then, on April 1, Bani Sadr announced the imminent transfer of the hostages away from the students, only for the Revolutionary Council to fail to take them back. Bani Sadr then accused the bewildered administration that it had failed to live up to its side of the bargain. Facing opposition from hard-liners and Khomeini, the president made it known that he wanted the hostages to stay with the "students."

One response, belated, on April 7 was to break diplomatic relations with Iran. Carter was now regretting his earlier lack of assertiveness. A few days later, on April 11, he began a series of discussions with the NSC, at which the military option was not only raised but enthusiastically promoted. Brzezinski insisted that it was time to "lance the boil," for U.S. honor was at stake. Others may have supported the proposed rescue mission because the only alternative appeared to be much more punitive military action. Once the idea took hold, the pressures to act quickly grew. Best to act when there was no moonlight and intelligence on the location of the hostages was still reasonably current. A plan had been developed, seemed now to have high-level military support (unlike earlier versions), and for want of anything better, Carter was prepared to give it a go. As Vance had not been present at the first meeting, another was held on April 15, in which the secretary of state could express his reservations. He pointed to the likely loss of life and denied that diplomatic possibilities had been exhausted. He had, however, no answer to Defense Secretary Harold Brown's immediate question, "When do you expect the hostages to be released?"[28] Vance, to Carter's dismay, then tendered his resignation, to be effective after the mission had been completed.

On April 16, the president met with mission commanders, and much of the discussion revolved around casualties. The possibility that rescuers and hostages would die was acknowledged. The president accepted the risks but warned against wanton killing, using the mission as a means of settling scores with the Iranians. Jordan had a final meeting with the Iranian foreign minister, at which it became clear he knew no more than Vance as to when the hostages would be released.

Because of the secrecy with which plans were developed and decisions taken, the operation was not subjected to critical scrutiny. The rescue faced formidable problems, in that Tehran was not the most accessible city and intelligence on where the hostages might be found and how well they would be guarded was sparse. The army's new Delta Force was to be airlifted at night into Tehran on navy helicopters (six, plus two reserves). A remote location 200 miles from Tehran was designated "Desert One." There the helicopters would meet up with C-130 Hercules transports carrying fuel bladders. Once refueled, they would fly to a remote location outside of Tehran ("Desert Two"), to arrive before dawn and hide during the day. Then CIA operatives would come and take them into Tehran on trucks. After assaulting the embassy and freeing the hostages, they would then take them to the soccer stadium next door, where they would be collected by the helicopters. From there they would go on to a nearby airfield, where they would be collected by a C-141 cargo plane with navy fighters providing cover. This was an extraordinarily ambitious plan, with uncertainties at each step, and allowed for no margin of error.

The flight was extremely difficult—at night, with radio silence, without lights, and at low altitude. A dust storm, a not uncommon feature about which more warning might have been given, reduced visibility and led to mechanical failure. By Desert One, only five helicopters were still functioning and then one collided with a C-130 as they were trying to leave, killing eight Americans. The mission was abandoned, leaving behind helicopters, weapons, maps, secret documents, and bodies. Carter was left desolate by the news of this calamity. The Iranians gloated. At a ghoulish press conference at the Tehran Embassy, the remains of the dead Americans were put on display. There were no further military options, and the subject was not raised again.

In place of Vance, Senator Edmund Muskie became secretary of state. He decided to take some intensity out of the American response. The government could get on with other business, suffering quietly rather than noisily. Soon, as if the Americans had used up their emotional energy on this crisis, Iran was out of the news and the country got on with other business. The hope was that the Iranians, too, would tire of this crisis. With the Americans not displaying their vulnerability daily, the affair seemed to lose its sense of purpose. As the months passed, Iran's position became economically more difficult and isolated internationally, and the students also wondered how this affair could be concluded. Eventually in September, Khomeini's grandson Sadeq Tabatabai said it was time for a deal. The conditions did not appear to be too onerous. But that month's Iraqi invasion of Iran was a large distraction. Moreover, neither the Majlis nor apparently Khomeini was ready for a deal.

It appears to have occurred to Khomeini that he could do to the United States as the United States had done to Iran. By holding on to the hostages, he could ensure Carter's defeat, just as the United States had once overthrown Mossadegh. It again showed a feeble understanding of American politics to assume that the defeat of Carter would result in greater respect for Iranian interests by the next U.S. administration. Only as Reagan was elected in November 1980 did it dawn on the Iranians that they would be unwise to leave this problem for Carter's successor.

Gary Sick later alleged that the Reagan camp knowingly conspired with the Iranians to keep the hostage crisis simmering to help ensure Carter's defeat.[29] The evidence suggests that this "October Surprise" was not a factor in the delay, although it might have been. Reagan's campaign manager, Bill Casey, tried to prolong the crisis, in itself a scandal, but the actual delays were mainly due to the practicalities of the final orchestration of the hostage release and the determination of the Iranians to humiliate Carter.

The deal was the one that had been available for some time. It began with a meeting in September in Bonn of Sadeq Tabatabai and deputy secretary of state Warren Christopher, and concluded in Algeria, where Christopher spent much of January. The United States promised noninterference and to release the Iranian assets that had been frozen when the crisis began (although some were held back to meet U.S. claims against Iran). On January 21, 1981, just as Reagan finished taking the oath of office, the plane carrying the hostages was allowed to take off. The hostages were free after 444 days of captivity.

Carter's presidency was irreparably harmed by being caught up in the tumult of the Iranian revolution. The administration first failed to appreciate the enormity of the upheavals underway in a state so important to American foreign policy, and by the time the seriousness of the situation was appreciated, it floundered around looking for an appropriate response and in the end was left chasing events. Afghanistan and then the Iraqi invasion would have offered incentives and opportunities for the regime to repair relations with the United States. By seizing the U.S. Embassy, the militants, at the same time, undermined the remaining pragmatists and moderates in Tehran and left the United States helpless in the face of a regime impervious to international entreaties or coercive pressures. The failed military operation just emphasized Carter's predicament. The Iranian desire to humiliate the Americans was helped by the speed with which the administration turned the seizure of the hostages into an emotionally charged national cause without a clear idea how they could get them back safely other than by paying an extortionate diplomatic price. This event poisoned relations between the two countries, and the effects are still felt to this day. Carter had not just lost a friend; he had gained an enemy. So, too, had Iran.

5

UPRISING IN
AFGHANISTAN

ON THE AFTERNOON of November 21, 1979, within days of the embassy in Tehran being seized, the Islamabad Embassy was also under attack, this time from students from Quaid-I-Azam University. This demonstrated Khomeini's potential appeal. Shias were a minority in Pakistan, at most 20 percent of the population, and the students were connected with the Islamic party, Jamaat-e-Islami, which was itself influenced by the Sunni Muslim Brotherhood. Nonetheless, the Ayatollah's ability to combine religious conservatism with political revolution, and then to humiliate a superpower, inspired young Muslim militants. As 15,000 chanting rioters occupied the grounds outside, setting fire to whatever they could find, 139 embassy personnel, including Pakistani employees, were stuck inside a basement vault, with one of their number, a young marine, already dying from a gunshot wound. Marines used tear gas to try to keep the rioters away, having been told that shooting would just make matters worse, but they could not prevent the rioters' setting the building alight.

According to Jimmy Carter's memoir, the situation was not too desperate because "President Mohammad Zia immediately dispatched Pakistani troops to protect our personnel and property."[1] This does not appear to be correct. For hours, away from the embassy, the ambassador and the CIA station chief got little response as they pleaded with the Pakistani authorities to clear the riot. A helicopter was sent to take a look, found the area covered in thick smoke, leading to the twin conclusions that it was impossible to make an assessment, but at any rate everyone was probably dead. The best course therefore was to wait until the rioters exhausted themselves. The rioters did become exhausted and eventually dispersed. By this time, another American had been beaten to death and two Pakistani employees had been asphyxiated. Fortunately, everybody else survived, but this was more because of fortitude and good luck than the help of the authorities. Understandably, Carter was relieved that he did not have a second hostage crisis on his hands, and phoned President Mohammed Zia-ul-Haq to thank him personally for his assistance. Better that the Pakistanis claim that lives had been saved because their troops acted promptly than that the Americans deserved all they got because of an iniquitous foreign policy.[2]

Like Iran, Pakistan had an Islamist government. Unlike Iran, it was not inherently anti-American and its ideology reflected a successful coup rather than a revolution. Zia, as army chief of staff, seized power in July 1977 from the leftist Zulfikar Ali Bhutto of the Pakistan People's Party (PPP). Bhutto had taken over after Pakistan, under its previous military dictator, was defeated in the 1971 war with India as East Bengal seceded to become Bangladesh. His socialist program produced economic chaos. A questionable victory for the PPP in the May 1977 elections was the product of flagrant manipulation. When in the face of popular unrest he resorted to martial law, Bhutto gave Zia his opportunity. The coup attracted less international attention and condemnation than Zia's subsequent decision to order Bhutto's hanging in April 1979.

As elsewhere in the Third World at this time, the failure of the left helped create favorable conditions for the growth of Islamic influence. The second radical wave was beginning to displace the first. This was already a strong factor in Pakistan. The country had been founded out of the British Raj, in opposition to secular India, as an expression of Islamic faith and identity. Even Bhutto had belatedly promoted notions of "Islamic egalitarianism" and promised the eventual introduction of Sharia law. Under Zia, however, the embrace of Islam was altogether more thorough. The Islamist party Jamaat-e-Islami was seen by Zia as the source of a political base he could not create by any other means. In October 1979, he announced that a "genuine Islamic order" would be established in Pakistan, without elections, but with the enthusiastic implementation of Sharia law. For Zia, Islam was a means of consolidating power, a source of national unity, and a barrier to insurrection. He remained pragmatic and had no intention of sharing power with the clergy. With a population of 121 million, almost doubled from twenty years earlier, he could claim demographic weight in the Islamic world. Foreign policy would still be based on national interests. Zia would contrast his careful promotion of Islam with the noisy and disruptive approach followed by Khomeini. Unlike Bhutto, who had toyed with nonalignment, he wished to be part of the Western camp, both to keep his armed forces equipped and because of India's close links to the Soviet Union.

As a military dictator who dealt harshly with opponents, Zia fell afoul of Carter's human rights policy. Evidence that he was continuing with Bhutto's efforts to construct nuclear weapons, which also emerged during 1979, did not help. Although there was an unavoidable cooling in U.S.-Pakistan relations, at a time when friends were hard to come by the Americans did not push their objections to Pakistani behavior too far. As they had done before, they made known their distaste but avoided a definitive break.

In the fevered context of late 1979, as Islam and anti-Americanism seemed to be walking hand in hand, this restraint may have been just as well. Iran and Pakistan were not the only countries giving Islam a more central political role. The events in Islamabad were triggered by a curious, troubling incident the previous day, this time at the Grand Mosque in Mecca in Saudi Arabia, where some 400 armed fanatics turned their weapons on pilgrims. This group was also a product of student activism, combined in this case with a religious fantasy based on the idea that one of their number was the returning Mahdi who offered all a hope of salvation. To the Saudi mainstream, this notion was preposterous, though the associated critique of the lifestyle of the royal family, and the material pleasures they enjoyed, was less so.

The initial confusion as to who had been responsible, coupled with the customary silence of the Saudis, encouraged rumors. On the campuses and in the bazaars, then as now, there was a tendency to blame all the most malign and otherwise inexplicable events on the United States (and Israel). Add to this the tension of the moment arising out of the Iran hostage crisis, which included reports of the U.S. Navy sailing into the Indian Ocean, rumors that the Mecca attack had been instigated by the Americans as a deliberate affront to the Muslim world soon took hold. It was this that triggered the Islamabad riot.

It took well over a week before Saudi national guardsmen were able to clear the Grand Mosque. After taking out most of the militants in a gun battle, they then, with the help of plans kindly provided by the Bin Laden Brothers for Contracting and Industry, scoured the tunnels and basements of the mosque for remnants.[3] Those who were caught were later beheaded. Unofficial accounts put the number of dead at 4,000—far higher than official estimates that were in the hundreds. In many ways this was an isolated incident, but it had a substantial long-term impact. This was already a torrid year for the Saudis, as past political certainties were lost. The fall of the shah, with the Americans apparently watching helpless, did not encourage confidence in their closest ally. Within the Arab world, Egypt's readiness to seek a separate peace with Israel had obliged the Saudis to make common cause with the secular, radical, antimonarchist Iraqis and Syrians. Within the Islamic world, they faced a challenge from the rise of Iranian-backed Shi'ism. From a Wahhabist perspective, this was a religious perversion to be opposed, especially with a restive Shi'ite community in their eastern provinces. Until this point, the Saudis had seen themselves as leaders of the Muslim world, reflected in their role as the founders and hosts of the Islamic Conference. Iran was claiming to be showing the way for Islam, and the influence of the revolution was evident as Muslim leaders everywhere rediscovered their religious convictions and began to court their clerics.

Now the Saudis were challenged from within, by a strange sect that castigated this most religiously conservative of regimes for its impiety. It dawned on the royal family that, having hitherto feared most attacks from the left, in the current climate they might be more vulnerable from the right, from those who presented themselves as being of an even purer faith. Theater and television entertainments were shut down, accompanied by a crackdown on laxity in social behavior, notably affecting the position of women. More power was given to the religious establishment. The scope for an independent intelligentsia as a source of fresh ideas was narrowed. "Saudi Arabia," observes Rachel Bronson, "has yet to recover from this turn to aggressive state-sponsored religious zealotry."[4]

Thus in two critical states, Saudi Arabia and Pakistan, there was a move in late 1979 to reassert their Islamic identity. The timing was crucial, for it influenced their responses, and that of the United States, to yet another major event of this tumultuous period—the Soviet invasion of Afghanistan. In the short term, the common Communist enemy obscured the full implications—for all three countries—of using religious faith as an organizing principle for a counterrevolutionary war.

*　*　*

The Soviet invasion of Afghanistan in December 1979 did almost as much damage to the Carter administration as the Iranian hostage taking. Both cases caught the president off guard, raised questions about his broad foreign policy strategy and grasp, and forced him into an unnaturally hawkish stance. In terms of our story, there was, however, an important difference. Whereas the Iranian revolution involved a skillful fusion of the first and second radical waves, as leftists and Islamists came together in their joint opposition to the shah, in Afghanistan the revolution came from the left and brought into being an Islamist backlash that the Soviet Union attempted, in the end unsuccessfully, to suppress. Whereas in Iran, the United States found itself working against the Islamists, in Afghanistan they supported them, in concert with Pakistan and Saudi Arabia.

Afghanistan is a landlocked country, bordered by Pakistan to the south and east, Iran to the west, and in the 1970s, the Soviet Union to its north, with an additional small border with China. In 1979, its population was around 13 million. Its strategic importance had long come from its position at the crossroads of Asia. Mountainous and tribal, it was never easy to control. During the nineteenth century, it was caught up in the "great game" between Britain and Russia, but once World War I was over, and after another war with the British, it effectively gained its independence. Until 1973, it was a moderately stable monarchy, until a coup led by the king's cousin, Mohammed Daoud Khan, a former prime minister. He ended the monarchy and attempted reforms. Initially, Daoud established close ties with Moscow, resulting in the equipping of the Afghan military forces with Soviet weapons, assignment of large numbers of Soviet military advisers to Afghanistan, and training of Afghan military officers in the Soviet Union.

There were at the time not one but two Communist political camps with similar ideologies, both supported by Moscow. The People's Democratic Party of Afghanistan (PDPA) was always a model of indiscipline. Its two factions reflect the rivalry of their leaders and were named after their respective newspapers. Moscow's—and Daoud's—preference was for Parcham ("The Banner") led by Babrak Karmal, partly because his ideological fervor was always subordinate to ambition. Khalq ("The Masses") was led by Noor Mohammed Taraki and Hafizullah Amin, both inclined to uncompromising, far left radicalism.

Other countries in the region were alarmed at the sudden emergence of what could become a new Communist satellite in such a sensitive strategic location. The shah of Iran was particularly concerned and led the efforts to provide Daoud with an alternative to dependence on Moscow. He apparently saw Daoud as a "country cousin, unsophisticated, backward and likely to be taken by the city slicker, in this case the USSR."[5] His efforts were backed by Kissinger, who made a point of visiting Kabul, in November 1974, to set in motion U.S. economic and technical assistance. This effort was hampered by continuing problems along the Afghan-Pakistan border. One reason for Daoud's support within the armed forces was his sympathy for the idea of a

Pashtun state emerging out of Pakistan that might one day unite with Afghanistan. This was not an idea that went down well in Pakistan. In retaliation, resources and weapons were provided to hard-line Islamic groups working against Daoud.

During the 1960s, in the universities of Afghanistan, as elsewhere in the Third World, students hotly debated the merits of the various forms of Marxism as an answer to the challenges of imperialism, poverty, and injustice. In Muslim countries, ideas developed under the aegis of the Muslim Brotherhood in Egypt started to offer a compelling alternative. The message was that only Islamic forms of government were tolerable and that everything else must be resisted. The Muslim Brotherhood remained a marginal political force in Afghanistan, but when faced by Daoud's left-inclined regime, its members gained in strength. By 1975, they were confident enough to launch an uprising, but were crushed. Those who were not caught and executed fled to Pakistan. They were allowed to stay, though Bhutto did not share their philosophy. He only supported them, with the shah's encouragement, to coerce Daoud to come to some arrangement to control ethnic nationalists. Using the carrot of generous aid as well as the stick of insurgency, Bhutto initiated talks in early 1975 with Daoud, for the two countries to resolve their conflicts.

As a result Daoud tilted away from communism. This was signaled by his denunciation of "imported ideology" and the start of purges against Communists, first in the government and then, more tentatively, in the military. It was almost as if he were starting to model himself on the shah, although his task, with a largely rural population (85 percent of total) and much power in the hands of mullahs and tribal chiefs, was harder. Daoud formed a new party and gained authorization for a new constitution that outlawed all other parties, including the PDPA. Officers started to be sent to non-Communist countries for training, including Egypt and the United States. All of this was viewed by Moscow with some dismay. Daoud was invited to Moscow in April 1977, where he was berated by Leonid Brezhnev for allowing NATO personnel—undoubtedly spies, according to the Soviet leader—into his country. After Daoud objected strongly, a superficial cordiality was restored but relations were now irreparably damaged. Daoud worked even harder to develop his links with other countries, notably Egypt. At the start of 1978, there were plans for a visit by the shah in June and for Daoud to visit Washington in September.

Moscow was already unhappy with trends in the region, especially after the overthrow of Bhutto by the rightist Zia. It now looked to get rid of Daoud and encouraged the Communist factions to unite, which they did, at

least notionally, in the summer of 1977. Plans for a coup were brought forward after the assassination of a Communist leader in April 1978. The PDPA
organized large-scale protests, which led to further arrests of senior party
figures. Before the arrests were complete, orders were sent to party supporters in the military. On April 27, army units surrounded key government
buildings, which were attacked by helicopter gunships and aircraft. Daoud
was killed in the presidential palace. The PDPA leaders were freed. Soon they
were in charge of the "Revolutionary Council" of the new "Democratic Republic of Afghanistan." The degree of Soviet connivance in this is unclear.
The Soviet news agency called it a military coup d'état, which was rarely an
expression of enthusiasm. Most likely, at the time they may still have been
hoping to work something out with Daoud.[6] Nonetheless, Moscow was the
first to recognize the new government and was soon back to sending advisers to Kabul and offering military assistance.

Taraki led the new revolutionary government with Amin as his deputy. By
July, Parcham elements in the new government had been purged. The Soviets helped Karmal avoid arrest and arranged for him to go into exile as ambassador to Czechoslovakia. The government was never going to be stable.
Faction fighting continued within the PDPA, narrowing its political and
military base even more, leaving it unable to see through a program of radical reform. Attempts to overturn the power of landlords and tribal chiefs,
and to give new rights to women, faced immediate resistance. This soon resulted in a cycle of repression and further resistance, leading to civil war. The
violence in the country was intense. Thousands were murdered by government forces, and many members of the old elite fled. The insurgency grew in
response, moving from the rural areas to the cities and taking in all ethnic
groups. The army could not cope, and its morale deteriorated. Alarmed, in
December 1978, Taraki and Amin flew to Moscow to get more support. They
signed a twenty-year treaty of "cooperation and friendship." The number of
Soviet military advisers grew sharply.

An important moment came in mid-March 1979, when there was an insurrection at Herat involving the local population along with elements of
the army. It lasted for four days before loyal Afghan units put it down. By
that time at least fifty Soviet citizens had been killed, along with many civilians, after Amin ordered the bombing of the town. Islamists were now playing a key role in the anti-Communist movement, with the familiar message
that the fault lay in corruption, injustice, and impiety. Although the Muslim
population was largely Sunni, Herat is close to the border with Iran and has
a substantial Shi'ite population. The educated knew Persian and had followed Khomeini's rise and understood his rhetoric of Islamic international-

ism and the need to fight the godless superpowers.[7] A report to the Politburo in April 1979 warned of the "flare up of religious fanaticism in the Muslim East." Yet even in this emergency, the government refused to work with the Parcham faction in an effort to broaden its base—let alone (as tentatively suggested by Moscow) Muslim leaders.[8] Instead, Taraki and Amin planned more purges and executions.

At this point the Politburo began to discuss possible combat operations in Afghanistan, and to make preliminary preparations. They were clearly of two minds. One day the starting proposition, from which there was no dissent, was that to lose Afghanistan, and have it turn against the Soviet Union, would be a major and intolerable setback, which had to be prevented even at the risk of being branded an aggressor. That would be difficult without an indigenous army capable of carrying the brunt of the battle. It was vexing to see a potentially favorable revolutionary movement falter so badly, especially in the context of a worsening international situation. Soviet influence in the Middle East was waning as a result of the defection of Egypt and continuing difficulties with Iraq. To be sure, Iran had been a setback for the United States, but thus far it was proving difficult to turn this into a gain for Moscow. Meanwhile, the crisis over Iran had led the Americans to increase their military presence in the Persian Gulf and arm Saudi Arabia. But then, almost immediately, anxiety surfaced about the potentially high political and military price, the prospect of fighting in terrible terrain against wily opponents, and the effect on relations with the United States when détente just about seemed to be back on track with the signature of a big nuclear arms control treaty that was going to the Senate for ratification.[9]

Unsure how to act, the Politburo decided to go no further for the moment than providing more military aid. The regular requests from Kabul for Soviet troops were equally regularly rebuffed. Only in late June was it decided to send the first combat unit, an airborne battalion, to protect Soviet air units at the Bagram air base near Kabul, the main Soviet operational base, in addition to between 2,500 and 3,000 military advisers in Afghanistan. More weapons were shipped to the Afghan army and air force. Soon the insurgency started to reach Kabul; the amount of territory under Afghan government control shrank ominously. The army was becoming mutinous, supply lines were tenuous, and munitions were falling into insurgent hands. Soviet advisers were expanding their roles in an effort to hold things together but were evidently failing. In August 1979, a group of army officers was unsuccessful in an attempt to seize the Presidential Palace, but mutinies had become regular events, hardly symptomatic of good morale. The Soviets could see the danger signs. They were trying to build up an army that might soon disintegrate.

Moscow judged that the problem was as much political as military. The Khalq faction in power was too provocative and needed to pull back from its extreme economic and social measures. A change in faction was needed, so military measures were geared to this end and not to an eventual occupation. However, any hope the message would get through to Khalq and cause a change in behavior was disappointed.[10] The government in Kabul wanted guns and showed little interest in Soviet lectures on the need to take note of popular concerns and demonstrate to Muslims that they would be beneficiaries of social and economic reforms. Taraki claimed to be following the Soviet example. He established a personality cult around himself and put the needs of the revolution above considerations of humanity. "Lenin taught us," he once explained to the KGB, "to be merciless towards the enemies of the revolution and millions of people had to be eliminated in order to secure the victory of the October Revolution."[11] He also played on Soviet fears about Iranian interference. When this issue was first raised in March 1979, not long after the shah had been overthrown, Moscow took the view that this danger was unlikely to materialize because of the chaos in Tehran. But with the passing of the months, the Soviets started to appreciate how Khomeini's influence might spread by other means.

From Moscow's perspective, the dogmatic Amin was even worse. Eventually Taraki understood that the only way to save his position was to deal with his partner, and with Soviet connivance began to plot his elimination. The scheme backfired and instead Taraki was the victim. His death of a "serious illness" was announced by Radio Kabul on October 10. The Soviet position was now even more desperate. Because Taraki was killed not long after he had been given a comradely hug by Brezhnev at Moscow airport, his death seemed a direct rebuff to the Soviet leader, who appeared to have been quite shocked by the turn of events. He now had to deal with a ruthless man— Amin—whose behavior was unpredictable and potentially disastrous in its effects. Yet the Soviet Union dared not pull out. There were more mutinies, while insurgents focused on supply lines, forcing the regime to use armored convoys or aircraft to move around the country. The only small victories came when Soviet military personnel were fully and directly involved. The whole infrastructure of operations depended on Soviet support. The larger the presence, the more likely that Soviet lives would be lost as the result of Amin's reckless ineptitude. Even more disturbing was the possibility that Amin might start to see the Soviet forces as useful hostages as he attempted to influence Moscow's policies.

Still the Afghan government efforts continued to be focused on internal power struggles, as Amin moved against his rivals, actual and potential. Soviet officials made little secret of their exasperation. Amin would never get a grip on the situation, and at worst he might even go the way of Daoud and decide that salvation required taking an anti-Soviet line. Moscow started to convince itself that this was what he might be doing. Speculation began about contacts with Pakistan, Iran, and China, and even with the United States. On this basis there was no prospect of success until Amin was out of the way. Changing notionally friendly regimes was a tried and tested technique for reversing deteriorating situations, so Moscow began to plan this for Afghanistan. The new regime would be led by Babrak Karmal, who had been exiled to Czechoslovakia as ambassador. He was brought to Moscow in October and prepared for his new role. A special unit was sent to Kabul, ostensibly to guard Amin's house (as he had requested) but in fact to move against him when the moment came. By late November, all Soviet units were in a constant condition of heightened readiness, others were being mobilized, personnel were being moved by stealth into Afghan cities, and senior Soviet military delegations visited Kabul.

The developing policy was spelled out by KGB chief Yuri Andropov in a letter to Leonid Brezhnev in early December. He warned that there was a risk of Amin's "political reorientation to the West." The evidence adduced for this was that he kept "his contacts with the American chargé d'affaires secret from us. He promised tribal leaders to distance himself from the Soviet Union." (None of those who dealt with Amin at this time actually saw any hint of him easing his hostility to the West.) With or without Amin, the situation was poor, and the wider political context made it more alarming. Iran was seen as an increasing threat as it backed the Islamists. There was concern that unsettling Islamist messages might begin to percolate into the Soviet Union's own Central Asian Republics, with their large Muslim populations. Meanwhile, détente was in poor shape: Congressional hostility to arms control; the continuing American courtship of China, the Soviet Union's Communist antagonist; and NATO's decision (taken on December 12) to deploy long-range intermediate nuclear weapons in Europe confirmed it.

Andropov argued they dare not lose "the domestic achievements of the Afghan revolution" or risk a "turn to the West." His remedy was to help Karmal and the Parcham faction get into power, with forces stationed on the border to help defend the revolution should it be attacked, and so resurrect "the Leninist principles of state and party building in the Afghan leadership and strengthen [the] Soviet position." His leading coconspirator, Defense Minister Dmitri Ustinov, wanted a much larger operation to ensure nothing went wrong and to guard against an Iranian or Pakistani intervention. The military was anxious but was overruled.[12] By late December, the number of

Soviet troops in the country was well over 5,000. The basic intervention plan was decided on December 8, when Andropov, Ustinov, and Foreign Minister Andrei Gromyko gained Brezhnev's verbal approval for a Parcham takeover before getting the full Politburo to sign up, despite the misgivings of some of their number. As Brezhnev seems to have been in an alcoholic haze for most of this time, his input was marginal.

Starting on December 24, military aircraft began to fly into Afghanistan. The plans for the introduction of troops do not seem to have been concealed from Amin. As he had asked for Soviet troops to support the counterinsurgency, it was easier for the general staff not to bother with deception and manage the logistics with their Afghan counterparts. Amin's initial reaction to the news was therefore to express pleasure and to urge that they be deployed quickly.[13] As late as December 27, he seems to have been unaware as to what was planned for him. On that day, he received a rude shock as his palace compound was attacked. There, after some fierce resistance, which was the only serious fighting of the whole occupation, he was killed. This was also after a broadcast announcing the new regime ostensibly from Radio Kabul (although the real Radio Kabul had not yet been taken). Karmal took over, claiming preposterously that he had formed a new government, and only then requested Soviet military assistance. Given the sequence of events, this was clearly incredible. Soon there was an invasion force of 30,000 combat troops. By the morning of December 28, Kabul, along with other major cities, was effectively under Soviet control. The mission of the Soviet troops was "rendering aid to the friendly Afghan people and establishing advantageous conditions to prevent possible actions by the governments of neighboring countries against Afghanistan."[14]

*   *   *

The cold war, which earlier in the 1970s had appeared to be effectively over, to be replaced by an era of negotiation and détente, returned with a vengeance. The sharpness of Carter's reaction to the Soviet invasion of Afghanistan, and the contrast with the administration's previous pronouncements, added to the sense of an abrupt shift in policy. The administration's impression of being caught by surprise by the Soviet intervention raised questions about whether it had been let down by the intelligence community. Yet according to Gates, "If ever there was a crisis foreseen well in advance it was the gradual but unmistakable growing Soviet involvement in Afghanistan."[15] All agencies were watching the developing situation closely during the course of 1979.[16] It was evident that the Soviet leadership faced hard decisions. They clearly had a stake in the country and would not wish to lose it. The question was not whether they might therefore intervene directly but how this might be done. Would there be a complete takeover of the campaign, and effectively the country, or could it be done incrementally, without great drama, by a gradual thickening of support for Afghan forces? Taking over the campaign seemed to be too large an undertaking, only to be contemplated if there was a real danger of either political breakdown or an anti-Soviet regime. The view that this was quite likely was represented in the intelligence community by only a small minority of analysts. For example, in September 1979, as the crisis in Kabul began to become critical, Director of Central Intelligence Stansfield Turner warned that the Soviet leaders "may be on the threshold of a decision to commit their own forces to prevent the collapse of the regime and to protect their sizable stakes in Afghanistan," but he then went on to explain that this could be done by expanding the number of advisers and getting more involved in established types of combat operations. Until late November, the intelligence reporting was reasonably accurate on Soviet anxieties about the political fallout—with Iran, India, and Pakistan as much as the United States—and the military practicalities. It was understood that Moscow wanted to replace the Khalq faction with Parcham in the hope that it would reach out to disaffected members of the political elite and the wider community.

By mid-December, the level of Soviet activity in and around Afghanistan could not but attract high-level interest. The CIA now suggested that although the Politburo had decided that a pro-Soviet regime must be kept in power, even at a political cost in relations with the United States, the current buildup was preparation for a later move rather than an immediate intervention. Soon there were indicators that something more serious was under way. The U.S. ambassador's attempt to raise the issue in Moscow met with a brusque response, leading to disagreements among both the analytical and policy communities on exactly what the Soviets were up to. Those suspecting a substantial and imminent Soviet move were growing in number. The majority still judged the Soviet mobilization to be at an insufficient level for a step change in its counterinsurgency role. This disagreement hampered the ability of the intelligence community to give policymakers a clear and timely message.

On December 22, the National Security Agency alerted Brzezinski and Defense Secretary Harold Brown that there was "no doubt" of a major Soviet intervention in Afghanistan within the next seventy-two hours. By Christmas Eve 1979, the United States had reports of the massive airlift by Soviet military transport aircraft to border air bases, but also to Kabul and Bagram airfields in Afghanistan. These were moving airborne divisions and special forces into position. Yet the Defense Intelligence Agency as much as the CIA still saw this as a relatively small-scale operation, designed to raise the regime's dwindling authority. This perception lasted until December 27, when the announcements came of Amin's death and Karmal's arrival. The next day, it was apparent that 5,000 extra troops had been airlifted into Afghanistan and another 30,000 were moving over the border. By now, according to Brzezinski, "All knew that a major watershed had been reached."[17]

So-called intelligence failures of this sort often result not so much from a lack of information on the moves being made on the ground (which were quite full in this case) or elite intentions (which were reasonably well understood almost until the point when key decisions were actually made) but from the difficulty of accepting that the other side had just made a self-evidently foolish decision. Perhaps because of Vietnam, with which it was not hard to draw parallels, the American analysts assumed the Soviets would not allow the cold war stakes to tempt them into trying to suppress an insurgency when local forces had failed. But, unlike Vietnam, Afghanistan was adjacent territory. There was a shared border of 2,500 kilometers. In addition, the Soviet elite still tended to see the problem more in terms of an incorrect policy line than a determined, wily, religiously inspired enemy. Force on a major scale was seen as a "last resort," but when force is kept as a last resort it is much more likely that it will be on a massive scale. This is the point, by definition, at which all other remedies have failed. As the United States had found in Vietnam in 1965, the very act of intervention, on behalf of a failing government when supposedly loyal forces are feeble and demoralized, further narrows the political base and requires taking full responsibility for the fight. When the last resort comes, there is no incremental option.

★   ★   ★

When Brzezinski posed the question in September 1979 as to whether a distinction could be drawn between "creeping involvement and direct intervention," he knew the answer had profound implications for the future direction of U.S. foreign policy. Superpower relations were then delicately poised. The background was one of growing suspicion of Soviet intentions. For some years, Moscow appeared to have compensated for its declining fortunes in the Middle East by building up a position in Africa, taking advantage of the opportunities provided by the collapse of the Portuguese empire in 1974, as well as the overthrow of Haile Selassie in Ethiopia. These moves were opportunistic, and in practice counterproductive, as they dragged the Soviet Union, and its East German and Cuban allies, into inconclusive civil wars in poor, weak states. Nonetheless these moves were presented at the time in the United States (particularly by Carter's opponents) as being linked in some grand strategy, directed against the West's oil vulnerability and geared to controlling vital sea lines of communication. Henry Kissinger, for example, safely out of office, described Moscow's "geopolitical" purpose in the Horn of Africa as "to outflank the Middle East, to demonstrate that the U.S. cannot protect its friends, to raise doubts in Saudi Arabia right across the Red Sea, in Egypt, in the Sudan and in Iran."[18]

When he became president, Carter's initial inclination was to wind the cold war down rather than up. He had plans to get troops out of South Korea, cut back on all forms of weaponry, and judge friends as well as foes by their performance against human rights criteria. "Being confident of our own future," he stated in one of his first major foreign policy speeches, "we are now free of that inordinate fear of communism which once led us to embrace any dictator who joined us in that fear."[19] Yet Soviet operations in the Third World ate away at his confidence. Brzezinski later suggested that détente had been lost in 1978, in the "sands of the Ogaden," where Soviet advisers had supported Ethiopia in its dispute with Somalia. At the time, Carter described the Soviet role in the Horn of Africa as "ominous" and soon was suggesting that it was up to the Soviet Union to choose "confrontation or cooperation," with the United States ready for either.[20] A major intelligence estimate of June 1978 described how "Soviet military assistance and support to proxies have come to be an effective form of bringing Soviet power to bear in distant areas." It reflected a foreign policy that was still "essentially revolutionary, resting on the expectation of fundamental changes in the international system and within the states that constitute it, and deliberately seeking—though cautiously and intermittently—to help bring these about."[21] By the start of 1979, the defense budget was rising.

Against this background, another major Third World crisis was bound to tip the balance in favor of the hawks. One member of the administration later recalled, "The Soviet invasion was the hope of one wing of our government, and the fear of another."[22] The top priority during the second half of 1979, at least until the hostage crisis, was to get Senate ratification of the Strategic Arms Limitation Treaty (SALT). The Iran crisis had already created particular difficulties because of the loss of intelligence positions within Iran that would have allowed the United States to verify Soviet compliance with the treaty provisions. With the battle for votes under way in the Senate, and with the opponents using Soviet actions in the Third World to demonstrate the one-sided nature of détente, talking up the danger of an intervention in Afghanistan would be tantamount to talking down the treaty. Carter and Vance therefore avoided suggestions of global confrontation. They assumed that the Soviet leadership also had a stake in SALT, and that so long as there was a real prospect of ratification, this should act as a restraint on Soviet behavior. By the same token, evidence that the treaty might fail anyway would remove that restraint.

When Daoud was toppled in April 1978, the U.S. response was calm, though it was undoubtedly a setback. Having weaned one potentially leftist leader away from dependence on Moscow, the question was whether it could be done with another, for Taraki claimed to be an independent-minded nationalist. Vance was willing to try with the new regime, and Brzezinski was skeptical. The State Department view was that economic assistance should continue in order to preserve what U.S. influence remained and no actions should be taken that might push Afghanistan even further into the Soviet camp. The new regime was recognized and an ambassador, Adolph Dubs, was sent to Kabul. Dubs by his very presence offered the new leadership an alternative to Moscow that they seemed pleased to keep. Yet by December, it was hard to be optimistic as the regime signed its treaty of cooperation with Moscow. Even worse, in February 1979, Ambassador Dubs was kidnapped by an extremist group and then died during a rescue attempt. At this point the administration effectively gave up on the regime, ending the small amounts of residual economic and military assistance.

The shift in U.S. policy came in the summer of 1979. It was proving impossible to have a serious discussion with Moscow on Afghanistan. Although the idea that Moscow was in serious difficulties was still a minority view, it was shared by Brzezinski, who saw a real dilemma. Afghanistan must be either abandoned by the Soviet Union or occupied—with all the risks of a quagmire. Even if such a stark choice could be avoided or delayed, the dilemma offered an opportunity to make life a bit more difficult for the cold war adversary. Although the doves preferred not to stir the pot too much, they could accept the logic of alerting Moscow to the dangers of pushing too hard in Afghanistan. After meeting with Brzezinski on July 23, Carter agreed that the issue could be raised publicly. On August 2, Brzezinski made a speech on the need for prudence in U.S. policy with regard to Iran, and the general wisdom of abstaining "from intervention and from efforts to impose alien doctrines on a deeply religious and nationally conscious people." No mention was made of Afghanistan, but newspaper reports made clear that this was directed at the Soviet leadership.[23]

By this time, Brzezinski had already obtained, on July 3, an initial presidential finding for covert—but nonmilitary—support to the Afghan insurgency to be channeled largely through Pakistan. In a later interview with a French newspaper, Brzezinski explained that he told Carter at the time that "this aid was going to induce a Soviet military intervention." If true, this would imply that all else that followed, from the Soviet intervention to the Taliban and al Qaeda, was somehow America's responsibility as a result of a covert operation. It was an admission that it was Brzezinski's intention all along "to provoke a Soviet invasion."[24] Some care is needed, as this statement can be overinterpreted. Brzezinski was reclaiming from Reagan and for Carter some of the credit for bringing down the Soviet Union, as the inability to cope with the Afghan insurgency was one factor in draining credibility from the Soviet leadership. But in 1979, the United States was at most a bit player in a local drama with its script written elsewhere. The conflict within Afghanistan was the result of a sequence of coups and uprisings in which the ambition of the Communists was matched only by their internal disarray and political incompetence. Nothing the United States did that summer led to the fiasco of Amin's victory over Taraki or to the Soviet misapprehension that if only they could engineer a takeover by more politically savvy Communists, then everything would be fine. Their anxiety about the American role was that some link was being forged with Amin. The American contribution to the insurgency was marginal—about $500,000 of financial support. Its significance was in providing something upon which to build, after the Soviet invasion, and in establishing the modalities of cooperation with Pakistan.

Moreover, despite what he said in this interview, Brzezinski appears to have been of two minds about encouraging a Soviet Vietnam. While the United States had been stuck in Indochina, Moscow had continued to supply its enemies and make life as difficult as possible. Soviet propaganda sent into Iran was encouraging anti-Americanism (and this continued during the hostage crisis). Afghanistan might be as disastrous for the Soviet Union as Vietnam had been for the United States—but not necessarily. The guerrillas, unfortunately, were "badly organized and poorly led"; lacked the sanctuary, organized army, and central government available to North Vietnam; and had limited foreign support. In addition, the Soviets were likely to act far more decisively than the United States had done in the 1960s. Although Brzezinski was eventually of the view that support for the insurgents had been well worth any unintended consequences, as it contributed to the collapse of the Soviet Union, his initial thoughts were that the immediate effects would be adverse. This would undoubtedly be a major propaganda blow to Moscow, causing outrage, particularly in Muslim countries. But at the same time, the domestic pressures on the American president would grow. A policy that previously passed for restraint would now appear as timidity.

More than others in the administration, Brzezinski had a conceptual framework within which these events could be fitted. As the shah fell, Brzezinski postulated an "arc of crisis" stretching "along the shores of the Indian Ocean, with fragile social and political structures in a region of vital importance to us threatened with fragmentation." The arc was marked by areas where there was intervention by the Soviet Union or its proxies, from the Horn of Africa to Indochina. The idea was picked up in a major essay in *Time* magazine, entitled "Crescent of Crisis," which was the phrase that stuck. At its center was Iran. In one direction was India ("politically divided and troubled"), Pakistan ("inept military regime"), and Afghanistan ("pro-Soviet junta . . . trying to rule over one of the world's most ungovernable tribal societies"). In another direction was Turkey (torn by religious unrest and social instability) and other moderate Arab regimes such as Saudi Arabia, Egypt, Sudan, and Oman, which had to cope with radical Libya or pro-Soviet South Yemen. While events in Iran had confirmed impressions of American weakness, and the whole area created opportunities for the Soviet Union, the *Time* analysis suggested that in the "long run," there were also opportunities for the West:

> Islam is undoubtedly compatible with socialism, but it is inimical to atheistic Communism. The Soviet Union is already the world's fifth largest Muslim nation. By the year 2000, the huge Islamic populations in the border republics may outnumber Russia's now dominant Slavs. From Islamic democracies on Russia's southern tier, a zealous Koranic evangelism might sweep across the border into these politically repressed Soviet states, creating problems for the Kremlin.[25]

Brzezinski had been seized for some time by the importance of the "nationalities" issue for Soviet internal stability, and he had set up an interagency group to study the matter. Specialists in the region, such as Zalmay Khalizad, saw how "Islamic consciousness," already a form of counterculture, might be stirred "if the Soviets continue to make war on their ethnic and religious counterparts across the border."[26]

In this region of weak states and social turbulence, where religion continued to have a powerful hold and where socialism and liberalism, the ideologies of the Enlightenment, appeared as alien intrusions, the great cold war confrontation between the two superpowers entered a new phase. Neither Brzezinski nor anybody else in the administration had any doubt that the Soviet Union was still the country's main antagonist. They also understood that the mujahideen were animated by beliefs similar to those that were causing the United States such grief in Iran. Nonetheless, the countries with whom the United States was working had their own reasons to be wary of Khomeini and seemed to confirm that it was possible to have such religious zeal translate into political action without it being directed at the United States.

In this context, the natural response in the administration, as the Soviet intent became apparent, was to make things as difficult as possible for Moscow, and in the first instance that meant supporting the resistance with money, arms, and technical advice. This in turn would require working with Pakistan and a review of policy toward that country. In addition, "we should concert with Islamic countries," Brzezinski suggested, both as a "propaganda campaign and in a covert action campaign to help the rebels." By the time the first stage of the combined Afghan coup and invasion was complete, on December 29, Brzezinski was noting that the United States had gotten into the habit of not following up "verbal protests" with "tangible responses," so "the Soviets may be getting into the habit of disregarding our concern." The United States must not "let the Soviets get away with this invasion with impunity."[27]

★　★　★

The invasion came at what was already a horrid time for the Carter administration, with the Iranian hostage crisis showing no sign of resolution. Although it had not been caught totally off guard by events in Afghanistan, the past inclination to stress a calm continuity in relations with the Soviet Union now aggravated the sense of a jerking, reactive, almost panicking foreign policy. The impression that the president was stumbling in the area of his greatest responsibility was not helped by a New Year's Eve interview with ABC television when Carter acknowledged that the Soviet intervention had "made a more dramatic change in my own opinion of what the Soviets' ultimate goals are than anything they've done in the previous time I've been in office." As Raymond Garthoff has noted, "so embarrassing was this comment that it was not included in the Weekly Compilation of Presidential Documents, and Vance and Brzezinski had the grace to exclude reference to it in their memoirs. At the time, political opponents seized upon it as a shocking example of Carter's naïveté."[28]

He was never adept at finding a middle way. Carter was prepared to give the benefit of the doubt to those he could trust, but once he felt that trust had been abused, he would respond with intense indignation. In June, he had met Brezhnev in Vienna for a summit meeting to sign the SALT II Treaty. When he reported back to Congress, he made a point of stressing the importance of "face-to-face" discussions as a means of reducing "the chances of future miscalculations on both sides." He added, "President Brezhnev and I developed a better sense of each other as leaders and as men." Once again he demonstrated his belief that relations between countries with distinct interests and governing ideologies could be managed through warm personal relations between their respective leaders.[29] At the time, there had been messages from Soviet sources on the dilemmas they were facing in Afghanistan, although no hints of a substantial intervention. Carter wrote to Brezhnev on December 28 about how the Soviet actions "could mark a fundamental and long-lasting turning point in our relations" and was furious at what he considered to be a mendacious reply two days later.

This added to his anger with Brezhnev for putting him in a position where he could be dismissed for relying too much on protestations of trust and goodwill from dictators. The result was a swing in the other direction, with extravagant descriptions of the situation. He spoke of the "greatest threat to peace since the Second World War,"[30] passing over Korea, the various Berlin crises, and Cuba. When addressing Congress, he referred to "the small, nonaligned, sovereign nation of Afghanistan."[31] Although Taraki and Amin claimed nonalignment at the time of their coup, this had not been taken seriously by the administration, especially after the December 1978 Treaty of Friendship with the Soviet Union. The description in his memoir of the aggression being directed "against a freedom-loving people, whose leaders have been struggling to retain a modicum of independence from their huge neighbor,"[32] hardly did justice to the continual requests of the Afghan leadership for more Soviet troops to help quell the insurgency, or Amin's initial welcome to the extra Soviet troops pouring into his country in December. In this respect, the Soviet move was neither an invasion (though Brzezinski had been prepared to label it this way even before Amin was deposed) nor an attack.

Soviet motives were said to be geared to the expansion of its influence into an area of vital interest to the United States, perhaps prompted by the Politburo's concerns over the decline in its own oil production and preparatory to a grab for Iranian or even Saudi oil. From the Politburo's perspective, the move was largely defensive, even desperate. Yet those who saw an aggressive intent were not wholly off the mark, for the Soviet leadership did not expect to fail; their confidence in military power as a policy instrument was still evidently high; and if they had succeeded, they would have a firm base from which to extend their regional influence. Nor was there much doubt that within Afghanistan very few saw the Soviet intervention as a friendly act. The sense of outrage was by no means uniquely American. The UN Security Council voted 13 to 2 in condemnation, forcing Moscow to use its veto, while the General Assembly vote was 104 to 18. This new "great game" was being played for high stakes.

Carter confirmed the sense of a turning point in U.S.-Soviet relations: "Soviet actions over the next ten to twenty years will be colored by our behavior." It was necessary to "do the maximum, short of a world war, to make the Soviets see that this was a major mistake."[33] When he met with the NSC to discuss a list of countermeasures, he did not pick from the menu but chose the lot. Even Brzezinski was worried that he was going too far. This included denying grain exports to Moscow and boycotting the Moscow Olympics scheduled for the coming summer; both were controversial moves, and the first, in an election year, involved a high political cost. SALT clearly had no chance of getting through the Senate. As he thought the signed treaty would be one of his biggest achievements, its loss would be one of his biggest disappointments. To ensure that it was not lost forever, he asked that its consideration be suspended. A trip by Harold Brown to Beijing in January suggested that the previously evenhanded policy of playing the two Communist giants against each other was now being tilted in favor of China. Relations with Moscow were frozen. At the end of January, Vance offered a series of proposals to reestablish some sort of dialogue with Moscow. Carter could write to Brezhnev; Vance could meet Gromyko; a special emissary should be sent to Moscow. Carter refused them all.[34] There would be no "business as usual." The sanctions would "remain in force until all Soviet troops are withdrawn from Afghanistan."[35] As with Iran, where the administration was waiting for the release of hostages, it was now waiting for the withdrawal of Soviet forces. Soviet compliance seemed even less likely than Iranian. This meant that important aspects of relations with two difficult and important countries were now dependent upon their decisions to reverse policy.

For the long term, Carter sought to demonstrate U.S. readiness to move into the Persian Gulf area if necessary. This was a signal that Brzezinski's analysis of the "arc of crisis" was being taken seriously. On January 23, 1980, in his State of the Union address, Carter announced a new policy that came to be known as the Carter Doctrine. Soviet troops, he explained, were beside a region containing two-thirds of the world's exportable oil. They were "within 300 miles of the Indian Ocean and close to the Strait of Hormuz." The Soviet position posed "a grave threat to the free movement of Middle East oil." He therefore warned:

> An attempt by an outside force to gain control of the Persian Gulf region will be regarded as an assault on the vital interests of the United

States of America, and such an assault will be repelled by any means necessary, including military force.[36]

On March 1, 1980, the U.S. Rapid Deployment Joint Task Force (RDJTF) was formally established, with a focus on deployment to the Middle East and Southwest Asia. By the end of Carter's presidency, it was made up of 200,000 troops, based in the United States. Although both the doctrine and the force were triggered by concerns about potential Soviet actions, they eventually derived their importance through enabling later responses to threats from within the region.

More immediately, the objective was to get the Soviets out but, if that proved impossible, to make their stay as uncomfortable as possible. Carter, pushed by Brzezinski, agreed that the best thing the United States could do was to keep the insurgency going through money and arms. This task fell to the CIA. This was not a good time for the Agency. It had been battered by scandalous revelations of dubious practice and congressional investigations in the mid-1970s, presented as a rogue arm of government that had to be reined in. As director, Admiral Stansfield Turner had cut back on covert operations. These were now far more tightly regulated, with assassination expressly forbidden. If anything was going to be done in Afghanistan, it had to be through Pakistan, even though it was a military dictatorship pursuing a nuclear capability.

For President Zia-ul-Haq, this was wonderful. He could develop links between his own and Afghani Islamists, with his Inter-Service Intelligence keeping control, and still get U.S. support. He even felt able to dismiss the initial U.S. offer of support to Pakistan ($400 million) as "peanuts" and demanded more convincing demonstrations of trust and reliability. This would take time. In one area, however, there was movement. In February 1980, Brzezinski went to Pakistan, where, in addition to overt military assistance, he discussed expanded covert operations with Zia and was photographed waving a Kalashnikov rifle in the vague direction of the border. Most important, he stopped en route in Riyadh, where he gained agreement for matching contributions to the mujahideen. For every dollar the United States was to provide, another dollar would come from the Saudis. Zia, who had been involved with training Saudi soldiers during his military career, developed his own links with Saudi intelligence chief Turki al-Faisal, and together they worked to keep under control the political character of the resistance. The United States, Pakistan, and Saudi Arabia were united in their determination to help resistance groups struggling to cope with Soviet firepower. In the face of the strategic imperatives of the moment, it did not occur to any of the three governments that they were creating a radical force that might one day come to challenge their own security.

After speaking in 1977 of the nation's welcome release from an "inordinate fear of Communism," Carter was now back to square one. Although Carter's instincts were to make up with enemies, when his readiness to forge new friendships was spurned, his irritation soon showed. Having started suggesting that foreign policy had been governed by unnecessarily dark, even paranoid, fears, Carter's credibility was never going to be strong once he began to suggest that the original fears, and the associated and often uncomfortable policy responses, might not have been so wide of the mark. His legacy was a revival of the cold war with the Soviet Union and a deep chill in relations with Iran. It was a legacy his successor, Ronald Reagan, cheerfully embraced.

PART TWO

RONALD REAGAN

★ ★ ★

THE MUJAHIDEEN

In the November 1980 presidential election, Ronald Reagan beat Jimmy Carter by 10 percent of the popular vote, and the Republicans also took the Senate. Everything seemed stacked against Carter. A faltering economy ensured that he was on the defensive. He had little answer to the question posed by Reagan to the electorate during the campaign debates: "Are you better off now than you were four years ago?" Yet foreign affairs provided the setting in which Carter could be portrayed by Reagan as ineffectual, a hapless figure, out of his depth, buffeted by powerful forces that he could barely understand, let alone control. Having started out urging Americans to put the cold war behind them, Carter had reappraised his own position after the invasion of Afghanistan and then toughened his administration's whole cold war stance, beefing up military expenditures and putting arms control on hold. Having described Iran under the shah as an oasis of stability, he could do little to help the monarchy's collapse or stem the anti-American tide of the revolution. The military operation he authorized in order to rescue the hostages ended in a miserable fiasco. The notable achievement of the Egypt-Israel Treaty was rejected by the rest of the Arab world, while only grudgingly accepted by the Israeli government. Not only economically, but also politically, America appeared to be in decline.

Carter seemed to project his own internal doubts and agonies onto the country, as if the United States had become so depressed and worried that it needed to go into therapy. He was rejected in favor of a genial man who spoke naturally in positive and uplifting terms about America as a great country with a wonderful future. Reagan's diaries reveal him to be more on top of what was going on in his administration or at least in those areas that interested him than seemed apparent at the time. He never felt it necessary to match Carter in his mastery of details or pretend that he was trying. His background in the movies left him not only with an ability to speak well to a good script, if awkwardly inarticulate without one, but with few qualms about blurring image and reality. He also had an instinctive readiness to describe the human condition in terms of a conflict against the perils and temptations of evil, with the United States and God coming together on the side of goodness.

Reagan did not see it as his job to drive policy forward, because he wanted government to do less and not more. His basic belief was that the country was most likely to enjoy prosperity and security if those who knew how to make money, generate energy, and fight wars were unencumbered by regulations and restrictions. In the economic sphere, this approach worked well, as it did in Britain. Although the economy at times seemed dangerously out of balance, it was helped by the combination of deregulation and the progressive fall in oil prices during the 1980s. These were good years for the American consumer.

During the 1980 campaign, the Reagan camp spoke in lurid terms about the Soviet military buildup and the readiness of Moscow to fight and win a nuclear war. The critique was not just of Carter but of the Nixon-Ford years and the attempt to establish a détente with Moscow. The Russians, it was argued, used the West's natural desire for a more peaceful world to pursue their traditional agenda. The Reagan team presented the invasion of Afghanistan as part of a systematic strategy, connected to the Soviet Union's meddling in the Horn of Africa and its embrace of radical Arab regimes. They saw Brzezinski's arc of crisis and assumed that it was all Moscow's fault. "Let's not delude ourselves," Reagan said while campaigning in 1980, "the Soviet Union underlies all the unrest that is going on. If they weren't engaged in this game of dominoes, there wouldn't be any hot spots in the world."[1] The alleged aim was to exploit the West's dependence on foreign oil, by getting in a position to walk into oil-producing countries and prevent vital supplies traveling by sea at times of war. If Moscow believed that its accumulation of raw military power enabled it to throw its weight around, then it could only be countered by a compensating revival of American military power. This would be the first priority of the Reagan presidency. "As a foundation to my foreign policy," he later wrote, "I decided we had to send as powerful a message as we could to the Russians that we weren't going to stand by anymore while they armed and financed terrorists and subverted democratic governments." The intention was "to spend whatever it takes to stay ahead of them in the arms race." Reagan would "not trust words or pieces of paper."[2] More so than many of his aides, he was also convinced that the Soviet system was so rotten that it was bound to fail.

He took it for granted that the Soviet Union ignored notionally legal commitments that got in the way of its interests. The United States therefore must not allow itself to be too fettered. This helps explain the latitude given to the CIA to engage in covert operations of the sort recently deemed improper and counterproductive in a number of congressional investigations, but also the lack of effort put into what had been basic goals of U.S. foreign policy, such as preventing the spread of nuclear weapons. From the start, therefore, all world politics tended to be viewed through the prism of cold war conflict. This provided a basic guide to the choice of friends and enemies. Reagan came to power as cold war tensions were rising and his tough stance on the "evil empire" initially aggravated them, to the point where some in Moscow feared that the United States really was looking for an excuse to mount a nuclear first strike. Only as the president realized that such fears were becoming commonplace at home and in Europe did he present his more conciliatory side. It was the consistency in his conviction about the Soviet Union's rottenness, and his eventual readiness to let it fail gracefully, that represented the great foreign policy achievement of his presidency.

Because of his movie career, it was easy to present Reagan as a cowboy figure, always ready for a fight with his hand never far away from a gun. The image may not have displeased him. In practice, handing over much of military policy to the professionals meant introducing a considerable degree of caution. The lessons drawn by the armed forces from Vietnam were to avoid complex conflicts in the Third World and stay focused on preparations for big wars against other great powers. Training and doctrine concentrated on exploiting new conventional technologies and concepts of maneuver, geared toward possible war against the Warsaw Pact countries. Armed force should only be used for a clear purpose and, when victory was possible, through the application of overwhelming force. During the Reagan years, the case for a more activist military policy came not from the Pentagon but from the State Department, and later, the National Security Council staff.

Over the previous decade, the conduct of American foreign policy had been transformed. The position of secretary of state had been progressively undermined by the development of the role of national security adviser to a figure of competing—and, in the case of Kissinger and then Brzezinski, greater—influence. Under Nixon, William Rogers had been completely marginalized until Kissinger took over his role, while also (until he was forced to give it up) holding on to the national security adviser role. Under Carter, Vance eventually resigned in frustration. Reagan's first secretary of state, Alexander Haig, was aware of the danger and insisted, in a curious phrase, that he would be the president's "vicar" (by which he meant deputy) in foreign policy. Haig, a former general who had worked for Nixon but more recently had served as NATO's top commander, was chosen as someone who would reassure Europeans that their concerns would be heard at the top of the administration. But Haig was never close to the Reagan inner circle and was judged to be too emotional, erratic, and egocentric to work as a team player. After he had failed to keep a lid on the 1982 Falklands conflict, which saw two allies—the United Kingdom and Argentina—pitted against each other, he was replaced with George Shultz. Shultz was more endowed with gravitas and was a more effective Washington operator, but he too struggled to exert influence over the president and was constantly irritated as other members of the administration stepped on his turf.

One source of frustration was Caspar Weinberger, secretary of defense, who had worked closely with Reagan in California. He soon enjoyed international notoriety as an uncompromising hawk, although he remained conventional and cautious in his foreign policy thinking, which was the basis for many of his disagreements with Shultz, who was much more activist. Another independent operator was William Casey at the CIA, an old friend of Reagan whose intelligence experience went back to the old Office of Strategic Services (OSS), the precursor to the CIA. The Pentagon and the CIA represented institutional challenges to the State Department that had been muted during the Carter period. As national security adviser, no figure of comparable stature to Kissinger and Brzezinski emerged. Nor was there a figure such as Brent Scowcroft, who had served during the Ford interregnum and later served George H. W. Bush, who made it his business to ensure that the president got the best possible advice and that different agencies worked together. Instead, there was a rapid succession of figures who saw their job as protecting the president and enforcing his will, to the extent it could be discerned.

The position was conspicuously downgraded from the start, and the first adviser, Richard Allen, made no mark whatsoever. He was replaced by Judge William Clark, a loyal friend of long standing with minimal foreign policy experience, who worked more to spare Reagan the fallout from the poor decisions of others than to ensure that the initial decisions were good. He began the practice of drafting presidential material without consulting the State Department. He was followed by a former marine, Robert McFarlane, and a serving admiral, John Poindexter. McFarlane had a breakdown, whereas Poindexter was introverted and uncommunicative. Overwhelmed by the numerous issues reaching his desk, Poindexter was always struggling to make an impact. One complication they both faced was Donald Regan, the president's chief of staff from 1985, who jealously guarded the access to the president. Poindexter was replaced briefly by Frank Carlucci (who went on to replace Weinberger at the Pentagon) and then came a serving general, Colin Powell, who took the opportunity to establish himself as a capable policymaker.[3]

✶   ✶   ✶

Reagan did not inherit a crisis over Iran. The hostages returned home the day of his inauguration. But he did inherit a freeze in U.S.-Soviet relations, which his election, if anything, intensified, and a commitment to support the insurgency in Afghanistan. This renewed focus on the cold war suited him fine and set the framework for his foreign policy. The most important tension points were no longer in Europe but rather around Brzezinski's "arc of crisis," although there was also a new fixation with Central America. The administration took the view that the Soviet Union was vulnerable to global overextension and this might be exploited by supporting their local opponents. This led the United States into some alliances with regimes and groups whose commitment to democracy and human rights was well hidden. Intellectual support for this came from neoconservatives, many of whom began to join Reagan because they thought the Democrats too soft on national security. The neoconservative argument was summed up in 1979 by Jeane Kirkpatrick, a Democratic academic who went on to become ambassador to the UN under Reagan and yet another cabinet-level irritant to the secretary of state.

She gained notoriety for an article in *Commentary* magazine in 1979 entitled "Dictatorships and Double Standards," in which she distinguished between totalitarian regimes, which could never democratize, and authoritarian regimes, which just might. She wrote in opposition to Carter, blaming his human rights agenda for destabilizing Iran as well as the Somoza regime in Nicaragua, when the main need was to fight against Soviet totalitarianism. The implication of this was that the United States should be much more prepared to support anti-Communist groups, even if their own practices were illiberal, and be far less tolerant of totalitarianism. She mocked the idea that it was possible to "democratize governments, anytime and anywhere, under any circumstances" and stressed the time it took for the "necessary disciplines and habits" to be acquired "for democracy to take root." Removing autocrats tended to leave Americans surprised at the speed with which "armies collapse, bureaucracies abdicate and social structures dissolve."[4] It was of course always possible to make a case that it was as well to work with the deeply unpleasant in pursuit of the truly dreadful, to work with allies whose domestic practices left much to be desired in order to deal with enemies who posed severe threats. Candor when talking about even short-term allies was always going to be difficult, and there would be a tendency to gloss over their faults.

In Afghanistan, the administration was initially content to continue with the policies of the Carter administration, pushing money into Pakistan to be more than matched by the Saudis and other Arab states and then passed on to the various mujahideen groups. They were prepared to improve on Carter's offers of military aid, even if this meant turning a blind eye to its nuclear program. This was, Haig told the Pakistanis, a "private matter," leaving them with the impression that the administration would be content if it became a nuclear power. The main advice from Casey was that the Pakistanis would be of most assistance to the president if they kept their nuclear activities hidden.[5]

What is striking in the memoirs of key administration officials is how few references there are to policymaking on Afghanistan. It appears as a regular propaganda point, demonstrating Soviet ruthlessness, but not as a matter for decision. Reagan only mentions his early decision to lift the grain embargo imposed by Carter because it had been hurting U.S. farmers as others filled the gap.[6] One reason for the lack of references was that action in Afghanistan was largely a continuation of covert operations handled by the CIA and set in motion under Carter. Another was the guilty secret that the administration was playing down just how far Pakistan had got in developing nuclear weapons, ignoring what it knew and exaggerating the difficulties and delays before it could build a deployable capability. Contrary to a number of State Department and CIA analyses, Reagan annually certified to Congress that Pakistan was not involved in nuclear weapons design.[7]

At root, the approach reflected the uncontroversial, self-evident quality of the policy. Russia was the cold war enemy and a way had been found to cause it hurt. Far less attention was paid to the agendas of those who appeared to be serving well as the causes of this hurt. They were simply "freedom fighters." This added to a rather pleasing sense for the administration that the boot was on the other foot. They had often been told that those harassing, ambushing, and killing their forces and those of friends were truly "freedom fighters" and not at all terrorists.

The general view at this time was that the Soviets could be discomforted but not beaten by these groups, and that the first priority was to contain them within Afghanistan. This meant shoring up relations with Pakistan, even if this also meant playing down the significance of its autocratic, harsh rule and pursuit of nuclear weapons. "Given the uncertainty and sensitivity surrounding certain areas of our relationship," Shultz wrote late in 1982, Reagan should "endeavor to convince Zia of his personal interest in these concerns and his sensitivity to Zia's views. . . . We must remember that without Zia's support, the Afghan resistance, key to making the Soviets pay a heavy price for their Afghan adventure, is effectively dead."[8]

✯   ✯   ✯

Zia welcomed the opportunity provided by Afghanistan. His oft-repeated preference was "to keep the pot boiling, but not boiling over."[9] He did not want the Soviet Union to attack Pakistan, but so long as the conflict could be contained, his economy would benefit from the inflow of funds and his political base would be reinforced through a war fought on Islamic principles. This would undermine the tribal nationalism that always threatened the unity of the country. To exercise maximum control over events, his instrument was the ISI, led over this period by General Akhtar Abdur Rahman. Rahman was pleased to take funds from the Americans and Saudis, but he also discouraged anything other than the most formal contact between the ISI and the CIA. As the CIA lacked both the capacity and the inclination to manage operations within Afghanistan, it was content with this arrangement, but it meant handing over large sums of money without any control over where it went.

The Afghans were not known for unity, discipline, and organization. To cope with the tendencies toward fragmentation, the ISI recognized six major émigré parties, all close to Jamaat-e-Islami, as the designated recipients for money, weapons, and ammunition. All refugees in Peshawar had to sign up with one of these six. Zia did not want an even more unified entity, for then there would be a possibility of an independent power base. So when, in August 1981, five of the parties formed an alliance, the ISI soon worked to break it up. The two largest, headed by Gulbuddin Hekmatyar and Burhanuddin Rabbani, each had 800,000 members. The Saudis insisted on a seventh party to represent their—and Wahhabi—interests. The seven leaders came to be known as the seven dwarves.[10] Excluded were those with royalist or tribal links, who were most likely to develop links with opposition or nationalist movements inside Pakistan. Only Ahmad Shah Massoud's group in the Panishir Valley had a degree of independence. The teeming refugee camps by the border broke down traditional cultural ties and saw the recruitment of volunteers for the war and the promotion of radical Islamist ideas.

There was another important motive informing Saudi policies—the desire to thwart any attempt by Shi'ite Iran to take advantage of the situation. We noted earlier the origins of the division between the Shia and Sunnis in the succession struggle that followed the death of the Prophet Muhammad in 632, over whether the Prophet's cousin and son-in-law Ali ibn Abi Talib should head the Islamic community (*umma*) because he was chosen by the Prophet, or because the elders of the community chose him as the best qualified. After three other caliphs, he eventually got his turn on the basis of qualification, but by this time the community was already disputatious, and Ali's time was marked by civil war and his eventual assassination. The dominant Sunni tradition thereafter looked to caliphs who could provide order and good government, accepting the authority of religious scholars (the *ulama*) on religious matters. The Shia were those who were unhappy with the separation of the religious and political functions and believed that the folly from the start was not to accept the sole authority of those who shared the Prophet's blood. This was an argument about leadership and explains why the Sunni caliphs always found the Shi'ite message threatening and subversive. The Shia were treated as second-class citizens and started to see themselves as the underdogs. Not all Sunnis, for example those in the Sufi tradition, found Shi'ite teaching anathema. Salafists, however, continue to treat it as a dangerous perversion.[11]

Sunnis make up 90 percent of the world's 1.3 billion Muslims. There are Shi'ite communities within the Arab world, but, other than Iraq, they are minorities. In all, they were excluded from political power, with the possible exception of the Alawite Assad in Syria. Sunnis had thus appropriated the Arab identity. This was contrasted with the Shi'ite Persian identity, for Iran is the most populous Shi'ite country, where they represent 90 percent of the population. The Salafic Saudis saw the rise of Khomeini and his aggressive promotion of Shi'ite ideology as extremely threatening. Their approach to Afghanistan, therefore, was influenced by the need to defeat not only one hostile power, the Soviet Union, but also another, Iran. In both Afghanistan and Pakistan, the Shia were about 20 percent of the population. Bhutto, the prime minister in the 1970s, was Shi'ite and the generals who overthrew him were Sunni. One part of the Saudi strategy was to encourage Zia in his embrace of Salafism. With Pakistan as a partner their other objective was to make sure that Iran was unable to take advantage of the situation in Afghanistan to extend its influence even more.

Saudi Arabia was therefore working with Pakistan to contain both communism and Shi'ism in Afghanistan. The Afghan incursion could also be used to isolate leftists within the Arab world (typically, Yasser Arafat was one of the few to find a good word to say about the Soviet invasion), and the Americans would not object to the use of Islamists in this way. The Saudi General Intelligence Department (GID) was headed by Prince Turki al-Faisal, an effective operator who understood U.S. society (where he had been educated). Like Pakistan, the Saudis remained confident that any tensions between a foreign policy dependent upon American support and a politico-religious movement that had strong anti-Western undercurrents could be managed.

To start with, the Reagan administration still associated terrorism with leftist, secular groups linked to nationalist movements, whether the Irish, Basques, or Palestinians. Haig even said publicly that the Soviets were behind most of what went on, though, as he soon discovered, there was little intelligence evidence to support a directing role.[12] Even in Beirut, the association was with Iranian-backed Shia. Little attention was paid to the possibility of groups emerging out of the Muslim Brotherhood with their own brand of strident militancy. Arab militants coming to support the jihad were seen at most as the equivalent of the idealists of the 1930s who joined the International Brigade during the Spanish Civil War.

★   ★   ★

Whatever their hopes in December 1979, members of the Politburo soon discovered that they had taken on an even weaker government against a much stronger insurgency. The PDPA's internal divisions and rivalries simply took on new forms as a result of the large Soviet political and military presence in the country and left the regime exhausted and incredible. Although Karmal was a more sympathetic leader than Amin, he was even less competent. He was prepared to broaden his government, but the circumstances of the intervention made it almost impossible for him to do so. His party was seen as no more than a tool of infidel foreigners. Potential partners were in exile, and his attempts to improve social conditions were undermined by the wretched security situation. In the camps in Pakistan, 1.5 million refugees were soon congregating (a number that was eventually more than doubled). They were full of angry young men prepared to fight. Throughout the Muslim world, Communists, and the left more generally, were undermined. Even more so than before, the language of resistance was religious.

After the initial Soviet buildup to 75,000 troops, the number rose to 120,000 (although some sources insist that the general staff rigorously capped the numbers at 108,800 after 1985, thereby reducing even further their chances of overwhelming the enemy).[13] The CIA was estimating that mujahideen casualties were around 40,000, whereas the combined Soviet and Afghan total was 92,000—unusual for guerrilla war, in which the insurgents normally suffer most. The best that Moscow could expect was continuing stalemate.[14] Soviet forces consistently failed to develop tactics that would enable them to take and then hold the main mujahideen strongholds. Only when Mikhail Gorbachev came to power at the start of 1985 was there a serious attempt to develop a new strategy. Soviet and Afghan forces then moved closer to the border in an attempt to interdict mujahideen supply lines. Border tensions with Pakistan were further aggravated by an active campaign, including regular acts of sabotage and murder, within Pakistan.

Gorbachev eventually concluded that the continuing intervention was allowing the Americans to "bleed" his country. He accepted that Afghanistan was an Islamic country and without that element no regime would be credible. Marshal Akhramayev explained that despite his forces solving every military problem faced, there was "still no result. . . . On occupied territory we cannot establish authority. We have lost the battle for the Afghan people."[15] In October 1985, Gorbachev told Karmal that he would have to find ways of struggling on with Soviet aid but not Soviet troops. This would be the equivalent of the "Vietnamization" Nixon had adopted in 1969 with South Vietnam. Gorbachev began to create the conditions for withdrawal in May 1986 by replacing Karmal with Mohammed Najibullah, the ruthless head of the secret police. Najibullah began to reach out to non-Communists and even talk with some of the resistance groups. Soviet relations with the Americans improved, but later that year the Iran-Contra scandal began to circumscribe Reagan's ability to support covert actions. Even so, Gorbachev found that neither the United States nor Pakistan was inclined to trust his intentions, suspecting that he was trying to get them to lower their guard, or end their support for the mujahideen so long as Najibullah was in power and received Soviet aid. There was no graceful way to withdraw, leaving a secure Afghanistan as a friendly neutral neighbor. It took until February 1989 before he got all troops out. By then 620,000 Soviet personnel had seen service in Afghanistan, suffering losses of 14,453 killed, 53,753 wounded, and 415,932 seriously ill (mostly from infectious diseases).[16]

*   *   *

The first estimates given to the Reagan administration about Soviet intentions in Afghanistan were that the Russians were prepared for the long haul but that they would be unlikely to take the war directly or at least very far into Pakistan. At the time, there were already 45,000 mujahideen fighters, mounting on average 500 attacks a month, and causing, in 1981, 4,500 deaths on the Communist side. The issue was whether it was worth pushing harder, and Casey, when first briefed, did wonder whether this was a place where the United States could "checkmate" the Soviets and "roll them back."[17] However, as with Zia, rather than a short, intensive push, he could see the advantage of a long, drawn-out campaign that would continue to hurt the Soviets without risking severe retaliation against Pakistan. At this time, the best advice was that the Soviets were resilient enough to cope with the mujahideen and eventually wear them down.

By 1983, the temptation to step up pressure on the Soviet position in Afghanistan was growing in Washington. Although Moscow was not making a lot of progress in pacifying the country, and in some areas had lost ground, its staying power was hardly being tested. Toward the end of the year Casey decided that the mujahideen, with proper support, might actually defeat the Soviets. In January 1984, he briefed Reagan and advisers. By this time, the CIA estimated, 17,000 Soviet soldiers had been killed or wounded by mujahideen, and they had lost numerous tanks and vehicles. The cost to Moscow was put at $12 billion, against which the United States had spent $200 million since the start of the insurgency, with an equivalent amount provided by the Saudis.[18] An intriguing coalition was supporting a stepped-up effort. Casey was as staunchly Catholic as anti-Communist and could appreciate the deep religious faith of the mujahideen. As his deputy, Robert Gates, later observed, Casey had come to the CIA not to be a better manager or quality controller of intelligence. "Bill Casey came to the CIA primarily to wage war against the Soviet Union."[19] By contrast, Representative Charlie Wilson (Democrat of Texas), who had emerged as the unlikely champion of the Afghan cause, had a personal lifestyle of drink, sex, and drugs that epitomized the sort of Western decadence that most appalled the Islamists.[20]

For the United States, pushing the resistance harder could lead to the intensification of the conflict with added loss of life and held the risk of provoking Moscow further without causing its defeat. It might also mean fewer opportunities to find diplomatic means to achieve a Soviet withdrawal. If the mujahideen were to be used, that meant they would take heavy casualties, only to be dropped when diplomatic circumstances changed and it was no longer expedient to continue to provide funds and supplies (as had happened, for example, with the Kurds in Iraq in 1975). A lot would depend on whether the Soviet Union was really vulnerable. The advocates of stepped-up action assumed that it was, buoying themselves with the thought that the United States was working with the tide of regional and international opinion. Those opposed warned that the Soviet position was solid and remorseless. If it would accept huge losses rather than succumb to a guerrilla war, then in the end the United States would be responsible for causing great pain to no strategic purpose. Additionally, neither side was showing great delicacy in the methods they were prepared to employ to hurt the other. A guerrilla war would inevitably lead into attacks on civilians that would equate to terrorism if experienced in Western cities. The CIA was nervous about getting into situations where it could be accused of taking aim at KGB personnel, even if only by encouraging and supporting the mujahideen, because of a tacit understanding between the two organizations not to kidnap or murder each other's officers. Since the mid-1970s, when there had been revelations about past "dirty tricks," there were official U.S. rules against assassination; distinguishing assassination from other forms of killing in a guerrilla war could be challenging.

National Security Decision Directive (NSDD) 166, "Expanded U.S. Aid to Afghan Guerillas," had established the aim of driving the Soviets out by "all available means." Funding was raised to $200 million per year. Congress (encouraged by Wilson) added more. The availability of large amounts of cash encouraged Afghan commanders to lobby Washington directly for resources, especially those who had been frozen out by the ISI. This set some alarm bells off in the administration and in Congress that the degree of internal cohesion among the rebels was not great. They were as susceptible to faction fighting and rivalry as the Communists. In addition to improved intelligence, the main benefit to the fighters was improved equipment. Supplies of old Soviet weaponry were running low.

During the summer of 1986, the mujahideen were struggling because of attacks from helicopters close to the border with Pakistan. The critical decision was to supply Stinger portable heat-seeking ground-to-air missiles to help the mujahideen cope with the Soviet helicopter threat. There were misgivings from the start about this move, including within the CIA. To date, no U.S. weapons had been supplied. Missiles were seen as dangerously provocative, with a risk that they might be diverted to groups whose aims the United States did not share. Zia was also wary about pushing things too far with Moscow until he could say he was no longer at risk from Soviet retaliation. Casey, with some support from Shultz, pushed against the opposition of his own staff and the military. Soviet helicopters were wearing the rebels down and the alternatives, such as the British Blowpipe, were of limited effectiveness. Against Stingers, Soviet pilots had no effective countermeasures and soon their helicopters were being shot down. A thousand Stingers were sent; about 350 were fired; others may have been used in training or lost in accidents. But there was soon evidence that the Iranians had managed to get hold of some, and after the war, the CIA scrambled around the arms market

trying to recover missiles, for which it paid inflated prices. It got 200 back—
leaving at least 200 unaccounted for.[21]

*   *   *

By the time it was all over and Soviet troops had left Afghanistan, Reagan's
vice president, George H. W. Bush, had taken over, and Casey had succumbed to brain cancer early in 1987. Zia died in a plane crash in August
1988, to be replaced by Benazir Bhutto, the daughter of the man he had executed. The Soviet exit exacerbated the differences between the various anti-
Communist groups, so the PDPA regime took far longer to collapse than
anticipated, lasting until 1992. The Communist Party of the Soviet Union
only managed to survive to December 1991. The conflict may not have been
solely responsible for the implosion of the Soviet Union, but it was certainly
a contributory factor. Afghanistan was in a mess and had years of civil war
ahead of it. In the largely Muslim republics of Central Asia, which emerged
from the ruins of the Soviet Union, Islamic parties were strong. Even as the
United States was stepping up deliveries of material, the leaders of the more
radical groups were telling their supporters that they were opposed to America as well as Russia. Meanwhile, in Pakistan's border regions, there were
complex social networks of refugee camps, relief agencies, charities, mis-
sionaries, intelligence officers, volunteers, and Wahhabi madrassas. In 1971,
there had been 900 religious schools in all of Pakistan. By the summer of
1988, there were about 8,000 official and as many as 25,000 unregistered
madrassas.[22] Zia had seen them, especially those on the border, as "a kind of
ideological picket fence between communist Afghanistan and Pakistan." The
Communists melted away; the madrassas did not.

7

IN AND OUT OF BEIRUT

By way of contrast with the covert and generally consensual approach to Afghanistan, the Reagan administration's approach to the Arab-Israel conflict was marked by constant disputes. With their normally strong Jewish support, Democratic presidents tended to be closest to Israel, but this was not the case with Carter because of his readiness to pressure Prime Minister Menachem Begin into what were alleged to be dangerous deals with the PLO. Reagan's intuitive pro-Israel position came through during the election campaign. As a result, Carter's percentage of the Jewish vote slumped from 80 to 60 percent. In addition, and though the State Department was expected to be pro-Arab, Haig was strongly pro-Israel, as was his successor, George Shultz. Other senior figures in the administration showed the more traditional Republican preference to avoid too close an association with Israel. Vice President George H. W. Bush and Secretary of Defense Caspar Weinberger argued the need for other regional allies, notably Saudi Arabia.

After the fall of the shah, Israel presented itself as a regional power that was ideologically congenial, as well as militarily dependable and capable, able to offer a strategic base from which core U.S. interests could be protected and further Soviet inroads could be prevented. The contrary argument, to which Bush and Weinberger were inclined, was that to the extent that American interests concerned oil, trade, and anticommunism, the Gulf monarchies, including Saudi Arabia, seemed a better bet. If this was the case, then too close an association with Israel became a liability, especially so long as relations with neighboring Arab states were hostile and the Palestinian question seemed far from resolution. Pushing the Israelis into further concessions did not always seem so sensible, however, when the beneficiaries were likely to be politically unstable, economically socialist, close to the Soviet Union, and sponsors of terrorism.

The Israeli government showed few signs of appreciating its good fortune in the president's attitudes or the extent to which opinion within his administration was by no means uniform. "Israel had never had a greater friend in the White House than Ronald Reagan," Haig later lamented, yet it "administered a series of violent shocks to the Administration and to public opinion."[1] Begin was stubborn, dogmatic, and shrill, and he tested the president's patience at every turn. There had been a shift in the internal balance within the Israeli government in late 1980, when two of the moderating influences on Begin—Moshe Dayan and Ezer Weizmann—resigned as foreign and defense ministers, respectively. Begin kept the defense portfolio for himself and brought in as foreign minister Yitzhak Shamir. Shamir, a fellow Pole who had been part of the anti-British Stern Gang in the 1940s, was if anything more hard-line than Begin. He had opposed the 1979 treaty with Egypt. When Begin won reelection in the summer of 1981, he appointed Ariel Sharon as defense minister. Whereas Shamir's toughness resided in his refusal to budge under pressure, Sharon's lay in his readiness to take bold and adventurous action. He was also a true war hero, and Begin deferred to his greater military knowledge.

The first argument between Begin and Reagan was over Saudi Arabia. Even before the Iranian revolution, Jimmy Carter was working to cultivate the Saudi regime, typically noting how his administration had not had "better friendship and a deeper sense of cooperation than we've found in Saudi Arabia."[2] This friendship was then disrupted because of Sadat. The Saudis were publicly supportive of Sadat's break with the Russians and quietly supportive of his push for a peace with Israel, but still wanted to maintain a united Arab front. They were unimpressed by his penchant for dramatic, surprising gestures and his reluctance to consult. The Camp David Accords, which offered the Palestinians so little, were the final straw. Although the Saudi royal family was split on the issue, the result was a complete break with Egypt, including a massive cut in economic aid, and an unnatural association with the radical camp.[3] Carter found himself using arms sales to sustain the relationship with Riyadh. A deal involving F-15 aircraft barely scraped through Congress in the face of opposition not only from the Israel lobby but also those among his supporters who were dismayed to find him using weapons to cement political relationships just as his predecessors had

done. The Saudis were also underwhelmed by Carter's fainthearted act of reassurance after the fall of the shah, when he had sent a dozen U.S. F-15s to
Saudi Arabia but without missiles so as not to appear provocative. This
pointless gesture sent exactly the wrong signal of tentativeness. The tougher
response to Afghanistan restored some faith in the relationship, especially as
there were now practical things the two countries could do together. By now
Iran was also becoming more of a worry, stirring up the Shi'ite communities
in eastern Saudi Arabia as well as in Bahrain and Kuwait.

Whatever their differences over Israel, the Reagan cabinet members agreed
on the importance of Saudi Arabia. It was a stalwart of the anti-Soviet camp.
To those nervous about too close an association with Israel, there was a
need, as Weinberger put it with some regularity, to have "more than one
friend in the region." Reagan considered it to be a "relatively moderate country" ready to resist Soviet expansion. "To put it simply I didn't want Saudi
Arabia to become another Iran."[4] Although the language in their statements
was convoluted, the Saudis also appeared to be prepared to accept Israel's
permanence. The centerpiece of the weapons package to reinforce U.S.-
Saudi relations was five sophisticated AWACS aircraft that had been half
promised by Carter. Israel and its congressional supporters threw everything
into opposition, arguing that Israel's technological edge over the Arabs was
at risk. The Saudis put on an impressive lobbying effort of their own, so that
for a while America's two closest regional allies were vigorously briefing
against each other in Washington. At one point it looked as if the administration would lose heavily, but eventually they got themselves organized,
pointed out the threat to the administration's foreign policy credibility, and
scraped through by 52 votes to 48 in the Senate on October 28, 1981. Reagan
recalled spending "more time on one-to-one meetings and on the telephone
attempting to win on this measure than on any other."[5] His displeasure at
the role played by the Israelis, including Begin himself while visiting Washington, was reflected in his observation "It is not the business of other nations to make American foreign policy."[6] As a result of this refusal to accept
the policy logic of cold war imperatives, Israel's claims to be a strategic asset
were undermined.

In the middle of all this, there was further flurry because of Israel's June
1981 attack on Iraq's Osiraq nuclear facility. Begin had seen a new holocaust
in the making. As he explained to Reagan, after the "million and a half children . . . poisoned with Ziklon Gas . . . Now Israel's children were about to
be poisoned by radioactivity." His timing reflected advice that it was best to
attack early rather than late (to reduce the risk of irradiating the surrounding population), rather than the coming general election, although the suc-

cessful attack helped. Up to this point, the opposition Labor Party had a comfortable lead in the polls, but the combination of the attack and the opposition to the AWACS sales helped put the electorate behind a government that was taking a firm stand on national security, and Begin won. Begin appears to have given no thought to the implications of launching the attack three days after meeting with Sadat, thereby making the Egyptian president appear complicit.[7] Nor on such matters was he bothered by any sense of equivalence, since Israel was already an implicit nuclear power. Other nations preferred to ignore Iraq's ambitions because Iraq had signed up to the relevant international treaty. Reagan was not unsympathetic to the Israeli position, especially when he found out that the issue had been discussed with Carter, if not with him.[8] Nonetheless, the administration could not condone unilateral military operations of this sort, and so backed the UN vote condemning it.

The biggest worry for the administration was that the Israelis would renege on Camp David and not complete the move out of Sinai, scheduled for April 1982. It would not be easy for Begin, as it would require the removal of well-entrenched settlers and abandoning a buffer zone. Anxieties on this score were not helped on October 6 when Islamists dressed as soldiers assassinated President Sadat while he was reviewing a parade. This was a tragic conclusion to Sadat's efforts to use the Muslim Brotherhood to counter the left's influence. His successor, the former vice president, Hosni Mubarak, promised to honor Camp David and follow the same line, but he was also aware of how isolated this had left Sadat at the end. Then, on December 14, 1981, Begin added further to Arab ire when he announced the annexation of the Golan Heights from Syria. Again this was done without warning the Americans, and against established American policy. The American sanction—the suspension of a recent agreement on strategic cooperation—may not have hurt much, but it demonstrated Washington's growing irritation and with it lapsed the idea that Israel had any useful role to play in the conduct of the cold war. When the U.S. ambassador came to complain, Begin read out a harsh statement, with charges of betrayal, condemning the United States for wanting the Americans to turn Israel into a "vassal state."[9] Reagan saw this as an attempt "to arouse our own Jewish community against us," noting later with relief that among American Jews in his own country as well, it was believed he had gone too far.[10]

Reagan was therefore relieved that Begin honored his commitment to withdraw from Sinai. Once that was done, to Begin's chagrin, the administration started to consider the next steps. In his first major statement of Middle Eastern policy, on May 26, 1982, Haig promised a growing engagement in the many problems in the Middle East, including Lebanon and the Iran-Iraq war, but also more efforts to push forward with talks on Palestinian autonomy. The key question was whether any progress on this could be made without the PLO. In the 1980 Venice Declaration, European Community members proposed direct negotiations between Israel and the PLO. As far as the Israelis were concerned, this statement removed the Europeans from any role as serious participants in the peace process. The Americans were not yet pushing for the PLO, but they did argue that the best way to marginalize the PLO was to allow the Palestinian people some semblance of self-government and stop encroaching on their land. This was the backdrop to the conflict in Lebanon.

★   ★   ★

Lebanon is a small country, bordered by Syria to its north and east, Israel to its south, and the Mediterranean to the west. The composition of the estimated 3.5 million population of Lebanon was around 70 percent Muslim to 30 percent Maronite Christian. There was a time, around the census taken in 1932, when the Christians made up 54 percent. The 1926 constitution divided the government up on a religious basis. An unwritten agreement at the time of independence from France in 1943, known as the National Covenant, required a Christian president, a Sunni Muslim prime minister, and a Shi'ite Speaker. Other than a supportive American intervention in 1958, most recently after the king of Iraq had been overthrown, when the pro-American president feared that he would be swept away by the Nasserite tide sweeping the Middle East, Lebanon had enjoyed a prosperous stability. Then, after September 1970, 350,000 Palestinians moved to Lebanon. This upset not only the balance between Christians and Muslims but also within the Muslim community. The activities of the Palestinian Fedayeen (Commandos) prompted a number of Israeli incursions into southern Lebanon. Serious clashes eventually erupted between the Fedayeen and Lebanese government forces in May 1973. In April 1975, after shots had been fired at a church, a busload of Palestinians was ambushed by gunmen in the Christian sector of Beirut. This incident is widely regarded as the spark that touched off the civil war.[11]

In October 1976, the Arab Deterrent Force (ADF), composed largely of 30,000 Syrian troops, moved in at the Lebanese government's invitation to separate the combatants, and most fighting ended soon thereafter. Then, after a Palestinian raid on a bus in northern Israel, Israel invaded Lebanon in March 1978, occupying most of the area south of the Litani River. The UN Security Council passed Resolution 425, calling for withdrawal of Israeli forces from Lebanon and creating the UN Interim Force in Lebanon (UNIFIL), charged with maintaining peace. When the Israelis withdrew, they turned over positions inside Lebanon along the border to their Lebanese ally, the Southern Lebanese Army (SLA), and formed a "security zone." Problems began again in 1981, when PLO rocket attacks led to devastating Israeli retaliation. The fighting was ended by a cease-fire arranged by Reagan's special envoy, retired ambassador Philip C. Habib, who was Lebanese American. The frustration felt by the Israelis at their inability to stop the rocket attacks was one reason they acceded, but it left Begin determined to move the enemy away from the border as soon as a decent plan was available. The sporadic, diffuse rocket attacks were an early indication that there were forms of warfare that Israel's policy of swift retribution to any attack was unable to deter.

With Syrian support, the PLO used the cease-fire to build up its capabilities on Israel's southern border as the Israelis plotted how to eliminate them when they got their chance. Alexander Haig understood the concern, but he could not sanction any unilateral Israeli breach of an American-brokered cease-fire. When the Israelis spoke about their need to address the threat, Haig's main guidance was that this should only be in response to PLO attacks and should be proportionate. In contrast to the PLO view that the cease-fire only covered the Lebanese border, Begin took the view that it covered any use of force anywhere, that proportionality is always open to interpretation, and that passivity risked disaster. He saw this as a turning point, the moment when a Jewish state could take its future into its own hands, no longer fighting wars as a last resort as enemies came upon them but proactively to remove a future threat. Drawing on a biblical distinction, which eventually came to acquire a wide currency, Begin spoke of a war of choice rather than one of necessity.[12]

The Israeli objectives went beyond the expulsion of the PLO. Sharon had in mind a complete reshaping of the geopolitical map. In his dreams, the Palestinians would be expelled from both Lebanon and the West Bank and pushed away to Jordan. In this scheme, he saw as allies the equally beleaguered Lebanon Christians. In September, presidential elections were due in Lebanon. One of the strong candidates was Bashir Gemayel, head of the Phalange Christian militia. Sharon was in regular contact with Gemayel and was convinced that he represented an opportunity to turn Lebanon into a partner of Israel.[13] It was the case that many Christians, though not all, did see Israel as an ally as they tried to maintain their position in fraught demographic circumstances. Their first priority, however, was their own security and not Israel's, and the Phalange was no different from any other militia in being concerned with loot and status as much as ethnicity, let alone ideology, and would have no compunctions about working with whatever external power served its purposes, including the Syrians.[14] Intra- as well as interfaith relations in Lebanon were never simple.

Sharon's plans therefore depended on optimistic assumptions about the response of the Lebanese Christians to the opportunities he would give them. It also depended on sustained American tolerance. There were suggestions that Sharon believed he was given a "green light" by Haig to invade. Haig vigorously denied this. It is doubtful whether it would have made much difference to Sharon if it had been shining red. Haig agreed that the PLO was behind much of Lebanon's instability, but not necessarily the corollary that their attempted expulsion by Israel would lead to stability. What the Israelis may have focused on was Haig's deep hostility to Syria, which he believed to be the Soviet Union's main instrument in the region. After Haig's first visit in 1981, they concluded that "with a man of Haig's bent running the State Department, Israel could definitely allow itself to adopt a militant posture vis-à-vis Damascus."[15] Even so, it is surprising that the Israelis did not qualify this optimism about Haig's support with some sensitivity to the balance of power within the administration, and the powerful group much less ready to assume an identity of interests with Israel.

*   *   *

On June 3, 1982, Begin and Sharon got their pretext, when there was an attempted assassination of the Israeli ambassador to London. Although the Abu Nidal group, which had been expelled from the PLO in the mid-1970s, was known to be responsible, Begin insisted that this was a detail. The Israelis attacked the PLO headquarters in Beirut, knowing that this would be followed by artillery attacks on Israeli towns in the Galilee, creating the opportunity for the big operation. On June 5, the Israeli cabinet approved a large-scale invasion, involving 70,000 troops, known as "Peace for Galilee." In the cabinet meeting, Begin and Sharon denied any intention of driving to Beirut or risking war with Syria. Their early claims of limited objectives not only gained the cabinet's support but also delayed the international response as the Israeli Defense Forces moved north. It quickly became apparent that the much larger objective of chasing the PLO out of Lebanon altogether was being pursued. The Americans felt deceived. McFarlane described this as the "worst case of bad faith on the part of Israel that the U.S. ever experienced."[16]

The Israeli army pushed past the small UN force and quickly through southern Lebanon. After encountering resistance around Tyre, the Israelis pressed on, looking to link with the Christian Phalange militia in Beirut. So far Syria held back, though extra troops had been moved into Lebanon, bringing its total to 40,000. Their control of the Bekaa Valley gave inevitable sanctuary to some PLO units based there. As the Americans were trying to keep the two apart, the Israelis attacked Syrian air defenses in the Bekaa Valley, destroyed much of their air force, with no losses of their own, and engaged with their army. By June 11, Syrian forces were held in an Israeli pincer. Anxious communications involving Damascus, Moscow, and Washington eventually led to a stern American demand for a cease-fire with Syrian forces.

Although their forces took substantial casualties in Tyre and Sidon, Israel was well on top militarily. The Palestinians were in full retreat, the Syrians were no longer a factor, and a wider war had been avoided. At this point Sharon appears to have assumed that Bashir Gemayel would finish the job and move his men into West Beirut to take out the remnants of the PLO. But these remnants amounted to thousands of fighters, and Bashir had an election in mind. A bloody urban battle did not seem like good electoral politics. This left the Israelis in a quandary. Their stated objective was to push the PLO out of Lebanon, but they had not thought through the end game. If the Christians would not act, they then must, but they were wary about entering West Beirut for the same reasons. The only alternative strategy to vicious street fighting was to make life as miserable as possible for the Palestinians through artillery barrages and air strikes, although this would inevitably also make life miserable for Lebanese civilians.

At this point, Haig attempted a complex diplomatic maneuver, by linking the efforts to end the impasse in Lebanon with those to revive the stalled Arab-Israeli peace process. This did not come off and led to his departure from government. "Dangerous and tragic though this turn of events was," according to Haig, "it provided a historic opportunity to deal with the problem of Lebanon by removing the causes of a national crisis that had long threatened to be mortal."[17] The starting point was that the only way to stabilize Lebanon was to remove the three foreign armies on its territory. The first step was to get the PLO out because that would remove the rationales for the Syrians and Israelis to stay. The Syrians were reeling from the humiliating loss of their aircraft and expensive, carefully constructed, Soviet-supplied air defenses around the Bekaa Valley (the Israelis claimed to have shot down twenty-three Syrian MIGs). In addition, this added strain to an already fragile alliance as accusations were traded between Moscow and Damascus as to whether the fault lay with the Soviet equipment or the Syrian pilots. Once everyone was out and its northern border was secure, then perhaps Israel might be persuaded to make more concessions to gain peace with Arab states and the Palestinian people. The last part of Haig's calculation was that if the legitimate government of Lebanon could be bolstered, then it, too, could play a constructive role in any peace process. This depended on quick action, and the Palestinian leadership accepting the hopelessness of their position. If the PLO believed that diplomatic pressure on Israel might let them off the hook, they would be tempted to wait, but the longer they waited, the harder Israel would push. At the same time, the harder Israel pushed, the more the diplomatic pressure against it would grow. For a fleeting moment Haig was convinced that a quick move in the president's name could be decisive. The PLO and Syria were reeling, Israel was uncertain about its next step, and Ambassador Habib was in place.

There were two problems. The first was that the PLO would only leave if it was assumed that nothing—including the Americans—would hold the Israelis back. By presenting its main objective in terms of ending the fighting rather than assessing the rights and wrongs of the Israeli advance, the United States was sheltering Israel from international criticism. "Above all," explained Haig, "we must not clarify our position publicly. We can tell the Israelis privately how upset we are with them, but we don't need a public break with Israel."[18] This was a challenging position for a secretary of state to take, especially one whose star was on the wane, which was the second problem. Haig's relations with the president were not good—Reagan sensed that Haig patronized him, and he had also unforgivably slighted his wife, Nancy. Relations with the White House staff, including William Clark, were even worse. The timing was also poor because the president and his entourage were in France for a summit.

All these tensions now overflowed as Haig was unable to get the decisions he wanted from the president. Only at the last minute did he get instructions to the UN to veto an anti-Israel resolution, which he thought spread the blame too unevenly but which the president's other advisers wanted him to accept. At the funeral of King Khalid of Saudi Arabia, who died on June 13, Bush and Weinberger apparently made known their unhappiness with Israeli tactics sufficiently for word to go to the PLO from Riyadh that American support for Israel was weakening. This encouraged a hardening of the PLO position just as Haig thought he had gotten their agreement to leave Beirut. For Haig, it was essential that the PLO did not believe that it could escape an Israeli attack. Haig complained to Reagan, but in a competition for influence with the president's close staff, there was no doubting the result. Haig's resignation was accepted while it was still being drafted. Reagan contrasted in his diary "how sound" Haig could be "on complex international matters but how utterly paranoid with regard to the people he must work with."[19] Although Haig stayed on for a few more days, soon George Shultz had taken over.

★ ★ ★ ·

On June 25, as Yasser Arafat declared his intention to make Beirut his Stalingrad if need be, massive Israeli air and artillery strikes were launched against West Beirut. A three-month siege of Palestinian and Syrian forces in the city began. As international opinion became increasingly disconcerted by these events, so did a number of Sharon's colleagues, who became uncertain where he was taking them. Particularly perplexing was the lack of evident results. Palestinian fighters were under siege, but they were far from surrender and their elimination would only come at a frightful humanitarian cost. By July, with the media reporting on the heavy human toll of the intensifying bombardment of Beirut, the Reagan administration stance began to shift. The Americans offered to provide troops to supervise the departure of the PLO from Beirut, although part of the problem was finding somewhere for them to go, because no Arab state wanted to host them. Habib worked to get a sufficiently robust cease-fire to make the evacuation possible. Sharon wanted the PLO and the Syrians to surrender and to this end, and with increasing desperation, kept up the pressure. When Reagan began to demand more compliance from Israel, Begin was at first defiant.

On July 30, Clark called Shultz to say, "The president's friendship for Israel is slipping. Enough is enough."[20] There was another cease-fire, but when this collapsed again, the president himself was involved. On August 12, 1982, first Habib called, frustrated that he could not make arrangements to get the PLO out because of an intensive Israeli barrage. He was followed on the phone by King Fahd of Saudi Arabia. Reagan was already deeply upset by a picture of a baby with its arm blown off. He rang Begin. "Menachem," said the president with a provocative but deliberate opening, "this is a holocaust." Reagan warned of the damage that was being done to U.S. relations with Israel. "It's got to stop." Begin then ordered Sharon to end the assault. The bombing eased, but then attacks began in northern Lebanon. Reagan followed up with a strong letter, demanding an immediate strict cease-fire and warning that future relations were "at stake if these military eruptions continue." Begin responded, expressing his deep hurt over the use of the word "holocaust" ("of which I know some facts") and insisting what was done was to deal with the "scourge of terrorism." He had relied on the same language too often to cover too many actions that the administration judged to be counterproductive to Israel and harmful to America. It was not even clear that Begin fully appreciated what was going on. His son later recalled his comment, "I know everything, sometimes beforehand, and sometimes post facto."[21] On August 15, a deal was struck, involving PLO evacuation and an Israeli cease-fire.

*   *   *

The American role in brokering this deal led to its direct involvement in Lebanese politics. Shultz, along with the NSC staff, saw this as an opportunity to play a creative role in regional politics. By negotiating an immediate local disengagement in Beirut, conditions would be created for a wider regional disengagement. Weinberger believed it unwise to intervene in "a small country, torn by civil war, without strategically important resources, whose main claim to American attention was its ability to serve as a breeding ground for trouble in a very volatile region of the world."[22] At the center of the internal debate was whether an American military presence could set in motion a virtuous cycle or instead, as the Pentagon warned, invite a Soviet response, create friction with the local community, and strain American public support.

Underlying this debate was a question of the proper role of armed forces in such situations. From the Pentagon perspective, military objectives should be set with a clear purpose in mind and be achievable. It was both futile and dangerous to send forces too small to make a major impact on the local situation but large enough to attract attention and animosity. The State Department saw the conspicuous deployment of forces as an adjunct to diplomacy, a means of shaping attitudes about American power and interests. Because of Vietnam, U.S. governments had been understandably reluctant to put forces into a combat zone. If this could be done successfully in Lebanon, then that would send a larger message that U.S. military power was coming back into the international arena. As one NSC staffer put it, "My goodness! Look what the United States is prepared to do. We're prepared to use power to advance our objectives as part of our political strategy."[23] The advantage of this case was that the risks seemed low because the role did not have to be too forceful. Moving into Beirut with the consent of the belligerents seemed a safer bet than a forced entry.

Reagan accepted that the United States should back a deal it had brokered and for which it took credit. The existence of the marines would make it easier for the PLO fighters to leave, as the Americans would provide some guarantee that the Palestinians left behind would be protected. So he agreed that 800 marines would be deployed to the Lebanese capital as part of a multinational force, along with French and Italian units. Yet he also made a fateful compromise. To meet Weinberger's anxiety about getting into an open-ended commitment, which was soon picked up by Congress, he agreed that the marines would stay for no more than thirty days, half the time proposed by the State Department. Congress got a promise that there would be no UN mandate and no central command. Each of the contributing countries would make their dispositions according to their own judgments and prefer-ences. The French and Italian contingents went to the Green Line, where Christian East Beirut was separated from Muslim West Beirut. Weinberger considered such a position far too exposed, and so the U.S. contingent was placed close to the port area.

Initially, all went well. The forces were in place as 15,000 PLO fighters and Syrian units left by sea. Arafat traveled to Athens for an official welcome, soon to be followed by an audience with the pope. He hoped to follow the Middle East tradition of turning military defeat into political victory, but the PLO's credibility as a serious army was now lost. Arafat had talked of martyrdom but had chosen retreat. As always, there were no limits to the rhetorical support from his fellow Arabs but few tangible signs of practical support. He relocated to Tunis.

The State Department argued against being in a rush to get the marines out of Beirut. The local situation was not yet stable, and also there was a pos-sibility for a close alliance with the new Lebanese government, formed after the election of a Christian leader, Bashir Gemayel, as president on August 23. As far as Weinberger was concerned, the mission was accomplished and the troops now could leave. Without consulting anyone else, he ordered the troops out. So, four days after the marines had arrived it was announced, to general surprise, that they would leave within fourteen days. The Italians and French had little choice but to follow. This left no time for their vacated positions to be taken over by the Lebanese Armed Forces.

On September 14, Gemayel was assassinated by a bomb explosion at his Phalangist Party headquarters, apparently by a Syrian agent. He had seemed well-placed to begin a process of reconciliation among the divided Lebanese community, but there were many scores being settled in Lebanon. If the international force had stayed, his position might still have become untenable, but without the forces, the consequences were much greater. Against American opposition, as a breach of the cease-fire, the Israeli gov-ernment took the assassination as a cue to enter Beirut. The ostensible purpose was to maintain order, but Sharon saw an opportunity to deal with unfinished business. Israeli forces surrounded the Palestinian camps of Sabra and Shatilla, where they believed many PLO militants had been left behind. They left the Phalange militia to sort out this last remaining problem. If the Israelis thought that the Phalange would behave as a "digni-fied" army and focus solely on PLO fighters, they were at best naïve and at worst knowing. While Israeli forces guarded the camps' exits, a massacre took place with at least 700–800 Palestinians murdered, and probably many more. Israel desperately tried to deflect blame—a "blood libel" according to Begin. The Israeli chief justice, Yitzhak Kahan, made the comparison with a pogrom and stressed the culpability of those who claimed responsibility for public safety. Begin was blamed for his indifference and Sharon and chief of staff General Eitan were charged with culpability for the massacre. When this came out in February 1983, Sharon was obliged to leave government. Begin, disillusioned with the turn of events and depressed by the death of his wife, followed in September.

*   *   *

The massacre was a devastating consequence of the evacuation of the PLO fighters. The Israelis had promised Habib that the PLO need not fear for its people, and now they had been complicit in a massacre. The international outrage was enormous. On September 20, Reagan received a formal Lebanese request for the return of peacekeepers, to which, along with the French and Italians, he acceded. The British joined in with a modest contribution.

Whether or not there was a link between the withdrawal of the first U.S. peacekeeping force and the disastrous events that immediately followed, the views of Weinberger and General John Vessey (chairman of the Joint Chiefs of Staff) were now discredited. This did not stop them from again objecting to the new multinational force. They complained about its poorly defined mission, which, when clarified, Weinberger disparaged as "demonstrably un-attainable."[24] Regardless, the advocates of intervention now had the political upper hand. They pressed forward their view that only a renewed American presence could calm a tense situation and get the Israelis and Syrians out of the country.

This, the NSC staff suggested, required a force of several American and French divisions, perhaps involving as many as 15,000 personnel. Wein-berger and Vessey once again, having lost on principle, won on practicality. To avoid an extended entanglement, they sought a small force, capable of quick introduction, inexpensive support, and easy withdrawal. As a result, the U.S. component of the Multi-National Force (MNF) was put at 1,200 men ashore. While the Pentagon won on keeping the force small, they lost on the schedule. The chiefs of staff wanted to set a deadline of sixty days, but on September 28, 1982, Reagan announced that the marines would remain until all of the Israeli, Syrian, and PLO forces withdrew, from all of Lebanon and not just Beirut, and the government of Lebanon was fully in control. As this would be a traditional peacekeeping role with the consent of the belligerents, the marines would not engage in combat, other than in self-defense and then with restraint, and would not move outside Beirut or support anybody else's forces. There must be no inference that they were responsible for anything other than their own positions or were taking sides. Their neutrality was to be maintained scrupulously. It would be up to the Lebanese Armed Forces (LAF) to suppress interfactional violence.

It was, however, one thing for the MNF to interpose itself between the warring parties to help them calm down and think about reconciliation and reconstruction. It was another to support the Lebanese authorities (or the closest approximation) as they tried to reunite the country and negotiate the withdrawal of the Israeli and Syrian forces. The only reason to believe that this package might work was the psychological state of Beirut at the time. Groups were both confrontational and insecure. They were looking to the MNF as a tranquilizer, but most of all as a guarantee of Israeli good behavior. If the MNF had to withdraw, the country would be in an even greater mess. So, the hope was that the prospect of a more desperate confrontation would create an incentive not to make things worse by attacking the modestly armed peacekeepers. But getting the Israelis to withdraw was already a demanding goal, and when this became apparent, the Americans became even more ambitious, working more closely with the Lebanese Armed Forces, and so upping rather than lowering the stakes and putting local consent at risk.

Initially, the troops were colocated with the LAF to demonstrate visibly U.S. intentions to support the government of Lebanon as the Israelis and Syrians withdrew. They deployed to the south of Beirut, away from Beirut's most populated areas. This area included an accessible shoreline and the international airport, simplifying the problems of introducing and extracting the marines. In other respects, however, it was unsatisfactory—the ground was low, flat, and indefensible.

Because the MNF was the main American lever in the developing situation, the State Department and NSC wanted to make the most of it by backing the new president, Amin Gemayel, the assassinated Bashir's brother. They were also optimistic that such a firm U.S. stand would help moderate Israeli intransigence. Political success, however, would depend on many factors other than the continuing presence of the MNF. Amin was to pick up where Bashir left off, but he was not of the same political caliber. He lacked his brother's experience and was more sectarian and less interested in reaching out to the various Muslim communities. The very fact of the assassination, in addition to the terrible events at the refugee camps, had left Lebanese society tense. Stability would require American (and French) economic assistance, but this could only be delivered once a local accord had been reached. If any accord was to last, the LAF had to provide local law and order and a unifying force in itself. In no way could it cope in a direct confrontation with either the Syrian or the Israeli army. Getting foreign troops out therefore required some diplomatically brokered deal. Nobody was in a position to push them out. Here the problem was that the Syrians wanted an unconditional Israeli withdrawal, but the Israelis had conditions. They were really after a peace treaty with Lebanon. But Bashir had told Begin and Sharon just before he died that he could not get Muslim support for such a step. It would leave Lebanon isolated just when it needed help from the rest of the Arab world. Amin's political position, and his credibility with Muslim segments of the community, were even weaker and were unlikely to get stronger until the Israelis were out.

*   *   *

The Israelis were attracting great hostility. Many Lebanese would have been more than content if the Israelis had pushed out the PLO and then departed, even if some PLO pockets had been left behind, but by staying they provoked local anger, aggravated by the damage they caused to Beirut and their negligence over the massacres in the two camps. As a result, the Israeli Defense Forces started to be attacked. The IDF not only blamed the U.S. marines for protecting those mounting the attacks but even began to harass the MNF. Most important, they refused to pull back sufficiently to allow the marines to get into a position where they could not be accused from the other direction of protecting the Israelis. The administration made known its mounting displeasure with Israel, within and beyond Lebanon.

If the Americans had demanded an unconditional withdrawal, there would have been a fierce argument, but Israel might have been hard put to resist for long, especially as its forces in Lebanon were becoming stressed and overstretched. Instead, Washington took the view that these developing difficulties would at least make the Israelis amenable to a negotiated withdrawal. Even though this would involve conditions unacceptable to Arab states, there was still hope that it might elicit some positive response from Syria, still recovering from its own battering at the hands of the Israelis. This was unrealistic. The Syrians had indicated some interest in a deal, with what sincerity it is hard to tell, but they gradually lost interest as the Israeli position began to look more parlous and Damascus patched up relations with Moscow. President Assad could see opportunities to make life miserable for the Israelis, and he could never tolerate the conditions that would prompt the Israelis to leave of their own accord.

*   *   *

A further complication at this point came with a broader American peace initiative. The administration had concluded that the situation was too dangerous to let fester and that it had to move the peace process along, even if the Israelis screamed all the way. Reagan's speech of September 1, 1982, the only one he ever made on the Middle East, tried to build on Camp David by finding a solution for the occupied territories somewhere between Israeli annexation and a Palestinian state, involving a form of association among the West Bank, Gaza, and Jordan but also a freeze on settlements and full Israeli withdrawal. Unfortunately, as a compromise it satisfied nobody. The Israelis rejected it immediately, furious with the last condition, while the Arabs, applauding the direction in which Reagan was moving, still argued for an independent Palestinian state. A lot of effort had been put into cultivating King Hussein, and though this was the optimum outcome for Jordan, he dared not go too far out on a limb, especially after seeing what had happened to Sadat. Over the next six months, he tried to find a way to gain the PLO's consent, but they refused to budge from a hard line.[25] The lukewarm Arab response worked to the Israeli advantage. The Arabs made Israel's departure for Lebanon a precondition for any progress. This suggested a simple strategy to the Israelis. Going slow on withdrawal would ensure that Reagan's initiative was stillborn.

Without the broader context of a peace process addressing the Palestinian issue, there was little chance that a narrow Israeli-Lebanonese treaty would hold, especially if obviously negotiated under duress. The Lebanese government was so weak and dependent on American support that it might be persuaded to agree, but in doing so it would alienate the Muslim population, which, up to this point, had taken a reasonably benign view of the American role. Yet over the first months of 1983, Shultz pressed ahead, now hoping that an Israeli-Lebanese treaty might somehow encourage a wider Middle Eastern peace. A series of concessions to Israel on technology for the Lavi fighter and strategic cooperation was followed by severe pressure on Lebanese prime minister Shafiq al-Wazzan to sign an agreement. The accord signed on May 17, 1983, allowed Israel to keep observers in Lebanon while the Israeli-backed militia, the Southern Lebanese Army, would be incorporated into the Lebanese Armed Forces. There were to be joint Lebanese-U.S.-Israeli security arrangements, while a commission would worry about Israel's northern borders. Even then, Israel did not have to withdraw fully unless Syria did at the same time. Once the IDF was withdrawn, then Lebanon was committed to normalize relations within six months.

This was a time-consuming and pointless exercise. The United States had not found a way to negotiate sensibly with Syria, relying on wishful thinking that the Saudis would encourage them to be reasonable. While Shultz had been pursuing this track, Assad had taken the opportunity to rearm, fully aware that no deal would work without his acquiescence. He now could make a similar judgment to Israel in favor of staying put. If the Israelis would not withdraw before Syria, and the Americans would not press them to do so, he had no reason to fear that intransigence would lead to isolation. Assad stated at once that Syria's army would stay unless and until the accord was repudiated by the Gemayel government. Worse still, Syria was actively inciting Lebanese Muslims to challenge the accord and the Gemayel government. As militant Christians were moving closer to Israel, and with the PLO now out of the picture, it seemed natural for hard-line Muslims to move closer to Syria.

*   *   *

This changed political context put the U.S. marines in danger. The IDF was on one side and increasingly hostile Shi'ites on the other. The Druze, a distinctive religious minority, were restive. As they lacked natural allies among the various confessional groups within Lebanon, they had always been politically agile when it came to the formation of coalitions. They had, however, a long history of vicious relations with the Maronite Christians, and this was now the major influence on their actions. The marines were giving noncombat support to the small Lebanese Armed Forces, with its predominantly Christian officer corps, supporting a government that had antagonized the Muslim communities. As the LAF took a bolder stance, the Americans found themselves coming in behind, without the implications of this extension of their role being fully appreciated. At first their "presence" alone was supposed to boost the government and the LAF. Then, in November 1982, their mandate was extended to cover limited noncombat-related support for the LAF, with provision of equipment and training. Next, in February 1983, "presence" was extended, at Gemayel's request, to include patrolling in East Beirut, which made it harder to claim neutrality in Lebanon's domestic disputes. There were joint checkpoints and on occasion joint patrolling. The line was still drawn against participation in direct combat support or antiterrorist operations, but the relationship was getting palpably closer.

The first U.S. casualties came on March 16, when five troops were wounded with a hand grenade. Soon the Italians and French were also being targeted. On April 18, the U.S. Embassy in Beirut was car-bombed, destroying the embassy and killing fifty-seven people, of whom seventeen were American. Among the dead were Robert Ames, a senior intelligence official, plus the local CIA station chief and his deputy. It was suspected—but not proven—that both the Iranians and Syrians had been involved.

This was a crucial moment for a reappraisal of policy. Congress was wary. It was prepared to vote more aid for Lebanon but not to authorize a greater role for the MNF unless President Reagan made a better case. Meanwhile, it placed restrictions on the size, disposition, mission, and employment of the force. Yet the inexorable logic of an expanding military role continued to work itself through. If American diplomats were to stay in an increasingly insecure Beirut, then they would need protection. The problem was later described as "mission creep"—the tendency for military roles to develop incrementally and move beyond previously agreed limits. The same modest, lightly armed force was being asked to take on a greater range of tasks in a deteriorating situation.

In July 1983, the Israelis destabilized the situation further by announcing a partial withdrawal to the Awali River. This meant abandoning the Shouf District (southeast of Beirut), where they had acted as a buffer between the Druze and the Christian militias. They left in August without coordinating their departure with the LAF. The Phalange prepared to enter in force against the objections of the Druze. Gemayel wanted the MNF to accompany the LAF into the Shouf. The aim was a classic peacekeeping operation, depending on the consent of the warring parties. The Americans sought an agreement between the Druze leader, Walid Jumblatt, and Gemayel. Syria wasted no time in persuading Jumblatt not to cooperate.

Thus the marines either had to abandon the LAF or follow them into the Shouf. They followed and were soon caught in cross fire. On September 5, two marines were killed and three wounded by the Druze militia. The frigate USS *Bowen* of the Sixth Fleet responded with five-inch guns, silencing the Druze artillery on the Shouf Mountains. After this demonstration of military power, Robert McFarlane, recently appointed the U.S. special negotiator, pressed for authority to commit the U.S. forces directly in support of the LAF. "I can't get it out of my head," confided Reagan to his diary, "that some F-14's off the Eisenhower coming in at about 200 feet above the Marines and blowing hell out of a couple of artillery emplacements would be a tonic for the Marines and at the same time would deliver a message to those gun happy Middle East terrorists."[26] On September 10, 1983, Reagan approved a more "active presence" in the greater Beirut area, including an "aggressive self-defense" against hostile or provocative acts directed against the MNF or

other governmental personnel operating in Lebanon, or both. The battleship USS *New Jersey,* with sixteen-inch guns, arrived off the coast, increasing
the number of U.S. warships offshore to fourteen. The marine contingent at
Beirut airport was increased from 1,200 to 1,600.

On the ground, the Phalange were no match for the Druze militia, which
began to move toward Beirut. Gemayel and the LAF decided to make their
stand at the town of Suq Al Gharb. This was declared vital to the "self-defense"
of the MNF, whose positions were close and would be vulnerable if the town
fell. This allowed the Sixth Fleet to provide air and naval gunfire support to
the LAF. Despite their misgivings, Weinberger and Vessey were unable to
prevent the increasing American entanglement in the developing civil war.
The MNF commanders were also alarmed; the militias might have no direct
answer to the heavy U.S. firepower coming from the sea, but they could always take their revenge on the vulnerable marines onshore.

On September 18, 1983, four U.S. warships unleashed the heaviest naval
bombardment since Vietnam into Syrian and Druze positions in eastern
Lebanon. This lasted for three days and, for the moment, Suq Al Gharb was
held. In the land battle, the LAF also did better than expected (though expectations had not been high). Encouraged, Shultz and McFarlane believed
that this showed how the Pentagon was exaggerating the difficulties and un-
derestimating American power. Another positive factor was that the French
had taken a similar position and had struck against Druze positions in the
Shouf with eight aircraft. Together, these events had had a salutary effect on
Syrian and Druze thinking to the point of stimulating interest in a cease-fire.
The Druze did not want to fight against hopeless odds, and Assad was wary
about committing the Syrian army, especially while there was a possibility
that the Israelis would join the fray. So, while Congress was not ready to
agree to augment the U.S. MNF, it was prepared to let it stay for another
eighteen months.

Weinberger remained unhappy. The United States was supporting not so
much a legitimate government as one side in a civil war. In his memoirs he
lamented how the State Department "stubbornly clung to its 'agreement' as
if it were a major diplomatic triumph" and played on the president's concern
that the removal of the MNF would appear as an American defeat. Using
phrases such as "cut and run" and "driven out" encouraged "the belief that
only if we stayed in Lebanon could we demonstrate our manhood or secure
any of our objectives." [27] In public, Weinberger stuck to the official line supporting the government and asserting the MNF's deterrent effect. In private,
he was seeking some way of reducing the size of the force ashore and their
concentration at Beirut International Airport. The Sixth Fleet's firepower

was more likely to make an impact if it could be used without concern for reprisals against the marines. He was prepared to provide material support to the LAF. In short, he followed the familiar formula of combining American firepower with indigenous ground forces. Unfortunately for his plan, the Syrians were also demanding the withdrawal of MNF, so to do that would look like giving in to their pressure, whereas the other contingents of the multinational force wanted the United States to stay. Control of the international airport might be very welcome under certain scenarios.

Although the mission was becoming more hazardous, it was not as yet alarmingly so. By October 22, the U.S. force of 1,600 had suffered seven killed and forty-seven wounded (in contrast to the sixteen killed and fifty wounded of the 2,000-strong French force). The fall of 1983 was calm enough to allow the second marine amphibious unit, which had been held in reserve, to steam home on October 9. Business was getting back to normal. The MNF contingents kept a low profile while material was transferred to the LAF. Yet the buildup of intelligence warned that terrorist attacks were being planned against the force, including with car bombs, although the reports were short on specifics. From August to October, the trickle of warnings started to become a flood.

On October 23, 1983, just before 6:30 AM, as the marines slept in their compound at Beirut airport, a Mercedes truck turned into the airport parking lot, circled the area twice, and then accelerated to crash through the barbed fence that surrounded the headquarters building, passing sentries before exploding with the force of 12,000 pounds of TNT. It was, according to the FBI Forensic Laboratory, the largest conventional blast it had ever seen. Witnesses recollect the driver grinning as he broke through barriers. Of 350 marines, soldiers and sailors in the building, 241 were killed as the structure collapsed upon them. At the same time, also in Beirut, another suicide bomber attacked the French barracks, where fifty-eight people were killed. Iranian-backed Shi'ites were soon held responsible. The then head of the Iranian Revolutionary Guards later cheerfully boasted about providing "both the TNT and the ideology."[28]

*   *   *

Until the 1978 invasion, the Shi'ite community in Lebanon showed no particular animus toward the Israelis. There was sufficient irritation with the arrogance, corruption, and heavy-handedness of the Palestinians that some even considered forming a common cause with the Israelis against the PLO. But the Israelis made no attempt to work with them and instead assumed Shi'ite complicity, which led to considerable local suffering. Even in 1982, the thought of getting rid of the PLO overcame misgivings as the Israelis entered southern Lebanon, but once again the Israelis became convinced that there were PLO sympathizers or militants everywhere. They took prisoners, pulverized houses, and acquired a new enemy. The Shi'ites had been represented politically by the Amal Party, founded when the civil war began in 1975 and relatively moderate, with middle-class leadership. Since 1979, Khomeinism had offered a rival appeal. Hussein Musawi, a chemistry teacher, split with Amal's leader, Nabih Berri, over Berri's readiness to engage in negotiations with the Americans. He founded "Islamic Amal," which led, in late 1982, to the formation of Hezbollah (the party of God). This was initially an umbrella organization for Islamists, committed to the view that even Lebanon, with its large Christian community, could and should be an Islamic state.

The Syrians had mixed feelings about all of this. In Syria, Shi'ites were in the minority, although President Assad's Alawite group had Shi'ite links. Since Assad took power in 1970, the Sunni Muslim Brotherhood had agitated against him. They had objected to his de facto support for the Maronites in Lebanon in 1976, and this was followed by assassinations. The campaign gathered momentum in 1979, especially after eighty-three Alawite cadets were killed in an attack on an artillery school in Aleppo in June, culminating in an attempt to assassinate Assad a year later. The army took revenge on Muslim Brothers already held prisoner, massacring up to 1,000. The violence continued, with regular car-bomb attacks. For the regime, this was now a fight for survival. In February 1982, the Brotherhood took control of the city of Hama. The Syrian response was brutal. The city was bombed incessantly, leaving as many as 25,000 dead. Unusually for these cases, the regime pushed the published numbers up, to make sure the Muslim Brotherhood and those who would support them got the message. They were not going to be loved, so they must be feared.[29] The regime was never troubled again.

Thus, Assad's was not a regime inclined to support Islamists. Within Lebanon, Assad preferred to work with the relatively moderate Amal Party. Although allied with the Iranians, up to the 1982 Israeli invasion, he discouraged their active engagement in Lebanon. He then relented and agreed that Iranian volunteers could go to Lebanon. These were members of the Revolutionary Guard: "Ostensibly meant to fight Israel, the guards were really political commissars for the Iranian Revolution."[30] Their natural partner was Hezbollah, and it was Iranian money and enthusiasm that helped Hezbollah's rapid rise. The regular shelling of Muslims by American battleships provided the rationale for stepping up attacks on the United States.

The devastating bombing of the marine barracks in October appeared to succeed in its mission of persuading the marines to leave Beirut. The reality is more complex. In the first instance, in the United States an expeditious withdrawal seemed politically impossible rather than essential. Reagan immediately sent 300 replacement marines and contacted leading figures in Congress to get their support for staying. When a visiting Lebanese dignitary in March observed that "past experience with A. [American] Presidents was that they advanced so far and then retreated," Reagan insisted he "didn't have a reverse gear."[31] This was exactly the reputation he was trying to change. He had also just approved the intervention in Grenada, which began on October 25, and he did not want this assertive message confused by a contrary one from Lebanon. Weinberger, who was now determined to get the marines out come what may, proposed an immediate cut in their numbers to 600; instead they were reinforced with a fourth infantry company to defend the airport, which Reagan said was now part of their mission. There was still hope that the LAF could turn itself into a serious army, especially backed by the firepower of the Sixth Fleet, while the MNF concentrated on its own protection. Even the chiefs of staff were coming around to the view that unless it was possible to withdraw completely, it was better to stick with the MNF so long as those forces could safely keep the airport under control. The aim was still to keep Gemayel in place, while encouraging him to agree to a more equitable distribution of political power and to develop a more sophisticated approach to internal Lebanese politics.

If there was, after October, a new imperative driving policy, it was the urge to retaliate. By November 8, the Sixth Fleet had been reinforced with a second aircraft carrier battle group, suggesting preparations for a retaliatory strike of significant proportions. There was excellent intelligence implicating Iran directly in the attack, for Iranian as much as Lebanese reasons. France, for example, was an important arms supplier to Iraq in its war with Iran. It was also known where the Iranian Revolutionary Guards were billeted. In his memoir, Reagan suggests that the reason for not striking was that "our intelligence experts found it difficult to establish conclusively who was responsible for the attack" and says that as he did not want to kill innocent people, he canceled the planned strikes.[32] McFarlane, who was now national security adviser, recorded that he convened a meeting on November 14 to agree on a retaliatory strike with the French on November 16. Although the president authorized the strike, Weinberger denied it. Reagan was disappointed, but it was not his style to come down heavily on insubordination, especially when it was from old colleagues.[33] Reagan's diaries confirm that targets had been identified but are silent on Weinberger's role. Instead, they note that the French attacked these targets without the United States on November 17 (at which Reagan expressed surprise).[34] In addition, the Israelis, following a painful attack on their headquarters at Tyre, were also attacking Shi'ite targets in the Bekaa Valley. Publicly, the United States could say there had been quite enough retaliation for the moment. On November 17, therefore, Shultz announced that there would be no further discussion of a U.S. retaliatory strike. Israel and France had done the job for them.

Early on the morning of December 3, Israeli air strikes again pounded targets in the Bekaa Valley. When an hour later U.S. F-14s flew over a nearby portion of the Syrian-controlled area in Lebanon, they were attacked by surface-to-air missiles and antiaircraft fire. The F-14s escaped, but it was the third attack in recent days. With Weinberger out of town, McFarlane encouraged the president to order an immediate response. At dawn the next day, aircraft from the carriers *Kennedy* and *Independence* struck three Syrian missile-launching sites. Two U.S. planes were shot down, with one airman killed and another captured. Reagan told the press that in the future, "if our forces are attacked, we will respond." Then, in retaliation, U.S. forces at the airport came under intense ground fire. Although the attacks were repulsed, one mortar scored a direct hit and killed seven marines instantly. This did not convey an appropriate image of overwhelming power and led to continual public bickering. Again Weinberger argued for moving MNF out; again Shultz felt that marines had to stay at the airport, which is also what the other MNF nations wanted. On December 14, Syrians again fired at U.S. aircraft engaged in reconnaissance. Almost at once the battleship *New Jersey* fired its sixteen-inch guns at Syrian targets. Weinberger considered all these actions "exercises in futility," because they had nothing to do with "winning."[35]

✶   ✶   ✶

It was an accumulation of events that made it apparent that the MNF as constituted could not succeed. The NSC and State still wanted to step up the military pressures against Syria, but the Pentagon argued against "pursuing fruitless tactics in pursuit of unreachable goals" and for disengagement. The May 17 accord between Israel and Lebanon was now irrelevant, and the crisis could not be resolved through the application of U.S. force. A plan for withdrawal was drawn up. On December 14, Reagan announced that the MNF would be withdrawn if the Gemayel government collapsed. This of course in itself made the event more likely, though as late as the end of January, Reagan was considering employing Israel's supporters to persuade an increasingly doubtful Congress to stay firm.[36]

Through January, the fighting in the Shouf and in South Beirut threatened the well-fortified marine positions with automatic and indirect weapons fire. The most significant change, however, was in the nature of the threat, for civilians now became targets. In the midst of other killings and kidnappings, Malcolm Kerr, president of the American University of Beirut (AUB), was assassinated. Meanwhile, at the start of February, Shi'ite militiamen surged into South and West Beirut, the LAF began to crumble, and brigades began to defect. The government began to collapse. On February 5, Reagan insisted that "the situation in Lebanon is difficult, frustrating, and dangerous. But this is no reason to turn our backs on friends and to cut and run." The next day, Professor Frank Regier, a U.S. citizen teaching at AUB, was kidnapped, the first of a series of kidnappings of Americans in Beirut that would hound the Reagan and later the Bush administration for years. That day also, Gemayel was confirming his readiness to scrap the accord, as his government unraveled. Regier's kidnapping was the last straw. On February 7, 1984, Reagan suddenly reversed himself and announced that all U.S. marines would shortly be "redeployed."

There then followed yet another compromise between two incompatible schools of thought. McFarlane agreed to the demand for withdrawal in return for a final show of muscle. The government and the LAF still had control of some areas, the Israelis still wanted to reinforce Christians against Syrian domination, and the Sixth Fleet was still ready to strike if the MNF was attacked directly. To warn off the militias, U.S. naval gunships began pounding enemy artillery positions with nearly 800 rounds of sixteen-inch and five-inch shells. The militias began to hold back, allowing on February 10–11 an evacuation from Beirut of 900 civilians, including 200 Americans. On February 14, as the militias took control of more of the city, confining the LAF to Christian East Beirut and Suq Al Gharb, Reagan agreed that the marines would be withdrawn. The Italians and French were not consulted (the British had already left). Just before the marines left, Reagan tried to explain that the United States was not "bugging out" because it was only redeploying to a safer place, ships offshore, where they would still be at hand. Only if they came "all the way home" would it be "an admission" that terrorist attacks could succeed.[37] On February 26, as the marines embarked on ships, the Gemayel government signaled that it was now looking to Syria rather than the United States to help sort things out. On March 5, Gemayel abrogated the accord with Israel.

*   *   *

The Beirut experience was sobering in a number of respects. The problems lay in the failure to integrate the political with the military strategy. The limited U.S. military presence was adequate for a peacekeeping job, but it was always going to be put under strain in such a fluid situation when other countries were occupying parts of Lebanon and militias were operating freely. Peacekeeping depends on the consent of the other parties. There was some consent at the start of the operation, but in many cases, it was only grudgingly supplied and was always liable to be withdrawn as the underlying configuration of forces changed. The attempt to push Lebanon in a direction that was bound to be resisted by a number of key parties exposed the limitations and vulnerability of the U.S. capability on the ground. By the time of the marine barracks bombing on October 23, there were many things going wrong with the mission, and Beirut had acquired a general sense of lawlessness. The United States was palpably failing to cope well with forces that lurked around the city. Out of the urban shadows, they would emerge without warning to assassinate, kidnap, snipe, ambush, and bomb— the collection of activities that tend to be lumped together under the broad category of terrorism.

The Reagan administration had entered office pledging to respond to terrorism through swift retaliation. Two large impediments had become apparent. The first was working out who was actually responsible. Could "irrefutable evidence" be gathered, especially when countries such as Iran and Syria were suspected to be pulling the strings? The second difficulty lay in designing a form of retaliation that was both proportionate and effective. If the retaliatory air strikes planned after October 23 had been canceled because of a lack of good evidence and precise targeting, the implication was that retaliation would normally only be occasional. The more the terrorists avoided leaving fingerprints and found sanctuary in civilian areas, the less likely a response. The greater the uncertainty, the less likely that the prospect of deadly reprisals would influence terrorist behavior. This logic pointed to the advantages of preemption. Better to stop terrorists as attacks were being prepared than to face the dilemmas afterward of working out how to respond.

Admiral Robert Long's official postmortem into the October attack on the barracks, which came out before the marines had been withdrawn, picked up on questions of objectives and poor protection, insufficient attention to warnings, and the concentration of such a large component of the force in a single building. The most important conclusion was that the United States was now at war with terrorism, requiring a shift in military doctrine and structure. The attack was described as being "tantamount to an act of war using the medium of terrorism," and thus representative of a distinct form of warfare "endemic to the Middle East" and "indicative of an alarming world-wide phenomenon." Since 1968, there had been a three- to fourfold increase in the number of worldwide terrorist incidents. During the previous decade, over half the recorded incidents were directed against U.S. personnel and facilities. Those in the military were particularly at risk. In 1982, they had been targeted sixty-seven times, up from thirty-four times in 1980. Another trend was that the attacks were becoming more deadly. Even excluding the marine barracks, 1983 was the worst year yet for deaths due to terrorism. Already that year there had been 666 fatalities due to terrorism, compared to 221 in 1982 and 374 in 1981.

This "systematic, carefully orchestrated terrorism" went beyond random political statements or occasional acts of intimidation. It was instead "an alternative means of conducting state business and the terrorists themselves are agents whose association the state can easily deny." For small states, this was warfare "on the cheap," with reduced risks because the covert attacks avoided the U.S. response that would come if they were overt. It was a severe threat with which the Pentagon was "inadequately prepared to deal." The Long Commission called for "an active national policy . . . to deter attack or reduce its effectiveness." It would need both political and diplomatic options and "a wide range of timely military response capabilities."[38] The implication was that the threat could be handled in military terms, so long as specialist doctrine, force structure, and training could be developed.

The Pentagon picked up this theme less enthusiastically than the State Department. Shultz felt thwarted by the turn of events in Beirut. He had returned from a trip to Latin America to find a "virtual stampede" to get out of Lebanon that he was unable to resist. Even after the troops had left, he did not want to abandon the country completely. The "appropriate punctuation to put after the word 'Lebanon' right now," he suggested in May, was "not a period—perhaps a comma, but certainly no more than a semicolon."[39] On April 3, 1984, Reagan signed National Security Decision Directive 138. This described the "practice of terrorism by any person or group in any cause a threat to our national security," considered force as an appropriate response, and, most important, looked for ways to take the offensive against terrorism. The next day, Shultz publicly spoke of the possible need to take "preventive or pre-emptive action." Over the following months, he took every opportunity to describe the nature of this new threat. His campaign culminated in a speech at New York's Park Avenue Synagogue on October 25, 1984, using language strikingly similar to that which would be employed two decades later.

Shultz described terrorism as a "contagious disease that will inevitably spread if it goes untreated." The democracies struggled "to understand the fanaticism and apparent irrationality" behind it, "especially those who kill and commit suicide in the belief that they will be rewarded in the afterlife."

There was "an unfortunate irony that the very qualities that make democracies so hateful to the terrorists—our respect for the rights and freedoms of the individual—also make us particularly vulnerable." Terrorists could claim no cause in justification. The "means discredit their ends." The United States would not be driven off course or change policy because of "terrorist brutality" and would seek to develop responses "beyond passive defense" to include "active prevention, preemption, and retaliation." This required better intelligence on what the terrorists were up to, but also a readiness to use force and accept sacrifice. Shultz expressed confidence that the U.S. military had "the capability and the techniques to fight the war against terrorism." It would require public understanding "before the fact that there is potential for loss of life of some of our fighting men and the loss of life of some innocent people." There could not be an intense debate after every attack or a search for the evidence that would stand up in a court of law. Morality must be a source of courage rather than paralysis. The United States must not

> allow ourselves to become the Hamlet of nations, worrying endlessly over whether and how to respond. A great nation with global responsibilities cannot afford to be hamstrung by confusion and indecisiveness. Fighting terrorism will not be a clean or pleasant contest, but we have no choice but to play it.[40]

Although this seemed to contradict Reagan's public line that the United States would retaliate only if civilian lives would not be endangered, and any controversy threatened distraction days before the 1984 presidential election, the president approved the speech prior to delivery and was said to be in accord. The speech alarmed the Pentagon because it seemed to promise the further reckless use of military assets to take on adversaries and pursue vague goals. Weinberger feared that the United States would find itself attacking cities in Syria and Iran out of revenge, thereby creating the risks of a wider war that would undermine the nation's ability to meet its security needs. Once Reagan was comfortably reelected, the secretary of defense delivered his riposte. His speech of November 28 had a more lasting impact, largely because it was seen as a reflection on the Beirut experience (rather than as a direct response to Shultz) and took the form of a doctrinal statement on the criteria for the use of armed force.

Weinberger talked about "gray area conflicts," somewhere between the black and white of peace and all-out war, as unusually difficult challenges for democracies. Like Shultz, he believed responses should be "clear and understandable." He was worried that the national will might be insufficient to sustain the effort and apply the resources required until the mission was complete. At times force would be needed, but he criticized "theorists . . . eager to advocate its use even in limited amounts simply because they believe that if there are American forces of any size present they will somehow solve the problem." This risked plunging the country "headlong into the sort of domestic turmoil we experienced during the Vietnam war, without accomplishing the goal for which we committed our forces." Such policies "would also earn us the scorn of our troops, who would have an understandable opposition to being used—in every sense of the word—casually and without intent to support them fully." The tests, to which regular reference is still made, were that (1) the United States should only commit forces to combat overseas when the particular engagement or occasion was deemed vital to national interests or those of allies; (2) unless combat troops were to be used wholeheartedly, and with the clear intention of winning, they should not be committed at all; (3) forces committed to combat overseas should have clearly defined political and military objectives; (4) the relationship between these objectives and the forces committed—their size, composition, and disposition—must be continually reassessed and adjusted if necessary; (5) there must be some reasonable assurance of the support of the American people and their elected representatives in Congress; (6) the commitment of U.S. forces to combat should be a last resort.[41]

Thus, in contrast to Shultz, who insisted on the importance of the United States adjusting to a world in which terrorism in a range of guises would provide one of the main threats and for which an adequate military response had to be fashioned, Weinberger saw U.S. armed forces as a valuable asset to be kept for use against the main threat and not to be squandered on missions that involved high military risks for low political returns. The main lesson of Beirut was to confirm that of Vietnam: It was always unwise for the United States to get involved in complicated civil wars in the Third World, to take on wars that would be protracted, complex, and indecisive. The implication of Weinberger's position was that enemies should be chosen with care. They should have earned the hostility of the American people and should be likely to be defeated by means available to the American military.

8

IRAQ

SHULTZ'S FRUSTRATION lay in the lack of consistency and staying power shown in the face of the Iranian challenge. Once again, Iran helped inflict further humiliation through the instrument of Hezbollah. Reagan's decision to abandon Beirut in February 1984, only a couple of weeks after he had insisted that the United States would stay indefinitely, presented the "quintessential symbol of American inconstancy."[1]

As first a Democrat and then a Republican president were caught out, loathing of Iran could at least serve as the basis of a bipartisan consensus. Such an intense antipathy created a natural temptation to view Iran's enemies as America's friends. In this respect, though not in any other, Saddam Hussein's Iraq was a natural ally. The United States had not had diplomatic relations with Iraq since 1967. Iraqi politics had long been violent and argumentative, certainly since the overthrow of King Faisal in 1958. The ruling Arab Ba'ath Socialist Party reflected the progressive politics of the time. Because Iraq saw itself as a natural alternative to Egypt as leader of the Arab world, it had never fallen under Nasser's spell. Nor had it managed moderately cordial relations with its fellow Ba'ath regime in Syria. The Soviet Union had been the main arms supplier, though Communists were not tolerated, and there was a close relationship with France (always ready for a unique form of regional influence) as an alternative source of weaponry.

Saddam Hussein's career began with plotting against the monarchy, to be followed by plotting against the new rulers once the monarchy had been overthrown, and eventually to plotting against anyone who might conceivably be plotting against him. After using the patronage of his uncle and eventual president, Ahmed Hassan al-Bakr, to establish himself in the Ba'ath Party hierarchy, he became interior minister, always a crucial role, and gradually established himself as the de facto leader. The British ambassador to Baghdad described Saddam as a new deputy to the president in 1969, as a "presentable young man" with "an engaging smile." He was a "formidable, single-minded and hard-headed member of the Ba'athist hierarchy, but one with whom, if only one could see more of him, it would be possible to do business." Although he was regarded as an extremist, "responsibility may mellow him." Such optimism lasted, despite the evidence, until 1990.

President al-Bakr was eventually pushed aside in 1979. Saddam, at only forty-two, established himself as supreme leader. The timing had a lot to do with the tumultuous period in regional politics. Saddam had not opposed Anwar Sadat's peace diplomacy during the 1970s. It suited him to have Egypt and Syria moving in opposite directions, as that maximized his own freedom of maneuver. His rivalry was greatest with Assad in Syria. With Sadat, he had also begun to ease away from the Soviet Union and toward the West, although not so dramatically. As Iraq did not share a common border with Israel, he was less anxious than Syria about the strategic consequences of Egypt's defection.

Nonetheless, he turned completely against Egypt as soon as it made peace with Israel. Saddam saw this as a great opportunity both nationally and regionally. In the immediate aftermath of the Camp David summit, Assad was invited to Baghdad. Saddam now proposed that the two countries put to one side their rivalry, including their recent support of opposing factions in the Lebanese civil war. Instead of the incessant diatribes, the talk was of rapprochement, even unity. An all-Arab summit was hastily arranged in Baghdad, with al-Bakr notionally presiding, to prepare for Egypt's expulsion from the Arab League. Saddam had positioned Iraq at the center of Arab affairs at a moment of crisis. The unity plans did not last long, as Assad soon drew away from the secondary role in the new entity to which he had been assigned by Saddam as his predecessors had drawn away from being subordinate to Nasser.

Enthusiasm for unity was already waning as 1979 began. It was soon overtaken by the Iranian revolution. Relations between Iraq and Iran—Persian and Arab with a disputed border—had long been strained. Iran had used support for Kurdish insurgents as a means of putting pressure on Iraq over a dispute connected with the 120-mile Shatt Al Arab waterway, which provided Iraq with its primary access to the sea. Saddam bitterly resented the 1975 agreement with Iran that left the waterway divided and Iraq the evident loser. Yet, in return for unwelcome concessions, relations between the two countries had moved to a new footing. Saddam's ambitions were in the Arab world. It suited him to have stability to his east and for the Kurds to be denied external support. He had developed a stake in the shah's survival, so much so that in October 1978, he had agreed to expel Khomeini from his Najaf base. Having made the wrong call, Iraq quickly sent good wishes and support to the new Iranian regime. Saddam sensed that now the whole region was in flux. It was time to consolidate his power, and for that he needed the presidency.

As al-Bakr stepped aside, ostensibly on the grounds of ill health, Saddam moved ruthlessly and quickly to remove dissent and potential rivals. He was a close student of the Soviet supreme leader Josef Stalin and even described this time as his "Stalinist era." He followed the well-tried method of a foreign plot uncovered, followed by staged confessions. "We shall strike with an iron fist against the slightest deviation or backsliding beginning with the Ba'athists themselves."[2] At a specially convened meeting of the Revolutionary Command Council that summer, the treacherous senior party members, who were all in the audience, were identified after one of their number admitted that he had been part of a pro-Syrian plot. As Saddam read from a list, sixty-six men were taken from the hall, one by one. Those spared proclaimed with ever greater fervor their loyalty to Saddam. A chilling video was made of the event for widespread distribution, to give pause to any other potential traitors. Not all of those taken were killed. Some were released and others put in prison, but the majority were executed, often by the more senior survivors at Saddam's invitation. From this point on, no hint of dissent was tolerated and the personality cult began in earnest.

Saddam had made himself supreme leader of a country whose prospects were good. At 6 million barrels per day, Iraq was second only to Saudi Arabia in oil production. Oil revenue of $1 billion a year in 1972 had become $21 billion by 1979 and was still on a rapid ascent. Living standards were rising fast in a booming economy. Health and education services were free and of improving quality. Following the standard path of the Middle Eastern oil producers, Iraq took the opportunity to transform its military capability. In 1970, military expenditure was running at around $500 million, with the equipment largely coming from the Soviet bloc. Five years later, the expenditure had increased to $4.5 billion, and, to Soviet irritation, the process of diversification had begun. By 1977, deals had been struck with France for fighter aircraft, attack helicopters, and air defense missiles.

During the mid-1970s, Iraq also pursued chemical and nuclear programs. Orders for massive supplies of the most toxic insecticides aroused suspicions among leading American and British companies. Eventually, Western companies were found that either did not ask the awkward questions or failed to appreciate that the items they were supplying were part of a bigger piece. On the nuclear side, France seemed the most willing country in the West to offer the most capabilities with the fewest questions. That Prime Minister Jacques Chirac had any illusions when he agreed to terms for the supply of French nuclear reactors, including some fuel, must be doubted. The total nuclear deal was worth £3 billion. One agreed stipulation was that "all persons of the Jewish race or mosaic religion" be excluded from employment with the project.[3] Somewhat ironically, France had been responsible for the Israeli nuclear program getting a kick start in the 1950s with a reactor of a similar type. Iraq claimed that the nuclear capability it sought was purely for peaceful purposes, but few Iraqis involved with the project acted as if they believed this. Iraq's 1976 signature of the international nonproliferation treaty was at most a cover for proclaiming good intent and finding out more about nuclear issues. Iraq's position within the International Atomic Energy Agency (IAEA), which monitors the treaty, was used to deflect attempts to monitor its facilities.

The French responded to international anxiety by reducing the quality of the fuel it was due to provide. The Iraqis were furious but soon compensated by sourcing uranium from elsewhere and setting out to construct their own enrichment capability. As already noted, in June 1981 the Israeli concern led to an audacious attack on the reactor at Osiraq, using a squadron of eight F-16As with fighter support, flying over Jordanian and Saudi airspace before reaching Iraq. There were reports that the Iranians, who had tried to do the same thing the previous September, provided the Israelis with helpful intelligence. Although the UN resolution that condemned Israel's attack was not particularly forceful, the lack of an American veto indicated the Reagan administration's developing mixed feelings with regard to both Israel and Iraq. When Saddam's intentions became even clearer, the Israelis claimed credit for their prescience. Yet while the attack may have delayed the nuclear program, it also pushed it underground and increased Saddam's commitment to deterring further Israeli attacks.

The origins of Iraq's chemical, biological, and nuclear weapons programs during the 1970s may have had something to do with hardheaded security calculations, but these were long-term programs for systems loaded with political significance. They were a dramatic way of demonstrating technological prowess and achieving status in the international hierarchy. The first Arab country to acquire nuclear weapons, and Iraq was not the only contender, would be in a natural leadership position. One of Israel's clear strategic advantages would be neutralized. The energy and resources put into these programs reflected Saddam's ambitions for Iraq. The Israeli raid on the Osiraq reactor was a setback but did not deflect Saddam's ambition. By 1981, he did, however, have other distractions. Iraq was at war with Iran.

$$\star \quad \star \quad \star$$

After the revolution, Iraq had been conciliatory and friendly toward the new Iranian regime, encouraging the break with the United States. As the influence of the Islamic radicals and their theocratic ideas grew, relations deteriorated. The Islamists wanted to extend their influence to the whole region. Iraq, with its majority Shi'ite population, among whom the Ayatollah Khomeini had lived while in exile, was a natural target. Efforts were made to stir up discontent. Khomeini was unstinting in his contempt for Saddam and regularly urged Iraqis to overthrow this "deviant." In April 1980, one of the radical Islamic groups supported by Iran, al-Dawa, attempted to assassinate Foreign Minister Tariq Aziz. Saddam observed maximum provocation from Iran at a time of maximum weakness. Iran was in postrevolution tumult, and its armed forces were in disarray. He saw his chance. If he did not seize it, he might not get another. Iran had three times the population (45 million as against 14 million) and a larger army. On the night of September 21–22, 1980, Iraq invaded Iran. The aim was at least to regain full control of the Shatt Al Arab, possibly some other oil-rich territory, while destabilizing or even toppling Khomeini's regime.

Whatever the provocation, which was considerable, this was a clear act of aggression. Over a decade later, in December 1991, when Iraq was viewed in a different light by the international community, the secretary-general of the United Nations issued a report on responsibility for the Iran-Iraq conflict. This concluded that the Iraqi attack showed a "disregard for the territorial integrity of a Member State" and could not be "justified under the Charter of the United Nations, any recognized rules or any principles of international morality and entails the responsibility for the conflict."[4] At the time of the invasion, however, none of the five permanent members of the Security Council were ready to antagonize Iraq. Whatever their misgivings about the Iraqi regime, other Arab countries feared Iran more, and this view was reflected in the nonaligned members of the council. The Iraqis were able to persuade the council to delay meeting until they had completed their thrust into Iran. This they hoped would not last more than a matter of days. When a meeting eventually took place, the war was described only as a "situation" and not even as a "threat to peace." By this time Iraqi forces had occupied a substantial part of Iranian territory, including Khorramshahr. The British ambassador to the UN later described the performance of the Security Council in response to the Iraqi invasion of Iran as "contemptible."[5] Brian Urquhart, then undersecretary-general, observed that the Security Council had "seldom seemed less worthy of respect."[6]

Resolution 479, adopted unanimously on September 28, called upon Iran and Iraq to "refrain immediately from any further use of force and to settle their dispute by peaceful means and in conformity with principles of justice and international law." This had the familiar problem of all cease-fire resolutions. The demand was for the fighting to stop while Iranian territory was occupied but not for an Iraqi withdrawal. By refusing to blame Iraq for starting the war or even to determine that there had been a technical "breach of the peace," there was no need to worry about mandatory sanctions—even if there had been any confidence that they would be honored. This pro-Iraqi line persisted within the Security Council. It did not return to the matter for another two years and only began to call for withdrawal from international boundaries once Iran was holding some Iraqi territory.

*　　*　　*

At first Saddam's bold opportunism appeared to be paying off. The Iraqi offensive prospered and extensive inroads were made into Iranian territory. But, as was so often the case, Saddam's gamble failed because he could not sustain the initial advantage. The Iranians turned the situation around, using nationalist appeals to mobilize an otherwise divided people. By November 1980, Iraq was essentially on the defensive. Soon it was Iran's turn to take Iraqi territory, and by the end of 1981, Iran held the upper hand. Khomeini demanded Saddam's removal and reparations for Iran. Before, Iraq wanted to be left alone to sort out Iran. Now it sought international help to cope with Iranian pressure.

Saddam was helped by Iran's arrogant and uncompromising attitude. The regime had reached that point in the revolutionary cycle when militants are to the fore and pragmatists keep quiet. All other governments were damned as corrupt and suspect, while great hopes were placed in the masses. Khomeini was becoming more strident. The readiness to throw poorly prepared young men into battle confirmed the regime's fervor. As Iraq faltered, other Arab regimes became anxious. In May 1981, six of them—Bahrain, Kuwait, Oman, Qatar, Saudi Arabia, and the United Arab Emirates—formed the Gulf Cooperation Council (GCC) in response to their shared fear of Iran. Among Arab governments, only Syria (with its own suspicions of Iraq) showed any sympathy.

The Soviet Union attempted to court Iran. After Iran's estrangement from its former superpower ally, it seemed natural to explore the possibility of bringing Iran into the Soviet camp. Ideologists worked out how theocracy might just be compatible with Marxism. When its established client, Iraq, went to war, Soviet strategists realized that it might be challenging to support both belligerents, but they soon noticed that Iran was much bigger and more important. Moreover, they were getting fed up with Iraq. A series of differences over foreign policy, for example Saddam's condemnation of the invasion of Afghanistan, along with purges of Iraqi Communists, had not gone down well. Moscow therefore signaled an interest in better relations with Iran by not actually endorsing the Iraqi invasion, though it hedged its bets by not condemning it either. More significantly, and not for the first time when it was angry with Baghdad, it cut off arms supplies. If Iran had been more responsive, then the ploy might have worked. But Khomeini was not about to ally with atheists fighting Islamic resistance fighters in Afghanistan. Moscow was swiftly rebuffed and so returned to Iraq.

The United States was not likely to give active support to Iran, but neither could it initially work up much enthusiasm for Iraq. Officially it wished both countries to be "secure, stable, prosperous and free of outside domination." There was a view, which never quite went away, that U.S. interests would be best served by the two sides hammering away at each other indefinitely, so long as the effects could be contained. At the time of Iraq's invasion, Carter was still in office and embroiled in the hostage dispute with Iran. By stating in early 1980 that there were no fundamental barriers to improved relations with Iraq, Brzezinski might have been attempting to add to the pressure on Tehran, but the administration had not had prior notice of the Iraqi invasion, nor was it welcome. The first consequence was to distract the Iranian government at a time when negotiations on hostages had been making some progress. Indeed, if there had been a breakthrough, the United States was prepared to hand over large amounts of military equipment, much of it already paid for by Tehran, but held back in the aftermath of the revolution. Here again a more pragmatic Iranian response to the new situation would have prevented the later U.S. drift to the Iraqi side. As it was, the continuing restriction on selling arms to either belligerent hurt the Iranians far more than the Iraqis because of the recent dependence of the Iranian armed forces upon the United States. They would be in trouble without spare parts and ammunition.

With the Reagan administration in place and the hostages home, there was more freedom of maneuver but no particular pressure to back one side rather than the other. The official position was one of neutrality, of a rather negative sort, with no significant relations, diplomatic or military, with either side. Iraq made the first overtures to the United States. The trigger was the futile and short-lived courting of Iran by the Soviet Union. Iraq was furious about a lack of support at such a critical moment. Unlike Khomeini, Saddam was pragmatic, especially when in a fix. Initially, therefore, the Iraqi approach to Washington was a classical cold war tactic, threatening one superpower with defection to the opposing camp in order to bring it to heel. It worked. Moscow was already giving up on Iran and resumed arms supplies in 1982. This was not, however, Saddam's only motive. The United States was also seen as a new source of invaluable practical support. Saddam was aware of the limits of Soviet capabilities and their inability to compete technologically with the United States. A country that wanted the best had to look to the West.

Washington was tempted. The congruence of antipathies to Iran provided a natural basis for reasserting the American position in the Gulf and weaning away another state from Soviet influence. Initially, there seemed to be little to lose. The process of reconciliation began with high-level official meetings in the spring of 1981, the first since 1967. From the start, there was a working assumption that this was a process that could, even should, end with the restoration of diplomatic relations. By the spring of 1983, Shultz was meeting with his Iraqi counterpart, Tariq Aziz. In September 1984, Iraqi officials at the UN made it known that Baghdad would like to resume full diplomatic relations with the United States. Shultz replied that the idea would be considered, and this was followed by a formal approach on October 12, 1984, to which Washington responded positively. On November 26, 1984, Foreign Minister Aziz met with President Reagan and Secretary Shultz at the White House.

A key figure in this process was Donald Rumsfeld. Although a private citizen, he was acting as a presidential envoy. In December 1983, he toured Middle Eastern capitals on behalf of the president. His instructions when he reached Baghdad were to establish direct contact with Saddam and hand over a letter from the president. There was a lot of talk about mutual interests, particularly in dealing with the Iranian threat and events in Lebanon, where there was a mutual hostility to Syria, and residual disagreements, including the one over the dispute with Israel. Saddam greeted Rumsfeld warmly, and the feedback from U.S. officials commented on how impressed the Iraqi dictator had been. The official photo shows Saddam wearing military dress and a pistol, as was Tariq Aziz. This image, and the records of the cordial discussions between the two men, with no mention of either human rights abuses or weapons of mass destruction, excited considerable comment two decades later. By this time, as secretary of defense, Rumsfeld was the public face of the

war to overthrow Saddam's regime. The contrast between the first conciliatory role and the second confrontational one was taken as a striking indictment of America's underlying hypocrisy or, less starkly, as evidence of the
difficulty of holding to a constant foreign policy course.

The records of these discussions reveal that the issues to the fore in the early
1980s were very much those of the early 2000s—oil supplies, international terrorism, weapons of mass destruction, the impact of revolutionary Iran and of
the Palestinian question. Nor was U.S. policy that different. The Reagan administration wanted secure oil supplies and was opposed to the promotion of
terrorism and the proliferation of weapons of mass destruction, while seeking
to contain the influence of Iran and of the Arab-Israeli dispute. The difference
with the early 2000s lay in the weight attached to these issues, which largely reflected the distinctive geopolitical context. In the 1980s, there was scant sympathy for either Iran or Iraq, and little to choose between them when it came
to support for terrorism (with Iran then more active), an interest in weapons
of mass destruction (here Iraq was in the clear lead), or even regular condemnation of Israel. But they were engaged in a bitter war, and the Reagan administration came to the conclusion that an Iranian victory would have the direst
consequences. At the same time, the United States did not want to get so tied
to Iraq that it could not take advantage of any openings to Iran, especially if
the influence of the mullahs began to wane.

Once that determination was made, then the question became one of
how to forge some sort of understanding with Iraq without conceding
ground on the issues in which they differed. The Iraqis had been told that
their defeat was not in U.S. interests and that efforts were being made to prevent weapons getting through to Iran, although not a lot could be done
about North Korea, which had become Iran's main supplier. There was no
U.S. disposition to sell military equipment to Iraq—at any rate, this was not
Iraq's main problem—and even less to send forces to defend Iraq. This left
keeping the Gulf open to help Iraq's oil export operations as the most useful
support. As two State Department officials noted in reviewing these options,
there were risks: "Either Iraq is able to force a level of U.S. support we may
not wish to provide (such as military protection of transport in the Gulf) or
that we become identified with a regime whose longer-term political
prospects remain uncertain."[7]

Caution turned out to be warranted, yet the Reagan administration
pressed on. At root, the decision was strategic. Against the arguments for
having nothing to do with either side in the Iran-Iraq war was the argument
that the United States did have a stake in the outcome. Iran was in the grip of
an extremist ideology that it aimed to spread through force. Iraq was ruled

by a typical Arab strongman whose methods might be unpleasant but whose calculations were at least crudely pragmatic. As Iran was closing down to Western influence, Iraq was opening up. It was Iran that had most recently engaged in an act of direct hostility to the United States. While Iraq was causing more disruption to oil flows, Iran had the capacity to do the most damage by closing the Strait of Hormuz. More seriously, Persian, Shi'ite Iran was perceived as a threat to the wider Arab world and thus to a number of states of consequence whose interests the United States felt obliged to protect. Shultz later recalled how this came to be viewed as a "strategic disaster" for the United States.

> Because of the hostage crisis going back to Iran's seizure of our embassy in Tehran in 1979, official Washington and public attitudes had been conditioned to view Iran as the primary threat and Iraq as a fragile counterforce holding back the tide of Khomeini's human waves. A defeat for Iraq would leave America's friends intimidated and even inundated.[8]

Although the inspiration was strategic, a potential motor was economic. It was possible to imagine other benefits resulting from a new relationship with Iraq, not least the economic opportunities that would emerge once Iraq was able to return to more peaceful pursuits.

*　*　*

The Iraqis understood both U.S. strategic and economic motivations perfectly well and played on them with skill. Although Iraqi vulnerability created the conditions for the tilt, at no point did Iraq ever admit to weakness. The briefings on the situation at the front were always upbeat; the effort to get a cease-fire through the United Nations was described as a magnanimous attempt to provide the Iranians with an escape route from the desperate situation in which they found themselves. When the United States warned against measures that risked escalation or set dangerous precedents, such as attacks on Gulf shipping or the use of chemical weapons, it was the Iraqis who became most angry and complained of betrayal. As trade opened up, the Iraqis managed to use the competition among Western companies for orders to get access to some of the most sensitive technologies on the most generous terms.

To start with, Iraq set the conditions, insisting that a shift in the American position on Israel was essential to a new U.S.-Iraqi relationship. By May 1983, when Iraq had much else to worry about, the priority given to the Palestinian cause as the key to Middle Eastern stability had subsided. After meeting Aziz, Shultz described the Iraqi foreign minister's discussion of the issue as "elliptical." The need for an equitable solution to the Palestinian problem was stressed, but the "focus was on the need for peace."[9] For the Reagan administration, the linked issues of Israel and terrorism were the most difficult because these most excited Congress. The first indication of the administration's reappraisal came in May 1982, when Iraq was taken off the list of countries supporting terrorism. With Syria, Libya, and South Yemen, it had been a founding member on the list. As it was removed, Iran was added.

This was presented as a reward for Iraq's shutting down the Baghdad headquarters of the Palestinian militant Abu Nidal. Nidal, who had first come to Iraq in 1970 as a representative of Yasser Arafat's Fatah group, broke away when he suspected his former colleagues of going soft on Israel. He had conducted assassination operations designed not only to attack the Zionist enemy and its supporters but also to assert his position in the Palestinian movement and undermine Syrian influence. Just as notorious was Wadi Haddad, who was behind the kidnapping of OPEC oil ministers while they met in Vienna in 1975 and had links with the various European and Asian revolutionary cells that regularly acted in the name of the Palestinian cause. Haddad died in 1978 and was buried in Baghdad with full military honors. The reason for Nidal being dropped was less to mollify the Americans than Arafat and Assad, as part of Saddam's repositioning himself in the aftermath of Camp David.

The administration could not claim that Iraq had renounced terrorism altogether—only that there had been steps in the right direction and incentives should be provided for yet more improvement. In practice what seemed to Americans to be support for terrorism, to Arab leaders was simply a way of keeping in touch with one strand of the Palestinian movement. This limited how far Saddam would go. In 1983, Shultz was still stressing to Aziz the importance of the terrorism issue—a "remediable impediment." Both countries, he argued, had an interest in dealing with the issue, as both suffered from "the same sources" (i.e., Iran). The secretary of state observed hopefully that Iraq was "approaching the conclusion that its interests are never served by international terrorists," yet "was hesitating to cut its threads to international terrorism." Pointing to congressional disquiet on this issue, he urged provision of evidence of a positive approach.[10] When Rumsfeld had his first meetings in December 1983, the only thing he spoke of forcefully was terrorism. "Nations which export terrorism and extremism ought to be recognized as such," he observed, specifically mentioning Iran, Syria, and Libya. "Terrorism adversely affects the sovereignty and independence of nations. We feel extremely strongly about it." A 1984 analysis did note a "marked reduction of Baghdad-supported terrorist operations,"[11] though as we shall see in the next chapter, Iraq never fully abandoned support for Palestinian terrorist groups.

The importance of the list of countries supporting terrorism lay in trade. So long as a country was included, certain exports were precluded and it could not gain access to credits. The main effect of the 1982 decision came later that year when Iraq was provided with $210 million in credits to purchase American wheat, rice, and feed grains, as well as access to Export-Import (EXIM) Bank credits and continuing financing of agricultural sales by the Commodity Credit Corporation. At a time when the normally reliable supply of revenue from oil sales had halved in two years, and a long and difficult war was in prospect, this was an important financial lifeline. At first, the most important economic benefit the Americans could offer was an oil pipeline. Iranian air attacks against Iraq's major oil terminals meant that it could not get its oil out through the Gulf and depended on pipelines. In 1982, Syria, Iran's only Arab ally, closed the Iraqi pipeline through its territory. Fortunately for Iraq, that same year a pipeline through Turkey began to carry 1 million barrels per day (bpd), later extended to 1.3 million bpd. Now there was a proposal for a new pipeline to run from Iraq through Saudi Arabia to the Jordanian port of Aqaba. The key problem in Saddam's eyes, after the Osiraq experience, was that the pipe would run close to the Israeli border. U.S. support was therefore seen as a factor deterring any Israeli attack. The American ability to gain explicit Israeli assurances was a major topic of conversation at both the Rumsfeld and Shultz meetings. In the event, the Aqaba pipeline was never actually built because of problems with gaining additional financing.

*   *   *

Both sides were dependent upon oil for revenues, and as the war developed into a bloody impasse, the ability to export was going to assume ever greater importance. The greater part of Iranian oil went by sea. Air attacks against Kharg Island, Iran's principal oil terminal, began in the spring of 1982. That August, Iraq declared a maritime exclusion zone that covered waters up to 35 nautical miles from Kharg. Any ship in the area was vulnerable to attack. Although to start with, more effort was put into frightening foreign tankers than destroying them, by the end of 1983 significant numbers had been sunk or damaged as a result of Iraqi actions. Saddam had a further objective, beyond putting an economic squeeze on Iran. He was seeking to draw external powers into the conflict, and he would not have been upset if this campaign provoked a harsh Iranian response, including closing the Strait of

Hormuz, that would in turn trigger intervention by oil-dependent Western countries.

In this he was encouraged by the evident preoccupation of the Western powers with the strait and the potential consequences of its closure. By 1984 the situation was ripe for escalation. Iraq's main weapons in attacking tankers were Exocet antiship missiles, received from France in the 1970s. These could be delivered by French "Super Frelon" helicopters. In April 1982, Iraq gained agreement to purchase Super-Etendard aircraft, soon to gain notoriety in the Falklands War because of the difficulty the Super-Etendard–Exocet combination caused the Royal Navy. The Americans had made an effort (with others) to persuade the French not to risk increased escalation by making the deliveries. This annoyed Iraq and only seemed to have a temporary effect on France. By the start of 1984, the aircraft were ready for operational use, and a stockpile of Exocets had been built up by Iraq. The first was used in March 1984 against a Greek tanker. Although the United States had urged the Iraqis not to go this far, so long as the action was in a known combat zone, then the inclination was to tolerate if not condone. By contrast, an Iranian effort to shut off the whole Gulf would be seen as a major threat requiring direct U.S. intervention.

As Saddam's position became even more desperate, he was prepared to resort to even more extreme measures. From late 1982, Iraq was using chemical weapons regularly to hold back the human waves of Iranian forces being thrown at its defenses. This was clearly forbidden by the 1925 Geneva Protocol, to which Iraq was a party. By late 1983, Iran was making repeated complaints about Iraqi chemical warfare, and in November 1983, it asked for a UN investigation. The Reagan administration was well aware that the Iranian complaints were justified. Intelligence reports confirmed use against not only Iranian forces but also Kurds. The weapons had been developed through "the unwitting and, in some cases, witting assistance of a number of western firms." Despite this, the State Department fretted about whether a public fuss should be made. To do so might involve compromising intelligence sources without necessarily restraining Iraq. To criticize Iraq would go against a trend in U.S. foreign policy; not to do so would be repudiating one of the established principles of policy. The issue was not going to get any easier, especially if Iraq continued to face the prospect of an Iranian breakthrough.

The United States decided on a private approach to warn the Iraqis of the damage that this issue could do to their developing relationship. A message was sent in Shultz's name to Tariq Aziz. On November 21, the United States presented a démarche in Baghdad telling the Iraqis that the Americans knew of the chemical use and were strongly opposed. The initial impression was that this had done the trick. This helps explain why Reagan's November 26, 1983, National Security Decision Directive (NSDD) 114, on policy toward the war, made no mention of chemical weapons. The focus was on defending oil facilities and ensuring the flow of traffic through the Gulf. Similarly, little was said about WMD during Rumsfeld's visit in December 1983. He referred to chemical weapons when talking to Aziz, without response, as part of a list, including possible escalation in the Gulf and human rights, of "certain things that made it difficult for us."

By the time of Rumsfeld's return to Baghdad in March 1984, the issue had rushed to the fore. A new offensive by Iran in February had triggered a series of chemical responses by Iraq. The United States had not only picked up evidence of this but had already taken steps to prevent Iraq from acquiring a precursor necessary for chemical weapons production. The Iraqi Ministry of Foreign Affairs was warned that the United States would seek to thwart attempts to manufacture chemical weapons and would condemn their use.[12] A press statement on March 5 confirmed that "the available evidence substantiates Iran's charges that Iraq used chemical weapons." In this context, the United States had little choice but to take a strong line. Although the Iraqis never publicly acknowledged use, their attempts at denial were rarely convincing, especially as they also sought to extract some deterrent value from their chemical weapons stocks. Little room for doubt was left by a February comment from the Iraqi military warning Iran "that for every harmful insect there is an insecticide capable of annihilating it whatever the number and Iraq possesses this annihilation insecticide." Meanwhile, the International Committee of the Red Cross had reported on the evidence of chemical weapons use. Iran continued to complain and in October demanded an investigation. Secretary-General Javier Pérez de Cuéllar eventually decided to send an expert UN mission on his own authority to investigate. This mission confirmed Iran's claims. Its final report concluded that lethal chemical weapons (both mustard and nerve agents) had been used but did not name Iraq. But it hardly needed to.

The Iraqis were furious. The United States was denounced for its March press statement as being hypocritical. It was "the last country with the right to speak about the ethics of war." The U.S. atom-bombing of Japan was recalled as a measure to shorten a war and reduce casualties. Saddam complained that the United States was supporting Iran by "repeating allegations which were used by Iran to cover its battlefield failures."[13] The UN Secretariat was chastised for concentrating on "the secondary aspects of the conflict" while ignoring the necessity of ending the war. Yet, realizing that the issue was not going to go away, the Iraqis worked at the UN and through

the United States to get a statement from the president of the Security
Council rather than a resolution, referring to chemical weapons but not any
country, mentioning former resolutions on the war (which were more hostile to Iran), and calling for an end to the war through a cease-fire or negotiations as well as adherence to the 1925 Geneva Protocol.[14]

While unable to let the matter pass completely, in the spirit of the muted
UN response, the United States tried to contain the issue. The theme of
diplomatic messages to Iraq was that the best interests of the two countries
would be served if Iraq made no further efforts to purchase these chemicals
from the United States. Neither side would want this issue "to dominate our
bilateral relationship nor to detract from our common interest to see war
brought to an early end." The theme of briefings around the March 5 statement was that there was no reason that the use of chemical weapons should
affect the effort to draw Iraq into a "closer dialogue." The statement was balanced by a denunciation of the "present Iranian regime's" determination to
eliminate "the legitimate government of neighboring Iraq." (Exactly why the
Iraqi government was more legitimate than the Iranian was not explained.)

It was part of Rumsfeld's job during his second visit to move the dialogue
on. There are no records of this second set of meetings, which took place
during difficult military times for the Iraqis. There have been suggestions
that this was when intelligence on Iranian dispositions was handed over to
the Iraqis. What is known is that Shultz's instructions to Rumsfeld told him
to stress, despite the arguments over chemical weapons, that "our interests in
(1) preventing an Iranian victory and (2) continuing to improve bilateral relations with Iraq, at a pace of Iraq's choosing, remain undiminished." Rumsfeld appears to have followed his instructions and concentrated on what the
United States could do for Iraq, in terms of export credits, the pipeline, and
what had now become "Operation Staunch," the effort to reduce arms transfers to Iran. On April 5, a further presidential directive (NSDD 139) pulled
these elements of the policy together. It emphasized the need to avoid an
Iraqi collapse and balance condemnation of chemical use with condemnation of Iranian offensives. "Our condemnation of the use of CW munitions
by the belligerents should put equal stress on the urgent need to dissuade
Iran from continuing the ruthless and inhumane tactics which have characterized recent offensives."[15]

*   *   *

In his memoir, Shultz reported that he "took the firm position that there
should be no deviation from our policy of seeking to deny arms to both
combatants and urging other nations to do so as well."[16] This may appear

superficially to be an important confirmation of neutrality. It was not, however, an evenhanded policy. In addition to the seepage into Iraq of American arms from Arab states friendly to Iraq, and also the provision of dual-capable technology by the United States, Iraq was already well plugged into the international arms market. It had no history of arms supplies from the United States, so denial of access to American weapons posed no serious problems for Iraq. Iran's armed forces, by contrast, had been built up on American weapons and therefore denial was a real handicap.

The United States had been the major supplier to Iran before the revolution. Britain also was no longer entering into new contracts with Iran. Meanwhile, the Soviet Union and France were established suppliers to Iraq, and continued to be so throughout the 1980s. For this reason, any American effort directed against the flow of arms to the region would have a disproportionate impact on Iran. The goal of Operation Staunch, launched by the United States in the spring of 1983, was described in 1987 by Secretary of Defense Caspar Weinberger as being

> to persuade Iran of the futility of pursuing the war by limiting its ability to secure weapons, ammunition, and other supplies. This effort is aimed specifically at Iran because that country, unlike Iraq, has rejected all calls for negotiations. STAUNCH entails diplomatic efforts to block and complicate Iranian arms resupply efforts.[17]

The United States was now taking sides. The Iraqis might not need actual weapons from the United States, but they welcomed information that helped them assess the Iranian military threat. The most important early support for Iraq lay in intelligence. In June 1982, Iraq was reportedly provided with satellite photography and other material indicating vulnerabilities in its defensive lines. In 1984, the U.S. government formally authorized a "limited intelligence sharing program" with Iraq. Iraqi officials began to meet with CIA director William Casey, who passed sensitive satellite reconnaissance photographs to assist Iraqi bombing raids.[18] Intelligence came initially from the AWACS supplied to Saudi Arabia, and later from American satellites passing over the battlefront.[19] This allowed Saddam to take credit for military victories. Information was provided for targets for bombing raids and data on the Iranian air force and troop positions. The provision of satellite photography continued thereafter. When Shultz met with Aziz in Washington not long after diplomatic relations had been established, Aziz explained how superiority in weaponry was working to Iraq's advantage. Shultz's reported reply was that "superior intelligence must also be an important factor in Iraq's defense. Aziz acknowledged that this may be true."[20]

*   *   *

Once diplomatic relations had been established, the United States did not start selling weapons to Iraq but did the next best thing. Iraq purchased transport planes, vehicles, and helicopters, all of which were useful to its war effort. Between 1983 and 1989, annual trade between the two countries grew from £571 million to $3.6 billion. From 1985, $730 million in exports of sensitive technology was approved.[21] Although Saddam Hussein promised that Iraq would use new equipment such as sixty Hughes MD-500 Defender and ten UH-18 helicopters only for civilian purposes, these had been used extensively by the United States in Vietnam, and they were used by the Iraqi armed forces.[22] In addition, the United States did not stop, and sometimes actively encouraged, others from selling weapons to Iraq.

This is the point at which the relationship took a new turn. Iraq appeared desperate for certain types of goods and ready to pay the price. Over the previous few years, the United States had moved from having nothing to do with Iraqi oil to being a modest importer. Iraq was becoming a major importer of American grain, winning it a powerful lobby in Washington. There were numerous opportunities for U.S. business. The more cautious observed that payment for U.S. goods and services was only possible because of credit terms that went well beyond normal levels of acceptable risk. The geopoliticians in the Reagan administration considered such views to be shortsighted. When the EXIM Bank, which had a responsibility to warn against taking on bad debt, suggested that Iraq would be unable to meet requirements for "reasonable reassurance of commitment," it was overruled, with Vice President George H. W. Bush intervening to insist on Iraq being provided with $484 million in credits.

At the same time, restrictions on sensitive technologies began to be relaxed. When there were no diplomatic relations, it was argued, concerned U.S. agencies were unable to follow up concerns about whether any dual-use exports had been diverted to improper use. Now that this was possible, there was a readiness to permit dual-use exports in nonnuclear areas. Within the Pentagon, this developing laxity met with considerable unease. Assistant Secretary of Defense Richard Perle, later to gain fame as a leading neoconservative and anti-Saddam campaigner, warned:

> There is a body of evidence indicating that Iraq continues to actively pursue an interest in nuclear weapons, that the large number of Warsaw

Pact nationals in Iraq makes diversion in place a real possibility and that in the past, Iraq had been less than honest in regard to the intended end-use of high technology equipment.

Perle lost this battle. After a July 1986 National Security Council meeting, a new National Security Directive was issued "enjoining all government agencies to be more forthcoming" on Iraqi license requests. As a result, the controls were eased significantly. During the last two years of the Reagan administration, 241 licenses were approved for dual-use export to Iraq and only six were denied.[23] According to Kenneth Timmerman, a regular pattern soon developed: "The reviewing agencies were wary about high-tech sales to Iraq, delaying approval if not rejecting the applications outright—until the early months of 1985, when the Commerce Department succeeded in overruling them. From then on, Commerce simply stopped referring critical Iraqi licenses to other agencies for review." If it did and objections came, they moved to a next level where they would expect a better decision.[24]

In this way the tilt to Iraq stored up trouble for the future. Any connection of this sort with a beleaguered belligerent at some point would raise questions about the extent of the commitment and its purpose. It was one thing to prevent a country from being defeated; another to help it to victory. Selling defense-related goods and services might have started as a concession, but once trade began in earnest, the United States had its own stakes. The United States was of course following where others had led. Arab governments backed Iraq as a bulwark against Iran's revolutionary, subversive thrust into their region. The combination of Iraq's oil wealth and belligerency created a dream market for arms firms. Some companies came with the active encouragement of their governments, others with a degree of connivance, and some against their government's wishes. Iraq's established partners, the Soviet Union and France, were pleased to sell arms and, with other European governments, turned a blind eye to those "dual-use" sales that allowed Baghdad to acquire some lethal technologies in the guise of sophisticated civilian purchases. Although later regularly accused of doing so, the Americans did not get into the sale of frontline combat equipment. The intelligence estimates of this time gave no hint of the trouble to come. They assumed that a postwar Iraq would be in recovery mode and in no fit state for any further adventures.

9

IRAN-CONTRA

ON NOVEMBER 25, 1986, President Ronald Reagan announced to an astonished press corps that Lieutenant Colonel Oliver North had been relieved of his duties on the National Security Council staff as deputy director for political-military affairs and that the assistant to the president for national security affairs, Vice Admiral John Poindexter, had asked to go back to the navy. Other than saying he was "deeply troubled that the implementation of a policy aimed at resolving a truly tragic situation in the Middle East has resulted in such controversy," Reagan left it up to his attorney general to explain what had gone wrong.[1] What made the developing scandal so extraordinary was that the wrongdoing went beyond the overzealous pursuit of the president's wishes into direct breaches of his declared policy. Having urged other countries not to sell arms to Iran and insisting that it was never right to trade with terrorists, the United States had tried to use arms sales to secure the release of hostages held in Lebanon and then moved funds to bankroll the Contra rebels in Nicaragua to get around a restriction imposed by Congress.

This link between Iran and the Contras gave the scandal its name and also its focus. The narrower the focus, the easier it was to claim that the president was not a party to the crime and could therefore be absolved from guilt. This in effect required his admitting to the lesser crime of having very little idea what his staff was up to. The presidential commission set up to investigate the affair euphemistically referred to Reagan's "management style," conveying a semidetached approach to the business of government, an attribute not normally prized in a president. Thus, the popular image of Reagan as barely in touch with the world around him may have spared him even greater embarrassment. Yet while Reagan was never a "detail man," he normally set the framework for policy, and in both the Iranian and Nicaraguan strands, the NSC staff was following the presidential will. With regard to the movement of funds, Poindexter took the blame by saying that he had never put the question to Reagan but accepted that had he done so, he would probably have received a sympathetic answer. Those who were known to be opposed to dealing with Iran—the secretaries of State and Defense—at times thought they had persuaded the president of the folly of swapping arms for hostages, only for the attempt to resume. The only senior figure in favor, the director of central intelligence, sustained his enthusiasm by ignoring the misgivings of many within his agency. A bizarre collection of characters, from ex-CIA agents to an Iranian arms dealer with a dubious reputation to a collection of Israelis, were involved in the operations, which were, as a congressional committee observed, "characterized by pervasive dishonesty and inordinate secrecy."[2]

The standard conspiracy question, "What did he know and when did he know it?" is less important than the conflicting interests playing upon U.S. policy at the time and the consequences of this curiously amateurish way of handling them. Once again, different agencies pursued policies they liked while obstructing those they did not. As the NSC staff was part of the problem, it could not provide the solution, in line with its supposed function, by pulling the competing strands of policy together. The result was that all strands were followed at the same time, leading inevitably to confusion and contradiction.

In Nicaragua, the administration was seeking to subvert the Sandinista regime by funding the rightist Contras, despite a congressional prohibition. Choosing Iran as an unlikely source of funds was opportunistic and, to those responsible, delightfully ironic. The Iran element requires a fresh look because the question, as is so often the case, is whether the problem was a policy that was flawed from the start or one that had potential merit but was implemented ineptly.

*   *   *

The context for this episode, and one reason the disclosures seemed so shocking, was the developing policy with regard to terrorism. A "war on terrorism" had begun to become a theme of Reagan's foreign policy after the Beirut debacle, when Iran was seen as one of the states, along with Syria, most responsible for inspiring and facilitating attacks on Americans. With

Shultz to the fore, the talk had been of preemption and retaliation, although the practical application of this policy was always going to be problematic because of questions of evidence and effects. Was the source of attacks sufficiently well established, and would any military response prevent or deter further attacks?

Certainly taking the marines out of Beirut had not solved the problem there, and there was a growing conviction that Iran was responsible for the ongoing violent instability. In March, the new CIA station chief, William Buckley, was seized almost as soon as he arrived. He had been sent to Beirut by Casey, despite having been outed as a CIA agent. This created a CIA interest in getting him back. Then in December 1983, al-Dawa set off a series of truck bombs in Kuwait. Targets included the American and French embassies, the control tower at the airport, and the main oil refinery. The attacks left six dead, including a suicide truck bomber, and more than eighty injured. Seventeen members of al-Dawa were imprisoned. They became a cause célèbre in radical Shi'ite circles and a justification for kidnappings and hijackings.

A truck bomb directed at the U.S. Embassy in Beirut in September 1984 killed twenty-four people, including two Americans. That December, just after the United States had restored diplomatic relations with Iraq, a Kuwait Airways flight to Pakistan was hijacked and diverted to Tehran. Again the demand was for the release of the "Kuwait 17," and again it was not met. Two American officials from the U.S. Agency for International Development were killed. After six days, Iranian security forces stormed the plane, released the hostages, and arrested the hijackers, who appear to have been connected to Hezbollah. They eventually left Iran without facing trial. In March 1985, in what appeared as attempted retaliation, in which the CIA may have been implicated, a car bomb in the Beirut suburb of Bir al Abed killed eighty people, although not the Hezbollah leader who was the main target.

On June 14, 1985, TWA Flight 847, with 153 passengers and crew, was hijacked en route from Athens to Rome by two Shi'ite gunmen. They were ordered to Algiers, but lacked sufficient fuel. They instead went to Beirut, refueled, released some women and children, and then went to Algiers, where they issued their demands for the release of 700 Shi'ite prisoners in Israel. After releasing another twenty-one hostages, they decided to go back to Beirut, which only became possible when one of the crew members stepped forward to pay for the fuel with his credit card. On return to Beirut, the saga became darker when Robert Stethem, who had already been beaten, was shot and his body dumped on the airstrip. Stethem was a U.S. Navy diver, who, unfortunately, given the Lebanon associations, had been assigned to the USS *New Jersey*. More militants with more weapons joined the plane, and then once again it set off for Algiers. Here the first deal was done when the Greeks released a man held for being part of the original plot in return for the freedom of Greek hostages on board. This man joined the hijacking party, and once again the plane went back to Beirut. This had all taken four days.

The plane was now settled on the ground, but the drama had another seventeen days left to run. Three crew members and a number of hijackers stayed on the plane, while the remaining thirty-six hostages, all male, were delivered to the Amal militia and distributed around Beirut. This was precautionary on two fronts. First, it reduced the ability of the United States to mount a rescue mission, and second, it protected them from Hezbollah, although four did end up in the more extreme group's hands. Hostages were a form of currency in Beirut. Amal's bargaining position depended on them being kept alive. The hijackers demonstrated refined media skills, with impromptu news conferences, sometimes at the point of a gun. For one bizarre moment, five hostages were put into the middle of a media scrum before being returned to captivity.

If the intent was coercive, the Reagan administration gave no hint that it would yield. In a firm statement on June 18, Reagan made it "plain to the assassins in Beirut and their accomplices, wherever they may be, that America will never make concessions to terrorists—to do so would only invite more terrorism—nor will we ask nor pressure any other government to do so." As it happened, the Israelis were planning to release most of the prisoners but now hesitated because this would appear to be giving in to terrorist demands. To get around this obstacle, Yitzhak Rabin (who was then serving a brief stint as prime minister as part of complex coalition arrangements) mused openly that the United States could ask for the prisoners to be released. This irritated Reagan, for it would require establishing a "linkage we say doesn't exist."[3]

It was hard, however, to see how a deal of some sort could be avoided. Initially, the United States had seen it as a chance to test out the new tough line on terrorism. The idea was to mount a rescue mission using the Delta Force, designed for such purposes. This was thwarted by the distribution of the hostages around Beirut. U.S. warships, including the carrier *Nimitz*, gathering off the shore of Lebanon added to the sense of military menace and the prospect of retribution if the hostages were harmed. In the end, the hostages were released because of the intercession of Syria with Amal, and intermediaries ensuring that Israel would do its share. The fact that it required Iran to persuade Hezbollah to release its four captives was significant in terms of the story being told in this chapter, although it was not fully appreciated at the time.

The episode demonstrated again the complexities of managing terrorist incidents and the difficulty of staying calm and assured when the lives of innocent individuals are being put at risk. The president made a point of staying in the White House, there were emergency meetings, and even Weinberger did his bit to raise the temperature by declaring, "It is a war and it is the beginnings of a war."[4] Democracies were clearly poor at showing insouciance in the face of such challenges, and the message for would-be terrorists seemed clear. It was obnoxious dealing with "thugs and murderers and barbarians," as Reagan described the hijackers (to which they took offense), but the military options remained unimpressive and elusive. The mixed messages became apparent when Reagan made the point of announcing to the American people that these hostages were on their way home, describing a "moment of joy." It was not, however, a "moment of celebration." Referring to those hostages still in Lebanon, he spoke of the need for "decisive action" against terrorists. Reagan's line was firm:

> The United States gives terrorists no rewards and no guarantees. We make no concessions; we make no deals. Nations that harbor terrorists undermine their own stability and endanger their own people. Terrorists, be on notice, we will fight back against you, in Lebanon and elsewhere. We will fight back against your cowardly attacks on American citizens and property.[5]

Two other dramas that followed this incident indicated the determination of the administration to find ways of getting at those responsible for terrorism. In addition to the Shi'ite, Lebanon-related activity already described, Palestinian groups and others sympathetic to their cause had been active. In October 1985, four men of the Palestinian Liberation Front, led by Abu Abbas, planned to get on a cruise liner, the *Achille Lauro*, in order to attack the Israeli port of Ashod on a planned stop. The four were discovered in their cabin attending to their guns and so instead decided to hijack the ship itself. Most passengers were onshore touring Egypt at the time. There were only ninety-seven on board, as well as a crew of 344. This time the demand was for the release of fifty Palestinian prisoners in Israel. Unable to hit out at Israelis, the hijackers did what was for them the next best thing, although it did little for their heroic image. While off the coast of Syria, which refused them entry, they murdered Leon Klinghoffer, an elderly, wheelchair-bound Jewish American. His body was thrown overboard.

The ship returned to Egypt, where PLO officials negotiated the release of the hostages in return for safe passage out of the country. Once Klinghoffer's death became known, the Americans decided that it was intolerable to permit safe passage. An airliner flying from Egypt on October 10, with the four men, plus Abu Abbas and one of his aides, was intercepted by U.S. fighter aircraft and forced to land at the U.S. air base at Sicily. The Italians refused to let the Americans transfer them all back to the United States for trial. They managed to move Abbas and his aide out of the country but did agree, after intense discussions between Reagan and the Italian prime minister Bettino Craxi, to try the four hijackers in Italy. Reagan was upbeat after the operation. He spoke of the demonstrable determination to counter "the scourge of international terrorism." A message had been sent to "terrorists everywhere." It was in a form that presidents in these circumstances seem to find irresistible: "You can run, but you can't hide."[6]

Somewhat awkwardly for the State Department, Abbas ended up in Iraq. During 1985, there had been an attempt to get Iraq renamed as a state sponsoring terrorism, but Shultz had deflected this by first contending that "Iraq has effectively disassociated itself from international terrorism" and any attempt to suggest otherwise would be deeply resented in Baghdad, and that should the United States conclude "that any group based in or supported by Iraq is engaged in terrorist acts, we would promptly return Iraq to the list." Yet when the American ambassador requested the arrest and extradition of Abbas, it was to no avail. Then came a report that a thwarted attack at Rome airport involved men who had arrived on an Iraqi Air flight from Baghdad, where they had bought their tickets. Such events, Shultz acknowledged, when explaining why Iraq was still not to be returned to the state terrorist list, are of "deep concern." The "depth and breadth" of these concerns were to be conveyed to the government of Iraq.[7] In 1986, an internal memo to Shultz described Iraq's retreat from terrorism as "painfully slow," and noted Iraq's reluctance to "cut completely its links with terrorist groups."[8]

A contrast with the reluctance to take on Iraq was the enthusiasm to strike at Libya. For the leader of such a small country, with a population of only 3.5 million, Libya's leader, Mu'ammar Qadhafi, had managed to cut quite a figure on the international scene since he had led a coup to overthrow the monarchy in 1969. Qadhafi's radicalism had led him to cast his favors widely, giving aid and assistance to a range of groups hostile to Israel and Western powers, including the Irish Republican Army (IRA). The Libyans had seemed to have a hand in most of the notorious incidents of the 1970s, bolstered by their oil revenues, which still left room for an advanced welfare state. Although originally inspired by Nasser, he had failed to forge close links with other Arab countries, despite a number of attempts. He had fallen out with the PLO and most bitterly with Egypt after Camp David. In

1986 it was reported that 7,000 terrorists were being trained in Libya at some 34 bases.[9]

He had been marked out for his belligerence and recklessness from the start of the Reagan administration. In August 1981, Reagan approved a challenge to Qadhafi when the Sixth Fleet conducted maneuvers in the Gulf of Sidra, which Qadhafi claimed as his "lake." Unwisely, two Libyan fighters fired on two from the U.S. Navy, missed, and were then shot down. A furious Qadhafi vowed to assassinate Reagan. In response, Reagan described him as irrational and difficult to take seriously. "I find he's not only a barbarian, but he's flaky."[10] Late in 1985, the very same Egyptian airliner that had been diverted by the Americans to Sicily after the *Achille Lauro* affair was hijacked by supporters of Abu Nidal, backed by Libya for his opposition to the PLO, and taken to Malta. There, Egyptian commandos attempted a rescue operation that ended in great bloodshed, with fifty-eight fatalities.

On December 27, 1985, in yet another operation mounted by Abu Nidal, simultaneous attacks using grenades and automatic weapons at El Al counters in Rome and Vienna led to twenty dead. Of the five Americans killed, one was an eleven-year-old girl shot at point-blank range. By association Libya was again implicated, especially when it commended the attacks as "heroic operations." At this point, plans began to be made for a military strike against Libya, but the consensus within the administration was that the evidence of culpability was not yet strong enough. So, for starters, economic sanctions were introduced against Libya. Then, in the full knowledge that it was bound to irritate Qadhafi, the Sixth Fleet was sent back into the Gulf of Sidra. This led to regular but restrained encounters between American and Libyan aircraft, until March 23, when two missiles were fired ineffectually at U.S. planes, which led to a retaliatory strike against Libyan radar stations and some boats.

Qadhafi decided to get his own back the way he knew best. Barely two weeks later, on April 5, a bomb exploded in a West Berlin discotheque frequented by U.S. military personnel. Three were killed, including two U.S. servicemen, and over 230 people were injured, fifty of whom were U.S. servicemen. Intercepted signals linked Abu Nidal and also Libya to the attack. Weinberger asked immediately if this was "our smoking gun." At last, here was "irrefutable evidence." This also came just a few days after an attack on another TWA plane, in which four Americans had died. Reagan was anxious to act at once. Libya was now set up to be the proving ground of the tough new attitude.

On April 14, 1986, Operation El Dorado Canyon was launched. After some persuasion that this was a legitimate act of self-defense, British prime minister Margaret Thatcher allowed twenty-nine USAF F-111s and twenty-eight tankers to fly from their bases in Great Britain to meet up with a large collection of naval strike and support aircraft off the Tunisian coast. Targets were attacked in the capital city, Tripoli, and the coastal city of Benghazi. In just over ten minutes, a large number of targets, largely military, were attacked, although Qadhafi's home was also hit, killing his eighteen-month-old adopted daughter and injuring others, leaving the Libyan leader shaken. Civilian casualties resulted when a populated area was hit by a stray bomb. Some 70 Libyans died.[11] The United States lost the two pilots of an F-111 that crashed. Reagan declared an immediate victory in the "long battle against terrorism." It was now Libya's choice whether to end its "pursuit of terror for political goals."[12]

Public opinion was overwhelmingly in support and the Reagan team considered this to be a success. Weinberger claimed in his memoir that as "nothing was heard from Qadhafi for many months after the attack," this was "all the vindication that anyone should need of our correctness in rebuilding our military strength and in deciding how to use it."[13] He might have stopped bragging, but Qadhafi was not deterred from revenge. After 1986 Libya responded with more terrorism, largely using the Abu Nidal organization, and still was a contender for top place among state sponsors of terrorism in 1987 and 1988. The immediate response was in Lebanon, and it may have been spontaneous. Here, within two days, four hostages (three Britons and one American) were murdered. But arms shipments to the IRA in Britain continued and then, notably, Libya played a role, allegedly the main one, in the explosion of Pan Am Flight 103 on December 21, 1988, over Lockerbie, Scotland, killing all 259 passengers and crew and eleven on the ground. Libya was also connected to the explosion on a French DC-10 over Chad, which killed 170 people the following September.

*   *   *

It was remarked at the time that Libya was an easier target than Syria, Iraq, or Iran. It was small and out on a limb, barely bothering to hide its terrorist connections. The intelligence that implicated Libya in Pan Am 103 had also implicated Syria, which appeared to have provided the actual explosives. Syria was also implicated in a failed attempt to get explosives onto an El Al plane at London's Heathrow Airport around the same time, leading the British to break off diplomatic relations when this was confirmed later that year at a trial. The Americans did not follow suit. There was a greater respect for Syrian military capabilities and its political linkages. Syria had been thanked publicly for its help in concluding the TWA 847 episode, and there was still a hope that it would be possible to establish moderately satisfactory relations. It was never the case that responding to terrorism was an overwhelming priority that overrode all foreign policy considerations.

With Iran, the same could also be the case but here the depth of the antagonism was much greater, sufficient for the United States to work with Iraq, with whom Iran was fighting a bitter and vicious war. Under Operation Staunch, the United States was regularly berating countries suspected of selling arms to Iran. At some point, the thinking went, it might be possible to do business with Iran but not while Khomeini and his militant supporters were in charge. There was no basis for a rapprochement. An interagency study completed in August 1984, just before the restoration of diplomatic relations with Iraq, concluded that little could be done to acquire influence in Iran. This was confirmed in a succession of CIA assessments. As important, it was the emphatic judgment of the secretaries of both Defense and State. For Weinberger, Iran's conduct during the embassy seizure "completely disqualified it from any civilized intercourse with other nations." It was "futile to expect any kind of agreement with such a Government to be either kept or of value."[14]

Not dealing with Iran, however, meant that there was no obvious way of rescuing hostages held in Beirut. At the start of 1985, two Americans were already in captivity—the Reverend Benjamin Weir and CIA Beirut station chief William Buckley. They were soon joined by journalist Terry Anderson; relief worker Father Lawrence Jenco; David Jacobsen, director of the American University Hospital in Beirut; and Thomas Sutherland, dean of agriculture at the University of Beirut. Reagan seemed at a loss about how to deal with this type of threat, just as Carter had been. Without any presence in Beirut, the United States had no obvious way of gaining the release of these captive Americans. Other than Iran, there was no natural intermediary.

There were other reasons to worry about a complete rupture in relations. Iran's size and location gave it a strategic importance far in excess of Iraq's. The early approaches from the Soviet Union to the regime had been rebuffed, but further approaches might come when the Iranians were desperate and had nowhere else to turn. An alliance would be a very big prize for Moscow. With its long shared border with the Soviet Union, Iran had long been seen as crucial in the containment of Soviet power. Thus, the United States had been reluctant to sever all relations with Iran. There are suggestions, which largely seem to be based on the claims of Mansur Rafizadeh, a former Iranian intelligence officer who worked with the CIA until 1983, that the Agency revived an intelligence connection with Iran after the diplomatic hostages were returned. This was in order to maintain the links, but also to set back the Communist cause. When a Russian agent in Tehran defected to the British, a list of Communist Tudeh Party members was obtained. Allegedly this was passed over to the regime, leading to many arrests and executions and the outlawing of the Tudeh Party on May 4, 1983.[15]

For the foreign policy specialists, the Soviet connection and ensuring the uninterrupted flow of oil out of the Gulf were reasons to reappraise Iranian policy, but for Reagan it was the hostages that mattered more than anything else. For a man who spoke so easily in terms of broad themes and clear principles, he often approached policy at a human level. Once he met the families of the hostages, he felt under an obligation. McFarlane recalled warning Reagan how the portrayals of his anguish encouraged the hostage takers, "making it clear there is real leverage." Reagan acknowledged the point but said, "I just can't ignore their suffering."[16] He placed great trust in the CIA, and in particular Director Casey, whose enthusiasm for covert operations harked back to the pioneering days of the Agency. So he could not understand why so little was happening. Casey's deputy, Robert Gates, later recalled Reagan's preoccupation with this issue, his inability to understand why the CIA could not find and rescue the hostages, and his continued pressure on Casey to do so. "Reagan's brand of pressure," he added, "was hard to resist." Not "the loud words and harsh indictments" of Johnson or Nixon. "Just a quizzical look, a suggestion of pain, and then the request—'We just have to get those people out'—repeated near daily, week after week, month after month."[17] Weinberger testified to the same fixation. Every time the possibility of getting the hostages out was discussed, Reagan would say, "Oh, that is what I most want to do."[18] It is hard to be a full-blooded enemy of a country that might help secure the release of people whose captivity is of such concern.

*　*　*

The other critical factor in the arms-for-hostages saga was Israel's decision, in contrast to the United States, to opt for Iran in its war with Iraq. The Americans had seen the tilt to Iraq as an opportunity to improve relations with Arab states. Although this could work to Israel's advantage, as it allowed for a growth of Egyptian influence, the Israelis never saw Iraq under Saddam Hussein as a likely peacemaker. In the past they had been able to forge a strategic partnership with Iran, on the basis of a shared distrust of Arab countries. This went back to the foundation of the Jewish state in 1948, reinforced for many years by concerns about leftist forces in the Arab world. The relationship was sufficiently important for most Israeli leaders to visit Tehran at some point. Many senior Iranians traveled to Israel. Although full diplomatic relations were never established, they existed in practice: Israel's de facto embassy in Tehran was its second largest after Washington. Israel became a major arms supplier to Iran and also provided training to Iranian military forces. Over the five years from 1973 to 1978, Israeli exports to Iran grew from $33 million to $225 million, much of which was military equipment.[19] While both enjoyed good relations with the United States, they were prepared to work together independently. At the time of the revolution, the two were cooperating on a surface-to-surface missile, a matter on which the United States was kept ignorant.[20] Israel was designing the missile—the Jericho 2—while Iran provided the financing. There was also a connection between the two intelligence agencies—Israel's Mossad and Iran's SAVAK.

In return, after the Soviet Union stopped supplying oil to Israel in the late 1950s, Iran became its major supplier. As with most of these types of relationships, there were doubts on both sides. The Israelis, to some extent before the Americans, became alarmed at the inner corruption and decadence surrounding the Pahlavi court, while the shah thought Israel unreasonable on territorial issues. After the mutual hostility with Egypt during Nasser's rule, he had become an active and enthusiastic supporter of Sadat, urging Israel to make concessions to obtain a broader peace settlement. After the Likud victory in Israel in 1977, relations became more strained, but were reviving because of the peace process when the revolution came.

This close connection with Israel was one of the major items in the opposition's indictment of the shah. Khomeini made anti-Zionism a prominent theme of his revolutionary campaign from the early 1960s. In exile, he worked closely with Palestinian groups. In addition to the clerical objections to partnership with Israel, many of the guerrilla groups active in Iran during the 1970s, from a variety of political persuasions, were trained in Palestinian camps. It was notable that even before Khomeini returned to Iran from Paris at the start of 1979, the Bakhtiar government had discontinued oil supplies to Israel. The new official line was that Israel was an illegitimate state that should be replaced by a reconstituted Palestine. Revolutionary forces took over the Israeli Interest Office on February 11 (the Americans having helped the Israelis still in Tehran to escape), and then handed it over to the PLO. Yasser Arafat was the first foreign dignitary to visit Tehran (apparently without invitation and in his own private jet). Arafat reported that Khomeini had assured him that the Iranian revolution could not be complete without a successful Palestinian revolution, although he did not mention the lecture he received on the need for a more Islamic orientation. The PLO had marked the shah as a vital ally of Israel, so his fall was seen as a victory and in some ways a compensation for the "loss" of Egypt.

Relations with the PLO soon suffered as a result of the Iran-Iraq war. For the PLO, the conflict was generally catastrophic. Its potential allies were split, with the bulk supporting Iraq and only Syria and Libya on Iran's side. It was scant consolation that the worst Khomeini and Saddam could say about each other was that they were shameful servants of Israel. Meanwhile, the war provided Israel with an opportunity to reinstate an arms relationship with Iran, if not quite on the previous scale. One factor in all of this was that the arms industry, a big employer in Israel, had been badly hit by the loss of the Iranian market. The desire to revive it should not be underestimated. Another important factor was anxiety on behalf of the substantial Jewish community in Iran. The regime did execute one of the community's leaders in 1979, at a time when executions were commonplace, but there was no widespread persecution. Israel hoped to provide an added layer of protection. Last, the Israelis took the view that although their best interests might be served if the war continued indefinitely, on balance they would rather the Iraqis lost. Their basic assumption was that Iran and Israel had shared strategic interests that would eventually reassert themselves. Khomeini was old and ailing, and at some point he would go. The revolution might be more than a passing aberration, and the virulence of its anti-Zionism was objectionable. But if the Iranians were prepared to maintain some lines of communication, there was no need for Israel to break them.

The Israelis took this view even when the PLO was riding high in Tehran. The passage of time provided some vindication. As usual, military equipment was the key. The bulk of the equipment used by Iranian forces was American. They needed spare parts, and the Israelis began to supply them. The Carter administration was furious when this was discovered, so for a while the Israelis desisted. The trade started up again in earnest in 1981 after the hostages were released, and with Iran now at war. By 1982, Israel was responsible for about half the military equipment reaching Iran, so that by the end of 1983, $500,000 worth of arms had been sold. Israeli politicians did not deny the sales.[21] Although American laws appeared to have been violated, Israelis suggested that tacit approval had been granted at the highest level, apparently by Casey. One reason for this was the need for intelligence. The United States had very little idea what was going on inside Iran, and Israel's network of old and new contacts gave the Americans some insight into the trends in the regime's thinking and the developing factional struggles.

The opportunity for a breakthrough came during the course of the negotiations over TWA 847 in June 1985. The Speaker of the Iranian Parliament, Hashemi Rafsanjani, traveled to Damascus for the final negotiations, where he distanced himself from the hijackers. This gave credence to the view that when the moment came, and despite previous proclamations, deals could be done with Iran over hostages. There was a growing concern in Tehran that at a time when the country was caught up in a long war, these disputes were not only a distraction but reinforced the coalition of supporters lining up behind Iraq. The isolation was hurting Iran, and elements within the leadership, led by Rafsanjani, sought to use the effort to resolve the TWA 847 hijacking to connect again with the Western world.

One very practical reason for this was that Syria and Libya were not much use as arms suppliers because they had long relied on Soviet equipment, whereas Iran's was of Western origin. The Israelis picked up on these debates. As they later argued to the Americans, a dialogue with Iran was not preposterous. The deadlock in the war and decline in oil prices was putting pressure on the already troubled Iranian economy. Rafsanjani was establishing himself at the head of a more pragmatic faction, and he had publicly compared Soviet and French weapons unfavorably with American. Combine all this with concerns about opportunities opening up for the Soviet Union, and a case could be made. Against this was the consensus view in Washington that nothing could be done until Khomeini passed on and that Iran did not deserve any help.

Similar thoughts led in 1984 to NSC-prompted investigations into whether there would be opportunities to influence a post-Khomeini Iran. The options appeared meager and the prospects bleak. There was talk of encouraging pro-Western elements but no credible ideas on how it could be done. The danger, if anything, appeared to be one of growing Soviet influence.

McFarlane picked this up in a draft NSDD of June 1985 that suggested that in order to reduce the attractiveness of Soviet assistance and trade, the United States should encourage its allies and friends to help meet Iranian needs, even including selected items of military equipment so long as they could work with pro-Western forces. This was strongly opposed by Weinberger and Shultz on the grounds that arms sales to Iran would be "seen as inexplicably inconsistent by those nations whom we have urged to refrain from such sales" and "would adversely affect our newly emerging relationship with Iraq."[22] No assistance could be contemplated to a government supporting international terrorism. A straight arms-for-hostages deal would be contrary to U.S. public policy, violating the Arms Export Control Act, as well as the U.S. arms embargo against Iran. They never wavered from this line. They were reassured by the president and McFarlane that this was all understood, but were unable to ensure that it was followed. Shultz was marginally less adamant in his opposition than Weinberger—who likened the idea to "asking Qadhafi to Washington for a cozy chat"—as he did not wish to fall out with the Israelis over the issue. His view was that if the Iranians really did want some sort of back channel, one could soon be established, perhaps through Pakistan. Alternatively, the Europeans could be encouraged to help the Iranians out of isolation.

*   *   *

The possibility of arms sales, especially with a country with whom there were no formal relations, was bound to attract middlemen. One was the Saudi businessman Adnan Khashoggi, who had made his fortune introducing foreign corporations to Saudi Arabia while helping the kingdom procure advanced weaponry. An even greater role was played by one of Khashoggi's contacts, Iranian businessman Manucher Ghorbanifar. He had used his roots in both Iran and America to considerable financial advantage during the shah's time. His trademarks were irrepressibility, persistence, and a readiness to tell stories with less regard for their veracity than their impact on his audience and his own reputation as a man of influence. After the revolution he was able to sustain some contacts within Iran, and he gained in value to the Iranians as they became desperate for arms. Khashoggi also was aware of Iran's appetite for weapons. Because of the shah's past purchases, these would have to be American. But there were two problems. First, U.S. policy was resolutely anti-Iranian, and second, Ghorbanifar had been judged to be a "fabricator" and wholly unreliable in the past by the CIA, which continued to want nothing to do with him.

The two decided to get at the Americans through the Israelis. They had contact with Israelis connected to the arms industry and, most significant, David Kimche, director general of the Israeli foreign ministry. Ghorbanifar persuaded them of rumblings of discontent within Iran sufficient to exploit. It was a message to which they were naturally receptive. The man who provided the link into the U.S. administration was Michael Ledeen, a sometime journalist and academic, working for the NSC as a consultant. He was later described by Shultz as having a "conspiratorial bent,"[23] and by others as indiscreet, verbose, and prone to exaggerating his own position.[24] Ledeen had no particular background in the Middle East, although he had some in counterterrorism. In the spring of 1985, he became interested in the possibility of upheavals in Iran. As U.S. intelligence was unusually poor on Iran and he had heard that Israel's was much better, he persuaded McFarlane to let him meet a former contact, Shimon Peres, then in one of his occasional stints as Israel's prime minister. His instructions were to do no more than inquire about Israeli intelligence on Iran, which turned out, according to Peres, to be as poor as America's. As they discussed the possibility of more pooling of intelligence, Peres, who was aware of the Iranian interest in American weapons, checked whether the United States would object if Israel acceded to a recent Iranian request to purchase artillery shells. Ledeen took the question back to National Security Adviser Robert McFarlane. By this time, Shultz had heard of Ledeen's visit, about which the U.S. ambassador to Israel had not been consulted, and sent off a furious missive to McFarlane, warning that "Israel's agenda is not the same as ours," which could skew any intelligence received; McFarlane sent back a defensive response and decided to pursue the matter anyway.

In early July, McFarlane met Kimche. Israel's understanding of the debate under way in Tehran came directly from Ghorbanifar (who in the correspondence was elevated to an adviser to the Iranian prime minister) and led to the idea of a revived dialogue with Iran, including the possibility of its intercession with the militants holding the hostages in return for arms, specifically 100 tube-launched optical-tracking wire-guided (TOW) missiles. After going through all the ways in which the pursuit of this matter could go badly wrong, McFarlane argued to Shultz that it would be worthwhile to see if an entrée to Iran could be found. At about the same time one of the Israelis, Al Schwimmer, was sent to Washington to meet up with Ledeen, who in turn passed on to McFarlane the idea of dispatching arms to demonstrate U.S. bona fides with Tehran, in order to persuade them to get the hostages released.

On July 16, 1985, McFarlane decided to put the idea directly to Reagan, who was at this time recovering from abdominal surgery at Bethesda Naval Hospital. The president was told that the Israelis had a contact who could reach certain people in the Iranian government who might help get hostages released. Reagan later said that "once we had information from Israel that we could trust the people in Iran, I didn't have to think thirty seconds about saying yes to their proposals." All this seems to be predicated on the untested assumption that there were moderate Iranians who both wanted change and at the same time had sufficient clout with Hezbollah in Lebanon to get the hostages released.[25] That day, Ledeen left for Israel to begin his long relationship with Ghorbanifar, whom he met there later in the month.

Kimche, who had been in on these discussions, was authorized by his government to go back to Washington, but also to gain assurance that Shultz knew what was going on, and Reagan approved. McFarlane, whom he met on August 2, gained the impression that high-ranking Iranians were already in on the scheme and wanted the weapons to demonstrate the value of their Western links. When McFarlane said that the United States could not transfer arms directly to Iran, Kimche came up with the answer: Israel would make the sales and then purchase replacements from the United States. After a number of consultations around the administration, on August 6 the president, still recuperating, met with his principal advisers. The scheme, with the Israelis actually doing the selling and the optimism about the benefits that would flow, was outlined. There was the customary dissent from Shultz and Weinberger, who believed they had killed the idea. Reagan was not prepared to let it die. McFarlane worked toward a position whereby the Israelis could proceed, so long as the weapons went to the right Iranians.

The position was bizarre. Just after the opening to Iraq, the idea had developed of a parallel track with Iran, possibly also extending to the sale of arms, which was actually further than the United States went with Iraq. This would confuse rather than qualify the established policy, as if the U.S. government could tilt in two opposing directions at once. To help those, including Reagan, who preferred to believe this was not a crude arms-for-hostages swap, the move was to be presented as an attempt to create the conditions for a step change in U.S.-Iranian relations. On this basis, hostage release was a means of showing good faith, though it was also bound to be for the Americans an end in itself.

★ ★ ★

The first shipment of ninety-six TOW missiles arrived in Iran on August 20. When no hostages were released, Ghorbanifar explained that these missiles had gotten into the wrong hands, but that it was worth trying again. By mid-September a further 408 TOWs had been sent. There was one hostage released but not the one asked for, CIA station chief William Buckley. Unfortunately (though this was not then revealed), he had died the previous June after being tortured. McFarlane was asked to choose, and so the Reverend Weir was freed. He had been held the longest but also, as McFarlane acknowledged, had the noisiest family support.[26] The note he carried from his captors demanding the release of the Kuwait 17 indicated that this was a complicated game. The release of one hostage at least suggested that it was worth staying in the game, although it also indicated that the Iranians were unlikely to release too many hostages all at once because then they would lose their leverage.

Ghorbanifar proposed diversifying into a range of advanced weapons, with the added bait of an introduction to a senior Iranian official, Hassan Karoubi with links to Khomeini. It was unclear how senior or how official Karoubi actually was. He was introduced to the Israelis in July and gave some corroboration to Ghorbanifar's claims. He explained the regime's need to cooperate with the West and his fear of the Soviets. The Israelis were impressed. Ledeen was increasingly of the view that the United States should not wait for Khomeini to die but should work to undermine the hard-liners in Iran while he was still in place.

In mid-November, Yitzhak Rabin, at this time Israeli defense minister, met first with Casey and then McFarlane to gain approval for a sale of HAWK (Homing-All-the-Way-Killer) antiaircraft missiles to Iran and their later replenishment by the United States. Once McFarlane determined that Reagan was content with this plan, the Israelis wasted little time and soon reported that eighty HAWKs were ready to go. At this point, irritating questions of logistics and legality started to intrude. This was only to be the first consignment, yet any more than eighty would exceed the U.S. capacity for replenishment. The Pentagon was objecting to the transfer of any HAWKs. In addition and contrary to McFarlane's understanding, the deliveries would precede any hostage release. Then the transfer failed to get the necessary clearances (despite attempted American help) to pass through Portugal, so that the aircraft carrying the missiles had to return to Israel. Eventually, with the aid of the CIA, eighteen HAWKs did reach Iran. The Iranians, with a welcoming party including Prime Minister Moussavi, were furious. Having paid out a lot of money, they had been sent a dated version of the missile, ineffective at high altitudes, and still marked with the Star of David. By sending the wrong missiles, the Pentagon had effectively sunk the deal.

The obvious implication of this fiasco was that the effort to make a good impression on the Iranians had backfired spectacularly. They were blaming Reagan personally for cheating them and not the sundry intermediaries who had actually put the deal together. This meant that there would be no freedom for any hostages. The best course was to abandon the enterprise and find alternative ways to talk to Iranians. This was McFarlane's view, but too many people now had a stake in trying again, so the Americans had another go. One influential factor, given the Iranian irritation with the previous delivery, was concern that without further action, one or more hostages might be executed in retaliation. On November 26, Reagan met Poindexter, who was in the process of replacing McFarlane as national security adviser, and decided to persevere, except that now they would take over control from the Israelis.[27] Trying again would in fact raise the stakes for the administration. The United States was now directly handling aspects of the transaction. Colonel Oliver North, the chief fixer on the NSC staff, had become directly involved. North, a decorated Vietnam veteran who had been on the NSC staff from early in the administration, was inexhaustible, competent, and loyal to the president. He gradually took on more responsibilities, including dealing with the Contras in Nicaragua, which is why he provided the link between these two otherwise separate strands of activity.

An additional potential for embarrassment came when it transpired that the CIA had failed to get a presidential finding that would make its role in this covert operation legal. One was drafted belatedly. Uniquely, it was retro-spective rather than anticipatory, based on an apparent "mental Finding" made by the president that he had unaccountably failed to write down. It was signed by Reagan on December 5, 1985. The finding specifically linked the CIA's activities to an arms-for-hostages deal. It noted "certain foreign materiel and munitions may be provided to the Government of Iran which is taking steps to facilitate the release of the American hostages."[28] No men-tion was made of moderate Iranians. Congress was not to be told.

Because Poindexter was overloaded, he let North get on with the busi-ness. North worked on a plan that had 1,500 TOWs delivered in stages dur-ing a single day, with hostages coming out in between shipments. On December 7, Reagan presided over a key meeting of his senior advisers. Mc-Farlane and Poindexter were both present, along with Shultz, Weinberger, and John McMahon of the CIA, deputizing for Casey. The two most senior figures, Shultz and Weinberger, expressed grave doubts about the wisdom and legality of arms sales to Iran, while McMahon queried the very idea that there were moderates to be found within the Iranian regime. But Casey had told Poindexter that he supported allowing sales to continue, using the Is-raelis as a conduit. Again Weinberger and Shultz believed, erroneously, that they killed off the escapade. The president, however, was not easily dis-suaded. According to Weinberger's notes: "President sd. he could answer charges of illegality but he couldn't answer charge that 'big strong President Reagan passed up chance to free hostages.'" Again Reagan appears to have rationalized it to himself on the basis that the weapons would go to the "moderate leadership in the army."[29] For the moment, the only decision was to convey to the Iranians a readiness to improve relations, which would be conditional on the release of the hostages and independent of any later deci-sions on arms sales. This did not go down well when conveyed to the Israelis, who believed in the possibility of causing a shift in internal Iranian politics, and Ghorbanifar, who saw future deals at risk and was still out of pocket from the last calamity.

North remained enthusiastic. He mooted the idea that it might be more straightforward if the United States sold arms directly to Iran, still using Ghorbanifar as an intermediary. North was quite persuaded of the unrelia-bility of the Iranians but also of the lack of any alternative. McFarlane, who remained involved as a private citizen, had confidence in neither Ghorbani-far ("a pathological liar") nor the value of the process.[30] Yet Reagan was re-luctant to let go of the possibility that out of all of this the hostages might be freed. As the NSC staff interpreted the president's will and his unhappiness that the hostages would still be in captivity over Christmas, they began to prepare the ground for direct sales to Iran. Casey was also committed, prepared to ignore his own analysts' extremely negative assessments of Ghorbanifar and not even pass them on to the NSC. Gates, however, suggested that Casey's motives were not altogether pure. Casey understood that this was something Reagan wanted to happen, and while he always suspected it would fail, by backing the president while Shultz was opposed, he acquired some political credit. The operation meant that he would no longer be nagged to free the hostages, and if it failed, it was the NSC's responsibility. In general, Gates contended that the "whole business was seen inside the government as a wacko, likely to fail NSC operation that the President wanted to pursue—and *no one* was willing to put his job on the line to stop it." He noted that CIA analysis suggested that any moderate faction referred to economic issues and not potential political deals with the United States. It was not that there was lack of information on internal Iranian affairs. "The intelligence we had was simply inconvenient."[31]

The Israelis were still pushing for a broader U.S. strategic relationship with Iran, even taking in Lebanon. They came up with a scheme to transfer 500 TOW missiles to Iran in return for the release of all hostages, to be followed by an Israeli release of some Hezbollah prisoners held in southern Lebanon. The next step would be 3,500 more TOWs in return for an Iranian pledge never again to take hostages or indulge in terrorism. This seemed to carry more promise and fewer risks than earlier proposals. North got to work, and this time a presidential finding was prepared so that any CIA involvement would be legal. On January 7, 1986, another NSC meeting was held. There was now no doubt that Reagan wanted to go ahead, and that the people closest to the president—Poindexter, Casey, and Donald Regan—supported him. Reagan records that Shultz and Weinberger "argued forcefully that I was wrong, but I just put my foot down."[32] On January 17, another finding was signed. Reagan agreed to sell TOWs to Iran.

The plan soon ran into trouble, as it became apparent that the numbers of missiles involved in replenishing Israeli stocks required Congress to be notified. At this point, the simplicity of turning the sales over to the CIA so that they could be both direct and kept covert began to look more appealing. By now North had hit upon the idea of using spare funds generated during this supply operation to support the Contras in Central America. The extra income was generated by a markup on the original cost of the missiles and the price paid by the Iranians. This became an added incentive to continue with the process. The involvement of Ghorbanifar in the transaction added a further markup, which led to the Iranians' balking at the price when the deal was offered. It took until February 18 to resolve the complex logistical and financial arrangements for delivery of the 500 TOW missiles.

One potential benefit was that North and other U.S. officials could meet directly with Iranian officials in Germany. The dialogue yielded little. The Americans, led by North, pushed for the release of hostages; the Iranians, led by Mohsen Kangarlou, who had a position of sorts within the Iranian government, pushed for more weapons. The Americans gave the Iranians snippets of intelligence information, and the Iranians promised to see if they could arrange for a high-level U.S. delegation to visit Iran. North seized on this promise with enthusiasm. He now had the idea that McFarlane, who would lead the U.S. delegation, would be meeting Speaker Rafsanjani. He felt they were on the verge of a breakthrough. At the end of the month, 500 more TOWs were delivered, but still nothing in response.

Before anything could happen, the United States had bombed Libya, because of its sponsorship of terrorist acts, which did not make it a propitious time for a sensitive mission to a country accused of the same thing. Then U.S. Customs arrested Ghorbanifar, which resulted in further delay, not least because it undermined his ability to raise the bridging finance. Nonetheless, he still managed to stay involved, promising access to Iranian interlocutors of considerable seniority and also that within three days of the U.S. team arriving in Tehran, all hostages would be freed. Despite his history of inconsistent and untenable promises to both sides, Ghorbanifar still managed to string everyone along. Only an unusually amateurish group, acting outside the normal bureaucratic constraints and practices, could ever have believed that so much could be achieved on such a flimsy basis. As Theodore Draper observed, when they were dealing with Ghorbanifar, "For their credulity, the Americans had only themselves to blame."[33]

Without any advance discussions between the two sides that might have helped warn of the later difficulties, an American team traveled to Tehran, led by McFarlane, with North; George Cave, a former Iranian expert for the CIA and translator; and NSC staff officer Howard Teicher. It also included an Israeli, Amiram Nir, who had been closely involved in earlier discussions and was posing as an American. The Iranians were unimpressed when his nationality was revealed by Ghorbanifar. They also had little idea who McFarlane was. As he was now a private citizen, it was not clear why the Iranian leadership should put themselves out to meet him. As was explained to McFarlane during the visit, the precedents were not encouraging. The last senior Iranian politician to meet with a senior American, Mehdi Bazargan, almost immediately lost his job. Nor at a time when a thaw was developing in U.S.-Soviet relations was it clear why the Iranians should take seriously warnings, which were fabricated, of Soviet plans for an invasion. Last, the Iranians had realized just how much they had been overcharged on the equipment they had received.

The visit, which lasted for just over three days in late May, was inevitably frustrating. In addition to a strange collection of gifts, including a cake in the shape of a key, symbolizing U.S.-Iranian relations being unlocked but unfortunately destined to be taken and eaten by Iranian border guards, the mission brought the first installment of spare parts for HAWKs. Soon they were told that the Iranians claimed they had never promised to do anything more than try to obtain the hostages' release. There were limits, they were told, to Iranian influence with the groups responsible. They suggested that if the Americans stayed longer, then they might secure the release of one or two hostages, but McFarlane and North were fearful that if they were away much longer, their absence would be noticed in Washington. McFarlane was also far more anxious about the whole process and was taking a tougher line than North on whether to demand that any deal depended on all hostages being released. In practice, a few days was too little time for the sort of negotiations required. Another plane from Israel loaded with additional spare parts departed for Iran but was ordered to return in midflight to Israel, because no hostages were to be freed. The American party departed on the morning of May 28, 1986.

Cave later took the view that the "major problems we encountered stemmed from the lack of prior preparation by both sides." He recalled being told by a member of the Iranian team that as they had not expected the Americans actually to come to Tehran, they only hurriedly sent someone to Lebanon to talk to the hostage takers after the Americans turned up. Even as the Americans left, the Iranians were asking for more time to secure the release of hostages.[34] The Americans were told that to get the hostages back, the Israelis had to withdraw from the Golan Heights and Lebanon, the Kuwait 17 must be freed, and the United States should pay for the costs of hostage taking!

The Iranians may have been getting concerned that this unexpected source of vital arms might now dry up. In July, messages came through more normal diplomatic channels of an Iranian interest in improved relations. On July 24, 1986, American hostage Father Lawrence Jenco was released, which created some optimism on the American side. Ghorbanifar cautioned that without a positive response to Jenco's release another of the hostages might be harmed. It turned out that without any authority, he had promised HAWK missile parts in return. In light of this, North proposed, and Reagan agreed, the remaining HAWK spare parts should be delivered to Iran. This took place in early August. Ghorbanifar was now revealed to have not only been telling tall stories but also lining his own pockets even more than had been supposed.

Another indication of Iranian interest in continuing the dialogue came with a proposal to set up a second channel, without Ghorbanifar. This involved a nephew of President Rafsanjani, Ali Hahemi Rafsanjani, a senior official in the Revolutionary Guard. Poindexter decided that he was worth cultivating. At this point, when something might have come of the effort, it fell victim to faction fighting within the Iranian regime. In September, two more hostages—Frank Reed and Joseph Cicippio—were taken in Beirut. In terms of the balance of gains and losses, the Americans were back where they started. Increasingly desperate, North's team met with the new contact to see if the deal could be revived. Now the possible release of the Kuwait 17 was developed as an alternative sweetener, although nothing came of this.

Rafsanjani visited Washington in September. The account of this meeting suggests a serious encounter of the sort that might have been productive had it occurred earlier in the proceedings. The Iranians were certainly not talking of overthrowing Khomeini, but they shared concerns about Soviet intentions and the unreliability of Ghorbanifar. North was worried that Ghorbanifar knew too much and could cause mischief. The Iranians seemed to think they had some leverage over him. The Iranians explained their strategy for the Iran-Iraq war. They did not need a complete victory, but they did expect to see the end of Saddam Hussein and suggested that the Americans try to arrange this through their Arab friends. Some hostages for some weapons were discussed. Further U.S.-Iranian talks took place in Germany in early October, in which North was exaggerating his links with the president and what the United States might offer, on the Kuwait 17 and intelligence information, and potential policy on the war and Saddam Hussein, without actually promising anything. The Iranians were doing the same with regard to the hostages.

At the end of October there was another meeting, with the exchanges becoming more detailed. The Iranians described the split within the regime, with Rafsanjani most favoring ties with the United States but others now coming along. Five hundred TOW missiles reached Iran via Israel, and soon another hostage, David Jacobsen, was released. A proposal was now put, through this channel, for a special commission to be created to discuss ways of improving U.S.-Iranian relations. Although it was claimed that this was a view with consensus support, that was clearly not the case. It was now known that the immoderate faction in Tehran led by Ayatollah Hussein Ali Montazeri was circulating details of the links and was intending to leak the information. When one of those responsible was arrested, his supporters gave an account to the Lebanese newsmagazine *Ash Shiraa,* which came out on November 3, 1986. McFarlane's visit to Tehran was admitted by Rafsanjani. His speech by necessity (for him) mocked the Americans and complained about their tactics, but did not actually close the door to further discussions. Prime Minister Moussavi, however, ruled out any improvement in relations.

* * *

The first official response in a White House press statement inaccurately insisted that "no U.S. laws have been or will be violated and . . . our policy of not making concessions to terrorists remains intact." As congressional demands for full disclosure grew, the administration appeared divided and confused. Many statements were made that were simply not true. The sudden revelations about first dealing with Iran and then, on the back of this, funding the Contras made any further dialogue with Tehran impossible. As more was revealed, in addition to attempts to destroy evidence in a "shredding party" in North's office, the scandal threatened to engulf the administration. Not only were Poindexter and North obliged to resign, but Reagan reluctantly agreed to a bipartisan special investigation chaired by former senator John Tower, including former secretary of state Edmund Muskie and former national security adviser Brent Scowcroft. Both the Tower Commission and a later congressional report criticized the president for his lack of control over the National Security Council staff.

The president described the initiative to the American people as part of a policy designed to bring the Iran-Iraq war to an end and deal with problems of terrorism, subversion, and hostage taking. This required signaling to Iran that its strategic importance was recognized and that improved relations were possible if these problems were addressed.[35] As the administration could provide little evidence that anything had changed as a result of its policy, the logical inference was that the policy's failure was Iran's fault. According to Shultz, a signal had been sent in the form of a transfer of arms, but that "did not elicit an acceptable Iranian response."[36] Reagan spoke of Iran as a "barbaric" country.

Was the attempt to establish a dialogue with Iran doomed from the start? It was hard for the Americans to make sense of the internal politics of a revolutionary state at a time of considerable turmoil. The regime did not speak with one voice. A hint of conciliation might therefore represent a significant policy shift, a tentative probe, or just deliberate dissimulation. Expectations should, however, have been kept modest. Khomeini was still alive and honored; his core principles could not be readily disregarded. The whole approach was instrumental, geared to getting weapons. Perhaps they found it curious that the only regional power courting them was Israel, but their main fight was with Arabs who had refused to be impressed by their noisy support for the Palestinian cause. The Israelis did not seem to mind dealing with them while being denounced. As this was how the Israelis always had to operate when talking to the neighbors, it did not discourage wishful thinking, an unrealistic desire to recreate the partnership of the shah's time, when the two countries could together hold the Arabs in check. The Israelis were seduced by the possibility that furtive conversations with a collection of Iranian fixers, albeit well-placed, could turn round a whole political system. For the Iranians the Israelis were simply a route to the Americans. Yet it took even longer for disillusion to set in with the Israelis than the Americans. When it did, however, they moved rapidly from making the case for dialogue to alarmism about this dangerous new threat.

The Iranian approach to the Americans was also instrumental. Arms were top of the agenda. Desperate, the Iranians might have been prepared to accept that a flow of arms would cement a wider political rapprochement, but it was only towards the late stages of the affair that such a possibility was properly addressed. Instead the Americans began the conversations at the wrong end, as if they were after only the narrowest of bargains, trading arms for hostages. This encouraged the Iranians to haggle. A more effective dialogue would have required more accomplished diplomacy and greater internal cohesion than either side could muster at the time. Nonetheless, the senior Iranian leadership probably hoped that more would come of the dialogue. The individual responsible for leaking the talks was executed.[37] They may also have thought that the Americans would be impressed by restraint, as if they would be satisfied by a terrorism cease-fire. Unfortunately, the management of the whole process was clumsy and inept. As James Bill has observed:

> It involved the wrong people (McFarlane, North, Teicher) advised by the wrong "experts" (Ledeen, Ghorbanifar) supported by the wrong allies (Israel); they went to the wrong place (Tehran) at the wrong time (during the month of Ramadan and after the United States had tilted to the Iraqi side during the gulf war) carrying the wrong tactical plan.[38]

The scandal caused immense political damage to the Reagan administration and had important consequences for American policy. As the relevant NSC officials left office, control over policy was reasserted by the secretaries of State and Defense, both of whom felt vindicated in their views of a duplicitous Iran and strongly supported the policy of tilting to Iraq.

10

THE TANKER WAR

THE REVELATIONS ABOUT the extraordinary undercover dealings with Iran did enormous damage to American credibility in the Arab world. The Iraqis bemoaned their betrayal, claiming that the covert deals represented the appeasement of Iran and proof of a U.S.-Zionist conspiracy. Relations with the Gulf countries had already been undermined by congressional rejection of a proposed weapons sale to Saudi Arabia in the spring of 1986. Faced with such a strong negative reaction, the Reagan administration went out of its way to repair relations with Arab governments, and in particular Iraq. The administration insisted that the unfortunate Iranian incident should not be taken as any lack of commitment to Saudi self-defense. Shultz reaffirmed to Congress that in general the war had "highlighted overlapping interests with Iraq." Although, he acknowledged, the news that there had been some arms shipments to Iran had put a "strain" on U.S.-Iraqi relations, nonetheless both sides understood that there was "an overriding common interest in finding an early end to the war."[1]

Privately, American officials acknowledged more of a crisis. Undersecretary of State Michael Armacost observed: .

> In light of recent events, Iraq and the other Gulf Arabs are looking for
> signs of American seriousness about their region. Tangible steps, such
> as breaking the logjam on licensing for Iraq, would give us something to

point to as we attempt to reassure the Gulf states about U.S. policy in
that region.[2]

As this quote indicates, compensation for a detour toward Iran involved
going full steam ahead with Iraq. As Reagan upped the rhetorical stakes, as if
the scandal were all Tehran's fault, the pressure to forge ever closer relations
with Iraq became even greater. Dubious requests for sensitive technologies
received even less scrutiny. The range and intensity of business contacts
grew. The most important developments were at sea, as the United States became a virtual ally of Iraq in its naval war with Iran.

★   ★   ★

During the course of the mid-1980s, the oil market was transformed. At first
the war resulted in a dramatic loss of production in both Iran and Iraq, with
the result that by the end of 1980, worldwide crude oil production was 10
percent lower than in 1979. The oil price reached $35 per barrel in 1981, ap-
proaching twice the level of 1978, before the Iranian revolution. However,
the price rises of the 1970s, reinforced by this second surge, had encouraged
greater energy efficiency, development of alternative energy sources, and ex-
ploration and production outside the OPEC area. This led to an additional
10 million barrels a day by 1986. The result was a crisis for OPEC. Not only
were two of its leading members at war, but the higher prices of the past had
lowered demand for oil while increasing supplies from outside the organization. The preferred method for dealing with this crisis was to set production
quotas for member states at a level sufficient to stabilize prices. Discipline
was poor, and overproduction by individual states became an additional
source of tension. It was one factor that led to Iraq's turning on Kuwait in
1990.

Saudi Arabia was best placed to manipulate its production to control the
price, and it attempted to play this role of the "swing producer." By late 1985,
the continuing fall in price and excessive production by others led the Saudis
to tire of this role. They increased their production significantly, with the inevitable result that by the middle of 1986, crude oil prices had plummeted
below $10 per barrel. The fall was sufficient to alarm all oil producers, in-
cluding those in the United States, as the economics of the industry was
turned upside down. It has even been suggested that this was one reason for
the United States to want to develop a dialogue with the Iranians in order to
influence their oil policy. For similar reasons, and to some surprise, the
Saudis talked to the Iranians. In September 1986, as the U.S. discussions

with Iran were reaching their own climax, the two countries agreed on lower production. By 1987, prices had recovered to $18 to $20 per barrel.

This was the context for the Iraqi-Iranian "tanker war." Both sides were seeking to secure their own oil production and distribution while disrupting that of their enemy's. Iraq's inability to get its oil out through the Gulf meant that it was dependent upon pipelines. Although the idea of a pipeline through Jordan was abandoned, the one through Saudi Arabia was given extra capacity and another through Turkey was agreed on. It was being completed as the war ended. The Iraqi effort to hurt Iran's oil economy involved attacks on oil tankers. Because of the pipelines, Saddam was not desperately worried about Iranian retaliation against traffic in the Gulf. Indeed, it suited his purposes, for this was one way of internationalizing the conflict. This would be most likely to occur if the Iranians decided to close the Strait of Hormuz, as this would trigger intervention by oil-dependent Western countries. Separating the Gulf of Oman from the Persian Gulf, the strait is twenty-one miles wide at its narrowest, overlooked by Iran to the north. For the local oil-producing states, this is a vital route. Through the strait came 17 percent of the West's oil (although only a small proportion of oil destined for the United States). Thus, when the Security Council addressed the tanker war in Resolution 540 in October 1983, it was not the Iraqi activity about which it was bothered but the possible Iranian response, and in particular the potential closure of the Strait of Hormuz.

There was actually no obvious reason for Iran to close the strait, even if it had the ability. Far more than Iraq, Iran was dependent upon the sea for oil exports and also for imports. The Iranians would be hurt by its closure without being helped in the ground war. As early as October 2, 1980, Iran denied that it intended to close the strait, stating that fears to the contrary were being "generated by governments intent upon interference in the region of the Gulf."[3] Rather than escalating, Iran worked to reduce the harmful effects of Iraqi actions by supporting those foreign tankers still prepared to operate from Kharg Island and by keeping its rates competitive, while building up its own tanker fleet. Later, it developed a shuttle service so that its tankers could ferry oil from Kharg to the lower Gulf, where it could be loaded safely into foreign tankers.

By 1984, the Iraqis had French Exocet missiles and were increasing attacks. Compared with forty-eight tankers in the first three years of the war, seventy-one were attacked in 1984. This was an inconvenience rather than a major threat. Tankers are not very vulnerable to missile attack, and stored oil is not particularly flammable. Yet the impact should not be understated. Sailors lost their lives, ships were damaged, insurance premiums went up, and traffic through the Gulf slowed down. Generally, Iraqi attacks outnumbered Iranian by about three to one and were more effective. At the time, the United States was prepared to argue that the Iraqi rationale for the "tanker war" was more compelling than that of Iran, as it was directed at a belligerent and limited to "legitimate military targets."[4] President Reagan observed, "I think we have always recognized that in a time of war, the enemy's commerce and trade is a fair target, if you can hurt them economically." He claimed that while Iraq confined its attacks to shipping vital to Iran's economy, Iran's response was geared to neutral countries, "like Saudi Arabia and Kuwait."[5] Few at the time would have described Saudi Arabia or Kuwait as neutral in this dispute. Furthermore, in its conduct of the tanker war, Iraq failed some basic tests in international law. It made no provision for safe passage routes; subjected merchant vessels, predominantly of neutral countries, to assaults without prior warning or concern for the safety of crew members; and launched a number of attacks outside the designated area.[6] The UN secretary-general explicitly disagreed with Iraq's contention that its attacks on shipping were justified by international law.

Iran's weapons were mainly suitable for harassment, and there were not even any commercial vessels of any kind sailing to Iraq. It lacked spare air capacity, and its navy was in a poor state, in both areas hampered by the Western embargo as it could not get new systems or spare parts. It did have British-made fast attack craft and could also use some helicopters to launch the Italian-made Sea Killer antiship missiles. When these missiles became operational in 1984, it had a greater capacity to damage rather than harass ships. In April 1984, attacks on neutral shipping began with the shelling of an Indian freighter, but the priority targets were soon Kuwaiti and Saudi oil tankers. Rather than close the strait, its preference appeared to be to disrupt the traffic of Iraq's Arab allies as they used the Gulf, to the benefit, the Iranians claimed, of Iraq's war effort. Their attacks had less impact than those mounted by Iraq and were largely in retribution for those supporting Iraq.[7]

In late 1986, as news of the Iran-Contra affair was breaking, the Iranian missile threat began to be upgraded. In terms of antipopulation attacks, Scud missiles from North Korea could be lobbed in the direction of Baghdad. For the tanker war, the Iranians had acquired the much more substantial and longer-range Silkworm antiship missile. Based on the veteran Soviet Styx, this was not a particularly sophisticated missile, but it could cover and potentially sink ships passing through the strait. Deliveries from China began in the summer of 1986, and one was test fired in late February 1987. A complicating factor in this story was that China refused to admit that it had sold the missiles to Iran. The missile story changed regularly. At one point, the North Koreans (who undoubtedly were active in the arms market) were blamed; later the Iranians claimed to have bought the Silkworms on the open market; then the story was that they had been captured from Iraq. The Americans warned that they would attack the Silkworm launching sites if there was any threat to U.S. forces or shipping; the Iranians promised unspecified retaliation if they were attacked.

*   *   *

In the face of what now appeared to be a more credible threat to navigation through the Strait of Hormuz, Washington revived a promise to assist members of the (anti-Iranian) Gulf Cooperation Council if this was their wish. The first time around, they had been unwilling to get too close to the United States, given the perceived inconstancy of its policy. Now their ships were in danger. Although the GCC states claimed to be neutral, Iran could argue with some justice that they were in fact allies of Iraq. They were pursuing what was described at the time as "defense by proxy" by providing "loans" to Iraq of at least $35 billion, allowing goods bound for Iraq to pass through their own ports and selling oil on Iraq's behalf. This was probably more important to the Iraqi war effort than any formal entry into the war as belligerents. Any actual military contribution would have been marginal. Of all these countries, Kuwait was the most important supporter, with 13 percent of the world's proven oil reserves and great wealth. It gave Iraq financial assistance and allowed the use of its territory as a land route for supplies to Iraq. It had taken sides. There was therefore a clear Iranian motive to act against Kuwaiti shipping.

In November 1986, aware of the threat, Kuwait approached members of the GCC about the idea of superpower protection for shipping in the Persian Gulf. The other states were doubtful but accepted Kuwaiti concerns. On January 13, 1987, Kuwait made a formal request to the United States for help in escorting its oil tankers through the Persian Gulf. The idea was to reflag Kuwaiti ships, so that the Iranians would have to fire against the Stars and Stripes. The initial American response was unenthusiastic. The Kuwaitis were told that reflagging would take six months under U.S. law and that only a few ships were available to help them. The U.S. Navy was "lukewarm," seeing such an operation as a "diversion of effort and potentially hazardous."[8] This position soon changed.

The Kuwaitis approached the Russians in the first instance because they thought that they would act more quickly and Iran-Contra had left them uncertain about American intentions.[9] Kuwait was the only Gulf state with good relations with the Soviet Union. Tentative agreement on a chartering plan was reached with Moscow in early December. As Kuwait undoubtedly understood, this made the matter of even greater interest to Washington, still heavily influenced by the priorities of the cold war. Weinberger immediately interpreted this as a challenge to the American position in the Persian Gulf: "I was . . . convinced," he later recorded, "it was not in our interest for Soviet forces to move into an area so vital to us. That was a major point in my calculation."[10] Shultz was more cautious. While Weinberger still viewed matters in terms of cold war rivalries, the secretary of state was becoming confident in the winds of change in Soviet foreign policy under Mikhail Gorbachev and saw the potential opportunities for future cooperation. "Despite strong feelings throughout the administration that we should not be part of an effort by the Kuwaitis to draw the Soviets into the Gulf," he later recalled, "I felt we should not object to some Soviet presence: to object would only heighten Kuwait's bargaining power with us."[11] He still went along with the policy,[12] as did Reagan when he met with his senior advisers on March 4, 1987. A month later, Kuwait formally proposed transferring registration of some of its oil tankers to American flag registry. President Reagan explained, "If we don't do the job, the Soviets will. And that will jeopardize our national security as well as our allies."[13]

The secretaries of State and Defense saw the operation as a valuable means of rebuilding support after the setbacks to America's credibility in the region. Assistant Secretary of State Richard Murphy acknowledged as potent an argument: "Frankly, in the light of the Iran-*contra* revelations, we had found that the leaders of the Gulf states were questioning the coherence and seriousness of U.S. policy in the Gulf along with our reliability and staying power."[14] Another reason for Kuwait's wanting to hold the United States "at arm's length," Weinberger suspected, was its "failure to support the Shah when Iran was in turmoil."[15] Iran would be encouraged to test American resolve by mounting attacks. If losses led to withdrawal, this would send unfortunate signals not only to the Iranians but also to the Soviets about whether interests in the Gulf were seen to be vital. Last, there was a determination to act against Iran. In part this was because of new factors that were perceived to have entered the equation—in particular the acquisition of Silkworm antiship missiles and preparations for their deployment, as well as apparent preparations for naval operations by a new branch of the Revolutionary Guard. The basic motivation, however, was much more political. Shultz reports that he saw the policy as "a way to thwart Iran's ambitions and possibly lead to an end to the long, bloody war."[16]

It may be that American policymakers did not see the policy change here as being "momentous." The limited significance was indicated by the lack of a requirement for an increase in the number of American ships in the Persian Gulf. At the time, the U.S. Navy had only four vessels in the area, plus a five-ship battle group nearby. This was considered capable of deterring Iran without provoking it. The starting assumption was that as Iran had steered clear of direct confrontation with the superpowers in the past, this would continue. Murphy told a May 21 press conference of the "numerous factors" that suggested Iran would not attack U.S. naval ships or flagships, as this would be a diversion from the war against Iraq and Tehran would have to be concerned about the American response.[17]

*   *   *

When the United States was attacked, the culprit was not Iran but Iraq. On the evening of March 17, 1987, radar operators on the frigate USS *Stark*, then seventy miles north of Bahrain, became aware of an Iraqi Mirage F-1 fighter jet 200 miles away. Although the captain had no reason to be alarmed when he requested identification from the Mirage pilot, he got no response. Suddenly the aircraft turned back to Iraq. Not immediately apparent was that in doing so, it released two Exocet missiles. None of the formidable array of defensive systems on board the ship engaged with the threat. One missile hit the hull on the port side, entering the crew's quarters and starting a fire that took time to get under control. Eventually, the wounded frigate returned to port, with thirty-seven of its crew dead.

The attack was viewed through the filter of the "tilt" to Iraq, so the inclination was to explain away the attack as "inadvertent."[18] The day after the attack, Iraq apologized, insisted it was an accident, proposed a joint investigation, and offered compensation. Saddam Hussein used the incident to illustrate the urgent "need for joint efforts to end the war and force the Iranian regime to agree to peace in accordance with the principles of international law and UN resolutions." Reagan's conciliatory response echoed these sentiments and met with widespread publicity in Iraq.[19] Weinberger stated that the incident "heightened perceptions that the situation in the Gulf is more dangerous now than before the incident occurred."[20]

Some U.S. officials were suspicious that "the *Stark* incident was not an accident, but a deliberate attempt on the part of the Iraqis to drag the United States into war."[21] There is no direct evidence for this, although elements of the Iraqi account were questionable. The House committee report on the incident described the Iraqi claim that the *Stark* was within the Iranian war zone when it was attacked as "facetious at best."[22] In addition, there were other examples of Iraqi military action against the assets of apparent friends and allies. In 1984, for example, Saudi ships using the Iranian Kharg terminal were attacked by Iraqi aircraft, though outside of the exclusion zone. Martin Navias and Edward Hooton asked whether the first such attack, on *Safina Al Arab,* was "an unlucky coincidence or a deliberate attempt to remind friends where their sympathies should lie?" Certainly, in reporting the attack Saddam Hussein made a point of urging "Arab brothers to avoid chartering their ships to foreign companies which load oil at Kharg Island." After the second tanker, *Al Ahood,* was wrecked a few days later, the Saudi oil minister, Sheikh Yamani, warned Saudi charterers not to send their ships to Iranian terminals.[23] According to one report, in 1986 Saddam Hussein sent two jets to bomb a couple of the United Arab Emirates' oil rigs because he felt that he was not getting enough support from the UAE against Iran.[24]

There is at least an indication here of a pattern of Iraqi behavior that would not preclude military action against apparent friends to achieve some desired effect. In this case, whether or not intended, the attack on the *Stark* served Iraqi purposes by leading the United States to move more firmly in favor of reflagging the eleven Kuwaiti tankers and providing navy escorts. In addition, and curiously, the *Stark* incident gave the exercise a much higher profile and anti-Iranian flavor. According to Shultz, the episode had sent a "signal" that "at the first sign of danger, Congress, the press and the public would cause us to pull back." In this case allies would fear that the prospect of casualties would render any U.S. commitments less firm while, for the same reason, enemies would be more likely to set tests. If an attack came, the United States would have to choose between escalating and abandoning the policy.[25] Casualties were not the only reason for objections in the United States. For one, the United States took little oil directly from the Gulf, although that point could be countered by noting that oil was still a fungible commodity in world trade, and the United States was still the largest user and importer of oil. Yet those allies who undoubtedly did depend on Middle Eastern oil were not rallying to America's side. Even local allies, such as the Saudis, would not allow planes to use their airfields as a base for providing air cover. Although Senate approval for the reflagging operation was obtained, this was with evident misgivings and after representations, expressions of anxiety, and calls for delay.

Within three days of the attack on the *Stark,* the U.S. force was increased from six ships to nine, then with pressure from Congress to reduce military risks and cover all possible contingencies, the force grew some more. On June 2, it was stated that the aircraft carrier *Saratoga* and fourteen smaller escort craft would leave U.S. ports to go to the area. By the middle of July, the fleet in or near the Gulf had grown to roughly thirty-three vessels. The administration also raised the stakes with heightened rhetoric, including talk of preemptive attacks on Iranian Silkworm missile batteries. The blame for continuing the war was put on Iran. Senator Sam Nunn observed the consequence of these developments: "What the Administration conceived as a quiet, tactical move overnight became a highly visible, although indirect, involvement of the United States in the Iran-Iraq war."[26]

✫   ✫   ✫

While all this was being debated in Washington, there was a shift in the balance of advantage in the war. When the reflagging policy was first mooted in early 1987, it was rationalized in terms of a growing Iranian threat. After a major offensive in January, the Iranians got even closer to Baghdad and Basra. Schultz portrayed the developing Iranian menace to commercial shipping in lurid terms. It was "threatening to close the Gulf and strangle the states of the Arabian Peninsula, let alone Iraq. Iran sought to position itself to dominate the entire region."[27] Somehow, despite its superior numbers and however hard it tried, Iran could never quite manage a decisive blow against Iraq. It had already passed the high point of its efforts, which came in February 1986, when it took the Fao Peninsula, in sight of the city of Basra. Young and poorly trained Iranian troops were thrown against the Iraqi lines at great sacrifice and to no avail. By the middle of 1987, Iran was facing increasing military difficulties, with its land offensives petering out.

Iraq was seeking to exploit the situation and expand the war by all possible means. It reopened the "war of the cities," using surface-to-surface missiles, and attacked Kharg Island. In May, Murphy drew attention to the high costs and limited gains made in Iran's January offensive and noted that during the July–November period Iraqi jets had "daily hammered at Iran's critical economic infrastructure." Crude oil exports had plummeted. Iran even had to import substantial, and costly, amounts of petroleum products. Iran was now virtually a nonplayer in the air war, so action against shipping was one of its few areas for developing new options. This explains the emphasis the administration was placing on the Silkworms. On June 28, Shultz still explained the policy in these terms when he told *Meet the Press* that "only the U.S. could defeat Iran's efforts to close down navigation in the Persian Gulf and choke off the flow of oil through that critical waterway . . . The immediate crisis lay in making Iran understand that it could not close the Gulf to commercial shipping."[28]

It is doubtful that this was a credible Iranian objective at this time. The Iranians proposed a partial cease-fire, confined only to the Gulf, but not affecting the land war. This obviously went against Iraqi strategic interests and was rejected by the United States on the grounds that the need was for a general cease-fire, but it indicated that a shipping war was not particularly to its strategic advantage. Unless Iran found a way to close the strait, and this was always improbable, there was no reason to suppose that its actions could do much more than impose some pressure on Kuwait and Saudi Arabia. Moreover, the actual U.S. maritime objectives stated were quite specific and modest. Weinberger stressed that the reflagging exercise was "*not* part of an open-ended unilateral commitment to defend non-belligerent shipping in the Persian Gulf," though he also claimed that the presence of U.S. forces "acts as a moderating element with regard to the Iran-Iraq War."[29] Only American ships were to be protected, except for those of other countries that were carrying military equipment to regional clients. With 600 monthly transits through the Gulf, protecting eleven tankers could only have a limited effect. There would be no shortage of alternative targets. Furthermore, if the concern was really the threat to Gulf shipping, then the main culprit remained Iraq. If the American objective was to end the tanker war, as Nunn observed, "the United States is encouraging a continuation of the war at sea by protecting a key Iraqi ally," thereby reducing Iraq's "downside risks" in continuing its attacks.[30] Iraq was now getting the internationalization of the conflict it had always sought. Little difference was made to the tanker war itself. After the policy was announced, the number of attacks attributed to both sides went up and not down.[31] As Weinberger acknowledged, "Our official policy was to remain neutral in this conflict, but the Iranian outrages against our people, beginning in 1979, made it difficult for me to remain neutral in any conflict to which Iran was a party."[32]

*   *   *

Pro-Iraqi diplomacy continued and was reflected in efforts at the UN. Security Council Resolution 598, passed by the Security Council on July 20, 1987, deplored all aspects of the conflict—its initiation and continuation, the bombing of purely civilian population centers, attacks on neutral shipping and civilian aircraft, violation of international humanitarian law and other laws of armed conflict, and use of chemical weapons. It demanded

> that, as a first step towards a negotiated settlement, Iran and Iraq observe an immediate cease-fire, discontinue all military actions on land, at sea and in the air, and withdraw all forces to the internationally recognized boundaries without delay.

The resolution was based on an original U.S. draft that followed lines said to have been agreed on by Richard Murphy in discussions in Baghdad in

May. The idea was to pass a resolution that Iran could not accept and then impose a mandatory arms embargo on Iran.[33] Iran was set up as the main obstacle to the war's termination. Iraq still held some Iranian territory, but the territory Iran held was more important—the Fao Peninsula and atop sizable oil deposits. Compliance for Iran would therefore mean relinquishing Iran's main bargaining card without any definite settlement. This strategy was made clear by the conjunction in Weinberger's description of an apparently evenhanded demand with a one-sided threat:

> The five Permanent Members of the Security Council agree that the war has gone on too long and that more assertive international efforts are needed to force the parties to end the conflict. As a means to do so, the United States strongly supports mandatory sanctions against Iran.[34]

In two key respects, however, the eventual resolution deviated from American proposals. First, the demand for mandatory sanctions was watered down to a requirement that the Security Council consider "appropriate action against any country that failed to comply within two months," and second, there was a nod in the direction of a key Iranian demand, that is, an "international body" to investigate and assign responsibility for the conflict. This initiative came from the secretary-general.

The American-Iraqi game plan at this point assumed that the resolution would be rejected by Iran. Instead the Iranians asked for further clarification and fixed on the idea of an impartial commission. There were indications that if the commission were established, then a cease-fire could follow. Iraq, however, insisted that all the steps covered in the resolution should follow in sequence, so that no commission could be set up until all measures had been implemented. Shultz acknowledged that there had been "signs of a shift in Iran's diplomatic posture," when a message came through to him that Tehran was "open to suggestions" about how to avoid escalation of the war and conflict with the United States.[35] While the diplomatic explorations continued, there was a lull in the tanker war. This suited Iran, which said that it would only resume attacks if Iraq did. It also indicated that it did not wish to provoke a clash with the United States. It was pleased to be able to export its oil without disruption.

Iran's failure to reject SCR 598, even while it refrained from accepting it, began to cause frustration on the Iraqi side. Saddam saw Iran using the lull to rebuild its economy while holding its gains. He therefore looked for ways to revive the pressure on Tehran. Meeting in Tunis on August 23–25, the Arab League set a deadline of September 20 for Iran to accept the resolution.

The United States was also reported to have urged the Security Council to come up with "enforcement measures."[36] Iraq took matters into its own hands. It had already resumed attacks on urban and economic targets on August 10, and revived the tanker war on August 29, on the erroneous grounds that Iran had de facto rejected Resolution 598. This interpretation was not universally embraced. On September 10, UN secretary-general Pérez de Cuéllar was still visiting Tehran and Baghdad to discuss the resolution. Nonetheless, the Iraqi action appeared to have had its intended effect of undermining diplomatic efforts.

The administration continued to seek an arms embargo against Iran. In February 1988, when the United States was president of the Security Council, it announced an intention to move to a "showdown" with Iran, but it could not get support. On February 28, the Iranian foreign minister sent a formal letter to the UN secretary-general confirming acceptance of his implementation plan for a cease-fire, claiming that this was "tantamount to the acceptance of resolution 598." The next day, Iraq fired eleven Scud B missiles against Tehran as the start of an intensive missile bombardment that caused many casualties and mass evacuations. The cease-fire offer was never explored.[37]

*   *   *

This was the background to the reflagging operations. The Rules of Engagement (ROE) were based on the "inherent right to employ proportional force as necessary in self-defense; this right will be exercised in the face of attack or hostile intent indicating imminent attack."[38] Little thought, however, had been given to the sort of attack that might be faced, and whether mines might be involved. U.S. intelligence information suggested that Iran had few mines and little effective ability to sow them. Weinberger failed to mention mines when reporting to Congress about the risks facing U.S. forces in the Persian Gulf, which he held to be "moderate,"[39] though warships are actually more vulnerable than tankers to mines.

In fact, key locations in the Gulf—Kuwait's Ahmadi channel, UAE's anchorage off Fujayrah, and the waters south of Fuarsi Island—had been laced with sixty mines. In some respects, it was odd for Iran to engage in mining, as its own interests lay in being able to export through safe channels. It may be that this was a response to the reflagging exercise, a means of demonstrating that Kuwaiti tankers would still be vulnerable. It might have been unauthorized action by militants. On July 22, just after UN Resolution 598 had been passed, three U.S. Navy ships escorted two reflagged tankers up the Gulf toward Kuwait. One of the tankers, the *Bridgeton*, was hit by an old,

World War I–vintage mine. The awkward truth was that the damage would have been much worse if a warship had been struck. As the American warships supposedly protecting the Kuwaiti ships actually had no antimine defenses, this led to the spectacle of the *Bridgeton,* crippled but still able to sail, leading the way through the channel believed to be mined, with three U.S. ships behind. They were being protected by the ship they were supposed to protect. All this suggested that the U.S. Navy had added to the risks in the Gulf rather than eased them. Help in minesweeping was sought from European allies, and although Britain initially refused, it eventually agreed. Without this support, the whole U.S. operation would have been impeded. The U.S. naval presence was increased again—up to forty-one U.S. ships.

A series of incidents then followed. On September 21, an Iranian boat, the *Al Fajr,* was hit by a U.S. Navy helicopter and was boarded the next day. Mines were found on board, leading to U.S. allegations, denied by Iran, that the *Al Fajr* had been engaged in mines at that time. In response, Iran attacked a British-flagged tanker, leading Britain to shut down Iran's London-based arms procurement office. A more serious response appeared in prospect when a flotilla of Iranian gunboats moved toward a Saudi-Kuwaiti oil facility, but they turned back after being buzzed by Saudi warplanes. In another move on October 8, one Iranian gunboat and two others were damaged after they had fired at, and missed, American helicopters.

Then Silkworm missiles hit and damaged the U.S.-owned Liberian supertanker *Sungari* and the reflagged Kuwaiti tanker *Sea Isle City* while in Kuwait territorial waters. It had been understood that protection of even U.S.-flagged ships in Kuwait waters was Kuwait's responsibility. Schultz described the attack as one "on Kuwait."[40] Yet although the attack on the *Sea Isle City* did not fall under the terms of the established policy, Weinberger and William Crowe, chairman of the Joint Chiefs of Staff, argued for a response designed to cripple the Iranian navy and its offshore guerrilla bases. According to Weinberger, "I felt that it was important to deny the Iranians some measure of capability and to impress upon them the fact that we were not going to yield the Gulf to them."[41]

The missiles had been launched from the Fao Peninsula, from where they could be moved before U.S. aircraft could reach them. Moreover, while pleased with a tougher American stance, the Kuwaitis and the Saudis were anxious not to provoke the Iranians further. An attack on an Iranian frigate was ruled out because of the prospect of too many casualties. The compromise was to attack the Rashadat oil platforms, on which Iranian forces were claimed to have been stationed. From this vantage point they monitored the movements of US convoys, coordinated mine laying, assisted small boat attacks against nonbelligerent shipping, and fired at U.S. helicopters. Because the facility was in international waters, it was not quite as provocative as a direct attack on Iranian territory. When U.S. warships fired their guns into the platform on October 16, they set the platform afire. An unexpected "target of opportunity" came when U.S. forces spotted Iranians fleeing another facility. No claims were made for military activities being supported from this platform. Reagan described this attack in a low-key way, reporting that "additionally, U.S. forces briefly boarded another platform in the area, which had been abandoned by the Iranians when the operation began."[42] He might have added that it had been largely destroyed.

One commentator described this as "an exercise in overkill."[43] American officials considered it "measured and proportionate." The argument was that the platforms were not vital to Iran, either militarily or economically, no lives were lost (prior warning was given to permit evacuation), and the point was made. Other targets, such as the well-defended Silkworm batteries in the Fao Peninsula, would have been more demanding militarily but also meant a more direct involvement in the hostilities. Although the events started with a Kuwaiti grievance, an engagement in international waters was also said "to avoid expanding the U.S. military commitment to include the direct defense of any Gulf nation."[44] The impression that this operation was part of a wider policy was reinforced by the attacks being accompanied by a total embargo on U.S. imports of Iranian oil and other products. This should be understood in the context of Richard Murphy's opinion of Iran's difficult economic situation. Reagan sought to reassure the public that there would be no escalation: "We're not going to have a war with Iran. They're not that stupid." Weinberger told a press briefing, "We consider the matter closed."[45] On October 22, another Silkworm missile launched from the Fao Peninsula hit Sea Island, Kuwait's only deep-water oil-loading facility, again raising the question whether it had been fired into the harbor area and allowed to home in on the nearest target.[46] This time there was no American response.

By the spring of 1988, the Iranian position in Iraq had deteriorated further and the likelihood of a victory had receded, let alone the dreaded drive into the Arab Gulf states. The Americans now believed that four elements were necessary to bring the war to an end. The Iraqis had to do sufficiently well to preclude any possibility of an Iranian victory, the war had to become more painful to Iran, the supply of arms to Iran had to be reduced further, and international pressure had to be maintained on a broad front. This was the background to the events of April 1988, culminating in attacks on Iranian oil platforms and also on Iranian naval vessels, just as the Iraqis launched an offensive to recapture Fao. Thomas McNaugher suggested that the United States wanted to demonstrate that Iran could not hide military forces behind economic assets, but he noted that in attacking a producing oil platform, "U.S. warships were now doing precisely what Iraqi warplanes had been doing for four years."[47]

On April 14, 1988, USS *Samuel Roberts,* one of twenty-nine American warships in the area, was damaged by a mine recently sown by Iran. In deciding on a response, the United States followed the line set the previous October but took it much further. On April 18, U.S. warships closed in on the Sassan platform and, following some exchanges of fire with Iranians on board, set it on fire. One hundred miles away, three more warships issued the same warnings to Iranian personnel on the Nasr platform off Sirri Island. According to an authoritative account, the objectives of the U.S. attack were to sink the Iranian Saam-class frigate *Sabalan* or a suitable substitute and neutralize the surveillance posts on the Sassan and Sirri gas-oil separation platforms (GOSPs) and the Rahkish GOSP, if sinking a ship was not practicable. The goal was to clear the platform, not destroy it. By warning the occupants and getting them to leave the platform, there should be time to "plant demolition charges and destroy the surveillance post."[48] The platforms were both larger than the Rostam and were working, producing oil at an estimated 150,000 bpd. The Nasr oil platform at Sirri Island produced almost 10 percent of Iranian oil for export. Because this was an active oil-producing platform, when one of the initial rounds hit a compressed gas tank, it set it ablaze. If the Iranian navy had not presented itself, there would have been an attack on the third platform at Rahkish.[49] Instead, there was a series of clashes between U.S. and Iranian forces. Iran's navy consisted of a few frigates and corvettes, eight fast attack craft, and thirty to fifty speedboats with small arms and antitank rockets. The United States sank or crippled six Iranian ships. Iraq retook the Fao Peninsula on April 18. The American loss was a Cobra helicopter carrying two American crewmen.

On July 3, the USS *Vincennes* shot down an Iranian airbus, killing 290 civilians, believing it to be an Iranian F-14 fighter jet. This tragic incident came as a direct result of the expansion of the reflagging policy to include coming to the aid of non-U.S. flagged ships, in this case the Danish tanker *Karama Maersk,* which had been attacked. The cumulative effect of the reverses in the land war and the bruising encounters with the United States helped persuade the Iranians to agree to a cease-fire, which was announced on July 18, coming into effect on August 20, 1988.

In terms of its immediate objectives, the United States could claim a geopolitical success. It had helped thwart Iranian ambitions and obtained a measure of revenge for earlier humiliations. In the process, it had regained lost ground with the Arab states. It had also established an effective working relationship with the most radical of the Arab states, Iraq. This had, however, required it to play down many aspects of Iraqi behavior that it would have been quick to denounce in other circumstances. Washington was not alone in hoping that with the war over, Baghdad could now turn to more peaceful pursuits. It was soon to be disappointed.

PART THREE

GEORGE H. W. BUSH

★ ★ ★

11

IRAQ TAKES KUWAIT

"REALISM" WOULD BEST DESCRIBE the foreign policy philosophy of President George H. W. Bush. There are many varieties of realism as political theory, but for the worldly wise practitioner, realism may mean little more than dealing with matters as they are found rather than how one might wish them to be. The first responsibility of government is to contain, deter, or deflect threats to national security, through a combination of military strength and artful diplomacy, acquiring allies and partners where possible while avoiding creating unnecessary enemies. Realists accept that they cannot be too choosy about those whose hands they have to shake or the deals that must be done in the name of the national interest, for they know all about human imperfection. They are therefore wary of grand schemes that rely on appealing to the better instincts of humankind or the ability to create new international institutions that will represent the common good and somehow push to one side the factors of power and interest that appear to animate states when acting unilaterally. An American realist acknowledges the country's privileged international position and that this creates a disposition in favor of the status quo, and the attachment of high values to stability and order.

Bush's career was tantamount to a training in realism. He worked for the Nixon-Ford administrations when realists were very much in charge. As ambassador to the UN, he could see great ideals mischievously manipulated. As ambassador to China, he watched the Communist Party of the People's Republic engaging in complex and cynical power plays. As director of the CIA, he focused on what was threatening in the world. As vice president, his influence was limited, but he could observe the consequences of excessive zeal and attempts to fit events into a preset worldview. To Carter and Reagan, in their different ways, the cynical maneuverings of the Nixon-Ford years undermined the ambition and the moral core that they thought should be at the heart of foreign policy. To Bush, their records vindicated realism. Affirmations of high principle and noble ideals were all very well, but not if they got in the way of the national interest.

Bush had been a last-minute choice to be Reagan's vice president after the breakdown of curious negotiations that would have seen former president Ford in the number two spot. Like Ford, Bush added traditional Republicanism to the ticket, lacking Reagan's charm and presence but pragmatic and safe. During the 1988 campaign, when asked why he did not talk about the long term, he acknowledged that he did not do the "vision thing." "I never felt comfortable with the flowery phrases dreamed up by a speechwriter," he acknowledged in his memoir. He knew he could not express himself as well as Reagan. "I was certain that results, solid results that would lead to a more peaceful world, would be far better than trying to convince people through rhetoric."[1] He could also claim to be on good personal terms with many key players around the world. At times of crisis, his first instinct was to pick up the telephone and talk directly to the people he needed to persuade.

Bush picked a team in tune with his philosophy. He had known James Baker, his new secretary of state, for thirty years. Baker had worked for Reagan as chief of staff and then treasury secretary. At one point Baker almost became Reagan's national security adviser, and Reagan later ruefully acknowledged his second term might have been easier if he had been. Brent Scowcroft, a former lieutenant general in the U.S. Air Force, worked under Kissinger and was Gerald Ford's national security adviser. Although Reagan's people saw him as too committed to détente, his reputation for good judgment meant that he was regularly called in whenever the administration needed someone reliable to be part of a bipartisan commission. He now reprised his former role in charge of Bush's National Security Council. He saw his job not as an alternative secretary of state, but as making sure the president got the best advice. Bush's foreign policy team was competent, professional, and unlike those of Carter and Reagan, of like mind.

This administration, geared to continuity and eschewing idealism and vision, found itself presiding over two huge upheavals that offered opportunities for a complete transformation of the international system. The first, which gathered pace during 1989, was the implosion of European communism. The Soviet leader, Mikhail Gorbachev, was convinced that his country

could only reform if it opened up to the West, stopped trying to run an economically ruinous arms race, and no longer tried to control countries against
their will. He hoped that allowing the members of the Warsaw Pact to follow
their own paths would help keep Communist parties in power and the Warsaw Pact intact, but this underestimated the deep disillusion that had set in as
a result of years of stagnation and repression. Where in the past, with Hun-
gary, Poland, Czechoslovakia, and East Germany any move out of orthodoxy
was suppressed rapidly and ruthlessly, Gorbachev watched benignly as one by
one the satellite countries of Eastern Europe abandoned the old ways. The
critical point came in November 1989 as the Berlin Wall was breached, and
soon East and West Germany were coming together, with, to say the least,
mixed feelings in the rest of Europe as political leaders contemplated a new
regional political configuration dominated by a united Germany. Bush may
have been slow to appreciate the enormity of the changes under way, but
once he did so, then, with Baker and Scowcroft, he worked effectively to manage them to get the optimum outcome and limit the impact of the convulsions that tend to accompany the collapse of empires. When the convulsions
began, however, in the former Yugoslavia in 1991, his instinct was to avoid
any deep American involvement. He was content for the Europeans to handle
the crisis. Here his vision let him down because, especially after the sudden
end of the cold war, with only one superpower left standing, a region in trouble would naturally look to Washington to help sort things out.

The same was true in the Middle East, where the second upheaval took
place, resulting from Iraq's invasion of Kuwait on August 2, 1990. Here local belief in "Arab solutions for Arab problems" lasted even less time than European
beliefs that they could cope with a fragmenting Yugoslavia all on their own.

*   *   *

The aftermath of the conclusion of the Iran-Iraq war was disappointing
both for Iraq and the countries that supported it during its long struggle.
Saddam saw his, and by extension Iraq's, future in terms of becoming a
dominant regional power. He still considered himself as Nasser's natural
successor to lead the entire Arab nation. To that end, there was no letup in
his military programs, and in particular those geared to biological, chemical,
and nuclear weapons. But now there was far less readiness in the Western
world to turn a blind eye to activities that could no longer be explained away
by reference to the Iranian threat. Particularly disturbing was Saddam's persistent pursuit of mass destruction capabilities and his readiness to use
them. It was just possible to rationalize the use of chemical weapons when
"human waves" of Iranian troops threatened to overwhelm Iraqi defenses,

but their use against the Kurdish village of Halabja in March 1988 was inde-fensible. The Kurds, who were always in revolt against Baghdad's rule, had taken advantage of Iraq's struggle with Iran to push hard for autonomy. As the Iranian threat began to subside, Saddam turned on the Kurds, destroying village after village, in the same spirit that Assad had turned on Hama in 1982, to ensure that he was feared where he would never be loved. There were two days of artillery bombardment on Halabja before Iraqi aircraft dropped canisters containing nerve agents. Some 5,000 died and many more were left injured or ill. Later, Iraqi forces destroyed the town completely.

The incoming Bush administration, like its predecessor, decided not to make too much of this atrocity or of Iraq's dubious military programs, but it could not ignore them altogether. Harsh congressional resolutions had been passed, and the established principles of national policy had to be upheld. Although the policy preference of the new administration was, as before, to pursue "normal relations" with Iraq while using "economic and political in-centives for Iraq to moderate its behavior and to increase our influence," this was easier said than done. Iraq was not a "normal" country, and Saddam saw nothing wrong with his behavior and dared not moderate it. To criticize Ha-labja was to side with the Kurds and thus seek the breakup of Iraq. Further-more, while he was capable of changes of course and about-faces, he would never concede weakness or vulnerability, even when he was potentially weak and vulnerable. He would always play the aggrieved party, whose would-be partners were not living up to their promises and expectations and who therefore did not deserve Iraq's friendship. When the Americans complained or sounded warnings, it would be Baghdad that would cancel meetings while Washington sought to continue the dialogue.

Saddam did not want to break with the United States and the United States did not want to break with him, but the issues of chemical weapons and nuclear proliferation that had been present through the 1980s could no longer be contained in the absence of the shared Iranian threat. Increasingly, the Americans wanted to retain influence in Baghdad, but not, as they had once hoped, to help Iraq with economic reconstruction and a moderate for-eign policy, because now there were evident tendencies toward immodera-tion, especially with regard to Israel.

As he pushed forward with his WMD programs, Saddam's statements and actions became more erratic. He realized that once his enemies, and in particular Israel, assessed the incontrovertible evidence that Iraq was on the verge of acquiring the most devastating weapons, they might be tempted to preempt, as in 1981. In April 1990, he warned Israel of the consequences of a repeat performance: "By God, we will make fire eat half of Israel if it tries to do anything against Iraq." It did not take much imagination to work out how this might be achieved. He tried to follow this with a reassurance that his purposes were only deterrent and defensive, but with more information of his military programs, and the execution of a British journalist who was inquiring too closely, the mood changed.

In February 1990, the best argument for continuity in U.S. policy was that withdrawing favors from Iraq would feed Saddam's paranoia. This was not a sufficient argument for sustaining some of these favors. This was particularly so with credit, the biggest of these favors. Saddam's ability to rely on Western companies to encourage their governments to go easy on Iraq so long as there were lucrative contracts to be had was gradually eroding as Iraqi credit dried up. He was concerned that his creditors might start to work together and his debt position would force him to go to the International Monetary Fund. The last thing he wanted was international auditors going through his books. With his overall sense of insecurity aggravated by the collapse of Communist governments in Europe, he was not at all inclined to abandon his military programs, but he was becoming desperately short of funds. The economy had yet to recover from the war, and the oil price remained depressed. In this context, the main American lever, when it came to showing disquiet and attempting to influence Iraqi decisionmaking, was agricultural credits. Another $1 billion had been agreed on for 1990, but the administration felt able to release barely half of this. This was a consequence of financial scandals surrounding past credits and their diversion into weapons deals as well as growing congressional hostility to Iraq. The Iraqi sanction was to threaten nonrepayment of past debts, but that would do further damage to their creditworthiness. The administration tried to override the resistance to reinstating the extra credits from within as well as in Congress on "foreign policy" grounds. Senators from farming states tended to agree. Five, led by Senator Robert Dole, visited Iraq in April and worked hard to distance themselves from the chemical weapons and human rights criticisms made by what they described as a "haughty and pampered" press and from a Voice of America broadcast, which had considered the implications of the fall of dictators in Eastern Europe for police states elsewhere (a subject on which Saddam was becoming extremely sensitive). Still, nothing the Iraqis did provided enough ground for releasing the extra credit.[2]

*   *   *

It was in this context that an invasion of Kuwait started to appear as a quick fix to Saddam's dilemma. There were a number of reasons to pick on Kuwait. The emirate was small in size (5,400 square miles) and population

(1.8 million, of which only around one-half were indigenous Kuwaitis) but large in oil reserves and pumping 2 million barrels per day (bpd). Iraq had claimed Kuwait from the moment it gained full independence from Britain in 1961, leading to a small British deployment to deter any action. Although Iraq grudgingly recognized the new state, the issue was never completely settled. Their border remained a lingering source of dispute. During the 1980s, the Iranian threat loomed larger than the Iraqi, so Kuwait backed Iraq with loans and permission to use its airspace. In return it took considerable pressure, including occasional military strikes, from Iran, hence the threats to its oil exports in the mid-1980s that led to the reflagging of its tankers by the United States. Its substantial Shi'ite minority had also been targeted, and it suffered many terrorist acts through the decade. Iraq's view was that Kuwait was not doing it any favors but was reflecting the broader Arab interest in the war and should show more gratitude to Iraq, the country actually doing the fighting. Nor did the Iraqis ever stop thinking of the emirate as really part of their proper inheritance from the Ottoman Empire. They compared their modern, secular state, with its well-educated population and rights for women, with the degenerate feudalism of Kuwait.

As far as Kuwait was concerned, the money handed over to Iraq during the war was a loan and therefore had to be repaid. Even if he had wanted to repay them, which he did not, Saddam was unable to do so. The fact that he was put in a position of having to admit his parlous financial position publicly fueled his anger. He therefore demanded that Kuwait forgive the loans. This was the core of the crisis of 1990. A second item on the charge sheet was encroachments into claimed Iraqi territory, including the extraction of oil from the al-Rumaila oil field. This "stolen" oil, it was claimed, was worth $2.4 billion. A third factor was that Kuwait was one of the worst offenders when it came to sticking to production quotas in what had been a series of futile attempts to raise the price of oil to at least $25 a barrel. Because Kuwait had invested in refining and other downstream activities, it had less interest than other producers in a high price. The warning shot was launched by Saddam on July 18, 1990, when he observed:

> War is fought with soldiers and much harm is done by explosions, killing and coup attempts—but it is also done by economic means. Therefore, we would ask our brothers who do not mean to wage war on Iraq: this is in fact a kind of war against Iraq.[3]

In mid-July, divisions of the Republican Guard began to move toward the border with Kuwait. As a result, the discussion of Iraqi grievances against Kuwait took place against a backdrop of military preparations. Whether Saddam intended to move against Kuwait come what may, or whether a more compliant Kuwaiti approach would have led him to call off his actions, his approach was deliberately intimidating. The coercive impact of the demands and the troop movements was dampened by the decision of Hosni Mubarak of Egypt to repeat to the Kuwaitis Saddam's reassurance to him that the military moves were largely bluff. This had the natural effect of reducing Kuwait's already limited readiness to contemplate concessions.

There was a first attempt at negotiation, presided over by the Saudis at Jeddah. By the time the talks collapsed on August 1, 100,000 Iraqi troops were fully primed and ready to go. They invaded the next day. Foreign Minister Tariq Aziz claimed that the decision was taken only on August 1, as it became apparent that further negotiations would be futile.[4] It is possible that major Kuwaiti concessions might have stayed Saddam's hand, though he would have later been back for more, but he was probably not too disappointed when few were forthcoming. The first objective of the invasion was to capture the emir quickly, but there was just enough notice of attack for the emir and the royal family to escape to exile in Saudi Arabia. Had they been captured, Saddam could have killed them or obliged them to agree to humiliating terms. As it was, the authority and legitimacy of the al-Sabah family remained intact. Within hours, the Kuwaiti crown prince was appealing to his people in a clandestine radio broadcast, calling upon them to resist "the Iraqi aggression." Opposition from regular Kuwaiti units was crushed by the afternoon, though the air force managed to operate until the next day, when its base was overrun. The occupation forces experienced continued harassment and sabotage. By September, this was largely over as a result of tough Iraqi policies. All Kuwaiti military men (including police and reservists) who failed to surrender and anyone found with weapons were executed.

The invasion was presented as a popular Kuwaiti response to the reactionary policies of the ruling al-Sabah family. A new "Free Kuwait Provisional Government" was said to be in charge, and the Iraqis promised to "withdraw as soon as things settle and when the temporary free government asks us to do so."[5] This would not take long. The provisional government, however, had clearly been concocted in a hurry, after the original plans for Kuwait had gone awry, and its members were evidently not Kuwaiti. All significant statements were coming from Iraqi television commentators. On August 8, Baghdad stopped pretending and annexed Kuwait. The Revolutionary Command Council spoke of "returning the part and branch, Kuwait, to the whole and the Iraq of its origins."

The free provisional Kuwaiti government has decided to appeal to kins-
folk in Iraq, led by the knight of Arabs and the leader of their march,
President Field Marshal Saddam Hussein, to agree that their sons
should return to their large family, that Kuwait should return to the
great Iraq—the mother homeland—and to achieve complete merger
unity between Kuwait and Iraq.[6]

As of August 28, Kuwait became Iraq's nineteenth province. The control
of security and administration was put in the hands of Ali Hassan al Majid,
notorious as the senior Iraqi official in Kurdistan, and responsible for the
brutal suppression of the 1987–1988 rebellion. Gradual "Iraqization" began,
including changing street names and issuing new currency. There were no
plans for the development of Kuwait. The aim seemed to be to encourage
depopulation and the transfer of anything portable to Iraq. Over 80 percent
of the Kuwaiti workforce was from overseas, and most fled the country at
the start of the crisis (other than Westerners who were held as hostages).
Iraq was more than happy for Kuwaitis also to leave and about one-third of
the indigenous population did so. All accounts of Kuwait under occupation
stress widespread pillaging and vandalism. Immediately after the invasion,
the key targets were the most prominent, such as the royal palace, the Treasury, the Central Bank, and the Kuwait National Museum. Then, in September, the Iraqis moved on to schools, research institutes, libraries, and
hospitals, as well as factories and many office blocks. Leaving aside items related to infrastructure and industrial production, one estimate suggested
that goods worth $1 billion were taken, many of which were later reex-
ported.[7] Efraim Karsh has described the transfer of the emirate's financial
assets, industrial and commercial infrastructure, transport, health, education, and communication systems as "one of the most striking instances of
national piracy in modern history." This policy continued until the bitter
end. As late as February 18, 1991, with a land war days away, forces in Kuwait
were ordered to withdraw "all valuable and necessary machinery and equipment from the Kuwait Governorate to other Governorates."[8]

★   ★   ★

The Americans watched the late July buildup of three Iraqi divisions on the
border with Kuwait with a degree of apprehension. By July 24, it was notable
that sufficient logistic support for an offensive had been added. None of the
intelligence information received was encouraging. The Iraqi military
preparations were serious and extensive, and disproportionate to an act of
bluff. The differences between Iraq and Kuwait on the debt issue were

known to be substantial, and the Kuwaitis appeared to be almost reckless in their disregard of Saddam's demands. As the Jeddah talks began, there were clear signs that the Iraqi forces were getting themselves into attack positions. Thus, on the basis of the raw intelligence and background information, the natural conclusion was that a high probability should be assigned to an Iraqi invasion. Why then was the U.S. response so sanguine?

Most important, in regular phone conversations, Arab leaders, such as Mubarak and Kings Hussein and Fahd, reassured Bush that all would be well. If Bush had gotten around to it in time, Saddam would also have received a personal call and no doubt further—but conditional—reassurances would have been offered. Mubarak's conviction that this was largely bluff was particularly calming. In addition, even if Saddam did act, it seemed likely that his targets would be confined to disputed territory rather than the whole country, in which case there were limits on what those who were not parties in the dispute could do. The Kuwaitis were generally unloved, and there would be more than a few in the Arab world who would be quietly pleased as they got their comeuppance for insufferable arrogance. Even if the plan was to take Kuwait, any American response would depend on regional attitudes. Furthermore, the Kuwaitis, who had shown no special gratitude for the efforts taken on their behalf during the reflagging exercise, were looking to fellow Arabs for cover during the crisis rather than to the United States.[9] For Bush to start threatening Saddam with dire consequences should he do something that other Arab governments said he was not going to do, on behalf of a country with which the United States had no defense agreement, would lack credibility. As the Jeddah talks collapsed, the United States issued a statement hoping that the next meeting would be more successful and conducted with less intimidation.

There is a question of whether Saddam felt he had a "green light" from the Americans. This is different from whether Haig gave one prior to the 1982 Israeli move into Lebanon, because there was no conceivable reason for the United States to support an invasion of Kuwait. The issue is only whether Saddam was encouraged to believe that the United States would avoid getting involved. The key episode here is a meeting Saddam suddenly called with U.S. ambassador April Glaspie on July 25, 1990. Although she had been in the post since 1987, this was her first such meeting with Saddam and she arrived without time to get new instructions. Saddam's main purpose in calling the meeting reflected his concern that the United States was already starting to raise its military profile in the Gulf and emboldening Kuwait and the UAE (which was also a target of Iraq's ire) to ignore Iraq's concerns. In the course of his complaints, he observed, "Yours is a society which cannot accept 10,000 dead in one battle," as if it was a commendation of Iraq's that it could. The thrust of his remarks was to warn the Americans that backing Kuwait and the UAE meant supporting and encouraging economic warfare against Iraq. If this led to a proper war, the United States would be advised not to participate because the conditions would not suit the Americans. He emphasized that Iran was defeated by Iraqi troops and not U.S. attacks on oil platforms. The ambassador went out of her way to insist that the United States sought friendly relations, sympathized with his hurt at attacks on his character from the American media, and regretted the Voice of America broadcast that had already caused such offense. She went on to proclaim her admiration for "your extraordinary efforts to rebuild your country" and to state the standard line that "we have no opinion on the Arab-Arab conflicts, like your border disagreement with Kuwait."

Saddam's opening rant should have left Glaspie with no doubt about the seriousness with which he viewed the confrontation. But then as the meeting concluded, in connection with the coming talks with the Kuwaitis, he observed that "when we see that there is hope, then nothing will happen. But if we are unable to find a solution, then it will be natural that Iraq will not accept death, even though wisdom is above everything else." According to the most used transcript of this meeting, released by the Iraqis and translated and published in September 1990 by the *New York Times*, this came after Saddam had taken a call from Mubarak confirming that talks would take place and that more substantive negotiations would occur thereafter in Baghdad. It was this last detail that probably was the most deceptive, because it still gave Iraq the possibility of surprise when nothing positive emerged from Jeddah. Saddam concluded this passage with, "There you have good news," and Glaspie expressed her relief.[10] This last-minute development in the conversation meant that the importance of most of what had been said was lost. The concluding message was that everything would probably be fine. There was no need for alarm. This meeting was followed by a further message to Saddam on July 29 to remind him of U.S. interests in the region, while conveying pleasure with moves toward peaceful resolution. King Hussein reported back that the message had been "well received and nothing will happen."[11]

*   *   *

When the invasion came, the United States felt duped. Although Bush had been to the fore in promoting better relations with the Arabs, even at the expense of Israel, and had supported working with Iraq despite Saddam's bad behavior, the invasion of Kuwait crossed a line that he could not ignore. The

Kurdish tragedy could come under the heading of Iraq's "internal affairs," but Kuwait was clearly aggression of the crudest sort. It was also in a part of the world of huge importance. It was later observed that Bush would not have responded so forcefully if Kuwait grew broccoli (his least favorite vegetable) rather than pumped oil. Yet by the same token, Kuwait would not have been occupied in the first place if it were not for its vast oil reserves and consequent wealth. No president would have been able to ignore the implications of Iraq turning itself into an oil superpower with 10 percent of the world's oil supply and exports of 4 million bpd. If, as seemed plausible, the next step was Saudi Arabia, then Saddam's influence over oil markets and regional affairs would be overwhelming. Even if he had not intended an immediate move into Saudi Arabia, he would have expected to be appeased. If the occupation of Kuwait had been allowed to stand, one way or another there would be more trouble to come.

Of the steps to be taken the first, getting international condemnation and a Security Council Resolution 660, was the easiest. Even Cuba joined in. Only Yemen abstained. Kuwait might have been imprudent in failing to give in to extortion, but this did not count as mitigating circumstances. Equally unsparing in condemnation was the Arab League in Cairo. Saudi Arabia was nervous about what would happen if Iraq continued to throw its weight around, while Mubarak was furious that Saddam had lied to him. The League proposed a summit of Arab leaders "to examine ways of reaching a durable negotiated solution." It rejected "strenuously any foreign intervention or attempt at intervention in Arab affairs."[12] Saddam was being offered a way out on the basis of an "Arab solution," but he was in no position to take it. Iraq suggested that it just might reconsider its position on Kuwait, but only on condition that Israel left the occupied territories and Syria left Lebanon.

Aziz later asserted, "We bet on the Arab world to find a solution. We thought that the Arabs, fearing the fatal consequences, not on Iraq, but to them, would tell the world OK, you have done your part, but we would like to find a solution. 'Til November we hoped that we could do something with Saudi Arabia."[13] He claimed the Americans refused to allow the Saudis to explore an agreement (and some in the Saudi elite would have preferred such explorations to a confrontation). It was, however, always difficult to define the nature of a viable settlement. Most of those proposed, often by self-appointed middlemen and envoys, assumed that in return for leaving Kuwait, Saddam must be offered some means of "saving face." Proposals included a possible change of regime in Kuwait, serious negotiations with the Kuwaitis on economic and territorial questions, progress on other regional disputes, and a promise that Iraq would not be attacked and American forces would leave the region following the evacuation of Kuwait. The more hawkish among the British and Americans were not inclined to go beyond a promise not to attack Iraq, while at times the French and Russians indicated that nothing should be ruled out and that these items were worth discussing. Regime change in Kuwait might have been of interest, as a satisfactory political solution would have been one that regularized in some way the "satellization" (and the eventual annexation of Kuwait), but this option was only available, if at all, in the days following the invasion. With all other options there was no guarantee that serious concessions would result. Abandoning Kuwait would have meant lost prestige and lost relief from Iraq's economic predicament. No face-saving measures could hide this problem. The starting point for all Saddam's calculations was his personal survival and the survival of his regime. He judged the risk of war to be less than the risk of withdrawal.

*   *   *

Early responses included the suspension of arms shipments by the Soviet Union, Iraq's largest supplier. France, the next-largest supplier, had already suspended them because Baghdad owed about $4.5 billion in debt. The United States, Britain, and France all froze Kuwaiti and Iraqi assets in their countries to prevent the Iraqis from gaining access. This was just in time. Iraqi telexes demanding access to these assets were soon on their way. On August 3, the European Community's foreign ministers met to coordinate a joint strategy, and by August 5, they had agreed on a series of tough measures against Iraq, including an embargo on oil exports and a freeze on Iraqi and Kuwaiti assets. By this time, Japan had fallen into line on a UN resolution, as had a number of other countries that had initially appeared reluctant to move in this direction. Resolution 661 was adopted on August 6, with Cuba and Yemen abstaining. It prohibited all trade with Iraq or Kuwait and any transfer of funds. The only exception was "supplies intended strictly for medical purposes, and, in humanitarian circumstances, foodstuffs." Soon, more than 90 percent of imports and 97 percent of exports were cut.

If an Iraqi aim had been to engineer an increase in the oil price, it succeeded. In the aftermath of the invasion, the price moved up to $25 per barrel. But if another aim was to increase Iraq's share of the oil market, that failed. Oil represented 95 percent of Iraqi exports. The two pipelines, one across Turkey and the other across Saudi Arabia, which had been built during the Iran-Iraq war as a means to circumvent Iran's naval blockade of the Persian Gulf, were soon closed. Once oil tankers were not loading at one end of the pipeline, there was little point in the Iraqis pumping oil they could not sell down the other. So Iraq requested as a "marketing" decision that they be shut. To reduce the impact of sanctions, Iraqis were told that hoarding foodstuffs for commercial purposes would be a crime punishable by death. Ration cards were issued, underutilized land suitable for agriculture was expropriated, and farmers were encouraged to increase their production. There was, in fact, a bumper wheat harvest in 1990. The assets plundered from Kuwait provided extra supplies and ensured that there was some return from the invasion.

Other than becoming more self-sufficient, there was not much Iraq could do against the pressure to start with. The only countermeasure that came easily to hand involved the use of Western nationals who had been caught in Kuwait at the time of the invasion as hostages. The Iraqis were aware of the potential value of their foreign "guests" from the start, and Bush recalled enough about the Iran hostage crisis to know how the fate of innocents caught in great international dramas could influence policy responses. After the imposition of economic sanctions, the Iraqis decided to hold on to their guests and began to move them to Baghdad. Although these measures were described by Aziz as "technical" and "temporary," soon a "strategic shield" policy was adopted by which the "guests" would guard vital Iraqi installations. The UN was informed that "if the United States of America and its allies should persist in their policy of aggression and attack Iraq with their military force . . . making Iraqi women, children and old men victims, then whatever the Iraqi people would be subjected to would also be applied to its foreign guests." This led to another UN resolution (the fourth of the series) expressing "deep concern" for the "safety and well-being of third state nationals in Iraq and Kuwait," demanding that Iraq accept its obligations under international law for their safety, security, and health and arrange for their immediate departure.

When there was no early military action, the Iraqis began to use the hostages more as inducements than shields. Selective releases or variations in treatment rewarded countries that hinted at a more flexible and accommodating attitude. A pattern began of allowing visiting dignitaries to take some hostages home as a sort of going-away present for making the pilgrimage to Baghdad. This began with President Kurt Waldheim of Austria, the former UN secretary-general. Just before a scheduled meeting on August 30 between Waldheim's successor at the UN, Pérez de Cuéllar, and Aziz, Saddam reported that he had been "deeply affected" by meeting Western families prevented from leaving Iraq and had ordered that "all women and children . . . be free to stay or leave." The male hostages were sent to "vital installations." By the start of October, well over 600 foreigners were being held—including 103 Americans, 260 British, 77 Germans, 141 Japanese, and 80 French.

✳   ✳   ✳

The question of armed force first arose over defending Saudi Arabia. If it had been posed in terms of liberating Kuwait, then nothing would have been done. The fact that a military option was available later was the result of an agreement to deploy U.S. forces in Saudi Arabia to deter further Iraqi aggression. This in turn depended on the United States convincing King Fahd that an Iraqi invasion was a distinct possibility. Bush's initial suggestion was to dispatch two squadrons of F-15 combat aircraft. This was too reminiscent of Carter's limp response to the Iranian revolution to impress the Saudis. As Saudi ambassador Prince Bandar Ibn Sultan explained, this would leave the Saudis facing a provoked Iraq with only token U.S. support. Yet the deployment of a substantial non-Muslim army would leave the Saudi government open to accusations of defiling Islam's holy places. It was a risk worth taking only if Riyadh was convinced that the threat was real, that Iraqi forces really were massing on the border with Saudi Arabia. On August 4, with the Saudis still equivocating, Bandar persuaded Bush to send a high-level team to Riyadh, led by Secretary of Defense Richard Cheney, to demonstrate the extent of the Iraqi threat. They arrived on August 6. Although by this time U.S. analysts had concluded that the Iraqi military effort was geared to holding Kuwait rather than advancing further, the briefing was based on now dated and therefore more alarming intelligence. It was sufficiently persuasive that by the evening, the king had agreed to the deployments.

Whether or not Iraq planned further moves, it was clear that if Iraq proved able to hold Kuwait, then Saudi Arabia would be vulnerable to later intimidation. As Defense Minister Prince Sultan later recalled, the question of Saddam ordering an imminent attack was "in a sense irrelevant. On all important matters—particularly oil policy and foreign affairs—he would be in a position to dictate terms."[14] For either the short term or the long term, the kingdom needed American support, but it also had to hope for a quick resolution of the crisis. The longer it dragged on, the more a garrison of 200,000 armed infidels so close to Islam's holiest places, soon being denounced in the mosques, would appear as a fixture. Yet if Saddam did not buckle under the weight of sanctions, then the use of foreign troops to oust Iraq by force from Kuwait would have to be accepted. In agreeing to American help to deal with an immediate threat from the secular left, King Fahd introduced an alien presence into the kingdom's affairs that would be exploited over the next decade by the religious right.

Offensive possibilities were inherent in the movement of substantial American forces to Saudi Arabia, even though the stated military purpose was defensive. This was because the Americans, with the British, had created a political objective that did not allow for compromise. If sanctions and diplomacy failed, then the choice would be between coming to terms with the incorporation of Kuwait into Iraq and resorting to force. When the news of the Iraqi invasion was first discussed by Bush and his advisers, the response had been cautious and tentative. Scowcroft recalled being "frankly appalled" at a discussion that suggested adapting to invasion. He sent Bush a memo: "I am aware as you are of just how costly and risky such a conflict would prove to be. But so too would be accepting this new status quo. We would be setting a terrible precedent—one that would only accelerate violent centrifugal tendencies—in this emerging post–Cold War era." If the United States was passive, U.S. reliability would be called into question, complicating any progress on such issues as the Arab-Israeli dispute.[15] By the time he met with British prime minister Margaret Thatcher, who was in the United States at the time, Bush had decided on a tough stance that was reinforced by the "iron lady," who was in no doubt that this was unacceptable aggression that must be opposed resolutely.

On August 5, Bush stated unequivocally, "This will not stand, this aggression against Kuwait." Colin Powell, the chairman of the Joint Chiefs of Staff, remarked to him that this was tantamount to a declaration of war.[16] It certainly concluded the internal debates. The president had set unequivocal objectives. With the deployment of troops to Saudi Arabia on August 8, Bush demanded "the immediate, unconditional and complete withdrawal of all Iraqi forces from Kuwait." For the moment he insisted that "the mission of our troops is wholly defensive. . . . They will not initiate hostilities, but they will defend themselves, the kingdom of Saudi Arabia, and other friends in the Persian Gulf." The British also agreed to deploy troops to the Gulf at this time.

It did not take long before forceful measures were under consideration, first in connection with economic sanctions. On August 19, an American frigate fired three warning shots at the *Bab Gugur,* an Iraqi tanker. The tanker did not stop. The United States held back from further escalation in order to allow for a negotiation with the Soviet Union. Bush agreed that Gorbachev would explore the possibility of an early settlement with Saddam. In return, should Saddam prove to be intransigent (which of course he was), then Gorbachev would agree to support enforcing the embargo under UN auspices. It was a crucial move, for it not only created authority for the use of force but also, in this first post–cold war crisis, established a pattern of regular consultation between the two former adversaries. Thatcher doubted the need for either consultation with Gorbachev or a new UN resolution. She was nervous that Gorbachev might work to protect Saddam, who had been a Soviet client. It was in this connection that she made her famous admonition to Bush against going "wobbly." Bush's method worked. The Soviet-approved naval operation to enforce the embargo began on August 25.

As U.S. troops began to arrive in numbers during the first weeks of August, there was widespread speculation in the Western press that a war might begin quite soon. This undoubtedly influenced Iraqi thinking. The Iraqi press began by dismissing the United States as a "paper tiger." Because of Vietnam, "no American official, be it even George Bush, would dare to do anything serious against the Arab nation."[17] From his comments to Joe Wilson, left in charge of the Baghdad Embassy, Saddam seemed to think that the most likely American action would be to use airpower against Iraq's economic and industrial base. His response was "The greater the damage you cause, the greater the burden to you." This was because it would inflame Arab opinion that the Iraqis could exploit: "In such a situation, we will not remain idle in the region."[18] Soon, the Iraqis were not so sure. All available Iraqi military resources were deployed to prepare for a seaborne assault by U.S. marines, along with air strikes. This early war scare lasted until around August 22. Iraqi troops were stationed at key government installations and most hotels. Tanks were placed along the beach, facing the sea. By the end of the month, fear had subsided and the Iraqis were preparing for a long political battle, in which the manipulation of Western concerns about hostages, and Arab concerns about Israel, was central to Iraqi strategy.

★   ★   ★

In late September, Bush became convinced of the need for an offensive military option. He could be confident about the defense of Saudi Arabia. Sufficient forces would be in place by the third week in October, and the initial buildup would be complete by late November. Meanwhile, the evidence of the plunder being carried out within Kuwait was having an impact on his perception of the problem. On September 28, Bush was visited by the emir, who told him "firsthand of the extent of the atrocities Iraqi troops were inflicting on his people." He now moved from "viewing Saddam's aggression exclusively as a dangerous strategic threat and an injustice to its reversal as a moral crusade."[19] If Iraq had operated a more benign occupation regime, or possibly moved less quickly to transfer all portable Kuwaiti assets to Iraq, then Bush might have been tempted to wait and see whether sanctions could eventually wear Saddam's regime down. Instead, the president concluded that the longer he waited, the less there would be left of Kuwait to liberate. The country would have been dismantled. To create an offensive option, Powell argued that the numbers had to be almost doubled. Scowcroft and Bush needed convincing. The U.S. military had a reputation for offering presidents the starkest options, with little between doing nothing and throwing everything at the enemy. In the end Bush was convinced. At the end of October, he decided to do what was necessary to create an offensive option.

The announcement of this decision on November 8, just after the 1990 congressional elections, caused considerable resentment and threatened the bipartisan approach to the crisis that had hitherto been evident. A meeting with senior figures from Congress at this time "made graphically clear," according to Scowcroft, "what we were up against." Although there were some stalwarts, "by and large, there was no appetite for forceful action." This created a political dilemma. To go for a congressional resolution against these odds risked defeat, in which case the coalition would be disheartened and Saddam encouraged. If it was ignored, there would be a "domestic firestorm."[20] An opinion poll reported that only 41 percent of the population felt that they had been given a satisfactory explanation of why extra troops were being sent to the Gulf, compared with 60 percent satisfaction with the explanations for the original deployment in August. Particular difficulties were caused for the administration by hearings held by the Senate Armed Services Committee, chaired by Senator Sam Nunn. A number of former senior officers spoke at the hearings and warned against hasty action. Former chairman of the Joint Chiefs of Staff General David Jones was concerned that raising U.S. force levels in the Gulf could "narrow our options and our ability to act with patient resolve." Those with this view argued for continuing with a combination of defense of Saudi territory and rigorous enforcement of sanctions. Nunn assumed that they were acting as proxies for the views of the current chiefs.

There were arguments that the emirate was not worth all this effort, that sanctions should be given a chance to work, and that the president was moving too quickly and risking large numbers of American lives. If, as Senator Daniel Patrick Moynihan suggested, this was "a small disturbance in a distant part of the world,"[21] then an embargo and defensive deployment might represent an appropriate level of cost, but a war would not. Former secretary of defense James Schlesinger observed that there was little doubt that the United States and its allies could inflict a crippling military defeat on Iraq. "The question is, at what cost, and whether it is wise to incur that cost." Then there were the risks of a wider war. In the congressional hearings, there were descriptions of how a bellicose policy would stir up anti-Americanism, turning Saddam into a great hero and complicating attempts to resolve the

Arab-Israeli dispute. Specialists in Arab affairs attached great weight to evidence of pro-Saddam and pro-Palestinian sentiment and concluded that this could render pro-American regimes highly vulnerable and lead to a radicalization of the region and further "disorder." The objections were summed up by Senator George Mitchell in the Senate on January 10, 1991. He complained about "a war in which Americans do the fighting and dying while those who benefit from our effort provide token help and urge us on." He enumerated the risks:

> an unknown number of casualties and deaths, billions of dollars spent, a greatly disrupted oil supply and oil price increases, a war possibly widened to Israel, Turkey or other allies, the possible long-term American occupation of Iraq, increased instability in the Persian Gulf region, long-lasting Arab enmity against the United States, a possible return to isolationism at home.

*   *   *

Yet despite these objections, Bush won the Senate vote. One reason for this was his use of international diplomacy to demonstrate to Congress that the country was not alone. Britain and France also sent forces to the Persian Gulf. To help pay for it all, the hat was passed to partners who were not able to contribute in other ways—Germany and Japan—and to the main beneficiaries of Western military action, Saudi Arabia and Kuwait. If the charge of being mercenary stung, it was not for long. The only Arab leaders who did not join in the anti-Iraq coalition were those whose dependence on Iraq gave them little choice—notably Yasser Arafat and King Hussein. For the normally pro-Western Jordan this was a difficult time, but it was vulnerable to quick economic strangulation if Saddam wished. Bush and Thatcher were pained by this, just as they were surprised to find themselves working directly with Syria and indirectly with Iran.

Other states unwilling or unable to take direct action were crucial in ensuring the passage of UN Security Council resolutions, China and the Soviet Union being the most important in this regard. The weakness of the Soviet Union was a key element in forging the anti-Iraq coalition. The USSR's economic troubles ensured a high stake in close and cooperative relations with the West. The coincidence of a visit by U.S. secretary of state James Baker to Moscow just as the crisis was breaking made possible a strong joint statement condemning Iraq's action and calling for an embargo on arms supplies to Iraq.[22] In early September, Bush made a point of meeting Gorbachev in an emergency summit. Treating the Soviet Union as an important player reduced the risk of it acting as a "spoiler" and left Saddam bereft of his most likely friend among the major powers.

For a president who prided himself on his realism and pragmatism and was reluctant to offer an idealistic vision, the combination of the collapse of European communism and aggression in the Middle East was something of a challenge. He was soon talking about a "new world order." In his speech to the American people explaining the decision to send troops to Saudi Arabia, Bush conveyed the essential idea of a "new era," which could be "full of promise, an age of freedom, a time of peace for all peoples," and which would be put at risk if there was a failure to resist aggression.[23]

The creation of a new world order became an explicit American objective on September 11, 1990, in a critical speech, the president's first formal address to Congress since the start of the crisis. The draft of the speech ready that morning contained the four core objectives of American policy—immediate and unconditional Iraqi withdrawal from Kuwait, restoration of Kuwait's legitimate government, assurance of security and stability in the Gulf, and protection of American citizens. Reviewing the draft, Scowcroft was concerned that not enough had been said about why the crisis mattered as opposed to how it was being conducted. This was, after all, the first great crisis since the end of the cold war, and its outcome could have consequences far beyond the Middle East. Now there was an opportunity for the UN to take center stage as a place where the Great Powers could work together. The idea of a new world order was already in the speech, but Scowcroft now worked to give it more definition. Bush accepted the new draft:

> We stand today at a unique and extraordinary moment. The crisis in
> the Persian Gulf, as grave as it is, also offers a rare opportunity to move
> toward an historic period of cooperation. Out of these troubled times,
> our fifth objective—a new world order—can emerge: a new era—freer
> from the threat of terror, stronger in the pursuit of justice, and more se-
> cure in the quest for peace. An era in which the nations of the world,
> East and West, North and South, can prosper and live in harmony.[24]

The natural emphasis was on the word "order." The cold war era was often tense and dangerous, but there was an underlying stability based on the standoff between two nuclear-armed superpowers. Over time they had learned to manage their crises and not provoke the other. The end of that era was welcomed, but there was a desire to find quickly a new "order" to replace the one that had just been lost, as durable as the one before but this time based more on shared values and interests. There was reluctance to acknowledge the possibility that the new era might be much more dynamic and fluid. Bush's concept for this new order essentially involved the old, post–World War II order, working as it should because now the United States and the Soviet Union could work together. This would allow for a reinvigorated United Nations. Confidence in this grew as the conflict developed, because of the role being played by the Security Council. What remained unclear was how much the focus on order could also combine with the promotion of "justice," which also figured in Bush's presentation. Holding together an international coalition required muting criticisms of the practices of particular states, and repairing relations with others whose past behavior had made them subject to strong criticism. This was particularly true in the case of China, which was in a position to veto Security Council resolutions and saw in the crisis an opportunity to end its post–Tiananmen Square isolation; Syria, condemned in the past for state terrorism but now valued as a radical member of the anti-Iraq coalition; and Iran, previously the bête noire of American policy, but now to be dissuaded from any alliance of convenience with its erstwhile Iraqi enemy. Many members of the coalition—including Kuwait and Saudi Arabia—had poor human rights records. It was therefore impossible to sustain such a wide-ranging coalition on the basis of the highest political standards.

Yet Bush was not content to let the case rest on the basis of the principle of nonaggression. It did not in itself seem to be sufficient to take the American people to war. The United States had an interest in the price of oil and security of supplies, but so far the conflict had pushed up the price and was aggravating the recession the United States was experiencing. When James Baker tried to suggest that the conflict was all about "jobs," this backfired, as the link was unclear and could hardly serve as a legitimate motive for war. On the other hand, the more general dangers posed by Saddam, especially his nuclear and chemical programs, were alarming. Past and rather complacent estimates of when Iraq could become a nuclear power were being revised, a prospect that would convince U.S. opinion that there was a real danger to be dealt with. Although the speed with which Iraq had reached virtual nuclear status was mocked by those suspecting that the administration was casting around for rationales for an unpopular war, postwar evidence suggested that this time the administration was closer to the mark than many of its critics.

Bush started also to make the almost instinctive comparisons with Hitler, referring regularly to the parallels he found in Martin Gilbert's *History of the Second World War*. The stories of Iraqi atrocities helped gain public and congressional support for military action. In one well-documented incident, a Washington public relations firm fabricated a story of Iraqi brutality with a case of babies being taken out of incubators, using the testimony of a supposed nurse who had witnessed the atrocity, who was in fact a Kuwaiti princess who had not. Other than to dramatize the point, there was no need for fabrication. There were enough terrible things going on in Kuwait. In addition to making a familiar, almost routine, observation about the dangers of appeasement, Bush does seem to have convinced himself that Saddam's behavior put him into a special category. "I think what he did," observed Bush in his memoir, "can be morally condemned and lead one to the proper conclusion that it was a matter of good versus evil. Saddam had become the epitome of evil in taking hostages and in his treatment of the Kuwaiti people."[25] Few leaders deserved the label "evil" more, but it had been deserved for some time. The only difference was that the people of Kuwait and Western hostages had been added to his already long list of victims. This lead to pointed political question: If he was evil now, why had the United States been working so closely with him before? It was hard to claim that some essential flaw in Saddam's character had only just been revealed, having been previously masked. If this really was about evil versus good, could all members of the anti-Iraq coalition be properly described as "good"? The strong moral tone may well have been sincere and also effective in shoring up domestic support, but it compromised the purity of Bush's realism. Realism implied restraint; a war against evil had an absolutist quality.

★ ★ ★

The oscillation between self-interested and idealistic rationales confused rather than mobilized public opinion. Those arguments that resonated most were the possibility of the hostages being harmed, and of Iraq acquiring nuclear weapons. Public support was secured by a UN resolution and an evident readiness to reach a negotiated solution that had been rebuffed by Saddam. Resolution 678, passed on November 29, 1990, allowed Iraq a "pause of goodwill" so that it had time to comply, but then authorized "Member States cooperating with the Government of Kuwait . . . to use all necessary means" to implement the successive Security Council resolutions and to "restore international peace and security in the area." Once this was passed, Bush later recalled, he felt "a huge burden had been lifted from my shoulders." There was no longer a need to wait for an Iraqi provocation to provide a pretext for action. "Although we didn't realize it at the time, it also changed the debate with Congress, creating a context for the use of force which helped bring it aboard. The Security Council had voted to go to war."[26]

Its effect on Iraqi perceptions was almost immediately qualified by Bush's promise to "go the extra mile" for peace and explore the possibility of a diplomatic settlement. If necessary, he would send Secretary Baker to Baghdad and receive Foreign Minister Aziz in Washington. He said at the same time, although this tended to be missed in the commentary, that this offer should not be construed as the initiation of negotiations. Rather, it would be a last attempt to drive home to Saddam the seriousness of his situation. The aim was still to bring about Iraq's unconditional withdrawal from Kuwait and the full release of foreign hostages. It did actually get the hostages back, although not because Bush was being tough but because Saddam suspected he might be going soft. He assumed that Bush was looking to climb down, reflecting the many doubts being expressed in the United States. Many of America's supporters were drawing the same conclusion, fearful that domestic opposition had weakened Bush's resolve. When the Iraqi president went on television on December 2, he put the chances of a peaceful solution to the crisis at 50–50, depending on whether or not the U.S.-Iraqi encounter was to be "a real dialogue."

To encourage this dialogue, Saddam made the concession on hostages. After first responding to the Security Council vote of November 29 with a ploy to use the hostages' vulnerability to undermine the coalition's willingness to use force, on December 6, following President Bush's offer to go the "extra mile," Saddam announced that all hostages could leave. In doing so, he mentioned the readiness of the European Community to talk to Iraq, following the United States, and the evidence of a strong feeling against war in the United States. At this time 3,400 foreign nationals were still trapped. This included 584 hostages at strategic sites and 1,200 Britons and Americans in Kuwait still hiding from Iraqi forces. The advice to make this gesture appears to have come from Yasser Arafat, who had effectively joined Saddam's court. His close association with Saddam did him no favors among the more conservative Arab states; the results of his advice on how to respond to Bush would also leave Saddam unimpressed.

When talks did take place between Baker and Tariq Aziz in Geneva on January 9, neither had room for maneuver so there was little to discuss, although they spent a long time discussing it. If Bush thought that the clarity of threat might give Saddam pause for reflection, or if Saddam hoped that the American public would resist a move to war, they were both disappointed. By now, public opinion had moved in Bush's direction. A poll released the previous day showed that a majority wanted Congress to back Bush. The president's approval rating for his handling of the crisis had picked up from its low point in December (from 61 percent to 67 percent), and readiness to go to war was up from 55 percent to 63 percent. Saddam was not incapable of the dramatic about-face, but the stakes were very high. He felt able to rely on his staying power and the reluctance of other countries to go to war. Should war occur, he might well view a stalemate as a likely outcome (as had been the case in the war with Iran) and that might raise the possibility of the partition of Kuwait. The talks gave the Americans a chance to show that they had tried to find a peaceful outcome but had been thwarted by Saddam's intransigence. It was also an occasion to deliver a specific warning. On January 9, Baker handed Aziz a letter from Bush to Saddam, which Aziz refused to take. In this letter, the president stated that

> the United States will not tolerate the use of chemical or biological weapons, support of any kind of terrorist actions, or the destruction of Kuwait's oil fields and installations. The American people would demand the strongest possible response. You and your country will pay a terrible price if you order unconscionable actions of this sort.[27]

This implied retaliation in kind, or even worse, although in the talks it became clear that the most likely form of retaliation, deadly enough to Saddam, would be to topple the regime. When Baker spoke to Aziz, the latter was told that if chemical or biological weapons were used against coalition forces

> the American people would demand revenge, and we have the means to implement this. This is not a threat, but a pledge that if there is any use of such weapons, our objective would not be only the liberation of Kuwait, but also the toppling of the present regime.[28]

The corollary of that was that if the Iraqis showed restraint and allowed themselves to be beaten on the regular battlefield without resort to irregular weapons, then the regime might survive.

Before he characterized Saddam Hussein as "evil," Bush had not intended to make him America's enemy. The policy, inherited from the Reagan administration, was to treat him as a potential partner. This was not on the basis that he was "good," but rather that he was flexible and had an interest for political and economic reasons in partnership with the United States. The invasion of Kuwait was not anomalous in terms of Saddam's past behavior, but it was against American interests and confirmed his disdain for the established rules of international order. For realists these were good enough reasons to accept Iraq as an enemy, but the remedies did not require regime change. Realist calculations now came up against the demonic qualities ascribed, justifiably, to Saddam Hussein.

DESERT STORM

THE PRESIDENT PROMISED the American people that this would not "be another Vietnam"; there would be "no protracted drawn-out war."[1] Nonetheless, Vietnam shaped the American debate. For every opinion on the Gulf
crisis, there appeared to be a "lesson" of Vietnam to support it. It was used by
left-wing critics to warn of the perils of military intervention in support of
nondemocratic regimes and by right-wing critics of the folly of letting "our
boys" fight others' battles. It was cited by reluctant allies as an example of the
dangers of getting too caught up with Washington's latest cause and by the
more enthusiastic as reason to get in a position to influence its crisis management. The Arabs who suddenly found themselves dependent upon
American military strength and those who opposed it could all look to the
Vietnam experience and wonder about the ability of the United States to
sustain a commitment when the going got tough.

In all material respects, the Vietnam and Persian Gulf wars were quite different. Vietnam was a civil war with a cold war twist. Although the United
States claimed that the non-Communist South was being undermined by
the aggression of the Communist North, in practice this was because of its
own weaknesses and the indigenous strength of the Communists. In 1990,
there was no doubt that Iraq had aggressed against Kuwait in an extraordinarily blatant manner. One consequence of this was that whereas in Vietnam
the United States was largely on its own, other than for some local regional
support, in the Gulf there was a remarkable United Nations consensus be-

hind the demand that Iraq should leave Kuwait, and a coalition was forged combining Western (United States, Britain, and France) and Arab (Saudi, Egyptian, and Syrian) forces. The burden of a flawed American strategy was carried in Vietnam by a draftee army, with the conscripts selected through a system that was widely believed to be unfair. By the time of the Gulf, this had been replaced by a volunteer army. Compared to Vietnam, the conditions were favorable. There was time to gather full intelligence, prepare plans, and bring in all types of capabilities to the requisite levels. With excellent bases, airfields, and ports, Saudi Arabia was well geared to the logistical demands of a major influx of forces. There was no need to worry about a "second front." No Arab country would take military action in support of Iraq. Most important, Iraq's umbilical cord to its former chief supplier, the Soviet Union, had been cut. In contrast to Vietnam, the Americans did not have to worry about provoking a Great Power that might enter the war on the enemy's side.

For the American military, the leaders of which in 1991 had almost all served in Vietnam, the key lesson was the need to avoid the strategy of graduated response that had been adopted by the Johnson administration. According to this sort of "turning the screw" approach, pressure is gradually ratcheted up until it becomes intolerable and the enemy gives in. Over two decades of Vietnam retrospectives, this notion was discredited on the grounds that instead of disorienting the enemy by intensive, shocking blows from day one, the incremental pressure allows time to adjust. Another problem was that taking escalation one step at a time did not necessarily reflect a steely but patient determination to find the enemy's pain threshold but might show uncertainty brought on by internal self-doubts, as was the case in Vietnam. The determination to avoid incrementalism of this sort was the starting point for the military planning of 1990–1991. It was reflected in the chosen name for the campaign—"Desert Storm"—and most notably and symbolically, in describing the air campaign as "Instant Thunder" as against the "Rolling Thunder" of Vietnam.

The second element of U.S. strategy was to accept that Iraq could not be defeated without a major commitment of ground forces. For Colin Powell, as chairman of the Joint Chiefs, the biggest strategic error would be to try to avoid casualties by relying on airpower alone. He had the soldier's distrust of the airmen's claims to be able to win wars all by themselves. Airpower could coerce and intimidate, but it could not force an enemy into surrender. The fundamental flaw with sole reliance on airpower, he argued, was that Saddam Hussein "makes the decision as to whether or not he will or will not withdraw." The U.S. Air Force could inflict terrible punishment but, he added, "One can hunker down. One can dig in. One can disperse to try to ride out such a single dimensional attack."[2] This meant sending troops against a supposedly numerous and battle-hardened enemy enjoying all the tactical advantages of the defender. In the prewar debates, estimates of the consequences of all-out assault on entrenched Iraqi positions suggested high casualties. Unofficial estimates ranged from a few hundred to up to 15,000. For example, one analyst, Edward Luttwak, argued that high casualties were "almost mathematically certain," even given what he deemed to be extremely optimistic assumptions. These would result from "the incidentals of war: troops stepping on unmarked mines, short fire-fights with stragglers and hold-outs, mechanical accidents, and the ragged fire of some surviving fraction of the huge number of Iraqi artillery tubes."[3]

The readiness to accept such risks challenged what many assumed to be the main political lesson of Vietnam—that the public could not support mounting casualties over time, especially when the losses were depicted nightly on television. In practice, the disillusionment with the Vietnam War had set in largely because casualties were being sustained to little evident point. The costs of war were certainly troubling, but their impact was magnified because there was no attainable political objective that might begin to warrant these costs. A political objective that was well justified and attainable ought to steady public support. Given the balance of forces, there seemed little reason to doubt that an eventual coalition victory was attainable. After all, any battle would be fought in the desert. This was not going to turn into a guerrilla war. Nonetheless, the memory of Vietnam, and for that matter, Beirut, was still that public support for any war could erode rapidly in the face of high casualties. A poll in early January showed support for the war at 63 percent but dropping to well below 50 percent once it was postulated that 1,000 troops might be killed, and if this number should rise to 10,000, as some claimed possible, then the support would drop to only one-third of the population.[4] Powell's answer to this was to opt for massive, overwhelming force to convince the Iraqis that their position was hopeless. The larger the army ready for battle, the fewer that would get hurt. Powell told Bush that he did not do "marginal economic analysis looking for crossover points. I go in with enough to make sure . . . we're not operating in the margin."[5]

*   *   *

The American strategic debate assumed a formidable foe. Saddam was terribly proud that a country of 19 million could generate an army of 1 million, the fourth largest in the world, though this was a quantitative, not a qualitative, measure. The American military was not disposed to play down its qualities. Iraqi performance against Iran suggested a professional, tough, and well-led army, numerically strong and with relevant experience, now bristling with modern equipment. This was against the normal, unflattering portraits of Arab armies, which reflected their regular defeats by the Israelis and characterized them as poorly trained, badly led, and prone to early surrender. By contrast, the more elite sections, such as the Republican Guard, were well motivated and trained, but the army numbers were made up by less committed conscripts, who were as weary of war as they were hardened. Some of the experienced commanders had been purged, especially if they challenged Saddam's rule. Such a political system, and the Soviet military command system that the Iraqis had been taught, discouraged local initiative and tended to a limited tactical repertoire. Western estimates, reinforced by Iraqi boasts, put the size of the opposing army in theater at 540,000, but the actual number was less than half by the time the fighting started, either because the units were never up to full strength or they had been depleted through desertions. If the larger number had been reached, the Iraqi logistical system would have struggled to cope even more than it did. In any case, it suited Saddam to emphasize the numbers to deter, and it suited those in the U.S. military to ensure that they got sufficient numbers on their side to be overwhelming.

Saddam was convinced that the war would be decided on the ground and that America's reluctance to accept casualties would be its main vulnerability. His strategy was calculated to accentuate the risk by using extensive fortifications to channel coalition forces into confined areas, where they could be picked off by well-protected Iraqi units. By developing this strategy in a conspicuous manner from August 1990, he hoped to deter an American ground attack. The Iraqis took heart from the substantial evidence of antiwar feeling in the United States and skepticism from military specialists exhibited during late 1990. If war came, so long as it could be dragged out for months, even years, then the will of the United States and its partners would soon be sapped. Aziz told Baker in Geneva that Iraq could cope with tests of endurance and was prepared for a long war; on the eve of the war, Saddam warned Bush that he faced not just a "second Vietnam" but the "mother of all battles."

Along with many in the United States, Saddam did not appreciate the transformation of the U.S. Army from the demoralized conscripts of Vietnam to the well-equipped professionals of 1990, who had been concentrating for the past fifteen years on how to deal with a force trained and equipped along Soviet lines. Moreover, while he was right that the war would ultimately be decided on the ground, that hardly made airpower irrelevant. If the Americans could achieve "command of the air," then the Iraqi army risked being pulverized from above as its troops moved into the open. Although aware of this possibility, Saddam tended to discount it. His confidence was in part based on his extensive air defenses. These had been built up over a decade and had elements bought from France, Yugoslavia, and the Soviet Union. In addition to numerous surface-to-air missiles, air defense guns, modern fighter aircraft, and an integrated command and control system, Iraq could boast many large airfields. Some of these were huge, with many runways to which hardened aircraft shelters were connected with multiple access lines. The main operating bases were backed up by numerous subsidiary bases, and even some roads seemed to have been fortified for aircraft use. Many of the systems were state-of-the-art, in service with Soviet and French forces. This network "constituted arguably the finest air defense technology available on the international market in 1991."[6] At the same time, it should be noted, the Iraqis often failed to master the technologies at their disposal. Systems constantly malfunctioned and broke down. In addition, Saddam had a rather dismissive attitude toward strategic airpower. His own air force was used during the Iran-Iraq war for attacks on shipping but had not played an important role in direct engagements with Iran. His intention apparently was to follow the same approach, avoiding an early commitment and holding it in reserve to intervene in a land war. Better still would be to keep it out of this conflict to sustain Iraq's regional standing. All this reflected an assumption that coalition forces would be unable either to destroy his air force on the ground or degrade his army to the point where it would be unable to resist a coalition offensive. He observed, for example, just before the war began that "extremely few of the thousands of tanks and million men" in the theater of operations could be seen, the rest being "dug in and fortified." When enemy forces moved in on the ground, his troops would be "safe and sound and ready for battle."[7]

★   ★   ★

American military strategy was well advertised in advance. Most publicity was given to the Senate hearings, which were largely concerned with the wisdom of going to war against Iraq and may have encouraged Baghdad to believe that there was limited domestic political support for the war option. The House hearings were more focused on the military options.[8] Les Aspin, chairman of the House Armed Services Committee, provided a guide based on the hearings held by his committee. He noted that the war would probably start on or about January 15, the date set in UN Security Council Resolution 678.[9] It would begin with "an air campaign against strategic and military targets in Iraq and then proceed to a sustained air campaign against Iraqi military forces in or near Kuwait." Only then would ground forces be committed. "Advocates of air power will likely get a full opportunity to see if air power can win it by itself. But the U.S. military has made sure that sufficient ground force capability is available to do the job, if air power does not force Iraq's withdrawal from Kuwait."[10] This would be "a phased campaign," which was not the same as a "graduated" campaign, for it would be geared from the start to creating the conditions for military victory.

If the Iraqis had acquired U.S. war plans in September 1990, they would have noted that the initial strategic air campaign was weighted toward the sources of Saddam Hussein's power, including weapons of mass destruction, with an initial focus on Iraqi air defenses and airfields. However, the target sets included only ten items for air defenses and seven for airfields, indicating that the American planners were prepared to take some risks in order to wage a short but intensive campaign. It was only later, as they became more prudent, that an air and ground force was assembled in the Gulf that would provide maximum freedom of maneuver. By December, the target sets for strategic air defenses had been expanded to include twenty-seven items, and twenty-five airfields were now to be struck.[11] In addition, an operations order of September 2, 1990, made it clear that "anything which could be considered as terror attacks on the Iraqi people will be avoided." This important restriction applied to cultural and historical sites, hospitals, mosques, and civilian population centers. Later restrictions included archaeological sites, foreign embassies, and camps holding Kuwaiti prisoners of war.[12]

Although the air campaign was supposed to be geared to the requirements of eventual invasion to liberate Kuwait, the U.S. Air Force had an extremely broad interpretation of this mission. Few could argue with the importance of suppressing air defenses and air bases, the disruption of command and control, or interdicting the supply lines between the rear and the front. There was a case for also disrupting the supporting infrastructure of production, fuel, power, and communications. Not to be forgotten were the facilities that appeared to be geared to nuclear and chemical weapons, and this was undoubtedly a good opportunity to deal with them. Then the air force suggested that what might really make the difference would be attacks on what were described as Iraq's "centers of gravity"—not only those elements of Iraqi economy and society critical to its military effort but also the sources of Iraqi state power. As the strategic air plan was developed, it soon had objectives beyond the expulsion of Iraqi forces from Kuwait and expanded to reducing the long-term ability to exert a regional military influence and weakening the regime's hold on power. Undoubtedly, not far from some of the planners' minds was the thought that if these objectives were to be achieved, Saddam might well either be caught or induced to surrender to preserve what he could of his power base prior to the onset of a ground war.

The one aspect of the U.S. strategy that was not well advertised was the readiness to envelop Iraqi forces by maneuvering around the main body of Iraqi forces, so that while they were being held at the Saudi-Kuwait border, forces would get into position to cut them off at the Kuwait-Iraq border. This strategy had two advantages. It should help avoid casualties by avoiding the frontal assaults that Iraq was expecting, while also encircling the main body of Iraq's armed forces, therefore weakening the regime and its ability to cause future mischief in the region.

★   ★   ★

As advertised, the air strikes began on January 16, 1991, with the passing of the UN deadline. Allied military planning focused on reducing the effectiveness of Iraqi air defenses as the first requirement of any military operation, and this is how the war began. The initial plan had two aspects. The first was to destroy the integrated command and control network. The second was to attack the airfields to prevent their being used. In the event, the first aspect succeeded better than the second. Allied air attacks effectively damaged the integrated air defense system, so that surface-to-air missiles (SAMs) could not be properly employed and only concentrations of anti-aircraft artillery (AAA) were at all effective. As a result, very few allied aircraft were lost to SAMs and ground fire, despite the extraordinary number of sorties flown. Although there were initially over sixty sorties a day against airfields and they continued to be struck until the end of the war,[13] the Iraqis barely tried to get their aircraft in the air. Only five of the possible sixty-six airfields available to the Iraqis were actually used during the first days of the war.[14] The few interceptors that flew against the coalition attempted to keep their distance, and when they got involved in dogfights, the results were invariably disastrous. Two Iraqi F-1s mounted the only evident attempt at an offensive air strike, probably against coalition shipping, but they were caught en route and destroyed by a Saudi F-15C. This lack of activity frustrated the coalition planners, as it created a risk that the air force would remain intact.[15] After three days, the coalition could only claim sixteen Iraqi aircraft destroyed. Meanwhile, the attacks on the runways were dangerous for coalition aircraft and yielded limited results.

On January 23, operations moved from runways to destroying aircraft shelters. There were 594 of these shelters, of which 375 were eventually severely damaged or destroyed. This was a slow process (as often only F-111F and F-117 aircraft could be used) but one that was bound to be successful over time. Two approaches were adopted by the Iraqis when faced with this problem. One was to make it difficult to attack aircraft on the ground by taking them out of shelters, dispersing them (so that one bomb could not destroy both a shelter and an aircraft) and moving them around (so that intelligence on their location was bound to be dated), and moving them off airfields and close to targets on the coalition's prohibited list (so that they would be spared for fear of collateral damage). The second approach was to escape. In a four-day period, beginning January 26, nearly eighty aircraft fled, and then more tried to escape during the first week of February. The extraordinary aspect of this was that the Iraqi pilots, for want of a better alternative, flew to Iran, a recent and bitter enemy. There appears to have been some informal understanding between the two countries before the war, but not surprisingly, the Iraqis experienced considerable difficulties in getting the aircraft back afterward. A number of Iraqi aircraft did "survive the war out in the open."[16] The coalition did not bother with them, because once dispersed they "were effectively out of the fight."[17] By the end of the war, Iraq still possessed 300–375 aircraft. ·

Progress through the target list was hampered by unusually poor weather and by the need to search for Scud missiles. Iraq's first serious riposte to the outbreak of hostilities, from January 17, was to launch Scuds against first Israel and then Saudi Arabia. During the conflict, Israeli targets, mainly Tel Aviv, were hit by forty missiles, and Saudi Arabia received forty-six. The aim of these attacks was to undermine the will of the Saudi people and to extend the conflict into Israel and, Saddam hoped, to transform the conflict into an Arab-Israeli war. The attacks were limited in their physical impact, with the bulk of the casualties coming later on from one chance direct hit on a U.S. barracks in Dhahran, when twenty-eight were killed and ninety-one injured. In Israel, a couple of people were killed by direct hits, while another eighteen died because of heart attacks and gas mask malfunctions. The main effects were psychological, along with disruption to everyday life as people sought safety, and the extraordinary exertions from the coalition to try to deal with the threat. In addition to sending British Special Forces into the desert to look for the Scuds, up to 40 percent of the strategic air campaign during its early stages was devoted to attempts to find and destroy the missiles from the air. The ability of the mobile missiles to avoid detection illustrated the problems that even the most sophisticated intelligence systems can have in pinpointing individual weapons on the move. The pressure did mean that numbers of missiles launched were cut from five to one a day. In addition, Patriot air defense missiles were deployed by the United States. As with the Scuds they were supposed to stop, the Patriots also had a psychological effect, in this case calming, disproportionate to their modest physical achievements.

For the Israelis, the Scuds were certainly a true provocation, and the idea of taking hits and not retaliating immediately on their own account went against the grain, especially when they lacked confidence in the American ability to find the Scuds. The administration had to work hard on the Israelis to hold them back. Saddam's strategy was transparent, so the most compelling argument for restraint was to ask what Saddam would want Israel to do. Even if the Israelis had responded, the interests of the Arab members of the coalition were completely bound up with the success of Desert Storm. It would have taken the most enormous provocations from the Israelis or shifts in American objectives to get them to defect. The Syrians, Egyptians, and Saudis would probably have tolerated a limited Israeli attack on Iraq. As the Syrians put it to Saddam: If Palestine was your top priority, what are your forces doing in Kuwait?

The more "strategic" aspects of the air campaign also had limited success. It was influenced by the thought that with such a centralized society, the loss of the top political and military command would paralyze the whole society and its military organization. For this reason, the air campaign included a set of "leadership targets." Command bunkers, Ba'ath Party headquarters, the Interior Ministry, and Saddam Hussein's palace were all on the target list. The awkward truth appeared to be that the loss of these physical assets was not as critical to a centralized political organization as had been supposed. The only time that these targets were noticed in media coverage of the war was when a bunker believed to be used for command purposes turned out to be providing shelter from air raids for women and children, about 400 of whom were killed when the bunker was struck. Having made a point of refusing to interfere with the detail of military planning and the choice of targets for the air campaign, Bush now was required to take notice. As a result, attacks on similar targets were stopped. In a war fought, in part, as a media spectacle and in the name of the UN Security Council, the loss of civilian life appeared as a failure of strategy.

It indicated the degree to which ideas about the proper conduct of air war had shifted since World War II. There were never any proposals, in public or private, to undermine Saddam's regime through direct attacks on the civilian population and its morale. Whether, as some anecdotal evidence suggested, threats to the Iraqi people unnerved Saddam and his colleagues, this was not a deliberate route that Western countries could follow. Relatively accurate strikes against specific targets were assumed at all times. In an age of precision weapons, excessive "collateral damage" was considered unacceptable. Yet even though the commanders insisted they were keeping clear of civilian structures, civilian and military facilities can be interchangeable. Oil refineries and electrical power installations were attacked. Officially, there was an attempt to leave some power for civilian life, but the power system still suffered badly. The efforts made to avoid civilians were not always successful, and clearly considerable damage was done to civilian life in Baghdad and elsewhere—but equally clearly, this was a fraction of the damage that would have been obtained if coalition forces had been ordered to inflict the maximum damage, as in the great air raids of World War II.

Nor was there ever any intention to use nuclear weapons, though there were some ambiguous statements. In late December 1990, Defense Secretary Richard Cheney observed that "were Saddam Hussein foolish enough to use weapons of mass destruction, the U.S. response would be absolutely overwhelming and it would be devastating." At the same time, he still insisted that the use of chemical or nuclear weapons "has never been on the table" and no preparations were made for any nuclear operations. According to a poll, 25 percent of Americans would have favored tactical nuclear use if it would end hostilities quickly and save the lives of American troops. Seventy-two percent were still opposed, even with this positive slant of the question.[18] The view of the military commanders, and certainly key allies, was that the potency of modern conventional munitions meant that there were no vital targets that could be destroyed only with nuclear munitions.

* * *

Those commanding the ground forces were concerned that the effort being put into the strategic campaign was disproportionate when compared with that put into "preparing the battlefield" for the ground offensive, as if airpower had to be given a chance to work before matters were handed over to this second-best form of warfare. It took time before the air strikes began to concentrate on the forward positions of the Iraqi forces and their supply lines from the Iraqi heartland, degrading the Iraqi capabilities and demoralizing their troops. This allowed time for calls for cease-fires and new diplomatic initiatives. The most important of these came from Gorbachev just before the ground war began. His emissary to Baghdad, Yevgeny Primakov, believed that he had evidence of Iraqi interest in a peace deal. Perhaps Moscow's assessment was that a ground war could be a prolonged and bloody affair for all concerned, and that Washington would be pleased if it could be avoided. But he may also have been responding to complaints in the Supreme Soviet over Moscow's support for a military campaign against a former client that was a pretext for the establishment of a Western military presence close to the Soviet Union's southern border. For his part, Saddam may have seen the sudden possibility of a conditional withdrawal and a possibility to play for time. By now he realized that his best card—his army—was no longer in a fit state to inflict punishment on a coalition offensive, let alone stop it.

On February 15, Baghdad Radio announced that the Revolutionary Command Council was now prepared "to deal with Security Council Resolution 660, with the aim of reaching an honorable and acceptable solution, including withdrawal." This was the first time since August 5, 1990, that the Iraqi president had referred to the possibility of withdrawal. Soon the conditions appeared, and the concession appeared to be less impressive. In return, the requirements were Israeli withdrawal from occupied territories; the cancellation of all UN resolutions against Iraq; international guarantees for "Iraq's historical rights on land and at sea," which implied general recognition of Iraq's claim to Kuwait; the cancellation of Iraq's $80 billion foreign debt; and the economic reconstruction of Iraq by the allied countries and at their expense. In Moscow on February 18, Gorbachev presented Tariq Aziz with a plan that guaranteed that the threat to Iraq and to Saddam's regime would be removed following withdrawal, an end to sanctions, and a loose linkage with the Palestinian question. The Americans were unhappy with this initiative and insisted that all UN resolutions had to be accepted. There was no response until February 21, when Saddam made a wholly rejectionist speech. The diplomacy continued, as the Palestinian link was dropped and Aziz offered withdrawal in return for all other resolutions being declared redundant. To avoid further procrastination, the coalition demanded full compliance with all UN resolutions and an ultimatum. Then news came in that the Iraqis were putting Kuwaiti oil wells to the torch. Soon, as many as 580 were destroyed or burning. This was not a last-minute stratagem to interfere with a coalition advance, where it made a marginal difference, but an act of vengeance. If Saddam could not have these wells, then neither could the emir. This news reduced the time for Iraqi compliance from two days to one, with the deadline set at 8:00 PM Iraqi time on February 23 to begin an "immediate and unconditional withdrawal from Kuwait." No such undertaking was received. The ground war began on February 24 and was effectively over within three days.

*　　*　　*

Saddam was now trying to salvage what he could from a hopeless military position. His air force was either destroyed, in hiding, or in Iran. He had explored forms of irregular war, all designed to undermine coalition confidence in the limited character of this conflict.[19] The most important instruments of this strategy were the Scud attacks. He also resorted to ecological warfare.[20] In addition to setting fire to Kuwaiti oil wells, during the air campaign the valves on the Sea Island Terminal were opened (which an air strike managed to close again) and tankers' loads were dumped into the Gulf. Terrorism was another possibility, but Iraq was largely relying on enterprise by sympathizers. Its own embassies were ill suited to terrorist activity. It was further hampered because Syria, with its rather full knowledge of the Arab terrorist network, was a member of the coalition, and last because the PLO was unwilling to add to the political costs already incurred by supporting Saddam by being seen to engage in terrorist activity. As a result, the amount of serious terrorism was minuscule compared with the intensity of hostilities within the defined combat zone. Over 160 attacks were recorded, with roughly half aimed at U.S. business enterprises or installations, but these were mainly freelance operations by local sympathizers. In practice, *fear* of terrorism was much more significant in its effects, as air travel was abandoned, than the actual practice.

Saddam had chemical munitions, but he did not fit them on Scuds or employ them during the ground war. This could have been because of a variety of technical difficulties; an awareness of the quality of Western chemical protection; general disorientation of Iraqi forces, and especially artillery units; fear of local commanders being branded as war criminals; or ambiguity surrounding possible American retaliation, including the threat to extend the war. As we have seen when Baker met Aziz at Geneva on the eve of the war, there was a clear warning that use of weapons of mass destruction would provide justification for a formal extension of the war aims to the elimination of Saddam's regime. Given Saddam's preoccupation with his survival, this could have been a formidable deterrent threat. The Iraqis themselves indicated that they were influenced by the prospect of nuclear retaliation, although as much from Israel as from the United States. There may have been an element of ex post facto rationalization here. After all, it suited Iraq to present its failure to use its chemical arsenal as a result of high strategy, exalting its position as a country that had to be deterred by the most powerful forces of the most powerful state, rather than because its local commanders were disoriented and frightened, or because its means of delivery were unsuitable and in disarray. For Saddam, the failure of his unconventional capabilities to deter or disorient put him at severe risk. By February 21, he may have been reconciled to losing Kuwait, which meant that his challenge was to hold on to Iraq.

*   *   *

This did not influence Bush's calculations, yet when the ground war came, Saddam was still able to hold on to power, if not Kuwait. Why? The simplest answer is that the United States never intended to topple Saddam unless he used chemical weapons. There were a number of reasons for limited war aims. Overthrowing Saddam was a result that could not be guaranteed; a drive to Baghdad would be a tougher fight than the liberation of Kuwait and would confirm accusations of neocolonialism and involve a costly and potentially difficult military occupation of Iraq. Once the United States arrived, Saddam might go to ground and then be hard to find. If Baghdad were taken, the United States would be responsible for replacing what it had just destroyed and for the governance of a stressed country that might break up.

Restraint was what domestic and international opinion appeared to want. Obtaining a consensus within the Security Council on direct military action against the Iraqi occupation of Kuwait depended on the cooperation of China and the Soviet Union. Both these countries had long championed the principle of noninterference in internal affairs, as they believed that it helped protect them from Western attempts to change their political structure. Neighbors of Iraq were nervous with regard to the potential consequences of its dismemberment. Turkey and Iran would give no support to any notion of an independent Kurdish state. The Saudi monarchy, fearful of Iranian-supported radical Islamic movements, was loath to see Iran's influence enhanced through its connection with Shi'ites in southern Iraq. The congressional resolution authorizing the use of force explicitly related this solely to "implementation" of the relevant Security Council resolutions. The *New York Times* editorialized that wider objectives would mean higher casualties and grave political risks. Saddam's martyrdom could fuel regional unrest, while a weakened Iraq would be prey to separatists and neighbors: "If Mr. Bush is waging war in the Gulf for the sake of regional stability, then the most sensible war aims are limited ones."[21]

This was a formidable set of reasons for restraint. Yet there was still a Saddam problem for Bush. Prior to the occupation of Kuwait, he had been willing to do business with a man now routinely described as a monster. Traditional diplomatic practice distinguished between the abuses a people suffered from their own government and those resulting from foreign occupation. There were limits to what the international community could do about the former; but it was basic to world order that every effort was made to prevent the latter. But Bush's immoderate language when comparing Saddam with Hitler sat uneasily with moderate war aims, and he personally believed that defeated regimes should end either with suicide in a bunker or at least an unambiguous, ceremonial surrender as had been required of the Japanese on the USS *Missouri* in 1945. He had already watched the passing of a collection of East European dictators and would have been happy to add another from the Middle East. On this he disagreed with Scowcroft. Through successive drafts of a paper on war termination, prepared by Richard Haass of Scowcroft's staff, recommending against seeking such a decisive conclusion, Bush asked, "Why not?" Eventually, on January 23, Bush met with Scowcroft and Haass, and acknowledged that their arguments could not be easily dismissed. Bush's instincts were in tune with public opinion, which seemed to consider the overthrow of Saddam as being critical to the success of the campaign. Seventy-one percent of the American people believed that the toppling of Saddam should be an allied goal, whereas only 29 percent of respondents in a *Newsweek* survey believed that an Iraqi withdrawal with Saddam still in power would constitute a coalition victory.[22]

Bush barely attempted to change his language to reflect limited objectives. He remained anxious that Saddam might survive unpunished. He continued to speak of a "war against Saddam." His diary entries conveyed frustration. On February 15, with Gorbachev making attempts to mediate, he confided to his diary: "I don't see how it will work with Saddam in power." Five days later he expressed the same thought again: "What is victory—what is complete victory? Our goal is not the elimination of Saddam Hussein, yet in many ways it's the only answer in order to get a new start for Iraq in the family of nations."[23] On February 15, he let his feelings show publicly. He invited the Iraqi people to "take matters into their own hands, to force Saddam Hussein the dictator to step aside." This was widely interpreted as revealing the true Bush "agenda" for the war. Precisely for that reason, the administration took steps to confirm that its policy had not changed. On February 20, the White House deputy press secretary, Roman Popadiuk, insisted, "We have never targeted or made Saddam Hussein an object of that mandate or this conflict." He added, "We support the territorial integrity of Iraq. We are not in this war to destroy Iraq."[24]

In the most explicit statement of war aims, set by Bush on January 15, after getting Iraq out of Kuwait, restoring the legitimate government, and protecting American lives came promoting "the security and stability of the Persian Gulf," which at least suggested reducing Saddam's capacity to cause future mischief, even if it did not mean removing him altogether. Little secret was made of the attempt to undermine the ability of the Iraqi leadership to control its force and assert its authority through the strategic air campaign, nor was the hope that Saddam might be sheltering in one of the command bunkers as it was struck much concealed. The sources of Iraqi military power were made an explicit target. The regime might survive, but it would be neutered. The administration asserted that Iraq's "capacity for future aggression" must be part of any settlement with Iraq.[25] In particular, Iraq's nuclear program was established as an objective. CIA director William Webster observed that the administration would have "no real confidence that the area will ever be secure again" unless Saddam were "disassociated from his weapons of mass destruction."[26] The administration wanted to see the back of Saddam, but it was not prepared to do the deed itself. There was an assumption that the fall of Saddam Hussein would be a natural consequence of Iraq's defeat. That, however, required that defeat be unequivocal, and that was what the ground war somehow failed to deliver.

✳   ✳   ✳

The U.S. commanders considered the ground war to be an unfortunate necessity that should be delayed until they were absolutely ready. Saddam, by contrast, had felt that it was his best chance and was impatient to get it started. He even tried to get one going before the coalition was ready by launching a surprise incursion toward the Saudi city of Khafji about a week into the war. This caught the coalition off guard, though it soon recovered. Meanwhile, to the U.S. commanders "preparation" of the battlefield essentially meant pounding away at Iraqi forces, knocking out their equipment, and disrupting their supply lines until they were thoroughly miserable and demoralized. A target was set for a properly prepared battlefield of 50 percent reduction in armor and 90 percent in artillery in those areas where Iraqi defenses would need to be breached at the start of the land campaign. As to when the critical moment would be reached when it was safe to attack, General Norman Schwarzkopf, commanding Desert Storm, reported that he was being deliberately conservative. Better to wait and get it right than to rush in and be sorry. The process of assessing damage from the bombing, however, was hampered by poor weather and the slow production of imagery. The analysis was inexact and often formulaic. Much to the irritation of the pilots who thought that they were doing rather a good job, the CIA remained skeptical of their achievements. This frustrated the generals and left the politicians impatient. In the end, it would only be possible to assess the state of Iraqi forces when they were engaged. Those that had been well dug in would only become fully vulnerable to airpower as they were forced to move into the open.

The plan still assumed that where the Iraqi forces were waiting for the coalition advance, they would be hard to dislodge. Iraqi strategy assumed the coalition traveling up the coastal highway or landing from the coast, but the Iraqis lacked the capacity to concentrate defensive forces all along the line. Also, the borders tended to be manned by less capable troops. If the coalition attacked in a surprising way, therefore, the Iraqis would be hard put to adjust. Of the forty-three committed divisions, seven were of the elite Republican Guard, far better equipped and trained, but they were held in reserve. Their position was such that they could mount a counterattack against a breakthrough but also, and as important, they could withdraw quickly should the battle shift to Iraqi soil.

The U.S. aim was to separate the Iraqi occupation forces from their home base and prevent them from being reinforced. The basic principle was expressed starkly by Powell when he explained, "First we are going to cut [the Iraqi army] off and then we are going to kill it." The Iraqi forces were going to be kept looking toward the expected line of attack by the marines, who would move against the main defensive lines while also giving the appearance of preparing for an amphibious landing. Their aim would be to keep the Iraqi forces in place rather than break them. Here the assumption was that the Iraqis would at least try to hold their lines, despite the bombardment they had just endured. Meanwhile, supported by the British and French, the relatively heavy Twelfth Corps would work to outflank and then destroy the Republican Guards, while the relatively light Eighteenth Corps would block Iraq's escape routes in the Euphrates Valley. This was what Schwarzkopf called his "Hail Mary" play. The metaphor was a football game in which a "quarterback is desperate for a touch-down at the very end ... he steps behind the center and every single one of his receivers goes way out and then they all run down as fast as they possibly can into the end zone, and he lobs the ball."

This was the right plan for a capable enemy, but overly elaborate for the Iraqis. The choreography broke down very quickly. As the marines' supposedly secondary operation moved forward, the men were soon pushing through fortifications and minefields, facing only a halfhearted challenge. Soon, far faster than anybody expected, they were on the outskirts of Kuwait City, waiting for the Arab armies to catch up for the honor of retaking the city. The movement of the large armored divisions was comparatively ponderous. With 235,000 troops and all their equipment, including 12,000 tanks and armored personnel vehicles, they were on a 500-mile journey. As far as they were concerned, when they did come across the enemy it had to be taken seriously. The Republican Guard established a blocking line to prevent American troops from getting through to the rear. Schwarzkopf was annoyed at the sluggish speed of the Seventh Corps, under which he wished to "light a fire," but the corps commander, General Fred Franks, faced real resistance. The movement could not be a dash, and the fighting was more than mopping up. Those Iraqi units that attempted to fight, however, had no answer to superior firepower, so after two days the Iraqi army was effectively beaten.

Saddam was left to salvage what he could. On the evening of February 25, hoping for the cover of darkness, the pullout from Kuwait City began. Soon Highway 6 leading north toward Basra was jammed with escaping vehicles, often crammed with plunder from Kuwait, slowed down by the volume of the traffic and a route of bombed roads and bridges. Early the next morning, U.S. F-15s bombed the front of the convoy to trap its vehicles in the Mutla Pass; they then flew south and attacked the rear with a convoy of 1,500 cars and trucks, now also trapped. They were given no opportunity to surrender. There was no one on the ground to take it. Most Iraqis prudently abandoned the scene. Those who stayed had little chance, as waves of aircraft attacked the stranded convoy.

Reports of the carnage were disturbing, with talk in the press of pilots boasting of "turkey shoots" and "rabbits in a sack." The United States risked losing the moral high ground, a factor that bothered Bush and his advisers. They also seemed to have achieved their objectives. In a press briefing on February 27, Schwarzkopf spoke of twenty-nine Iraqi divisions rendered ineffective. "The gate is closed," he announced, "there is no way out of here." He added that nobody would be "happier than me" if the decisionmakers opted for a cease-fire. This encouraged Bush and his advisers in the belief that this was exactly what they should do. Kuwait was liberated and the Iraqi forces were trapped. There was no external pressure to cease hostilities. The Arabs had no stake in anything other than Saddam's complete humiliation. The British assumed that the current operations would at least be concluded. Senior staff had not been asked for their views and analyses. The only person consulted was Schwarzkopf, whom Powell phoned from Bush's office. He was told of the developing disposition to announce a cease-fire. For "all intents and purposes" the enemy forces had been destroyed. "I'll check with my commanders, but unless they've hit some snag I don't know about, we can stop." It was soon agreed that a cease-fire would be called for the next morning. They noted that would allow the ground war to last a neat 100 hours. The only problem was that the Iraqis were not trapped. This required another day. After checking with his commanders, Schwarzkopf did report back that the position was not as complete as he had suggested. Iraqi forces could still escape. The president's group decided that this did not make too much difference. They still did not want to be seen to be engaging in "a battle of annihilation," as Powell saw it, with unnecessary human cost. So the Iraqi forces did escape. Although there were some engagements after the cease-fire, the surprised U.S. field commanders held back as 100,000 Iraqi soldiers, including Republican Guards, with well over 8,000 tanks and 14,000 armored vehicles, streamed back.[27]

An ad hoc, haphazard set of cease-fire talks followed, where Schwarzkopf operated without full instructions, seeing himself engaged in a military conversation apart from politics. Schwarzkopf wanted to separate forces, exchange prisoners, and identify minefields. In part because of disagreements in the Pentagon, the Iraqi commanders could soon conclude that the Americans had no intention of pressing on, and because they could claim that they could not get their troops home any other way, they were allowed to fly helicopters. There was no formal document of surrender.

Did all this matter? Powell argued that it did not, and letting some troops escape made no difference to Saddam's later conduct.[28] Yet the testimony of Waffiq al-Samarrai, Saddam's director of military intelligence, is eloquent. He reported how tense and tired Saddam was, sensing imminent doom and close to tears. Then came the cease-fire announcement. He now considered himself a victor and a hero. "Soon he was laughing and kidding and joking and talking about Bush."[29] He immediately broadcast claims that the cease-fire had only come because Bush needed to "preserve the forces fleeing the fist of the heroic men of the Republican Guard." The Iraqis had demolished the "aura of the United States, the empire of evil, terror and aggression."[30] Bush picked up these notes with a degree of alarm. "It hasn't been a clean end—there is no battleship Missouri surrender. This is what's missing to make this akin to WWII, to separate Kuwait from Korea and Vietnam."[31] His frustration was reflected in the title of one of the first accounts of the war to be published: *Triumph Without Victory.*[32] Because the battlefield success had seemed so easy, it was hard to escape the conclusion that more should have been done with it, even if the actual goals had been reached.

★   ★   ★

As the war ended, there was an uprising by Kurds in the north and Shi'ites in the south. As he no longer had to worry about coalition forces, Saddam was able to cope. Aware of the risk, he had held twenty-six divisions back in Iraq. He then encouraged those facing the coalition to avoid gallant last stands in Kuwait in preference to a quick retreat. He was relieved to see returning tanks and artillery as well as troops. When the insurrection came, his forces were ready and the response was vicious. Although Schwarzkopf claimed he had been "suckered" by the Iraqis into letting them use their helicopters, the Bush administration did warn that their use against the rebels violated the spirit if not the letter of the cease-fire agreement. Some U.S. armor was moved back into Iraq, and a couple of fixed-wing aircraft were shot down. On March 26, the ever cautious Powell believed that Saddam had plenty of firepower other than helicopters. The administration did not want to be seen to be challenging Iraqi territorial integrity. Because both Kurdish and Shi'ite leaders had associated themselves with the Iraqi opposition, formed in Damascus in December 1990, it was even more difficult to attend to the humanitarian needs of repressed Iraqis without appearing to interfere in Iraq's domestic affairs. Reinforced by coalition passivity, Saddam stepped up his offensive against the rebels, who were soon crushed.

This episode had three consequences. First, the emergency helped Saddam reinforce his position within the Sunni minority. Whatever their misgivings, this was a man who knew how to protect their interests. So the obvious presumption that no leader could fail so spectacularly in war and then survive in power turned out to be false. As before in the Middle East, military defeat did not inevitably lead to political disgrace, so long as somehow it could be claimed that dignity was maintained. However furious the military might be with Saddam for putting so much at risk in a futile war with a superpower, they rallied to the survival of the state. Scowcroft later confessed that he wished that the uprising had not happened. "We clearly would have preferred a coup," he acknowledged, because "it's the colonel with the brigade, patrolling his palace, that's going to get him."[33] Coups tend to be triggered by factional infighting. In Iraq, unfortunately, any competitive factions had long been suppressed.

The second consequence was that the United States could not disengage. The plight of the Kurds became desperate, as refugees were pushed into the mountainous border with Turkey, which they were not allowed to enter. Suggestions from the administration that this really had nothing to do with them, that they did not ask for an insurrection, sounded hollow and heartless, and soon it accepted that the only way it could get the refugees away from the border was to guarantee that they would be safe at home. Creating and then sustaining these "safe havens" ensured that the United States was now involved in Iraqi internal affairs.

The third consequence was that it could not be said with complete confidence that Saddam's regime was no longer a threat to the peace and security of the region. The United States might want to disengage and leave the local countries to sort out their own defenses against a resurgent Iraq, but it would be hard now to avoid maintaining garrisons in not only Kuwait but also Saudi Arabia. In a January 1996 interview, Cheney repeated the reasons for restraint in 1991. Most important, the United States did not expect to need to do anything to be rid of the Iraqi leader: "The assumption from the experts was that Saddam would never survive the defeat." This reduced the risk of forcing the matter by trying to "topple the regime." Getting rid of him would have required "a very large force for a long time into Iraq to run him to ground," which could have taken many weeks and casualties. This would have risked getting "bogged down in a long drawn out conflict" in a "dangerous, difficult part of the world" and taking on "responsibility for what happens in Iraq." When asked whether he found Saddam's continuation in power frustrating, Cheney answered that he did not, that "if Saddam wasn't there that his successor probably wouldn't be notably friendlier to the United States than he is." He was just one among a "long list of irritants in that part of the world."[34]

13

INTIFADA

On March 6, 1991, in the full afterglow of the successful prosecution of the war with Iraq, Bush declared: "The time has come to put an end to Arab-Israeli conflict." U.S. regional prestige was high. Working relations with local regimes were good. The PLO was suffering for its unwise support for Saddam Hussein, but that might make it more pliable. Israel's government was hard-line, but there was hope that an uprising in the territories—the intifada—might have encouraged greater flexibility.

It is always hard to argue against trying to resolve bitter conflicts that have unsettling regional, and in this case wider international, effects. The key to success, however, lies in getting the timing as well as the tactics of peace right. Get this wrong, and the whole effort can backfire. An authority on this topic was one of Bush's top advisers on the Middle East. Before he joined the Bush administration in 1989, Richard Haass wrote a book exploring when and how outside mediation can help resolve conflicts. He focused on "ripeness," the point when both parties are hurting so much that they are prepared to make the compromises necessary to bring their conflict to a closure and understand how bad things might get if they fail to do so. This requires the availability of sufficiently and persuasively "rich" compromises, procedures to identify and agree on them, and leaders with the internal capacity to make compromises and then deliver. When the time is ripe, mediators can move the process along, but when unripe, too much activism can lead the parties to avoid painful decisions. "Paradoxically," observed Haass, "outside activism can actually discourage the emergence of a situation in which outside activism might be highly productive." Premature or inappropriate activism can generate actions by one of the disputants to frustrate the process or embark on unilateral measures that make matters worse.[1] The notion of ripeness can be dismissed as tautology, as a claim that a conflict is ripe for resolution when it can be resolved. Yet there is clearly something in the argument that certain necessary conditions have to be in place before mediation will be worthwhile, but that these conditions will not be sufficient if the mediation is ill judged and clumsily conducted. It is not just that both sides want relief that makes mediation possible but also that they can work out how to get it and how to sell it to their publics.

Waiting until all conditions are in place may drain urgency from a process that will never ripen on its own accord. Moreover, on the metaphor of the life cycle of a piece of fruit, after ripe comes rotten. Haass's purpose was to argue for caution, against rushing in with ambitious plans before the parties were ready. Better instead to work to build up confidence to achieve the right conditions. When he was writing, the Middle East was an example of a conflict he judged unripe, yet this was the time when it was becoming apparent to the Israelis that they could not suppress Palestinian aspirations indefinitely, and to the Palestinians, that they needed to talk to the Israelis. The problem was that the readiness for compromise was uneven and unstable. When one party was ready for compromise, the other was not.

*　　*　　*

The international consensus, almost from the day that the Six Day War ended, was that the solution to the Arab-Israeli conflict was very simple—a return to the borders of June 4, 1967, except that now Israel must be recognized by all Arab states. One of the clearest expressions of this view came with the 1980 European declaration, which was a deliberate if implicit criticism of the failure of the first Camp David Accords to deal with the problem of Palestinian self-determination. This argued for a comprehensive settlement based on "two principles universally accepted by the international community: the right to existence and to security of all States in the region, including Israel, and justice for all the peoples, which implies the recognition of the legitimate rights of the Palestinian people." Most controversially, it argued that these principles must be "binding on all the parties concerned, and thus on the Palestinian people, and on the PLO, which will have to be associated with the negotiations." It argued against any unilateral change to the status of Jerusalem and against Israeli settlements, as illegal under international law, but also for the renunciation of force.[2] This illustrates the problem of offering mediation when the conditions are unripe. The Israelis interpreted the European statement as evidence of a bias resulting from overdependence on Arab oil. This reinforced their belief that only the Americans could have a credible mediating role.

Even those Israelis who worried about the logic of settlement construction did not accept that there could ever be a return to the position of June 4, 1967. Although Article 2 of the UN Charter prohibits "acquisition of territory by the use of force," the Israeli view was that the prewar borders were in themselves arbitrary, reflecting no more than cease-fire lines, and had never been recognized by Arab states. Borders in this area had long been settled through force and superior power. What mattered at any time was who was in control, not who should be in control according to sets of principles that were rarely applied in any region of the world, and certainly not this one. Insisting on international law to define borders seemed even more unwise if it was just going to re-create the conditions for more conflict at a later date. A small country in a hostile neighborhood needed secure borders. Moreover, if the Europeans really wanted to return to the status quo ante, why did they want to include the PLO? Until the war, the West Bank had been Jordanian. The Israelis tried a number of times to deal with Jordan, and Jordan in many furtive conversations with Israeli leaders showed itself willing, but these efforts were always thwarted by the hostility of other Arab governments as well as the PLO. It was fine for the Europeans to argue for a comprehensive settlement, thus damning the separate treaty with Egypt, but the alternative was to make the process hostage to the most intransigent elements on the Arab side.

On this much most Israelis could agree. Where they disagreed was on the status of the land seized in 1967. The Likud Party believed that the war completed a historic mission to reestablish biblical Israel. Even if Arab pledges on peace and recognition could be trusted, which they did not believe for one moment, it was impossible to contemplate the abandonment of Judea and Samaria. This was the emphatic conviction of Likud's leader, Yitzhak Shamir, who was prime minister for most of the 1983–1992 period and was still in government as part of a power-sharing arrangement when he was not prime minister. He was most explicit about his views after he lost the 1992 election. When in power, it suited him to appear as a cautious, stubborn man who was working for the best deal for Israel but not opposed to deals per se. Once out of power, he explained to the Israeli newspaper *Ma'ariv* that moderation "should relate to the tactics but not to the goal." His regret was that losing the election meant that in the coming years, he "would not be able to expand the settlement in Judea and Samaria and to complete the demographic revolution in the Land of Israel." He revealed that he would "have carried on autonomy talks for ten years" and while this was going on would have built up the Jewish population in the West Bank territories to half a million. Shamir acknowledged that a majority of the Israeli public did not support this expansionist vision, but he believed that this could have eventually been achieved.[3]

Even the figure of half a million represented a scaling down of aspirations from the 2 million Jews in Judea and Samaria by the end of the century envisaged by Ariel Sharon as the settlement movement's main champion after the Likud government came to power in 1977.[4] In government, Likud found the issue more complicated than anticipated. There had been from the start tension between the security imperative for new settlements in occupied territory and the Zionist imperative. The security imperative, which had first been embraced by Labor governments, reflected a desire to make it harder for Arab armies to get across the Jordan River or dissect the country at its thinnest points. The Zionist imperative was to create as large a state as possible, reflecting at least the biblical borders. To start with, the two imperatives might reinforce each other, but at some point they would come into tension. Seizing land would preclude harmonious relations with the Palestinians, leading to a potential counterreaction that would make security more difficult. That there could be a choice between settlements and peace had been illustrated by the disengagement from Sinai as a result of the treaty with Egypt, which Sharon had implemented despite the fierce opposition from the settlers' movement. The settlers' movement irritated the more moderate elements in Begin's government with its insistent demands and expectations of a first claim on national resources, though it remained a small minority. The rabbis who gave the movement religious legitimacy could be compared with the Islamic clerics who claimed that they spoke for a higher law than those laws of mere men. After 1980, there was even a Jewish underground prepared to force the pace by engaging in its own campaign of terror against Arabs.

Despite the equivocation, the direction was clear. During the first decade of the occupation, twenty-two settlements were approved. During the Likud government, until the end of 1983, 103 were approved. The majority of these were the result of a burst of activity after July 1982, when Professor Yuval Ne'eman of the ultra-right Tehiya Party became head of the settlement committee. The numbers at this time were still relatively small: 22,800 inhabitants, up from 7,400 in 1978. Under Ne'eman, scant regard was paid to planning procedures or the resource implications, with the costs of the program at $250 million a year. Many of the sites were isolated and of no obvious strategic value, except as a colonizing enterprise for young zealots. After that burst of activity, the movement seemed to run out of steam. The national unity government formed in 1984 led to a degree of deceleration, so from 1985 to 1990, fourteen new settlements were added, with the number of inhabitants up to 81,600. This excluded the 120,000 Jews who now lived in and around East Jerusalem. By 1989, however, fewer people were choosing to live in the settlements, despite the subsidies. That year, five new settlements were approved and the number of inhabitants grew by only 5,000. The sources of new immigrants into Israel had also dried up, to just over 10,000 a year. By this time, the total population of Israel proper was 5 million, of which about one-fifth were Arab. There were over 1 million Palestinians living in the West Bank and over 600,000 in Gaza. It is hard to see how even Shamir's half million settlers would really have changed the demographic balance or the fundamental problem of the choice between the democratic character of the state and its Jewish character.

The only way to avoid this choice was either to expel Palestinians or to allow them self-determination. In the early 1980s, with Sharon to the fore, the expulsion option had a hearing, although few Israelis took it seriously and it declined along with Sharon's own career following the Lebanon debacle. Consideration of withdrawal was frustrated by Likud and the settler community, not only intensely opposed to any territorial concessions but also ready to resort to extralegal methods. The deep divisions within Israel were fully reflected in the composition of the Knesset. Israel's almost exact system of proportional representation election encouraged small parties, fragile coalitions, and therefore weak governments. After the 1984 election, Likud and Labor entered into a power-sharing arrangement. As Likud and Labor each took its turn, the emphasis of Israeli policy changed, but basically the arrangement institutionalized paralysis so that the core dilemmas at the heart of Israeli policy were not definitively addressed.

★   ★   ★

For the first ten years after the 1967 war, the Israelis had left the Arab populations of the West Bank and Gaza largely alone, but as settlement activity gathered pace, local anger and resentment grew. This in turn led to more heavy-handed policing by Israel, which added to the bitterness. Israeli politicians comforted themselves with the thought that the population was largely quiescent. The 100,000 Palestinians working in the Israeli economy seemed to have more of a stake in the status quo than the extremist PLO leaders in exile in Tunis. The Arab world was focused on the battle between the Iraqis and the Iranians, and the resistance in Afghanistan. The PLO could only imagine what might have been done with a small portion of the funds that had gone to the mujahideen. All this encouraged complacency among Israelis and despondency among Palestinians.

The frustration was felt most deeply by the young. The territories' birthrate was among the world's highest. Half the population was under fifteen: 70 percent were under thirty. Many were well educated, yet all they could look forward to was unemployment or menial work in Israel. In December 1987, at the funeral of four Palestinian youths killed by an Israeli car, anger erupted. A Palestinian threw a stone at an Israeli soldier and was shot dead instantly. Soon the territories were engulfed by full-scale rioting. This "intifada," or uprising, was generally spontaneous, with broad support and an unprecedented intensity and range. The Israelis were caught by surprise. Rowdy and angry, it was not exactly nonviolent. Stones were thrown along with Molotov cocktails. But the violence was an expression of resistance rather than a deliberate strategy. The rioters could not be readily dismissed as terrorists. The Israeli dilemma was aggravated. Any response risked appearing disproportionate; failing to respond risked a loss of control. Yitzhak Rabin, at this stage defense minister, may not have actually told the Israeli Defense Forces to break the bones of the rioters, though this was widely reported. He might as well have done so, because that was the spirit with which soldiers set about the task of restoring order. Soon the international media were reporting rough tactics. The Israelis identified Abu Jihad, a member of one of the Palestinian groups in Tunis, as masterminding the intifada. In a typically audacious raid, they assassinated him, but without any evident effect on the rioting. The Palestinian flag flew regularly in the territories: From now on, the authenticity of the cause of self-determination could not be denied.

With the PLO absent and the local leadership inchoate, space was created for new movements. The most important of these was Hamas—the Islamic Resistance Movement. This was essentially the local branch of the Muslim Brotherhood. The Brotherhood's first members could be traced back to the mid-1930s; the first branch was established in 1945 in Jerusalem. The Brothers in Gaza, while it was under Egyptian jurisdiction, suffered from Nasser's deep hostility. Those in the West Bank, under Jordan, had a comparatively easy time, in part because of their opposition to Nasserites, then seen as the main threat to the kingdom. After 1967, the Brotherhood was left relatively untroubled in the West Bank. The Israelis saw it as a largely nonviolent religious group, opposed to the PLO, that built mosques and engaged in welfare and educational activities.

This method of influencing political consciousness through communal activities was always good strategy in countries where state institutions were weak and failed to provide proper welfare. The number of mosques in the territories doubled in the two decades after the 1967 war. The most substantial of the social welfare organizations was the Islamic Center in Gaza, founded by Sheik Ahmed Yassin, a quadriplegic religious teacher. From the early 1980s, a parallel security organization was established on the basis of small cells of militants. This led to Yassin's arrest, but he was released by the Israelis in a prisoner exchange in 1985. The Muslim Brotherhood published a communiqué on December 15, 1987, signed by the Islamic Resistance Movement, calling for the intensification of the uprising. They were still tentative, wishing to avoid excessive provocation to the Israelis so as not to give them an excuse for repression.

At the start of 1988, the organization announced itself as Hamas. Its covenant, published on August 18, 1988, offered an alternative manifesto to the PLO's, conveying its ideological wellsprings as well as its uncompromising vision. It describes itself as "one of the wings of Muslim Brotherhood in Palestine." Article 11 states: "The Islamic Resistance Movement believes that the land of Palestine is an Islamic Waqf consecrated for future Muslim generations until Judgment Day. It, or any part of it, should not be squandered: it, or any part of it, should not be given up." Under Article 13: "There is no solution for the Palestinian question except through Jihad. Initiatives, proposals and international conferences are all a waste of time and vain endeavors. The Palestinian people know better than to consent to having their future, rights and fate toyed with." The role of the PLO is acknowledged, but the secular nature of the organization was seen as its main weakness: "The Islamic nature of Palestine is part of our religion and whoever takes his religion lightly is a loser." Article 32 warns that "the Zionist plan is limitless. After Palestine, the Zionists aspire to expand from the Nile to the Euphrates. When they will have digested the region they overtook, they will aspire to further expansion, and so on. Their plan is embodied in the 'Protocols of the Elders of Zion,' and their present conduct is the best proof of what we are saying." This reference to a famous forgery, first published in Russia in 1903 to demonstrate a Jewish and Masonic plot for world domination, is used as evidence that Hamas is anti-Semitic as well as anti-Zionist.[5]

The other movement to emerge at this time was Islamic Jihad. This had been founded in the 1970s among Palestinian students in Cairo, some disillusioned with the secular PLO but also with the Muslim Brotherhood. They considered the Brothers to be too fixated on the need to return Muslim states to Islam, starting with Egypt, before anything could be done about Israel. Fathi Shiqaqi, its founder, was expelled from Egypt in 1981 after Sadat's murder and returned to Gaza, where he established Islamic Jihad. He was not particularly interested in educational or welfare projects. His aim was to use spectacular terrorist attacks to inspire a wider Palestinian revolt. In the early 1980s, after falling out with the PLO because of its support for Iraq, Iran backed Islamic Jihad as its best bet among the Palestinian groups. After operations began in the mid-1980s, Shiqaqi was arrested by the Israelis and spent two years in jail before being deported to Lebanon, whence he made his way to Syria. Islamic Jihad's headquarters were established in Damascus, which facilitated direct links with Iranian officials. The movements' activists soon began to train in Hezbollah camps under the guidance of the Iranian Revolutionary Guards. Islamic Jihad was torn apart by Israeli raids in early 1988, which left the field wide open for Hamas. In May 1989, the potential of Hamas dawned on the Israelis and they arrested Yassin and 200 other leading activists. This, if anything, elevated Hamas's standing.

In the competition between the PLO and Hamas for control over the intifada, Hamas had the tougher fighters but the PLO enjoyed greater authority. Arafat was still a commanding figure in the territories, and though the PLO was unimpressive, it did not actually have a state of its own to demonstrate fully its potential for corruption and incompetence. Over time, these Islamist movements grew in importance, but to start with they appeared to be on the margins of the struggle. If anything, the greater threat to the PLO from the intifada appeared to be the possibility of a local leadership emerging ready and willing to negotiate with Israel. The question for the PLO was how to use the intifada. It had rattled Israelis and revived American interest in the peace process. But neither was prepared to talk to the PLO, so it was hard to see how to set in motion a political process able to take advantage of the evident untenability of the Israeli occupation over the long term. Stuck in Tunis and still discredited by the flight from Beirut, somehow the PLO had to get itself back onto center stage. For this, it needed to talk with the Americans.

The moment was propitious. Without a political process, the prospect was of violence and radicalization gathering pace in the occupied territories. A number of unofficial groups, including some American Jews working with the Swedish government, began to explore the possibility of U.S. recognition of the PLO as a prelude to their direct participation in talks. Secretary of State George Shultz had not planned any more Middle Eastern initiatives, but he now saw a possibility to create the conditions for serious progress once Reagan's successor took over in 1989. Nonetheless, he had to stick to the official U.S. view that nothing could be done until the PLO renounced terrorism, embraced diplomacy, and accepted Israel, at least in its pre-1967 form. The Palestinians wondered what they would get in return. Would the United States, for instance, accept the principle of Palestinian self-determination? But they had no other obvious means of advancing the Palestinian cause. For Arafat, giving up on the armed struggle would be a wrench. This was how he had made his name. His world was one in which words were always backed by threats of force, and to abandon them when in an inferior position was asking for trouble. The armed struggle had, however, achieved nothing except pain and isolation. It had made it easier for the Israelis to disregard Palestinian rights and had reduced the level of Arab governmental support. To have any hope of progress, he needed the Americans, and these were the American conditions.

This led to a curious diplomatic dance whereby Shultz tried to get Arafat to make unambiguous statements, and the Palestinian leader always tried to leave room for doubt. Eventually, he managed to say that he "accepted the existence of Israel as a state in the region." When it came to renouncing terrorism, he almost, but not quite, said the right words in a speech in December 1988. Rather than read out what was in front of him, he transposed the words so the meaning became ambiguous. Shultz later recalled explaining to Reagan: "In one place Arafat was saying 'Un . . . Un . . . Un' . . . in another 'cle . . . cle . . . cle . . . ,' he has yet to cry 'Uncle.'"[6] In a following press conference, Arafat managed to get it right. The PLO condemned "individual, group and state terrorism in all its forms and would not resort to it." At last the United States and the PLO could talk to each other.

Within the constellation of Palestinian politics, Arafat was not particularly extreme. He had also made himself unassailable as the embodiment of Palestinian hopes and aspirations, but this had been achieved through a lifetime of maneuvering through Arab politics. Although he had few natural allies and was widely despised among Arab leaders, he had managed to survive. He had made his name as someone able to take the fight to the Israelis and had always presented himself as a military commander, although his successes in this guise had been few and far between. To re-create himself as a man of peace and dialogue was an extraordinary risk for him to take. While trying to convince the Israelis that he had forsworn terrorism, he needed to deny his Palestinian rivals reason to challenge his authority. He never quite pulled it off.

* * *

Whatever view the Reagan administration might be taking on the PLO, the Israelis were certainly far from convinced that it had turned over a new leaf.

The constant line from Shamir as the PLO sought to render itself respectable was that this was all a sham, a propaganda exercise designed to convince the feebleminded that there was hope for peace when with such people there could be no peace. They wanted a Palestinian state, and as this was unthinkable, they were clearly unrealistic and extreme. Yet the Israeli government was in a quandary as it tried to cope with the uprising. Its methods were deplored internationally and also by Israeli human rights groups. Members of the IDF began to complain. This was not the task for which they had trained, and many felt it was illegitimate. With even Israeli Arabs starting to be affected, it dawned on the Israeli elite that over the long term they could not hold down the whole Palestinian nation. From the state's foundation, they had been fixated on hostile Arab states as the greatest security threat. Now by mishandling the occupation and allowing settlers to set the agenda, they had created an internal security problem. A strong peace movement came into being, pointing to the damage to Israel's reputation caused by beatings, the use of live ammunition, the deportation of suspected troublemakers, and the disillusion among many of the IDF reservists called upon to administer these harsh methods. Once again, when it came to the crunch, Israel appeared to have no answer but displays of military might, no matter who got hurt. This time, the displays just made the problem worse. Rabin belatedly but profoundly got the lesson. Something had to be done to give these people hope and to recognize their rights. Polls suggested two-thirds of Israelis were ready to explore previously precluded options, including talking to the PLO.

The Israelis and the Jordanians would have preferred to have worked out a deal together. But the PLO claimed independence from Jordan as well as from Israel, which limited King Hussein's freedom of maneuver. In private he could conjure up a variety of credible deals with Israel, but in public he needed cover from other Arab governments. To provide this cover the best approach was an international conference, at which a number of Arab governments would be present, thus legitimizing negotiations with Israel. As the PLO could not agree to this, Syrian acquiescence was required. In 1987, this appeared to have been obtained by Jordan. Although some in the Reagan administration were wary of Syria, still seen to be too close to the Soviet Union, Peres saw the possibilities and so did the king. They met secretly in London and reached agreement on the scope and nature of a conference. But under the power-sharing agreement, Peres was now only foreign minister. As Shamir was bound to be hostile, Peres urged Secretary of State George Shultz to embrace this as a U.S. initiative. Unfortunately, as soon as Shultz raised it with Shamir, it was rejected. Soon the effort faded. At the Algiers summit of July 1988, Hussein relinquished all legal and administrative ties to the West Bank, handing the problem over to the PLO. This was the effective end of the dream, harbored by Labor for two decades, of using Jordan to pacify Palestine. In practice, peace with Jordan would require a prior peace with the Palestinians.

But if not the Jordanians, then who? Shamir toyed with the idea that elections in the West Bank and Gaza might lead to a relatively moderate leadership, separate from the PLO, which might then negotiate along the Camp David notions of autonomy. Yet even this vague plan was sufficiently alarming for it to be challenged by members of his party, leading to a quick shift into reverse gear. It was because of this that the national unity coalition with Labor collapsed. The assumption that a local leadership would be more moderate and malleable was at any rate self-deluding. There was a Unified National Leadership of the Intifada, and there were some tensions with the PLO leadership, although never a suggestion that they could not work together. At most, local leaders might focus more on improving conditions over the short term than the more unrealistic long-term demands of the PLO, such as the return of all refugees. But the PLO claimed to be the "sole, legitimate representative of the Palestinian people" and was not going to be displaced by some new grouping, even if one were to make the attempt.

The Israeli election of November 1988 reflected the split in Israeli society, between those who saw the intifada as a threat to be crushed and those who saw that it demanded a reappraisal of past policies. The result was once again inconclusive, with the religious parties slightly stronger and Labor slightly weaker. Once again a national unity government was formed without real unity. The background of continuing unrest in the territories was exposing the lack of creative ideas. Moreover, further problems were being caused by the increasing readiness of the settlers to take matters into their own hands, pressing for mass expulsions of Palestinians. They were acting as if they were living in a lawless state where almost any act of violence on their part could be justified as self-defense. Palestinian villages were invaded to cause mayhem, while the IDF stood by, uncertain what to do. Although this behavior earned up to 75 percent disapproval rates from their fellow Israelis, the fear of a Jewish civil war paralyzed the government.

Even members of Likud, including new foreign minister Moshe Arens, believed that some response was needed to a new political situation. With Rabin, Arens argued for an initiative based on a cessation of violence followed by elections and then talks. Without anything better to offer, and with a new U.S. administration in place, Shamir went along with the majority. On May 14, 1989, he announced the proposal. Secretary of State James Baker welcomed the very fact that Shamir was taking such action, but it was hard to see how the proposal could prosper unless the Israelis moved beyond symbolic concessions and addressed the hard questions of territoriality. Before anything else, it was necessary to stop new settlement activity. Baker expressed himself without equivocation in a speech to the American Israel Public Affairs Committee (AIPAC), the main Israeli lobbying organization, in May 1989. This was a worrying time for the organization, as a result of the negative publicity generated by the intifada and the political advances being made by the PLO. Addressing such a supposedly powerful lobby, Baker hardly played to the gallery. He left them in no doubt as to what the new administration expected. He referred to the need for negotiations and "territorial withdrawal" as a probable outcome.

> For Israel, now is the time to lay aside, once and for all, the unrealistic vision of a greater Israel. Israeli interests in the West Bank and Gaza— security and otherwise—can be accommodated in a settlement based on Resolution 242. Forswear annexation. Stop settlement activity. Allow schools to reopen. Reach out to the Palestinians as neighbors who deserve political rights.[7]

Although Baker got a less than warm response from the delegates, he continued to make the point. Shamir was being put on the spot. He could either go where Baker wanted to take him, knowing that he would infuriate his traditional supporters, or resist the pressure, knowing that Labor would leave the coalition. Hard-liners within the Likud set conditions to kill off his initiative, which Shamir decided not to resist; and so he rejected his own proposals. Baker was furious. As he spoke to the House Foreign Affairs Committee, Baker addressed Israeli officials. He gave the number of the White House switchboard: "When you're serious about peace, call us."[8]

Provocatively, Shamir started to talk about diverting Russians who were now arriving en masse to Israel from the Soviet Union into new settlements in the territories. Bush now joined his secretary of state in criticizing the settlement policy. In March 1990, Labor left the coalition, but Peres could not take the small religious parties with him, which tended to see coalition formation as an opportunity to pursue parochial interests, such as funding for religious schools. Instead of new elections, there was a narrowly based and hard-line government. Shamir no longer had to pretend. He insisted that all the occupied territories were truly Israeli. The United States and Israel were on a collision course.

Before the Americans could put Shamir on the spot, events took over to keep the PLO on the margins. In May 1990, a seaborne attack was launched against Israel by Palestinians operating out of Libya. Six small boats were sent toward Tel Aviv's beach. Four failed for technical reasons, and the Israeli military blocked the other two. In a short battle, four Palestinians were killed and twelve captured. The raid was carried out by the Palestine Liberation Front, led by Abu Abbas (which was responsible for the *Achille Lauro* affair). The United States called upon the PLO to condemn the attack, disassociate itself from the PLF, and take steps to discipline Abu Abbas. Meeting in Baghdad in June, the PLO refused to do so. The Americans misunderstood, they explained. Ending terrorism referred only to attacks mounted outside of Israel; those within Israel were acts of resistance. The Americans were unimpressed. Bush suspended the dialogue with the PLO.

After the invasion of Kuwait at the start of August 1990, Arafat allied the PLO with Iraq, applauding the linkages Saddam made with the Palestinian struggle. This was a big mistake. The principle of one Middle Eastern state gobbling up another was not one for him to applaud. Bush was infuriated, and so were the conservative Gulf regimes. One of Arafat's deputies, Abu Iyad, expressed concern about the alliance with Iraq. In January 1991, he was murdered by a member of Abu Nidal's group, presumably on Saddam's orders. A number of groups affiliated with the PLO threatened to retaliate against the U.S. for attacks on Iraq. During the war, Israelis noted the enthusiasm with which Palestinians cheered the Scuds coming down on Tel Aviv.

As the Israelis had never approved of the U.S. courtship of Iraq and were seriously worried about Saddam Hussein's ambitions, they were pleased to see Saddam being taken on. They also had a demonstration of their argument that it was ludicrous to suggest that Israel was the only or even the main source of regional instability. While all the big powers were preoccupied with Iraq, they might be left alone. At the same time Bush's determination to sustain a broad-based international coalition, including Syria, meant keeping a distance from Israel. For a country claiming to be a unique strategic asset to be treated as a liability was galling, however much the rationale was understood. Shamir complained that while Bush was making constant personal phone calls to heads of government, only he and Arafat appeared to be off the list.

The logic of the American position became clear after Israelis fired into a crowd of demonstrators on Temple Mount (Haram al-Sharif, containing the Dome of the Rock and the al-Aqsa Mosque), the holiest of the Muslim religious sites, on October 8, 1990, killing twenty-one Palestinians and injuring more than 150. They were protesting about the antics of a Jewish extremist group that had been trying to assert Jewish control of the area. There were Palestinian demands that the Security Council investigate the issue and condemn Israel for a "criminal act." Bush would not go so far, yet at such a tense point in the confrontation with Iraq, he knew that Arabs were watching out for double standards. He did not want to appear uncaring about the loss of Palestinian life by having to veto a resolution, so, with the British, the Americans presented their own resolution, which condemned Israel's use of excessive force, but in less harsh language, and called for a more restricted UN mission. This mission was still rebuffed by Israel. As Scowcroft noted, this brought relations with Israel to "a new low," adding that the U.S. Jewish community was "surprised, hurt and furious."[9] During the war, when Scuds started to fall on Tel Aviv, Shamir accepted the American view that it would just be serving Saddam's purposes to get involved. The Israelis left the military business to the Americans, and while they got thanks and praise from Washington for their restraint, the political credit was limited.

*   *   *

After the Persian Gulf War, Bush declared that it was the time to move forward to a peace that would guarantee Israel's security and Palestinian rights. At last the conditions appeared ripe for a political breakthrough. The working relationship established between Bush and Gorbachev during the Gulf crisis meant that there seemed to be no special dangers in having the Soviet Union act as cohost. The evident collapse in Soviet power meant that its former clients were already assessing the implications. Those who had relied on Soviet support, particularly Syria and the PLO, felt abandoned as Moscow argued against rejectionism and urged negotiations for peace. Arms transfers to Syria dropped. Syria and Libya became friendlier to Egypt than they had been since Camp David. The credibility of Marxism and socialism was further dented. Iraq, the most powerful and aggressive of the rejectionist states, was broken. The intifada had subsided, its participants exhausted and battered. Jordan was grateful to be included and welcomed help in repairing relations with its erstwhile Arab benefactors, such as Saudi Arabia, which were still furious over the support given to Saddam Hussein. With the PLO even more in the doghouse, the Palestinian issue could be handled by finding credible Palestinian leaders who were not part of the PLO, though not unacceptable either, and who could attend as part of the Jordanian delegation.

In his memoir, Baker described in painful detail the effort required to get Syria and Israel to the negotiations. "I don't believe in territorial compromise," Shamir explained in July. "Our country is very tiny. The territory is connected to our entire life—to our security, water, economy. I believe with my entire soul that we are forever connected to this entire homeland. Peace and security go together. Security, territory and homeland are one entity."[10] Baker faced objections to everything. "They constantly raised procedural roadblocks, debating points, reservations, and new concerns. The haggling seemed endless to me, a calculated exercise in obfuscation to play for time and avoid coming to grips with the hard choices required."[11]

Assad's favorite tactic was endurance, based on his remarkable ability to sustain marathon negotiations in stuffy rooms without ever needing a comfort break. Baker called this "bladder diplomacy." In this uncomfortable setting, Baker's main effort was to convince Syria that here was a historic chance, and that he would be left isolated if he did not take it. This required persuading Assad that there had to be real negotiations with the Israelis. It was no good assuming that a satisfactory solution could be found simply by demanding it from Israel, and threatening to withdraw American financial and security support if it was not forthcoming.

Shamir was not expecting Assad's acceptance and was both shocked and suspicious when it was reported to him. He now had no choice but to attend. On October 30, 1991, the conference opened in Madrid under the joint chairmanship of Bush and Gorbachev. For the first time, Palestinians were speaking on their own behalf. All parties were reluctant attendees, and none expected much from the occasion. In that respect they were not disappointed. The most useful aspect was to find procedural devices for Israel to engage in bilateral discussions with its neighbors. Politically, the victors were the Palestinians. Instead of Arafat, with all his political baggage, their cause was expounded by fresh, articulate people of evident moderation who could speak of peace in terms impossible for the PLO. By contrast, the Israeli and Syrian contributions conveyed intransigence. Shamir gave his standard anti-Arab speech without any hint of compromise. The Syrians managed to score a point off Shamir by displaying an old wanted poster from the British mandate of the man wanted for assassinating Count Bernadotte. Shamir was accused of being a terrorist who "killed peace mediators." They did not, however, take the opportunity to demonstrate new thinking on their side. Israel and Syria were the two most reluctant participants at the conference. In bilateral discussions afterward, the only significance lay in the fact that the conversation was taking place at all.

Moreover, by way of taking a reward for agreeing to attend, Shamir decided to announce new building in the territories, calculated to double the Jewish population over four years. This brought the collision with the United States closer. From the start of the Bush administration, Shamir had tried to argue with Bush that the settlements were an internal matter. When Bush demurred, noting the $1,000 in aid to Israel contributed by every U.S. taxpayer, Shamir said, "You can rest assured, this will not be a problem." This was an ambiguous statement. The assurance Shamir was offering was not that settlements would stop but that there was no need for the Americans to worry about their continuation.[12] In 1991 the Israelis argued that they needed to build wherever they could. After low levels of immigration during the 1980s, the collapse of European communism brought a surge of new immigrants at levels in 1990 and 1991 not far short of 200,000 a year. The Israeli budget for 1992 assumed that U.S. guarantees would make it possible to finance the new housing. In April 1991, Sharon announced construction of another 13,000 housing units in the territories over the coming five years. The next month, $10 billion in American loan guarantees were requested to help absorb the Soviet Jews.

By now, Shamir had a history with the administration, and it was not inclined to give him the benefit of the doubt. After the last grant of $400 million in loan guarantees for housing, American conditions on how the money could be spent had been ignored. So had a suggestion that new construction be halted as a goodwill gesture for peace. This came just after Baker had almost declared the Israeli ambassador persona non grata after public comments to the effect that the United States was giving Israel the "runaround" and was not compensating Israel for its losses during the Gulf War, and after the secretary of state had refused to meet with Sharon during a visit to Washington. Now the administration insisted that settlement construction must be halted before more guarantees could be approved. Baker stated bluntly, "I don't think that there is any bigger obstacle to peace than the settlement activity that continues not only unabated but at an enhanced pace."[13] Congress was asked for a 120-day delay before considering the Israeli request.

The Israeli government decided to try to get around the administration by using Congress to force its hand. AIPAC, the Israeli lobby, in turn convinced the Israelis that it had the muscle in the legislature to overturn the president's wishes and that once Bush realized this, he would accede to their requests. By September, with the peace conference close, Baker was determined that the administration would not budge. To do so would confirm Arab prejudices about the U.S. bias and reinforce the rejectionists. Baker pressed Shamir for a short delay and then, after he thought he had gotten some agreement, Shamir told him that he could not accept any delay. Baker later discovered that Shamir had been assured by his American supporters that Congress would approve the guarantees. AIPAC had thrown down the gauntlet, in effect asking the Congress to choose between the president and Israel. This was a high-risk domestic battle. The president was not pleased: "I heard today there were something like a thousand lobbyists on the Hill working the other side of the question. We've got one lonely little guy doing it." He noted that he was "up against some powerful political forces."[14] Although he later apologized for slighting the lobby, Bush did not back down from his demands. This jibe rankled with Israel's supporters. More serious was the allegation, vehemently denied, that at a White House meeting, Baker had said "F—— 'em. They [the Jews] didn't vote for us."[15]

At a time when economic conditions were hard, there was limited public support for unconditional handouts to foreign governments. By this time in its history, Israel had received $77 billion in aid, and was getting an extra $3 billion a year. Nor would Bush expect to get much Jewish support, anyway. Some in Congress were questioning whether Israel should be treated so generously, and with the cold war over, talk of Israel as a strategic asset seemed dated. Asking for a four-month deferral on a loan to see what happened in the peace process did not seem unreasonable or warrant the accusations being made by AIPAC. On October 2, the Senate backed the president. By relying on the lobby to deliver, Shamir made an error that strengthened the administration's hand and reduced the aura of invincibility surrounding AIPAC. Within Israel and the American Jewish community, sentiment was already moving against Shamir's unyielding stance.

Yet Shamir was still unwilling to concede the point. Bush effectively trapped him by attaching conditions on settlement construction to the loan guarantee, putting the onus on Shamir to reject it, which he duly did. In April 1992, after the administration rejected compromises that contained enough loopholes for settlement construction to carry on regardless, a foreign aid bill was passed without any loan guarantees for Israel. In the run-up to an election, this was bad news for Shamir. The prospect of a dispute with the United States and no end to the conflict alarmed the electorate. In June 1992, Labor united behind Rabin as a leader who was both tough and ready to take risks to end the conflict. Likud was comprehensively defeated, getting 25 percent of the votes to Labor's 35 percent. Rabin became prime minister, with Peres as foreign minister. A relieved Bush met Rabin in August and described the meetings as "a consultation between close friends and strategic partners." Settlement construction would be slowed down; loan guarantees would go forward.

While Shamir was in power, little was achieved. But once Rabin took over, there were possibilities. Unfortunately the momentum was lost when Baker was taken away from State to run Bush's faltering reelection campaign. The perception that in some sense Bush was anti-Israel did not help—his share of the Jewish vote went down from 30 percent in 1988 to 12 percent in 1992, and Bush later claimed he had paid "a hell of a price" for his stand against Shamir. But in the context of a presidential election, the Jewish vote is small, and the campaign was in trouble because of poor organization and a weak economy. His opponent ignored foreign policy, where Bush was still generally considered to be successful, and focused relentlessly on domestic issues. Furthermore, the election was confused by the intervention of Ross Perot as an independent candidate, who took 19 percent of the vote. Clinton got 43 percent, Bush 38 percent.

In some ways Bush's foreign policy had been too successful for his political good. During his presidency, the adversary that dominated U.S. thinking for over four decades had imploded. The Soviet Union had left Afghanistan in chaos but there was no hint as to where that chaos might lead. Iraq came and went as a new adversary, cut down almost as soon as it directed its aggressive tendencies against Western friends in a war in which the United States had received tacit support from its other main regional adversary, Iran. The PLO's self-inflicted wounds meant they needed to redeem themselves, while Israeli politics was veering away from Shamir's dogmatic stubbornness. America's international environment was as benign as it had ever been. It was safe to take risks when choosing a president.

PART FOUR

WILLIAM CLINTON

★ ★ ★

14

DUAL CONTAINMENT

FEW PRESIDENTS EPITOMIZED change as much as Bill Clinton. The two Republicans he defeated—George H. W. Bush in 1992 and Robert Dole in 1996—had proud records of service in World War II. Bill Clinton's war was Vietnam and his record of service, not at all uniquely for his generation, was one of avoidance. Until he became president, he showed scant interest in foreign policy or military affairs. His 1992 election campaign was governed by the slogan "It's the Economy, Stupid." He correctly saw the depressed economy as Bush's greatest vulnerability and exploited it mercilessly. Bush's foreign policy experience and success were turned against him with the suggestion that he worried more about what was going on outside America than inside. His acceptance speech contained 4,250 words, of which 141 were devoted to international matters, and then a key theme was that the world "needs a strong America, but we have learned that strength begins at home."

During the cold war, Clinton's apparent indifference to external challenges and global strategy would have been a severe handicap. In 1992 he appeared as a risk worth taking. It was time to enjoy the peace dividend and relax after the tense decades of confrontation with communism. Those who grew up in the harsh years of depression and war, hot and cold, had dominated government. Now it was the turn of the baby boomers, with their expectations of affluence and personal freedoms and a post-Vietnam suspicion of military adventures. The old left-right divisions could be recast in the light of social and technological change. Clinton also understood the new media and the premium it placed on quick sharp messages—sound bites—and control of the policy agenda. With his intelligence, charm, and eloquence, he was a master of communication. His political antennae were the sharpest of his generation, and they combined with a capacity to empathize with the tribulations of ordinary people and a desire to please and be liked. Like Carter, his experience was as a liberal governor of a southern state. He had learned the political arts of compromise and presentation in a hard school, and preferred not to make a move without consulting pollsters and focus groups. His political skills were not always matched by managerial skills. The White House was disorganized, chasing crises that screamed for attention while other issues got caught up in inconclusive debates.

Clinton's lack of interest in foreign policy was reflected in the somewhat haphazard way he put together his foreign policy team.[1] Because Democrats had been in charge of the White House for only four of the previous twenty-two years, Clinton had to stock his administration with people who gained their experience under Carter. Thus his first secretary of state was Warren Christopher, who held the deputy position in 1980, and his national security adviser was Tony Lake, who had worked in the 1970s under Brzezinski. Christopher was in his late sixties, experienced and disciplined without being demonstrative, and acceptable to the different strands of party opinion. In a talkative administration he followed his own advice to say little. As a lesson from public service he concluded that silence "begets confidence as well as confidences" and a presumption of wisdom.[2] But at a time of great change, he was also a figure from an earlier generation and lacked any grand theory to help make sense of the moment.

For the second term, Christopher was replaced by Madeleine Albright, an academic who had advised Clinton during the 1992 campaign and whose first job was as ambassador to the UN. Lake, who had trouble establishing a rapport with his president and also with his staff, struggled to move the foreign policy agenda forward. For the second term, he was replaced by his deputy, Sandy Berger, a lawyer and old friend of Clinton's. By now the president was starting to get the hang of foreign policy and make the commitments of time that were lacking in his first years. Unlike Lake, Berger had the sort of access that enabled him to discern and communicate the president's wishes. Albright was mainly preoccupied with the Balkans, so in practice after 1996 the locus of policymaking on the Middle East shifted to a much sharper White House operation.

The first secretary of defense was Les Aspin, who had worked in the Pentagon in the 1960s before becoming a congressman and an effective chair of the House Armed Services Committee. He was intelligent, popular, and knowledgeable but wholly undisciplined, lacking the management skills to run an extraordinarily demanding institution, and plagued by ill health. He left in 1993 and died from a stroke in 1995. William Perry took over. Perry's scientific background and organizational skills made him much more effective, reassuring to both Congress and allies. As a gesture toward bipartisanship, Perry was succeeded by William Cohen, a Republican senator, for the last years of the administration. Clinton's own relations with the military were poor from the start. The corporate preference was for the Republicans, who were thought to be closer to military values and to appreciate how best to use the military and keep it properly equipped. Clinton appeared as unpatriotic, of lax personal morality, and apt to take the idea of a peace dividend far too seriously. His inability to grasp military culture was confirmed when his first priority appeared to be to make it possible for gays to serve openly in the forces. When he took over, Colin Powell was still chairman of the Joint Chiefs, by far the most experienced person in the team and a man already being touted as being of presidential timbre. For Powell, the American military was a fine instrument to be used with care and only when appropriate. He resisted interventionism to the point where Albright, in an argument over Bosnia, challenged him to explain, "What's the point of having this superb military you're always talking about if we can't use it?" Powell recalled that he almost had "an aneurysm," although Albright could later argue that the value of limited force had been demonstrated in the Balkans.[3]

One area where Clinton had problems was with selection of the director of central intelligence. The first—James Woolsey—was given the job as a sop to neoconservatives, but he rarely met with Clinton, who lacked confidence in him. After Woolsey was perceived to have mishandled the discovery of a Soviet spy at the heart of the Agency, he was fired in January 1995. His successor, John Deutch, really wanted to be secretary of defense, and left in 1996. Clinton nominated a man he could trust, Tony Lake, to replace him, but Lake was unpopular among Senate Republicans and could not get confirmed. Eventually the job fell to George Tenet, who had been deputy director during this time and at least knew the Agency well and was liked within it. As a result, the CIA was "rudderless and undermanaged" for much of the 1990s.[4]

* * *

Clinton appeared disengaged from foreign policy issues for much of his first term, seeing it more as a nuisance than a challenge. He was happy to let the professionals get on with their business. Yet he also faced foreign policy challenges quite different from those of his predecessors. His team saw the old models, still influential under Bush and Scowcroft, as obsolescent. Realism as traditionally conceived seemed to be diverging from reality. Classic state-centered, balance-of-power thinking was being undermined by the new types and structures of power arising out of the swirling patterns of international trade and financial markets that were coming to be described as "globalization." The contemporary international script was moving on from one where big states had all the main parts. There were many other important actors, above and below the level of the state. The old models of sovereignty, stressing the principle of "noninterference in internal affairs," were also being challenged by the growing importance of the norms of human and minority rights when pitched against those of states. Whereas the old security agenda was dominated by the distribution of military power, the new agenda was full of proposals for eradicating disease and poverty and preventing environmental catastrophe. These issues were beyond the capacity of individual states to resolve and could only be addressed at a global level.

The abrupt end of the cold war and the collapse of Soviet power suddenly removed the old strategic imperatives. The United States was left in a class of its own, not even primus inter pares but the lone superpower—a hyperpower. Everything was working in its favor: the implosion and then apparent taming of its main adversary; established alliances with the majority of the other candidate Great Powers; the demonstrated superiority of not only its armed forces but also its political principles, social values, and economic philosophy. Liberal capitalism had acquired the aura of progress, having demonstrated after more than half a century of ideological competition in Europe that it could offer more freedom and more prosperity. This was reinforced by the economic recovery the United States enjoyed under Clinton, as a result of the impact of new information technologies at a time of low commodity prices. A more confident and internationalist outlook contrasted with the sour protectionist mood of previous decades, when the Americans felt that they had been overtaken by the Japanese and risked losing out to the rest of Asia. Now there was no real alternative model for other states to adopt. Even advanced industrial economies, such as Germany and Japan, were obliged to follow the American example. Those largely Asian countries still claiming to be Marxist sought access to international markets and started to achieve extraordinary levels of economic growth. With free markets came the movement of people and ideas. For optimists, this promised a new golden age. Closed states would be opened up by the need to attract investment and the logic of trade. The battle to control information, vital to the success of authoritarian regimes, was being lost to the Internet and mobile phones. More states would be obliged to become more democratic and, if international relations theory was to be believed, more peaceable in their relations with each other. Close attention to the economic fundamentals would create irresistible demands for freedom and human rights, expanding the community of democracies and ensuring that conflicts were managed without violence.

Therefore, when Clinton defined the promotion of democracy and human rights as a core foreign policy objective, he could claim to be riding the crest of a historical tide. The hegemonic impact of American power—and that of its closest allies—limited the capacity of states to mount serious opposition. In this way a system that encouraged individualism in politics and trusted self-interest as a guide to economic policy acquired a visionary aspect and even idealism of its own. The vision was of a world of democracies governed through cooperative multilateralism, in which old power struggles had been transcended by the search for comparative advantage, and sovereignty was pooled to address shared challenges where no state, even a superpower, could expect to act alone. War would be left without a constituency or a purpose. Instead of working to maintain the established order, the erstwhile status quo powers of the West, led by the United States, would be occupying the position of the radicals, subverting regimes they found disagreeable and demanding changes in economic practices they found inefficient.

There was a particular set of problematic states connected with the aftermath of decolonization (especially if the collapse of the Soviet empire in Europe was seen as the last great act of decolonization). They were marked by weak political institutions unable to generate viable economies, and with populations caught by deep social cleavages, poverty, and the spread of disease. During the 1990s, as the other side of the coin to globalization, the restricted competence of such states resulted in the growth in power of the shadowy and unaccountable, from messianic cults to those settling ethnic scores, from warlords to organized crime. It was hard to respect the sovereignty of such states, especially when they were no longer able to manage their internal affairs. A regard for human rights made it hard to stand aside when those rights were being violated on a large scale.

Realists would argue that however much civil wars and humanitarian catastrophes in distant places were terrible for those caught up in them, fortunately there was no need for the United States to get involved. There was often little that could usefully be done without a disproportionate commitment of resources. Even those, including Clinton, who found indifference troubling and saw real opportunities for effective interventions recognized that there was always a discretionary element in any application of armed force. These would not be wars of necessity, with the nation's core values and way of life at stake in the face of a rising and rival Great Power, but wars of choice.

Here the hegemonic logic of a universalist philosophy came to be qualified profoundly by the more parochial concerns of a self-interested state with limited resources to spare for external affairs. Tendencies toward caution were reinforced by a widespread sense in the United States that too great a price had already been paid for the former role of "Leader of the Western World." The political elite had become convinced of a declining social tolerance for the sacrifices entailed in substantial military interventions, although the evidence suggests that the key factor here was whether American casualties were incurred to no obvious purpose. The United States could, for the most part, pick and choose which crises to become involved in because most would have scant impact on the way of life of average Americans. It was not so much that the potential costs of taking an initiative were high in absolute terms, but they seemed to be relative to the narrowly defined national interests involved.

By his second term, Clinton was celebrating the American role as the country that could make the difference in a great range of international issues. In his 1996 acceptance speech he spoke of the United States as "the world's indispensable nation, to advance prosperity, peace and freedom, and to keep our own children safe from the dangers of terror and weapons of mass destruction." He used the term again in his second inaugural address.[5] Yet when it came to armed force, there was always a degree of tentativeness in Clinton's approach. He could see how operations undertaken for short-term expedience, perhaps reflecting media pressure, could turn into long-term commitments. After an inherited role in Somalia turned bloody, Clinton pulled out quickly and then avoided getting involved in Rwanda as genocide got under way. In the former Yugoslavia, which produced some of the greatest pressure for intervention, his initial preference was to advise Europeans on what they should do, and as he accepted the need for U.S. involvement, he concentrated on airpower and avoided putting the army in too much harm's way.

∗   ∗   ∗

This was a world in which the main foreign policy challenges seemed to come from inside failing states rather than the expansionist urges of strong states. No Great Power now demonstrated a visceral anti-Americanism. Those looking for candidates to challenge American predominance on the assumption that a new Great Power challenger *must* emerge looked to China or even to the possibility that Germany and Japan might reprise their past performances in this role. Others thought different types of transnational threat might emerge, with most speculation focusing on "Islamic fundamentalists."

After the Iranian revolution, Muslims suffered from poor press. One 1981 survey showed that Arabs/Muslims/Iranians (by now a somewhat blurred category) were considered "barbaric" and "cruel" by 44 percent of Americans, "treacherous and cunning" by 49 percent, and "warlike and bloodthirsty" by 50 percent. During the 1990s, polls showed most Americans believed that "Muslims tend to be religious fanatics" and that the religion was "basically antidemocratic."[6] Among policy elites, there was a readiness to consider "Islamic fundamentalism" a serious national security threat. This was in many ways an unfair and unfortunate legacy of the regular troubles with Iran. In addition, "Islamic fundamentalism" was a misnomer. Fundamentalism refers to intense piety and literal readings of sacred texts, which can affect Christians and Jews as well as Muslims, whereas the real issue was Islamism, which is a political project designed to replace all secular law with Islamic law.

If Islamists could be the new enemy, the era's strategic threat, then this was because of their influence in the Middle East, because of the importance of the oil reserves and the prospect of fanatics getting hold of weapons of mass destruction. Specialists in the Islamic world could point to its fragmented nature, with elements that were positive as well as negative to American interests, and note that where the more radical Islamists made progress, it was often because of corrupt and repressive local regimes that had been unwisely supported by the West. It was wrongheaded to try to fit all of this into a cold war–type global confrontation between good and evil.[7]

Israelis, regularly castigated even by moderate Muslims, tend to be wary about fine distinctions between forms of political Islam and, with their U.S. supporters, regularly urged American policymakers to take the threat seriously and not be beguiled by promises of democracy to come or conciliatory language. In 1992, President Herzog of Israel, speaking to the Polish Parliament, described "Islamic fundamentalism" as a "disease" that was "spreading rapidly and constitutes not only a danger to the Jewish people, but to humanity in general."[8] This led some commentators to blame the Israelis for poisoning the American mind on the topic, but even though the political link between Israel and the United States is always to the fore in Islamist rhetoric, the perceptual damage was really done by the Ayatollah Khomeini. Moreover, the most influential American commentary on the subject took the issue well beyond the Middle East. Samuel Huntington used a striking phrase for his 1992 article "The Clash of Civilizations?" which was generally pessimistic on the ability of the benign processes of globalization to overcome deep cultural divides. He reported that "this century-old military interaction between the West and Islam is unlikely to decline. It could well become more virulent." At the time it was the violence in Bosnia, at the fault line between the old Austro-Hungarian and Ottoman empires in Europe, that helped make his point.[9] The slogan "clash of civilizations" was in fact borrowed from another influential article published in 1990 by Bernard Lewis, a leading figure in Middle Eastern studies, who wrote of Muslim rage against America and modernity, based on the revival of "ancient prejudices" among extremists.[10]

The Bush administration was aware of this issue but stepped carefully around it. As an administration committed to close relations with the conservative Arab states, it was wary about encouraging anti-Islamic feeling. This extended to avoiding any meeting with the author Salman Rushdie, who was denounced throughout the Islamic world, including a fatwa calling for Rushdie's death issued by Khomeini in 1989 just before his own death, for the irreverent depiction of the Prophet in his book *The Satanic Verses*. Clinton did meet him. As Sunni Islamists made advances, notably in Sudan and Algeria, the Bush administration barely reacted. With regard to Algeria, where elections were canceled by the military in time to stop a victory by an Islamist party, it was content to let France take the lead, which meant in practice supporting the generals. This position was taken without much deliberation and probably with some relief, in that the French were taking the heat for disregarding democratic norms when they looked like they were producing the wrong result. Secretary of State Baker was quite open about the dilemma posed when movements that cannot be trusted to be democratic look to be gaining power by democratic means. In a later interview, he acknowledged that "generally speaking, when you support democracy, you take what democracy gives you. If it gives you a radical Islamic fundamentalist, you're supposed to live with it." In this case, however, the Americans went along with the French and decided not to live with it because the radicals' views "were so averse to what we believe in and what we support, and to the national interests of the United States."[11] The administration saw the potential for Algeria to become another Iran.

A June 1992 speech by Edward Djerejian, assistant secretary of state for Near Eastern affairs, alluded to the Algerian dilemma by distinguishing "one person, one vote" from "one person, one vote, one time," but also made a point of stressing that the administration did not see Islam as "the next 'ism' confronting the West or threatening world peace." Islam was recognized as a "historic civilizing force among the many that have influenced and enriched our culture."[12] The Clinton administration took a similar stance. In May 1994, Lake sought to cast the divide in the Middle East between those who supported violence, repression, and isolation and those more inclined to peace, freedom, and dialogue. This was a tricky distinction to sustain, especially when it came to democracy. Clinton picked up this theme when speaking to the Jordanian Parliament in October 1994. Here he disagreed with those "who insist that between America and the Middle East there are impassable religious and other obstacles to harmony, that our beliefs and our cultures must somehow inevitably clash." They were wrong. "America refuses to accept that our civilizations must collide. We respect Islam. Every day in our own land, millions of our own citizens answer the Moslem call to prayer. And we know the traditional values of Islam, devotion to faith and good works, to family and society, are in harmony with the best of American ideals." The real contest in the Middle East, as elsewhere across the world, he argued, was not between civilizations but "between tyranny and freedom, terror and security, bigotry and tolerance, isolation and openness."[13] Such rhetorical devices, not unique to Clinton, could mislead by suggesting that the positive attributes would come together as a sort of benign package deal, while in practice there would be a range of permutations.

If this was the real contest between good and evil, the administration had no evident strategy for bringing it to a decisive conclusion. In practice the distinction was going to be between countries with a pro-Western or "moderate" foreign policy and those that were hostile; and though questions of tyranny and freedom could be addressed with friendly states, this was not going to be to the point where there was a risk of undermining their stability. At the same time, when it came to enemies, the United States did not so much try to bring them down as to keep them in check.

The only possible success in this regard was Libya. After Lockerbie, evidence was gathered pointing to a strong Libyan role, and by 1991, warrants had been issued for the arrests of two Libyan suspects. In a series of resolutions over 1992 and 1993 the Security Council demanded that the Libyans hand them over and backed the demand with sanctions, the first time they were adopted on a terrorism issue. There were soon indications that Libya was interested in talking. The collapse of oil prices had weakened its economy, with rising inflation and unemployment. In a familiar symptom of trouble, there were a number of attempted coups. Despite claiming Islamic credentials for everything he did, Qadhafi was considered by the clerics to have a rather singular understanding of the religion. There was trouble with the Muslim Brotherhood and militant Islamist groups were suppressed only with difficulty. Qadhafi appears to have decided that the game was getting too dangerous. After 1994 it no longer used terrorism as a weapon of state policy. It opened up conversations with the Americans and British over Lockerbie in 1998, expelled the Abu Nidal organization in 1999, broke ties with radical Palestinian groups, and stopped supporting efforts to bring down the Egyptian, Jordanian, and Yemeni governments.

★   ★   ★

The 1991 Persian Gulf War left the United States in an extraordinarily strong position in the Middle East. It no longer had to worry about the Soviet Union and the price of oil was low. There were a variety of security arrangements with the main oil producers, other than Iraq and Iran, in the Gulf Co-operation Council, making it easier for the United States to project power into the region, should it choose to do so. In the case of both Iraq and Iran, a deliberate decision was made not to seek to overthrow the regimes, on the assumption that there was lack of popular appetite and international support for such ambitions. Instead, their influence would be contained, allowing them to manage their own internal affairs in the hope that one day common sense would prevail and it would be possible to restore a degree of normality to their relations with the United States. In both cases, sanctions were the main forms of containment, backed up by a substantial local military presence and, at least in the case of Iraq, occasional operations.

As an approach to awkward countries, containment had a decent track record. When Harry S Truman concluded in the 1940s that the Soviet Union's dominion could not be rolled back but must not expand further, he adopted containment as the only option. Successive administrations came to the same conclusion. This doctrine was of little comfort to those stuck in Warsaw Pact countries yearning to be free and required all sorts of adjustments in the face of Soviet power. In the end, however, patience was rewarded and the doctrine was vindicated when the Soviet system imploded; any attempt to bring matters to a head before then would have risked a calamitous nuclear war. Containment, as Sandy Berger observed, was "aesthetically displeasing but strategically sufficient." Clinton's second national security adviser was replying to critics who argued that the administration seemed content merely limiting Saddam Hussein's ability to cause trouble. Removing him from power, acknowledged Berger, "would be emotionally gratifying, but the costs of it would be greater than our national interests."[14]

The difficulties with containment went beyond aesthetics. It was realist in accepting that an inability to eliminate a hostile power required a degree of accommodation. The aim was to set limits, accepting that within those limits its influence could be malign. A problem contained, therefore, was not a problem solved. As we have seen, at the end of the 1991 Persian Gulf War the Bush administration did not so much opt for containment as decide against toppling Saddam Hussein. This reflected a prudent understanding of the risks involved in taking responsibility for the governance of a potentially turbulent and fractious country as well as a more optimistic conviction that regime change would come from within. Yet as we also saw, the United States was unable to manage a clean break with Iraq after Kuwait had been liberated. Under the Cease-fire Resolution 687 of April 1991, the so-called mother of all resolutions, there were still requirements to disarm Iraq and continue to protect Kuwait. In addition, the obligations to the Kurds, including the "no-fly zone," in the north meant that Iraqi forces must not be allowed to regain lost territory. The line of containment therefore was already being drawn within Iraqi sovereign territory rather than at an international border. UN authority for the no-fly zone was normally taken to flow from UNSCR 688, also of April 1991, although the actual resolution was quite weak. It was weaker still for the southern no-fly zone, which was established in August 1992, following continuing Iraqi military attacks against the Shia, whose plight had, until this time, not attracted the same degree of international attention as had the Kurds' situation.

In terms of a possible revival of hostilities, the most serious issue was ensuring Iraqi compliance with the provisions of Resolution 687, which required the destruction of Iraqi mass destruction facilities and weapons. Iraq was obliged to destroy, unconditionally and under international supervision, all its nuclear, chemical, and biological stockpiles and research facilities, as well as its ballistic missiles with a range greater than 90 miles, and to undertake not to "use, develop, construct or acquire" any such weapons or subsystems or facilities related to their production. The UN established the Special Commission (UNSCOM) with the authority to inspect any location in Iraq, to operate in conjunction with the International Atomic Energy Agency.

These demands provided Saddam with an opportunity to demonstrate that he could still resist the international community. With some regularity he refused to allow inspectors the documents or access they needed, leading to coalition threats of force, followed by some concessions before the whole process repeated itself. Saddam's tactic became known as "cheat and retreat." Iraqi officials would claim that nothing existed, or what was there was for peaceful purposes, or whatever had been there had been destroyed by allied bombing during the war, or, if it had not, that there was far less than alleged. Claims of this sort were made about ballistic missiles, chemical weapons, and the nuclear program. All these came under the heading of "weapons of mass destruction," a term that has now passed into popular use, so it is impossible to avoid but is seriously misleading. Not all the capabilities under this heading were of equal seriousness. It takes special circumstances for chemical or biological weapons to cause mass destruction, and there were forms of protection. Nuclear weapons were altogether more serious, unequivocally devastating even when used at low yield and in small numbers.

After the war, it became clear that Iraq had been far further down the road to a nuclear device than previously understood. At the end of June 1991, an IAEA team was sent to inspect the newly discovered nuclear sites. They were soon playing hide-and-seek with the Iraqis, and though unable to enter key sites, they recorded frantic attempts to hide uranium enrichment equipment. After an emergency Security Council session on June 28, a delegation went to Baghdad to convey the seriousness with which the international community viewed the Iraqi actions, consisting of Yasushi Akashi, UN undersecretary-general for disarmament affairs; Hans Blix, the head of the IAEA; and Rolf Ekeus, the head of UNSCOM. They explained that there could be no compromise over full implementation and that noncompliance would entail "serious consequences." Saddam gave ground, providing a detailed list of nuclear activities, but also arguing that eighteen of its twenty-four nuclear facilities had been destroyed during the war, and though it had thirty calutrons, only eight were functioning, producing barely half a kilogram of enriched uranium.

This first Iraqi admission of a nuclear weapons program was proof that it had been lying all along. As a result, international support for continued UN scrutiny was galvanized. Further demands were made on Iraq to provide irrefutable evidence by July 25 that it was not hiding any nuclear sites. Now Saddam acknowledged having extracted three grams of plutonium from spent fuel rods at the Tuwaitha reactor in violation of the safeguards agreement governing those facilities. As a show of goodwill, he declared his readiness to accept another inspection team, which indeed arrived in Iraq in late July. This team found yet more evidence that the disclosures to date had been incomplete, about the chemical as well as the nuclear programs. At the beginning of August, the U.S. Senate voted 97 to 2 to grant the president full authority to resume bombing, if necessary, to ensure Iraqi compliance. As a result the U.S. Air Force redeployed to Saudi Arabia. Yet the issue remained unresolved. The threat of force was invoked but that was all. The next crisis came in September, when for four days an inspection team of forty-four UN personnel was besieged by Iraqi troops in a Baghdad parking lot. Despite the insistence by members of the Security Council that the inspectors be allowed to leave, Baghdad demanded that they return the documents they had found. The team sent the documents back to the UN, using portable satellite communications, and Iraq backed down.

Saddam took great heart from the fact that Bush was defeated in the November 1992 election, not least because his durability was one reason for Bush's defeat. Sensing a changing power balance, he once again decided to try his luck, this time by testing the no-fly zones. On December 16, 1992, after at least fifteen trucks were damaged or destroyed by bombs planted by Iraq, humanitarian convoys to the Kurds had to be temporarily canceled. Then on December 27, two Iraqi aircraft crossed the southern no-fly line and flew right out again as they were approached by two U.S. F-15s. This was repeated, except that this time the Iraqis turned to fight, with the result that one of their aircraft was shot down. These violations, along with evidence of anti-aircraft systems being readied for action, led on January 6, 1993, to the American, British, French, and Russian representatives (but not Chinese) at the UN demanding no more threats to coalition aircraft or violations of the no-fly zone.

At first it seemed as if the SAM batteries had been dispersed. But then on January 10, 1993, the day after the ultimatum expired, Iraqi troops crossed the recently revised border into Kuwait to repatriate equipment, including four Silkworm missiles, from bunkers in the old naval base at Umm Qasr, now on Kuwaiti territory. The next day, there were further intrusions into Kuwait. SAMs were moved to south of the 32nd parallel and other systems were placed on operational footing. Bush decided to strike against Iraqi targets, with no more ultimatums. On January 13, 114 coalition aircraft attacked Iraqi air defense and command and control facilities in southern Iraq, along with other air defense installations. Fighting resumed on January 17, when Iraqi air defenses attacked a number of aircraft, leading to the sites being attacked. An Iraqi MIG-19 aircraft was shot down. Cruise missiles hit a plant near Baghdad that had made components for Iraq's nuclear enrichment program, though it was no longer doing so. The next day, there were further strikes against air defense and command and control facilities in southern Iraq. Last, on January 19, aircraft attacked air defense facilities that had been targeting them. This was George Bush's last day in office. While this was still going on, before the inauguration, Clinton signaled that the matter was less personal for him than for Bush and that there was an opportunity for Saddam to turn over a new leaf. He told the *New York Times*, "I am not obsessed with the man," adding, "I believe in deathbed conversions. If he wants a different relationship with the United States and the United Nations, all he has to do is change his behavior."[15] The Iraqis issued a statement as a "gesture of goodwill" to incoming president Bill Clinton, blaming the military engagements on Bush and offering a cease-fire.

Saddam, however, did not believe in opponents leaving office and enjoying retirement. In April 1993, the former president George H. W. Bush, with members of his family and close associates from his administration, visited Kuwait to be honored by the emir. Just as he was preparing to accept an honorary degree at Kuwait University, security forces came across an Iraqi on his way to the same destination in a vehicle packed with explosives. The bomb was designed to revenge Saddam by wiping out Bush and his entourage. The Kuwaiti authorities eventually acknowledged the discovery, after first trying to keep it quiet. Clinton recognized that he had to respond to such audacity, but the aim was to send a warning rather than cause real harm. Only one target—the Baghdad headquarters of the Iraqi intelligence services—was to be attacked, and on a Saturday night to minimize casualties. On June 26, the building was destroyed by U.S. cruise missiles. This was containment in practice. Saddam was being told that if he overstepped certain boundaries, he would be punished; if he stayed within them, he would be safe. The administration also hoped that now that the new president had made his point, the Iraqis would settle down.

This was always unlikely. In October 1994, Clinton was looking weak. He had taken fright over troop losses in Somalia and withdrawn U.S. forces in a hurry, and now he was distracted by difficult congressional elections. The Iraqis deployed 80,000 troops north of the border with Kuwait. The U.S. response was swift. In Operation Vigilant Warrior (a good containment-type name) the Twenty-fourth Mechanized Infantry Division and a few hundred extra combat aircraft were sent back to Kuwait. Iraqi forces withdrew, and by the end of the year the crisis was over. There was, however, another consequence. In 1991, there had been half a million American personnel in Saudi Arabia. Before this latest crisis, the numbers had fallen to fewer than 1,000. This time, the numbers did not go down after the crisis subsided. To sustain deterrence the U.S. numbers in Saudi Arabia steadily rose to a more conspicuous 7,000.

*   *   *

Soon, however, containment was facing a challenge from another direction—dissident Iraqis who were expecting support in their efforts to topple Saddam. These efforts went back to George H. W. Bush. Although unwilling to take direct U.S. responsibility for regime change, Bush was disappointed by the failure of the anticipated postwar coup to materialize. He had therefore succumbed to a familiar temptation in such circumstances by signing a "lethal finding" in May 1991, authorizing the CIA to "create the conditions for removal of Saddam Hussein from power." When Frank Anderson, the responsible CIA division chief, received this finding he was unimpressed. He scribbled on the paper, "I don't like this." As he later explained, "Like any bureaucrat, I was reluctant to be responsible for bringing about an objective for which the means were not at hand." He could not see where to get the necessary overwhelming force to "defeat even what was left of Saddam's army" without "really significant outside military assistance."[16] The United States had just demonstrated that this was what it was not going to provide.

Moreover, following standard CIA rules, it was forbidden to suggest that the United States would back an insurrection with force or get involved with assassination plots. In the miserable aftermath of the uncoordinated acts of rebellion of March 1991, the optimum approach appeared to be to develop a serious and coherent opposition able to maximize impact and attract international support. With an initial budget of $15 to $20 million, Kurdish, Shi'ite, and other opposition elements were brought together in the Iraqi National Congress (INC). The first meeting was in June 1992 in Vienna, where the two main Kurdish militias—the Kurdistan Democratic Party (KDP) of Masud Barzani, and the Patriotic Union of Kurdistan (PUK) of Jalal Talabani—agreed to work together. The next meeting of 600 people was held in October in Kurdish-controlled northern Iraq when the major Shi'ite groups joined the coalition. This in itself was something of a risk. The meeting was conducted in a hurry, lest Saddam pick up on what was going on and take the opportunity to strike at all his internal enemies at once.

The impresario was Ahmad Chalabi, who became chair of the INC's Executive Committee and would be a controversial figure over the coming decade. A secular Shi'ite Muslim who left Iraq in 1958, Chalabi trained in the United States as a mathematician and then went on to make money in Jordan, running a bank, until he fell afoul of Jordanian authorities, who accused him of financial malfeasance (a charge he claimed was based on Iraqi pressure). Chalabi brought to his role a good grasp of the U.S. political system and how it could be swayed. The INC's platform included all the right sentiments about democracy, pluralism, and territorial integrity, though cynics might wonder if they were included only to keep the Americans content.[17] The INC had some credibility because of its base on Kurdish-held territory and access to the Kurds' substantial militias. Another advantage was its diversity, though that was also its weakness. The two Kurdish groups were the product of the split in Kurdish ranks in the 1960s, when the PUK broke away from the KDP. In addition to the constant risk of interfactional rivalry, there were suggestions that CIA funds were providing comfortable conditions for exiles without seriously inconveniencing Saddam Hussein.

When it came to office, the Clinton administration could not and did not disown the INC. In April 1993, a meeting was arranged between an INC delegation and Vice President Al Gore. On August 4, 1993, Gore wrote to the INC, on behalf of Clinton, with an "undertaking . . . to prevent Saddam Hussein from oppressing the people of northern Iraq" and "solid assurances" to "do whatever it can to assist you, to overthrow Saddam and establish democracy in Iraq."[18] The only firm commitment here was deterrent. The United States would prevent the Iraqis from retaking the now effectively autonomous Kurdish areas. When it came to taking the war to Saddam, the INC could expect only assistance, offered with lashings of skepticism about their chances. A National Intelligence Estimate of December 1993 noted that the INC "does not have the political or military clout to bring Saddam down or play an important role in a post-Saddam government."[19]

Regardless, plans were developed on the basis that an insurrection might be set in motion that would gather momentum, spread, and eventually overwhelm the regime. There was increasing evidence of discontent in Iraq, with reports of mutinies and desertions in the army and regular plots. Still, attempts to trigger spontaneous uprisings tended to fizzle. A lot of combustible material was needed to turn a small spark into a mighty explosion. Robert Baer, a CIA official who established a small headquarters in Salahuddin, near the Kurdish capital, Irbil, in January 1995, later described Chalabi's agenda as convincing the United States that the Iraqi regime was a "leaking warehouse of gas, and all we had to do was light a match." Yet the intelligence upon which this was based was a concoction of assertions. According to Baer, "There was no detail, no sourcing—you couldn't see it on a satellite."[20] This raised the question of how far the Americans should encourage people to take great risks against a ruthless regime, especially if they were unprepared to support them if they got into trouble. This was an obvious question for a potential defector, mutineer, or rebel to ask. It was not one that Americans could ever answer with confidence. Baer felt that Washington was uninterested in what he was trying to achieve in Iraq. He kept them informed of the various plans and asked questions of his superiors but got little response. On the evidence, Iraqi dissidents had no reason to trust the Americans. Add conspiracy theories, to the effect that the Americans actually wanted Saddam to stay in power and assisted him deliberately (rather than inadvertently) at key moments, and the task became harder.

The plan was to start a revolution from the north, where there was a firm base, some protection from the U.S. no-fly zone, and anti-Saddam sentiment was running high. The hope was that early success might lead to the revolt spreading to the south. There were three handicaps, however. First, given Washington's reluctance to commit, it was hard to offer anything beyond good luck. Second, there was a complex interaction between plans for a coup involving Sunni generals, and the uprising that would start from the Kurdish areas. They were being developed in parallel, and it was always likely that they would compromise and undermine each other. Third, the continuing feud between Barzani and Talabani, aggravated by arguments over control of the smuggling routes, regularly led to pitched battles. Chalabi pressed the two leaders to unite to fight Saddam, like squabbling parents being urged to come together for the sake of the children. He persevered even when the rivalry reemerged in May 1994 over arguments about revenue from smuggling at the Turkish border and control over the Kurdish enclave's government, based in Irbil. To no avail. By the end of 1994, Barzani was smarting because his forces had been pushed out of Irbil by Talabani's. He was already skeptical about whether the Americans could or would make this work. His father had been sold out in 1975 when a revolt against the Ba'ath regime, backed by the CIA and the shah of Iran, had been abandoned abruptly when the shah had made peace with Iraq. This was typical of Kurdish history, in which the Kurds had been regularly used by outside powers for their own plans and then forgotten.

Chalabi intended to strike on March 4, 1995, but the imminent event sharpened the Kurdish differences. The KDP described his plan as "child's play." "Imagine," observed a senior party figure later, "a few hundred armed people with the Kalashnikovs taking on Iraqi army outposts, one after another, from here to Baghdad. This is unbelievable. So of course, we wouldn't take part in such little silly things."[21] The CIA had also been skeptical. Their doubts about whether anything would come of the plan meant that senior policymakers, including National Security Adviser Anthony Lake, were not fully informed. According to one story, General Adnan Nuri, who had been recruited by Chalabi but then moved over to the rival Iraqi National Accord (INA), spilled the beans. When the March offensive was imminent, he flew to Washington to warn Lake that the INC was preparing to draw the United States into a new war with Iraq. Another story is that Chalabi told two Iranian officers that the U.S. government had decided to get rid of Saddam Hussein and had asked them to contact Iran to gain support. Chalabi reportedly showed the Iranians a letter on NSC stationery that asked Chalabi to provide the NSC team leader, Robert Pope (actually Robert Baer), "all assistance" required for the mission. Chalabi was presumably trying to get the Iranians to come behind him by claiming more support than was the case. This led to Baer's being brought back to Washington for investigation for plotting assassinations.

Whatever Lake was told, he was unimpressed. He assumed Chalabi was trying to get one up on his rivals. He saw a looming "Bay of Pigs," the tragic episode at the start of John F. Kennedy's administration in April 1961, when a gallant but weak group of Cuban rebels took on a well-entrenched Fidel Castro. The risk for the United States in 1995, as in 1961, was that it would be damned if it left the rebels to defeat but damned also if it escalated by joining in the fight. The danger now was even greater, as it appeared that Saddam knew what was coming. His forces had gone on full alert at the end of February. Lake sent, uniquely for someone in his position, an urgent message: "The action you have planned for this weekend has been totally compromised. We believe that there is a high risk of failure. Any decision to proceed will be on your own."[22] Chalabi decided it was too late to stop, and Lake's message left the final decision to him. With Talabani he launched the initial attacks. The American anxiety confirmed to the KDP that it was right to back away. Although initially the remaining INC forces made some progress, overrunning some of the poorly motivated and less well-trained Iraqi units on the front lines facing the Kurds, they could not be reinforced and soon ran out of steam.

Preparations for a coup involved Mohammad Abdullah al-Shawani, formerly a commander of Iraqi Special Forces. He suggested that if Saddam faced a crisis, he would retreat to his Tikrit stronghold, so plans should be made for a final, decisive blow to be struck there. But after the debacle in the north, the coup was also doomed. Al-Shawani aborted it and fled to Syria. U.S. attention now switched to the INA.[23] This predated the INC, and was supported in London by Britain's Secret Intelligence Service (SIS) and led by Dr. Ayad Allawi, a former Ba'ath Party official. The INA's link to disaffected former civilian and military members of the ruling group created suspicions in the INC and risks of penetration by Saddam's spies, but it also meant that there was a substantial network within the Iraqi elite, including in the security organizations. Within Iraq, the INA had some minor operational successes. It stole radios from army stockpiles in the south, smuggled gear to the Kurdistan area, and started a car-bombing campaign in Baghdad and Tikrit.[24]

This was still an uneasy time for Saddam. In August 1995, two of his sons-in-law defected, probably out of fear that Saddam's even wilder son, Uday, was about to turn on them. Jordan's King Hussein, who had been cautious up to now, broke completely with Saddam and began to encourage the opposition. In March 1996, a former chief of staff of Saddam's army, General Nizar Khazraji, defected and threw his support to the INA. There were other silent military backers, along with some tribal leaders. The United States encouraged Shawani to come back into the frame and coordinate his efforts with Allawi. The INA opened an office in Jordan. Once again, Saddam Hussein was underestimated. He had written the textbook on how to survive in power against the odds. His intelligence service had penetrated the operation at an early stage. Some accounts suggest that already by January, agents had captured the secure communications equipment used by Shawani. The Iraqis rolled up the network, executing around 100 of the participating officers. This undermined further the credibility of the United States as an effective anti-Saddam force within Iraq.

Things went from bad to worse. The antagonism between the two Kurdish parties deepened. As the KDP could not expect the Americans to do much, it looked instead to Baghdad for armed support to retake Irbil from the PUK. With enthusiasm, Saddam dispatched 30,000 to 40,000 Iraqi troops with 350 tanks to deal a blow against the PUK and strike down the INC base in Salahuddin, as well as what was left of the INA network in northern Iraq. Although the United States had worked with the INC to try to prevent open conflict, by the time the administration got the two Kurdish parties to meet at the U.S. Embassy in London, Iraqi forces were moving toward Irbil. Once news of this came through, the meeting ended in disarray. The CIA agents and some of the INC leaders escaped (to be resettled back in the United States), but the Iraqi forces shot ninety-six Kurdish dissidents immediately and took a further 2,000 back to their headquarters, where they were tortured or shot.[25]

As the United States deliberated over whether and how to respond, Iraqi forces withdrew. All that happened was that the Southern Watch no-fly zone was extended to include all areas of Iraq south of the 33rd parallel, one degree further north, to take in the range of all Iraqi air defense missiles, allowing cruise missiles to attack these missiles on September 19, 1996. This was a gesture. Matters had reached the point where air defenses were being attacked, not to gain air superiority in order to attack high-value targets that were now unprotected but because air defenses were military targets that tended to be free of civilians. They could be attacked safely to prove a readiness to use force, but the underlying message was that the administration was only interested in risk-free displays of military strength. The only effect on Saddam was to prompt him to boast even more about his successful defiance.

Iraqi Kurdistan became divided into two regions, administered separately by the two parties. It took until 1998 before the Americans managed to persuade them to work together again. Saddam meanwhile restored his position in Iraq with his customary thoroughness and viciousness. The two sons-in-law were gunned down after they had been persuaded to return. This was followed by an almost successful assassination attempt on Uday. Eventually, as a means of reasserting his power, Saddam ordered a plebiscite on his presidency, turning in a modest 99.96 percent support.

☆   ☆   ☆

Meanwhile, the sanctions regime was losing its coercive effect, subverted through smuggling and corruption. Iraq was now a poor shadow of the economy and society of 1980, with per capita income down to less than one-fifth of the earlier level. Many sections of society were in desperate straits. The infrastructure bombed in 1991 was largely unrepaired. Saddam's calculations were based on the survival of the regime rather than the welfare of his people, whose wretchedness he blamed on the coalition and the UN. After a time, the link between the sanctions and Iraqi noncompliance with a series of UN resolutions was forgotten. Saddam successfully deployed the argument that whatever he did, the United States and the United Kingdom would maintain sanctions because of their hostility to Iraq. When proposals were made in 1991 to ensure humanitarian supplies of food and medicine got through by allowing oil to be sold to pay for them, he resisted because of the implications for Iraqi sovereignty. Eventually he relented, and humanitarian conditions did improve under the oil for food program. But because Iraq was able to choose its own suppliers and oil traders, he used the opportunity to strengthen the regime. His ability to control smuggling into the country and the distribution of resources added to the levers at his disposal, and he made sure that the key elements of the elite, including the Republican Guard, had priority. Postwar investigations confirmed allegations that the regime received kickbacks from contractors, members of the UN Secretariat were complicit, and France and Russia were rewarded with contracts for being supportive of the regime.[26] Most of the rest of his military capability remained in a poor state. The sanctions regime succeeded in denying Iraq new military equipment and spare parts.

During this period, with France and Russia arguing that sanctions no longer served a useful purpose, America and Britain were accused of using the Iraqi people as pawns in a pointless campaign of coercion. In this propaganda war, an unusually unfortunate moment came in May 1996 when Albright, then UN ambassador, was being interviewed on the CBS show *60 Minutes*. When asked by reporter Lesley Stahl about the sanctions, she defended them as forcing Saddam to yield on both his weapons programs and Kuwait's independence. Then Stahl asked, "We have heard that half a million children have died. I mean that's more children than died in Hiroshima. And, you know, is the price worth it?" "I think this is a very hard choice,"

replied Albright, "but the price—we think the price is worth it." The implication, quickly picked up in the Arab world, was that Americans attached
minimal value to the lives of Iraqi children in pursuit of their selfish strategic objectives.

"I must have been crazy," Albright observed in her autobiography. "I
should have answered the question by reframing it and pointing out the inherent flaws in the premise behind it. Saddam Hussein could have prevented
any child from suffering by simply meeting his obligations." As soon as she
uttered the words, she wanted them back again. "My reply had been a terrible mistake, hasty, clumsy and wrong. Nothing matters more than the lives
of innocent people. I had fallen into a trap and said something that I simply
did not mean." She explained, but did not justify, the lapse by her exasperation with CBS for what she considered to be Iraqi propaganda, having taken
viewers on "a visual tour of Iraqi health care facilities, with pictures of starving children and denunciations of UN policy by Iraqi officials." There had
been no "effort to explain Saddam's culpability, his misuse of Iraqi resources,
or the fact that we were not embargoing medicine or food."[27]

She could also have challenged the figure of 500,000 child fatalities, which
had appeared the previous year and tended thereafter to be used uncritically.
Later studies suggested that it was significantly inflated, although of course
there was undoubtedly a serious problem even if the numbers were halved.
The methodology relied on calculations of child mortality rates, where there
had been significant deterioration throughout Iraq. Once the oil for food
program began in 1996, the Iraqi government repeatedly disrupted the flow
of revenues and refused to use all available funds for humanitarian supplies
and civilian goods for its people. Nonetheless, the health of the population
improved, notably in the more autonomous Kurdish region, where the UN
handled the aid. Here mortality rates went down.[28]

With the sanctions regime increasingly seen as punitive, further difficulties developed around UN inspections and Iraq's weapons programs. The
defection of Saddam's son-in-law, Hussein Kamel, in late 1995 had focused
attention on biological weapons. It led Saddam to update his declarations to
the UN in a conspicuous and humiliating refutation of what he had said before. Yet Kamel also reported that as a result of UNSCOM's efforts, the
whole WMD enterprise had been attenuated. He told the UN that the
regime had destroyed all its stocks of chemical and biological weapons in
1991, though this could not be proved. Nor was it widely reported. The basic
point was not that the regime was innocent but that large, retained stocks,
for which Iraq would pay a heavy price if they were discovered, were useless

without a decent delivery capability. The strategy was to keep the scientists and technology in reserve, so they could resume their programs when the pressure was off and try to reconstruct a delivery capability. Kamel confirmed that the interest in acquiring WMD in the future had not been jettisoned along with the old stocks.

While Ekeus was coming to this correct analysis of the situation, his successor as head of UNSCOM, Australian diplomat Richard Butler, was far more skeptical. He noted Iraq's continuing difficulties with truth telling and assumed that this was because weapons that had yet to be accounted for were hidden. In particular, he suspected it was hoarding a biological weapons production capacity and stockpile. Large questions also remained unanswered about chemical weapons. Unfortunately, unlike nuclear weapons and missiles, these items were potentially portable and concealable. This led to demands that when there were grounds for suspicion, UNSCOM should be able to visit any site anytime. When these demands were resisted, Butler found the Security Council no longer so supportive.[29] Russia and China were challenging his judgment at every turn, while France seemed to share their view that the 1991 policy had been taken as far as it could go. It was now necessary to end sanctions and just hope that Saddam would not be so bold as to flaunt any residual capacity for mass destruction. America and Britain were therefore already becoming isolated.

Certain compounds were described by the Iraqis as "presidential palaces" sites, though together these included over 1,000 buildings and storage sites. Palaces, insisted the Iraqis, were inappropriate places for inspectors to visit. UN secretary-general Kofi Annan and Iraqi deputy prime minister Tariq Aziz agreed that Iraq's sovereignty and territorial integrity would be respected, and presidential sites would be treated with dignity, though the inspectors would carry on with their work. The limits on access, including the need to give notice, reduced the likelihood that the inspectors would discover much, assuming that there was something still to be discovered (but if not, why was Saddam being so awkward?). In late 1998, Butler reported on continuing Iraqi obstruction. There was then a series of arguments about whether force should be used to enforce UN resolutions, prefiguring in many respects, though not their intensity, those of 2003.

Just before Christmas 1998, in Operation Desert Fox, the United States and Britain launched strikes against targets in Iraq. Of the 325 sea-launched and ninety air-launched cruise missiles, 90 percent were said to have reached their designated targets. About 650 air sorties were flown, and around 600 bombs were dropped. The original target list for the campaign included 250 targets, but this was reduced so that the strikes would not continue long into the holy month of Ramadan, though they did not stop for the start of the festival. The campaign lasted four days, against a background of complaints and demonstrations in the Arab world and objections from Russia, China, and France. During the operation, U.S. Air Force and Royal Air Force aircraft attacked ninety-three targets in Iraq, destroying fourteen and severely damaging another twenty-six. The targets included thirty missile and warhead development and manufacturing facilities, twenty-seven air defense sites, and six airfields. In addition, ten Special Republican Guard units and Republican Guard barracks were attacked, possibly killing as many as 1,600 troops. Although at issue was the continued maintenance of an arsenal of chemical and biological munitions, possible storage sites were not targeted, lest toxic substances get into the air. The effectiveness of the strikes was also apparently reduced as a result of the advance warning of likely targets, allowing for personnel, materials, and equipment to be dispersed to safer sites. For these reasons, they were only advertised as helping "degrade" Iraq's WMD capabilities.

The operation was largely justified in terms of reinforcing the policy of containment, reminding Saddam that the coalition was prepared to act if he attempted to break out of the boundaries set for him. This, Clinton said, required "a strong military presence in the area, and we will remain ready to use it if Saddam tries to rebuild his weapons of mass destruction, strikes out at his neighbors, challenges allied aircraft, or moves against the Kurds." Britain's prime minister, Tony Blair, also defended the action, criticizing those who argued that because it was not possible to "get rid of Saddam Hussein there is no point . . . in trying to contain him." Just "because we can't get in the cage and strike him down it doesn't mean we should leave the cage untouched and the bars too fragile to hold him. What we have done is put him back securely and firmly in the cage."[30]

Both leaders found that a policy poised between passivity and greater belligerence was difficult to sell. Consider an American poll of mid-November 1998, when the crisis was coming to a head. It confirmed a view from the previous February that Saddam Hussein had been the winner in the confrontation between the United States and Iraq in the "last year or so" and revealed doubts that any attacks on Iraq would achieve significant goals for the United States. If force was to be used, then the majority by far wanted it to overthrow Saddam rather than support the UN (70 percent as against 25 percent). When Desert Fox began, polls showed general support for the military action, with approval levels of about 70 percent, even though most assumed that this would be at best a temporary solution to the Iraq problem. These numbers would have been higher if the main aim had been to remove Saddam from power.[31]

*   *   *

The second challenge for containment was Iran. With its population of over 65 million, Iran was larger than the other Gulf nations combined. A sensible strategy toward the region depended on sorting out relations with Tehran, but recent history weighed heavily on attempts to do so. This worked both ways. In the United States, the debate was over whether the undoubted value of a rapprochement was worth the sort of exasperating and fruitless negotiations that had characterized the hostage crisis and then the arms-for-hostages fiasco. Iran was also actively hostile to the Arab-Israeli peace process and was supporting terrorism. In Iran the debate was over whether economic and political good sense required some sort of understanding with the world's only superpower, or whether the integrity and security of the revolution demanded constant resistance to the Great Satan.

The end of the war with Iraq was followed almost immediately by Khomeini's death. Whether or not he would have moderated his legacy in the light of the new circumstances of the early 1990s, he did not have a chance to do so. His legacy of anti-Americanism, anti-Zionism, and export of the revolution was fixed and could not be updated. It was something to which the radicals could always return when they wished to resist attempts at pragmatism. Khomeini's successor as supreme leader, Ayatollah Ali Khamenei, was the ultimate power in the land, whatever the results of the occasional elections. He was more cautious than the radicals but essentially conservative when it came to sustaining the broad themes of the 1979 revolution. The president, Hashemi Rafsanjani, was counted as a pragmatist but was also cautious when it came to challenging the prevailing power balances in Tehran.

During the Bush administration, some thought was given to the possibility of improved relations, but with a crowded foreign policy agenda there was little time to pursue it and Tehran showed little interest. Yet there was unfinished business, notably the hostages still in Beirut, and after Desert Storm there was an opportunity to open discussions again. The Iranians were quite cheerful about Iraq being hammered by the coalition, once they were convinced that they were not the main target for American forces. Yet they also noted the reluctance to support the Shi'ite uprising of March 1991, which indeed in part reflected the residual American anxiety about providing opportunities for Iranian involvement in Iraqi affairs. If the Americans were considering some opening, they were quickly put off by the murder in

August of the former Iranian prime minister Shapour Bakhtiar in Paris, from where he led an opposition movement. There was little doubt that Iranian agents were responsible.

The day after the assassination, the British hostage John McCarthy was released from Beirut, the start of a process that saw all remaining U.S. hostages, including five Americans, released by early December. They were soon followed by the bodies of the murdered Americans, CIA station chief William Buckley and Lieutenant Colonel William Higgins, being dumped on Beirut streets. Critical to the conclusion of the process was UN secretary-general Javier Pérez de Cuéllar and his envoy, Giandomenico Picco, who dealt with all the major players.[32] Iran made much of its role in getting the hostages released, and the timing of McCarthy's release suggested at least some effort to provide a distraction from Bakhtiar's murder. The capture of a French aid worker a few days before the assassination and his immediate release also indicated a link. In practice, the hostages had long since outlived the original reasons for their capture. The "Dawa 17" had been released from imprisonment in Kuwait during the Iraqi occupation; Hezbollah was trying for respectability in Lebanese elections. Syria also wanted improved relations with the West after the loss of the Soviet Union as its major benefactor. There was also an opportunity to get the release of imprisoned Shi'ites. The main thing the Iranians got was the release of a UN report that unambiguously blamed Iraq for starting the 1980 war. This set in motion the release process. With Bakhtiar's murder in mind, the Bush administration took the view that the return of the hostages was about time rather than a positive gesture that required reciprocation.

Could a more positive U.S. response to the hostage release set in motion a virtuous cycle of détente? Rafsanjani would not disavow the Khomeini legacy but he was after some economic breathing space that in turn required a calmer strategic environment and in both these quests the American position was critical. The Iranians were impressed by the speed with which the United States cut through Iraqi defenses in Desert Storm and concerned by its new security role in the Gulf. What was there to contain Iraq could equally well be used to coerce Iran. Rafsanjani let it be known that if Iran was treated as a responsible regional player it would respond constructively, for example, as a participant at the Madrid Conference. It was not, however, only the Americans that assumed that Tehran had little to offer, so the invite to Madrid never came. Iran therefore saw the peace process in an entirely negative light. Its residual regional influence was at risk in a process that might extend American hegemony, allow Israel to make up with its neighbors, including Syria, so that both countries could withdraw from Lebanon.

This prospect reinforced the radical arguments in Tehran that the priorities had to be to derail the peace process and make the American position in the Gulf as uncomfortable as possible.

⋆   ⋆   ⋆

The Clinton team was naturally wary of Iran, given its role in the demise of the Carter administration. Secretary of State Warren Christopher had dealt with the final stage of the hostage crisis as his last job in government. The passage of time had not made him more sympathetic to the regime. Iran was an "international outlaw," a "dangerous country" because of its support for terrorism. Tony Lake was also a veteran of the Carter years and had seen the damage caused by even tentative contacts with Iran to the Reagan administration. Tehran had a seduction technique that could tempt policymakers into offering favors in return for a hypothetical turn to moderation that would never actually materialize.

Policy toward Iran was one of a number of reviews ordered by Clinton on taking office. It was heavily influenced by evidence of Iranian support for terrorism, involving training camps in Lebanon and Sudan; support for Islamist groups in Egypt, Algeria, and Tunisia; and direct links to Hezbollah in Lebanon and Hamas in Palestine. There may have been a suspicion that Iran was implicated in the first attack on the World Trade Center, weeks into the Clinton presidency, on February 26, 1993. Although this was not the case, to the extent it was believed it would certainly have added to the determination to keep Iran isolated.[33] Little optimism was placed in opposition groups to overthrow the regime, especially as some had been backed by Saddam Hussein. There were no obvious carrots to be offered in return for good behavior. The core strategy was to deny Iran access to the money and weapons needed to rebuild its military capabilities. This would not include an oil embargo because it could not be enforced. By contrast, it was possible to deny a proposed sale to Iran of twenty Boeing 737 jetliners, in a deal worth more than $750 million. From the start, it was evident that the real problem would be in persuading other countries to join in.

The policy of dual containment was set out not by the president or the secretary of state, but instead by the special assistant to the president for Near East and South Asian affairs, Martin Indyk. He spoke on May 18, 1993, to the Washington Institute for Near East Policy, an institute he had helped found. Looking back over the previous decade when the approach appeared to balance Iraq against Iran, the current American strength in the region meant that this was now unnecessary. Rather than depending on one to counter the other, the United States could contain them both. Whereas Iraq's regime was described as "criminal" and "irredeemable," Iran was recognized to be more problematic. It was not yet as great a threat as Iraq had been, but it could become so if it continued with its current efforts. Sanctions against Iraq had international support, but those against Iran did not. The problem was not Iran's governing Islamic philosophy, but its support for assassination and terrorism; evident interest in chemical, biological, and nuclear weapons; acquisition of sufficient conventional capabilities to threaten the GCC countries; hostility to the Arab-Israeli peace process; and a history of human rights abuses. For all these reasons, the United States was opposed to military transactions or "normal commercial relations" with Tehran. This was not a regime that any responsible member of the international community should invest in—either for commercial or strategic reasons.[34]

The administration's conceptualization of the broader problem of which Iran and Iraq were parts was set out by Lake in an article in *Foreign Affairs*. Lake used the term "backlash states," one that, unlike "rogue" or "outlaw," has not quite lasted. The list was familiar: Cuba, North Korea, Libya, Iran, and Iraq. Their shared characteristics were that they were

> ruled by cliques that control power through coercion, they suppress basic human rights and promote radical ideologies. While their political systems vary, their leaders share a common antipathy toward popular participation that might undermine existing regimes. These nations exhibit a chronic inability to engage constructively with the outside world; they are often on the defensive, increasingly criticized and targeted with sanctions in international forums. Finally, they share a siege mentality. Accordingly, they are embarked on ambitious and costly military programs—especially in weapons of mass destruction (WMD) and missile delivery systems—in a misguided quest to protect their regimes or advance their purposes abroad.

At some point, they would join the "community of nations committed to democracy, free markets and peace." The basic objective of the administration was to enlarge this community as a route to stability and prosperity.[35]

Despite this ambition, in practice, as Pollack has noted, dual containment was more defensive than offensive, more declaratory than operational.[36] The basic hope was that Iran would not continue to interfere in Middle Eastern peacemaking. During 1994, the policy began to harden because of the Iranian association with terrorist offenses geared to disrupting any moves toward a Middle Eastern peace. Hezbollah demonstrated its ability to operate at a distance when it detonated a bomb in 1992 at the Israeli Embassy in

Buenos Aires, killing twenty-nine. This was probably triggered by Israel's assassination of Abbas Musawi a month earlier, ending his brief period as head of Hezbollah. In July 1994, a combined effort of Hezbollah and local neo-Nazis saw a Jewish community center in Buenos Aires bombed, killing eighty-five and wounding 200 others. In both cases, evidence pointed toward Iran as well as Hezbollah, but in neither was anybody brought to justice.

Evidence of its complicity in such attacks and its hostility toward the peace process provided a formidable indictment of Iran. In 1995, Christopher wrote, "The enemies of peace are determined to kill this historic chance for reconciliation. As we promote peace, we must also deal with the enemies of peace." For this reason, the dual containment policy was geared toward creating "the secure environment in which Arab-Israeli peacemaking can succeed." Iran was the "most significant state sponsor of terrorism, and the most ardent opponent of the Middle East peace process." A "concerted international effort" was necessary to "stop it."[37]

★　★　★

The basic problem with the policy was enforcement. The American sanctions were incomplete and international sanctions were nonexistent. Just before Clinton's inauguration, the Europeans came up with an alternative approach described as "critical dialogue," which essentially meant the Iranians would be able to trade with Europeans so long as they listened to complaints about terrorism and the death threats against Salman Rushdie. American objections to this process, which seemed basically designed to protect lucrative trading relations with Iran, lost their impact as it became apparent that, by 1995, the United States was Iran's third-largest trading partner and largest purchaser of oil. Either the United States was going to have to tighten up its own sanctions or stop criticizing the Europeans.

The issue came to a head after the November 1994 congressional elections. After his uneasy first years in office, Clinton now faced a well-organized and hostile Republican Congress. One early proposal was for full sanctions on Tehran. Rafsanjani saw the danger and decided to offer a large carrot in the form of a new oil production contract to the U.S. firm Conoco, which had been assumed to be going to the French oil company Total. During the negotiations, Conoco was assured by State Department officials that there were no objections, but when the contract came to the administration for approval, it was denied. Christopher said the contract was "inconsistent" with containment. If it was intended as an overture by Tehran, that is not how it was seen in Washington, where it had the effect of drawing attention to an unwelcome fact about American trade with Iran, which was presumed to see the advantages in hard currency and U.S. technology. The oil dimension of the conflict was further demonstrated when the administration persuaded Azerbaijan to exclude Iran from an international consortium developing an offshore oil field. It also argued, against the Europeans, that oil and natural gas from the Caspian Sea should go via the more complex and expensive route from Azerbaijan through Georgia and Turkey to the Mediterranean rather than by the more direct route through Iran to the Gulf.

Under pressure to extend sanctions, Clinton decided to make the best of a bad job by taking the initiative before Congress forced his hand too publicly and announced his decision to the World Jewish Congress. On May 6, 1995, Clinton signed an executive order that prohibited all trade, trade financing, loans, and financial services to Iran. This included the purchase of Iranian oil, and new investment by American companies in Iran. The United States could no longer be accused of double standards, but it made no difference to anybody else's actual behavior. The European countries and Japan, which held much of Iran's considerable short- and medium-term debt, had an interest in the country's economic health. Most countries quietly explained that they did not believe in embargoes, including the Arab allies that were supposedly being protected, so trading opportunities for Iran hardly dried up. For weapons, Iran turned to North Korea and Russia, which were willing suppliers.

The temperature was also raised by a rather public congressional discussion of the virtues of a covert program to destabilize the regime. The CIA thought public disenchantment with the Iranian regime would not benefit from any association with the United States. The possibilities were also limited by the advance notice given to Tehran, which proceeded to milk the propaganda advantage of further evidence of American dirty tricks. The Iranians protested to the Security Council, while Hezbollah announced that its fighters were just waiting to be told by the Iranians when to go, for "each of us is a powder-keg and the United States is very vulnerable." With pressure from within the United States to keep on pushing against the regime, Iranian actions did not help. First, Rafsanjani welcomed Rabin's assassination in November 1995. Iran supported the suicide bombings by Islamic Jihad and Hamas against Israeli citizens in early 1996 and also encouraged Hezbollah's attacks in southern Lebanon.

The most serious developments, which almost led to a war between the United States and Iran, came in June 1996. Although Shi'ites constituted a majority of Bahrain's population of 550,000, they considered themselves to be victims of discrimination. The disaffection spilled over into rioting, including a wave of arson attacks in May. The ruling al-Khalifa clan accused Iran of being behind the recent unrest. Saudi Arabia also had an interest because of the risks that unrest might spill over into its Shi'ite Eastern Province. After Bahrain announced that a plot had been uncovered involving forty-four people conspiring with Iran to overthrow the government, in June 1996, the GCC issued a statement expressing concern about the Iranian role in Bahrain. On June 25, 1996, just after this statement, a truck bomb exploded at the Khobar Towers housing complex in eastern Saudi Arabia, where many American military personnel lived. The attack killed nineteen Americans and wounded another 372. It could have been worse; the truck carrying the explosives had been denied access to the main compound and prompt action by an air force sergeant on sentry duty led to some evacuation.

The intelligence evidence that the attack was Iranian-inspired was strong, although not sufficient to satisfy a court of law. The Saudis had the evidence, and though they were also sure where it pointed, they were nervous about handing it over to the Americans. The issue went to the heart of the American role in the Gulf. There was no doubt that the Iranians were fomenting subversion in the region, using local Shi'ite populations. At most they wanted to expand the scope of the revolution; at a minimum they wanted to make life as uncomfortable as possible for the Americans. To the Americans, the logic of this situation was straightforward. They wanted the culprits. If the evidence was compelling, they were prepared to strike hard against the Iranians. By this time Clinton was exasperated with the Iranians, blaming them for the setbacks suffered by the Middle East peace process over the previous six months. He told his counterterrorist adviser, Richard Clarke, "I don't want any pissant half-measures." Options from all-out invasion to cruise missile strikes were under consideration, but the preference was growing for large-scale air and naval attacks against Iranian coastal facilities.[38]

Potential problems with the evidence were illustrated when the 9/11 Commission raised questions about whether al Qaeda was involved in the Khobar Towers attacks. This was not wholly implausible, given bin Laden's animus toward the American presence in his country, although the evidence is sparse and circumstantial. Clinton's FBI director, Louis Freeh, had no doubts about Iran's culpability. Freeh, who became so obsessed with the issue that he became effectively the case officer, has described how with the help of former president Bush in 1997, he eventually got proof from the Saudis. By this time, he claimed, Clinton and Berger "had no interest in confronting the fact that Iran had blown up the towers." If the evidence had been obtained when it was first requested, it would probably have been acted upon; but by the time it was received, the political context had shifted.[39] In

2001, the U.S. Justice Department announced a forty-six-count indictment against thirteen Saudis and one Lebanese man in the bombing. They claimed a link to Hezbollah, which in turn was linked to Iran.

Saudi attitudes were shaped by the debate on military action. Some in Riyadh were against encouraging the Americans to strike at all. They were worried that they would suffer the brunt of Iranian retaliation, including stirring up further unrest among their Shi'ite population. There were others who would have wanted a major American assault on Iran, but worried that they would have the sort of pinpricks with which Clinton was becoming associated—actions that would have all of the negative consequences but none of the more positive, such as giving the Iranian regime a real fright. They therefore procrastinated. Prince Bandar, the well-connected Saudi ambassador to Washington, pressed Berger for detail on American plans before he would hand over information. Berger consistently replied that until he had seen the evidence, he could not know what the plans might be.

The Europeans for their own reasons were also getting fed up with Iran. They shared the distaste at Iranian celebrations of Rabin's assassination and complicity in 1996 terrorist attacks. They objected to assassinations of Iranian Kurds in Germany and were irritated by the withdrawal of a promise to repeal the fatwa against Rushdie. Yet they still were against sanctions. In 1995, Clinton had persuaded Congress not to extend U.S. sanctions provisions to subsidiaries of other companies operating in other jurisdictions. Extraterritoriality was a sensitive issue with allies. In 1996, Congress was even less inclined to hold back. The extension of sanctions to companies that invested in Iran's oil industry passed with massive majorities in the House and Senate. Imposing U.S. law on other countries was forbidden under the rules of the World Trade Organization, and this created another issue in an already crowded trade agenda. Because of his own frustration with Iran, Clinton decided against a veto, and on August 5, 1996, he signed the Iran-Libya Sanctions Act (ILSA) into law (Senator Edward Kennedy had added Libya for good measure because of the Lockerbie air disaster, for which Libya was generally blamed). As anticipated, the allies were furious, and once again the United States faced charges of double standards, this time because it had fought against the Arab boycott of Israeli goods. The European Union (EU) forbade companies from complying with ILSA and began proceedings against the United States in the WTO. When, despite some ugly threats, a German court decided in April 1997 that Iran's Committee for Special Operations had ordered assassinations of Iranian Kurdish leaders, the result was the suspension not of trade but only of the "critical dialogue" that had been used to give it respectability. In 1998, to end the impasse, the United

States agreed to grant waivers for European companies from ILSA in return for an agreement to toughen the EU's position on nonproliferation and counterterrorism.

*   *   *

By this time, there seemed to be some possibility of a thaw in U.S.-Iranian relations. Iranian foreign policy could hardly be considered a resounding success. The United States had not been persuaded to leave the region, the revolution had not spread, and relations with Arab states were poor. The economy was suffering from high debt and high inflation, and corruption was rife. Young Iranians, with no strong memories of the shah or the revolution, wanted more personal freedom and some escape from the stifling demands of the clerics. Presidential elections are supposedly controlled by the Council of Guardians, which allowed only men fit to be president of an Islamic republic to stand for office. Their preferred candidate was Majlis Speaker Nateq Nuri. He was endorsed by everyone who mattered. For the appearance of democracy, three nonentities were also allowed to stand. To everyone's surprise, one of them, Mohammad Khatami, won on a platform of reform and a reduced role for government. Despite attempts to silence him during the campaign when it became apparent how effective his message might be, he got the support of the pragmatists as well as the reformers, reflecting the widespread frustration with the old establishment: "We are in favor of relations with all countries and nations which respect our independence, dignity and interests."

Khatami got off to a flying start, while the establishment was still in shock and absorbing the evidence of its own unpopularity. He managed to get reformers into some, if not all, key positions and began to explore how to open up the economy. He spoke about improving relations with the United States, initially at a human level through exchanges of academics, authors, and athletes as much as diplomats. He avoided all the vituperative rhetoric about the United States, and even Israel, which had become commonplace in Tehran—as if there was no other form of discourse. Iranians began to visit Washington in an informal diplomatic offensive with the message that they needed help if they were to fight off the conservatives' counterattack. Clinton recognized what Khatami was trying to do and was attracted by the idea of making up with Iran. He started to sound out congressional figures as well as Israelis. None was of the view that Khatami could be any worse than his predecessors. Albright spoke of the need to draw up "a road map leading to normal relations." In order to give Khatami something more than eased visa restrictions, Clinton provided the next best thing to a public acknowledgment that Iran really did have legitimate grievances against the United States for its past behavior. It was in the middle of this process that the United States received evidence that Iran had masterminded the Khobar Towers atrocity, but rather than a belated retaliation, a message was sent through Oman that the United States now had the evidence, but, as Khatami had not then been in office, there would be no direct action; but Washington did expect perpetrators to be put on trial or extradited to Saudi Arabia.

Khatami moved to ease social and political restrictions, but he made little impact on economic policy and never gained control of security forces. In July 1998, a test of the Shahab missile demonstrated that there had been no letup in attempts to develop a strategic weapons capability. By late 1998, hard-liners were harassing, often violently, newspapers and politicians associated with reform. Ayatollah Khamenei complained about "creeping excesses." Allies of Khatami lost their posts and some were imprisoned.

Speaking to the UN General Assembly in 2000, Khatami urged a "dialogue among civilizations." His rhetoric, however, was already becoming more careful, and therefore more typical of previous Iranian pronouncements on Israel and the United States. At a press conference, he rejected government-to-government talks and complained about all the measures still in place, from the economic embargo, to the opposition to the oil pipeline from the Caspian Sea traveling through Iran, to hostile broadcasts from U.S.-sponsored radio stations. The only real concession was to appear to lift the fatwa against Rushdie, declaring the issue "completely finished." This in itself led to further attacks from his critics in Iran. The conservatives' tactics led to street demonstrations by the reformers. At this point, Khatami took fright. He was not ready to lead a counterrevolution and was fearful of the consequences of full-scale violence if the matter were left to the Revolutionary Guards to sort out. Khatami denounced the "rabble rousers," and the security forces moved in to break up the demonstrations. Although the reformers remained a political force, for example winning the 2000 Majlis elections, the hard-liners had the power, knowing that Khatami would not challenge them on the streets.

The Clinton administration continued to explore the possibility of a rapprochement and offered to move from containment to engagement. On March 17, 2000, Albright spoke to the Iranian-American Council and offered both an apology for the 1953 Mossadegh coup and dialogue with the United States with no preconditions. From the Iranian perspective, there was a curiosity in a speech which began with an apology for interfering in Iran's internal affairs and then continued with the tradition by complaining about how the "military, judiciary, courts, police remain in unelected hands."[40] After a number of positive responses, Khamenei stepped in to suppress the initiative with some dismissive comments. Indyk observed that the Iranian response had been to say, "be patient; we can't do it now, whatever." This meant that the United States had little choice but to continue with containment. Indyk concluded, "But, whereas what we're saying is on the Iraqi side it's containment plus regime change, we're saying on the Iranian side it's containment until they are ready for engagement."[41]

"Dual containment" put together two states that were similar only in their names and had recently been at war. Each required quite different policy responses, and these would differ from the containment policy pursued against the Soviet Union. One feature of that policy combined deep antagonism with regular communication, facilitating crisis management, avoiding unnecessary upset, and, over time, identifying shared interests (most notably preventing nuclear war). In addition, so long as the Communist Party maintained its tight grip on internal affairs, there was no question that the Soviet side could abide by any undertakings. Containment was therefore the means by which the United States could work out the terms of mutual restraint with its fellow superpower.

In the case of both Iran and Iraq communication was lacking. Without the normal forms of diplomatic intercourse there was no way to regulate, let alone move beyond, the antagonism. With Saddam no accommodation was likely. Containment here was a form of constant pressure to impose restraint on Iraq. With Iran, communication might have helped, although its competing power centers and independent militias made it hard to move to any political agreements and then ensure that they stuck. Containment during the cold war was geared to the long term; the Soviet collapse was unexpected. This dramatic and welcome event allowed the unrealistic inference to be drawn that if the United States contained Iran and Iraq for long enough, these enemies would follow the Soviet model and implode, to be replaced by more amenable regimes.

RETURN TO CAMP DAVID

THE AREA WHERE CLINTON made a real effort to move matters to a resolution was the Arab-Israeli dispute. As with Carter, some of the most dramatic moments of his presidency came as he brought antagonists to the presidential retreat at Camp David. The summit of July 2000 was as fateful as that of September 1978. It was also a turning point in contemporary Middle Eastern history, but this time in a wholly negative way. After this point, everything got worse.

The summit was called by Clinton as a means of reaching an agreement on the "final status" of the Palestinian territories, something that the Palestinian leader, Yasser Arafat, had long been demanding and the relatively new Israeli leader, Ehud Barak, believed to be desirable. Why this effort failed is the subject of vigorous controversy.[1] The immediate Israeli view, confirmed by the Americans, was that when it came to the crunch Arafat could not bring himself to grasp a deal that was as good as any he could have expected before or since. Regular references were made to the quip of Abba Eban, Israel's former foreign minister, to the effect that the Palestinians never miss an opportunity to miss an opportunity. A much more nuanced view of events has emerged since, recognizing that Barak may have missed an opportunity but also that neither the buildup to nor the timing of the summit was particularly propitious. The controversy arises because in this arena more than most, the narratives of the past became crucial to the politics of the present as a way of addressing whether the Israelis or Palestinians were truly interested in peace and whether the Americans really acted as honest brokers or effectively as agents of the Israelis. These narratives could appear as cynical mythmaking, designed for propaganda purposes, but to the extent they were believed, they influenced not only the blame game but also contemporary policymaking.

The experience of the 1990s demonstrated that there was no sure way to peacemaking in the Middle East. In 1991, in the context of Secretary Baker's efforts to get to the Madrid Conference, the U.S. Institute of Peace published the results of a study group, including a couple of the eventual Camp David negotiators, entitled "Making Peace Among Arabs and Israelis: Lessons from Fifty Years of Negotiating Experience." The report stressed the importance of timing and the vital role of mediators, with the United States "the essential third party." To play this mediating role successfully required "tedious, prolonged renegotiation," narrowing the agenda to keep it manageable, while reducing political risks and developing an outline of the eventual agreement. The president would have to be involved and deal directly with the leaders. Little could be achieved at the foreign minister level. The report drew attention to the ease with which verbal compromises could evaporate, the need to avoid public surprises when a new U.S. proposal was introduced, and for perseverance and continuity once mediation began. American leverage, the report suggested, only made itself felt when the process was advanced and a final agreement was in reach. During the prenegotiation phase it was easier for parties to walk away. Another recommendation was to deal with the government in power in Israel as the responsible decisionmaker and not to get involved in Israeli politics. It was best to work on the basis of established guidelines, such as UN resolutions, rather than try to establish everything anew, and to avoid public rejection of any ideas, as you never know when they might become useful again.[2] The events of the 1990s confirmed that these lessons were both wise and easily ignored. Policy choices tended to present themselves at inopportune moments in a suboptimal form.

☆   ☆   ☆

The trail that led to Camp David began with secret and direct talks between Israelis and Palestinians in Oslo, with support provided by the Norwegian government. For both sides, the Scandinavian setting allowed issues to be explored away from publicity, domestic constraints, and the uncertainties of American politics at a time of transition to a new administration.[3] It all began with a private initiative on the Israeli side, masterminded by a junior minister, Yossi Beilin, a protégé of Foreign Minister Shimon Peres. In May

1993, in order to assuage Palestinian concerns that informal talks were being used to test their flexibility, Israeli officials attended. Prime Minister Rabin was skeptical, and therefore initially content for the dialogue to be associated with his rival Peres in case they failed. He took it on as the other peace track, with Syria, seemed stalled. The initiative developed an approach based on a progressive handover of the territories to the Palestinians. The Americans were aware of this, but they were only formally contacted late in the process and then asked to endorse the effort. There were obvious flaws, but Clinton had little choice but to embrace the Oslo Accords as his own. He spent the rest of his presidency trying to make them work. The fact that the two sides had engaged in direct discussion and reached agreement on a process was a remarkable breakthrough, given all that had gone before. This was also an optimistic time. The international climate was unusually benign, with both the cold war and apartheid in South Africa at an end. That one of the most persistent and corrosive international disputes was also coming to a reasonable conclusion seemed almost too good to be true, which it was.

On September 13, 1993, Rabin managed, with evident distaste, to shake Arafat's hand at a ceremony on the White House Lawn, to sign the Declaration of Principles (the official name of the Oslo Accords) between Israel and the PLO.[4] Under the accords, Israel would begin a staged withdrawal from the West Bank and Gaza Strip, starting with Gaza and the Jericho area. A new Palestinian Interim Self-Government Authority (PA), accountable to a democratically elected council, would govern the vacated territory. It would be self-governing in terms of raising taxes and taking responsibility for health, education, and welfare, and would also have a strong police force, although Israel would continue to guard against external threats. The West Bank and Gaza would be divided into one zone (Area A) where the PA would exercise full control, another (Area B) that would combine Palestinian civil control with Israeli security control, and a third (Area C) that would be under full Israeli control, although not over Palestinian civilians. Over a five-year interim period, a permanent agreement would be negotiated that would deal with all the tricky but core matters not covered by the accords—delineation of borders and the position of Jerusalem, the rights of Palestinian refugees and Israeli settlers, and long-term security. Letters were also exchanged, by which the Israelis recognized the PLO as the legitimate representative of the Palestinian people, while the PLO recognized Israel's existence, renounced terrorism and violence, and promised not to continue to work for Israel's destruction.

The risks in the deal were evident from the start, and opponents on both sides immediately began to pick away at them. A vicious cycle driven by a loss of momentum, recrimination, and disillusion was always as possible as a virtuous cycle of growing confidence, as land was progressively swapped for peace. The Palestinians embarked on a process without any guarantees that the final outcome would provide a return to the pre-1967 borders and full statehood. Nor was there anything in the accords that actually prevented the Israelis from expanding settlement activity. This astonishing lacuna was the result of the Palestinian negotiators coming from among the exiled leadership in Tunis, with a prime objective of establishing a process in which they played a central role. In the territories, priorities were set by the continual encroachment of the settlements. "It's clear," objected Hanan Ashrawi, "that the ones who initialed this agreement have not lived under occupation."[5] There was no control over the cause of so much Palestinian discontent, and should a final agreement look possible, an incentive was created to construct even more frenetically in order to put more immovable "facts" on the ground.

This omission did little to pacify the settler movement and its allies, because the Israeli government was clearly committing itself at some point to withdrawal from the bulk of the territories, and the logic pointed to a Palestinian state and a divided Jerusalem. Moreover, they had to deal with Arafat, a man who had made a career out of denying the legitimacy of the Israeli state, using the most hateful language while encouraging murderous terrorism. To the extent he had recanted, this was not because of some visionary turn in his thinking but because unnaturally conciliatory words had been extracted from him by the Americans. It was hard to trust such a man. They would be relying on the Palestinians to help look after their security, which would involve them developing a police force. When Oslo was debated in the Knesset, Rabin barely won with 61 out of 120 votes. The critical military view, from Chief of Staff Ehud Barak, was that no territory should be handed over to Palestinian control until there was a complete settlement. He was not alone in the military in believing that it would have been better to persevere with the Syrian track.[6] Barak remained consistent in his views, even when he became prime minister six years later.

★   ★   ★

The key three players—Arafat, Rabin, and Clinton—all adopted the Oslo Accords for want of anything better. Arafat's position in 1993 was dire. None of the region's Arab leaders wholly trusted him. Because he backed Iraq's takeover of Kuwait, the Gulf monarchies were furious and withdrew funding. Saddam was so constrained that he could barely offer rhetorical support, while poor relations with Assad in Syria went back to clashes over Lebanon. Russia and the former Warsaw Pact countries were making up to

Israel. Arafat was stuck in Tunis, notionally presiding over a collection of militias that had never achieved much militarily, while Israel gradually colonized the West Bank and made inroads into Gaza. On the ground in Palestine, the PLO was being challenged by Hamas, coming from a quite separate tradition, which as a former member of the Muslim Brotherhood Arafat well understood (in his youth in Cairo). He had given Hamas a boost simply by recognizing Israel and talking to the Americans, as this risked abandoning his original constituency of dispossessed Palestinians, whose refugee status went back to the 1940s. In short, he was in a political and financial mess. Scanning the wreckage of the faded ideologies of Arab nationalism, collapsed superpowers, fragile alliances and enduring antagonisms, terrorist operations and intifadas, charters, resolutions, and summit communiqués, the only thing left to try was a direct deal with the Israelis.[7]

At least Oslo allowed Arafat to be a person of standing and consequence again and offered a point of entry into international discussions on the future of Palestine. If all went well, he would have his own state and army, if only in embryonic form. Whether he actually believed in the bargain at the heart of the accords is another matter. He wanted a state but had little grasp of what proper states required, including the importance of addressing his people's social and economic needs. The Israelis can point to post-Oslo statements that suggest he was at the very least trying to reassure constituents that he had not given up on the PLO's most ambitious goals and still looked forward one day to the full defeat of the Israelis. As always, it was never clear whether the true Arafat was revealed in the modest or the extreme guise, or indeed whether he really knew himself.

For Rabin, whose personal biography was wrapped up at every stage with the Israeli state, this was also a moment of truth. In military and economic terms, Israel was far stronger than seemed possible during the first years of fragile independence, and he was to preside over impressive rates of economic growth. As chief of staff he could claim credit for the victories of 1967 and had adhered consistently to the firm belief of the founding generation that in the face of unremitting Arab hostility, and with the memory of the Holocaust, Jews must never again allow themselves to appear weak and vulnerable. The state would survive only so long as its many enemies understood that it could not be beaten. In many respects this was now understood in the Arab world, especially with the unspoken Israeli nuclear force available for the direst emergencies.

Yet it was hard to say that Israelis felt more secure. In large part this was because Israel had overextended itself in two directions. The first was into Lebanon, where it was still bogged down in the south and trying to cope with Hezbollah. The second was into the occupied territories. When, in the 1970s, he had a chance as prime minister of a governing party rather than a fragile coalition to do something about this, Rabin had been uncertain and overcautious. This led to Likud dominating the political scene for fifteen years, during which time the situation got immeasurably worse. Instead of allowing security to be the governing principle of every move, Likud had seen the takeover of the territories as the fulfillment of a historic, sacred mission. Whereas a more sensitive approach to local Palestinian needs and respect for their rights might have made possible a relatively tranquil coexistence, especially in the light of a strong Israeli economy that offered employment and markets, the expropriation of land and the accompanying colonial attitudes and practices had created a bitter and hostile population. The intifada had come as a shock. Rabin had played his part in the crude attempt to suppress it, but the basic lesson was clear. Israel lacked the military and political capacity to annex Judea and Samaria. With the 1992 election, the dream of a Greater Israel effectively died, although the dreamers refused to accept this.

Although by Israeli standards, Labor's victory had been decisive, the country was still divided. Moshe Dayan once observed that you make peace by talking to your enemies and not your friends, but talking to Arafat would be controversial enough and making the sort of concessions he (and the Americans and Europeans) would expect would be more controversial still. In principle, the Syrian track should be easier. Although Begin had annexed the Golan Heights and there were some settlements there, this was largely a security issue. For a former soldier such as Rabin the attractions were obvious. If a return of territory could remove the other main traditional military threat, then that would be a clear security gain. A deal with Syria should help make possible a relatively graceful withdrawal from Lebanon, as well as further isolate the PLO.

Rabin certainly initially gave no hint of a developing moderate streak with regard to Palestinians. In December 1992, members of Hamas kidnapped two Israeli border policemen and demanded the release of their founder, Sheikh Yassin. When their murdered bodies were found, Rabin was furious and decided to expel 415 Hamas activists who had been rounded up after the kidnapping. He went ahead, despite being warned that this would make them heroes and was also illegal. In the process he raised Hamas's profile, put Arafat in the position of having to defend them, and then had to agree to a compromise. If Syria had made progress, he would have offered a withdrawal from Gaza as a start for the Palestinians and checked how that worked out before taking any further steps. But the Syrian track looked slow and uncertain, so he instead devoted his energies to this more far-reaching project. Rabin's approach remained cool and calculating. He never shared Peres's enthusiasm for bridging the communal divide through shared economic endeavors. He was looking for a way to disengage as painlessly and cleanly as possible.

For Clinton, Oslo hardly constituted a diplomatic triumph, for the deal was done by others. He could not, however, be churlish about a move that seemed to be so self-evidently in the right direction, and he accepted that he must now try to make it work. In this he was encouraged and supported by two men who were at the heart of the administration's policymaking and played a larger role than either of Clinton's secretaries of state. It was often noted, not least by Arabs, that both Dennis Ross and Martin Indyk were Jewish. Ross came from a nonobservant Jewish background and had made his name as a Soviet specialist, valuable during his stint as director of the State Department's Policy Planning Office under Baker. As he also knew something of Middle Eastern affairs, he worked closely with Baker on the Madrid Conference negotiations. When Clinton came to power, he recognized Ross's expertise and kept him on as his special coordinator on the Middle East. Indyk's biography is more intriguing. Born in England, he grew up in Australia. There could be no doubting his commitment to Israel. He began his American career as research director for the American Israel Public Affairs Committee (AIPAC) and then founded the Washington Institute for Near East Policy. He acquired considerable knowledge of all aspects of Middle Eastern affairs and was therefore appointed to work in the National Security Council under Clinton, quite soon becoming the first Jewish American ambassador to Israel.

Ross and Indyk are naturally held up as examples of the influence of the Israel lobby on American policy. This is the line taken by John Mearsheimer and Steve Walt.[8] The position, however, is not so simple, because it fails to locate them in the ongoing policy debates under way in both Israel and the United States. Israel's right to exist is not in contention in the United States: the issues surround the condition of Israel's existence. There was a longtime American commitment to the land-for-peace formula, and there was always going to be tension with Israel over the risks to be taken when returning land. This tension became acute after Likud came to power in 1977, and worse once the Lebanese dimension was added. The American Jewish community was unavoidably affected by these developments. Some sections were wholly sympathetic to Likud's ambitions; others felt it was their duty to defend Israel, whatever their private misgivings; while others were far more open in their anxieties and their hopes for peace. The sense of frustration bordering on disillusion is captured most effectively by Thomas Friedman's book, *From Beirut to Jerusalem*. Friedman, a friend of Ross, represented a group that combined considerable knowledge of the region, including good contacts in the Arab world, with a conviction that the security of Israel could no longer depend on military strength alone but must involve reaching out in some way to its neighbors. Although Indyk had once worked for AIPAC, he had also left it because he did not want to speak up for Likud, and when ambassador to Israel, he was so anti-Likud that he had to leave after Likud returned to power in 1996, only to return to the same job in 1999 when Labor came back. Labor was also wary of AIPAC's pro-Likud tendencies.

The important point therefore about Ross and Indyk (and Friedman in his influential columns for the *New York Times*) was not that they were Israeli agents in the American system but that they were in many respects partisans in the Israeli debate, and to an extent American agents, for they could shape American interventions. For this reason, and precisely because they were Jewish, they were considered to be particularly dangerous by Likud-niks, as their views could not be dismissed as evidence of a deep-rooted anti-Zionism. The complication this introduced into American policy was not so much one of bias but of alignment. For an American president, especially a Democrat who would want to stay close to the Jewish community but also had to think about broader foreign policy considerations and good relations with Arabs, the best hope was a Labor government in Israel that accepted the principles of land for peace. That created a stake in the political success of Labor, lest it be replaced by something worse. This meant that the administration was always less likely to put Labor under pressure than Likud, even when it was taking steps the administration thought unwise.

This had important consequences for the American role in the process. Other Arab states helped fund the Palestinians and offered unlimited verbal support but showed no inclination to put themselves out on their behalf. They ruled out going to war, and oil embargoes were a nonstarter in the prevailing market. Other than non-Arab Iran and Syria, who stirred the pot with their support for Hamas and Islamic Jihad, the Arab states largely mounted protests when the Israelis were being visibly brutish, pointing to the anger in the street, but with the main objective of getting the Americans to do something about the terrible situation. They could not expect the Americans to act as impartial, evenhanded mediators, only that they get the Israelis to show restraint and bring them to more conciliatory positions than they might reach on their own accord. This would be a sort of "tough love." There was no doubt about the sincerity of the U.S. commitment, but Israeli governments needed help to reach unpalatable positions. In practice, successive American governments had experienced the difficulties of trying to persuade and pressure Israeli governments to accept proposals that they believed to be inimical to their core interests. Now that Labor was in power, the problem was no longer fundamental disagreements of principle but the party's domestic political weakness. The question for Washington was how much to push Rabin into positions that would inflame the Israeli hawks, with the risk of the political tide turning again and having to deal with Likud.

* * *

In terms of peacemaking theory, Oslo came at a time when conditions were as ripe for an agreement as they were ever likely to be. In terms of peacemaking methodology, Oslo was in the incremental rather than the comprehensive category. Merely getting the two sides to acknowledge each other's legitimacy was a huge step. The further steps involving actually addressing the core issues that divided them could not be taken until the parties were ready. The familiar problems with gradualism soon reasserted themselves. Slow speed provides opportunities for destroying as much as constructing confidence.

The first stages were promising. On May 4, 1994, the Gaza-Jericho agreement between Rabin and Arafat was concluded, establishing the Palestinian Authority, which meant that Arafat could show an Israeli withdrawal and had territory to control. There was also a significant bonus, at least for the Israelis, in that it proved possible to sneak in the sort of Israel-Jordan treaty that had proved impossible before. King Hussein wanted this in part as a means of countering what he saw as the inevitable growth in Arafat's influence, including in Jerusalem, where he had taken responsibility for the upkeep of the al-Aqsa Mosque, but also potentially across the Jordan River into his kingdom. He could also see the economic opportunities opening up in tourism and cross-border trade. He could achieve this while the Palestinians were in no position to complain. Just after the Gaza-Jericho agreement, the king and Rabin met in secret in London without the Americans present. Once the Israelis agreed to Jordanian concerns about the delineation of the border between the two countries and water issues, and American support was obtained, largely in terms of forgiving Jordanian debt, it was possible to move swiftly to a treaty. After it was signed on October 26, 1994, Clinton addressed both the Jordanian Parliament and the Knesset. This turned out to be the most lasting achievement of the Clinton era, though much was directly negotiated between the Israelis and Jordanians.

The Palestinian-Israeli process soon ran into trouble. To the extent that Rabin and Arafat tried to control the more unruly members of their communities, neither was successful. Although the Palestinian transgressions were more deadly, the Israelis had less excuse, as they already had a proper democratic state with accountable armed forces and police. Ross suggested that Arafat let his deputies lead the complaints about the settlements as if there was a sort of deal with Rabin: "You don't push me beyond where I can go with my opponents and I won't push you beyond where you can go with your settler constituency."[9] If so, this was a huge mistake. To make progress, the opposition on both sides would at some point have to be confronted, and the longer this was delayed the harder it would become.

Arafat's political position was always compromised by rivalries and in-fighting among the various factions within the PLO. All members had their own militias, and there was no tradition of accepting political defeat grace-fully. More serious, the PLO itself, which still represented old pan-Arabism, was being challenged by Islamic Jihad and Hamas. Encouraged by Iran, these groups saw their role entirely as spoilers. The easiest way to embarrass Arafat was to attack Israeli civilians. The day before the Declaration of Principles was signed, Hamas killed three Israeli soldiers in Gaza; the day after, a suicide bomber self-exploded in an Israeli police station, also in Gaza. To the Israelis, Arafat's normal response to requests to crack down on extremists was to offer vague promises. Only when he saw his own position under threat would he get his security forces to arrest known militants. Often, after the fuss was over, those arrested would be quietly released. This left the Israelis nervous about the training and weapons being handed over to the Palestinian police. Faced with terrorist provocations, Rabin took the line that terror should not stop the pursuit of peace, and peace should not stop the fight against terror. Given the aims of the terrorists, the logical response was to refuse to allow terrorism any influence, but in practice this was difficult, for many in Israel saw this as a grisly vindication of their worst fears. With some 300 Israelis dead from ter-rorist attacks between 1993 and 1996, it was hard to claim that the peace pro-cess was a net gain in security. In addition, even while continuing to talk and avoiding crude collective punishments, fighting against terror still meant cur-fews and arrests. The terrorist activity meant that Israel demanded more on security and added where it could more checkpoints, multiplying the frustra-tions of everyday Palestinian life.

At the same time, the settler population grew by almost 50 percent in the West Bank and over 60 percent in Gaza, without apparently a worry about what this did to Palestinian perceptions of the peace process. Just as Arafat feared a Palestinian civil war, Rabin feared a Jewish civil war. The settlers were well established as a political force—far more than a renegade element whose illegality must be reversed. If anything, they challenged Rabin's legiti-macy as the leader of a Jewish state because he governed with the support of

Arab parties in the Knesset. With bitter polemics, they denounced Oslo for squashing their dreams of a Greater Israel, with rabbis joining in the denunciations of the government and easing the religious consciences of those prepared to work outside the law. The extent to which matters had gotten out of hand was demonstrated in February 1994, when one of the Hebron settlers, Baruch Goldstein, showed his anger by murdering twenty-nine Palestinians in Hebron's Ibrahami Mosque, only stopping when he was himself killed by Palestinians. As frightening as the act was, more distressing was the willingness of many hard-liners to turn Goldstein into a martyr rather than accepting Rabin's description as a "disgrace to Judaism." This was a critical moment when Rabin could have confronted the settler movement directly or at least this group of settlers, which was demanding a presence in one of the Palestinian cities. He was irritated by Arafat's use of the incident to internationalize the dispute, but most of all he was fearful of the reinforcements that the settlers might bring in if the IDF were sent in to remove them. After prolonged vacillation, and in the face of extravagant threats of civil disobedience and violence, he decided to let the settlers stay. Although Rabin had always been hostile to the settlers' movement and understood the damage they were doing, he always feared the consequences of direct confrontation. In this case his restraint was hardly appreciated, for a government even talking to Palestinians was tantamount to treason. One young man, Yigal Amir, who attended Goldstein's funeral, later told police that then it "dawned" on him that he must "put down" Rabin. As the oppositional fury gathered even more intensity, Amir shot the prime minister dead at the conclusion of a pro-peace concert in Tel Aviv in November 1995.[10]

Peres became prime minister. The nation was in shock and the right was on the defensive, indicted for inciting Rabin's murder through rhetorical excesses. Peres wanted to press forward with peace deals, and in principle he had time to do so, but he was persuaded to go for early elections in May. By the time they took place, Peres's political credit had run out. He had tried for a quick deal with Assad but, like Rabin, quickly became discouraged by the Syrian leader's tedious mode of negotiation. He had hoped that Assad would use his influence to stop Hezbollah from raining down Katyusha rockets on northern Israel from southern Lebanon. When, despite Syrian assurances, the rockets kept on coming, he launched the unfortunately named "Grapes of Wrath" operation in late March. This started well enough with precision attacks against Hezbollah offices in Beirut, but they also attacked Lebanese power plants in a futile attempt to persuade the Lebanese government to deal with the Shi'ite militia. As the fighting continued, 400,000 Lebanese fled their homes. When the IDF saw Katyushas being launched from a UN refugee camp at Qana, the Israelis fired artillery shells, avoiding the Hezbol-lah gunners and hitting instead the refugees, killing 102 innocent people. Peres was forced to make a hasty retreat, resulting in an operation appearing to be a complete failure.

What most undermined him, turning a commanding lead in the polls into electoral defeat, was a deadly campaign by Hamas, using suicide bombers against busloads of Israeli civilians, with fifty-eight killed in four attacks over nine days. This was in retaliation for the assassination of a Hamas leader, Yehya Ayyash, known as "The Engineer," who had been re-sponsible for many terrorist episodes. The extent of the retaliation suggests that Hamas was content to see Likud return to power. Polarization suited it, and would further undermine Arafat. Islamic Jihad was headquartered in Damascus and taking credit for the attacks. Not a word from Syria regretting or condemning the bombings suggested that the Syrians had no strategy for reaching out to Israel. Clinton tried, rather blatantly, to intercede on Peres's behalf, with a variety of joint activities, including a conference with Arab leaders at Sharm el-Sheikh to denounce terrorism. Peres added to his diffi-culties by fighting an ill-judged campaign. Likud just managed to get enough votes to squeeze back into power.

*   *   *

As Likud's leader, Benjamin "Bibi" Netanyahu was quite unlike his predeces-sors. Begin and Shamir were products of the dark days of the 1940s and were tough and dogmatic. Netanyahu was too young to have pioneering creden-tials and was the brother of a war hero rather than being one himself. He had spent time in the United States, and his fluency in English had proved very effective when pleading his country's case during the 1991 war. Ne-tanyahu's evident intelligence and apparent pragmatism went together with a sly and slippery reputation. His judgment was often questionable—for ex-ample, jeopardizing the treaty with Jordan by authorizing a failed attempt to assassinate a Hamas leader in broad daylight in Amman.

Given Clinton's evident bias toward Labor, relations were bound to be poor. Netanyahu followed through the logic by developing close relations with Clinton's opponents in the United States. To the extent he had a vision, it was influenced by the developing ideas of an unavoidable civilizational conflict between Islam and the West, in which Israel had a special role as a frontline state and an outpost of democracy. These were very similar to the ideas being developed by neoconservative groups in the United States at the time. This link was made more explicit after the election, when a right-wing Jerusalem-based think tank commissioned a report through its Washington office, apparently at Netanyahu's request, chaired by Richard Perle and including a number of neocon luminaries. This report advocated a clean break with the socialism of the Labor Party and also with the Oslo process, along with more aggressive policies toward both Syria and Iraq. The report appeared more significant later on, when some of the study group members gained posts in George W. Bush's administration, and was taken as an indication of what they had been plotting. The real significance lay in the developing convergence of views between an ascendant political tendency in the United States and Likud, in contrast to the convergence between more centrist U.S. views and Labor:

> In recent years, Israel invited active U.S. intervention in Israel's domestic and foreign policy for two reasons: to overcome domestic opposition to "land for peace" concessions the Israeli public could not digest, and to lure Arabs—through money, forgiveness of past sins, and access to U.S. weapons—to negotiate. This strategy, which required funneling American money to repressive and aggressive regimes, was risky, expensive, and very costly for both the U.S. and Israel, and placed the United States in roles it should neither have nor want.[11]

Netanyahu was tempted on occasion by his right-wing friends to test his support in Congress against the president's, but in the end he realized the dangers of siding openly with a president's political opponents.

Similarly, on the American side there were real doubts as to whether it was possible to work with Netanyahu. He had campaigned openly against Oslo, and Albright and Berger were of the view that he wanted to destroy the process, despite the president's evident commitment to its success. When he visited Washington, he was "insufferable," lecturing the president about how to deal with the Arabs. Yet, argued Ross, it would be a mistake to shun him. His problem was not that he had a dangerous grand design but that he lacked any design and tended to use his intelligence to get himself out of scrapes. "I had no illusions about Bibi, but also believed we could not wish Bibi away. He was Israel's Prime Minister for two years and [we] could not shun him unless prepared to do so indefinitely."[12]

Netanyahu's basic problem was that he did not know how to provide security for Israel without concessions to the Palestinians. For example, in July 1997, he gave an interview on Israeli TV, declaring the end of "the game of tipping the wink to Hamas and to Islamic Jihad and telling them they may go ahead and blow up buses in Israeli cities." They will no longer "get off scot-free. That is why the Palestinians have taken measures to restrain them."

Two days later, on July 30, twin suicide bombings in a Jerusalem market killed sixteen and wounded 178.[13] When such incidents occurred, Netanyahu tended to use them to deflect and delay American pressure to agree to proposals that would involve some concessions on his part.

The first signs of the potential dangers of an uncompromising stance to the Palestinians came when his government decided in September 1996 to open up an archeological site under the Dome of the Rock. This led to Palestinian rioting, with fifteen Israelis and seventy-five Palestinians killed, and ominously, at one point the Palestinian police sided with the rioters. Although the Americans superficially kept the process on track by patching together deals and keeping the parties in conversation, the effort was being drained of credibility. In Hebron, Netanyahu instinctively supported a militant band of settlers determined to prevent any concessions to the Palestinians, and the eventual compromise symbolized the unequal power relationships in the territories. Four hundred and fifty settlers held 20 percent of a city of 140,000. Then Netanyahu refused to abandon settlements close to East Jerusalem, continuing with housing demolitions and land expropriation. In October 1998, after considerable pressure, Clinton got Netanyahu and Arafat together at the Wye Plantation in Maryland to agree on how to implement the previous interim agreement of 1995, which was in itself a renegotiation of what had been anticipated in Oslo. Under the Wye River Memorandum, Israel would relinquish 13 percent of the West Bank, release 750 prisoners, allow for the operation of Gaza's air- and seaports, and create a corridor between the West Bank and Gaza. In return, the Palestinian Authority was to take concrete measures to reduce terrorism, collect illegal weapons, and reduce the size of Palestinian police. In addition, Arafat would reaffirm the letter of January 13, 1998, to nullify all provisions of the Palestinian Covenant inconsistent with commitments to live in peace with Israelis.

In December 1998, Clinton even went to Gaza. Read retrospectively, an edge of desperate pleading comes through in his speech. He asked the Palestinians about the peace they wanted—"grudging and mean-spirited and confining" or else "generous and open." He asked how they would wish to be judged and view each other's children. "Will they feel your pain and will you understand theirs?" "Surely to goodness," he concluded, "after five years of this peace process, and decades of suffering, and after you have come here today and done what you have done, we can say, enough of this gnashing of teeth, let us join hands and proudly go forward together."[14]

Likud received the same message. Netanyahu disliked the process but dared not abandon it if this meant a public break with the Americans. His discomfort was evident, as the right accused him of dangerous concessions and the left complained about his lack of commitment to peace. His political base shrank, and in January 1999, his government collapsed.

★   ★   ★

For the 1999 election, the Labor Party chose Ehud Barak, and so did Clinton. Barak recruited Clinton's advisers, including his pollster, Stanley Greenberg, and many of his campaigning techniques. He was projected as a soldier statesman in the Rabin mold. In some ways he was Rabin plus. The country's most decorated soldier, who had engaged in brave special missions, was an accomplished musician and known for his brilliant mind. He also had immediate credit in the Clinton administration simply as a result of not being Netanyahu and having campaigned successfully on a peace platform. He was in a hurry and set out an ambitious agenda involving withdrawal from Lebanon, a peace treaty with Syria, and a final status agreement with the PLO. It was hard to disapprove of such ambition.

Unfortunately, Barak was not a natural politician and lacked the ability to empathize with the problems of other politicians. Charm, courtesy, and respect were not weapons in his diplomatic armory. Even when he was being relatively generous, he tended to make offers on a take-it-or-leave-it basis. Clinton's description fits those of others. Although brilliant and brave,

> he had a hard time listening to people who didn't see things the way he did, and his way of doing things was diametrically opposed to honored customs among the Arabs with whom I'd dealt. Barak wanted others to wait until he decided the time was right, then, when he made his best offer, he expected it to be accepted as self-evidently a good deal. His negotiating partners wanted trust-building courtesies and conversations and lots of bargaining.[15]

With a comfortable majority, this lack of political aptitude might not have mattered too much, but his victory was narrow, and for a general, he was unnaturally anxious about the opposition. He did not want to be seen to be relying on Arab votes in the Knesset, which made the postelection horse trading even more difficult and left him with a government dependent upon seven parties, two of them religious, for its survival.

The debate in Israel was deeply polarized. Israelis needed to be convinced that they were no longer to be treated as an aberration. They wanted Palestinians to stop dwelling on victimhood and claims of heroic resistance, and to recognize their own contribution to their tragic circumstances. If they did not, how could Israel be sure that after a deal, the Palestinians would not revert to their old ways? But at the same time there were other grounds for fear, a lack of conviction that military strength alone was the key, or that a large, angry Palestinian population could be suppressed indefinitely, and embarrassment at trying to excuse human rights abuses and the harsh treatment meted out in the occupied territories. Barak knew that concessions were needed but he wanted to avoid early agitation of the hawks. So after all the hopes invested in his election by the Americans, and for that matter the Palestinians, Barak's first speech was entirely negative, setting out his red lines—on Jerusalem and the return of Palestinian refugees. To some extent this was tactics, and the Americans decided to treat it as such, but it alarmed the Palestinians without mollifying Israel's hard-liners.

This political tentativeness, which might have encouraged gradualism, was combined with rejection of an incremental approach. A succession of modest concessions with a short half-life led to constant bickering over the meaning of words and whether promises had truly been implemented. A proper negotiation, he believed, would conclude with a definitive agreement and the peacemakers' work would be done. Rather than have a series of disputes over small measures, each raising the same issues of principle, better to have one major fight over a suitably substantial deal and then declare the process over and the conflict at an end. His tight coalition could not survive too many debates about the direction of an incomplete peace process. He judged Oslo to have been misguided because it lacked any sense of an end point. Rather than moving forward tentatively from the position as he found it, Barak preferred to agree on the conclusion and work backward.

Barak never quite found the tactics to match his strategy. He knew where he wanted to get to but did not know how to adjust his vision to the needs of his negotiating partners. It was almost as if he wanted to make peace by stealth, in the hope that his opponents at home would not notice exactly what he was up to until he could present them with the fait accompli, bound to be embraced by the majority of the population. But as Barak had made no secret of his intentions, the opposition was never likely to go easy on him. He was subject to the same level of vituperation as Rabin had been. His imminent betrayals were regularly denounced. Rather than deal with this by shoring up his political base and negotiating with urgency while he had the chance, this political storm led him to hesitate and backtrack at critical moments. Like Rabin, he tried to calm the opposition by allowing new settlement activity, justifying it on the grounds that what he had permitted would never happen, because before settlement construction could begin, a peace settlement would stop it. Such tactics impressed nobody. The settlers remained suspicious but pressed ahead, while the Palestinians became more disillusioned.

★   ★   ★

As with Rabin, he wanted to get a deal with Syria before moving on to Palestine. The dispute over the Golan Heights was conceptually simpler. Although Assad was a harder nut to crack, he was in complete political control. As with Rabin's efforts, Barak's negotiations faltered on the basis of what seemed to be a comparatively trivial strip of land. There was no agreed June 4, 1967, boundary, although there was a reasonable approximation. There were other available boundary lines, including the international line agreed to in 1923. Assad wanted the more recent one. It gave him an extra 7 square miles and, more important, an actual physical connection to the Sea of Galilee. Without this connection, he could not accept that he had recovered his land. Israelis felt uncomfortable with the Syrians on the edge of their inland lake.[16]

As soon as Rabin returned to power in 1992, he signaled his readiness to do a deal by accepting, unlike Shamir, that Resolution 242 applied to the Golan Heights, and publicly linking the "depth of withdrawal to the depth of peace." The Israelis had been aware of a Syrian option since 1992, when the possibility of a deal was raised, via James Baker, after Rabin had been elected. Rabin demonstrated his interest in the matter by putting Itamar Rabinovich, a leading academic specialist on Syria, in charge of any talks. With Clinton in power, this track moved along. Rabin wanted normal relations, including an exchange of ambassadors, some understanding on trade and tourism, security measures, of which the most important was an early warning station on the Golan, and no linkage with any other disputes. Assad acknowledged the importance of Rabin's offer but was soon fussing over details. In August, Christopher was to go to Damascus to explore Assad's willingness to deal. He would want to know how far Rabin would go. Rabin was ready to accept full withdrawal, without specifying quite what this meant. At any rate, he wanted Christopher to keep this in his "pocket" so that it could be revealed only as Syria offered reasonable terms in exchange. He did not want Assad to "pocket" it before offering anything in return or for news of this concession to leak and lead to a political fuss back home. Unfortunately, Christopher not only revealed the existence of the "pocket" but also failed to appreciate the importance of the nuance over 1923 versus 1967. Assad now believed he had full withdrawal in his "pocket" and insisted that must be the starting point for future negotiations. Rabin was furious, and with the Palestinian option now available, decided to work on that instead.

When Peres came into office, he decided to make a push for peace with Syria, but again he found the pace of negotiation frustrating. He tried for a summit with Assad, but the Syrian leader was wary. Rabin and Assad at least agreed that they did not want to become friends, but just coexist without war. Peres's more expansive talk of closer economic ties to Assad threatened too much Israeli influence in Syrian affairs. If a breakthrough was imminent, Peres might have been less tempted by the opinion polls into an early election. Netanyahu did not ignore the Syrian track, and used Ron Lauder, an American businessman, to act as an intermediary rather than Clinton. He found some flexibility in Assad's position, but any deal was thwarted because of Sharon's objections.

Aware of Lauder's belief that there was some give on the Syrian side, Barak decided to investigate whether he could bring these spasmodic negotiations to a successful conclusion. This was based on a suggestion from Lauder that Assad was prepared for a withdrawal to the 1923 rather than the 1967 line, and an Israeli early warning station. This was not, however, based on Assad's preferred draft, in which he accepted neither. Going forward on the basis of what turned out to be a misapprehension, and against the urgings of his advisers, Barak decided to speak positively and openly about Syria while keeping the Palestinians waiting. By now, Assad was ailing and seemed more bothered about the legacy he would leave his son. The son he had groomed for succession, Basil, had been killed in a car accident in 1994. The second son, Bashar, was now preparing for a role he had never expected to take. A man famous for his patience now sensed the end of time. The Syrians seemed responsive, ready to explore compromises. There was talk of a shift from a conflict that was now territorial rather than existential, and being transformed from one of "struggle to competition."[17]

Barak saw the opportunity but was not quite sure how to take it. He had a tactical fixation with keeping his concessions in reserve, in this case confirmation of the "pocket." Avoiding early commitment, he hoped, would deflect opponents while softening up the target to be more receptive to the final package. Though these tactics rarely worked, Barak refused to allow talks to get going on the border question. He wanted to keep this for his own direct negotiations with Assad.

Clinton, a master tactician, understood these flaws but, nostalgic for Rabin and frustrated by Netanyahu, he was anxious for Barak to succeed. This meant that he kept on giving Barak the benefit of the doubt and was prepared to make allowances for his odd behavior. After what had happened to Rabin, it was hard to blame the prime minister for being cautious in the face of a vituperative opposition, but Clinton took this to mean the best option would be not pushing him to go further than local politics would bear, rather than applying the pressure in favor of American proposals that would make it easier for Barak to shift the blame. It was standard for Israeli prime ministers to ask the United States to try out positions on their behalf. This could be frustrating for the Americans, when they believed that the proposals were insufficient or would benefit from a different emphasis. It was even more frustrating, as kept on happening with Barak, when the Israelis suddenly concluded that their own suggestions went too far. Clinton kept on putting his prestige on the line for little reward.

Direct talks were arranged for the start of 2000 at Shepherdstown, West Virginia, hosted by the president. All the advance publicity suggested that they would succeed. Although Assad knew that Barak had yet to make a commitment and must have been aware that the Israelis expected the detail to be a matter of negotiation, he was still expecting the 1967 line to be endorsed. In essence this is what the Americans and Barak were also expecting. At this point, Barak lost his nerve. It was relevant that his three predecessors had each explored a deal with Syria and each concluded that Assad's quid pro quo for the return of the Golan Heights was vague and insufficient. The military was also cautious and this shift in elite opinion, reflected in newspaper columns and Knesset speeches, turned public opinion. Perhaps also reflecting the influence of American politics on Israeli, Barak was a great consumer of opinion polls and the conclusions of focus groups. Polls from the preceding weeks had told him that Israelis thought he was going too fast with Syria, were worried about Syrian control of the northeastern shore of the Sea of Galilee, especially when so little was being offered in return, and felt that he was not bargaining hard enough. He was warned explicitly by his American pollster, Stanley Greenberg, that he lacked majority support and that the "public wants to see tough, cautious negotiations in connection with such critical issues."[18]

Musing on all this en route to Washington, Barak's first comment to Indyk when he got off the plane was "I can't do it." He was desperate not to show weakness. At the very least he had to put on a show of being tough and difficult. Barak, looking over his shoulder, told Clinton that he "needed the appearance of a fight, he needs to have this dragged out longer."[19] The appearance of a fight was helped by a tough speech from the Syrian foreign minister, which was hardly conciliatory. Both Clinton and Albright use the term "slow walk" when describing Barak's approach.[20] In practice he did not walk at all, leaving the Americans angry at having made a great effort themselves when the prime minister made none at all. The longer he did nothing, somehow the more he could claim to have fought, but it left the president occupied with his other guests while they fumed. Albright was particularly forthright. According to one account, she yelled at Barak, "You humiliated us, you humiliated our President. You wasted our time. The President of the United States and all his staff sat here hour after hour and you said nothing. What are we going to say to Assad? Only you will be responsible if these negotiations become ruined."[21] "To put it mildly," said Clinton in his memoirs, "I was disappointed."[22]

Barak concluded after the fiasco of Shepherdstown that he must work to change Israeli opinion, letting it be known how far his predecessors had been prepared to go on the withdrawal line. But Assad, in increasingly poor health, was angry at the turn of events, and angrier still when an Israeli paper reported the details of the draft treaty with the language on the border bracketed as undecided. Despite this, Clinton again agreed to entreaties from Barak to have another go. Once again his advisers were dubious, but Clinton hoped that if Barak really could bring himself to offer full withdrawal, a deal might still be done. Barak vetoed a proposal that Albright travel first to Damascus. Part of his theory of negotiations was that Arab leaders would only draw back from long-held positions as they realized that they had just been offered the best offer they would ever get, even if it fell short of their past demands. He did not believe in prior negotiations on the most challenging issues. Yet Clinton had used the Saudi ambassador, Prince Bandar, as an intermediary, and Assad gained the impression that he was going to get exactly what he wanted.

"You will hear what you expect to hear," Clinton told Assad, seeking to persuade him to listen to the latest Israel proposals. And so the weary and wary Syrian leader made his way to Geneva, where he met with Clinton on March 26, 2000. It seems improbable that a man so ill would have made the effort if all he intended to do was deliver a negative judgment on the process. He was prepared to negotiate, but only after hearing that Israel would withdraw to the 1967 border. When he heard something different, he could not be bothered to continue. Barak, as before, had asked Clinton to convey a nuanced position that gave Assad his 1967 border, with adjustments that would have the effect of keeping the Syrians away from the shoreline. The formula was to offer Assad a "commonly agreed border," based upon the June 4, 1967, line. But it was not so well based that it made any sense when shown to Assad on a map. If anything, it was worse than the 1923 line.

Assad concluded that Barak "doesn't want peace." The fact that he did not bother to continue negotiating has been criticized as suggesting that he was the one who did not want peace. A better explanation is, as Clinton put it, that the Syrians had "been burned once by being flexible and forthcoming, and they weren't about to make the same mistake again."[23] Assad's goodwill, always a commodity in short supply, had been exhausted at Shepherdstown. He wanted peace, but he no longer believed in the process. Barak also wanted peace but had an exaggerated belief that he could design a process that could cause Assad to budge from a position on which he had been both consistent and rigid. On June 10, 2000, Assad died. His son Bashar stepped into his place, but it would take time before he could establish his authority to do any deal, let alone one that went beyond what his father had been prepared to accept. For the Americans and Israelis, the Syrian track died with him.

When he was trying again to cope with Barak's theories of negotiation at Camp David in July, Clinton reportedly told the prime minister, "I went to Geneva and felt like a wooden Indian doing your bidding."[24] But there was no need for Clinton to do Barak's bidding. He could have said that the exercise was pointless or else insisted that it be left to him to work out a package with Assad. If Barak wanted to show that he had fought the good diplomatic fight, then it was not going to help if he still succumbed to Syrian demands. Better that he succumb to American pressure, although of course, given the attacks Clinton faced at home from Republicans for consorting with tyrants who were hostile to the United States, he also did not want to appear to be coming down hard on Barak. The other problem was that Clinton, who was undoubtedly persuasive, believed that he could talk his way through most problems and so would always rather be engaged and in conversation than keeping a distance and refusing to talk. After Shepherdstown, he could have avoided the ignominy of a pointless confrontation with Assad by insisting on Barak's being explicit on the June 1967 line. If Barak did not feel he could count on domestic support, then it would have been better to have waited until he could.

*   *   *

What is even more surprising is that given this experience, Clinton announced on July 5, 2000, that a summit meeting involving Israeli and Palestinian teams would convene on July 11 at Camp David. This was the last moment in his presidency to conclude a process that had begun with such promise in his first year in office and which, in the absence of any further American intervention, could go badly wrong. If nothing was done, then it could be another year before a new administration would be in a position to engage with the process. Moreover, Barak was pressing hard for the effort, and however disappointing his performance over Syria, it was hard to turn down a man who claimed to be prepared to make concessions for peace.

Clinton's own stock of political capital was pretty low by this time, but at least he did not have to worry about reelection (although he was concerned about his wife's first election as a New York senator). He knew that he was embarking on a gamble that might make things worse, but the alternative was a virtual certainty that the situation would further deteriorate.

Clinton's main challenge was to persuade Arafat to attend. Everything since Oslo had been a disappointment to the Palestinian leader. He was being asked to move to a "final status" agreement, which is something he wanted, but previous "interim" agreements had been ignored. Every time there was a change of government, there was a demand to start again as if previous agreements had no standing because they had been negotiated by someone else and did not deserve implementation. So Barak had not redeployed troops out of the West Bank, handed over to the Palestinian Authority three villages close to Jerusalem, or released prisoners. With economic conditions poor and the occupation as intrusive as ever, Arafat was finding it progressively harder to convince his people that the effort was worthwhile. Meanwhile, the settlements had expanded, with a great rush under Netanyahu, so numbers had grown to over 250,000. The problem was not only the amount of land taken but its quality and the network of Israeli-only roads that crisscrossed the territory. Although Barak opposed "wildcat" settlements that lacked political authority, by the end of December 1999, well over 3,000 invitations to tender for settlement construction had been issued, and the number of settlers was growing even faster than under Netanyahu.

Then there was Lebanon. An important consequence of the failure to get a deal on Syria was that it undermined Barak's attempt to get a negotiated exit from southern Lebanon. He intended to leave anyway, but if this were done unilaterally, without any quid pro quo from Hezbollah, then it would encourage militants who could point to Israel's vulnerability to the continuing pressure to which Israeli troops had been subjected. Northern Israel would also be left at risk from cross-border attacks, which is why the IDF had entered Lebanon in the first place. Despite the concerns of the IDF, which had worked to prevent Netanyahu from trying something similar, Barak pressed ahead. Although the withdrawal on the night of May 22–23 was efficient and involved no casualties, Hezbollah claimed this as a great success for its armed struggle. The obvious conclusion was that the Israelis were vulnerable to persistent military pressure. Arafat had assumed from the start that Barak's giving Syria the highest priority had been intended to undermine him. It also meant that valuable time had been lost. Now it was humiliating to watch Hezbollah's gun-waving militants cheer the Israelis out of their territory, while he had spent years in fruitless negotiations. His militants wanted to follow Hezbollah's example.

Moreover, discussions thus far with Israel had been restricted and desultory. There was no prepared package ready to unveil at Camp David, leaving only a few outstanding issues to be addressed at the summit. If the Americans really wanted success, then they should insist on more preparatory work. When the Syria negotiations had been going on, it had been "slow-slow," Arafat complained to Albright, and "now you are rush-rush."²⁵ Arafat told his team, "We're going to face a disaster. We are being set up. . . . They want to take us for a summit so they can blame us."²⁶ In the end, he went along because he had little choice. Albright explained forcefully that the president was not going to spend his final months on another interim accord. He was never going to get a president as sympathetic again, and Barak was sincere in his readiness to make peace. In June, when Arafat visited Clinton, he expressed exasperation with Barak for not implementing any of the interim agreements. He saw no reason why the Palestinians should accept any of this: "I think Barak has decided to put us in the position of the guilty party, and I need your promise that wherever we go with the negotiations, you won't shift the blame for failure on to us and won't back us into a corner." "I promise you," Clinton replied, "that under no circumstances will I place the blame for failure on you."²⁷ But whatever Clinton said prior to the summit, the commentary afterward was bound to be based on how the parties had behaved. Arafat went to the summit with low expectations, little preparation, and no particular endgame. If anything, he wanted to prevent the summit from becoming what both Clinton and Barak seemed to think it was bound to be—a make-it-or-break-it situation for the whole process.

There is no evidence that Barak was not genuine in his pursuit of a peace deal or that he was not prepared to offer major concessions to get one. It would have been pointless for Barak to go to Camp David just to demonstrate Arafat's bad faith, because with the Americans there and committed to the process, there was always a risk that Arafat might actually accept what was on the table. The problems came with Barak's strategy rather than his sincerity. As his foreign minister, Shlomo Ben-Ami, put it: "He expected his interlocutors to fall in with his wishes, according to the scenario that he had prepared for himself and for them, and when this did not happen he tended to lose his composure, to entrench himself in his positions, thus, in effect, helping to block the dynamics of negotiation."²⁸ This was as true with Arafat as it had been with Assad.

Barak's approach was shaped by essentially correct assessments of the political positions of the three players. He could not but be aware that his own position was fragile. Just before the summit, he lost a vote of confidence in the Knesset, although not sufficiently to force him out of office. A summit was the only way he could get a deal without being cut off by the opposition, but an expansive show of goodwill to the Palestinians would leave him even weaker. Any deal he could sell was going to have to emerge, and be seen to have emerged, from tough bargaining. For all these reasons, an incomplete conclusion that revealed how far he was prepared to go without anything confirmed in return would be the worst outcome for him.

As for Clinton, Barak assumed that this was the last moment he could exercise real influence over the future course of the Middle East, just before the nominating conventions signaled the formal start of the presidential election campaign. With regard to Arafat, he was least sure. Like most Israelis, he did not have high regard for the Palestinian leader. Whether or not his slipperiness was due to a defect of character or the complexity of Palestinian politics, the question was whether he could ever commit to a definitive deal that would settle the issue once and for all. In this respect, he saw Camp David as above all a test for Arafat. If he rose to the challenge, then Barak was prepared to be generous, but if he did not, then the only conclusion was that there was no point in pretending any longer that he could deliver. For Barak, therefore, the task of Camp David was to set a test for Arafat without, at least in the first instance, setting too severe a test for himself. This required him to keep control of the process, in particular avoiding a situation whereby the Americans, anxious to secure a deal, put him on the spot and let Arafat off the hook. His tactics were therefore to avoid substantive negotiations prior to the summit because that would detract from the psychology of the encounter he was planning, and to take a tough and sullen stance at the summit, only allowing concessions to be extracted from the Israeli side as and when they became necessary to keep the process going and to ensure that Arafat faced a proper test. Arafat must therefore be persuaded that what was on offer was the best that he could possibly expect and that he should grasp it while he had the chance.

Clinton had enough experience with Barak's idiosyncratic approach to negotiations to assume that the Israeli prime minister would not open proceedings with attractive proposals and lively conversation. He was also well aware of Arafat's anxieties and that Palestinian attitudes had become angrier and more militant. Whatever the promises made to Arafat about blame, Clinton was always going to be more attentive to Barak's political position. They shared pollsters, so he was well informed about the pressures Barak faced. One example of this was his readiness to accept Barak's argument that a certain amount of settlement activity was a necessary price to keep the Israelis in the process, because when the eventual "final status" agreement was signed, the settlements would go anyway.

As neither side was in a fit state to make bold gestures on its own, the American management of the summit would be crucial. Clinton was in no doubt of the importance of his personal role, and he prepared extensively by absorbing detailed briefs on the history of the conflict and attempts to negotiate an outcome. He had a good legal mind and enormous persuasive ability. But he was also wary of trying to impose an American plan on the parties. Politically, this was always a risky step because if he pushed too hard, especially on the Israelis, the reverberations would be felt back home. But it was also because he saw his job as finding and building on points of agreement, encouraging each side to meet the other's concerns, rather than insisting on an American plan. This meant that Clinton was unable to create any sense of irresistible pressure. According to Ben-Ami:

> Clinton had an extraordinary capacity to untie diplomatic knots; he uniquely combined the vision of the statesman with the skills of a negotiator capable of mastering the most minute details. Brilliant, passionate, humane and hardworking, proverbially patient, tolerant and good-humored, always shunning confrontation with his days at the White House numbered, Clinton was not a president who was capable of browbeating opponents.[29]

For his approach to work, Clinton needed at least to manage the process so that when concessions were made or creative solutions suggested, they would be captured quickly and set down accurately. Clinton had high-level support, but there were tensions between the State Department and NSC teams. By virtue of the years he had spent as the president's special envoy for the Middle East, Ross was bound to play a crucial role, and Albright was dependent upon his expertise. Yet the Palestinians believed that Ross was too committed to the Israeli perspectives, and some Americans were concerned that his own investment in the process affected his judgment on what was the best strategy for the United States. Although Jewish Americans made up two-thirds of the American negotiating team, this did not result in any unanimity of view, other than a desire for the summit to succeed.

At the first Camp David summit, Carter's team kept control of the process by drafting a text upon which all sides could work until final agreement was reached. Something similar was attempted in this case, but it was an untidy cut-and-paste effort. The Israelis insisted on amendments before it could be shown to the Palestinians, who then saw it as an Israeli rather than an American text and therefore unsuitable as a basis for negotiations. "After three days," as Albright recalled, "we had drafted one paper rejected by Barak and a second rejected by the Palestinians."[30] Thereafter, further communications were either verbal (and thus subject to both misinterpretation and later denial) or notes brought out of meetings at various levels of informality. Barak's negotiating approach was deliberately antisocial, while Arafat liked to keep his underlings at odds with each other. In addition, the Palestinian team, in comparison to the Israeli, lacked technical and legal expertise. Officials spent much time coming up with agreements that their seniors were unable to accept. After nine days, Clinton left for a summit at Okinawa, lamenting that "I had left Madeleine and the rest of our team with a real mess."[31] He returned on the thirteenth day and found that little progress had been achieved.

Despite the summit's haphazard organization and the many discordant notes struck, what is surprising is not that it failed but that it got as far as it did. There were three core issues: the extent to which occupied land would be returned to Palestinian control, the status of Jerusalem, and the prospective return of the Palestinian refugees from the time of Israel's creation. The expectation was that if the summit failed, it would be on the first of these issues. Barak's starting point—a return of barely two-thirds of the territory— was risible from a Palestinian perspective. Yet by the end, Barak had agreed—at least verbally—to hand back over 90 percent of the West Bank and compensate the Palestinians for the rest with some Israeli land from elsewhere. Such a withdrawal would not have allowed Israel to keep Palestinian territory fragmented, even if it had wanted to. Interestingly, Arafat did not seem sufficiently bothered to haggle about the precise amounts of returned territory. His mind was elsewhere—on refugees and Jerusalem.

To the Palestinians, there was a fundamental inequality. Jews from around the world were allowed to come to a land with which they had at most a sentimental association, while the right of Palestinians who had fled in the 1940s to return to homes was considered unreasonable. For the Israelis, the Palestinian refugee problem was a consequence of the Arab refusal to recognize the legitimacy of Jewish aspirations and their failed wars. To be sure, many Palestinians had left their homes because of the conflict, but so had many Jews (including from neighboring Arab lands). If they wanted to return, they should return to the new Palestinian entity that would result from the current negotiations. This was an issue that both the Americans and Israelis thought it wise to postpone, other than to offer a "satisfactory solution," which would involve some help getting back to the new Palestinian entity, financial compensation, and possibly a symbolic return for a small proportion, perhaps in order to reunify families. Beyond that, once the principle of return was conceded, there was no logical place to stop. As the total number of claimants could be in the region of 4 million, the Israelis saw a potential for demographic swamping. The Palestinians understood the politics, but for Arafat to accept any restrictions was symbolically of great importance with the core Palestinian constituency of refugees upon which the PLO was founded.

Even more serious was the question of Jerusalem. The city had been divided before. Now it was united under Israeli rule. The Palestinians wanted at least the return of Arab East Jerusalem. For the Israelis, the symbolism was painful, but gradually they accepted that to deny the Palestinians sovereignty over the Arab districts would preclude a deal. Crossing one of his own red lines, Barak conceded seven out of the nine districts of East Jerusalem to Palestinian control. What was most difficult in this was the holiest area of the city—the area from the remaining wall of the old Jewish temple leading up to what Israelis called Temple Mount, and Arabs called Haram al-Sharif. This complex includes the al-Aqsa Mosque, after Mecca and Medina the third holiest site in Islam, where the Prophet ascended to paradise. This is where Arafat was at his most obstinate. As arguments were traded on how to satisfy both sets of religious claims without offending either, he simply denied that this was the site of the Jews' Temple. Attempts to agree on neutral custodians foundered on his insistence that nothing was possible other than Palestinian sovereignty. The implication was that here he feared more than anywhere else an Islamic backlash if he conceded any Jewish rights. "Do you want to come to my funeral?" was his main response when asked to compromise. Berger recalled Clinton trying to impress upon Arafat that this was an unrepeatable opportunity. "Every key, every note, he was cajoling, he was persuading, he was in some case intimidating a bit. At one point he's leaning over Arafat. And Arafat listened mostly. I thought he looked like he was overwhelmed by this looming six-foot-four presence who was leaning, getting closer and closer and closer to his face as he was talking about this being an historic moment."[32] Arafat just saw traps. He wanted more time, more clarifications. Almost by definition, everything put to Arafat fell short of what he wanted, even when it got tantalizingly close.

*   *   *

The blame game over Camp David became a matter of historical inquiry but began as a matter of practical politics. It was soon the conventional wisdom in the United States and Israel that not only was Arafat responsible for the failure at Camp David but this was because he had already decided on a campaign of violence to enable him to extract even greater concessions from the Israelis. Clinton was unimpressed by Arafat's lack of movement. "Perhaps," he mused in his memoirs, "his team hadn't worked through the hard compromises; perhaps they wanted one more session to see how much they could squeeze out of Israel before showing their hand." He was aware of the political risks Barak had taken and wanted to give him cover, so in his assessment he said that Arafat had shown that he wanted to stay on the path of peace, but Barak had shown "particular courage, vision, and an understanding of the historical importance of this moment."[33] There were two other ways of describing the outcome. The more optimistic was taken by Saab Erekat, the chief Palestinian negotiator. He spoke of how much progress had been made, perhaps more than was realistic to expect in two weeks of unprepared negotiations, and that after this excellent start another summit was needed to finish the business. Barak's assessment was both pessimistic and devastating. He had conceptualized this encounter as a test after which it would be known whether Arafat was truly prepared to reach an agreement, not just an agreement with Barak on the terms proposed in the summer of 2000 but almost any agreement at any time. His media advisers had prepared plans to sell success to the Israeli people and plans to blame Arafat for failure, but no plans to address how remaining gaps between the two sides might be filled. And so Barak gave his judgment, "There is no partner."[34] It was as if his strategy all along had been to unmask Arafat.

Yet this was a judgment picked up and taken more seriously by his political opponents than by Barak himself. This need not have been presented as a make-or-break summit. In fact, after Camp David, not only did Barak and Arafat meet for a reasonably convivial dinner but there were in total fifty-four meetings between the two sides of one sort or another. On December 23, Clinton put his "parameters for peace" to Arafat, demonstrating that Camp David was not the best deal Arafat would ever see. This time sovereignty was pushed to 94 to 96 percent of the West Bank and an amount of Israeli pre-1967 land, almost but not quite equivalent to the land conceded in the West Bank would be handed over in return. A formula was reached on the Palestinian right to return. Refugees would have the right to live in the new state with a controlled flow into Israel. The Arab and Jewish districts would be the basis for determining sovereignty over Jerusalem, while the Palestinians would control Haram al-Sharif and the Israelis the Western Wall. Among the Israeli security establishment, there was fear that the Americans were now getting too close to Palestinian positions for comfort. They were relieved that Arafat could still not grasp an even better deal. The Palestinians were by now suspicious that Clinton was buying them off with proposals on which he could not deliver. Even as Clinton was leaving office, with Barak now a caretaker prime minister facing a tough election just two weeks later, the two sides met at the Egyptian resort of Taba on January 21, 2001. Here they reached the outlines of an agreement, but back in Israel this was castigated as the last desperate act of a failed government.[35]

However problematic Barak's negotiating style might be in the end, he took a position that was politically courageous. Arafat played a more passive role, taking concessions as they came his way but not offering much in return, although the readiness to accept a border different in material respects from that of June 4, 1967, and something less than a complete return to Palestinian control of East Jerusalem was important. Nonetheless, Arafat had chosen his sticking points because of their symbolic political significance, and he milked his obstinacy when he returned from Camp David by claiming heroic status for not abandoning the Palestinian right of return or the demand to control Haram al-Sharif.

Arafat could not have been cheered by the prospect of Sharon defeating Barak in the coming Israeli election, but Bush replacing Clinton might not be so bad. After all, Bush's father had been well disposed to the Arabs and notably argumentative with the Israelis. More importantly, he may well have thought that the second intifada, now gathering pace, would strengthen his hand further. If so, he was tragically mistaken. This leads on to the second great controversy around this period, which was whether the upsurge in violence that followed Camp David was preplanned by Arafat for bargaining purposes or was essentially spontaneous, in reaction to Ariel Sharon's provocative visit to Haram al-Sharif that September.

*   *   *

Arafat had warned the Americans that a grand summit that failed would discredit the Oslo approach, strengthening the position of all those who argued that nothing could be expected from the Israelis unless the Palestinians began to put up a fight. His problem was that he dared not stay too far apart from those inclined to this view. Even before the summit, he had been considering how he might exploit Palestinian anger to sustain his own position and possibly use it to persuade the Israelis and the Americans that unless more was on the table the levels of violence were bound to rise.

Arafat had two potential instruments at his disposal. The first was the one thing he had gotten out of Oslo—a security apparatus..As so often in the Middle East, there was no single organization with a clear line of command (always considered a coup risk) but a number of different and overlapping organizations, each under Arafat's personal control, and numbering 40,000 armed Palestinians. He also had his own Mukhabarat (intelligence service). These operatives kept control in the territories, by their own methods, partly to satisfy the Israelis that they were keeping their side of the bargain but also to check any challenges to Arafat's leadership. The less the process delivered to ordinary Palestinians, the more this system seemed like an instrument of Israeli occupation.

Of the militant groups Arafat was supposed to hold down, Palestinian Islamic Jihad existed for little else other than terrorism, was small and vulnerable, and was largely financed by Iran and Syria. Hamas was of a different order. It was increasingly being seen as more of a champion, precisely because it was prepared to attack the settlers. Arafat began to understand that there would be no support if he tried to take it on. He had made some effort after the four bus bombings that finished off Peres, but he largely confined himself to saying the right things in public while doing as little as possible in private. By late 1999, there was evidence that Hamas was gearing up again for a major escalation in its campaign, taking bombs into Israeli cities and using the Israeli settlement drive as a rationale.

By the time Barak returned to power, the friction between Palestinians and the settlers was growing, and armed clashes were becoming more regular. By late 1999, Arafat was beginning to prepare for a return to armed struggle. In contravention of the Oslo Accords, weapons were being smuggled in to the security forces. To divert disaffected youth into an organization over which Arafat had some control, Fatah had set up Tanzim (the "Organization") in 1995 as a rival to Hamas. The aim was to deflect anger away from the Palestinian Authority and to compete with Hamas. In the event of a return to armed struggle, the focus would be on the IDF and the settlers.[36]

The mood on the Palestinian streets was sour. The peace process had brought nothing, while they could look with admiration at the success of Hezbollah in Lebanon. Emulation was a natural temptation. These factors had already led to a mini-intifada in the spring. Then Marwan Barghouti, a possible successor to Arafat and head of Tanzim, organized demonstrations on the streets to protest Barak's failure to release prisoners. They involved largely rock throwing, with the occasional Molotov cocktail, and a degree of competition between the Fatah element and Hamas. IDF troops responded strongly, with rubber bullets and live ammunition. Once this polarization began, the Palestinian police would have to work out whom to defend and it would be unlikely to be the Israelis. Barghouti had said in March, "Whoever thinks it is possible to resolve issues such as the refugees, Jerusalem and the settlements and the borders through negotiations is under a delusion." He was not, however, against negotiations, only for waging a "campaign on the ground" alongside them.[37] The mini-intifada might have served as a warning of the opposite effect. Barak had just steeled himself to hand back villages to the Palestinian Authority, prior to a summit, but Sharon, now leader of Likud, used the occasion to denounce this move as giving in to rioters.

The Israelis were aware of the preparations for a revival of the fighting. Just before Camp David, on July 10, the newspaper *Ma'ariv* carried a story, "Arafat to His People: Prepare for Confrontation with Israel."[38] In such tense circumstances, Sharon's visit on September 28, 2000, to Temple Mount was provocative. Its purpose was to establish him as leader of Likud. Arafat warned Barak that it would have an explosive impact. Barak said he had no basis to prevent his visit, and Clinton advised Arafat to play the whole thing down or even embarrass Sharon with an extravagant welcome. After an agreement, Israelis would want to feel that they were not precluded from the area, and Sharon did not enter any of the holy buildings. But with tensions so high this was not a time for pragmatic responses. Given that control over this area was also the issue on which Camp David had broken up, Arafat might well have hoped that once Sharon appeared, and having warned against the visit, a demonstration of Palestinian feeling would be eloquent and persuasive. This was therefore initially not about a mass rebellion but about asserting control over a particular area, along the lines of the 1996 tunnel episode, hence the term "al-Aqsa intifada." Once the rioting began, however, matters soon got out of control.

The next escalation was an Israeli responsibility. The contingency plans for another intifada involved swift and ruthless suppression, including the use of live ammunition, which was responsible for a number of the next day's grimmer images and the anger that raised the level and intensity of the violence. The second intifada might have picked up where the first left off, but it was not an "uprising" in the same sense. It only featured demonstrations and rioting for a few weeks, after which it started to take on the appearance of guerrilla warfare. In one of the most devastating Palestinian critiques of Arafat's approach, Yezid Sayigh argued that Arafat's problem was not a prior strategy based on the use of force, but the absence of any strategy, and his inclination when in trouble to "flee forward," to aggravate a crisis rather than step back. The sharpness of the Israeli response on September 29 gave Arafat an opportunity to reinvent himself once again as the leader of a people under fire. He went off on an international trip, leaving it understood that every effort would be made to keep the situation simmering. He seems

to have hoped that Clinton and Barak would come up with more concessions, and in this he was right, but he overestimated Barak's durability and
the continuity in American policy once George W. Bush took over from
Clinton. Only belatedly did he realize that he had given Sharon a boost, so
that days before the Israeli election he was urging votes for Barak to "save
peace." Sayigh had many criticisms, from the failure to address the settlements issue head-on or to mobilize Arabs in Jerusalem in support of the
Palestinian position, to the counterproductive use of firearms during the
early stages of the second intifada. His most serious criticism was that there
was no "sustained effort to deliver a specific political message to the Israeli
government, parliamentary parties and voting public." The result was that
the Israeli debate developed without any clear view about what would bring
peace and reinforced the inclination to assume the worst.[39] This of course
would also involve preparing Palestinian opinion for a deal that would leave
some historic claims unmet.

It could be added that from the Israeli side, there was also a failure to
think through what sort of deal would actually work and meet legitimate
Palestinian aspirations rather than what might be extracted from a weakened Palestinian leadership or what would keep the hard-liners calm. In the
end, this was also Clinton's failure. As a master politician he understood that
it was necessary to find positions that could keep the negotiating parties in
the game, gradually focusing on what could realistically be achieved rather
than maximum demands, but he never quite worked out the method or the
moment to insist on both sides adopting an American analysis and peace
plan that not only would recognize their respective domestic political positions but would in key respects be durable.

By this stage such an optimum outcome may no longer have been possible. Clinton pushed hard with the summit not so much because he was confident that he could get an agreement but because he feared the resurgence
of violence if nothing was done. He was right to be fearful, though more
handshakes around another contested piece of paper still might not have
prevented violence. The worn hopes of peaceful coexistence between Israelis
and Palestinians suffered further blows. The impact was felt more widely as
the profile of the conflict within the Muslim world was raised to new
heights. Powerful images of Israeli brutality became a staple of the new Arab
media outlets, from TV stations to the Internet. The second intifada was not
the reason for the surge in Islamist activity in the 2000s. Its roots lay elsewhere. But it made for a potent rallying call.

16

CHOOSING AMERICA

ALTHOUGH THE SECOND radical wave in the Middle East had begun in Iran and spread through Shi'ite organizations, a potentially more virulent strain was connected with the more populous Sunni communities. Those of this persuasion, many of them alumni of the war in Afghanistan, also chose the United States as their special enemy. As with the Iranian-inspired strain, the urgency and focus behind this campaign were derived from the apparent consolidation of the United States as a regional power through military bases in Kuwait, and especially Saudi Arabia. One difference was that it gave a lower priority to the Palestinian cause, at least until the second intifada.

It was not obvious why the United States should be chosen by al Qaeda, and the decision was controversial. It came after Islamists had suffered heavy defeats in some high-profile struggles, notably in Egypt and Algeria, and seemed foolhardy to many of those under the al Qaeda banner. As they had yet to succeed at a national level, why suppose they could succeed at the global one? The view of the group's leader, Osama bin Laden, and his closest associates was that the United States was at the same time the main barrier to Islamic advance but also in key respects the weakest. In developing this position, of particular importance was the Egyptian physician Ayman al-Zawahiri, who shocked many of his own supporters by shifting from his previously dogmatic insistence that national struggles must come first. The new line was that Islamists would only be able to triumph when the United States stopped interfering in the disparate conflicts in which they were engaged. The first task therefore was to develop tactics to compel the United States to abandon support for corrupt and apostate local regimes, along with the Zionists in Israel.

The story of al Qaeda's emerging out of a complex interplay of personalities and theological-strategic disputes has been well told. The theology of killing became something of a preoccupation of the writing and preaching of this time, as justifications were found for targeting ever widening categories of people. Mainstream Islam might be opposed to killing innocents, fellow Muslims, and oneself. Yet once it was accepted that Islam was in peril, and jihad was essential, then not only nonbelievers but also traitors and apostates must be targets. In the name of such a cause, willingly embracing death was not suicide but martyrdom. We will concentrate less on the theological and more on the strategic side of this debate, and consider the development of al Qaeda in two stages. The first leads up to August 1988, when the name was first used to describe a group led by bin Laden. The second covers the next decade, which concluded in August 1998 with al Qaeda bursting onto the global scene with attacks on two U.S. embassies in East Africa. These attacks were not the first to be backed by bin Laden or undertaken by associated Islamist groups, but they followed a declaration of war to which they were meant to direct attention.

★   ★   ★

The crucible was Afghanistan. This had encouraged the spread of the austere Saudi Wahhabist doctrine into Central Asia, propagated through numerous Saudi-funded madrassas in Pakistan. Many enthusiastic young Arabs volunteered to join the mujahideen, notionally as a religious duty. By and large, the contribution of these "Afghan Arabs" to the conduct and outcome of the anti-Soviet campaign was minimal, though the numbers passing through were significant—perhaps by the end of the war up to 6,000 Saudis, 4,000 Egyptians, 2,000 Algerians, and 1,000 Yemenis. But many of these rushed in for the denouement, coming to get a glimpse of jihad in practice before the opportunity passed, and these numbers have to be set against the hundreds of thousands of Afghan fighters. The Afghans saw the Arabs as often ineffective and self-indulgent, at times acting as if a glorious martyrdom was as much of an objective as actual victory, leading to excessive displays of rapture when one of their number got killed. For their part, the Arabs found the Afghans tending to the irreligious and chaotic.

Bin Laden acknowledged the poor fighting qualities of the Afghan Arabs. From 1984, he was convinced that the remedy lay in better training and preparation for those who wished to be soldiers in this cause. He wanted to create a proper jihadist army and persisted with this conviction, even though the initial results were unimpressive. This ambition was behind the formation of al Qaeda. This entity had existed in an embryonic state since 1984, when Abdullah Azzam as leader and bin Laden as financier had founded the "Bureau of Services for Arab Mujahideen." This became al Qaeda on August 11, 1988, when the leaders of the Afghan Arabs met in Peshawar, Pakistan, to ponder the future, now that Soviet forces were clearly on their way out. Already there was evidence that the always uneasy alliance among the various mujahideen was breaking up, and that there was a risk that the Arabs might start fighting each other. Benazir Bhutto was now in power in Pakistan and wanted the foreign jihadists to move on before they could stir up more local trouble. The conclusion of the meeting was that a new group was needed to keep jihad alive after the Soviets left. This was to be named Al-Qaeda al-Askariya (the military base). The base was necessary because jihad required more than a militant vanguard. It also needed a proper organization and a training camp. From the start, al Qaeda was a grouping of factions and individuals coming together for mutual support rather than a rigid hierarchical organization with a uniform ideology.

The ongoing ideological debate within this grouping can be traced back to those who had developed in and around the Muslim Brotherhood in Egypt. The key ideologist of the Brotherhood, until his execution in 1966, was Syed Qutb. He was executed because he declared illegitimate any regime not based wholly on Islamic law and declared them unbelievers *(takfir)*, thereby inciting believers to seek their overthrow. His prison writings prior to his execution reflect the intensity of his anger and his vision, pushing his logic to a global conclusion and the elimination of all those who usurped the laws of God. So incendiary were Qutb's ideas that the Muslim Brotherhood could only survive in Egypt by denouncing them. The Brothers stuck to nonviolent tactics and concentrated on their underlying religious message. The leadership's focus on organizational survival softened the harsher edges of the message, thereby creating a space for the militants inspired by Qutb. However carefully phrased, this message still retained its subversive content.

The tension grew following the easing of the restraints on the Brotherhood under Sadat, and then the attempts to contain the militants as Sadat belatedly appreciated their danger. The most important ideological output of this period was a book by Mohammed Abd al-Salam Faraj, called *Absent Duty*, which insisted on the importance of jihad as a duty for all Muslims. This was something more than an inner striving to be pure and good. It was more a determination to protect Islam from all its enemies. In the past, such a jihad would be invoked if Muslims were threatened by an external enemy.

Faraj identified the enemy as the current regime in Egypt. Although they pretended to be Muslim, in practice they were apostates, collaborating with colonial forces "of the crusading, the communist, or the Zionist variety." These were the "near enemy," and they must be the main priority of jihad. Meanwhile, the "far enemy" could be left alone.[1] The underlying strategic judgment was that the Islamists lacked the wherewithal to challenge big and powerful states. If, however, they could introduce proper respect for Islam into state structures, then Western influence was bound to decline. This judgment dominated Islamist discourse until the mid-1990s.

This defined the way forward for the Islamist groups in Egypt that had broken away from the more passive strategies of the Brotherhood. The most substantial was Gama'st al-Islamiya, or the Islamic Group, which emerged out of the student movements of the 1970s. It was led by Omar Abdul Rahman, blinded at birth through diabetes and therefore known as the "Blind Sheikh." After being thrown into jail under Nasser for his denunciations, under Sadat he developed a complex, well-resourced, and extensive organization. When Sadat began his peace overtures to Israel, the Islamic Group led the protests. The resultant suppression inflamed militant sentiment, and pushed activity underground and then into violence. Rahman, who had moved to Saudi Arabia, returned in 1980 to declare that heretical leaders deserved to be killed. This declaration got him arrested after Sadat's murder, but as he had been careful not to mention the actual leader he had in mind, he was not executed. When released from prison, Rahman went to Saudi Arabia, and then into Pakistan, before requesting asylum in the United States in 1990.

In prison at the same time as Rahman was Ayman al-Zawahiri, who had also come into politics through the Brotherhood, but then fell out with the leadership because of their pragmatic approach to working with Arab rulers. They had become "a tool in the hands of tyrants." His way was to renounce "constitution and man-made laws, democracy, elections, and parliament."[2] He was a leader of al-Jihad, a rival to the Islamic Group. While the much larger Islamic Group could follow traditional forms of guerrilla warfare, harassing and ambushing representatives of the state apparatus, his preference was to infiltrate the army to create the conditions for a military coup. Both groups, in their focus on seizing the state to turn it into an instrument of religious direction rather than raising consciousness from below through preaching and civic action, were far more influenced by Lenin's notion of a vanguard Communist Party than perhaps they realized. In addition to substantive differences, their natural rivalry for the leadership of Egyptian Islamists colored Zawahiri and Rahman's relationship. Although Zawahiri was ambivalent about whether it was wise to attempt to murder Sadat, he gave some support to the plot. In 1986, further radicalized by the brutal treatment he received inside prison, he returned to Pakistan, where he had spent some time in the summer of 1980 tending refugees from the war. He saw Afghanistan as a means of finding a secure base from which he could work to revive al-Jihad from its post-Sadat trauma. His commitment to Afghanistan, therefore, was temporary and expedient.

Up to the meeting in August 1988, the natural leader of the Afghan Arabs was Abdullah Azzam. He left Palestine after the 1967 war for Jordan and then moved on to Egypt, where he gained a doctorate. He returned to Jordan, where he was considered too extreme, and eventually moved to Jeddah. He knew Qutb's family, and even in Palestine had connections to the Brotherhood. He was a critic of the PLO for the religious laxity of their fighters and the downgrading of the overriding cause of Islam in any secular national liberation struggle. For Azzam, the ultimate objective had to be a caliphate spanning all Muslim lands. Lawrence Wright has described him as the embodiment of the "warrior priest," known for his courage and oratory, combining "piety and learning with a serene and bloody intransigence." Azzam opposed all talk of conferences and dialogue, relying on "Jihad and the rifle alone."[3] He moved to Pakistan in 1981 to get closer to the action as the Afghan resistance took shape, drawing inspiration from the purity of this conflict between the worlds of belief and unbelief.

There he met up with Osama bin Laden, from one of Saudi Arabia's wealthiest and best-connected families, the seventeenth son (of fifty-two children) of a construction magnate. He was educated by disciples of the Muslim Brotherhood, including Qutb's brother, and graduated from Abdul Aziz University in 1971 with a degree in economics and public administration. He made his way to Afghanistan after meeting mujahideen and coming under the influence of Azzam's teachings. There he soon made an impact, not because of his religious learning or fighting qualities but because of the resources at his disposal and his knowledge of construction. The 9/11 Commission stresses that al Qaeda was not funded through bin Laden's personal fortune. He never received a massive inheritance and many of his businesses were not viable.[4] Nonetheless, the importance of bin Laden's wealth in his rise through Islamist ranks should not be underestimated. The $1 million annual income received from his family until 1994 was hardly trivial. Even when he was not using his own money, he had access to prosperous individuals in the Gulf states who saw his causes as worthy of charitable support.

Azzam was attracted by the unifying symbolism of Arabs being spread among the various Afghan groups, but bin Laden, more practical, wanted to keep the Arabs together and turn them into a serious and durable fighting force, to overcome their reputation for cowardice and incompetence. Their numbers would be grown by offering to pay travel costs and living expenses. They would also be inspired by a fatwa issued by Azzam, calling for jihad in Afghanistan as obligatory to prevent a Muslim state falling into the hands of unbelievers. This gained high-level clerical support in Saudi Arabia, but the call was only a modest success. As a member of a leading Saudi family and a conduit for substantial funds, bin Laden appears to have been seen by Prince Turki al-Faisal, head of the Saudi intelligence services, as in effect a Saudi agent helping keep the flow of people and funds in order.

It is often alleged that bin Laden and other Afghan Arabs were subsidized or supported in some way by the CIA over this period. At this point, neither bin Laden nor Azzam was that interested in the United States. Although bin Laden later claimed that it was the events in Lebanon in 1982 that made him hate Americans, other sources suggest he did appreciate the American backing for the Afghan resistance. Also, he wanted to stay close to the Saudi elite. Overt attacks on the United States would not have been welcomed. So, while in a manner of speaking the United States and bin Laden were on the same side in this war, those who looked for evidence of any direct links did not find them, and they were strenuously denied by both parties. The CIA was able to work with Afghans and had no need for the Arabs, who tended to be unpopular. The Arabs were not short of funds and would not have seen Americans as a natural source of strategic advice, especially in light of their own particular agenda. As Coll observed, "If the CIA did have contacts with bin Laden during the 1980s and subsequently covered it up, it has so far done an excellent job."[5] All that can be said is that at this time bin Laden showed no unusual animosity toward the Americans, beyond the normal level of disdain to be found in the circles in which he moved.

It was Azzam who argued that jihad had to move on to all Muslim lands where Islam had been in retreat, which covered many African and Asian countries, and even Andalusia in Spain, from which Muslims had been expelled in 1492. Given his own background, as a Palestinian with connections to Hamas, not surprisingly he put Palestine to the fore and wished to bring brigades of Hamas fighters to Afghanistan for training. He was opposed to purely national struggles, but also to attacks within the "community of believers" and against innocent civilians. In these respects, Azzam's philosophy was quite distinct from that of Zawahiri, who only really cared about Egypt and was not too fussy about methodology. Zawahiri was a relatively recent arrival to this circle. His medical skills were part of his attraction, notably for bin Laden, who suffered from a variety of ailments. In return, Zawahiri, always strapped for cash to keep his organization alive, was undoubtedly attracted by bin Laden's wealth. This put bin Laden in the middle of these debates, and he became increasingly uncomfortable as his old mentor's leadership position was challenged directly. Zawahiri's associates brought charges against Azzam for working with Christians or even Americans. The Saudis were also worried about his links to the Muslim Brotherhood.

Bin Laden had not been seen as a natural leader, but rather as apt to be controlled by stronger characters. But he had the money, was considered to be a reassuring presence by the Saudis, had not fallen out with any of the main players, and did not offer a distinctive philosophy of his own to which others might take exception. He was not the first person with such attributes to rise to the top of a group because he was the least unacceptable to others. So in August 1988, bin Laden emerged as the leader of the nascent and inchoate al Qaeda. The next year, Azzam was murdered along with his two sons. There is no certainty on culpability. Bin Laden is one possibility, as Azzam was now a rival, and Wright suggests that Zawahiri was to blame. It seems most likely that he was caught up in faction fighting between Afghan warlords. At any rate, by this time there was not much to lead, as the post-Soviet chaos and lawlessness engulfed the Arab contingent as much as everybody else. The various Islamist groups were skirmishing, often viciously, with each other.

★   ★   ★

Everybody was caught out by the failure of the Communist government in Kabul to collapse as predicted after the Soviet departure. There were many mujahideen factions, but the two major ones were led by Gulbuddin Hekmatyar, which was Pashtun and backed by Pakistan's ISI (and by implication the Saudis), and by Ahmad Shah Massoud. By common consent Massoud, a Tajik from the Panjshir Valley north of Kabul, was the most talented of the mujahideen leaders. He had stayed clear of Peshawar during the war and had not courted the outside powers. Part of Azzam's supposed heresy was that he was also impressed by the more focused and disciplined, but more ideologically suspect, Massoud, and this is what probably led to his murder. By now the country was awash with weapons and men who had done little for a decade but fight. Without the common enemy, all the old divisions opened up as competition began for a share of the postwar spoils, and the various external powers with an interest in the outcome meddled and manipulated the various factions to maximize their own influence.

With the Soviets beaten, the United States had no particular policy at all, and far more to think about in terms of the implications of Gorbachev for

Central Europe before they could worry about Central Asia. They were content to see if the Pakistanis could sort out the scramble for advantage in the new Afghanistan, acknowledging that Islamists might come out on top and just hoping that they would not be as extreme as the Iranians. They were increasingly aware that this might not be the case. Hekmatyar's ideological roots, for example, were in the Muslim Brotherhood, and he was linked to Jamaat-e-Islami. Not only did he show no gratitude for the American money that had helped keep him going, but his attitudes were consistently anti-American. Those whose political inclinations were more Western had been consistently sidelined by the Pakistanis, whose main objective was to have a friendly and compliant state as neighbor. They now felt abandoned by the Americans.

Meanwhile, Pakistan was further complicating matters. The continuity in Pakistani political life was provided by the military and ISI. Their view was that instead of being accountable to the politicians, which was how the West understood civil-military relations, the politicians should be accountable to them as custodians of national security. Even democratically elected prime ministers such as Benazir Bhutto and Nawaz Sharif, who alternated in the role during the 1990s, were considered to be there on sufferance and only allowed to stay so long as they did the bidding of the security establishment. Bhutto later recalled that when she became prime minister, only 2.6 percent of GNP was spent on education and 6.7 percent on the military, while soldiers outnumbered doctors by 10 to 1.[6]

At the start of the 1990s men of Islamist sympathies were in the senior echelons of both the military and ISI. They believed that Islam was the basis for national salvation and mobilization, and a means of reaching out to people well beyond Pakistan's borders. The country was much smaller than the old enemy, India, but it could gain distant friends and local supporters on the basis of a shared faith. The other requirement was a nuclear capability, which had been energetically under development and would soon be ready for testing. This had been kept hidden to placate the Americans, but there was no point in having nuclear weapons unless they were known; otherwise how could they have a deterrent effect? They also required getting aircraft and missiles, and since the 1980s they had been developing links with other Muslim countries that might be interested in acquiring nuclear technology for a suitable price, including Iran and Libya. They also looked to countries such as North Korea, who might be helpful with missile technology.[7]

By the end of the decade, when the weapons were tested following Indian tests, these activities led to a crisis in relations with the Americans and then a crisis that got perilously close to a nuclear war with India. The crisis came over yet another local campaign, begun in late 1989 in the excitement of the Soviets being chased out of Afghanistan. ISI decided that as it now knew all about insurgencies, this was the moment to inflict one on India. This was also a means of undermining Bhutto's attempts at a rapprochement with India. The Indian stake in Kashmir, however, was far greater than that of the Soviets in Afghanistan. India claimed this to be an integral part of the country. A country with multinationalism as a governing ideology saw no problem with the fact that this was largely Muslim territory. Yet another bloody front for the Islamists opened up as the Indians imposed direct rule in the face of demonstrations and violence.

In Afghanistan, the triumphal next step was to be an assault on the Communist stronghold of Jalalabad, where the remnants of the old regime could be smashed and a new one established before the succession struggle got out of hand. Everybody wanted a piece of this action, including the CIA. The internal divisions and complacency among the mujahideen hampered what was supposed to be their final push against the Communists. It was hopelessly commanded, with sets of uncoordinated attacks involving disastrous frontal assaults. The city held, and a siege began. As the Soviets began to have confidence that the Communists might hold, sparing them the embarrassment of an early capitulation, they kept supplies coming forward. The result was a fiasco, including for bin Laden, who lost eighty of his fighters and only just escaped. This was all the more bitter because of the advance publicity that had described the coming triumph, thereby encouraging the arrival of extra Arabs to help in the final defeat of the Communists. This led to recriminations, against bin Laden as well, for his misplaced enthusiasm over an ill-prepared attack that led to the unnecessary sacrifice. The failure over Jalalabad meant that a struggle between Hekmatyar and Massoud was inevitable, and this soon turned into open civil war. Although both sides were Islamist in persuasion, each denied the legitimacy of the other. Denunciations became more vitriolic, and the killing became ever more inclusive. Hekmatyar even tried to get one up on Massoud by trying to organize a coup against the Communist leader Najibullah, in cahoots with a dissident Communist. This also failed.

*　　*　　*

Despite their investment in the Afghanistan struggle, it is striking how quickly the Arab mujahideen began to lose interest. This comes across in an al Qaeda document captured after 9/11. Although dated from the early 1990s, it makes most sense as a compilation of views from the late 1980s, perhaps just after the formation of al Qaeda, as it includes references to the views of the assassinated Azzam. A number of leading Arab individuals and organizations were asked why they were participating in combat in Afghanistan. Azzam suggested only token participation to raise Afghan morale and Arab training and consciousness, "with the long-term goal being the waging of jihad against the Jews in Palestine." Zawahiri's Tanzim al-Jihad (Islamic Jihad) saw the value of participation purely as training. "Nothing is to be hoped for from the war in Afghanistan, nor will there arise an Islamic State there, on account of doctrinal/ideological defects among the leaders and the masses. Egypt is the heart of the Islamic world and it is necessary to establish the Caliphate there first." Others thought fighting in Afghanistan to be a religious duty, though a lost cause. The idea that a political and military victory might yet be achieved to transform it into an Islamist base was clearly a minority view. Bin Laden's reported contribution was curious: "deep participation in the battles in accordance with the political and strategic vision of the leadership in Peshawar [suggesting this is pre-Jalalabad], with the long-term goal being the liberation of South Yemen from communism."[8]

Thus, while Zawahiri's agenda was still Egyptian, bin Laden's was Saudi. He even tried to organize a jihad in South Yemen until the Yemenis picked up members of his advance unit and complained to Riyadh. Marxists certainly had been in control of South Yemen since it gained independence from Britain in 1967, and there were close ties with the Soviet Union and the PLO. It was an irritant to Saudi Arabia, although by this time the Saudis saw no need to wage military campaigns of their own, a point they made to bin Laden whenever he raised the matter. Nonetheless, his interest in this issue reveals the extent to which he still viewed the world through Saudi eyes. For their part, the Saudi elite saw him as wayward and overzealous but potentially useful. During the 1980s, members of the Saudi elite, including Prince Turki al-Faisal, kept in regular touch, and bin Laden went back and forth to the Saudi Embassy in Pakistan. There are other indications of his keen sense of Saudi identity, including his later defensiveness about the number of his compatriots at the higher reaches of al Qaeda compared with Egyptians. If anything, the image he was trying to project at this time was of a unique Saudi hero. This might be based on little more than having survived intense Soviet fire for a few days in 1987 before being forced to withdraw, but this was sufficient for a transformation from the helpful man of money to a brave and inspiring commander. Showing his early sensitivity to the importance of powerful images and good stories, he commissioned a recruiting video that showed him acting out his new role in heroic guise.

His Saudi patriotism was particularly evident in June 1990, when Saddam invaded Kuwait. Whereas some Islamists instinctively took a pro-Saddam line, bin Laden, who was then back in Saudi Arabia, was clear that Saddam must be opposed. Orders were sent to the Afghan Arabs to prepare to form an army to protect Saudi Arabia from a continuation of Iraqi aggression. He met with the Saudi minister of defense and promised 100,000 capable fighters in three months. "You don't need Americans," he claimed. "You don't need any other non-Muslim troops. We will be enough." Noting the absence of caves in Kuwait, the minister asked about how he would cope with chemical and biological weapons. "We will fight him with faith came the reply."[9] All this reinforced impressions of bin Laden's naïveté, in supposing a fight could be waged against such impossible odds, and his exaggerated belief in his own abilities. At such a tense time, the regime was unlikely to want to import thousands of fanatics from Afghanistan.

For a man who was cultivating a reputation as a gallant Saudi leader, who had personally engaged in jihad and helped defeat the mighty Soviets, this was something of a snub. Even worse than having his own scheme summarily rejected was the preference for the Americans as defenders of the Kingdom of Saudi Arabia. This confirmed all of bin Laden's worst fears about what had happened to his country under a corrupt royal family. Bin Laden was not alone in expressing displeasure at the arrival of Christian, even Jewish, forces close to Islam's holiest sites of Mecca and Medina. Although the grand mufti was prevailed upon to issue a fatwa permitting the entry of foreign forces, to many younger and more radical clerics this merely demonstrated a loss of independent religious judgment. Anxieties about the infection of Western ideas were confirmed as demands were heard from within Saudi society, soon suppressed, for greater liberalization and more rights for women (including the right to drive cars). The U.S. presence became an occasion for virulent denunciations of the oil-hungry Americans and their decadent way of life that was now said to be infecting Saudi Arabia in a far more deadly way than Iraq's occupying of Kuwait. Having worked hard to direct the zealots outward, toward spreading Wahhabism and waging jihad, the Saudi elite could now see the risks to themselves.

This was the principal cause of the turn in bin Laden's worldview, leading him to concentrate on the malevolent international role of the United States and develop a seething contempt for the supine way that the Saudi elite had collaborated. After returning to Pakistan to try to join efforts to sort out the faction fighting among the mujahideen, bin Laden made his way to Sudan, one place where Islamists were in command. This was a divided country, Arab and Muslim in the north but African and Christian in the south. From the late 1970s, it had a government supported by pan-Arabists and Communists, but its desperate need for financial support had allowed the Saudis to enjoy greater influence, and in the early 1980s there had been a not wholly convincing turn toward Islam in an effort to hold the country together at a time of economic stress. In June 1989, the army took control. General Omar Hasan al-Bashir was in charge, but the most prominent figure was Hasan al-Turabi. Turabi had been leader of the Muslim Brotherhood in Sudan in the 1960s and turned it into a political party, the National Islamic Front. He had spent time in the United States, London, and Paris and offered, in his own way, an internationalist vision. In some respects he was even progressive, seeking to heal the Sunni-Shia breach, find roles for women, and allow modest entertainments. Anticipating the prestige that could flow from being the only Sunni Islamic movement actually in control of a state, Turabi opened doors to extremist organizations from around the world. The disaffected and the unwanted soon began to arrive.

In Sudan and Afghanistan, the Saudis were appalled to find that movements to which they had given some help and encouragement in the past showed no gratitude when the kingdom was in peril and instead supported Iraq. The position taken by Afghan leaders such as Hekmatyar and Abdul Rasul Sayyaf was particularly shocking, given the extent to which they had been bankrolled over the years. Turabi saw this as an opportunity, for he wanted the radical wing of the Muslim community to have its headquarters in Sudan. In April 1991, after Saddam's defeat, the Arab and Islamic Conference was hosted in the Sudanese capital of Khartoum for those with pro-Iraq sympathies, as an alternative to the Saudi-dominated Organization of the Islamic Conference.

Bin Laden arrived in Sudan in 1992 with four wives and seventeen children. Soon he was joined by other former colleagues, including members of Zawahiri's and Rahman's groups, although by this time Rahman himself was in the United States. This mingling, combined with the experience of Afghanistan, led bin Laden to consider a more unified approach to jihad. He was ready to make approaches to Shi'ites, including opening up lines of communication with Hezbollah, whose success against the Americans in 1983 earned the group a special place in Islamist narratives. Bin Laden was now involved in refashioning himself again as a leader of the Saudi opposition, writing tracts about the venality of the Saudi regime and the shame of the American occupation of his homeland. The Saudis sent his family to Khartoum to persuade him to come home and apologize to the king. He refused. Instead, in August 1995 he accused the Saudi king of being corrupt and denounced the presence of "filthy, infidel Crusaders" exploiting the country's oil. In November, five Americans were killed when a U.S.-Saudi training facility was attacked. Six months later, without telling Washington, the Saudis captured and executed four suspects who claimed to have been inspired in their hostility to the American presence by bin Laden.[10] At the same time, he was supporting propaganda from the exile public relations machine that had established itself in London.

Sudan began to pay a price for having bin Laden and other Islamists as guests. The Saudis were exasperated and the Egyptians were furious as Sudan became a base for those trying to kill Mubarak and overthrow his regime. By April 1996, Sudan was completely isolated, and Turabi decided that bin Laden should be sacrificed. Some reports say that the Sudanese even offered to hand him over to the United States, but the opportunity was missed because bin Laden was still seen by the United States as more of a nuisance than a threat, a financier rather than a leader, and there was no evidence that he had harmed U.S. citizens. Richard Clarke has said this was a "fable" and has remained adamant that no such offer was ever made. He also claimed that the break between Turabi and bin Laden was something of a sham and that bin Laden left simply because he was too vulnerable in Khartoum.[11] Yet there is evidence that the two men did not get along, that bin Laden found Turabi irritating, while Turabi saw bin Laden as a potential rival as well as a risk. For whatever reason, in April 1996, bin Laden took a plane out of Sudan back to Afghanistan. As he had to sell his business to the Sudanese at unfavorable rates, he was almost bankrupt.

*   *   *

By this time the conflict in Afghanistan had taken a new turn. In early 1992, Najibullah tried to persuade the Americans that they should support him as a bulwark against fundamentalism, but he had no internal support. He decided that it was best to quit and hand over to a new government. The hostilities between Massoud and Hekmatyar had not abated and attempts to mediate between them, which appear to have included bin Laden, floundered. Massoud, who was best placed, eventually simply took Kabul and then turned his forces against Hekmatyar's men. This was no basis for an orderly transition in a country awash with weapons and without a functioning economy. Over the next two years, alliances formed and re-formed and re-formed again, with the militias losing any sense of ideological purpose, turning to crime, and picking on anybody unfortunate enough to get in their way. Thousands died and the already primitive infrastructure gave up altogether. It was worst in Kabul but not confined to the capital. Kandahar was particularly grim. And it was from Kandahar that the Taliban emerged.

The Pakistanis felt that they had both the right to control events in Afghanistan and a clear interest in doing so, to open up trade routes and introduce calm into their border areas. They struggled along with everyone else, until in 1994 a group of students (Talibs) raised in the refugee camps and outraged by the depravity of mujahideen rule presented themselves as a new, idealistic, and disciplined force. Their leader was Mullah Mohammed Omar, who had lost his right eye in an artillery explosion in the Jalalabad battle of 1989. He had the triple attributes of scholarship, piety, and military experience. Against the backdrop of the chaos and corruption of post-Soviet Afghanistan, he recruited from the largely Wahhabist madrassas around Kandahar, where he was a teacher. He began with about 200 activists, but the numbers grew as he attracted people desperate for order. With support from Pakistani intelligence, a militia rabble was trained in guerrilla tactics, and it did not take long before they were 24,000 strong and moved with startling speed to take control of much of the country. In the final battle, the old enemies Massoud and Hekmatyar came together in an uneasy and futile alliance.

Benazir Bhutto—now back in power—wanted to use the rise of the Taliban to get a broadly based government in Kabul, but this was not what the Taliban wanted, nor did its supporters in ISI, who saw the chance at last to get the friendly government in place that had eluded them in 1990. Once again they went to the Saudis to help them reshape Afghan politics, at least promising that this would limit Iranian influence. The Saudis hoped that the responsibilities of power would tame and mature the Taliban. They also hoped that unlike the discredited old warlords, who had supported Saddam despite all the Saudi resources that had come their way, the Taliban would show proper gratitude. As the Taliban moved into Kabul, they imposed their religious will in an uncompromising fashion. Women had to cover their faces; men had to grow beards. By prohibiting schooling and work for women from the first day, they crippled health and education services. Anything that implied fun was banned. At the same time, they encouraged opium production as a source of revenue. By 1999, Afghanistan was the source of almost 80 percent of the world's opium, only cutting back when overproduction pushed prices too low. Saudi Arabia and Pakistan recognized the new government, but nobody else, other than the UAE, followed. The Taliban never quite managed to gain control of the country. Although Hekmatyar ended up in Iran, with many of his fighters going to the Taliban, Massoud continued to deny the Taliban some 15 percent of the country.

This was the position when bin Laden arrived in 1996. Omar's interests then did not extend much beyond Afghanistan. He accepted bin Laden and noted the advice from the Saudis that he should be kept quiet. This turned out to be easier said than done. Bin Laden continued to make vitriolic statements about the Saudi royal family and the Americans, and claimed responsibility for terrorist events overseas. Omar had mixed feelings toward him. He was not the easiest guest, but he was impressively religious and had access to resources and know-how that could be useful. For bin Laden's followers and associates, the return to Afghanistan was not desperately popular. They complained about the wretched infrastructure of the shattered country and were contemptuous of the Afghans, who were lacking in education and reliability.[12] Over time, there were grumbles that al Qaeda's camps were poorly organized and the systems for handling new trainees inadequate, a matter in which bin Laden did not appear to take much interest. Bin Laden's relatively pragmatic approach to political relationships meant that he was far less bothered about a close relationship with the Taliban than those in al Qaeda who saw it as an instrument of the Pakistani government. Whatever the complaints, here was a perfect sanctuary in a country he knew and an opportunity to create the headquarters and training facilities for an international movement with him at its head. The camps filled up with enthusiastic and tough fighters. Estimates of the numbers passing through from 1996 to 2001 are anything from 10,000 to 20,000.

Omar was uneasy about bin Laden because of his strident anti-Americanism and the way he continually annoyed the Saudis. In 1997, he required bin Laden to relocate from Jalalabad to Kandahar, which made it harder to execute operations. Now, there were risks that he might be kicked out of Afghanistan for the same reasons he had been kicked out of Sudan. So bin Laden worked on his uncertain host to make sure that Omar did not view him as a rival. He flattered him as the new caliph and put his men at the service of the Taliban's defense and in conflict with Massoud. When the Saudis and Pakistanis demanded bin Laden's expulsion, Omar demurred. By now he was drawing closer to bin Laden and imposing Sharia law with even greater rigidity. Evidence of bin Laden's growing influence is seen in the April 2001 destruction of the ancient and magnificent Bamiyan Buddhas as false gods. Also, the size of the al Qaeda presence meant that it had to be taken seriously. Al Qaeda is often described as a nonstate actor, but by the time of 9/11, it was closely enmeshed in the Afghan state, which was, bin Laden claimed, "the only Islamic country."

*　　*　　*

In August 1996, not long after the Khobar bombing, *Al Quds Al Arabi*, a London-based newspaper, published "Declaration of War Against the Americans Occupying the Land of the Two Holy Places," by bin Laden. This mentioned a long list of places where Muslims had been "massacred." The "latest and greatest of these aggressions, incurred by the Muslims since the death of the Prophet," was "the occupation of the land of the two Holy Places . . . by the armies of the American Crusaders and their allies." Bin Laden's group had also been the victim of injustice, having been "pursued in Pakistan, Sudan and Afghanistan." This explains the "long absence on my part." Now, bin Laden wrote, he had a safe base "in the high Hindukush mountains." "Today," he announced, "we begin the work, talking and discussing the ways of correcting what had happened to the Islamic world in general, and the Land of the two Holy Places in particular. We wish to study the means that we could follow to return the situation to its normal path."[13] This manifesto was followed by interviews and statements. In one of the most significant, with CNN's Peter Arnett in March 1997, he was explicit about his intentions with regard to the United States. The "driving-away jihad against the U.S. does not stop with its withdrawal from the Arabian peninsula, but rather it must desist from aggressive intervention against Muslims in the whole world."[14]

In February 1998, another and much shorter fatwa was issued at a press conference in Afghanistan. It referred to three facts: the U.S. occupation of "the lands of Islam in the holiest of places," its use as a staging post against Iraq, and its service of "the Jews' petty state" by destroying Iraq and fragmenting the other Arab states. "All these crimes and sins committed by the Americans are a clear declaration of war on God, his messenger, and Muslims." The ruling issued by the signatories was that "to kill the Americans and their allies—civilians and military—is an individual duty for every Muslim who can do it in any country in which it is possible to do it, in order to liberate the al-Aqsa Mosque [Jerusalem] and the holy mosque [Mecca] from their grip, and in order for their armies to move out of all the lands of Islam, defeated and unable to threaten any Muslim."[15] The signatories were bin Laden, Zawahiri as leader of Islamic Jihad, Rifai Taha for the Islamic Group (who later withdrew), and leaders of the Islamist groups of Pakistan and Bangladesh. They did not refer to themselves collectively as al Qaeda but as the International Islamic Front for Jihad against Jews and Crusaders.

This fatwa came after what had undoubtedly been a busy period for Islamists. They had been engaged to varying degrees in a number of conflicts, including those in Algeria, Bosnia, Chechnya, Egypt, Kashmir, and Somalia, yet had precious little to show for their efforts. In this respect the timing of the fatwa was curious, because it came when Islamists were licking their wounds and many were seeking to give up on violent action. To declare war on the United States from an isolated camp in a broken country ravaged by war struck many, even potential supporters, as foolish and reckless bombast. Zawahiri's role, as he drafted the declaration, was particularly surprising. As late as 1995, he insisted that "the Road to Jerusalem Goes through Cairo."

Many of his erstwhile comrades were shocked at the turn in his thinking. After a period of minimal success with a series of "near" enemies, why decide to take on the "far" enemy?

To answer, it is necessary to look at their recent experience in two Arab conflicts. The first was in Algeria and was particularly intense and nasty. After gaining independence from France in 1962, the National Liberation Front (FLN) held on to power in Algeria, acquiring a reputation for corruption and repression. As with many North African countries, it struggled with a young and angry population. Some 40 percent of a population of 24 million was under fifteen. The young were largely urban, unemployed, and disaffected. Until the mid-1980s, discontent had been bought off using oil exports, but when the price collapsed there was nothing to fall back upon. Unlike other repressive regimes, the FLN's Marxism deprived it of tame clerics able to give it legitimacy. President Boumedienne tried to respond in 1985 by displacing the original Marxist orientation in favor of a more Arabic and Islamic approach. This was, however, already the ideology of protest. The normal alternative of socialism had for so long been the official ideology that it could not also serve in this role.

In 1989, the Front Islamique du Salut (FIS) was legalized. A relatively new party with strong Saudi backing, it claimed respect for the democratic process and no greater ambition than replacing the FLN in government and establishing a state true to Islamic law. In this it reflected the traditional focus of Muslim groups in Algeria on piety among leaders rather than creating Islamist states or nationalist struggles. There were, however, more radical elements in the movement that lacked confidence that winning elections would be sufficient to cleanse Algeria of its impure elements. To the fore of the radical segment were veterans of Afghanistan. One reason for the relatively large number of Algerians who had traveled to Afghanistan to fight was the close association of the Soviet Union with the FLN, which made the Soviets more despised than in other Arab countries.

In March 1991, the FIS won municipal elections. As its members took control of local councils, they began to impose Sharia law and pass funds to Islamist organizations. The FLN took fright as demonstrations were organized demanding their overthrow. There was slippage in the FIS's support, but the group did sufficiently well in the first round of national elections in December 1991 to be on the verge of taking democratic power. To thwart this, the military took control, called off elections, dissolved the FIS, interned its members in camps, and put mosques under surveillance. The FIS had no response. Its members were imprisoned. Many went underground and began to organize themselves into opposition groups.

Although some FIS activists were prepared to explore negotiations with the authorities, bin Laden urged them to avoid dialogue and overthrow the regime. Whatever bin Laden's role, there is no doubt that it was the Afghan veterans who were at the heart of the Group Islamique Armé (GIA), which emerged as the leading opposition group. By May 1994, it managed to get all of the jihadist groups to come under its banner and was said to be able to call upon as many as 20,000 fighters. It began by killing non-Muslims, then journalists and intellectuals, and moved on to anybody who seemed interested in participating in a normal political process. Rather than taking on the army, it sought to use terrorist methods, including car bombs, to create a climate of fear among the civilian population. It also internationalized the struggle—picking on France in particular as the perceived power behind the government. French nationals were murdered in Algeria, and in 1995, Paris suffered a number of outrages.

By this time the GIA's influence was spreading through North Africa, including Morocco and Tunisia, and then into France, Italy, and Spain. By the end of 1995, the Algerian government looked vulnerable to a final push. The GIA's leader, Jamel Zituni, unusually, was not an Afghan veteran, which he suspected made him vulnerable to a coup. He began a purge, which, as was increasingly the pattern, led to his murder by other Islamists. The GIA was gripped by internecine fighting that damaged its reputation. So did its readiness to engage in ever more brutal massacres of civilians. The population started to swing behind the government, whose own methods had been vicious enough. They did not, however, as was often claimed at the time, engage in large-scale massacres to discredit the GIA. The GIA discredited itself. This was a classic case of a revolution consuming its own. The leadership kept on passing to ever younger and more extreme militants, who eventually reached the inevitable conclusion that anyone who had not joined the GIA deserved execution just for that lapse. By 1997, it had become apparent to many of the original FIS militants that they were also vulnerable to the GIA and that their attempted revolution had taken a terrible turn. At the end of a decade in which an estimated 200,000 lives were lost, a truce was signed. The GIA, depleted and despised, just vanished, until it returned as a branch of al Qaeda.

The Egypt struggle was not as deadly but was more consequential because this was Zawahiri's fight. In the immediate aftermath of Sadat's death, there were a number of Islamist uprisings in Egypt. Although not suppressed with the bloody efficiency of Assad in Hama, they nonetheless required determined action, often using paratroopers. Mubarak hoped, as had Sadat, that Afghanistan could provide diversionary activity for the jihadists, which is why he went along with support for the mujahideen. This enabled him, in 1984, to ease some of the political restrictions, thereby creating opportunities for the Muslim Brotherhood to expand in numbers and influence, notably in the universities and professional associations. Even the "moderate" preachers, of course, were deeply hostile to the Christian community and to secular intellectuals, and challenged all legislation deemed inconsistent with Islamic law. Yet this was still too tame for the Islamists, who were looking for more direct means to create an Islamic state. Zawahiri condemned the Brotherhood because of its misplaced belief in democracy. Yet he lacked a credible strategy. Originally, he hoped to develop support in the military in order to prepare the way for a coup. Insurgency in Egypt was difficult because of the country's flat terrain: The narrow valley of the Nile between two deserts "made guerrilla warfare in Egypt impossible."[16]

When the Islamic Group renewed its campaign, with foreigners and tourists as special targets, it was Zawahiri's Islamic Jihad group that got caught when the police stumbled on its membership list, with the result that 800 of his members were captured. After a 1993 attempt to assassinate the Egyptian interior minister, which instead killed a schoolgirl, still more of his people were arrested. From Sudan, where he survived an Egyptian assassination attempt, Zawahiri lashed out in retaliation and frustration. His activities put Turabi in a difficult position. His neighbor was already suspicious of Sudan's seditious activities. In 1995, an attempt on Mubarak's life while he was visiting Ethiopia almost succeeded. Turabi showed an undiplomatic lack of sympathy, praising the attempt, and said of Mubarak that he was "very far below my level of thinking and my views, and too stupid to understand my pronouncements."[17] Egypt turned on Sudan for its complicity. Realizing that he had overreached himself, Turabi expelled Zawahiri. Even bin Laden was nervous when Islamic Jihad used suicide bombers to attack the Egyptian Embassy in Islamabad, leading to sixteen deaths. In 1995, Zawahiri, isolated and with many of his activists incarcerated, concluded that he had to suspend operations. He sent word to this effect to his cadres inside and outside Egypt. But he did not publicly declare an end to hostilities. The Islamic Group was much larger and accounted for 90 percent of the attacks in Egypt during the 1990s. When the group started to debate, more publicly, its own cease-fire, Zawahiri felt able to denounce it for doing so.[18] The mood in the country was for some tranquillity after a testing period, and so in July 1997, the Islamic Group declared a cease-fire and urged its followers to end hostilities. The news stunned hard-liners living in exile. Furious at this betrayal, a number mounted one last attack. On November 17, 1997, six members casually killed fifty-eight tourists and four Egyptians at Luxor. Both Zawahiri and bin Laden were implicated, but if they thought this would inspire militancy, it had the opposite effect. After Luxor, support for the Islamists within Egypt declined.

This was a low point for Zawahiri. He was completely out of cash, his organization was broken, and his ambitions for Egypt were shattered. He had little choice but to bring the remnants of Islamic Jihad together with the Islamic Group and link up with bin Laden. In his memoir, he explained that he had to conclude it was impossible to overthrow local regimes because the "Zionist-Crusader alliance" would not permit it. There was therefore no choice left but to bring forward the struggle against the far enemy.[19] More positively, the various struggles of the 1990s in the Caucasus, the Balkans, Central Asia, East Asia, and the Middle East, and the movement of militants through bin Laden's camps in Afghanistan, had created a sort of global Islamist consciousness. One complaint about bin Laden from the other militants was that he was basically a publicist, with little grasp of organizational or doctrinal matters. In a way this was true, but it also meant that Zawahiri and bin Laden were in tune with the times, picking up on the new information technologies and ready to take advantage of opportunities to reach out to mass audiences that would previously have been inaccessible. In 1996, Al-Jazeera, an Arab satellite station, began to broadcast material that was not controlled by the main regional powers. By 1999, it was so successful that it was offering a twenty-four-hour news service.

✴   ✴   ✴

To argue for taking on a superpower when it had proved impossible to upend relatively minor regimes required a certain faith in the vulnerability of the superpower. Bin Laden was not unusual in drawing the conclusion from Vietnam and then Beirut that the United States lacked staying power in the face of casualties. His confidence was reinforced by his ability to mythologize his own role in the Soviet failure in Afghanistan, which showed that superpowers were not invincible, and then the role of his followers in Somalia.

It would have been surprising if bin Laden had not been interested in Somalia. From his perspective, this had obvious potential: a poor country in a strategically sensitive position on the Horn of Africa. The population of some 9 million was almost entirely Sunni Muslim, as Christians had been chased away during the 1970s. It was a country for whom the term "failed state" might have been invented: None of the normal state institutions functioned, and society was falling apart. In such a setting well-trained, highly motivated, and comparatively well-resourced activists ought to be able to make a difference without being harassed by the sort of ruthless local security apparatus that caused so much trouble elsewhere. The promise was of a new safe haven in which to train and to plan. The added attraction was that as al Qaeda moved militants into Somalia, the Americans were also dispatching a large force to the country. This meant that as well as trying to move the Somali people toward true Islam, it was important to get the Americans out, both to demonstrate once again their vulnerability to the righteous anger of believers and to stop them from establishing a presence in the region that could threaten bin Laden's sanctuary of Sudan. It was hard to get at the Americans in Saudi Arabia. This promised to be much easier.

Somalia's government, such as it was, had collapsed at the start of 1991. Rival militias competed for power while bandits took advantage of the general chaos. Combined with a terrible drought, this created a humanitarian catastrophe, threatening half the population with starvation and disease. In response, the UN tried to organize relief with a small peacekeeping force to monitor a supposed cease-fire and help get assistance to the people. But the international community could not cope with the continued violence and at the end of 1992, President Bush authorized a substantial U.S. force of 25,000 troops to intervene and work with the UN to attempt to ease the suffering. Operation Restore Hope was undoubtedly a response to the publicity surrounding the dreadful conditions in Somalia, but it also deflected attention from the administration's reluctance to get involved in Bosnia, then an apparently more dangerous arena for intervention. Moreover, Bush might have reasoned, with the presidential election already lost, this was a problem he was handing over to his successor, Bill Clinton. Clinton was less than pleased with this legacy and immediately ordered a reduction of troops and a handover of responsibility for the operation back to the UN.[20]

The most troublesome of the warlords was General Mohamed Farah Aidid, whose militia had been fighting since the 1980s to take power. He now opposed the outside forces. When, in June 1993, a number of Pakistani peacekeepers were attacked and killed, orders were issued to capture or at least contain Aidid, but they were ineffective and the local situation remained insecure. To address the Aidid problem, the United States sent U.S. Army Ranger units to the capital, Mogadishu, outside of the UN command. On October 3, 1993, the Americans launched an operation to capture some of Aidid's key aides, but it went badly wrong. Militiamen shot down two helicopters, killing eighteen U.S. soldiers and leaving seventy-five wounded. The bodies of some of the soldiers were publicly violated on the streets of Mogadishu.[21] In this battle, anywhere from 500 to 1,500 Somalis also lost their lives. According to Clarke, Clinton was irate at the mess. He pronounced that "we are not running away with our tail between our legs." Nor would they be going "to flatten Mogadishu to prove we are the bad-ass superpower." More troops would be sent in and food would be delivered. "If anybody fucks with us, we will respond, massively." But whatever the impression all this created, the telling fact was still that U.S. forces would withdraw by the end of March 1994.[22] The unavoidable conclusion was that once again the United States had been chased away as soon as its forces faced serious resistance. This was not necessarily how it was viewed in the United States, where many in Congress saw the main fault as having allowed U.S. forces to serve as part of a UN mission.

The episode revealed the inexperience and lack of coordination among the Clinton team. They had accepted too easily the idea that they should go after Aidid without providing the necessary military strength or thinking through the implications of the effort. Defense Secretary Les Aspin took the responsibility, and for other reasons it was time for him to go, but the blame should have been widely spread. Clinton drew the conclusion, soon evident as genocide unfolded in Rwanda, that whatever awful things were going on, the wisest course politically would be to stay clear.

Bin Laden claimed a critical involvement, with as many as 250 agents engaged in forcing the Americans out. One thorough study of the episode, for the U.S. Army, agrees that there was an al Qaeda presence but judges its role to have been marginal. This study put the arrival of al Qaeda into Somalia (and the neighboring and disputed Ogaden region of Ethiopia) at February 1993, just as the U.S. force was settling down. Twelve al Qaeda militants established three training camps, working with a Somali group known as al-Ittihad al-Islami (AIAI). This was an amalgamation of many small Islamist groups, some going back to the 1980s, all of which had trouble surviving independently. In 1991, they had reached a fighting strength of about 1,000 men, but the resurgence of internal divisions and poor command meant that by 1992, they were not in good shape and were uncertain about whether Somalia was really ripe for jihad.

When al Qaeda arrived, it faced not only this skepticism born of setbacks but also many of the factors with which other external actors struggled. The lawlessness of the country created enormous logistical problems and extra costs; notional local supporters turned out to be unreliable; and, despite a shared religion, al Qaeda had no means of bringing the warring clans together. Even when financial inducements were offered, tribal loyalties still proved to be stronger. The Somali brand of Islam was much more moderate and less demanding than the austere message of al Qaeda. Only where al Qaeda men could provide basic security was a durable presence created. One such area was around Ras Kamboni, where guards allowed people to get on with their daily life. This area stayed loyal to the Islamists, even until the 2000s, when it was a stronghold of the Islamic Courts Movement.

If the aim was to take on the Americans, then that required working as partners with one of the more substantial factions, including the secular General Aidid, who had inflicted earlier defeats on the AIAI. One al Qaeda official noted: "I do not mind cooperating with Aidid if you have made sure that what he is doing with the Americans is not staged."[23] If there was cooperation, the contribution to the embarrassment of the Americans in Mogadishu and their eventual departure was still marginal. Moreover, there was no lasting advantage to al Qaeda. As one member noted in 1995: "The West was defeated and fled Somalia. . . . [But] the original problem that you went to address still exists. What happened to the Somali Salafia and where is it now . . . ? Did you suddenly go to Somalia and suddenly withdraw, as happened in Afghanistan?"[24]

No matter. In bin Laden's thinking, this episode confirmed a compelling pattern of American behavior, which gave credibility to the strategy of attacking the far enemy, and in his mind, or at least his propaganda, he could claim some part in this, which gave credibility to his organization. He was quite prepared to take credit for any attack on the Americans, including the assault on the Khobar Towers: "We incited and they responded."[25] A 2000 recruiting video for al Qaeda brought these themes together. Already one superpower had been dealt a mortal blow: "Using very meager resources and military means, the Afghan Mujahideen demolished one of the most important human myths in history and the biggest military apparatus. We no longer fear the so-called Great Powers." Then after references to Vietnam and Beirut, comes the assertion "that America is much weaker than Russia." To support this, evidence is cited from Somalia: "Our brothers who fought in Somalia told us that they were astonished to observe how weak, impotent, and cowardly the American soldier is. As soon as eighty American troops were killed, they fled in the dark as fast as they could, after making a great deal of noise about the new international order."[26] He had made the same point in his 1997 interview with Peter Arnett, when he remarked on how those of his comrades who had fought in Somalia had been surprised by the "low spiritual morale" of the Americans, even compared with the Russians. He noted how "the largest power on earth" left "after some resistance from powerless, poor, unarmed people."[27] The Americans did not have to be hit too hard before they would run away.

*   *   *

On February 26, 1993, a Ford van packed with explosives was detonated under New York City's World Trade Center basement parking garage. It had been planted by Ramzi Yousef, born of a Palestinian mother and Pakistani father, animated by the Palestinian cause as much as by Islamist ideology. His aim was to topple one tower onto the other, hoping to kill tens of thousands of people. In the event, six were killed and 1,042 injured. The towers shook but they did not fall. Given that bin Laden was prepared to take credit for attacks on Americans where it was not due, it is notable that he denied involvement in this attack. This may be because he realized that claiming responsibility for direct attacks on U.S. territory might be too provocative. He was certainly linked with Rahman, the "Blind Sheikh," who was also linked to Yousef. When Rahman was arrested in the United States, bin Laden proposed attacking the U.S. Embassy in Saudi Arabia. This made not only some of the factions in al Qaeda nervous, but also his Sudanese hosts at the time.

From New York, Yousef flew back to Pakistan, where he tried to assassinate Bhutto, and then on to Manila, where he met up in 1994 with his uncle (although only three years older) Khaled Sheik Mohammed. Mohammed, born in Kuwait of a Pakistani family, had lived and worked in the United States and also spent time with the mujahideen in Afghanistan. When he and Yousef met up in the Philippines, they started to think through the idea of attacks designed as grisly media spectacle, commanding attention through their audacity and shock value, rather than following the patient path of guerrilla warfare, wearing down the enemy through the cumulative impact of ambushes and continual harassment. With such tactics, civilian casualties were not an unfortunate consequence: They were the central objective. His first plot was to destroy twelve commercial airliners over the Pacific, and they got as far as testing a bomb on a Philippine Airlines flight in December 1994, which killed an unlucky Japanese passenger. Soon afterward, the plot was uncovered and Yousef was captured in Pakistan. As a fugitive, Mohammed made his way to Afghanistan, where he met the newly arrived bin Laden in late 1996 and outlined his ideas for a multiple attack on the United States, which became the basis for 9/11. He initially resisted full membership in al Qaeda until bin Laden's first major operation.

This was in East Africa. On August 7, 1998, two trucks loaded with explosives went to U.S. embassies in Dar es Salaam, Tanzania, and Nairobi, Kenya. The bomb in Nairobi was the most deadly, killing 213, many from a secretarial college, and twelve Americans. There were 4,500 injured. The death toll in Tanzania was eleven dead and eighty-five wounded—all Africans. The rationales referred to Somalia, Sudan, and Rwanda, but the best explanation was that this seemed an effective way of putting al Qaeda on the map. There was an opportunistic aspect to the operation. These were African countries with no history of Islamist terrorism but with large Muslim populations. As Steve Simon and Daniel Benjamin put it, the "East African bombings were the companion piece to the fatwa."[28] When the Americans responded by sending cruise missiles to catch bin Laden at one of his camps, he was somewhere else. The public relations advantage was with bin Laden. He was now established as a survivor as well as a leader.

This does not mean that bin Laden's leadership position was undisputed. Although the August 1998 cruise missile attacks annoyed Omar, hardening attitudes to the United States, there was continual concern among the various groups working out of the Islamist camps in Afghanistan that if the Taliban were exposed too much to international anger, they might be obliged to expel them. Bin Laden had his loyal followers, who were obliged to swear their fealty to him, but others, often with their own jihadist histories and agendas, kept their independence. Many now were non-Arab, drawn to the Islamist cause through the conflicts in Chechnya and Kashmir. Not all in the camps were convinced of the need to mount spectacle against the Americans, as they saw these efforts as putting them in jeopardy and distracting from training for more local conflicts. They did not share bin Laden's confidence in the inner weakness of the United States: On the contrary, they thought it a "ruthless rival" that was dangerous to underestimate. In the fascinating collection of material taken in Kabul in 2001 from Zawahiri's discarded computer, there is a complaint, from July 1999, that bin Laden "has caught the disease of screens, flashes, fans, and applause."[29]

The proposal that eventually led to 9/11 did not enjoy widespread support among the broad leadership of al Qaeda, but bin Laden pressed ahead anyway. The plot was first hatched in meetings involving Mohammed and bin Laden in the spring of 1999. The concept was Mohammed's. The men who would carry out the attack were also recruited that year. The leader would be Mohammed Atta, born in Egypt of a Saudi family. For most of the 1990s, Atta was based in Hamburg, Germany, where he was a student of urban planning. His house became the base of a cell of young Arabs committed to the idea of jihad. They had planned to go to Chechnya to fight the Russians, but they were persuaded instead to go to Afghanistan. Atta was now marked out as a serious and competent leader and was given responsibility for a scheme that was now focused on crashing aircraft into symbolic sites in New York City and Washington, D.C. By the summer of 2000, he was in the United States, and soon he and his colleagues were enrolled in a flying school. Bin Laden was impatient. The political message would benefit from a link to the early stages of the second intifada in Palestine. He would have been content if the planes had just crashed in American cities without worrying about specific targets. Mohammed urged patience: He needed a larger team, and the flying training had to be completed.

In October 2000, al Qaeda did manage one attack, when the destroyer USS *Cole*, which had launched cruise missiles against al Qaeda's camp in August 1998, was attacked by a small craft carrying explosives off the Yemeni coast. Seventeen sailors were killed and a large hole left in the side of the warship. As with the later 9/11 attack, al Qaeda did not claim to be responsible, although the Islamist community assumed it was, and bin Laden's standing was boosted accordingly. The Americans made the same assumption, but they found it difficult to get definite proof. For this reason, and apparently to bin Laden's frustration, there was no retaliation.

★   ★   ★

By this time, the members of the Clinton administration who followed these matters were getting the measure of al Qaeda, but they were still not sure what to do about it. Part of the problem was making sense of radical Islam. Its rejection of modernity, human rights, and international institutions, and its obscurity of language and practice, all went against the progress and optimism bound up with the post–cold war world and globalization. The sense of a relatively coordinated network rather than a series of disparate operations undertaken by independent operators took time to develop. There were continuities in the terrorist activity associated with the more radical Middle Eastern states such as Libya and with groups such as Abu Nidal. With Libya suffering international isolation and sanctions, Iran was considered to be the growing and most dangerous threat. Then there were some strange new outfits, such as the Japanese cult Aum Shinrikyo, which released sarin nerve gas on the Tokyo subway in 1995, thereby forging a link between terrorism and weapons of mass destruction that encouraged worst-case thinking in the policy community. Organizationally, counterterrorism was given a higher profile. Richard Clarke, a tough, experienced, and driven official, was the first coordinator for counterterrorism on the National Security Council staff. He was hampered, as were all those who worked in this area, by the traditional rivalries between the FBI and the CIA, aggravated by the problems of finding demarcation lines between the domestic and the foreign.

In 1995, when Clinton imposed sanctions on groups linked with terrorism for disrupting the Arab-Israeli peace process, bin Laden and al Qaeda received not a mention. A 1995 National Intelligence Estimate on terrorism that also made no mention of bin Laden or al Qaeda nonetheless recognized Yousef as representative of a "new breed" of radical Sunni terrorist that might well have designs against the United States. This could include "na-

tional symbols such as the White House and the Capitol, and symbols of
U.S. capitalism such as Wall Street. . . . civil aviation will figure prominently
among possible terrorist targets in the United States." Even worse, if the terrorists were at all methodical, "they will identify serious vulnerabilities in the
security system for domestic flights."[30]

Only at the start of 1996 did the CIA start tracking bin Laden seriously. By
then he was off to Afghanistan. Intelligence cooperation with the Saudis and
Pakistanis who might be expected to have the best grasp of Sunni Islamists
was never straightforward: There were always areas of policy and activity into
which they did not want the Americans to pry. After the Soviet withdrawal
from Afghanistan, the CIA maintained a presence in Afghanistan, but the effort was drawn down in the face of the bewildering circumstances of the early
1990s and the inability to establish a durable partnership with any faction.
The initial reaction to the arrival of the Taliban was neutral, even mildly positive, as it seemed the best hope for restoring a modicum of order. But it was
not an easy group to talk to, even when amenable to dialogue, and its treatment of women (a matter on which the first lady and the secretary of state
had particularly strong views) meant that it seemed best to keep a distance.
At the same time, neutrality was maintained in the battle between Massoud
and the Taliban. This reduced American leverage with the local figure most
opposed to the Taliban. Meanwhile the CIA had no agents within either the
Taliban or al Qaeda. As bin Laden's role became more prominent and the potential for mischief recognized, there were plans to kidnap him, but they were
rejected as having all the ingredients of a first-class fiasco.

Clinton's growing interest in the topic was reflected in a 1996 speech not
long after the Khobar bombings. The president set down his strategy for
dealing with terrorism, a problem to which nobody was immune—an "equal
opportunity destroyer, with no respect for borders." Measures were required
at home and abroad, from better intelligence gathering and sharing to making life hard for the terrorists and ensuring that they were denied sanctuaries. In language that could be used a decade later, he spoke of "a long, hard
struggle" with "setbacks along the way." The United States, however, would
"not be driven from the tough fight against terrorism today. Terrorism is the
enemy of our generation, and we must prevail." He concluded:

> But I want to make it clear to the American people that while we can
> defeat terrorists, it will be a long time before we defeat terrorism. Amer-
> ica will remain a target because we are uniquely present in the world,
> because we act to advance peace and democracy, because we have taken
> a tougher stand against terrorism, and because we are the most open

society on Earth. But to change any of that, to pull our troops back from the world's trouble spots, to turn our backs on those taking risks for peace, to weaken our opposition against terrorism, to curtail the freedom that is our birthright would be to give terrorism a victory it must not and will not have.[31]

It was really only after the August 1998 attacks that there was a determination to do something about bin Laden. Then, according to Clinton, he "became intently focused on capturing or killing him and with destroying al-Qaeda."[32] He demanded the destruction of al Qaeda to be "one of our top national security objectives and an urgent one." He wanted to "get rid of these guys once and for all." Sandy Berger is said to have put it even more directly when he met with the heads of the key agencies at the White House: "I spoke with the President and he wants you all to know . . . this is it, nothing more important, all assets. We stop this fucker."[33]

While Clinton saw the August 1998 strikes as designed "perhaps to wipe out much of the al-Qaeda leadership,"[34] the result if anything boosted the organization and added to its legend. There were five unfortunate features of the strikes. First, the timing. The scandal was breaking around the president's affair with a former White House intern, Monica Lewinsky, and anything he did was bound to be judged in this unseemly light. Second, the worry about the link with WMD led to a cruise missile attack on a pharmaceutical factory in Sudan. Intelligence suggested that bin Laden sought to develop chemical weapons while in Sudan and that this factory was the site. This also assumed, which Clarke believed, that bin Laden had not broken with the Sudanese regime. To check the intelligence, the CIA managed to get a soil sample which, when analyzed, showed traces of chemicals used for making a nerve agent. This was probably an inadequate basis for firing thirteen cruise missiles into Sudan to attack a plant that by then was claimed to be producing medicines and without any residual al Qaeda connection. Third, when sixty-six cruise missiles were also sent into two al Qaeda training camps near Khost in Afghanistan, this time on the basis of only slightly dated intelligence, they might have caught bin Laden and key members of the al Qaeda leadership, because their decision not to visit the camps was taken at the last minute. In the end, as was later lamented, the main consequence of the strike was to "rearrange the sand." Fourth, neither the Saudis nor the Pakistanis were warned of the impending strikes (in part because they could not be trusted with the secret), which they saw as typically half-hearted American efforts, failing to deal with the problem while provoking Muslim opinion. Fifth, the strikes were optimistically named "Operation Infinite Reach," whereas the net effect was to expose the limits of the American reach, the poor quality of American intelligence, and the haphazard nature of some operational planning.

Elsewhere there was some success, including getting the mujahideen and Iranians out of Bosnia. When it looked like nobody else was going to come to their assistance, the largely Muslim Bosnian government was ready to accept all comers to help in the fight against the Serbs. The United States tried to make it clear to the Bosnians that American support was conditional on getting rid of the Islamists. Long after the peace accords were signed at Dayton, Ohio, at the start of 1996, NATO forces made finds of men and materials and uncovered plots. The Bosnians did not make removing these people a high priority. There were, however, too many NATO troops around to establish a base, and it was hard to stir up anti-Western feeling when the survival of the mini-state had depended on Western intervention.

Elsewhere, even in apparently friendly Arab states, evident cooperation with the United States in arresting terror suspects always seemed a risky business, so operations were often leaked or aborted before anything was achieved. And the cells were proliferating. Kashmir and Chechnya had become new fronts in the war. Activists were popping up in a range of countries, agitating among local Muslim populations and recruiting through mosques and religious schools, disseminating an antimodern message with the most modern of communication techniques. By the end of 1999, the CIA estimated that there were cells in sixty countries. There was a growing sense of foreboding about the ability of these groups to carry out more spectacular attacks, possibly—even probably—in the mainland United States. Yet there was increasing frustration about the ability to prevent such attacks by getting at bin Laden and his associates before it was too late. In part this was because of the general loss of authority Clinton suffered as a result of the Lewinsky scandal, as well as the unsatisfactory nature of the August 1998 attacks. It was also partly because of the poor relations between the White House and the military, with senior officers distrustful of schemes from civilians that willed the political ends without willing sufficient military means. Recent history was littered with examples of humiliating failures as soon as the military moved out of its comfort zone of large-scale conventional operations. The military showed no enthusiasm for long-distance commando raids, especially when intelligence was patchy and dated and CIA connections were limited and unreliable.

The diplomatic option was to put pressure on the Taliban to hand over bin Laden, but that required cooperation with Pakistan. Whatever the Pakistani leadership might say, the ISI continued to look after its assets and was playing Afghanistan for the long term, so it was not inclined to sacrifice its position to meet the transient American anxieties. By 1999, the Pakistani government of Nawaz Sharif was incredibly weak, unwilling to stand up to the military and ISI, which were looking to extend control over Afghanistan and undermine the Indians in Kashmir. After the military got deeply involved in Kashmir, Sharif was put under enormous international pressure to order a withdrawal. His acquiescence sealed his fate, and he was overthrown by a military coup led by General Pervez Musharraf.

The remaining military option depended on high-quality intelligence arriving in time to warrant a cruise missile strike, which would require bin Laden to stay put for two hours until the missiles arrived. This almost happened three times. But after August 1998, high standards of trustworthiness were required for intelligence and avoiding innocent casualties. Clarke's advice was just to keep on attacking the camps and not worry whether bin Laden was present or not. "We have to stop this conveyor belt, this production line. Blow them up every once in a while and recruits won't want to go there." The military pointed out the relevant value of each cruise missile ($750,000) as against simple buildings that would be easy to replace. Defense Secretary Cohen was reluctant to add another burden to an overstretched military, while Albright worried about an outcry in Pakistan in the event of regular bombing of Afghanistan.[35]

But the floundering demonstrated the basic problems of preemption. Strictly speaking, as Attorney General Janet Reno pointed out, preemption requires stopping an imminent attack. But in this situation, the difficulty with imminence as a concept was that once set in motion, these attacks developed in slow motion, away from those who had ordered them and always potentially frustrated by good police and intelligence work. Was not an attack on the supposed source rather drastic? And how could you be sure of culpability? Or that the target had been properly identified when a strike was ordered, or was still there when the strike arrived? Was the aim to capture or kill, and if the latter, how to be sure that innocents would not be killed? This was especially true if using Afghans as agents. How reliable would they be and what assurances would there be that they would not do too much, that is, cause a massacre of bystanders, or too little, and simply take money while doing little in return?

Bin Laden's choice of America as his main enemy was understood, and the dangers he could pose were recognized. It was hard, however, to grasp the potential impact of the threat, to think of it as a deadly and professional organization rather than as a ramshackle outfit with a fantastical worldview that aimed for targets of opportunity and sometimes struck lucky.

PART FIVE

GEORGE W. BUSH

★ ★ ★

17

THE WAR ON TERROR

GEORGE W. BUSH achieved little during the first decades of his life. During Vietnam, he managed to put on a Texas Air National Guard uniform but never got close to combat. He later acknowledged his irresponsible youth and admitted to drinking too much until he turned to Christianity. His first forays into politics, like those into business, were not particularly successful. Yet in 1994, he won a surprise victory to become governor of Texas. When he decided to run for president in 2000, his advantages were partly dynastic, but he also had a reasonable record as chief executive of a large state, an understanding of the need to appeal to the center as a "compassionate conservative" and to social conservatives as a conspicuous Christian, with the appropriately tough positions on gun control, abortion, and capital punishment. Neither articulate nor intellectually curious, he was easy to underestimate, which was the mistake made by his opponent in 2000, Vice President Al Gore. Gore should have benefited from a strong economy and the Clinton political machine, but after the Lewinsky scandal, he decided to distance himself from the president and came across as patronizing and ponderous during the campaign. Even so, it was Gore who won the popular vote, and it was only the peculiarities of how votes were counted in Florida and the Supreme Court's view of the proceedings that allowed Bush to squeeze in as president.

There was an early presumption that the younger Bush would pick up where the elder Bush had left off. Leaving aside psychological explanations of the determination of the son to distinguish himself from the father, there is little doubt that the son was influenced by what he saw as the two most damaging features of the father's presidency—raising taxes after promising not to and failing to topple Saddam Hussein when he had the chance. Looking at his team, however, the best assumption was of continuity, with one exception. That was Donald Rumsfeld, the new secretary of defense, a man the father disliked as a rival and excluded from his administration. Rumsfeld was returning to a post he had held under Gerald Ford, thereby making him both the youngest and the oldest man to run the Pentagon. He saw his task as transforming the American armed forces so that they were taking full advantage of the technical developments summed up under the heading the "revolution in military affairs," and getting away from the lumbering military formations of the cold war days. He was known as an acerbic activist, unlikely to respect an opinion just because it came from a man in uniform. Soon into his tenure at the Pentagon, he was in an adversarial relationship with senior officers.

Rumsfeld enjoyed his position as a result of his close relationship with vice president Richard Cheney, who, perhaps unfairly, was suspected of choosing himself as Bush's running mate. He added weight to the ticket, having had a spell in Congress in the 1960s and thereafter been in and out of government, peaking as secretary of defense under the elder Bush. His heart troubles meant that he could not be an aspirant for the presidency himself and could therefore concentrate on his executive role. The most formative political experiences for both Cheney and Rumsfeld went back to the Nixon administration. The trauma of those years of withdrawal from Vietnam and Watergate had left an impression. Both had seen power suddenly drain away from the executive branch, and they were determined not to let it happen again. Rumsfeld was unavoidably answerable to a Democratic Senate for the first two years, but Cheney was answerable only to the president. For Cheney, concepts of transparency and accountability held little sway. The point of power was to get your way, and that meant keeping tight control over decisionmaking and the information upon which it was based. He would not suffer the normal fate of vice presidents and be marginalized in the policymaking process. He expected to be involved in everything, including foreign policy, and unlike Gore, soon hired a substantial foreign policy team of his own. His approach to how the United States should exercise power internationally flowed from his personal approach to how it should be exercised in Washington—assertive and self-centered.

The tough, combative combination of Cheney and Rumsfeld was always going to be hard to beat in any debates over national security. The man who would be taking them on was Secretary of State Colin Powell, whose association with Bush during the campaign was offered as an assurance of heavyweight foreign policy advice. Powell was internationally respected for his caution and moderation, qualities that are admirable in a diplomat, though often of less value when it comes to hard political infighting. In addition, he was never close to any of the other key figures in the administration, including the president. National Security Adviser Condoleezza Rice had a stellar academic background and was a protégé of Brent Scowcroft, for whom she had worked when he held the same position. She had also become Bush's tutor in foreign affairs and a family friend. A Powell-Rice combination might have been a match for Cheney-Rumsfeld, but they were neither as close nor as ruthless. It was only with some effort that Rice managed to hold on as chair of the Principals Committee of the senior national security advisers, after Cheney asked for the task. Rumsfeld saw her as a lightweight and barely deigned to keep her informed of what he was up to. Rice was unable to control the big beasts of the administration, all of whom had served at the highest level in previous administrations and divided not only on personal but on philosophical lines that became progressively sharper. As a result this NSC was matched by only Reagan's in its dysfunction. Whereas with Reagan this resulted in policy paralysis, with Bush the result was policies not subject to effective scrutiny. Only during Bush's second term was a degree of order restored. Rice became the secretary of state. Rumsfeld's reputation was on the wane because of the mismanagement of post-war Iraq. The new national security adviser, Stephen Hadley, who had been Rice's deputy, was a more effective manager, albeit of a more compliant team.

Bush always made it clear that he was the "decider," and that he did not delegate responsibility for the big decisions. His sense of responsibility inevitably grew after 9/11 because all the decisions appeared bigger and more consequential. Any political leader at such a time would have some sense of destiny. Bush's feeling of destiny and his confidence that the right decisions were made may have been enhanced by his religious beliefs, but he never suggested that decisions came to him through divine revelation rather than the normal processes of weighing the pros and cons of alternative courses of action.

The other controversial influence on Bush's foreign policy (besides God, potentially) was neoconservatism. To the extent that this was a coherent philosophy, it involved a combination of causes normally associated with the left—overthrowing tyranny, easing humanitarian distress, and promoting democracy—and methods normally associated with the right, meaning relatively early resort to military force and distrust of international institutions and treaties. The most senior neocon in government was Paul Wolfowitz, deputy secretary of defense, and he had a number of associates in policy positions in the Pentagon and also in the vice president's office. Some of the elder statesmen of the neocon movement, such as Richard Perle, lurked around the edges of the administration. Neocons were apt to be confident and articulate in the presentation of a clear worldview, and polemical in style. These qualities tended to exaggerate their influence in practice. None of the senior figures in the administration were neocons. They might all agree that U.S. power was a great asset to be nurtured and savored, not carelessly shared with others or needlessly squandered, and that threats to national security had to be taken seriously and, where necessary, dealt with robustly. They might even take it for granted that American power would work for the betterment of humankind. But the neocons had a project which assumed that American power could and should be used to create a different kind of international system. They saw themselves engaged in a struggle with realists who prided themselves on their lack of radical goals, and felt that they had the critical advantage after 9/11, when U.S. policy was forced to take a radical turn and engage actively with the international system at its most dysfunctional points. Their agenda seemed appropriate to such a moment, both idealistic and hard-line at the same time. Yet while they provided the language with which policy was described, they did not provide the actual policy direction. For Cheney and Rumsfeld, the objective was to deal with threats to national security; everything else was secondary.

*   *   *

Initially neocon ideas, or any expansive agenda, were hardly apparent. Nor was there any reason to suppose that foreign policy would be a disputatious arena for the new administration. The positions Bush set out during the 2000 campaign were safe and conventional. The prospect seemed to be of a traditional realist approach—main priorities directly related to American interests, strong defense, suspicion of rising big powers, such as China, wariness about participation in Third World conflicts and nation building, and support for missile defenses, always a Republican Party favorite. Rice summed up the prospective attitude to armed force in a much quoted article for the journal *Foreign Affairs:*

> The president must remember that the military is a special instrument. It is lethal, and it is meant to be. It is not a civilian peace force. It is not a political referee. And it is most certainly not designed to build a civilian society. Military force is best used to support clear political goals,

whether limited, such as expelling Saddam from Kuwait, or comprehensive, such as demanding the unconditional surrender of Japan and Germany during World War II.

From this, Rice drew the conclusion that U.S. intervention in "humanitarian" crises would be at best "exceedingly rare." The criteria for getting involved were familiar. The president should ask "whether decisive force is possible and is likely to be effective and must know how and when to get out." Humanitarian interventions were thus largely jobs for allies.[1]

The most important example of caution when it came to the international agenda was the administration's attitude toward the Middle East peace process. As Bush entered office, Israeli and Palestinian negotiators were struggling to keep the damaged process alive at Taba. No American representative was sent to the talks, no replacement was found for Dennis Ross as the president's Middle Eastern envoy, and no commitment was shown to the "Clinton Parameters" of December 2000, which both Arafat and Barak had accepted as a basis for future territorial division. Although Clinton expected Bush to persevere with the process, when the two men met prior to the inauguration, he did not offer an encouraging description of Arafat as a partner. Moreover, Ariel Sharon defeated Barak in elections held just a few weeks after the inauguration, and Sharon had no interest in talking with Arafat. Powell expressed the American position: The United States cannot want peace more than the parties themselves, and the U.S. role in the past was not one of making the case for peace but of helping to find a means of achieving peace. As far as Bush was concerned, Clinton had spent an inordinate amount of time to no effect trying to broker a peace and seemed only to have made the situation worse. He was not going to follow this path. When in June the escalating violence required some response, Bush confined this to sending George Tenet to Israel, who had gotten to know the parties well during Clinton's time, to see if he could broker a cease-fire. At a time when a decade's worth of endeavors appeared to be collapsing, the preferred response was to stand back rather than engage.

From the perspective of Washington during the first eight months of 2001, the world did not seem unduly troubling. American power had reached a new peak, offering enormous range and flexibility in the potential conduct of foreign policy. If anything, the international concern was that the Bush administration would attempt to do too little rather than too much, but at least there were no great surprises. Contrary to some European fears, there was no precipitate withdrawal from peacekeeping responsibilities in Bosnia and Kosovo. Although he pushed the case for national missile defense, Bush tried to win over Russian president Vladimir Putin and even claimed to have "looked the man in the eye" and got "a sense of his soul." There was a spat with China over a reconnaissance aircraft, but it was managed through sensible diplomacy. Then came the attacks of September 11, 2001, and suddenly this was a war presidency, with a new internal balance. Foreign policy became national security, drawing in Cheney, who had been mainly involved in energy matters up to this point, and Rumsfeld, who had been trying to impose his will on the Pentagon with his agenda of military "transformation."

*   *   *

The transformation that Rumsfeld had in mind involved turning the armed forces, and especially the army, from something large and lumbering, with its ponderous buildups and demanding logistics, into a lighter, quicker, more agile instrument of policy. Whether because of organizational inertia or his bullying manner, he soon faced resistance and was scrapping with the service chiefs. Where he was not seeking a transformation was in the dominant scenarios that guided American force planning. These still pointed to proper wars between the armed forces of major powers, with far less attention being given to lesser types of combat. When thinking about asymmetrical conflict, in which the enemy adopts forms of warfare designed to avoid fighting the Americans on their own terms, the major threat appeared to be "superterrorism" of the most catastrophic kind, launched by "rogue" states rather than radical groups.

Powell was associated with the view that American military power was best employed, if at all, in an overwhelming manner to achieve clearly defined objectives with both speed and minimum casualties. Anything that threatened another quagmire, with murky purposes, was best avoided. Such interventions should never be started without a strategy for their conclusion.[2] Out of this came the critical distinction between "war," defined in terms of "large-scale combat operations," and "operations other than war," which included shows of force, operations for purposes of peace enforcement and peacekeeping, and counterterrorism and counterinsurgency. The military saw its role as preparing for proper war, which would be a climacteric, capital-intensive, high-technology, militarily decisive contest for political dominance between major powers. The other type, thrown up by the upheavals of a postimperial age, were localized, labor-intensive, socially devastating, never-ending struggles that gained international significance only to the extent that the major powers chose to take an interest.[3] Since the Soviet collapse, it was hard to imagine the United States being defeated in proper war, which for that reason alone became even less likely to occur.

Ample preparations were thus made to deal with adversaries aggressing against the United States and its allies. Communism had proved to be more durable in Asia than in Europe, and commitments to South Korea and, more ambiguously, Taiwan must be honored. With the status of conservative Gulf states upgraded to allies after 1991, containing Iraq was an additional commitment. A "two major wars" standard was set for defense policy, whereby at any given time the United States should be able to cope with aggressive action by both Iraq and North Korea.

Yet the Clinton administration discovered a variety of reasons that armed force might be used short of proper war. A growing amount of international business appeared to involve states suffering from internal wars, in which the United States had no vital interests. Clinton's embrace of humanitarian interventionism was only tentative, but even that went too far for a military establishment that preferred to stay well clear of Third World turbulence, where operations were apt to be irregular, protracted, complex, and indecisive, against an enemy that could merge with its surroundings. U.S. personnel could become caught in vicious cross fire while conducting largely political business of marginal relevance to U.S. interests. There was therefore an inbuilt reluctance to prepare for operations of this sort, and more effort was put into setting tough criteria for entrance and easy criteria for exit than into consideration of their special demands on regular armed forces. From the military perspective, for which they could expect strong congressional backing, it was best to avoid this lesser type of conflict, but if the United States chose to get involved, it would do so with the types of forces developed for repelling major aggression. There was little recognition that these operations required their own distinctive doctrine and training. When the issue arose, therefore, the preference was for allies and clients to offer the close combat, while the United States provided intelligence and logistics support and, possibly, airpower. As U.S. air capabilities were in a completely different league than all other nations, the United States could have a major impact without requiring the army to get involved in a type of operation it treated with disdain and for which it was not prepared.

Desert Storm had convinced the armed forces that they were on the right track. This campaign was the culmination of the trends in U.S. military planning since the Vietnam debacle, which had encouraged a return to the campaigning comfort zone of technically superior, skillfully orchestrated, and highly mobile firepower geared to eliminating the opposing force. This approach was marked by the adoption of the doctrine of AirLand Battle in

1982. Intended from the start to set broad principles for any war and not just NATO's central front, the doctrine renewed emphasis on maneuver after a past preoccupation with attrition, so the battlefield was seen in the round. The critical attributes of successful operations were stressed as "initiative, depth, agility and synchronization."[4] Even the 1986 Field Manual 90-8, *Counterguerrilla Operations*, dealing with action directed against armed antigovernment forces, claimed that the "basic concept of AirLand Battle doctrine can be applied to Counterguerrilla operations,"[5] demonstrating the extent to which this was seen as a secondary type of warfare that an army geared to proper war could take in stride.

Extrapolating from the success of AirLand Battle in Desert Storm led to claims of a "revolution in military affairs" riding on a technological dynamic that promised the domination of the information environment and thereby the battle space. The Bush administration took up this theme. Thus in May 2001, Bush asserted a preference for "future force that is defined less by size and more by mobility and swiftness, one that relies more heavily on stealth, precision weaponry and information technologies."[6] The very success of Desert Storm, however, made it less likely that future enemies would fight in a way that so conformed to American preferences: accepting a conventional battlefield where they would be comprehensively destroyed by superior firepower.

The expected adversary response would be to opt for asymmetric warfare. By definition, the weak have to employ asymmetrical methods against the strong, and the methods chosen will depend on how the weak analyze the vulnerabilities of the strong. As we have seen, one vulnerability that the weak noticed was the U.S. aversion to casualties, and it was on this precept that Saddam Hussein and Osama bin Laden had based their distinctive strategies. They found some support for this assumption in suggestions that advanced Western countries had entered a "postheroic" phase, leading to an increasing reluctance to put the young generation at risk in war, even with all-volunteer forces.[7] This was the lesson drawn from Vietnam, Beirut, and Somalia: The United States has such a low tolerance for casualties that it will abandon campaigns that it might otherwise have won to avoid severe losses. The strength of this presumption is illustrated in the U.S. Army's 1993 Field Manual 100–5 *Operations:*

> The American people expect decisive victory and abhor unnecessary casualties. They prefer quick resolution of conflicts and reserve the right to reconsider their support should any of these conditions not be met.[8]

The result was what Jeffrey Record described as "force-protection fetishism," in which lack of loss—not mission accomplishment—becomes the standard for judging an operational success. The 1999 Kosovo war demonstrated the impact of this concern. Because of the ability in this case to rely on the U.S. air contribution, there was a pleasing lack of American casualties but an added delay in easing the humanitarian distress.[9] Although there was evidence that the American people were far more robust than their leaders gave them credit for, in that accumulating casualties necessarily raised questions about the wisdom of a particular campaign but did not inevitably drain support,[10] the notion of casualty intolerance became so internalized that military and political leaders were loath to put it to the test.

Although terrorism was a political preoccupation through the 1990s, it was not really seen as a form of asymmetrical warfare. The disconnect was evident in the military's disinclination to put itself out to deal with al Qaeda in Afghanistan. Although in popular fiction and policy analysis, there was an awareness of the possibility that terrorists might be able to cause thousands of casualties using readily accessible instruments, including hijacked aircraft, the only scenario that created real anxiety was that weapons of mass destruction might be employed.[11] Analysis suggested a sharp distinction. "Normal" terrorism, relying on conventional explosives, would be capable of causing casualties in the low hundreds, of which the worst example was the 1988 bombing of Pan Am Flight 103 over Lockerbie, Scotland, which took the lives of 278 people. This could be the responsibility of terrorists representing a nonstate group or a state sponsor. On past experience it could be shocking in the short-term but of limited consequences as the impact could be absorbed. "Superterrorism," relying on chemical, biological, or even nuclear weapons, would cause casualties in the low thousands and upward. But this would probably only be within the capacity of a state and so would be an example of asymmetric warfare.

Such superterrorism would have severe consequences but it would also have a low probability, and the skeptics argued that it made more sense to concentrate on the higher-probability events. If anything, during the 1990s, the greatest speculation revolved around how a wily opponent would recognize the importance of information technologies to the nation's critical infrastructure and target them accordingly. In a culture that had assumed that the best military strategies were those that caused the minimum casualties, the thought that an enemy would aim for the support systems of modern societies was both comforting and alarming at the same time. The direct harm would be slight, while the indirect harm, as transportation, banking, and public health systems began to break down, could be substantial. An enemy able to mobilize an army of software wizards could subvert an advanced society by the most insidious electronic means. The threat gained credibility from the frequency with which companies and even high-profile networks, such as that of the U.S. military, were attacked by a variety of hackers. But much of this was "hacktivism," a way of making political or cultural points rather than threatening the economy or social cohesion, and even if more determined adversaries were prepared to try something more substantial, the result was likely to be "mass disruption" rather than "mass destruction," with inconvenience and disorientation more evident than terror and collapse.

Weapons of mass destruction did not appear to be those of choice for terrorists, and it seemed they would have problems handling them. Assuming that the terrorists had clear strategic purpose, their interest would be, as Brian Jenkins put it in a much quoted phrase, in getting "a lot of people watching, not a lot of people dead."[12] There was talk in the 1990s of a new terrorism that would move beyond occasional assassination and localized explosions to chemical and biological weapons and objectives that went off the normal political scale, the products of some private torment or zany cult as much as an organized movement for change.[13] Attempts to put al Qaeda in the same box as the Aum Shinrikyo sect in Japan, however, missed its distinctiveness. It went for spectacular deeds, because it wanted to catch attention, and was operating at a global rather than a national level; its aims were neither mystical nor obscure, despite the language in which they were often couched. In addition, despite the fear of mass terrorism, incidents in this category remained comparatively rare, so that by 2000 it was being noted, even by some of those who had taken the threat extremely seriously, that the "new era . . . of terrorism has failed to materialize."[14]

Moreover, following the 1995 Oklahoma City bombing, mass casualty terrorism appeared as much a domestic as an international problem. A 1996 nationwide survey found that 72 percent of Americans believed that there was a chance that terrorists could use a weapon of mass destruction to attack a U.S. city but only 13 percent worried about it. Two out of three declared themselves not much or not at all worried about terrorism in public places, and most saw the risks more likely to emerge from inside the United States than outside (49 as against 39 percent).[15]

Even studies that could later claim to have been prescient in their warnings about the hazards of superterrorism tended to discourage a focus on al Qaeda. Thus the Hart-Rudman Commission, which had identified "unannounced attacks on American cities" as the gravest threat, also suggested: "Terrorism will appeal to many weak states as an attractive, asymmetric option to blunt the influence of major powers. Hence state-sponsored terrorist attacks are at least as likely, if not more so, than attacks by independent, un-affiliated terrorist groups."[16] North Korea and Iraq once again appeared as likely culprits, so this threat could also be seen as having its most credible form as a derivative of the standard scenarios.

The framework within which the danger of superterrorism was viewed reinforced established defense thinking in another respect. In an influential article, Richard Betts drew on a 1993 estimate of millions of casualties resulting from the release of anthrax spores over Washington, D.C. He raised the issue of whether retreat might be the best defense, if faced with such dangers: "The United States should not give up all its broader political interests, but it should tread cautiously in areas—especially the Middle East—where broader interests grate against the core imperatives of preventing mass destruction within America's borders."[17] Thus if superterrorism might be an unwelcome by-product of an activist foreign policy, then a prudent policy would eschew too much involvement in the affairs of other states.

*   *   *

During the transition from the Clinton to the Bush administration, the terrorism issue was stressed repeatedly. Sandy Berger is said to have told Rice that she would spend more time "on terrorism generally and al Qaeda specifically than any other issue."[18] The two figures that had been most vocal about the danger of al Qaeda under Clinton were kept in their posts by Bush: Richard Clarke, the White House counterterrorism specialist, and CIA director George Tenet. Clarke passed a memo to Steve Hadley, Rice's deputy, setting out what was known about al Qaeda, the U.S. strategy for dealing with it, and success so far. There were warnings about sleeper cells in the United States and the risk of a major attack, but a lot of the focus was on how to squeeze bin Laden out of his privileged position in Afghanistan, which required finding ways of putting pressure on the Taliban and its sponsors in Pakistan. The basic message was "Continued anti–Al Qaida operations at the current level will prevent some attacks, but will not seriously attrite their ability to plan and conduct attacks."[19] The principals' meeting Clarke urged did not take place, and he and his function were demoted within the NSC structure. Rice wanted a comprehensive new plan, not just a leftover from the Clinton administration. Clarke was judged to be excitable and alarmist, and also pushing ideas left over from the previous administration rather than reflecting the thinking of the new. Clarke was focused on Afghanistan but to Rice there could be no progress until a way was found to deal with Pakistan's role in the region and its support for the Taliban.

In February 2001, Tenet reported publicly that the threat from terrorism was his priority, noting that terrorists were becoming "more operationally adept and more technically sophisticated," looking at softer civilian targets as military targets came to be better protected. "Usama bin Laden and his global network of lieutenants and associates remain the most immediate and serious threat . . . capable of planning multiple attacks with little or no warning."[20] Yet Tenet found it frustrating getting the new team to tune in to his concerns. They were focused on more traditional sources of threat—rising great powers such as China or states with well-established hostility to the United States such as Iraq. Nonstate actors whose rhetoric always seemed to be well ahead of their capabilities just did not seem to deserve such high-level effort and attention. Over the summer of 2001, intelligence, backed often by Arab media reports, picked up increasing activity and speculation about al Qaeda. But signifying what? The information was confused, often contradictory, and therefore rarely wholly reliable.

Al Qaeda's attacks had generally been directed against U.S. assets abroad, and this is what concerned most of these reports. The cumulative effect was to warn that something big and unpleasant was being planned but not exactly where and when. The CIA reports that warned of imminent al Qaeda and possibly "spectacular" attacks got lost among the blizzard of paper circulating around any governing warning of one calamity or another, with varying degrees of urgency and evidence, losing a bit of credibility every day that nothing happened. After one of Clarke's reports suggested that an attack might occur within the United States rather than overseas, representatives of the many domestic agencies were assembled on July 5. Having been given the warning, which they were told was highly secret, nobody was quite sure what to do with it and no action was taken.[21] Then, on July 10, a top-level briefing organized for Rice and headed by Tenet started with the dramatic opening line "There will be a significant terrorist attack in the coming weeks or months!" The objective of this briefing was to urge offensive action against the al Qaeda network rather than predict and prepare for a specific contingency. The main result was to step up deployment of the *Predator* unmanned aerial vehicle (UAV), which could be useful for targeting Osama bin Laden if the administration decided it had to go on the offensive.

However, there was one report, on August 6, 2001, entitled, "Bin Laden Determined to Strike in U.S." This was an answer to a query from Bush, and it warned that al Qaeda did indeed want to bring the fight into the United States and might have the support structure within the United States to do so, although there was no corroboration for the "sensational threat reporting" about hijacking aircraft. Nothing seems to have been done with this report. Only at the start of September was the administration starting to focus on the issue. As Bush later remarked, prior to 9/11 he would have approved a plan to go after al Qaeda, but "I didn't feel that sense of urgency, and my blood was not nearly as boiling."[22]

*   *   *

When the attack came on September 11, 2001, neither the public nor the government had a frame of reference to make sense of the events. Low technology was used to turn the West's own high technology against itself. The box cutters used to capture the hijacked aircraft served as advanced versions of the knife, the weapon of choice for street brawlers throughout the centuries. The direct cost of the operation was under $1 million. The expected result for that investment would be not only terrible human costs but also damage valued in the billions, causing an economic downturn, with particular harm to airlines and tourism, and generating a requirement for massive additional expenditure on internal security as well as on the subsequent military operations to close down the threat. The objectives of the attack were not so much material as psychological. It was to create an aura of power around al Qaeda and an audience for its demands. If there was a model, it was the old anarchist notion of the "propaganda of the deed."[23] This notion justified acts of terrorism (usually assassinations) as a means of undermining the old order by demonstrating that those who claimed to be all-powerful were really vulnerable. Dramatic deeds would cause the ruling classes to lose their nerve while at the same time inspiring the masses. Part of this strategy assumed that the ruling classes would lash out to preserve their position. In the process, so the theory went, they would diminish themselves further. Every punitive attack would open the eyes of the masses and feed their clamor for justice and an end to oppression. The global scope of the media meant that the "deed" of September 11 had the largest ever audience for a deliberate act of war. The political impact of this, and the images resulting from the subsequent unfolding drama, would be felt in all those individual conflicts that al Qaeda was seeking to influence.

Al Qaeda's readiness to take the initiative, and to accept the certain death of its own militants in operations, meant that the U.S. government found itself pondering how to defend a country where millions of people live and work in dense urban areas, reliant on complex and sophisticated systems of energy, transportation, and communication. When the tactical objective is to kill large numbers of people in spectacular fashion and cause panic and disruption, the United States constitutes a "target-rich environment" with many choices, even if individual buildings and facilities were well protected.

Alerts warning of further attacks soon began. The first came on September 24, concerning the possibility of attacks using crop-dusting aircraft to distribute chemical or biological weapons, following information that Mohammed Atta, one of the suspected 9/11 hijackers, had been investigating such aircraft.[24] On September 24, traces of anthrax turned up at ten different locations in Washington, including the State Department and the Supreme Court, resulting in five deaths. The culprit was never caught. As preparations began for attacks against al Qaeda–Taliban positions in Afghanistan, concern grew about possible retaliation. U.S. intelligence officials reportedly believed that Osama bin Laden had "long ago" begun "orchestrating a significant terrorist counterpunch to the expected U.S. retaliation for the attacks on New York and the Pentagon." An anonymous official was quoted as saying, "He has gamed out the next two or three moves already. He expects us to respond to the World Trade Center, and he has the next move planned after that."[25] The *Washington Post* reported that "credible new information" had led the FBI and the CIA to assess "the chances of a second attempt to attack the United States as very high"—indeed, one intelligence official was said to put the chance at "100 percent," should the United States strike Afghanistan. The potential targets could be in the "hundreds or thousands," from government buildings to "centers of entertainment" to natural gas lines, power plants, and other examples of "exposed infrastructure." President Bush telephoned congressional leaders on October 29. Governors were told that the government had "new, credible information of the possibility of another terrorist attack," but "no states were named, no location indicated."[26]

This was the backdrop against which the "war on terror" was launched, with the country in shock, mourning its losses, fearful of another attack, and overflowing with patriotism. There were questions as to whether this was really a war. Describing obnoxious criminal acts as warlike dignifies them and allows the perpetrators to enjoy an unnecessarily heroic status and become a matter for armed force rather than law enforcement.[27] War suggests that the gloves are off and governments can do things that would be unacceptable when problems are described in more civilian terms, for example, in finding ways to bypass the rights of those suspected of being implicated in terrorism. It also encourages a harsher foreign policy with scant scope for diplomatic initiatives, let alone attention to the conditions that breed terrorism. The validity of these concerns became apparent as the "war on terror" became associated with restrictions on civil liberties, detention without trial, and a toleration of interrogation techniques that were as near as made no difference to torture. War also gives a president a special standing as national leader. After the attacks, Bush's approval ratings soared to dizzying heights, above 90 percent. To his political advisers such as Karl Rove, a war allowed Republicans to avoid awkward domestic issues and stress their special qualifications for looking after the nation's safety. It also lent the opportunity to castigate Democrats who dared to dissent from the tough administration line as being divisive at a time of national peril and next to traitorous. The "war on terror" and the Republican Party's platform became indistinguishable.

The exploitation of the war atmosphere would not have been possible had it not felt, in 2001, like a war. Yet the enemy appeared to be shadowy, lacking conventional military capabilities, a capital city, or even, despite the focus on Osama bin Laden himself, a supreme leader and hierarchical chain of command. Yet this impression was wrong. Al Qaeda was not really a non-state actor. It had a base and sanctuary in Afghanistan, and its politics and fighters were integrated with those of the Taliban. Osama bin Laden had already declared war, but he had not been taken seriously until he surpassed previous levels of terrorist achievement. This was more than just a large crime or an affront to common decency. The U.S. government could also point to the limits of an alternative approach. It had dealt with the 1993 attack on the World Trade Center through the courts with a successful prosecution, but this had palpably failed to stop a second attack. It was hard now to take seriously calls for hard evidence before any action was taken or to figure out how a broad-based militant movement, with many activist cells dispersed around the globe, could be put in the dock. An attempt was therefore made, although without great conviction, to ask the Taliban regime in Afghanistan to hand over the prime suspect before military action was begun. This was rebuffed. In practice, the Taliban and al Qaeda had fused over the previous few years. It was impossible to deal with the terrorists without first overthrowing the regime.

Al Qaeda did not, of course, claim to be fighting a war for terrorism, but one that pitted true Islam against Christianity, Judaism, and apostates. Bin Laden did not speak for Islam, but he wanted to do so, which meant that this was a war about the future of Islam, and therefore about the governance of all states with Muslim populations and all conflicts in which Muslim groups were directly involved. These conflicts occupied much of the contemporary international agenda, taking in the Middle East, the Gulf, the Balkans, Central and East Asia, and parts of Africa. North American and West European countries have large Muslim populations, many drawn from these troubled regions, and the conflict highlighted their sensitive position, especially as members of the al Qaeda network hid themselves within them as they planned and mounted operations. According to al Qaeda and its ideological fellow travelers, the United States deserved to be a target because it was an overweening, hegemonic, and profoundly decadent power, acting on behalf of the enemies of Islam or apostate regimes.

Bin Laden wrote to Mullah Omar on October 3, 2001, urging him to stand firm and warn the Americans that they would "not be able to dream of security until Muslims experience it as reality in Palestine and Afghanistan." He urged the Taliban leader to "keep in mind that America is currently facing two contradictory problems." On the one hand, it did not dare respond to "*jihad* operations" lest its prestige collapse, "thus forcing it to withdraw its troops abroad and restrict itself to U.S. internal affairs. This will transform it from a major power to a third-rate power, similar to Russia." On the other hand, campaigning against Afghanistan would "impose great long-term economic burdens, leading to further economic collapse, which will force America, God willing, to resort to the former Soviet Union's only option: withdrawal from Afghanistan, disintegration, and contraction." His strategy, from this document, appeared to depend on U.S. vulnerability to further blows, which would undermine investor confidence, combined with "a media campaign to fight the enemy's publicity," to cause a rift between the American government and its people. This would come about by demonstrating how more money and lives would be lost, that this would be to "serve the interests of the rich, particularly the Jews," and that the war was all about protecting "Israel and its security." Omar must also "imply that the campaign against Afghanistan will be responded to with revenge blows against America."[28]

★   ★   ★

From the U.S. perspective, the prospective fight was to take place over a landlocked country, ravaged by decades of civil war, full of militias of uncertain loyalties. It would have to be entered from Pakistan, which had helped create the enemy that the United States now sought to overthrow. At least Musharraf was promising cooperation. Just as Zia had seen an opportunity in 1980 to turn around the Carter administration, he realized that he might now do the same with Bush. As he dared not oppose the Americans, he could make a virtue out of necessity and ensure that all those aspects of Pakistani behavior that had been irritating the Americans could be quietly forgotten. From senior military and ISI officers he was advised to "Let the US do its dirty work. Its enemies are our friends." No, he countered, "We should offer up help, and mark my words, we will receive a clean bill of health."[29] His judgment was exactly right. Sanctions imposed after the 1998 nuclear tests were lifted, military and civilian aid was lavished, and the Americans desisted from commenting on how Musharraf ran his country.

There were few developed military options. The Clinton administration had relied on cruise missile attacks against al Qaeda assets, but this had not achieved anything. Bush told General Henry Shelton, chairman of the Joint Chiefs, "I don't want to put a million-dollar missile on a five-dollar tent."[30] The CIA did, however, have a plan. A couple of days after 9/11, Tenet was describing how paramilitary teams along with Special Forces could work with the Afghan opposition and draw upon U.S. airpower to get rid of both the Taliban and al Qaeda. It was a clever plan, both in exploiting assets that were available and in playing to the American preference for using allied ground forces to work alongside allied infantry. There were still evident problems. With a lack of suitable bases close to Afghanistan, air raids would have to be mounted over long distances or from carriers. It was just as well that the air defenses of the Taliban were meager, because it would not be possible to mount many daily sorties. The infrastructure of Afghanistan was so wretched and primitive that there were few suitable targets to be attacked. What was the point of aiming for power plants in a country where only 6 percent had electricity?

Compared with the confidence with which the administration later went to war against Iraq, the initial objectives in Afghanistan were cautiously phrased, in terms of disrupting enemy operations and causing them to "pay a price" for past operations. Although Bush had spoken of getting bin Laden "dead or alive," precise objectives against which to judge operational success were not set, producing an improvised quality to the whole campaign. There was no bullish disregard of the possibility of convincing the Taliban to abandon al Qaeda in order to preserve its regime, even once the war had begun. At the same time, there was a degree of wariness about getting too tied to the Northern Alliance and the ambitions of its constituent warlords. The best-known and accomplished of its leaders, Ahmad Massoud, was murdered by bin Laden's agents, posing as reporters, just two days before 9/11. In addition to their dubious histories, the remaining warlords were Uzbeks and Tajiks and not Pashtuns, and thus unacceptable to the majority of the population, and certainly the Pakistanis.

The Pakistanis realized that they had no choice but to support the Americans, even if this meant upsetting their own Islamists and turning on their erstwhile Taliban clients, but they became even more anxious at the prospect of the war giving power to forces they had long sought to marginalize. The fighting record of the Northern Alliance was mixed and certainly did not impress General Tommy Franks at CENTCOM, who was in charge of developing the war plans on the military side. By contrast, the CIA was more comfortable working with the Alliance, so it prepared to fight its own war, which would be loosely coordinated with CENTCOM's. The alternative was to get U.S. troops into the country, which would be a long and difficult process, and Afghanistan was notably inhospitable to foreign armies. The Americans might face the Soviet problem of holding only cities and roads, while swaths of the country were occupied by stubborn, hostile fighters.

Because of the Northern Alliance, the Taliban and al Qaeda were not geared to a guerrilla campaign. The tactics of a guerrilla campaign, for which Afghanistan offered excellent terrain, are to trade space for time. With time sufficient attacks can be mounted against the enemy to drain it of patience, morale, and credibility. Instead, the Taliban and al Qaeda prepared to defend fixed positions that would be vulnerable to bombing and meant that they might be drawn into an open battle. This, therefore, need not be the asymmetrical war the Americans feared. The enemy was prepared for a conventional battle, albeit one that at times bore more resemblance to the nineteenth than to the twenty-first century.

After discarding the religiously loaded name "Operation Infinite Justice," the United States embarked on "Operation Enduring Freedom" on October 7, 2001. The initial strategy was essentially political and heavily influenced by Pakistani considerations. Now that Musharraf had purged the ISI of its Taliban supporters, the aim was to develop resistance to the Taliban in the south, within the majority Pashtun population close to Pakistan, and so avoiding too close an involvement with the disreputable Northern Alliance. There were a number of problems with this strategy. There was a lack of credible local leadership to challenge the Taliban on their home turf. The most likely candidate was Abdul Haq. In his day he had been a popular and effective mujahideen leader. He entered Afghanistan from Pakistan in October to trigger a popular uprising. The Americans were concerned that this was premature, and so it proved. Possibly betrayed, he was found by Taliban and, after a dramatic chase, captured and then executed on October 26. This setback confirmed that a southern strategy would have to be slow, with very little useful to be done militarily. Because the Taliban had not felt vulnerable in the south, with Pakistan to their backs, they had concentrated their forces in the north.

There was therefore only a limited number of targets to bomb. During the first twenty-five days, there was an average of only sixty-three combat sorties a day, mounted against the rather negligible fixed assets of the Taliban rather than their troops in the field.[31] After a point, it became unproductive to bomb the small number of "strategic" targets such as al Qaeda camps and attack the Taliban's primitive air defenses and command and control capabilities. Northern Alliance commanders were incredulous as the

United States kept returning to bomb airports that had already been destroyed, a result of the complex and demanding rules of bomb damage assessment. By late October, the air raids were doing more harm than good. The Afghan people were getting angry with the Americans because of civilian deaths, while the Taliban fighters were feeling even more confident because they had largely survived unscathed. American troops were "creatures of comfort" and would provide no match for fighters who had already seen off much tougher Soviet soldiers.[32] Columnist Maureen Dowd captured the frustration: "We're sophisticated; they're crude. We're millennial; they're medieval. We ride B-52's; they ride horses. And yet they're outmaneuvering us."[33] Journalists were starting to use the word "quagmire" and make comparisons with Vietnam.[34] A nation that invented the art of public relations and dominated the world media was being bested by a group that communicated only through melodramatic statements dispatched from a country that banned TVs. Journalist Nik Gowing, noting the challenge to "the complacent assumption of information supremacy," observed, "Low-cost video cameras and mobile phones can nimbly upstage billion-dollar information-processing systems and hierarchical command-and-control structures."[35]

With little to show for its efforts, the United States found itself at risk of losing the propaganda war. Al Qaeda had a well-prepared audience for its radical message in countries where the local media has little diversity and regularly denounces Western policies. The spectacle of the strongest nation in the world beating up one of the most wretched was uncomfortable. The impression gained ground that the bombing continued not because there was much of value to hit but because Washington could not think of anything better to do. Anxious correspondents reported back from the noisy streets constituting the Islamic front line that America and Britain were hated even more than before. Every expression of doubt and concern from a supposedly friendly government was cited as evidence that a coalition once so full of solidarity was now wracked by internal tensions and risked falling apart. Even if Bush was determined to mount a substantial land offensive, problems of logistics meant that little could be done before the winter was over. The Pakistanis, who had approved the strategy, had no real incentive to make it work, so long as the United States could be persuaded to keep a distance from the Northern Alliance. Their inclination was to wait and see, and the early signs were that the Taliban would not be moved easily.

In late October, the Bush administration decided on a new approach.[36] Despite doubts about its combat capability and the narrowness of its political base, the offensives on the ground would be the responsibility of the Northern Alliance. Although there was no great optimism in Washington, the results were immediate and impressive. The Taliban's defensive positions were geared to dealing with militia battles. They were often easy to spot and soon subjected to intensive air attack, using daisy cutter bombs with their loud, ferocious, and extensive effects. The Taliban was frozen in position. Its forces could hide, but if they moved out to fight they would be hit. All this encouraged the Northern Alliance, which now felt the Taliban was truly vulnerable. On November 10, the first major Taliban stronghold in the north, Mazar-i-Sharif, fell, providing control of major highways and two airports. Once enemy fighters realized that they were beaten, then defections and desertions began in earnest. Although for political reasons the administration would have preferred a less frantic pace—so that Pashtun forces as well as the Northern Alliance could liberate Kabul—the Northern Alliance pressed on regardless. There was some serious fighting in Kunduz in the north, where the Afghan Arabs made their stand. Kandahar in the south, the heart of the Taliban regime, was abandoned by Mullah Omar on December 7, 2001, who slipped away.

It then became apparent that as many as 2,000 al Qaeda fighters, including bin Laden, had moved to Tora Bora, where a network of caves and passages had been prepared for sturdy defense. The Americans decided to use the same formula as before, but the conditions were far less propitious. First, it was hard for aircraft to pick out targets in mountainous Tora Bora. Bin Laden told his men to spread themselves out so that single bombs could not take out more than one man. For a campaign that began with the president concerned about expending million-dollar cruise missiles on five-dollar tents, enormous quantities of expensive ordnance were spent hitting far less. Second, and more important, the United States expected the Northern Alliance to go into the mountains to extract the enemy, but the Alliance members lacked the interest in this fight that they had shown in overthrowing the Taliban. Using the pretext of considering surrender, and often paying their Afghan pursuers more for their freedom than the Americans were offering as bounty, al Qaeda fighters made their way out on December 12. When the Americans asked for more urgency, the Afghan response was essentially "If you want them, then you go and get them." Although American troops were available, U.S. commanders had gotten out of the habit of using their own forces even for the highest-priority missions. By the time the last cave was cleared on December 17, bin Laden was nowhere to be found. He was assumed to be moving around the Afghan-Pakistani border, an area not short of sympathizers, where the local tribal leaders were a law unto themselves.[37]

The next time U.S. forces came across a substantial al Qaeda force—in the Shah-i-Kot Valley at the end of February 2002—they decided to rely much more on their own capabilities. Operation Anaconda involved 1,400 soldiers, plus 200 Special Forces and about 1,000 Afghan fighters. The aim was to surround the valley with rings of forces to trap and then capture or kill the couple of hundred al Qaeda fighters believed to be there. This time, the operation had different problems than Tora Bora. The size of the enemy forces had been underestimated, and when cornered, they were prepared to fight hard rather than try to slink away. One possible lesson for the future was drawn by Stephen Biddle: "[A] combination of cover and concealment can allow defenders, though battered, to survive modern firepower in sufficient numbers to mount serious resistance."[38] In another reprise of anti-Soviet operations, the enemy managed to damage five of the seven helicopters initially assigned to Operation Anaconda. When the Afghan forces came under heavy fire, they retreated precipitately, while American forces were sent to a spot near an al Qaeda stronghold, where there were 600 of the enemy instead of the expected 150. There had also been poor integration of airpower into the early planning. The result was some of the heaviest fighting—and largest American casualties—of the whole campaign, as an operation that had been expected to take three days took seventeen. This time, however, al Qaeda took heavy casualties, with at least 500 killed, and a remaining base was eliminated.

★   ★   ★

The speed with which the Taliban was overthrown suggested that the United States might have hit upon a new form of warfare. Powell noted the connection of "a First World air force" to a "Fourth World army—B-1 bombers and guys on horses."[39] Bush spoke enthusiastically about the combination of "real-time intelligence, local allied forces, special forces, and precision air power" that had produced this victory in the first round of the war, adding that this conflict "has taught us more about the future of our military than a decade of blue ribbon panels and think tank symposiums."[40] Much of the success, however, was because the war was fought in a tried and tested Afghan way of warfare as much as a new Western way. The Afghan way depended on sparring to see who had superior power before the hard bargaining began on the terms of surrender or, as likely, defection. It only got really nasty when the outcome of battle was uncertain. Should victory come through brute force, little mercy was shown to the losing side to help impress any watching waverers.

To be able to achieve so much with so few forces on the ground—316 Special Forces and 110 CIA agents—pleased the Americans, but this also meant that the U.S. command came to rely on Afghan irregulars to take on tasks in which they had no interest. The United States had impressive new kits to help them operate in unfamiliar terrain, including UAVs that could help them spot the enemy, but a critical item in their armory was large wads of dollars that could provide a formidable inducement. For those with the sense not to fight to the bitter end, defeat became rather like insolvency, with the faction in question soon trading under another name. Trading was often the operative word, for with territorial control comes the ability to take a share of all economic activity, including trafficking in guns and drugs. Surrender was conditional. Many Taliban fighters drifted back, still armed, to their villages or into banditry. Many foreigners were able to slip away, and those able to use cash to gain safe passage could escape. The Americans were relieved by the speed of the Taliban surrender, but they did not always appreciate its conditional quality.

There was a striking lack of appreciation of the need to integrate considerations of postwar needs into military planning. At the end of November, Franks was postponing all these issues while still focusing on military operations: "The United States has one goal: Attack al Qaeda and get the job done. And they're not too worried about the rest of it right now."[41] From the Pentagon perspective, talk of postwar reconstruction appeared almost as a distraction. Rumsfeld's view was that there was no "responsibility to try to figure out what kind of government that country ought to have."[42] At various points, Wolfowitz said the objective was to find al Qaeda and "stop giving Afghanistan as a safe harbor for terrorists" rather than to reconstruct Afghanistan, stating that "we have to keep a focus on what are our main objectives in that country." He observed, "One of the lessons of Afghanistan's history, which we've tried to apply in this campaign, is if you're a foreigner, try not to go in. If you do go in, don't stay too long, because they don't tend to like any foreigners who stay too long."[43] But if the problem was not to recur, that required making sure that the Afghans could run the country themselves.

The basic aim was to destroy as much as possible of the al Qaeda infrastructure and kill or capture as many as possible of its fighters. Bringing down the Taliban was a plus, but that had not been a central objective, which in part explains why plans to replace it with a better regime took so long to develop. It was not until October 4 that Bush asked about "who will run the country." His advisers do not even appear to have considered the issue, never mind found an answer.[44] Ideas had not really progressed much beyond achieving the best military result possible and then handing over the problem to the UN. By mid-October, two experienced and senior officials in the State Department, Richard Haass and James Dobbins, were working with

UN special representative Lakhdar Brahimi to devise a government that might be moderately effective and sufficiently representative. Perhaps because of the lack of Pentagon interest, they were given considerable latitude, and thus involved the Iranians in the process. By the time the Taliban fell, a transition process was in place. By early December, Hamid Karzai, a capable and presentable Pashtun leader with a natural dignity and excellent English, was able to take over. He had fought against the Soviets and came from a leading Kandahar family. His father had been assassinated by the Taliban.

Unfortunately, inadequate consideration was given to the needs of a country devastated by years of war, with a large part of the population living as refugees and heroin the main cash crop. Only modest funds were set aside for reconstruction and no attempt was made to establish an international presence throughout the country. As the warlords returned to their own provinces, Karzai was left in control of Kabul but not much else. There a cobbled-together International Security Assistance Force was left to maintain order, without U.S. participation. The Bush administration was still in the mindset that saw postconflict peacekeeping as an inappropriate and inessential role. After the fighting had subsided, it gave little support to Karzai and moved on to other business.

As insensitive to the larger implications of policy was the manner by which Bush agreed to one of the most controversial strands of his policy. A group organized to consider what to do with prisoners captured during the war on terrorism met under White House Counsel Alberto Gonzales during the fall of 2001. It included representatives from Defense and Justice but none from State or the NSC, despite the potential consequences for foreign policy. By November the group had concluded that anybody who had "engaged in, aided or abetted, or conspired to commit" terrorism should not have constitutional guarantees or access to federal courts. Instead, the military would hold and interrogate them for as long as desired and then convene special tribunals for their prosecution. Cheney, who was driving the process, took the proposed directive to Bush on November 13 at their private lunch and got him to sign the directive without even sitting down to read it. Rice was "incensed" and Powell astonished at the way the decision had been taken.

It was then decided to use the U.S. naval facility at Guantanamo Bay in Cuba, which was both secure and not on U.S. soil. Proceeding along this line, in January the conclusion came back from the Justice Department that the non-Afghans captured in Afghanistan were stateless and were not prisoners of war and need not enjoy the normal protections provided by the Geneva Convention. The State Department's lawyers were appalled and protested. The United States should and could follow its obligations under international law. They lost the argument. Powell made a last-minute effort to persuade Bush to go back on a decision he had already made and at least, for the first time, have his advisers debate the issues in front of him. The conclusion, as announced on February 7, was that the Taliban prisoners would come under the Geneva Conventions, but others, "unlawful combatants," would not, although they would be afforded "humane treatment, and, to the extent appropriate and consistent with military necessity, in a manner consistent with the principles of" the Geneva Conventions.

This language had been carefully drafted. The CIA had alerted the Justice Department on the limitations resulting from current rules on interrogation when seeking "actionable intelligence." Cheney wanted the rules eased to allow for more coercive methods. This led to fine distinctions between "cruel, inhuman, or degrading" methods and torture, which involved pushing these methods to the extreme. The presidential statement of February 7 provided cover by making respect for the Geneva Conventions conditional on military necessity. In line with Cheney's theory of unlimited executive power, if the president as commander in chief chooses to permit forms of interrogation tantamount to torture, he has the legal authority to do so. Although this began as a dispensation to help the CIA, it was soon passed on to all military interrogators.[45] The State Department and NSC were carefully excluded from the development of this policy. Other than Iraq no set of decisions did more to damage the reputation of the United States over the coming years.[46]

The problems this policy created were for the future. For the moment the loss of Afghanistan as a proper Islamic state and a training and planning base for operations around the world was a major blow to al Qaeda. Bin Laden had made the familiar mistake of assuming that because the Americans were tentative when committing forces in areas of marginal concern, they would also shrink away when vital interests were at stake. His calculation was that if the Americans were hit hard enough, they would recoil from international engagement. Instead the opposite happened. First they moved into one Muslim country, and then they moved into another.

18

REGIME CHANGE

SUGGESTED REASONS FOR George W. Bush's choice to go to war against Iraq in 2003 abound. The simplest view is that, as claimed, Saddam Hussein was in defiance of UN resolutions in pursuing weapons of mass destruction, and there was a serious risk these weapons one day might find their way into terrorist hands. Then there was the unfinished business of 1991. Bush was outraged that a tyrant who had tried to kill his father was still in place and as defiant as ever. Another popular theory is that U.S. foreign policy was effectively hijacked by a group of neoconservatives with a grand design to reshape the Middle East. A conspiratorial version of this theory argues that the aim was to help Israel, by removing a leading rejectionist state from the scene. More positively, it is possible to point to idealistic if muddled notions about creating a model "democratic" Middle Eastern state that would set the standard for the many local autocracies. Last, there is the default explanation for almost anything the United States does in the Middle East, which is to put the whole enterprise down to exercising hegemony over a region that contains almost 70 percent of the world's known oil and natural gas reserves. The oil issue was not a trivial one but secondary in American policymaking. At the very least the administration assumed that because of Iraq's oil wealth there would be no need for excessive American subsidy of reconstruction. There should be opportunities for American oil companies when it came to developing the oil fields. Some geopoliticians might have dreamed of substituting Iraqi oil for Saudi oil, although given the state of Iraq this was always implausible.

If we look at the arguments actually made to justify regime change, by far the most common was that Saddam was a brute who was regularly, even routinely, compared to Hitler (although Stalin was far more appropriate, not least because he was Saddam's real inspiration). Evidence of WMD was not found after the war, but evidence of mass cruelty was, including mass graves.[1] Although human rights activists tended to be against using the repressive nature of the regime as an argument for war, for Saddam's most bitter opponents there seemed to be no other way.[2] Certainly, for the Iraqi exiles, all that really mattered was getting rid of a tyrant. Their activities to enlist the support of Western governments must be understood in this light. After Saddam was toppled, many of those who accepted war as the only way to eliminate a cruel dictatorship were furious at the failure to plan properly for the introduction of something better, suggesting their agenda was not quite the same as the government's.[3] Equally, the prominence of neoconservatives among the advocates reflects their prominence as prolific writers and outspoken agitators rather than their actual influence. In addition, the obvious concern about continuity of energy supplies did not by itself mandate any course of action when those supplies were not under direct threat.

During the prewar controversies, the desirability of regime change was not really in dispute. Most of the war's opponents acknowledged the frightful nature of Saddam Hussein's regime and its catastrophic consequences for Iraq and the Iraqis. The controversies were over whether this was really the business of the United States and then over timing and method. Regime change had long been U.S. policy for Iraq, but not by means of invasion. The key question is therefore not why did the United States seek to change the regime, but rather why at this time and by this means?

The basic problem here is that there does not appear to have ever been a formal decisionmaking process leading up to the decision to go to war. According to Powell, there was never a "moment when we all made our recommendations" to be followed by a presidential decision.[4] Rice had the same recollection: "There wasn't a flash moment. There's no decision meeting." As another policymaker put it, the decision "kind of evolved, but it's not clear and neat." During the early stages there was no consultation with allies, members of Congress, senior officers, or the intelligence agencies (no special National Intelligence Estimate was commissioned), barely even a paper trail.[5] What appears to be the case is that after 9/11, an established policy of regime change in Iraq was given added salience to the point that it was possible to contemplate military action to achieve this, and by the spring of 2002, military action was starting to appear to be the only credible option. Only belatedly was it recognized that the case in terms of the "war on terror" was flimsy, which required a focus on the established issue of Iraq's failure to abide by UN resolutions. This case was also subjected to vigorous challenge, especially internationally, which pushed questions of American power to the heart of the controversy. If there was an actual decision to go to war, it was taken by Bush alone at the start of 2003.

★ ★ ★

The Iraqi National Congress (INC) was created to topple Saddam Hussein. After the shambles of the failed insurrection and coup of the mid-1990s, the Clinton administration was inclined to give up on the INC, and the feeling was reciprocated. Its leader, Ahmad Chalabi, blamed the administration and especially the CIA. He turned his attention to creating broad-based political support. He noted Israel's success in creating a strong lobby with support in the media and Congress and set about doing the same. In particular, he realized that he had a ready-made audience among neoconservatives. The realist Republicans, such as Baker and Scowcroft, were still adamant that they had done the right thing by not trying to topple Saddam in 1991. They were not at all apologetic. The neocons, however, were scornful of this attitude, describing it as conciliation bordering on appeasement, which they compared to the realists' approach to the Soviet Union during the cold war. The claim that containment was ultimately successful against the Soviet Union was dismissed with the observation that it was only Ronald Reagan's readiness to raise the stakes that caused the Soviet collapse. They saw parallels with Iraq. Here was another rotten regime that survived on bluster. By raising the stakes, it could be brought crashing down. Instead of waiting for an inherently undemocratic coup, a popular insurgency should be encouraged. If Chalabi was to be believed, this would not only see off Saddam but usher in a new age of Iraqi democracy that could serve as an inspiration for the rest of the Arab world.

One of the first successes of the new campaign was the "Open Letter to the President" of January 1998, produced under the aegis of the neoconservative think tank Project for a New American Century, although by no means all the signatories, including Donald Rumsfeld, were neoconservatives. The letter to Clinton described the continuing danger posed by Saddam Hussein and the erosion of containment. A new policy was required, with the aim of "removing Saddam Hussein and his regime from power." This would "require a full complement of diplomatic, political and military efforts." The signatories expressed themselves to be "fully aware of the dangers and difficulties in implementing this policy," but they believed "the dangers of failing to do so are far greater." Existing UN resolutions provided the authority for the necessary steps. "In any case, American policy cannot continue to be crippled by a misguided insistence on unanimity in the UN Security Council."[6] The next month, in another letter to the president, Rumsfeld and Paul Wolfowitz joined with a wider group of signatories as the Committee for Peace and Security in the Gulf, established in 1990 to back action against Iraq. Warning that "sanctions and exhortations" were inadequate, this letter called instead for "a determined program to change the regime in Baghdad." Congressional support for the INC was now growing, and funds kept being pushed in its direction for propaganda activities, including a radio station, and to operations inside Iraq.

The administration was unconvinced. On February 26, 1998, Secretary of State Madeleine Albright confirmed the containment policy before a Senate committee. She noted that removing Saddam from power would "require a far greater commitment of military force, and a far greater risk to American lives, than is currently needed to contain the threat Saddam poses." Encouraging the "Iraqi opposition to initiate a civil war" suffered from the problem that the opposition was divided. It "would be wrong to create false or unsustainable expectations that could end in bloodshed or defeat." The United States was left with an unsatisfactory policy—a "real world" policy, but not a "feel good" policy.[7] The president, becoming engulfed by the Lewinsky scandal, decided against resisting the pressure completely. The bipartisan Iraq Liberation Act of 1998 (ILA) was signed into law by Clinton on October 31, 1998. It supported "those elements of the Iraqi opposition that advocate a very different future for Iraq than the bitter reality of internal repression and external aggression that the current regime in Baghdad now offers."[8] The case for the awfulness of the Iraqi regime was made by recalling every act for which it had been condemned in the past. Clinton was urged "to take appropriate action, in accordance with the Constitution and relevant laws of the United States, to bring Iraq into compliance with its international obligations." Once Saddam Hussein was removed from power, the United States "should support Iraq's transition to democracy."

The main support was expected to go to Chalabi's INC, which was now promoting the idea of using U.S. airpower to protect opposition-controlled enclaves, with U.S. ground forces used only as a last resort. In the course of an INC visit to Washington in May 1999, the administration announced it would draw down $5 million worth of training and "nonlethal" defense equipment under the ILA. The administration continued to insist that the opposition was insufficiently organized to deserve lethal equipment or combat training. This left the United States rhetorically in support of overthrowing the regime but unable to do much about it. Iraqi opposition groups were said to be at "one of the lowest ebbs in their history, hit by defections, foreign aid cuts and Iraq's army and secret police." For official Washington, a coup was still more likely than an uprising. One official was quoted as saying that Saddam's departure would probably come "from the inside, from the circle around Saddam. That's the nature of the system."[9]

The Republican Party platform in 2000 called for "a comprehensive plan for the removal of Saddam Hussein" but did not specify a method. It was not a big issue during the campaign. Gore presented himself as ready to go further in giving "robust support to the groups that are trying to overthrow Saddam Hussein."[10] Bush kept his options open. When campaigning for the Republican nomination in December 1999, just before Operation Desert Fox, he issued a clarification to be sure his reference to "take 'em out" was clearly to WMD rather than the Iraqi regime.[11] Rice, in an article intended as a preview of Bush's foreign policy, was notably relaxed. Weapons of mass destruction would be unusable "because any attempt to use them will bring national obliteration."[12] Deterrence could still rule.

Although reference is often made to Treasury Secretary Paul O'Neill's recollection of his first National Security Council meeting in January 2001, which was about discussing how to effect change in Iraq, this only confirms an interest in change, not that there was any idea how, or if at all, it might be done.[13] At the Pentagon, Wolfowitz still wanted to be rid of Saddam and to work with the INC but acknowledged that there was "no cost-free or risk-free option in dealing with that regime."[14] In his confirmation hearings, he remarked that he had yet to see a "plausible plan" for changing the regime. At most, Iraq was presented as the sort of long-term threat that might justify investment in ballistic missile defenses, then Rumsfeld's and Wolfowitz's main cause. Rumsfeld had used the possibility of an Iraqi ICBM ten years hence in an influential report of 1998 that argued for a major investment in missile defense.

At the State Department, the old policy was pursued. Powell was happy to describe the Iraqi regime as likely doomed by the onward march of history, but as for immediate policy, he considered containment a success because Saddam lacked the ability to pose conventional threats to his neighbors, let alone the United States. There were no doubts that WMD programs were being pursued, but they had not been terribly successful. If Saddam allowed UN inspectors back to check on all of this, then sanctions might be lifted. The main problem was that the sanctions regime was continuing to unravel, with Saddam International Airport in business once again, Syria reopening its pipeline with Iraq, and Jordan no longer cooperating with monitoring trade. A Brookings Institution study spoke of a move from "sanctions fatigue into sanctions defeatism."[15] So Powell was looking to "smarter" sanctions, eliminating items of civilian use and concentrating exclusively on those directly related to the prohibited weapons. Regime change was a separate policy and a secondary priority. Although he supported the INC, he indicated doubts about its effectiveness.[16] Nor was there much going on behind the scenes. The early NSC discussion led to an August 2001 paper on a "liberation strategy." This envisaged a phased process of pressure directed against Saddam using the INC. It was not in a form suitable for presentation to the president.[17]

*   *   *

The change came with 9/11. Bush later observed that prior to this day, "we were discussing smart sanctions. . . . After September 11, the doctrine of containment just doesn't hold any water. . . . My vision shifted dramatically after September 11, because I now realize the stakes, I realize the world has changed."[18] The attacks affected policy on Iraq, not because of the unsupportable thesis that Iraq was culpable, which if believed would have led immediately to war, but because it changed the terms of the security debate, in establishing the notion that potential threats had to be dealt with before they became actual, and because of the consequential power shift within Washington that strengthened the hand of those who had long sought to topple Saddam Hussein. Tough talk from the Pentagon found a receptive audience, whereas caution from the State Department no longer seemed careful but just complacent in the face of a terrible danger.

Powell won the first round of this argument because the president believed that it was sensible to focus on one campaign at a time, and the first priority was to deal with al Qaeda and the Taliban. Rumsfeld and Wolfowitz do appear to have planted a seed, so that the idea that the next round could be against Iraq took root. Cheney, who had never questioned the 1991 decision not to go after Saddam, was also starting to come to this view. An interesting aspect of this discussion was the assumption that there was going to be a next round. The United States was starting to dabble in other conflicts where Islamists posed a problem, such as the Philippines. There was some talk of a return to Somalia. Other countries, such as Yemen, from which the attack against the USS *Cole* had been launched in 2000, came to deals with the United States to help uproot the terrorists in return for intelligence support and other favors. In none of these cases, as with most operations undertaken in this "war," was large-scale military action likely.

In late November 2001, as the Afghan campaign seemed to be moving to a successful conclusion, Bush reintroduced the Iraq issue into the public debate. In a question-and-answer session with reporters, he made it clear that the "war against terror" would not stop with Afghanistan ("Afghanistan is still just the beginning") and that this could include states that held weapons of mass destruction ("So part of the war on terror is to deny . . . weapons to be used for means of terror getting in the hands of nations that will use them"). Both North Korea and Iraq were mentioned, and it was required of both countries that they let inspectors back in to assess the state of their WMD programs. When asked what would happen if Iraq did not do this, Bush said Saddam Hussein would "find out."[19] When Powell was asked what this might mean, he linked it with the efforts to get UN inspectors back into Iraq.

The secretary of state was seeking to get the Security Council to agree to a new line, a context in which Bush's harsh public comments on Iraq were actually quite helpful. On November 29, 2001, the day after Bush spoke, a new resolution was passed unanimously. A Goods Review List was adopted, with the objective of streamlining the process of selling civilian goods to Baghdad. This list contained weapons-related and dual-use items that would require UN approval before being exported to Iraq. Unlike before, all other items could be imported without restriction. The Goods Review List would be implemented on May 30, 2002, when the current phase of the oil for food program expired. On December 2, Iraq's ambassador to the UN signed a memorandum of understanding accepting the resolution. It was remarked at the time that the "new scheme follows more than a year of haggling at the UN, and represents something of a victory for the U.S. and Britain."[20] When the policy was confirmed in May, there was even hope that Iraq might now agree to the return of weapons inspectors. The fact that the Security Council was still holding to the old line on inspectors and sanctions, albeit with a modified regime, meant that it was always possible to return to a set of internationally backed demands.

On November 21, Bush agreed that Rumsfeld and the CENTCOM commander, General Franks, might review the plans.[21] He understood that this might be the "first step" on the road to war, and his main interest was in assessing the available options. War was his "last option," so he wanted this exercise to be tightly held to prevent political speculation from getting out of hand. CENTCOM was less than happy with this task as it still had its hands full with Afghanistan.[22] The existing plan was cumbersome and involved some 400,000 troops. On December 28, 2001, Franks presented Bush with a concept of operations involving independent and simultaneous attacks on air and land, which, if allies and opposition elements within Iraq were used, could get the force requirements down to just over 100,000. During the first months of 2002, however, war plans were not at all firm but were largely framed in terms of principles and frameworks.

The State Department was aware of the political hazards of appearing too cautious as well as the international dangers of recklessness. Powell's deputy,

Richard Armitage, tried to find the right balance in an interview on December 1, 2001, claiming that the United States was on "a roll" in its campaign against the Taliban and that "President Bush intended to use the momentum to force Iraq to open its borders to United Nations inspectors looking for weapons of mass destruction." The options now were to continue with smart sanctions, try to build up the opposition, and explore military options.[23] There was clearly little international support for the military options. Joschka Fischer, Germany's foreign minister, said, "All European nations would view a broadening [of the conflict] to include Iraq highly skeptically—and that is putting it diplomatically."[24] British comments remained cautious. Afghanistan was not yet over, and there was no specific evidence linking Baghdad with 9/11. Blair, however, was always wary of letting a gap develop with American policy, and he had already shown in 1998 that he was prepared to use force in the event that Saddam continued to defy UN resolutions.

The emphasis on regime change became explicit at a press conference after the president met with Tony Blair at Crawford, Texas, in early April. Bush said "the policy of my government is the removal of Saddam and that all options are on the table." Blair responded by stressing the desirability of the end of the regime, the need to look at options, and the importance of the threat of weapons of mass destruction.[25] The next month, to demonstrate Bush's conviction on this score, a *Time* magazine article described a March meeting between Rice and a bipartisan group of senators at the White House. The president joined in and started to discuss Iraq. Instead of discussing what to do about Saddam, "he became notably animated, according to one person in the room, used a vulgar epithet to refer to Saddam and concluded with four words that left no one in doubt about Bush's intentions: 'We're taking him out.'" Late that same month, Cheney was reported to have met with Senate Republicans. After telling them to put down their pens and pencils, he asserted that the "question was no longer if the U.S. would attack Iraq," he said. "The only question was when."[26]

*   *   *

But there was also a question of how. Up to this point, regime change had never been synonymous with a military invasion. The preferences had been for a coup or a proxy battle using local forces. Few placed much reliance on a coup. There had been at least six attempts in the 1990s, all of which had failed, ending with the plotters being murdered or fleeing the country. This was the sort of threat for which Saddam Hussein was well equipped. A proxy battle using local forces was a more serious possibility and appeared to have been given a significant boost by events in Afghanistan, when the United

States had largely Special Forces and CIA agents on the ground working with the Northern Alliance and backed by substantial airpower.

Something similar had been proposed for Iraq since 1998, called the "Downing Plan," after its author, General Wayne Downing, who was an avid supporter of the INC. He had been instrumental in getting the Iraq Liberation Act passed and developing programs for training and arming the INC. After 9/11, he was appointed the president's military adviser on counterterrorism, replacing Richard Clarke. His credentials included his Special Forces background, but he was also known as the INC's "mentor—and biggest cheerleader."[27] In the White House he had the opportunity to promote his plan. He could assume a receptive audience to any scheme that would get Saddam out of the way without a massive commitment of U.S. troops, especially from Wolfowitz, who had in the past been an advocate of this approach. Moreover, the model appeared to have been confirmed in Afghanistan with the Northern Alliance, and it was possible to envisage the Kurds in the north and the Shi'ites in the south playing the equivalent role in Afghanistan, drawing out the Iraqi forces to expose them to air attack and encouraging their demoralization and collapse. Chalabi was said to call this the "end game." Even as late as April 2002, it was one of the options Bush and Blair were considering.[28]

Unfortunately, the Iraqi opposition was fragmented and untested. The relevant forces would be insufficient to bring a change in power. There was still the problem of the long feud between Kurdish leaders Jalal Talabani and Masud Barzani. The Kurds, whose forces numbered about 85,000, could act as a proxy army in the north but were wary of sacrificing their newfound autonomy (their land was protected by the northern no-fly zone) for vague promises of a better future. Meanwhile, as with the Shi'ites, there were bitter memories of being left to cope with Saddam's forces all on their own when the Americans decided not to help. There was unlikely to be much spontaneous response to any American calls for an insurrection. In CENTCOM, the idea that the Afghanistan model could be applied to Iraq was treated skeptically. The Northern Alliance was battle-hardened. The INC was just not as capable. Saddam's forces had such a military advantage that they might be able to avoid operating in the open where they would be vulnerable to American air attacks. The end of this option was signaled by Downing's resignation from his White House job after ten months, in late June. At the same time, the INC made it clear that it was only expecting to perform a political role in the event of a change of regime.

By the end of April, it was evident to the administration that if the aim was regime change, then the only sure way to achieve this was through an invasion, and that this could involve well over 200,000 troops. Soon it was also clear that senior officers were very nervous that the risks were being underplayed by civilians, including the logistical demands, getting caught by chemical or biological weapons, or getting stuck in urban warfare. Elsewhere in government, there were concerns that a push against Iraq would alienate many in the Arab world and, even if successful, create a major headache in the management of an occupied Iraq. Of particular importance was a forceful, and prescient, article in August by Brent Scowcroft, the elder Bush's national security adviser and Rice's former mentor. He warned of an unnecessary diversion in the war on terrorism, the danger of a "virtual go-it-alone strategy against Iraq, making any military operations correspondingly more difficult and expensive." His preferred strategy was to insist on international inspections of Saddam's WMD capabilities. If Saddam refused, "his rejection could provide the persuasive casus belli which many claim we do not now have. Compelling evidence that Saddam had acquired nuclear-weapons capability could have a similar effect."[29] As these doubts reached the press, support for war against Iraq fell during August from close to 80 percent to 56 percent.[30]

*　*　*

The issue was now being posed in terms of what to do about Iraqi WMD rather than what to do about Saddam's tyranny. As a result of 9/11, worst-case analysis had gained a new credibility. Any terrorists determined to inflict mass casualties on the United States and its allies were bound to seek the most efficient means of doing so. In late May 2002, Rumsfeld asserted that "inevitably" terrorists would acquire and use chemical, biological, or nuclear weapons. There was evidence of an al Qaeda interest in chemical or biological weapons, and a reasonable assumption that if acquired these weapons would be used; there was no reason to suppose that such attacks would be of a high probability. Even when a scare was raised over a suspected plot to explode a radiation bomb, something that clearly interested al Qaeda from 1993, reports suggested that this was at an elementary stage and that even if some device were constructed, the effects would be modest, and only severe if panic ensued.

In June 2002, in a speech to the graduates of the U.S. Military Academy at West Point, Bush warned that now the "gravest danger to freedom lies at the perilous crossroads of radicalism and technology. When the spread of chemical and biological and nuclear weapons, along with ballistic missile technology—when that occurs, even weak states and small groups could attain a catastrophic power to strike great nations. Our enemies have declared this very intention, and have been caught seeking these terrible weapons. They want the capability to blackmail us, or to harm us, or to harm our friends—and we will oppose them with all our power." Such enemies were beyond containment. Nor did the United States dare to place "faith in the word of tyrants, who solemnly sign non-proliferation treaties, and then systematically break them." His conclusion: Waiting was dangerous. "We must take the battle to the enemy, disrupt his plans, and confront the worst threats before they emerge. In the world we have entered, the only path to safety is the path of action. And this nation will act."[31] In September, the National Security Strategy of the United States was released, addressing the issue of preemption directly as well as the claims that U.S. power was not used for unilateral advantage but against tyranny and to promote liberty.[32] Around the foreign policy bureaucracy, there was some disquiet about making a case for a strategy of preemption and taking a relaxed view about the circumstances when use would be legitimate, when this could set precedents for states with more malign motives. Officials suggested that preemptive actions did not have to be wholly military and that preemptive decisions would be few and far between, but Bush himself seemed content that a readiness to take such action would be, post-9/11, a defining feature of his presidency.

In terms of international law, preemption can be justified, as anticipatory self-defense, if an enemy attack is imminent. It was one thing to postulate a dreadful conjunction of terrorism and weapons of mass destruction, but quite a different matter to assert this as an imminent danger. The scenario constructed to provide an empirical case for war involved two propositions that were widely believed, that al Qaeda was interested in WMD and Iraq was developing WMD. It also involved a third proposition: Demand and supply might well meet, should al Qaeda and Iraq come together in a wicked alliance. Reports from the undergrowth of international politics spoke of networks of nuclear smuggling, of terrorists and criminal gangs and rogue states interacting in complex but indubitably malign ways. Yet al Qaeda's links with Saudi Arabia and Pakistan, or the possibility that Russia might, inadvertently, come to be a source of WMD for terrorists, did not acquire the same purchase in Washington as the potential Iraqi connection.

Given their quite distinct philosophies, it would be surprising to find significant links between Osama bin Laden and Saddam Hussein. This was the general view within government up to 2001. It was known that there had been desultory contacts early in the 1990s, possibly including an al Qaeda interest in using Iraq as a safe haven, but without much resulting. There were also reports of groups based in Iraq with some al Qaeda associations. Reference was made to the Jordanian Abu Musab al-Zarqawi, leader of an Islamic group in northern Iraq called Ansar al-Islam with links to al Qaeda, although his group was unaffiliated and largely based in the Kurdish north.

After the war, Zarqawi emerged as the greatest thorn in the American side. Over time, the CIA was prepared to acknowledge, these contacts might get closer. For the moment al Qaeda showed little interest.

The CIA view was that the Iraqis saw their WMD arsenal as having defensive value, not to be used unless attacked. It would invite trouble to make them available to an independent and unpredictable group, for not only would this be an admission that the arsenal existed but it would be sufficiently inflammatory to bring down the wrath of the United States. At most, if the regime concluded that the United States could no longer be deterred, it would be less constrained in adopting terrorist means, as it tried to do in 1991, this time possibly with chemical or biological weapons. Anything might be contemplated as a last act of vengeance when close to defeat.

The contrary view was that not only was there a link, but Saddam might even have been responsible for 9/11. The influence of Laurie Mylroie of the American Enterprise Institute on Paul Wolfowitz was mentioned in Chapter 1. Her 2000 book pulled together circumstantial evidence connecting Iraq with the February 1993 bombing of the World Trade Center. After 9/11, Wolfowitz encouraged James Woolsey, a former director of central intelligence and a long-standing advocate of regime change in Iraq, to go to London to meet with Iraqi exiles to get support for the theory and check with British intelligence, which strongly disagreed. His office also asked the Defense Intelligence Agency (DIA) to see if it could prove the allegations in Mylroie's book, but the Agency's analysts were unable to substantiate them. The other critical allegation, which had emerged not long after 9/11, was that Mohammed Atta, the ringleader of the attacks, met with an Iraqi agent in Prague in early 2001. This story came from Czech officials who appear to have overinterpreted meager evidence. Its meaning, even if true, was unclear, and by and large the administration was circumspect in using it, without ever quite denying its possible truth. When voters were asked in August 2002 why the United States might take military action against Iraq, as many believed this was because of terrorism as because of WMD.[33]

Yet while such suggestions helped create a political climate in favor of war, they could not sustain international diplomacy. By the summer of 2002, it was apparent that there was no clinching evidence demonstrating a link with al Qaeda. Woodward reported Rice's view that it would be impossible to get international support on Iraq's human rights record, and the terrorism case seemed "weak or unprovable." This meant that the argument was based not on the dread scenario but on the apparently more reliable proposition that Iraq was in violation of numerous UN resolutions in its pursuit of WMD. This change removed dependence on demonstrating an intent to pass weapons over to terrorists. This, Rice concluded, was the only issue that had any "legs."[34] Wolfowitz later acknowledged that the campaign against Iraq had to move forward on this issue and be one that everyone in "the U.S. government bureaucracy . . . could agree on." With the terrorism issue, there was "the most disagreement within the bureaucracy." The other potential reason that was not to be presented as "core" was "the criminal treatment of the Iraqi people."[35] In September, after meeting Bush, Canadian prime minister Jean Chrétien told reporters that when he asked about links between al Qaeda and Iraq, the president replied, "That is not the angle they're exploring now. The angle they're exploring is the production of weapons of mass destruction."[36]

Blair had also been pushing in this direction. A Cabinet Office memo of July 2002 noted, "The US Government's military planning for action against Iraq is proceeding apace. But, as yet, it lacks a political framework. In particular, little thought has been given to creating the political conditions for military action, or the aftermath and how to shape it." It also reported that Blair's support for "military action to bring about regime change" was on the condition that "efforts had been made to construct a coalition/shape public opinion," which included trying to calm down the Israel-Palestine crisis and exhaust the "options for action to eliminate Iraq's WMD through the UN weapons inspectors."[37]

The combination of Scowcroft's intervention, Blair's need for a compelling rationale for further action, and Powell's advocacy persuaded Bush to go back to the UN and build up a coalition against Saddam, as his father had done. Powell warned the president that such a step would mean that the administration would not get the outcome it sought: "If you take it to the U.N., you've got to recognize that they might be able to solve it. In which case there's no war. That could mean a solution that is not as clean as just going in and taking the guy out."[38] The pro-war camp, now led by Cheney and Rumsfeld, was opposed to this move for that reason. If Saddam faced clear demands with which he could comply, then he might indeed opt for compliance or give the appearance of doing so. In late August, Cheney sought to prevent this move in a speech, arguing that inspections would provide an illusory reassurance and that the dangers of inaction would outweigh those of action. One of the important though unintended consequences of this speech was to help polarize the European debate. It appeared toward the conclusion of a German general election and was used by Chancellor Gerhard Schröder to help boost his antiwar credentials and so obtain reelection. Nonetheless, in September Bush accepted the Blair-Powell view and on September 12, 2002, in a speech to the UN General Assembly, he made the case for a new UN resolution on Iraq.

The uncertainty about where this was leading was reflected in a book published by Bob Woodward, the reporter closer than anyone to administration thinking at this time. The president proceeded "as if he were willing to give the U.N. a chance and his public rhetoric softened." There was less talk of regime change. The president told an audience on October 1 that a "military option is not the first choice but disarming this man is." A few days later, Bush was describing war as avoidable and not imminent, adding, "I hope this will not require military action." Woodward's own uncertainty as to where this was leading was apparent. The shift in tone, he wrote, "was all a victory for Powell, but perhaps only momentarily."

> The scaled-down rhetoric did mean that the president could say no to
> Cheney and Rumsfeld, but it did not mean a lessening of Bush's fierce
> determination. As always, it was an ongoing struggle for the president's
> heart and mind as he attempted to balance his unilateralist impulses
> with some international realities.[39]

★   ★   ★

Whereas the discussion of the terrorist link was deeply controversial, that was not the case with the assumption that Iraq had stocks of WMD and was engaged in an active process of deception. Iraq was indeed still pursuing a WMD program. For 1996–2003, the Iraqi Military Industrialization Commission's budget was increased a hundredfold, to reach $500 million by its final year, largely using money from illicit oil contracts. There were materials that the Iraqis wished to deny to the UN inspectors, because deception techniques were continually being developed and practiced. Dual-use technologies helped prepare for the resumption of chemical and biological weapons production when the time came. Some research was still under way on nuclear weapons.

It would not have taken much time for Iraq to reconstitute stocks of chemical weapons. The main constraint on an operational capability was some means of delivering them to targets. This was in fact the area with the clearest violations of UN Resolution 687, as the flight testing of missiles and UAVs exceeded the set limit of 90 miles. Research was under way to extend missile range, and there were discussions with North Korea on the acquisition of the No Dong missile with a range of 800 miles.[40] Efforts began in 2000 to develop long-range missiles, though these were poorly organized and unsuccessful. Another constraint was that in order to challenge the coalition's dominance of the airspace over his country, Saddam's short-term priority was to find ways to shoot down American aircraft. This led to resources being diverted into invariably futile programs.

Having something to hide was not the only reason not to cooperate with the UN. It showed that Saddam had not been cowed. Capitulation to international pressure would mean that the great costs associated with sanctions, incurred through defiance, would have been to no purpose. In addition, if the absence of the awesome capabilities that had set Iraq apart from other regional powers, and upon which the regime had depended at moments of crisis, became explicit, Iraq would be more vulnerable to attack. A lingering element of deterrence would be lost. Iraqi commanders appeared to have been reassured by the presumed availability of chemical weapons, even if they did not have their own stocks. Moreover, if, as assumed, the inspectors doubled as American spies, then there were sound security reasons for preventing them from roaming around sensitive installations as widely as they wished and talking to anyone they wished. Last, Saddam saw no reason for further concessions, doubting that the United States would ever allow the sanctions to be lifted while he remained in power. But he could draw comfort from the help that the Russians and French would provide in easing the constraints under which he was operating.

Deception had been so integral from the start that it may well have affected both internal and external communications. Few, if any, senior Iraqis would have a full idea about what was going on. Record keeping was haphazard and undermined by the loss of documents seized by UNSCOM. Those responsible may have preferred their masters not to know that assets carefully hidden had not actually been properly maintained or that the technical claims behind ongoing programs had been exaggerated. There are suggestions that Saddam himself was promised that some activities were in good shape when they were not, particularly with regard to the speed with which production of chemical and biological weapons could be restarted, leading to the intriguing possibility that Saddam himself was among those surprised by how little the postwar survey group actually found.

Although the Iraqis denied there was anything left, they were unable to prove their point, with significant question marks against such items as precursor chemicals for the nerve gas VX and growth media for anthrax. These materials were unaccounted for, and given Iraq's record, it was not unreasonable for the inspectors to assume that this was because they had been hidden away. This was, however, still an assumption. The available information could support at least four possibilities. The first was that there was little left to worry about. This was the view of former inspector (and former hawk) Scott Ritter:

Most of UNSCOM's findings of Iraqi noncompliance concerned either the inability to verify an Iraqi declaration or peripheral matters, such as components and documentation, which by and of themselves do not constitute a weapon or program. By the end of 1998, Iraq had, in fact, been disarmed to a level unprecedented in modern history, but UNSCOM and the Security Council were unable—and in some instances unwilling— to acknowledge this accomplishment.[41]

The second possibility, and the one closest to the truth, was that the Iraqis no longer had any serious capability but were looking to recover when they got the chance, starting with delivery vehicles. There was also an important technical point: Stocks of weapons were likely to deteriorate or become hazardous, especially if they were left in populated areas. This was the view taken by Rolf Ekeus, the first head of UNSCOM. In 2000, he wrote:

In my view, there are no large quantities of weapons. I don't think that Iraq is especially eager in the biological and chemical area to produce such weapons for storage. Iraq views those weapons as tactical assets instead of strategic assets, which would require long-term storage of those elements, which is difficult. Rather, Iraq has been aiming to keep the capability to start up production immediately should it need to.[42]

The third possibility was that Iraq had retained some capability, hidden from the inspectors, and was looking to reconstitute them, and the fourth was that reconstitution was well under way. This was the view of Ekeus's successor, Richard Butler, whose analysis undoubtedly influenced the thinking of the American, British, and Australian governments. This was his view as he resigned from UNSCOM in June 1999:

I believe they have worked hard on increasing their missile capability, the range of those missiles and probably the number of them. I'm sure they've asked their nuclear team to start meeting again, and I feel certain, too, that they have commenced work again on making chemical and biological warfare agents.

Although he did not think they would find nuclear progress straightforward, he judged the Iraqis to be quite skilled in the chemical and biological areas. He therefore agreed that the priority would be missile delivery systems, but disagreed over the possibility of Iraq waiting before it rebuilt its chemical and biological weapon stocks.[43]

UNSCOM reports provided the starting point for all analyses, but not much new information had come in since 1996. Western governments therefore had to rely on their own intelligence agencies. There was not much to go on. In 1998, two separate U.S. government panels reportedly concluded that allegations about the state of Iraqi WMD were based on reasonable suspicions rather than hard facts. In late 1999, the CIA acknowledged in its biannual report to Congress on the acquisition of WMD that little could be said about reconstitution since Operation Desert Fox of December 1998.[44] It remained reluctant to declare categorically that Iraq had WMD. In the late 2000 National Intelligence Estimate (NIE), for example, it assessed Iraq as having retained a small stockpile of chemical weapons (CW) agents (not warheads), and possibly precursors for more, while it continued development work.[45] Yet the trend in analysis, which included Butler and senior officials from the Clinton administration, was to firm up the estimate in this direction. In June 2001, the CIA, accepting that it lacked hard evidence, asserted, "Given Iraq's past behavior, it is likely that Baghdad has used the intervening period to reconstitute prohibited programs."[46]

The assumption that Iraq had hoarded chemical and biological weapons in a deployable form influenced Western diplomacy and military operations, and even opponents of the war. Intelligence agencies around the world seem to have been caught up in a massive exercise in groupthink. President Chirac told Hans Blix that he did not share the view of France's intelligence agencies that Iraq had proscribed weapons. The intelligence services, he observed, "sometimes intoxicate each other."[47] In September 2002, the independent, London-based think tank, the International Institute for Strategic Studies (IISS), published a dossier providing a thorough published guide to the consensus view of the period. It described the toxic materials still unaccounted for, and then moved on to the more speculative area concerning what had happened since 1998. It was possible, but not proven, that production of both biological and chemical weapons had resumed. On the nuclear side, there were no facilities to produce fissile material in sufficient amounts, and these would require several years and extensive foreign assistance to build. Only if Iraq could obtain fissile material from foreign sources could it assemble nuclear weapons. Then it could be done quite quickly.[48] What changed in the official presentation of intelligence in the autumn of 2002 was that such reconstitution moved from conjecture to fact. This was reflected in the October 2002 U.S. National Intelligence Estimate, which was presented as the revelations of an "array of clandestine reporting" and was put forward with "high confidence."[49] This served as the basis for American government presentations.

What was the basis for these assertions? There was activity in relevant areas, though much of this was "dual-use," and so inherently ambiguous. One charge is that the Pentagon served as a conduit for dubious intelligence provided by the INC. In the past, INC material was discarded by other agencies as poor and self-serving. The State Department ceased supporting the INC's intelligence work. The Pentagon did not stop its support. Wolfowitz denied that he had been "mainlining" INC-derived materials into the intelligence process, but they undoubtedly achieved more circulation than before. The INC's Washington adviser was quoted as urging, "Go get me a terrorist and some W.M.D., because that's what the Bush administration is interested in."[50] On December 20, 2001, Judith Miller of the *New York Times* published a front-page story describing twenty secret WMD sites in Iraq, at least one under a hospital. The source for this was an Iraqi engineer whom, Miller explained, the INC had managed to help leave Iraq. She noted the INC's political agenda and that officials were still trying to confirm the claims. They seemed, however, to "be reliable and significant." Unfortunately, they weren't. After the war when the defector was taken back to Iraq, he was unable to locate any of the facilities to which he referred. The *New York Times* acknowledged then that it had not weighed the claims of defectors sufficiently against their desire to have Saddam ousted. "It looks as if we, along with the administration, were taken in."[51] Information from dubious defectors, of which the most notorious was known as "Curveball," often coached by the INC, found its way into the estimating process. Because the provenance of some of the material was obscured and the same sources could appear under a number of guises, at times they were providing self-corroboration.[52] The October 2002 NIE referred to an "array of clandestine reporting" put forward with "high confidence."

These stories would not have worked had there not already been a disposition to believe them, a widespread conviction that Saddam was hiding active weapons programs. On balance, the agencies came down with few reservations in support of the view that the regime was making a determined effort to use the end of inspections and the general decline of containment to rebuild its WMD capacity. Once active reconstitution was assumed, material being gathered by satellites and other technical means was interpreted with this in mind, leading to more innocent explanations being discounted. The political climate of the time encouraged this. The estimating processes that were designed to provide policymakers with private guidance became used to support controversial policies. In Washington the key audience was Congress, especially as the president had also determined that he would need both chambers to pass a resolution supporting military action if this became necessary. After a request from the Senate Intelligence Committee, Tenet refused to provide a broad assessment of the likely impact of the administration's policy but did agree, unusually, to bring forward the next NIE on Iraqi WMD.

For the intelligence agencies, this was one of those unique moments when they take center stage. There is a natural tendency for intelligence agencies to hedge their bets, and there is an extensive range of nuanced drafting language available to enable this. In such circumstances, however, equivocation can appear almost a dereliction of duty. Woodward reported that senior officials in the United States felt that in this case the policymakers were entitled to a strong judgment, so the normal caveats had to be reduced.[53] There were extensive debates on the appropriate language, and certain claims were discounted. Much of the detail on close examination was tentative and circumstantial. When the NIE was declassified, there were an unusual number of dissenting and qualifying footnotes.

Serious complaints were later made against the American process, that intelligence professionals were put under pressure to conform to the new line and present the Iraqi threat in as lurid terms as possible. Those who failed these political tests found their documents returned on a regular basis, with numerous detailed points on sources and content being raised, until the "right answer" was reached. Vice President Cheney made regular and intimidating visits to CIA headquarters.[54]

In an interview published in 1996, when out of government, Wolfowitz observed that "policymakers must become, in effect, the senior analyst on their core accounts. Above all, they must become adept at the analytic techniques for doing battle with incomplete information and contradictory assumptions."[55] Against this background, it is not surprising that the Pentagon's Office of Special Plans attracted attention as the source of intelligence mischief. Those involved have sought to play this down, pointing out that this office largely dealt with postwar planning, and that there was confusion with a separate, small intelligence cell, which was mainly concerned with the relationship between Iraq and terrorism.[56] A network of individuals who had worked closely in the past with Wolfowitz was used by Douglas Feith, undersecretary of defense (policy), and it was in touch with "Scooter" Libby, Cheney's chief of staff. Their major effort was geared to proving the link with al Qaeda.

Few nuances or equivocations bothered policymakers. "We now know," said Cheney in August 2002, that "Saddam has resumed his efforts to acquire nuclear weapons." "There is no doubt," said Powell the next month, "that he has chemical weapons stocks," followed soon by Bush's claim to the UN

General Assembly, "Right now, Iraq is expanding and improving facilities that were used for the production of biological weapons."[57]

✶   ✶   ✶

From the summer of 2002, therefore, Bush's diplomatic strategy depended on the widely accepted but essentially unproven assumption of a developing Iraqi WMD capability. This was not in itself an argument for war. Indeed, if it had been easy for Iraq to use chemical weapons, then this could be an argument against war, because of the danger posed to troops engaged in operations in Iraq. (Coalition forces always operated under the assumption that chemical weapons could at any time be used against them.) The reported view of the CIA was that available WMD would only be used in the event of an attack on Iraq. That would have fitted in with the Iraqi strategy of 1990–1991, when there was some link between chemical weapons and direct threats to the regime.

The case for believing that Iraq might be reckless with its WMD, even in the absence of a direct attack, assumed that Saddam Hussein and his regime were inherently unpredictable and aggressive, so that this was a man in some sense beyond deterrence. Kenneth Pollack wrote that this would be "unusually difficult" because of Saddam's "pathologies"—a "fundamentally aggressive," "inveterate gambler and risk-taker who regularly twists his calculation of the odds to suit his preferred course of action." When nothing was discovered, the same author was arguing that reducing WMD to the bare minimum without letting on was another one of Saddam's "famous gambles."[58]

Such character traits might explain why Saddam was hard to read, but they did not put him beyond deterrence.[59] Whether Saddam's personality was reckless or cautious, and therefore deterrable, it was his persistence in power that meant that the 1991 war could not be considered truly over. Iraq was left in a continuing dispute with the UN over a range of issues that could not be readily resolved. Containment eroded during the 1990s because members of the Security Council became increasingly unwilling to sustain a porous and counterproductive sanctions regime and endorse enforcement action that appeared to be more punitive than decisive. Because the pressure had been ratcheted up, containment returned as an option, but only fleetingly, because the main effect was to bring the crisis to a head. The regime was still cheating, in which case it should be overthrown, or it was not, in which case sanctions should end. Unfortunately, the crisis came to a head before the claims could be properly tested. If the pressure had not been ratcheted up in 2002, the most likely prospect was of the regime feeling increasingly unconstrained, until at some point Iraq's inherent fragility would have produced yet another crisis, perhaps involving the Kurds or real evidence that WMD programs were being reconstituted. The Iraq problem was the Saddam problem, and one was not going to be resolved without the other.

Since the opponents of the UN route, notably in the Pentagon, were pushing for a resolution couched in terms that could never get past the Security Council, Powell this time could demonstrate that such terms could not even get British support, never mind the more skeptical member states. In November 2002, Resolution 1441 was passed, the latest of forty-nine resolutions passed from 1990 to 2002 on the subject of Iraq, thirty-five of them after 1990, seventeen of them in which Iraqi compliance could be seriously doubted. The new resolution required that Iraq allow inspectors back in and provide a complete and final disclosure of its WMD activities, past and present. It recalled that the Security Council "has repeatedly warned Iraq that it will face serious consequences as a result of its continued violations of its obligations." Any technical violation could provide legal grounds for war, although whether without real substance this could legitimize war was another matter. [60] When presidential spokesman Ari Fleischer briefed the press on December 2, he described the trap supposedly set. If Saddam admitted weapons of mass destruction, then "he is violating United Nations resolutions" and had "deceived the world." If he said he had none, then he "is once again misleading the world." That was because "we have intelligence information about what Saddam Hussein possesses."[61] The trap, however, could work both ways, for if the assessments were wrong then the strategy could soon unravel. Although he may have been confident that Saddam Hussein would be unable to comply, Bush was effectively handing over judgments on compliance to the special UN inspectors (UNMOVIC), set up as the successor to UNSCOM, and the International Atomic Energy Agency.

Resolution 1441 required a full statement by Iraq demonstrating compliance. When this arrived on December 7, 2002, it was widely judged to be incomplete, thereby rendering Iraq noncompliant. Initial reports from the UN inspectors confirmed this attitude. So it seemed that Saddam Hussein was playing to the script. In his first report to the Security Council on January 27, 2003, chief inspector Hans Blix reported that "Iraq appears not to have come to a genuine acceptance, not even today, of the disarmament that was demanded of it." Blix's intention, with what he acknowledged to be a hawkish line, reflecting his own "gut feeling" that some WMD were being hidden, was to bring home to the Iraqis the danger they faced. Combined with his direct encounters with Iraqi officials, this may have had the desired effect, and thereafter Iraqi cooperation improved.[62]

The immediate Iraqi response convinced Bush that Iraqi behavior was as before and that there would be little reason to wait before overthrowing the regime. Part of the problem was concern about sustaining forces overseas and the imminent hot weather. According to Woodward, Bush decided on war by January 13, 2003. "Time is running out on Saddam Hussein," remarked Bush the next day. "He must disarm. I'm sick and tired of games and deception. And that's my view of timetables."[63] On January 15, he agreed to a further meeting with Blair, who came to Washington at the end of the month. Blair did not agree to abandon the UN process on the grounds that it was not going anywhere. For domestic political reasons, he wanted a second UN resolution, and with the evidence of Iraqi noncompliance he felt reasonably confident. However, just as Bush was making his decision, President Chirac of France was making his, which was to oppose war. The evidence of American forces moving to the Gulf ready for an assault may have had a coercive effect, but it also suggested that the Americans had given up on coercion and were bent on invasion.[64] On January 20, this led to a diplomatic argument between the United States and France in New York.

These positions were taken before the claims and counterclaims had a chance to be tested via the inspections. The Americans and British in particular were responding to Iraqi behavior but not UNMOVIC evidence. They therefore fell into their own trap. Their unqualified and strident assessments had raised the stakes, yet even they were becoming uncomfortably aware that they were on less than firm ground. Blair is said to have had doubts that the evidence was "rock solid," which he dared not share because that would make war "harder to sell." One of his entourage recalled, "We hoped we were right . . . We felt we were right."[65] In December, when Bush received a full briefing on the quality of the intelligence, he was reportedly unimpressed. "I don't think this is quite—it's not something that Joe Public would understand or gain a lot of confidence from." He asked Tenet if this was the "best we've got" and was told, "It's a slam dunk case."[66]

If the administration had wanted to backtrack, this was the point to do it. The UN process could test the evidence. There had been some mobilization of troops but the main buildup, which created its own pressure for action, would not start until the new year. Bush wrestled with the thought. Just before Christmas he asked Rice, without warning, "Do you think we should do this?" Rice said yes, because if Saddam did not respond there was no choice.[67] But the much harder question was what should be done if Saddam responded to a degree and if the intelligence turned out to be vacuous.

Instead of backtracking, the administration sought to bolster its case, perhaps in order to convince itself as much as the outside world, by seizing on any piece of potentially corroborative evident, even before it had been properly evaluated.[68] The claim that uranium was being sought from Niger, which embarrassingly made its way into Bush's 2003 State of the Union Address, was based on a forged document and had not been supported in the NIE. Ambassador Joseph Wilson had been asked to travel to Niger to see if this was true, and he had reported that it was not.[69]

The vulnerability of the United States on this score explains Colin Powell's address to the Security Council in February 2003.[70] Considerable care went into this speech. Powell felt that his credibility was being put on the line. His task was to demonstrate that the case against Iraq held up, despite the growing doubts, and that the inspectors were being fooled. All accounts of the preparation of this speech convey a growing sense that the case lacked a hard core of fact, and in key respects relied on inference and innuendo.[71] Powell did his best with what he had, toning down rather than discarding allegations, but highlighting areas where he felt the evidence was strongest. Most important, he refused to include the bulk of the material provided to him on the relationship between Iraq and al Qaeda, yet he did include some. He offered evidence that the Iraqis were still playing games with the inspectors, and also made some specific claims about capabilities, of which the most important (and unfortunately erroneous) related to the identification of two portable laboratories that could be used for biological weapons. Although first impressions were positive, this speech had the paradoxical effect of undermining the American and British position, for UNMOVIC was not able to validate these claims.

Blix reported being surprised at the modesty of this new material from Powell. When Blix gave his second report, on February 14, he conveyed not only doubts about some of Powell's allegations but his view that Iraq had decided to cooperate with inspectors. By now, UNMOVIC inspectors were starting to visit sites identified by the British and Americans and finding little,[72] while the IAEA was able to declare that Iraq was not in the process of reconstituting its nuclear program. In areas where the October NIE had been challenged from within the intelligence community, the dissents turned out to be correct. Attempts to obtain aluminum tubes for centrifuge rotors had been presented as evidence of a uranium enrichment program, except by the State Department and the Department of Energy (which might have been assumed to be in a position to know). The doubts about UAVs as offensive weapons rather than means of reconnaissance, apparently shared by the U.S. Air Force, were reinforced even as Blix was being chastised for not making more of this issue. Dramatic revelations turned out to have been clutching at straws.

The whole post-1998 reconstitution hypothesis was now looking fragile, although questions on the pre-1998 chemical and biological inventories had yet to be answered. The only area where the American and British claims stood up at all was delivery systems, which would be consistent with the view that this would be the first priority for the regime if there had been any hope of reviving a deployable capability. UNMOVIC revealed that there had been a surge of activity in this field over the previous four years, and then UNMOVIC began to destroy Al Samoud 2 missiles. These were not "toothpicks," Blix reminded Powell, when the significance of this move was played down. It was not surprising that in these circumstances, there was a developing view in the Security Council that at best the case was not proven and that the inspectors needed more time.

An awkward relationship had developed between the UN inspectors and Western intelligence. When UNSCOM was founded in 1991, it lacked its own intelligence sources and therefore had to rely on information from member states, and in particular the United States. In return, it was understood that there would be feedback on the reliability of the information received. Because of the Iraqi efforts to thwart the inspectors, intelligence became more important, in particular, interception of Iraqi communications. This always made it likely that the countries involved would get additional intelligence benefit in areas beyond UNSCOM's remit. As the inspections regime collapsed in 1998–1999, it was alleged that U.S. intelligence had used the UNSCOM cover to insert listening devices that went far beyond those needed for UNSCOM purposes and that this information might have been used during Operation Desert Fox.[73] Blix wished to demonstrate his independence of Western intelligence. He refused, for example, to have an American as his deputy. This was also reflected in his reluctance to interrogate key Iraqi witnesses outside of Iraq, without which the Americans, reflecting the past impact of defectors, insisted it would be impossible to rely on their evidence. It was bound to be difficult to formalize arrangements for such interrogations when the individuals involved had no desire to leave Iraq and would still be anxious about their families if they were suspected of handing over secrets. The UN was concerned about the legality and morality of what could appear as abduction.[74] Nonetheless, Blix was still expecting to be guided by Western intelligence to the sites where they assumed incriminating evidence would be found.

The riposte was that it was not up to the coalition to prove anything. There were still many reasonable suspicions, and Saddam had done little to dispel them. The skepticism became a recurring theme even after the adoption of UNSCR 1441. Wolfowitz, in a speech on January 23, 2003, noted that it was not the inspectors' job to find anything: "When an auditor discovers discrepancies in the books, it is not the auditor's obligation to prove where the embezzler has stashed his money. It is up to the person or institution being audited to explain the discrepancy." They were being expected to search every potential hiding place "in a country the size of France, even if nothing were being moved." Yet, he claimed, American intelligence was aware of great activity, involving items from documents to prohibited material being moved from one site to another where it would not be found, such as private homes, mosques, and hospitals: "It is a shell game played on a grand scale with deadly serious weapons." In the past, UN inspectors had been recruited as informants. Those Iraqis interviewed by the inspectors could not believe in their confidentiality and risked punishment if they cooperated. The Iraqis were practiced liars. Wolfowitz's conclusion: "We cannot expect that the U.N. inspectors have the capacity to disarm an uncooperative Iraq, even with the full support of American intelligence and the intelligence of other nations."[75] In the end, if Saddam Hussein was unable or unwilling to prove that his regime no longer had weapons of destruction, there was little choice but to assume that it had. As Rumsfeld later put it, "absence of evidence" was not the same as "evidence of absence." Nor was it evidence of concealment.

An interview Cheney gave on the eve of war indicates the reluctance of the administration to accept the judgments of the inspectors or even a completed disarmament process. The problem was, as before, that Saddam would still be in power. "Even if he were tomorrow to give everything up," Cheney remarked, "if he stays in power, we have to assume that as soon as the world is looking the other way and preoccupied with other issues, he will be back again rebuilding his BW [biological weapons] and CW capabilities, and once again reconstituting his nuclear program." He explicitly disagreed with the IAEA's view on the lack of a nuclear program:

> if you look at the track record of the International Atomic Energy Agency and this kind of issue, especially where Iraq's concerned, they have consistently underestimated or missed what it was Saddam Hussein was doing. I don't have any reason to believe they're any more valid this time than they've been in the past.[76]

France, Germany, and Russia argued strongly for giving the inspectors more time and not rushing to war. Blair, who most needed a second resolution, eventually used the uncompromising nature of French opposition as an argument for pushing ahead anyway with the United States, but it represented a big political gamble for him. Even until the last moment, there was some hope that the pressure on the Ba'athist regime would generate either a coup or some move organized by other Arab states to ease Saddam and his closest associates into exile. When none of this was forthcoming, war did become inevitable. It remains an interesting question as to what might have happened had France and Germany decided on a different strategy, perhaps following the line the British unsuccessfully promoted toward the end of the UN process, with a deadline and clear benchmarks of progress.[77] Possible compromises, involving an extended timetable with agreed means of evaluating compliance and the possibility of a UN-sanctioned war, failed because of French and German refusal to contemplate force under any circumstances. Whether Blair could have persuaded Bush to accept a further delay was never really put to the test. The breakdown of good working relations between America and Britain on one side, and France and Germany on the other, was both a symptom and a cause of the mismanagement of the UN process.[78] As the diplomatic debate raged and demonstrators marched, the war acquired a degree of inevitability. The military mobilization that Rumsfeld had set in motion at the start of January created its own timetable. By early March, the troops were in place. Last-minute appeals were made and ignored. On March 19, one day earlier than planned, the fighting began.

There is much to be said for Thomas Power's view that the most remarkable aspect of the Bush administration's adventure in Iraq was "the degree to which it has been driven by theory—general ideas about things that might or could happen."[79] The case for war moved forward on a series of propositions—about the nature of the Iraqi regime, its interest in deadly weapons and ability to deceive inspectors, its readiness to cooperate with terrorists of a different philosophical hue even to the point of handing over instruments of mass destruction, the fragility of its popular base, and the consequences of its overthrow, for Iraq and for the wider Middle East. These propositions drew on intelligence information, but they could rarely be refuted or confirmed in a definitive manner until they faced the supreme empirical tests of war and its aftermath. Some of these propositions, for example, about the likely course of an Iraq still governed by the old regime, will remain forever matters for conjecture. In the end, this war was something of an experiment, an unusual example of Western countries taking the initiative rather than responding to events. As with many experiments, the results were both surprising and disconcerting.

INSURGENCY

THERE WERE TWO distinctive influences on the U.S. conduct of the war in Iraq. The first concerned the possibilities of fighting and winning a war with far fewer forces than would hitherto have been thought prudent. This was bound up with the "transformation agenda" Rumsfeld was pursuing. The second was about creating conditions for democracy to take root and flourish in postwar Iraq. Thus, the first was about removing a regime, the second about inserting a new regime. If the two concerns had been mutually supportive, together they would have been about regime change. Unfortunately, the opposite was the case. Although in the first instance Rumsfeld made his transformational point, in that the regime was toppled with a remarkably small force, the consequence of this was that there were too few troops to provide the secure conditions necessary to complete a smooth process of transition. The problem was not only numbers. U.S. forces lacked the training and the doctrine to manage the transition from combat to nation building. The ensuing conflict and violence that engulfed Iraq in turn did not so much undermine the transformation agenda as render it irrelevant because it was geared to the wrong sort of enemy.

From one perspective, the Iraq project was doomed from the start, and the administration's ineptitude merely added extra misery and chaos to what was inevitably going to be a grim tale. According to this view, only the politically naïve and the historically illiterate could have contemplated constructing a working democracy out of the ruins of Saddam Hussein's tyranny. A moment's reflection on the problems that generally accompany violent regime changes, especially those triggered by outside forces, or a passing acquaintance with Iraq's history, including the United Kingdom's attempts to pacify the country in the early 1920s, should have chastened even Washington's most eager advocates for intervention. No region offered a more forbidding setting for experimentation with democratization than the Middle East, with all its ethnic and cultural divisions, and no country within the region held less promise than Iraq, brutalized as it was by decades of oppression, wars, and sanctions.

Claims about the positive value of regime change were made during the course of the buildup to war, but they were always secondary to those about the need to deal with Iraq's WMD. In principle, if Saddam had complied with UN resolutions, he would have been off the hook and these other benefits forgone. Even before the war began, the failure of the UN inspectors to find any WMD sites of significance had been troubling to the war's supporters, but it could be explained by Iraqi deception or the inadequacies of the inspectors. The Iraq Survey Group began its work soon after the war, in a massive effort to find those elusive WMD, led by David Kay, a former inspector who had an impeccable record for finding hidden nuclear programs. After six months he made the dramatic and politically damaging announcement: "We were almost all wrong." His work was completed by Charles Duelfer, who demonstrated just how wrong so many of the assertions on which the case for war had been built.[1] By this time, the administration was starting to stress the promotion of human rights and democracy as rationales for war. For a while, these motives became the war's defining cause. Unfortunately, the insurgency then grew so serious that the central justification for continued U.S. involvement became defeating terrorism within Iraq—a problem that had never been mentioned before, for the distressing reason that it was a product of the war's botched conduct.

To the extent that this was a bold experiment in evaluating the possibility of societies escaping the constraints of their past, the methodology was extraordinarily rigorous. The administration went out of its way to make the project as difficult as possible to test fully the underlying hypothesis. Advisers and observers who warned early on of the hazards of occupation and argued that such a bold undertaking called for special efforts were disregarded and often derided. Instead of mobilizing the whole U.S. government to ensure that the hard questions were asked and answered, the principal figures in the Bush administration made a determined effort to ignore available expertise, including serious preparatory work by State Department officials and others. The people whose opinions were sought were chosen on narrow grounds and often despite patent self-interest. Promises that the liberated people of Iraq would cheerfully cooperate with the occupation were taken far too seriously. To the Bush administration's cavalier assumption that Iraq could be transformed without any extraordinary effort, other charges can be added: the divisive diplomacy that accompanied Washington's rush to war, which tarnished the invasion's legitimacy and then limited international support for an extended occupation; disregard for the prospects (and the consequences) of the looting and disarray that followed the fall of Saddam's regime; the decision to disband the defeated Iraqi army; the failure to fully appreciate the implications of excluding numerous former members of the ruling Ba'ath Party from state institutions; the inability to foresee the public relations disaster and the ethical morass that would inevitably result from treating Iraqi prisoners in ways reminiscent of Saddam's methods. The list is not exhaustive.

*　*　*

At first, things seemed to have gone as well as could be expected. On May 1, Bush landed on the aircraft USS *Abraham Lincoln*. The impression that this was something of a stunt was enhanced by the fact that although his helicopter would have sufficed, he arrived on a jet wearing a flight suit. A background banner proclaimed "Mission Accomplished," though Bush did not actually use those words in his speech. This was the closest he was going to get to the "USS *Missouri* moment" that his father had been denied in 1991. His speechwriters actually began with General MacArthur's address on taking the Japanese surrender in 1945. The draft was toned down by both Powell and Rumsfeld, who worried about an "implication of finality."[2] The speech acknowledged "difficult work" still to do in Iraq, but also claimed, "In the Battle of Iraq, the United States and our allies have prevailed."[3]

The success of the military campaign to occupy Iraq was also seen as a vindication of Rumsfeld's transformation project. Since planning began at the end of November 2001, he had consistently pressed General Franks for a fast and light campaign, with as few troops as possible.[4] The war was scheduled to start on March 20, but the previous day, intelligence was received suggesting that Saddam was meeting with key aides and family at the al-Dora farming community close to Baghdad. Bombs and cruise missiles were dropped on the compound, but the intelligence was inaccurate and the promise of a swift and surgical act of regime elimination was dashed. The next day, conventional military operations began. Unlike 1991, when there was a long period of air activity before there was any engagement on the ground, Iraqi air defenses in 2003 were in a poor state after years of coming off second best in engagements with coalition aircraft, and coalition command of the air could be assumed from the start. The essence of the plan was to bypass civilian areas and peripheral areas to isolate Iraqi forces and prevent them from coordinating counterattacks. Air attacks focused on military targets and what were assumed to be the sources of Saddam's power.

It had been hoped to have a separate move from the north, but Turkey refused to serve as a base for offensive operations against its neighbor. Nonetheless, Special Forces did work closely with the Kurdish militia and used air strikes to prevent Iraqi forces from opening up a new front in Kurdish areas. Out of Kuwait, the British First Armored Division moved forward to clear the Fao Peninsula and move toward Basra. The First Marine Expeditionary Force first secured the Rumaila oil fields and then moved toward Baghdad, traveling up the Central Highway. To its left, the U.S. Army Fifth Corps, with the Third Infantry Division to the fore, also advanced. The advances were slowed by sandstorms, logistical bottlenecks, and occasional battles. In particular, at the cities of Nasiriyah, Najaf, and Samawah, sites of critical river crossings, Iraqi resistance stiffened. After some time, at a heavy cost to the defenders, this resistance was broken and the advance pressed on. One worrying portent of things to come was the presence of the Saddam Fedayeen guerrillas, who were able to mount occasional ambushes and began the process of creating suspicion within the local population. Certainly, there was no rush of cheerful Iraqis greeting their liberators. The Shi'ites had too many memories of being let down in the past to make any move before they could be sure that Saddam was finally on his way out.

A rather meticulous plan was developed to take Baghdad. Armored units would surround the city and then, starting on the outskirts, they would push forward, so that enemy units would be gradually forced to retreat toward the center. The plan changed as first the Republican Guards were engaged to the south of the city and lost most of their armor, and then a small army unit of tanks and armored fighting vehicles was sent to probe the remaining Iraqi defenses, and after some resistance got to the airport. The same technique—known as "Thunder Run"—was tried a couple of days later, when an armored unit reached the palaces and government offices of central Baghdad.[5] As this was broadcast live, official Iraqi resistance collapsed and by April 9, Baghdad was firmly in U.S. hands. It took until April 13 before Tikrit, Saddam's hometown, fell to coalition control. Although operations took far less time than those in 1991, casualties on the Iraqi side were high, with the numbers of military dead normally put at over 9,000 and civilian dead at over 7,000. The United States lost 139 dead, the British thirty-three.

The swift and decisive conclusion did not prove much about the transformation project because the enemy was so weak. The "thunder runs," for example, would have been foolhardy against opponents who were properly trained for urban warfare and knew how to direct their fire more accurately.[6] Prior to the war, the only real issue to most observers was the effort and cost involved in the defeat of Iraq and not the final result. The conclusion demonstrated the difference that airpower could make in supporting a professional regular force against a poor opponent.

The only believer in Iraqi victory was Saddam, which perhaps explains why he did not avail himself of opportunities for a safe exile. First he assumed that war would not come because France and Russia would prevent it, and then, once it started, he anticipated enormous pressure for a cease-fire. As none of his underlings dared be candid about how the reality fell far short of the grandiose claims made about industrial advances and military preparedness, he had no idea about the true state of affairs. He was told such lies about the state of his forces that he confidently believed that coalition forces would not be able to make it to Baghdad. At least this confidence in his survival meant that he did not ruin the country further by torching oil fields or opening the dams. Because he believed he could stop the coalition on the ground, he ordered his air force to be kept hidden so it would not be destroyed by the Americans, or confiscated by the Iranians, as had happened in 1991. As the fighting progressed, he lapped up stories of heroic resistance, to the point where he urged France, Russia, and China not to push for a cease-fire because that would allow the coalition to hold on to Iraqi territory they might otherwise be forced to leave.

Saddam took his role as supreme commander seriously. This was in part because he did not want any capable military figures to position themselves to mount a coup but also because he fancied himself as a strategist. The result was inappropriate plans and orders that could not be implemented, passed through a desperately sycophantic officer corps. His force planning was more affected by the Kurdish and Shi'ite uprisings of 1991 than by Desert Storm (the official line was that Iraqi strategy and tactics were vindicated when the Americans offered a cease-fire). He wanted politically reliable forces available to deal with any repeat performance. In the West, the Republican Guard was assumed to provide the most important guardians of his regime, but he could not be sure that they were coup-proof, even when his son Qusay was put in charge, and with lackluster commanders beneath him.

New militias were formed to provide truly loyal forces. Of these, the Saddam Fedayeen were the most formidable, a permanent force available to deal with whatever happened to be the most severe security challenges, where necessary reinforcing the Ba'ath Party militia. They took on the regime's nastiest assignments. The al Quds (Jerusalem) Army was more numerous, at about 500,000 strong. This was a part-time militia geared to the more troublesome regions, but with training and commitment, more rudimentary than the Fedayeen. Over the 1990s, these militias were preferred over the army in terms of recruitment and equipment. Although they were established with internal need in mind, as Saddam saw the trouble that militias could cause Western armies, as in the Palestinian intifada, he increasingly believed they could play a role in the face of foreign attack. Although no deliberate preparations were made for this role against the coalition, it does appear that the ammunition had been distributed by way of preparation for a long campaign against forces trying to reach Baghdad. Thus, the army was much reduced since 1991, now having old equipment and poor logistics. Saddam professed to believe that the military's commitment to the cause could compensate. The prospect of a peremptory execution for commanders at any level who showed hesitation or permitted defeat seems to have acted as an incentive of sorts.[7] The paramilitaries were the major new element, and though they were geared primarily to enforce internal order, they could also serve as the foundation for a later insurgency.

In February 2002, Ken Adelman, a former official in the Ford and Reagan administrations and a member of the Defense Science Board, published an op-ed piece in the *Washington Post* criticizing a previous piece that had appeared in the same pages by two Brookings analysts, Philip Gordon and Michael O'Hanlon, who had argued for persisting with a policy of containing Iraq. This was not because they did not accept a case for Saddam's overthrow or believe that, if successful, it would not be popular internationally, but because of the military risks. They argued that at least 250,000 troops would be needed and that "American casualties surely would be much higher than in Desert Storm."[8] Adelman took issue with such warnings. Instead, he suggested the demolition of Saddam's power and the liberation of Iraq would be a "cakewalk." He gave four reasons: "(1) It was a cakewalk last time; (2) they've become much weaker; (3) we've become much stronger; and (4) now we're playing for keeps."[9] As U.S. troops moved into Baghdad, Adelman enjoyed the moment, noting the campaign had gone better than planned without any of the predicted disasters, though he did mention the impact of the Fedayeen and the lack of Iraqi celebrations for their liberation. Having "worked for Don Rumsfeld three times," he said, he knew "he would fashion a most creative and detailed war plan," hence his confidence in the outcome.[10] By the end of November 2006, his assessment was less generous of his country's national security team. He had assumed great competence.

Instead, "not only did each of them, individually, have enormous flaws, but together they were deadly, dysfunctional." He recalled that Rumsfeld had said "that the war could never be lost in Iraq, it could only be lost in Washington. I don't think that's true at all. We're losing in Iraq . . . ."[11]

The point about Rumsfeld's Washington focus is telling. Policy analyses and prescriptions were judged by how well they worked within the American political system rather than by their direct relevance to the situation in Iraq. Not only did officials give little forethought to the difficulties Iraq might face after the war, they did not want others to reflect on those issues for fear that such attention might undermine the claim that a short, decisive victory could be achieved with remarkably few troops. Rumsfeld and Cheney dominated the policy process, marginalizing potential critics and drawing on their formidable expertise in the exercise of power. They were helped by Bush's insouciance and chronic lack of curiosity even when embarking on the greatest gamble of his presidency. Those officials appointed by Bush to get things right in Iraq reported on how little the president probed them about their opinions when they met him, how few questions he would ask about what was really going on. He seemed content to congratulate them for a "great job" as if he did not want to be told that the outcome might not be so great.[12] The result was that the administration came to live in a make-believe world removed from the deadly serious business it had set in motion. While worst-case analysis was rampant on Iraq, WMD, and terrorism, best-case analysis was equally rampant on the consequences of regime change.

In August 2002, Cheney set out the positive case for regime change:

> Middle East expert Professor Fouad Ajami predicts that after liberation, the streets in Basra and Baghdad are "sure to erupt in joy in the same way the throngs in Kabul greeted the Americans." Extremists in the region would have to rethink their strategy of Jihad. Moderates throughout the region would take heart. And our ability to advance the Israeli-Palestinian peace process would be enhanced, just as it was following the liberation of Kuwait in 1991.

Cheney spoke of the opportunities that could outweigh the dangers, and in particular the possibility of transforming the Middle East—"where so many have known only poverty and oppression, terror and tyranny." He opened up the prospect of people living "in freedom and dignity and the young can grow up free of the conditions that breed despair, hatred, and violence." The model of the past, confirmed by Afghanistan, was that after the

"United States defeated fierce enemies," it "then helped rebuild their countries." With Iraq, this would be less difficult than elsewhere. This was a country "rich in natural resources and human talent." The goal, according to Cheney, would be:

> an Iraq that has territorial integrity, a government that is democratic and pluralistic, a nation where the human rights of every ethnic and religious group are recognized and protected. In that troubled land all who seek justice, and dignity, and the chance to live their own lives, can know they have a friend and ally in the United States of America.[13]

Here then are the main planks of the optimistic scenario: The invasion would be popular; the Americans, recognized as the friends of those seeking justice and dignity, would be welcomed as liberators; with the jihadists defeated, there would be new opportunities to pursue an Arab-Israeli peace; with American help and its own rich resources, the reconstruction of Iraq would proceed apace and this would serve as a positive demonstration to the whole region of the possibilities of freedom.

A deep dissatisfaction with the Middle Eastern status quo and a conviction that a new and more optimistic regional order could emerge as a result of demonstrative effects of a reformed Iraq were an important strand in administration thinking. It reflected a critique of decades of American foreign policy based on taking the line of least resistance. Previous administrations had tried to conciliate the unreasonable, to mediate between the irreconcilable, to contain the undeterrable, and as a result now faced deep and disturbing trends that, if left unchallenged, would develop into a force that could cause social upheaval, economic dislocation, and political turmoil on a global scale.

In an influential article and then in a 2002 book, Professor Bernard Lewis asked the question, What went wrong in the Middle East? His answer was complex, but at its core he thought the lack of basic freedoms had stultified the region's development.[14] In October 2001, Lewis had dinner with Cheney. He took the view that the United States had let the Iraqis down by not supporting past insurrections. He observed that the defeat of Germany and Japan in 1945 was not about domination but instead offered "the Germans and the Japanese the chance to redeem and liberate themselves. The long-oppressed people of Iraq, the first and greatest victims of Saddam Hussein, deserve no less."[15] Fouad Ajami, the leading Arab-American scholar mentioned by Cheney in the earlier quote, warned the Americans not to be put off by the negative responses by Arabs to the occupation of

Iraq. He described it as "the 'road rage' of a thwarted Arab world—the congenital condition of a culture yet to take full responsibility for its self-inflicted wounds." This was still a case where "a reforming foreign power's simpler guidelines offer a better way than the region's age-old prohibitions and defects.[16]

Part of the background was a much quoted report of July 2002 issued by a UN-commissioned panel of thirty Arab experts from a variety of disciplines. The Arab Human Development Report (AHDR)[17] described a region facing a set of political, economic, social, and demographic challenges. It was unsparing in its criticism, gaining impact because of its Arab authors. It delineated miserable rates of economic growth, low and declining productivity, a youthful population (38 percent under fourteen) with few opportunities for employment and little preparation to take the opportunities that were available, and chronic deficits of freedom, women's empowerment, and knowledge (with less than 1 percent of the population using the Internet). The report challenged Arab governments to accept the rule of law, honest elections, an independent judiciary, removal of gender bias, and encouragement of the "knowledge sciences." It was seized upon by Western policymakers as an example of independent Arab thinking. "If you want to understand the milieu that produced bin Ladenism, and will reproduce it if nothing changes," enthused Tom Friedman, "read this report."[18] This enthusiasm was one reason the report was dismissed so readily in the Arab world as reflecting the views only of pro-Western secular elitists. It was not going to help the cause of reform to be so readily embraced by an American administration viewed with such suspicion and hostility in the Arab world. A follow-up report in 2003 appeared to be trying to reconnect by lambasting the policies of the United States and Israel.

★ · ★ · ★

The optimism about the enthusiastic Iraqi welcome awaiting their American liberators contradicted the advice coming from more detached Iraqi experts.[19] Most seriously, the CIA had been "utterly consistent in arguing that reconstruction rather than war would be the most problematic segment of overthrowing Saddam," pointing to the probability of "obstruction, resistance and armed opposition." [20] This potential tension between the needs of war, which Rumsfeld correctly judged to require modest numbers of troops, and postwar, which he incorrectly judged to require fewer, became evident in congressional hearings in February with the war less than a month away. Army Chief General Eric Shinseki, when pressed by the Senate Armed Services Committee on troop requirements for the occupation of Iraq, suggested "something on the order of several hundred thousand soldiers." Wolfowitz, before the House Budget Committee, described such "higher-end predictions" as "wildly off the mark." It was hard to conceive that more forces would be needed to provide stability in post-Saddam Iraq than to conduct the actual war. He cited northern Iraq, although here the local population had good reason to be friendly toward the United States, and the lack of the sort of ethnic rivalries that had caused so much trouble in the Balkans. The Iraqis would provide troops themselves and so would other countries. He was aware of the danger of being viewed as occupiers, but that was best dealt with by an early departure. Meanwhile, he was confident that initially, U.S. forces would be greeted as liberators.[21]

This assumption simplified planning assumptions for war and put those for postwar into a wholly unrealistic realm. Liberators do not have to face resistance, nor do they have to worry about running a state or even about rudimentary public safety and a modicum of law and order. Nor would anyone need to worry about those laws of war that reflect on the responsibility of occupying powers. Plan A therefore was an unguided and benign flowering of democracy. In the event this did not transpire, there was no Plan B.

It was not that the issue had been ignored within government. During the course of 2002, the State Department conducted a Future of Iraq project, including more than 200 Iraqi lawyers, engineers, businesspeople, and other experts, organized into "17 working groups to study topics ranging from creating a new justice system to reorganizing the military to revamping the economy." This study drew attention to a number of the problems that would face the occupying forces: the dilapidated state of Iraq's electrical and water systems and the brutalized civil society. The prescience and precision of these studies were variable, and they did not provide definite plans and action points, but they drew attention to the issues that would need to be addressed. Winning the war would be easier than occupying the country, and there were severe risks of a breakdown in public order.

Why, then, were these studies not acted upon? The Pentagon disliked them because of their focus on the problems of occupation, which was deemed to be too negative at a time when the decision to go to war was not yet firm. Warnings of a costly and difficult enterprise could be "an impediment to war."[22] A more influential factor was probably the Pentagon's assumption, as the provider of forces and infrastructure, that it should be in charge of all aspects of postwar Iraq. On January 20, 2003, somewhat late in the day, Bush signed National Security Directive 24, giving postwar control of Iraq to the Pentagon. In principle, this would ensure unity of command and the integration of civilian and military functions. Unfortunately, the senior commanders had no recent experience in this role and no evident interest in its effective execution. Wolfowitz still believed that the political answer for Iraq lay in the INC. This went against the view of Rice and Bush, who was emphatic that this was not "his man," that a much more broadly based coalition would be needed. The CIA and the State Department were said to consider Chalabi to be "a divisive, autocratic blowhard."[23] Even Rumsfeld was wary of him. If there was a neocon project for Iraq, Chalabi was at the heart of it. Chalabi's backers managed to get him flown into southern Iraq as soon as possible after the start of hostilities to help him establish himself, although in practice he was left rather stranded, with a small force of men but few supplies.[24] Here was an irrepressible man who was never completely out; never acquiring a large local following; sustaining setbacks, including the distrust of a large part of the U.S. government and financial investigations; yet he still hung on as a player in Iraqi politics.

Further complicating matters was the assumption that the problem was humanitarian assistance rather than reconstruction. The country was already in a mess, with many displaced people and 60 percent dependent upon the oil for food program for survival. Prior to the war, there was a general apprehension about the viciousness of urban warfare, which might prompt Iraqis to flee from the cities, thereby triggering a major humanitarian crisis. The dreadfulness of the war itself, rather than its aftermath, was also a major theme of much of the antiwar movements. The antiwar worst case was less the sudden lawlessness and subsequent resistance likely to accompany the collapse of the old order but massive casualties and humanitarian distress caused by war. There were fears that the war would displace as many as 2 million people and lead to a breakdown in power and water supplies and a potential public health crisis. Bush later recalled, "We spent *hours* talking about refugee flows and hunger, or what happens if Baghdad becomes a fortress."[25] He directed that plans be well developed for such contingencies. These concerns, and the involvement of international agencies, meant that relief plans were far more advanced than reconstruction plans.[26]

Both tasks were given to retired general Jay Garner. His dual role was described in the title of his unit, the Office of Reconstruction and Humanitarian Assistance (ORHA). Nora Bensahel compared the fifteen months of planning by a large and professional staff that went into the military campaign with the eight weeks of work by amateurs that went into reconstruction.[27] Garner's group only learned about the State Department project in February. Aware of a woeful lack of in-house expertise, they sought to employ Tom Warrick, the official who had overseen the report, only for this to be blocked by Pentagon officials. The result was that Garner was ready for problems that did not occur, such as oil fields aflame, refugees in flight from cities, and revenge killings. His group was ill-prepared for the looting and collapse of law and order, although this had been predicted. The Future of Iraq Project did draw attention to the risks of postregime lawlessness. Saddam had purposefully set free many criminals just before the war. The project warned that these criminals would see opportunities in postwar confusion to "engage in acts of killing, plunder and looting." This would best be prevented by "military patrols by coalition forces in all major cities to prevent lawlessness, especially against vital utilities and key government facilities."[28]

As the campaign moved toward its inevitable victory, ORHA members were kicking their heels, excluded from top-level discussions about what turned out to be the wrong questions (such as how to cope with refugees fleeing urban combat). When the looting began, U.S. troops watched passively, without plans or orders to guide any response, without a capacity for basic policing and crowd control, as a combination of criminals and Ba'ath loyalists tore down what was left of the structures of the Iraqi state. Of Iraq's twenty-three ministry buildings, seventeen were completely gutted.

Franks seems to have viewed ORHA as a potential nuisance and did not even want its staff in the country until he sorted out the military situation, because he did not have the resources to devote to the protection of civilians. Eventually, ORHA got to Baghdad on April 21, after much of the damage by looting and sabotage had already occurred. The effort to mend Iraq was begun in the looted shells of government buildings, relying more on idealism than on relevant experience, with none of the information or systems required to run a state. Almost as soon as he arrived, Garner was told he was going to be replaced by the new Coalition Provisional Authority (CPA), to be headed up by a tough diplomat with a background in counterterrorism, L. Paul Bremer. This was announced on May 12, the first formal acknowledgment that the United States now had to act like an occupying power. The CPA never had enough staff, and those recruited were often young, with no relevant experience and on short tours. It soon became stuck in the international and relatively safe area of Baghdad that became known as the Green Zone, with hardly a presence in the rest of the country, rarely daring to venture out and lacking contact with ordinary Iraqis and their problems. It had responsibility for all reconstruction efforts, even those started by the military, but had no capacity to deliver support. Despite the promise of unity of command, Bremer was reporting back to Washington, and links with the local military command were at best confused.

Iraqis waited for the all-conquering Americans to turn on the electricity, get the water to run, fix buildings, and keep the streets safe. Here the lack of planning told, as targets were set in an ad hoc fashion, in terms of the politics of the moment rather than maximizing efficiency, for example, by spreading the power supply to all regions rather than the critical arena of Baghdad. Much of the infrastructure had been looted and was then bombed, and equipment had to be found and funded. Optimistic targets were set and not met.

Meanwhile, U.S. officials dealt warily with the would-be Iraqi politicians (also neophytes and also suspicious of their counterparts) who had materialized from among the ranks of exiles based in the West or from the more enclosed world of local clerics. Saddam had destroyed Iraqi civil society: "Iraqi politics began from scratch in April 2003."[29] To organize a new government, the coalition needed international assistance to provide some legitimacy. The arrival of the UN's Sergio de Mello gave some hope, but on August 19, 2003, al Qaeda managed to blow up his poorly protected headquarters. A quick move to elections was problematic because of the lack, at one level, of an electoral register and at another, of democratic political organizations. In July 2003, the Iraqi Governing Council (IGC) was established as an advisory body. Although it contained representatives of the key groupings, it was also top-heavy with exiles. By late 2003, it was clear that the country needed elections, even if only on an interim basis. The UN returned again, this time with a small mission under Lakhdar Brahimi, who managed to organize a compromise solution. In June 2004, there was a handover to an Iraqi government, led by Ayad Allawi, who had run the Iraqi National Accord and was a direct rival of Chalabi's from their days in exile.

Elections were held in January 2005, but with one nationwide constituency, which meant that politicians were not addressing local issues and were largely following sectarian banners. Only Allawi tried to organize a nonsectarian list based on the secular middle class and an appeal to Iraqi nationalism. The Sunnis did not participate. They realized their mistake by the time of the ballot for a full-term government on December 15, 2005. The elections produced an impressive 76 percent voter turnout, with just under 50 percent for main Shi'ite parties, 20 percent for Kurdish, 20 percent for Sunni, and only 10 percent for Allawi's National Iraqi List. These divisions led to extraordinary delays in the construction of a new government. The new prime minister, Ibrahim al-Jafari of the al-Dawa Party, was incapable of providing leadership. During the 1980s, it will be recalled, Dawa was viewed in the West as a terrorist organization, uncomfortably close to Iran. One of its parliamentarians, elected in 2005, had been convicted in Kuwait for planning bombings of the French and American embassies in 1983. It also had close links, though also politico-theological differences, with another group, the Supreme Council for the Islamic Revolution in Iraq (SCIRI). This party could also be traced back to the 1980s, when it was set up as an instrument of Iranian influence over Shi'ite opposition groups in Iraq. In April 2006, Nuri al-Maliki, also of the Dawa Party, became prime minister. He made more progress but was still hampered by sectarian divisions and the consequential inability to punish incompetence or corruption.

At least in this case, Saddam Hussein was not able to taunt the coalition from an unknown sanctuary. In late July 2003, both his sons, Uday and Qusay, were killed in a raid, and that December, Saddam himself was hauled, ignominiously, out of a hole in the ground near Tikrit. After a chaotic trial, Saddam was executed at the end of 2006.

∗   ∗   ∗

As soon as Bremer arrived in Baghdad in mid-May 2003, he released the first two orders to the CPA. The first barred members of the Ba'ath Party from all but minor government posts, and the next was to disband the Iraqi army and security services. According to his memoir, he got his orders from Douglas Feith, who worked for Wolfowitz, and was allowed no flexibility.[30] In most accounts, the reason for this was to show that the old order and its repressive instruments were truly gone. Yet while this makes it sound like a Pentagon decision, Woodward suggested it came from the White House. But in a book published in 2007, Bush seemed to distance himself from the policy, saying, "The policy had been to keep the army intact; didn't happen."[31] This does indeed appear to have been the policy prior to the invasion, where the thinking was more along the lines of a South African–style Truth and Reconciliation Commission to root out the most noxious members of the Ba'athists, whereas those who had simply joined the party because their careers required membership could still play a role. On the same basis, the Republican Guard, which was assumed to be full of Saddam loyalists, would go, but the army could stay.

By May, two factors influenced thinking. The first was the apparent evaporation of the Iraqi army. It no longer existed as an organized force, and its barracks were bombed-out ruins. It could not therefore make up for the lack of coalition forces on the ground. Perhaps more important, key figures in the Shi'ite community were deeply hostile to forces that had largely Sunni officer corps, and they were urging a much more thorough purging of state institutions to remove what they saw as a malignancy. It may be that the ubiquitous Chalabi played a role here. For a short time he was at the head of the official de-Ba'athification commission, where he was notable for the ruthlessness with which he purged Ba'athists. On May 20, 2003, Bremer wrote to Bush, saying, "We must make it clear to everyone that we mean business: that Saddam and the Baathists are finished." This would go in parallel "with an even more robust measure" to dismantle the Iraqi military. Bush wrote back, thanking him for his letter and his leadership, although it is by no means clear that he had read the contents.[32] Powell was not consulted, nor were the senior military commanders in Iraq. Garner and the local CIA chief warned that this was a terrible idea and would create a large pool of hostile individuals, especially once they were denied pensions.[33] Ignoring some 250,000 former soldiers, leaving them feeling discarded, without income but with weapons, meant that they were natural recruits for the insurgency and the militias. Turning away functionaries, though there were no competent people to replace them, might have reassured the Shi'ite community but convinced many Sunnis that the new order would be hostile to their interests.

The mainstream Sunni resistance drew on the support of those who felt humiliated by their country's being occupied and fearful of the loss of their power. Their numbers were swelled by the disbanded military and volunteers from the many unemployed young men. Comprising only 20 percent of the population, the Sunnis may not all have fully appreciated just how much of a minority they actually were, until the revelation of elections, and for a while they comforted themselves with the thought that the numbers were being artificially inflated by Iranians pouring over the border. Whatever the true proportion of the population, they were threatened by the ascendancy of the Shia. They had clung to the Ba'ath regime in 1991 because of the same fear. Then they could draw on the armed forces to suppress the insurrection. This time, the insurrection would have to be theirs. The Sunni leaders tended to hedge their bets, talking to the coalition while staying close to the resistance. Until the spring of 2004, the majority of Sunnis wanted to stay clear of the violence and get on with their daily lives. Massive amounts of ordnance were looted, combined with arms caches already prepared by the old regime to serve as the basis for resistance. The early attacks came from the Saddam Fedayeen, using improvised bombs and rocket-propelled grenades (RPGs). They were able to prevent the infrastructure from working, so that the material benefits that might have been expected from the Americans failed to appear, and the economy could not be sorted out because oil pipelines kept being blown up. By the end of 2003, U.S. artillery and airpower were being used again, to try to take out insurgent positions. Soon, regular attacks were being reported against U.S. troops, especially in the area known as the "Sunni triangle."

The second large factor in the insurgency was the Islamists. Here the key figure was the Jordanian Abu Musab al-Zarqawi. He was in Afghanistan in

1990 too late to join the fighting against the Soviets but did connect with bin Laden. From 1992 until 1999, he was imprisoned in Jordan for conspiring against the monarchy. Once released, he immediately tried to blow up a hotel before fleeing to Afghanistan, where, with bin Laden's support, he set up a camp largely for fellow Jordanians. He fought against the U.S. invasion of Afghanistan, and by 2002 was back in northern Iraq, working with the Islamist group Ansar al-Islam that was fighting Kurdish nationalism. He was well-placed to take a leading role in the insurgency after Saddam's forces had been defeated. By October 2004, he was calling his organization al Qaeda in Iraq. For bin Laden and Zawahiri this was a risk, as it meant handing over the brand to Zarqawi's care. Even for Islamists, his views were somewhat extreme.

These were set out in a long letter sent to bin Laden and Zawahiri in early 2004. He assessed the positive opportunities posed by being able to mount a jihad in the Arab heartlands, close to both Saudi Arabia and Palestine. He derided the Americans, the "most cowardly of God's creatures," who offered "easy and mouth-watering targets for the believers." What comes over most strikingly is his real hatred of the Shia ("the insurmountable obstacle, the lurking snake, the crafty and malicious scorpion, the spying enemy, and the penetrating venom"), whom he saw colluding with the occupier while wearing "the garb of a friend." The "Crusader forces will disappear tomorrow or the day after," he predicted, although elsewhere in the letter he seemed to think that they would stay in their garrisons while the Shia did their work for them in reconstituted army and police forces. In an important misjudgment, Zarqawi concluded that the Shia were trying to prevent an open, sectarian war because they would lose. Although Sunnis were the minority within Iraq, once a civil war began, many in the Islamic world "would rise to defend the Sunnis in Iraq." He reported that the numbers of foreign mujahideen were still negligible, whereas the local mujahideen were too preoccupied with their own safety and had yet to understand that this was incompatible with victory and "that people cannot awaken from their stupor unless talk of martyrdom and martyrs fills their days and nights." It was necessary to target and hit them to "bare the teeth of the hidden rancor working in their breasts." The only solution, he concluded, was "for us to strike the religious, military, and other cadres among the Shia with blow after blow until they bend to the Sunnis."[34] Evidence that he was putting his beliefs into practice came with attacks on Shi'ite shrines at Karbala and Baghdad in March 2004.

Steadily, the security situation deteriorated, as American troops fell victim to ambushes while high-profile international and Shi'ite buildings and

individuals were picked upon by the Islamists. From the start there was reluctance to admit the truth about what was going on, which did not facilitate an effective response. The resistance was presented as being holdouts
from the old regime, and undoubtedly many of them were, but new groups
also joined. In July, as the attacks multiplied, Bush tried to argue that it was
fine to fight the militants in Iraq rather than have to deal with them in the
United States. When challenged on whether the United States could cope, he
answered with another statement he would come to regret: "My answer is,
bring them on. We've got the force necessary to deal with the security situation."[35] By the end of the year, the coalition was clearly struggling. The aim
had been to cut back numbers dramatically rather than replace with fresh
troops. With so few troops, with such inappropriate training, there was an
argument for caution, yet with U.S. authority being challenged there was a
contrary tendency for displays of force and a generally tough stance. It was
particularly frustrating that the Americans had no real idea what was going
on, and in their efforts to gather intelligence, large numbers of Iraqis were
rounded up, many sent to the old prison at Abu Ghraib. The desperation for
useful intelligence led to a lax attitude toward interrogation techniques.

What was going on in Abu Ghraib went beyond extreme interrogation
techniques to cruel and casual abuse of prisoners. It was only when the holiday snapshots taken by soldiers showing how they were routinely humiliating prisoners were published at the end of April 2004 that it became
apparent just how bad things had become. There were images and stories of
forced sexual degradation, beatings, and the use of dogs to intimidate prisoners. It was only small consolation that the army had already been investigating the stories of abuse, and the report, by General Antonio Taguba, was a
vital source for journalists such as Seymour Hersh, who made the scandal
known. Although the Pentagon had been aware of the problem since the
start of the year, it wanted to keep it under wraps. The president had not
been alerted to the potential scandal and struggled to respond when it
broke.

The administration acknowledged these were shameful acts but claimed
that they were the responsibility of a few characters who had gotten out of
control and were not at all representative of U.S. forces. Undoubtedly, however, part of the problem was that the administration had convinced itself
since 9/11 that strict rules on torture and inhumane treatment could impede
the war on terror and had gotten into the habit of making fine distinctions
that could not be sustained in practice (and went against received wisdom
that information gained through torture is inherently unreliable). Attempts
to get around the Geneva Conventions by declaring prisoners to be "unlawful

combatants" were both legally dubious and politically disastrous, as they took away U.S. claims to be occupying the moral high ground. Rice's first impression was that "we really have no chance to recover from this."[36]

The release of the images from Abu Ghraib concluded a disastrous month for the United States in Iraq. First, a challenge arose from an unexpected direction. The leadership of the Shi'ite community was generally benign under the Grand Ayatollah Ali Sistani. He had spent much time in Iran but was never a follower of Khomeini and believed clergy should not become politicians. He avoided positioning himself as pro- or anti-American and used democratic rather than crudely sectarian principles to push forward his community's claims. Shi'ite politicians worked with the coalition and avoided violence, as the natural beneficiaries of the toppling of the Ba'ath regime. Moqtada al-Sadr, the son of an influential cleric murdered by Saddam, was the exception. He saw an opportunity to challenge for the leadership of the Shia, taking populist and anti-occupation stances and establishing his own militia—the Mahdi Army—in Baghdad and in the south. His actions became sufficiently provocative for Bremer to decide to shut down Sadr's main newspaper and arrest one of his key lieutenants. This led to an immediate eruption of protests, many extremely violent. The coalition lost control of Najaf and struggled in many southern cities. Although Sadr had few allies, the tough measures used by coalition forces to reassert control meant that the more moderate Shi'ite leaders said little. The episode left the coalition politically undermined and militarily stretched.

Then the city of Fallujah, in Anbar Province, became a focal point for a challenge to the occupation. Almost a year earlier, as American forces were consolidating their hold over the Sunni heartlands, twice they had fired with deadly consequences into mass demonstrations in Fallujah, immediately helping the resistance to garner support. At this point the insurgency was still relatively small, but U.S. forces were too thinly spread to be able to get a grip as it started to become better organized, especially in some of the major Sunni cities such as Fallujah. This was also a center of Islamist activity, whence Zarqawi organized his activities. By the end of March 2004, the First Marine Expeditionary Force operating in the area was working on a plan to find moderate Sunnis with whom it could work to clear out the Islamists. After four U.S. civilian security contractors were murdered and their bodies hung from a bridge over the Euphrates River, to evident popular enthusiasm, senior U.S. commanders took the view that there had to be a robust response, lest the United States be viewed as feeble in the face of such blatant effrontery.

Rumsfeld was also demanding quick action, and not the plan being carefully worked up by the marines. Bremer told Washington that the United

States had to assert itself in Fallujah against the Sunnis as well as in the south against the Mahdi Army if it wanted to keep a grip on the security situation.[37] But Bremer had poor relations with the military commanders and was not au fait with the situation on the ground. The marines believed that they lacked sufficient men and proper plans for a major urban operation, in addition to evacuating the civilian population, but having been ordered to advance into Fallujah, they did so. Additional insurgents, including many local Sunnis, poured into Fallujah. The offensive began on April 6 and soon led to heavy fighting. The supposedly loyal Iraqi forces working with the marines either deserted or refused to engage. Fighting spread around the rest of Anbar Province. Inside Fallujah, there was much damage to buildings, including mosques, and hundreds of civilians died. The battle soon started to turn into a propaganda disaster for the coalition, even forging links between Sunni insurgents and the Mahdi Army, leading to members of the IGC calling for a cease-fire. There were complaints from the UN and also from the British. The Iraqi Governing Council was barely consulted and was already in a delicate state owing to the contradictory pressures it faced; it was unlikely to endorse any firm action. If the council resigned, the United States had no political cover at all. After the marines were ordered to cease offensive operations on April 9, a face-saving device was found that established a local Sunni militia that was ostensibly prepared to take on the Islamists. By now, support was drained dramatically away from the coalition, which had demonstrated weakness rather than resolve in a fight it had picked. The conclusion drawn was that the Americans could be defeated, thus leaving more moderate Sunnis fearful of the consequences of collaborating with what might already be a spent force. Fallujah became even more important as a base for insurgents.

*　　*　　*

The next two years were essentially lost. Progress on the political front was slow, while economic and social reconstruction was hampered by the dire security situation. The United States was caught in the classic trap of counterinsurgency. It could clear towns and villages of insurgents by sweeping through with superior forces, but as it lacked the troops to leave behind, the enemy would soon return, and, aware of this, the local population would make no effort to work closely with coalition forces. The task of creating a new Iraqi army and police force was begun, but the initial targets were too ambitious, so recruits were neither properly vetted nor trained before being rushed into duty, while as often as not the police forces came under the control of local militias.

Having been imbued with the notion that they were helping the Iraqis, U.S. troops began to consider the local population ungrateful. Robert Kaplan reported meeting up with U.S. marines prior to the Fallujah battle and finding them sporting moustaches to identify with the local population: "When they prepared for the battle, angry at recent events, they shaved them off."[38] British army brigadier Nigel Aylwin-Foster observed that American anger led to a "kinetic" rather than a strategic response, which, in the event, was not followed through to its logical conclusion because of the evident political backlash that resulted. The inclination was to intimidate opponents rather than win over waverers. An analysis of operations conducted from 2003 to 2005 suggested that most were "reactive to insurgent activity— seeking to hunt down insurgents. Only 6% of ops were directed specifically to create a secure environment for the population." Unfortunately, the damaging political consequences of these actions were not always appreciated. Because the cause was just, it was assumed that the actions would be understood even when they resulted in tragic errors.[39]

The strategy of "cordon and sweep" reflected the familiar military view that ultimately, physical force is all that matters in war, that the basic objective is to hold territory and to kill the enemy. It is, of course, much harder to train soldiers to withhold fire, not to rise to provocations, and to reach out to a wary local population when this might put them in danger. Montgomery McFate, with the unusual status of cultural anthropologist working for the Pentagon, identified three examples of mistakes in Iraq that resulted from a lack of appreciation of Iraqi culture. First was a failure to grasp that the civilian apparatus of the country would not survive the loss of the regime, as power would revert to the tribes; second, there was a presumption that key communications would flow through the broadcast media rather than coffee shop rumors (and U.S. force protection doctrine meant that coffee shops were out of bounds); third, an Iraqi propensity to get physically close to those they were addressing was found threatening by American troops, while the hand gestures for stop were reversed in the American and Iraqi cultures, leading to tragic misunderstandings at roadblocks.[40] David Kilcullen, an Australian officer on loan to U.S. forces, also with a background in anthropology, drew on the past history of counterinsurgency. If al Qaeda wanted to present itself as a global insurgency, then its opponents must work to disaggregate into separate, manageable pieces. If this insurgency prospered by operating effectively within the information environment, then its opponents must also recognize this to be as important as the physical environment.[41]

The army field manual for counterinsurgency operations of 2004 barely addressed political issues and was largely about tactics for seeking out enemy fighters, rather than how to isolate the militants. Over this period, officers coming back from Iraq, and also drawing on Afghanistan, started to argue that counterinsurgency needed to be taken far more seriously and began to form a lobbying group within the U.S. Army to encourage doctrinal reform.

A key figure in this effort was Lieutenant General David Petraeus. In an article published at the start of 2006, he observed that the recent wars were not those for which the army had prepared. Among the lessons learned were the importance of giving Iraqis a stake in the political process and high-quality intelligence. In addition, though a "statement of the obvious," Petraeus emphasized the limits of what military operations could achieve: "Counterinsurgency strategies must also include, above all, efforts to establish a political environment that helps reduce support for the insurgents and undermines the attraction of whatever ideology they may espouse."[42] Petraeus had been a successful divisional commander over 2003–2004 and was in charge of the U.S. Army Combined Arms Center, developing a new doctrine. The 2006 *Counterinsurgency* Field Manual, released on December 15, 2006, completely shifted the balance between tactics and politics, stressing the importance of understanding the culture in which operations take place and developing narratives that make sense to those to be influenced.

The changing approach came just in time. The strategy that General George Casey, the senior American commander in Baghdad, developed over 2005–2006, with the backing of Rumsfeld, was to hand over responsibility for security to Iraqi forces as soon as possible and get U.S. troops out. This accepted that the American presence was one of the factors driving the insurgency, and assumed that once the troops were clearly on their way out, the situation would calm down. Launching the National Strategy for Victory in Iraq in November 2005, Bush reported that his commanders had told him "that as Iraqi forces become more capable," the U.S. mission would "shift from providing security and conducting operations against the enemy nationwide, to conducting more specialized operations targeted at the most dangerous terrorists." The United States would "move out of Iraqi cities, reduce the number of bases from which we operate, and conduct fewer patrols and convoys." As Iraqi forces gained experience and the political process advanced, "we will be able to decrease our troop levels in Iraq without losing our capability to defeat the terrorists."[43]

General Casey told Bush in June the aim was to reduce the number of U.S. brigades from fourteen to twelve by September and possibly ten by December, by which time the Iraqis should have six combat brigades of their own. But by this time it was evident that the strategy was not going to work.

The insurgency was growing in strength while the Iraqi army was still far from possessing the capabilities required. Most importantly, Iraq was moving perilously close to civil war.[44] This followed the destruction, on February 22, of the Golden Mosque in Samarra. The Shi'ite leaders in Iraq continued to urge their people not to respond to these provocations, but patience had now worn thin and there was a demand for vengeance. Shi'ite militias turned on Sunnis, who soon found they were getting little protection from government forces. Over 2006, as many as 35,000 civilians and members of Iraqi forces died. Sectarian violence also meant that tens of thousands were forced to leave their homes, while the middle class fled to neighboring states.

The passivity of the Iraqi government led Rice, with her British counterpart Jack Straw, to go to Baghdad in April to explain to Prime Minister Jafari that he was a failure and had to go. He took some persuading. There are indications that a back-channel negotiation with Sistani, who generally kept a low political profile, helped ease the transition to Nuri al-Maliki.[45]

In September 2006, with the position looking generally dire in Iraq, Bush agreed to a review of policy. A bipartisan commission chaired by James Baker and Lee Hamilton was established. There was a developing view that the United States was stranded in Iraq without any easy way to make progress or get out without making matters even worse. The obvious remedy, which had been pursued for some time, was to hand over power to a plausible Iraqi government with sufficient forces of its own to allow for a steady reduction in the American commitment. This was where the commission came down: moving to a support role, with talks with local powers, even Syria and Iran, and conditional aid to the Iraqi government. Others were arguing for partition, dividing the country as neatly as possible (which unfortunately would not be very neat) into Kurdish, Sunni, and Shi'ite entities. Either way, so long as there was uncertainty about when the Americans would leave, the general view was that Iraqi politicians would avoid the hard choices needed to quell sectarian violence.[46]

After the Democrats took both the Senate and the House of Representatives in the November elections, Rumsfeld was summarily dispatched as secretary of defense, to be replaced by Robert Gates, associated with both the elder Bush and a realist philosophy. It seemed as if Bush would accept the need to bow to the inevitable and try to find a graceful way to exit a failed policy. When he spoke to the nation in January 2007, he described the situation in Iraq as "unacceptable" and agreed that "we need to change our strategy." He was not, however, ready to contemplate failure in Iraq. This would strengthen radical Islamists and destabilize the whole region. The risks were greatest in the Baghdad area, where 80 percent of the attacks took place. He acknowledged that past attempts to pacify Baghdad had failed because of too few troops. To remedy this situation, the Iraqi government was going to deploy more troops and so would the Americans—another 20,000. The Iraqi government also understood that no neighborhoods could be precluded from operations. After Baghdad, the other main target area was Anbar Province, which served as al Qaeda's base in Iraq, and where local tribal leaders were showing increasing irritation with the Islamists. Here, the United States would commit another 4,000 troops.[47]

General Petraeus was put in charge of what became known as the "surge," although he believed this exaggerated the importance of numbers as opposed to a changed approach to the use of force. This was a high-risk strategy. There would be additional early losses, as troops were required to live and operate among the population, thus offering extra targets. Once tried, there were no other options. This meant that Petraeus was given a heavy political as well as military burden, responsible for the reputation of the Bush administration. This put him in a tricky position when dealing with Congress, where he needed bipartisan support. This became evident in exchanges during hearings in September 2007, where he argued for continued support for the new approach, although results were still limited.

By this time, however, the situation on the ground was showing signs of improvement. The new initiative was better judged than those that had gone before. The message sent to Iraqi politicians was that Bush would stick with his project for the remaining two years of his presidency, but that pressures to pull out would clearly not abate. With violence getting out of hand, this was their last best chance to hold the country together. As important, the various groups causing the violence were having their own problems.

*   *   *

This was particularly true with al Qaeda in Iraq, as Zarqawi had named his group in the fall of 2004. This link with bin Laden appears to have been as much from strategic convenience as from a coincidence of views.[48] By this time, al Qaeda had little else going for it, so an association with a serious and apparently effective insurgency gave it continued international credibility. But Zarqawi's strategy of taking apostates and Shi'ites as more serious threats than Americans was not bin Laden's. In a letter of July 2005 to Zarqawi, Zawahiri took exception to the attacks on Shi'ite civilians, noting that his many Muslim admirers "among the common folk are wondering about your attacks on the Shia," and specifically their mosques. "I say to you: that we are in a battle, and that more than half of this battle is taking place in the battlefield of the media. And that we are in a media battle in a race for the hearts and minds of our Umma." He was also worried about the dangers of provoking the Iranians.[49]

Zawahiri's argument that attacks should concentrate on the United States and their local military allies fell on deaf ears. In November 2005, for example, three hotels in Amman, Jordan, were attacked, with one bomb exploding among a wedding party. This had the effect of alienating further potential Arab supporters. A document seized from a safe house gives a sense of an organization under pressure: irritated by the success of Iraqi forces and the ability of the Americans to hide behind them' under pressure because of financial restrictions and bad press; and weakened by internal divisions. The proposals were for an effective media campaign to improve the image of the resistance, infiltration into the Iraqi National Guard, more unity, and fewer mistakes. As a sign of desperation, the document suggested entangling "the American forces into another war against another country or with another of our enemy force, that is to try and inflame the situation between America and Iran or between America and the Shi'a in general." This included plans for fabricating an Iranian role in offenses within Iraq and "disseminating bogus messages about confessions showing that Iran is in possession of weapons of mass destruction or that there are attempts by the Iranian intelligence to undertake terrorist operations in America and the west and against western interests."[50] In July, Zarqawi was killed in an American air strike. There was a continuity in strategy. On November 23, a number of car bombs and mortar rounds in Sadr City in Baghdad killed at least 215 Shi'ites. It led at once to mortar rounds being fired into the holiest Sunni mosque in Baghdad and random murders of Sunnis.

Many Sunni resistance leaders found these activities both disturbing and dangerous. They began to criticize al Qaeda and its foreign members for attacking civilian targets. In September 2006, a new alliance called the Anbar Salvation Council was formed in Anbar Province to counter al Qaeda, and it began to cooperate with the government and U.S. troops. This precipitated al Qaeda attacks on the Council. The power struggle developed further during the course of 2007, when al Qaeda established its own Islamic State of Iraq, in preparation for the breakup of the country. Al Qaeda seems to have been sufficiently sensitive to the argument that the insurgency was being run by foreigners (Zarqawi's successor was an Egyptian) that they invented a fictitious Iraqi leader to make pronouncements on behalf of a proclaimed Islamic State in Iraq.[51] More evidence that the Sunni militia working with the Americans had rattled al Qaeda came when bin Laden devoted much of his end-of-year message to "hypocrite chieftains of tribes" and denounced plots to "steal the fruit of blessed jihad" in Iraq.[52]

At the same time, there were demands that Moqtada al-Sadr rein in his militants. As the number of attacks on Shi'ite sites declined, there was less excuse for revenge attacks on Sunnis. Sadr was being put under pressure by mainstream Shi'ite groups, which did not share his view that the first priority was to expel the Americans and also disagreed with his more nationalist approach. In addition, his Mahdi Army had gotten out of control, descending into criminality and not acting at all as the disciplined military arm of a political movement. Sadr's August declaration of a freeze on operations was an important factor in slowing the violence. Sadr appeared to have changed his strategy, intending to follow Hezbollah's example by concentrating on developing political support by dispensing services to communities that government could not provide while holding his militia in reserve. Here Iran may have helped, after promising Prime Minister Maliki that it understood that it was not helpful to a government in which it enjoyed potential influence, if it kept supporting militias just to aggravate the Americans.

By the end of 2007, the surge was being touted as a great success, which ought to lead to the Iraq issue fading as a major political issue entering the election year. American military deaths in December were at twenty-one compared to more than 100 in December 2006. Since June, violence had fallen by 60 percent. Nonetheless, 18,000 people were killed in 2007. The 899 Americans killed that year brought the total toll since the start of the campaign in 2003 to just over 3,900.[53] The most wide-ranging survey of Iraqi deaths estimated that 151,000 Iraqis died from violence in the forty months from March 2003 to June 2006. Men between fifteen and fifty-nine accounted for 83 percent of the deaths, children under fifteen for 10 percent.[54] Thus any measures of improvement were from a very low base. In effect, levels of violence were back to the summer of 2005. Petraeus was careful not to make exaggerated claims: "Nobody says anything about turning a corner, seeing lights at the end of tunnels, any of those phrases," he told journalists in early December. "There's nobody in uniform who is doing victory dances in the end zone."[55]

Some of the vital signs of Iraqi life were flickering. Some refugees were returning home, although barely 30,000 out of the over 2 million who had fled. But 2.4 million Iraqis remained displaced within Iraq because their communities had been divided along sectarian lines. Oil production was up, and the economy was starting to stir. However, electricity at eight hours a day in Baghdad was at half the prewar levels. Corruption was rampant. Politically, there was little progress. The government still pursued a largely

Shi'ite agenda and had made little effort to seek reconciliation with Sunnis. The government seemed unable to address issues that touched on the sectarian divide, or even pass a budget. Only in January 2008, after much U.S. pressure, was agreement reached on allowing former low-level Ba'ath Party members back into office, although still only on a restricted basis. Effectively, politics had become more localized, with American forces working with whoever had the greatest interest in stability in a particular area. This left uncertainty as to what would happen once the Americans left. The Sunni militias armed by the Americans to fight al Qaeda could find themselves also taking on Shi'ite militias, a thought that worried the government.

Iraq no longer represented the sort of regional threat it had posed under Saddam, and the administration could claim that persevering with the "surge" in 2007 produced a better outcome than would have been the case if there had been a rush for the exit in 2006. It looked less likely that Iraq would unsettle the whole region and serve as a staging post for Islamist operations in the wider Middle East and into Europe. That things might have been worse, however, hardly counted as a resounding success given the optimistic assertions with which the Iraq experiment had been launched. Five years after the invasion, Iraq remained in a fragile condition, dependent for its stability on war-weariness and a fear of even greater instability. Democratic elections had thus far done as much to divide as to unite the country. The relative calm was sufficiently tentative to leave little scope for major cuts in U.S. forces, leaving difficult decisions for the next administration. With the American public wary about further foreign adventures, it would also be left to the new administration to apply the lessons learned from Iraq about the limits of power. The potential for disruptive lawlessness was illustrated by the Kurdistan Worker's Party (PKK), which used northern Iraq as a base from which to launch attacks into Turkey on behalf of an autonomous Kurdistan, leading Turkish forces to engage in hot pursuit into Iraqi territory.

20

SUICIDES AND ASSASSINATIONS

WHILE THE UNITED STATES was struggling to quell an insurgency in Iraq, the Israelis were also struggling to cope with the second intifada. Before 9/11, Bush's understandable instinct had been to keep his distance from a conflict that had always been greedy of presidential time without commensurate results. After 9/11, his instinct was to back a friendly country being battered by regular acts of terrorism. Domestic politics suggested no other choice. Foreign policy, however, complicated matters. The unyielding approach of Israel to Palestinian demands and the harsh methods employed to suppress the intifada dominated the Arab media. At a time when he needed support in general for the war on terror and in particular for his Iraq project, he sought to demonstrate concern about the costs of the conflict and offer initiatives to find a way out. Bush's pronouncements, which accepted the need for a Palestinian state and the need for Israel to freeze and eventually roll back settlement activity as the Palestinians worked to end the violence, put him in line with mainstream international opinion. Yet he managed to give the impression that his pronouncements were largely designed to calm his relations with Arab governments rather than set priorities for action. His most original contribution to the issue was to suggest that progress depended on the Palestinians getting better leadership. When the opportunity came for an injection of democracy into Palestinian politics, as a result of

Arafat's death in November 2004, the results were not quite what he expected. Over this time, while the Palestinian Authority and its guiding party, Fatah, were being steadily enfeebled, the most effective driver of Palestinian militancy was Hamas. And far from being an instrument of Arafat's strategy, Hamas was a rival. In addition, unlike Fatah, it had strong connections to Iran and Syria, the two countries in the region with which American relations were most tense.

The origins of the intifada lay in the breakdown of the bargain at the heart of the Oslo Accords—increased Palestinian autonomy in return for reduced violence. It suited the Israeli government to present the violence that broke out in September 2000 as a deliberate element of Arafat's grand strategy, geared to extracting more and unreasonable concessions, despite the generous offer put to him at Camp David. The idea that Arafat could turn the violence on and off at will, which was a persistent Israeli theme over the years of the intifada, was always misplaced. There were many groups insisting that violence was the only way forward, and they could take advantage of the seething discontent in the West Bank and Gaza, to which Israeli tactics greatly contributed. Yet Arafat believed that somehow he could ride the violence and turn it to his advantage in the negotiations, by reminding the Israelis of the risks they ran without a deal.

This approach was unrealistic. If the episode had been confined to Haram al-Sharif, it might have served as a demonstration of Palestinian feeling, but the impact was wholly negative as it escalated and lost a specific focus. Guerrilla campaigns are not waged to tidy up second-order technical points in negotiations. It was at any rate going to be hard to improve substantially on what was agreed at the Taba meeting in January 2001. This was the last gasp of the Barak government. Once Barak had been replaced by Ariel Sharon, who did not feel bound by any past concessions, it was evident that violence was not going to help extract a better, or indeed any, deal from the Israelis. Furthermore, for the violence to work as a bargaining tool, it had to be disciplined and precise in its targeting. The various militias, including Tanzim, which came under the Fatah umbrella, let alone Islamic Jihad and Hamas, were not under central and coordinated control and adopted distinctive strategies. The Hezbollah model, which so impressed Palestinian activists, worked because of the relentless focus on patrols by the Israeli Defense Forces in southern Lebanon and demonstrated that there were limits to the sacrifices the Israeli population was prepared to make to stay in places where they were not sure they should be. The same model, which was the one to which Fatah and Tanzim were inclined, would have a Palestinian guerrilla war targeted against settlements and the military presence in Gaza and the

West Bank. The more radical strategy argued that the more pain inflicted on Israel proper, the more the public would demand a political solution. There was also an element of revenge, to make the Israelis pay for all the suffering of the Palestinian people over the previous decades. Groups such as Islamic Jihad and Hamas had no interest in negotiations with Israel. They saw the current battle as part of a long war in which they would steadily undermine the very foundations of the Israeli state. As all of Israel was illegitimate, all of Israel could and should be attacked.

Whatever strategy was being pursued and for whatever reason, success would depend on finding tactics with which Israelis could not cope. It was true that they had difficulty with the first intifada because they were then using disproportionate force against youngsters armed largely with stones. Once suicide bombs exploded in the heart of Tel Aviv, however, then this would represent a threat to the state's very existence and no measure would be excluded.

* * *

After winning the February 2001 election, Sharon formed a government of national unity, inviting Labor to join. After his tumultuous career, becoming prime minister represented an extraordinary achievement of political endurance. He was as responsible as anyone for the worst calamities of Israeli strategy—the colonization of so much Palestinian territory and the push into Lebanon. He offered no optimistic manifesto for the future, presenting himself as a man who could always be relied upon to put security first. As former foreign minister Ben-Ami put it, his support "was always the result of the hopelessness and despair he himself had generated."[1] Sharon's approach to the territories was to use settlements and the roads that connected them to keep the Palestinian areas fragmented, unable to come together in a critical mass. This, however, did not reflect an ideological conviction about Greater Israel, and when it suited him he could show surprising flexibility. Indeed, his approach to politics was always to try to stay a step ahead of his opponents, if necessary taking initiatives of his own, to sow confusion and change the framework of debate. This cultivated unpredictability affected all his political dealings. He was always trying to create the maximum room for maneuver and tried to avoid getting tangled up in prolonged negotiations.

Added to Sharon's natural disinclination to make deals with Arabs was a grudge factor in his relations with Arafat, the man he had chased out of Beirut in 1982 but whose organization he could not squash, and who was presiding as a self-styled president of a nascent Palestinian state. Sharon remained focused on the old enemy, determined to bury the Palestinian

Authority and Arafat's claims to be an interlocutor for peace. His fixation on Arafat led to what was in some respects the major Israeli miscalculation in handling the intifada, which was the assumption that Arafat was always the ringleader and that all violence could be traced back to him. Sharon's view was shared by the leadership of the IDF. The chief of staff observed in January 2001 that the Palestinian Authority was becoming "a terrorist entity."[2] Barak's insistence that Camp David had revealed Arafat's true intentions contributed to the consensus view. As the intifada took hold, the peace camp in Israel was left isolated and disillusioned, many feeling deep betrayal that the Palestinians had not only spurned a generous offer but then turned to terror in response.

Arafat contributed to the perception of the centrality of his role. There was nobody else who could claim to speak for the Palestinian people and he could not allow it to be thought that he was anything other than in charge. As the prospects for a return to negotiations dimmed, he reverted to his old role of guerrilla leader and encouraged talk of the violent expulsion of the Israelis from occupied territories, which reinforced Israeli views of his culpability. His actual control of events was tenuous, especially when it came to the Islamist groups. Hamas was growing in influence, as much because of its social welfare work and apparent incorruptibility as its operations. Hamas's leader, Sheik Yassin, indicated that Arafat was now leaving it alone: "The resistance is legitimate and the authority shuts its eyes and does not pursue the fighters."[3] Punishing the Palestinian Authority for all attacks, including those committed by Hamas, on the assumption that Arafat could clamp down on the Islamists if he were so inclined, was both unrealistic and reduced the Palestinian Authority's capacity to act. By shattering the Palestinian Authority, Israel made it less likely that it would have a secular Palestinian government, capable of both negotiating and implementing an agreement.

This problem was aggravated by the IDF's approach to counterinsurgency. All Israeli strategy, reflecting the vulnerability of a small country surrounded by hostile populations, started from the assumption that no weakness must be shown in the face of enemy hostility and that there must be a vigorous response to any attack. The position did not translate easily into a counterinsurgency doctrine, which depends on separating militants from their natural sources of support and recruits. This is normally assumed to require political carrots and the careful use of military sticks in order to isolate the militants. In principle, such tactics would argue for a major political initiative, including territorial withdrawal, combined with military measures that would only affect those determined to cause violence. But any territorial withdrawals could be presented as a victory for terrorism, and thus be seen as a sign of weakness. The IDF accepted that counterinsurgency strategy should influence the consciousness of the Palestinian people, but their aim was not to convince them that there would be benefits from desisting from violence but rather to persuade them of the hopelessness of their situation so long as violence continued. The net effect of the measures taken tended to reinforce the bonds between militants and population.

*   *   *

During the first months of both Bush's and Sharon's tenure in office, Bush left the Middle East alone. Nor did Powell make it a high priority. The administration showed understanding for Israel's predicament, but there was no change in the view that Israel could help itself by moderating its treatment of Palestinians and freezing both new settlements and growth in those already established. Clinton had invited former senator George Mitchell, who had played an important role in the Northern Ireland peace process, to try to find a way out of the impasse, but Bush was not inclined to back his predecessor's initiatives. Mitchell's report was full of good advice and was generally accepted, but it was left unimplemented because no weight was put behind it.

The attacks of 9/11 had a mixed impact on the situation. From Sharon's perspective, the most worrying aspect was Bush's apparent need to court Arab and Islamic opinion. If this was so, then Bush could not appear uncaring about events in Palestine. Sharon's reading was confirmed when, almost immediately after 9/11, Powell got in touch, urging Sharon to make conciliatory moves. The prime minister argued that there was no distinction to be made between good terror and bad terror, and that Israel should not be expected to respond in ways that the United States would find unacceptable on its own account. He even earned a public rebuke from the White House by suggesting that Israel was being cast in the role of Czechoslovakia in the 1930s, a potential victim of American attempts to appease the Arabs. In Washington, there was some sympathy for Sharon's view and doubts that there was much the Americans could do to change the situation with the Palestinians. The Israelis offered solidarity in the war on terror and could claim that they were on the front line. A decade of attempts to find a way forward with Israel's adversaries, including summits with Assad and Arafat, had produced no tangible results and, on the basis of most polls, had done little for America's reputation in the Arab world. With U.S. subsidies to Israel running at some $3 billion a year, Arabs took it for granted that the interests of the United States and Israel were intertwined. The administration veered to the view that the fault for the lack of progress lay in Arafat's refusal or inability to control the violence. It was coming to share Sharon's low opinion of the Palestinian leader.

At the start of December 2001, after a weekend that saw twenty-five Israelis killed in bombings, and following a hurried meeting with Sharon, Bush demanded that Arafat break up those responsible, Hamas and Islamic Jihad. Powell spoke of a "moment of truth" for Arafat, as he needed to demonstrate that he was willing or able to control extremists. As a *New York Times* report noted, the language used deliberately mirrored that adopted when demanding that the Taliban deal with al Qaeda the previous September, including jailing the terrorists and going after their training camps. New York senator Charles E. Schumer was explicit about the link: "The P.L.O. is the same as the Taliban, which aids, abets and provides safe haven for terrorists. And Israel is like America, simply trying to protect its home front. To ask Israel to negotiate with Arafat is like asking America to negotiate with Mullah Mohammed Omar, the chief of the Taliban." The analogy was a false one. Unlike the Taliban and al Qaeda, which were allies, Fatah and Hamas were rivals, so that if Arafat were toppled by way of punishment, it would strengthen the Islamists. In addition, the Palestinian cause was far more popular in the Arab world than al Qaeda's. The low opinion of Arafat was spelled out by Rumsfeld: "If one looks historically, he has been involved in terrorist activities. We all know that. That's been his background. We also know that he is not a particularly strong leader. And I don't know that he has good control over the Palestinian situation. He has not ever delivered anything for the Palestinian people throughout history."[4] The next day, Sharon told the Knesset, "The true Arafat is being discovered by all."

Arafat recognized the danger, some arrests were made, and for a few weeks there were no attacks. He was, however, soon undone when the Israelis intercepted a freighter, the *Karine A,* full of Iranian weapons, including rockets, mortars, and missiles. Despite suggestions that the weapons were destined for Hezbollah, an established Iranian ally, the captain of the ship was a Fatah activist and implicated members of the Palestinian Authority in the deal. As bad for Arafat as the evidence of planning for terrorism was the link with Iran, soon to be marked by Bush (in part because of this discovery) as a member of the "axis of evil." The timing was so bad for Arafat and Iran, leaving both discredited in Bush's eyes, that an Israeli hoax was alleged. The allegation was not substantiated. Khatami denied Iranian responsibility, but he did not control the radicals for whom undermining his foreign policy would have been a bonus.

Israeli tactics still made the Americans uncomfortable. The level of Palestinian casualties was rising steadily and the Israelis seemed to have no alternative approaches. "Frankly," observed Bush in mid-March, "it's not helpful what the Israelis have recently done in order to create conditions for peace."[5] In March, Cheney traveled around the Middle East, trying to drum up support for taking on Iraq, but found that all his Arab hosts wanted to talk about was the terrible things being done to Palestine. The vice president began to wonder aloud whether the parties to this conflict could resolve it if left to their own devices.

Arab governments could claim to have shown some forbearance, especially Egypt and Jordan, which faced regular demands to renounce their treaties with Israel and break diplomatic relations. In October 2000 at an Arab summit, these two worked hard to avoid unrealistic statements of support for the Palestinians. Mubarak warned that "with respect to what is happening between the Palestinians and the Israelis, war will not help and will not achieve the necessary security and peace." He made it clear: "The Egyptian army has no interest or goal other than to defend its country, guard its borders, and warn against any aggression toward Egypt."[6] They were now looking for ways to calm the situation, including taking the initiative in moving forward a peace process. The most interesting initiative was revealed by columnist Tom Friedman in a February interview with Saudi Arabian crown prince Abdullah, raising the possibility of all Arab states recognizing Israel in return for the withdrawal from lands occupied since 1967.[7] This was taken forward in an Arab summit at the end of March. Sharon was urged by senior advisers not to dismiss this opening lightly. This was a more serious prospect than continual and fruitless sparring with Arafat. Public opinion was getting restive. The violence was intense, the economy was in decline, and life was miserable.

Then on the evening of March 27, 2002, as families gathered to celebrate the first night of Passover at a Netanya hotel, a suicide bomber struck, killing twenty-nine people and wounding 150 others. Four days later, fifteen were killed at a restaurant in Haifa. This was a terrible month, which saw 127 Israeli deaths. Sharon felt under no obligation to take any notice of demands for new political initiatives or to go easy on the Palestinians. Operation Defensive Shield, a plan that had been under development by the IDF for some time, involved the reoccupation of the territories that had been under the Palestinian Authority, the Area A of the Oslo Accords. Sharon had promised Bush that he would not harm Arafat, and he was persuaded not to expel the Palestinian leader over the prospect of him going around the world lambasting Israel. But Arafat was left trapped inside his Ramallah headquarters, parts of which were bulldozed down, surrounded by tanks and soldiers. Arafat was soon basking in international sympathy. He was under siege, but with a telephone. He called world leaders and spoke enthusiastically to the media. "Thus far," he reported, "I have seen seven martyrs and over forty wounded persons. However, morale is high because we are all potential martyrs. To Jerusalem we are marching, martyrs in the millions."[8]

The proclaimed aim was to "systematically dismantle terrorist infrastructures in the entire region," confiscate weapons, and find munitions factories, as well as neutralize and capture potential suicide bombers and their masters. Powell made worried comments, deploring the heavy Palestinian casualties. The Israeli right to deal with terrorism was acknowledged. Sharon was, however, urged to consider the consequences of his methods. In the Security Council, rather than risk total isolation, the United States voted for a watered-down resolution calling for an Israeli withdrawal from Palestinian cities, but without giving a deadline. Sharon concluded that he had time to continue with the operation. The imagery did not get better. The Church of the Nativity in Bethlehem, serving as a sanctuary for fighters who had barricaded themselves inside with priests and nuns, was put under siege. Refugees were fleeing from the Israeli tanks; water shortages were developing; hospitals could barely cope. Palestine was paralyzed, both as an economy and as a society. From the beginning of March until May 7, 497 Palestinians were killed, 1,447 wounded, and another 6,000 arrested.

On April 4, Bush demanded an end to the operation and supported yet another Security Council resolution that now demanded Israeli withdrawal "without delay," though he also blamed Arafat for not controlling the terror. Two days later, Israel was still showing no signs of withdrawing. Bush took a sterner public stance. "I meant what I said to the Prime Minister of Israel. I expect there to be withdrawal without delay."[9] The next day, a pullout began from two towns close to the border, but elsewhere the operation continued. Powell was sent to the Middle East to get a cease-fire and find a way to get negotiations started again. Neither Powell nor Bush thought there was much to be done, and Bush was reluctant to put too much pressure on Sharon, but he dispatched Powell to give a show of concern and activity. "You've got to go," the president told Powell. "It's going to be ugly, you're going to get beaten up, but you've got a lot of fire wall to burn up." But as he traveled, the message from the White House, through Rice, was to slow down and not put too much pressure on Sharon.[10] To some extent Powell added to his problems by talking too publicly and too explicitly about his mission. He raised unrealistic expectations on the Arab side, gave Sharon a reason not to cooperate because that way he could also avoid unwanted peace talks, and was also misleading about the administration's intentions. As Powell later admitted, his main role was to "relieve Arab pressure" by showing "some action."[11]

On arrival in the Middle East, the secretary of state moved at a leisurely pace from capital to capital, leaving Israel until the end. As he traveled, there were reports of more forceful actions by the Israelis, with the entry into Jenin, where buildings had been booby-trapped in preparation for the arrival of the IDF, providing some of the bloodiest fighting. Palestinians claimed massacres of 500 dead, repeated uncritically by the media and non-governmental organizations (NGOs), which led to a UN inquiry that showed (despite a lack of Israeli cooperation) the casualties to have been exaggerated by a factor of ten.

By the time Powell reached Israel, expectations were being played down for any diplomatic breakthroughs. Meanwhile, pro-Israel groups in Washington began to gather support for Operation Defensive Shield, with speakers presenting it as Israel's contribution to the war on terror. Paul Wolfowitz was sent to show the underlying administration sympathy for Israel. But Wolfowitz, despite the stereotypes of neocon views, was not insensitive to the Palestine condition. "Innocent Palestinians are suffering and dying in great numbers as well," he told the audience. "It is critical that we recognize and acknowledge that fact." He was booed.[12] After appearing to agree to withdrawal, Sharon insisted that operations would continue for some time longer. After "ten of the most miserable days imaginable," Powell left the region having failed in his original mission.[13] He warned Arafat that he had nobody left to talk with in Washington and that he had to change. Powell asked Israelis to consider whether they could look beyond settlements and occupation to a comprehensive peace.

The United States was being blamed for its inability to rein in Israel. The administration was under pressure to respond to international criticism that it was indifferent to the plight of the Palestinians and had no plans to meet their aspirations. Cheney was opposed to any explicit support for a Palestinian state, on the grounds that Israel could not be expected to support a likely bastion for terrorism. The circle was squared by stressing the idea that the Palestinian Authority had to transform itself into a body that deserved to have its own state. In a speech on June 24, 2002, Bush insisted on the need for change. "It is untenable for Israeli citizens to live in terror. It is untenable for Palestinians to live in squalor and occupation. And the current situation offers no prospect that life will improve. Israeli citizens will continue to be victimized by terrorists, and so Israel will continue to defend herself." His alternative vision was "two states, living side by side in peace and security." This was an important statement for an American president. Critically, however, this required a "new and different Palestinian leadership. He called "on the Palestinian people to elect new leaders, leaders not compromised by terror. I call upon them to build a practicing democracy, based on tolerance and liberty. If the Palestinian people actively pursue these goals, America and the world will actively support their efforts."[14] Exactly how this might be achieved, or what possible next steps might be, he did not say. Bush had provided a new twist to a familiar tale, ratcheting up the threshold for the Palestinians to get what they considered to be their basic rights. So long as Arafat was notionally in charge, the Palestinians could not readily respond. It remained the European view that only Arafat could ever deliver peace, and therefore it was unwise to add to the pressure on him. The Americans did not now believe he could deliver anything. They made the same point to the Israelis when, that September, tanks again surrounded Arafat in Ramallah trying to extract from the compound men allegedly responsible for terrorism. With some effort Rice got the Israelis to desist. "Arafat is not a ticking time bomb," she told an aide of Sharon. "To me, he is not important."[15]

✦   ✦   ✦

Among the more grandiose claims for the Iraq war was that somehow the road to peace in Israel would come through a transformed Iraq. Saddam was undoubtedly a nuisance factor in the Arab-Israeli dispute, seeking to gain Palestinian backing by giving bounties to the families of suicide bombers. His removal would see the end of one of the Palestinians' more consistent supporters. Beyond that, regime change in Iraq would make little difference. Once Chalabi was discounted, it was always unlikely that a new Iraqi regime would make peace with Israel. The last thing the fragile governments in Iraq wanted was for the Americans to ask them to sound positive about Israel. The only reason to put Iraq before Palestinian was that there seemed to be no basis for any progress in 2002. The idea was that the United States could create such a secure environment that Israel could afford to take risks for peace, but the main risk now was not from an external force but from an angry local population.

Following the Iraq war, when there was briefly enhanced U.S. prestige, there seemed to be a possibility of political progress. Drawing on work over the previous year, the "Quartet" (the United States, the European Union, Russia, and the UN) unveiled in April plans for a "Road Map" that was supposed to lead through a series of incremental steps to a Palestinian state in three years. Bush was wary, but he went along because Blair had made joining that initiative part of his price for supporting the Iraq war. Militant organizations must be disbanded and all settlement activity (including organic growth of established settlements) frozen, with a view to establishing a democratic and peaceful Palestinian state.

Moreover, there seemed to be movement in Palestinian politics. By now most Palestinians wanted the violence to end and get back to their normal lives. They supported and admired those fighting on their behalf and derived some satisfaction from Israeli suffering. But their suffering was much greater. Palestinian workers were no longer being employed inside Israel, and unemployment reached 70 percent, with 50 percent of the population in the West Bank and 80 percent in Gaza below the poverty line. The first intifada had sown divisions within Israeli society and created majorities in favor of withdrawal from the territories, but this time the effect was to unify the Israelis behind intransigent positions. By the middle of 2002, Palestinian intellectuals were condemning the suicide bombings and warning of just how much damage was being done. In March, Arafat agreed to appoint one of the intifada's critics, Mahmoud Abbas (Abu Mazen), as prime minister of the Palestinian Authority.

Sharon was less than enthusiastic about the Road Map, but he was well aware of the danger of rejecting it. He needed something more than the basic mantra of Israel's right to exist and to defend itself from terror and vague promises about Palestinian self-rule in contained enclaves. There were hard questions to be faced about where Israel was going and the basis of coexistence with a population that was angry and distressed. In a speech on December 4, 2002, he accepted there would be a Palestinian state "with borders yet to be finalized" and placed emphasis on setting conditions based on Palestinian performance in stopping violence. By playing on his tough stance with the intifada, he then thrashed the Labor Party in elections at the start of 2003, leaving the opposition with only nineteen of 120 Knesset seats. Yet within months, his hard-line government was under strain as he asked them to accept the Quartet's proposals, and was then denounced by his colleagues for being prepared to reward terror, surrender sacred territory, and go blindly to a new holocaust. As he tried to explain realities, he uttered words that few ever expected to hear from Ariel Sharon: "It is important to reach a political settlement . . . the idea that it is possible to keep three and a half million Palestinians under occupation is wrong for Israel, for the Palestinians and for the Israeli economy."[16]

The problem soon came over the ability of the Palestinian Authority to clamp down on terror. One problem was that Abbas was not given full control. Arafat wanted to clear all decisions and keep control over the various security organizations connected to the PA. The basic problem was the PA had been so weakened itself that it was in no position to risk a direct confrontation with the Islamist groups, so Abbas sought instead to agree to a cease-fire and no more attacks on Israeli civilians. In June, a *hudna* (temporary truce) was declared by Hamas and Islamic Jihad for forty-five days. Violence declined but by no means came to an end. Israel was unconvinced, suspecting that without arms and militants being seized, a cease-fire would just allow the enemy to lick its wounds and replenish its stocks. The Israelis therefore continued with their own efforts to deal with Hamas. Almost immediately, one leading militant, Abbedalla Qawasameh, was killed in a gunfight as he resisted arrest. When a bus bomb exploded in Jerusalem in mid-August, Hamas described this as a retaliation for his death. The bombing in turn led to a general crackdown against all Hamas leaders in Hebron and the Gaza Strip, which left the organization damaged, particularly in Hebron. As before, the Israeli attitude was to wait and see before relaxing their standard security practices, fearful of the consequences of easing up at all. So Abbas was given nothing by way of prisoner releases or help to get the economy moving. No cities were evacuated by Israel troops. Eventually, caught by Israeli inflexibility and Arafat's reluctance to relinquish power, Abbas gave up. He was replaced as prime minister by Ahmed Querei (Abu Ala), who made even less impression on events.

✦   ✦   ✦

Although it was not apparent until 2005, the harsh measures Israel took did have the effect of suppressing the second intifada. The raw numbers tell the story. During 2002, 451 Israelis died as a result of terrorist attacks, many in the first months of the year. The next year saw 214 die, and in 2004 the numbers halved again to 117. They halved once more in 2005 to fifty-three. A number of points emerge from an analysis of these statistics.[17]

The total number of attacks against Israelis was highest in 2001, when there were 7,634. The numbers declined to 5,176 in 2002, and then to 3,941 in 2003. One explanation for this is that the gradual Israeli restrictions, particularly after Operation Defensive Shield, made it increasingly difficult for militants to operate freely and also put them on the defensive as they tried to avoid detention. The number of "preventive arrests" shot up from under 2,000 in 2001 to almost 4,700 a year later. There was a sharp decline in Israeli deaths during the second half of 2002. The changed political context made a difference, as in 2003 the Palestinian Authority presented a moderate face and could embrace a more serious political process. As the Islamists opposed any negotiations, they would be expected to increase their activity. This seems to have happened. Both Hamas and Islamic Jihad doubled their number of attacks (a combined total of 656, up from 352). This of course could also be in retaliation for the increased Israeli activity directed against their leaders. It was also now easier to operate from Gaza than from the West Bank.

Their increasing role was reflected in the greater number of attacks using suicide bombs. In terms of causing maximum pain to Israelis, they were far more efficient than any alternative method. As other types of attacks declined, attempted suicide attacks grew, peaking in 2003, when 210 were attempted. By this time, however, the bombers were starting to face difficulties. Only twenty-six of these bombers reached their targets, although individually they were deadlier. The previous year, 2002, sixty suicide bombs were successfully detonated out of 172 attempts, causing half the total Israeli fatalities for that year. By 2004, the number of successful suicide bombs was down to fifteen out of 134. In 2005, there were just fifteen attempts, out of which seven were successful.

The most effective means the Israelis had to bring down the number of successful suicide attacks appears to be murder of top military and political figures, either by air attacks in Gaza or through undercover agents in the West Bank. By and large, the success of these operations was admitted by Hamas. When the attacks missed and innocent civilians were killed, there was uproar. Otherwise the martyrs' identities tended to be acknowledged and their achievements eulogized. Assassination was not a new Israeli tactic, having been adopted during the early days of the second intifada in 2000. In 2001, thirty-one Palestinians were assassinated, but this became a much more systematic campaign in 2002, when there were seventy-eight assassinations, with fewer killed in subsequent years. Although the Israelis have insisted this is a matter of last resort, if only because those arrested can be interrogated, and the general assumption has been that these killings just encourage a cycle of violence, there is evidence that in this case the net effect was to disrupt the terrorist campaign. Daniel Byman, commenting on the striking correlation between the assassinations and the decline in Israeli deaths, observed, "Contrary to popular myth, the number of skilled terrorists is quite limited. Bomb makers, terrorism trainers, forgers, recruiters, and terrorist leaders are scarce; they need many months if not years, to gain enough expertise to be effective." This campaign succeeded because it was so ruthless. In contrast to a previous campaign against Hezbollah, which was "desultory," the relentlessness of this campaign rocked Hamas, with known militants having to spend time protecting themselves, while it was hard to find substitutes for those killed.[18] The campaign culminated in March 2004, when the Israelis caught Hamas leader Sheik Yassin. After Hamas tried and failed to respond with suicide bombings, less than a month later they also killed his successor, Abdel Aziz al-Rantissi. Hamas decided against naming its new leader publicly, and despite the dire warnings of a terrible retribution, its response was limited. The next February, Hamas announced that it would accept a temporary period of calm.

Although targeted killings raise important questions of legality and morality, they could be justified as focusing on the perpetrators of violence. They took place, however, against a background of intense surveillance and restriction of Palestinian life. The IDF's approach was to take a tough line from the start, and at times the forces went further than politicians intended. Bulldozing houses, establishing curfews, destroying crops, and imposing collective punishment and economic hardship added to the rage of the local population. Around and between cities, travelers had to pass checkpoints, causing delays and making normal business at times impossible. The violence that occurred as Israelis fought with militants or tried to cut them down took a heavy toll.

The idea of a wall separating Israelis from Palestinians was an idea that originally came from the left, as an alternative to the incorporation of Judea and Samaria into the state. Rabin toyed with the idea in the early 1990s. Now Sharon picked it up, despite the affront to the concept of Greater Israel. However the line was drawn, some settlements would be left isolated. That is why Sharon had opposed the idea, but there was strong public support for it. Although there was some evidence by this time that other measures were reducing the violence, 2002 had still been a tough year. It was hard to believe that Israel would not be living with terrorism indefinitely. The economy had suffered, and the public was becoming demoralized. To avoid upsetting the right too much, Sharon wanted the security fence, which would be 560 miles in length, to be built as far as possible inside Palestinian territory, skirting around settlements rather than confirming their isolation from Israel. This was bound to have a detrimental impact on Palestinians working in and around the area, who would be separated from their land and have a further imposition on their landscape. While the Israeli Supreme Court accepted the legality of the fence as a defensive measure, it demanded regular amendments to mitigate the impact on Palestinian life. The International Court of Justice in the Hague simply declared the barrier to be illegal and ordered it to be moved back to the 1967 border or dismantled. Although this did not happen, the route of the fence became less ambitious.

Another consequence of the success of Israel's offensive measures, and the improved defenses, was for the militants to move to rocket attacks. Qassam rockets were nothing like as deadly as the suicide bombings, but they were a nuisance. They were brought in through tunnels under the Egypt-Gaza border, along with other weapons and much consumer-oriented contraband, including cigarettes, currency, and drugs. It was a regular struggle for Israel to find and destroy these tunnels—ninety were shut down after 2000. In addition, the rockets were mobile and tended to be fired from highly populated areas, reducing Israel's capability for dealing with them.

★   ★   ★

A senior officer from the IDF observed that "the IDF had defeated all the terrorist gangs in Gaza save one: the population at large."[19] The missing element in Israeli strategy remained political. Sharon's strategy appeared to be geared toward agreeing in principle with the need for a Palestinian state while delaying any serious discussions. The peace camp in Israel was now recovering its voice. It demonstrated the possibilities of an agreement with Palestinians at a carefully orchestrated meeting in Geneva in December 2003, with the Israeli side led by Yossi Beilin. Sharon sought to regain the initiative in a way that would help Israel internationally and give him greater freedom domestically. He also at last understood that the logic of a Greater Israel could no longer apply. It had been undermined by the strain of imposing Israel's will on a hostile population, and this strain could only grow. By now only half of the 10 million people between the Mediterranean and the Jordan River were Jewish, and the demographic trends were inexorably in favor of the Arabs.

On February 2, 2004, the prime minister announced that all Jewish settlers would be transferred from the Gaza Strip. At the time there were twenty-one settlements with 8,500 inhabitants, as against 1.3 million Palestinians, living in this small strip of land, twenty-five miles long and six miles wide. The military had the same reservations it had with the unilateral withdrawal from Lebanon, fearing that it would give the impression of having been chased away and there would be no way to obtain a political quid pro quo. The reaction was astonished and venomous in Sharon's party and among his former supporters. All the vitriol that his predecessors faced as soon as they threatened to touch the settlements was directed against the man who had championed them so fervently in the past.

Skeptics assumed that Sharon intended to sacrifice Gaza in order to hold on to the West Bank. The Americans pushed to make sure that this was a complete break—initially the intention was to hold on to some settlements— and then gave Sharon strong support, in the hitherto unlikely guise of an agent of positive change. He was urged to coordinate his plans with the Palestinians, so that the effort had a semblance of negotiation. In an exchange of letters, the two leaders agreed that Israel would continue to work within the Road Map, with the standard proviso that the Palestinians would first need to dismantle the terrorist organizations. As Sharon did not believe that Arabs could ever agree on a nonviolent path toward Israel, this let him off the hook. Particularly important for Sharon, Bush also agreed that if progress were made, the United States would accept that Israel retain major settlement blocs in the West Bank and that the new Palestinian state would be the destination for any returning Palestinian refugees and not Israel proper.

Meeting with Sharon at the White House in April, Bush committed the United States to Israel's security "as a vibrant Jewish state," thereby precluding mass refugee return. With regard to the borders, he insisted that the fence, still under construction, should be "a security, rather than political, barrier" and "temporary rather than permanent," not prejudicing any final status issues. The outcome of negotiations on borders would be up to the parties. "But the realities on the ground and in the region have changed greatly over the last several decades, and any final settlement must take into account those realities and be agreeable to the parties." It was unrealistic to expect that there could be a simple return to "the armistice lines of 1949."[20]

At home, these significant diplomatic triumphs were less appreciated than the fact that territory was being abandoned. Hard-liners threatened to quit the government if Gaza was evacuated, and the splits within Likud grew. Sharon pushed through with his plan despite considerable opposition from the right, with the result that he needed to reconstruct a coalition with Labor to be sure of the Knesset votes. To encourage settlers to leave without too much fuss, compensation packages were offered. Those who refused to accept them would be evicted by force. Against the original plan, but in recognition of the practicalities, it was necessary to agree to let the Egyptians manage their border with Gaza and not to demolish all the buildings to be left behind. As the eviction of settlers got closer, the public became more apprehensive over the implications of handing over the territory to Palestinian control, while there were calls from the settlers for resistance. In the end, the IDF managed the evacuation forcefully but efficiently, using 14,000 soldiers, with many scenes of distressed settlers but less violence than anticipated. Rice put a considerable effort into an agreement between the Palestinians and Israelis to give the withdrawal a semblance of coordination. It made very little practical difference. Hamas was now seeking to emulate Hezbollah, claiming the Israeli departure as a victory and looking forward to the next stage of the struggle.

In the middle of the Israeli debate on disengagement, the politics changed. Stuck in his Ramallah compound, Arafat went into decline and died, after being taken to a French hospital on November 11, 2004, aged seventy-five. He was replaced by Mahmoud Abbas, who had long been opposed to the intifada and was considered a moderate, although also without a large popular following. This came just after Bush had been reelected for a second presidential term. When Condoleezza Rice was made secretary of state, she made it clear that she expected the Middle East to be a top priority.

Sharon realized that he should show some courtesy to Abbas, but he did nothing to ease the everyday burdens and humiliations of Palestinian life, while his view on the way forward was now increasingly unilateral. He started to talk about disengagement from the West Bank as well, picking up on a mood within Israel that wanted to be done with the Palestinians, leaving them to get on with their lives on the other side of a security fence. However limited and modest, any serious evacuation of Judea and Samaria went to the heart of the foundational beliefs of Likud. In a dramatic move, in November 2005, Sharon and key allies broke from Likud to set up a new party, Kadima (Forward), taking some support from elsewhere. This included Shimon Peres, who had just been ousted as leader of Labor by a left-wing union leader, Amir Peretz. Netanyahu, who had taken an increasingly rejectionist stance, was left in charge of the rump Likud. The first proposition in Kadima's platform was "The Israeli nation has a national and historic right to the whole of Israel. However, in order to maintain a Jewish majority, part of the Land of Israel must be given up to maintain a Jewish and democratic state." A new centrist party with such a strong leadership looked like it would sweep the board in elections planned for March.

Then, a few weeks after the party's formation, on December 18, 2005, Sharon suffered a minor stroke. He was scheduled to have a major heart operation on January 5, 2006, but the day before he suffered a massive stroke, putting him in a coma from which he did not awake. His deputy, Ehud Olmert, a former hard-line mayor of Jerusalem, who had been moving to the center for some time, succeeded him as leader of the party. Without Sharon's charisma, he led Kadima to a respectable, but not overwhelming, showing in the March elections, and formed a coalition with Labor.

* * *

By the time of the Israeli election, the political context had shifted again, this time as the result of a Palestinian election at the end of January 2006. The election had been championed enthusiastically by Condoleezza Rice. She felt committed to the "democracy in the Middle East" agenda. For Rice, as much as the president, democracy was the only way to go. Initially Bush might not have shared Clinton's enthusiasm for democracy promotion, but after 9/11 democracy was one of the qualities that distinguished the forces of good from those of evil. As early as 2002 he was musing at an NSC meeting on how much easier it would be to get peace if both Israel and Palestine were democracies. In his second inaugural address in January 2005, he spoke of little other than the virtues of freedom and liberty as the keys to healthy democracy and as a source of peace and security. It was U.S. policy "to seek and support the growth of democratic movements and institutions in every nation and culture, with the ultimate goal of ending tyranny in our world."[21]

What better place to start than the Middle East. Rice was clearly influenced by her own experience growing up as part of a community denied democratic rights, and of blacks being patronized as "not ready" for democracy. She was also impressed by the 2002 Arab Human Development Report, convinced that there was a groundswell of opinion in the region, yearning for a new, freer, and less corrupt direction. Free elections in Lebanon and Iraq gave grounds for hope. In *Foreign Affairs,* Fouad Ajami, largely drawing on events in Lebanon, wrote optimistically of "The Autumn of the Autocrats." In the same issue, with the salutary Iraqi experience in mind, Bernard Lewis wrote more cautiously of "Freedom and Justice in the Modern Middle East." The advantage of fundamentalists, he noted, is that they had the language and the imagery to make popular appeals and had made genuine efforts to alleviate the suffering of the common people. The new game suited them. Democrats must allow fundamentalists freedom, but the fundamentalists are not under the same obligation. In this respect a "genuinely free society in Iraq would constitute a mortal threat to many of the governments of the region—including allies as well as enemies of Washington."[22]

Rice made her pitch in June 2005 at a speech in Cairo. "For sixty years," she acknowledged, "my country, the United States, pursued stability at the expense of democracy in this region here in the Middle East—and we achieved neither. Now we are taking a different course. We are supporting the democratic aspirations of all people." She challenged the view that "democracy leads to chaos, or conflict, or terror," claiming the opposite to be true: "Freedom and democracy are the only ideas powerful enough to overcome hatred, and division, and violence." This was on the assumption that democracy could be inclusive and interactive, could build trust and settle disputes in a dignified manner. She looked forward to the Palestinian Authority's taking control of Gaza as "a first step toward realizing the vision of two democratic states living side by side in peace and security." Her only qualification was that "the democratic system cannot function if certain groups have one foot in the realm of politics and one foot in the camp of terror."[23]

That was hardly the only problem. For democracy to produce better government also requires the leavening of law and liberty, protection of minorities, free speech, and high levels of tolerance. Otherwise, it can turn into the tyranny of the majority or a means of sharpening social divisions, as happened in Iraq. It was hard to commend the traditional forms of government in the Middle East, which had produced stagnation, corruption, and disaffection, but that did not mean that an injection of democracy would bring with it an equivalent dose of liberalism and effective institutional reform.

Regional leaders contained their enthusiasm for this new message, trying to think of gestures that would placate this latest American obsession. Nor was this an area where the United States was following Israeli preferences. The only Israeli politician of any standing who thought democratization was always a good thing was Natan Sharansky, who first attracted international attention as a leading dissident in the Soviet Union.[24] The consensus view was that popular movements were invariably destabilizing and should not be encouraged. Exhibit 1 was the fall of the shah, whose loss had affected Israel more than any other international event, turning one of its few friends in the region into an implacable foe. Autocrats who were firmly in control could do deals and deliver on them, and would not get swept along by mass anti-Israeli fervor. In principle they might accept that it would be better if the people of the region were freer, but it helped to be able to make the contrast with their own lively democracy, and there was always a disposition to suggest that something in the Arab culture mitigated against the embrace of liberal democracy. In the Middle East, the choice, observed Israel's former foreign minister Shlomo Ben-Ami, was really between "secular authoritarianism and Islamic democracy."[25]

This debate was relevant to the future of Palestine. Abbas had been elected president of the Palestinian Authority but, in the aftermath of Arafat's death and with Hamas abstaining, this was not a particularly significant victory. To mark the new stage in Palestinian history, Rice wanted legislative elections in the West Bank and Gaza. At a time when Hamas was already getting credit for pushing the Israelis out of Gaza, and Fatah was looking tired and feeble, this was a gamble. The Israelis and Fatah agreed, along with Egypt and Saudi Arabia, that this was a bad time for elections. But Rice was adamant. It would be good for Fatah to be shaken up a bit and bring forward a new generation of leaders, and meanwhile Abbas needed a mandate to take forward in a negotiating process with Israel. Given what she had said about the difficulties of combining democracy and terror, there was an opening to exclude Hamas. But doing so would drain any election result of credibility. On this Abbas agreed. "I can't be a legitimate leader. They will say we were afraid of them. It would seem like a typical Arab election."[26] Moreover, as in the Northern Ireland experience, there could be advantages in gradually drawing Hamas into a democratic process.

All that was fine, so long as Hamas came in second. But instead, on January 26, 2006, it won. Rice was completely unprepared. By her own account, she first learned of the result in a television headline: "In wake of Hamas victory, Palestinian cabinet resigns." And she thought, "Well, that's not right."[27] Unfortunately it was, and while Rice acknowledged that the United States had failed to pick up the pulse of the Palestinian electorate, those paying close attention to local attitudes were not surprised. This created a general crisis in the American push for democratization. When she went back to the region after the elections the autocrats were smug. She had to explain why America was so enthusiastic about democratic elections but not about the results. Mubarak began to introduce constitutional amendments to hamper opposition movements and, unlike in 2005, paid no attention to American statements in support of the jailed opposition leader Amyan Nour. The elections that had been held had shown significant gains for the Muslim Brotherhood, underlining the point about the likely beneficiaries of any further moves to democracy.[28]

The immediate problem was what to do with Palestine. Abbas had to try to form a new government. The new prime minister, Ismail Haniyeh, was head of the Hamas list for the election and a man who would not apologize for what he considered acts of resistance or suddenly declare himself reconciled to Israel's permanence. The only way any political process could carry on would be for Abbas to continue to represent the Palestinians in negotiations, while Haniyeh governed as well as he could. His first trip abroad was to Iran. Abbas insisted on keeping control over the Palestinian Authority's elaborate security forces, but this created an inevitable tension, for they would function side by side with Hamas's own military organization.

All this confirmed Israel's worst fears about a Palestinian state under the control of a terrorist organization. There was no doubting the authenticity of the results and the legitimacy of the new government. But that did not require Israel, or for that matter, the United States and the European Union, to cooperate with the new government if it pursued unacceptable policies. Until terrorism was renounced, Israel recognized, and past agreements honored, no funds would be transferred to the new government, a stipulation that made it almost impossible for it to function. To ensure that the Palestinian people had food and medication, financial support would be delivered directly through humanitarian agencies. Conversations continued with Abbas, but the circumstances were hardly propitious for a diplomatic breakthrough.

In late June, a group linked to Hamas entered Israel and kidnapped an Israeli soldier. Coupled with regular rocket attacks, Israel decided it had to go into Gaza to try to retrieve the soldier and suppress the rocket fire. After a week that had seen no results, the IDF expanded its operation by attacking Hamas's civilian and military institutions. This was the context for Hezbollah's emulation of the combination of kidnapping and rocket attacks on July 12, 2006, which led to Israel's major operation in Lebanon. While this operation caused Israel a number of headaches, as we shall see in the next chapter, it did have the effect of distracting attention from Gaza, where Israel continued operations. Although the Israelis failed to get the soldier returned or stop the rockets, they had one weapon here that they lacked with Lebanon—their ability to close the border crossing, letting through only the most essential food and medical supplies. Prime Minister Haniyeh tried to bring an end to the crisis by persuading the militants to stop the rocket attacks and offering Israel a prisoner exchange, but he was undercut by Hamas's even harder-line political leadership in Damascus. Equally, proposals from Abbas to put PA security forces along the borderline were rejected by the various Islamist groups. Gradually, as the Lebanon war wound down, so did the rocket attacks, and Israel eased its grip. In September, Haniyeh again showed interest when Bush offered to recognize the unity government if the known conditions were met, but again the political wing of Hamas vetoed any positive gestures.

None of this helped the cause of unilateral disengagement. The events in both Gaza and Lebanon demonstrated a new strategic reality, that Israel was finding it extremely difficult to defend its borders. This was not in the traditional sense of being able to stop invading armies, which it could do readily, or even terrorist attacks, which it could frustrate. Now it could not repel rocket attacks from dedicated militias with mobile and concealable launchers. This required occupying large swaths of hostile territory, the strain of which had led Israel to abandon southern Lebanon and Gaza in the first place.

Moreover, there were signs of U.S. impatience with Israeli policy. The inept Lebanon operation combined with the continuing Palestine occupation to encourage claims that Israeli policy was callous, unimaginative, ultimately self-defeating, and making the United States suffer through guilt by association. Former president Carter published a book using the word "apartheid" to describe the way Israel had acquired and held on to Palestinian land.[29] This created the expected political storm, but the book still rose in the bestseller lists. A sign of a lobby whose influence is on the wane is normally the publication of books exposing its extraordinary and malign influence. Right on time, Mearsheimer and Walt published first an article and then a book (also a best-seller) on the Israel lobby.[30] Issues once on the margins of American political discourse were moving toward the center. Bush now accepted that he needed a more active Middle East policy and that it was not good enough to assume that all Israeli actions were reasonable and sensible, especially since Israelis themselves were no longer so sure.

*   *   *

A struggle for power was now developing between the two strands of the Palestinian movement. Having spent five years undermining and restraining Fatah, the Israelis and the Americans were suddenly desperate for it to hold its own in a coming clash with Hamas. The civil war that Arafat and Abbas had both been desperate to avoid was looming, now not because of Israeli demands to crack down on terror but because of its own struggle for survival. Abbas was conscious of the disparity in power, so during the summer of 2006, he resisted American calls to confront Hamas directly or dismiss the government because of its inability to function effectively. Hamas was content to hold on to power, blaming international sanctions for the wretched conditions in which its people were living and offering no compromise on the points of principle. Although he was being urged to take on Hamas, Abbas lacked the wherewithal to do so. Only in December 2006 did modest amounts of small arms get through to the Fatah units in Gaza, under the control of Mohamed Dahlan. Hamas, meanwhile, was smuggling in more arms from Syria and Iran. Serious fighting broke out in the West Bank after Hamas accused Fatah of trying to assassinate Haniyeh. Hamas also rejected Abbas's call for new elections. The fighting continued into the new year.

Arab governments watched the developing situation with alarm. The economic conditions for Palestinians were deteriorating, and fighting had begun between them. In February 2007, the Saudis invited Fatah and Hamas to Mecca to see if an agreement could be brokered. Out of this emerged a national unity government, subsidized by the Saudis, and with no concessions from Hamas on the fundamental points of principle that had led to the international boycott. Furious with Abbas, Olmert urged Bush not to change policy. Washington developed plans with active Arab, particularly Jordanian, and passive Israeli support to prepare Fatah for the clash by supplying arms and training for its security force. The idea was to build up Fatah forces enough to hold the streets when Hamas posed a direct challenge to Abbas's authority, for example, after he called new elections. He could then declare emergency rule. The Israelis were always extremely wary of this, for they recognized Hamas's strength in Gaza and feared that they would get hold of any weapons supplied to Fatah.

As little of this was secret, the net result was that Hamas was alerted to a coming power play for which it was better prepared. Even after the Mecca deal, fighting continued. It began again in earnest in mid-May, when more than fifty died in a series of clashes in Gaza, in which it was already clear that Hamas was the better organized. In mid-June, Hamas made its push. The Gaza headquarters of Fatah, including 500 fighters, were surrounded and then seized. After four days of fighting, and with 110 killed, Hamas soon had Gaza largely under their control and with its own government.

This was seen as a deep blow to American plans and the peace process in some respects, but it brought a new clarity to the situation. Although Fatah was outgunned in Gaza, it was far stronger in the West Bank, where Hamas was more on the defensive. Abbas's response was to dissolve the unity government, declare a state of emergency, and make a well-respected economist, Salam Fayyad, prime minister. His weakness was now his greatest strength. The Israelis and Americans realized that what they had previously pulled down they must now build up—for if control of the West Bank was lost, then chaos would result. It was now far easier to provide financial assistance to the PA. Tony Blair, having stood down as British prime minister in the summer, became the special envoy of the Quartet, his mission being to find ways of reviving the Palestinian economy. Hamas, with few resources of its own, 80 percent of its population reliant on foreign aid, and dependent upon Israel to keep the electricity on, demanded attention but refused to change its position. Abbas was insistent that the Israelis must not open up a dialogue, however informal, with Hamas, because that would give them credibility in the battle for Palestinian opinion. Instead, Hamas denounced Fatah, began to implement Sharia law in Gaza, and continued to send barrages of rockets across the border, leading to occasional Israeli raids.

To demonstrate that it was possible for a Palestinian leadership that had renounced terror to make advances toward its own state, a conference was organized by the United States at Annapolis on November 27, 2007. The aim was to agree on a document to take forward the 2003 Road Map, which essentially required regular meetings between Abbas and Olmert, with American support. The goal was to set the terms for a final status solution. There were positive aspects to the conference. The Palestinians were able to speak for themselves rather than as part of somebody else's delegation, as had been the case at previous international conferences. There was good representation from the Arab world (including Syria, but not Iraq) and a general consensus among the members of the Quartet about the way forward. At last Bush had accepted that the United States had to take an active role in making peace happen, and Olmert was prepared to speak up forcefully for a two-state solution. And yet the Palestinians were weak, and it was understood that whatever might be agreed on could not be delivered so long as Hamas was not involved. The Israelis could accept that Abbas was negotiating in good faith, but Fatah was still divided and the West Bank was hardly in a tranquil state. Olmert seemed wary of touching even the few outlying settlements he had agreed to dismantle early on as a sign of good faith. The Israelis remained caught in the catch-22 of their own making. So long as they maintained an overbearing presence in the territories, the Palestinians could not develop economically and politically; but as the Palestinians had not yet so developed, the Israelis were scared to let up.

For Abbas there were few options left other than to keep the lid on violence and hope that his forbearance would be rewarded by a relaxation of Israeli restrictions and some tangible moves to a proper state before Hamas began to get a grip on the West Bank. For Hamas, too, there were choices between taking every opportunity to discomfort Israel and addressing the problems of the people of Gaza, whose life support depended on international assistance. If Israel was prepared to open a dialogue at a strategic level, as it was constantly urged to do, would Hamas be prepared to talk? The United States and the other members of the Quartet were left clinging to the formula that had been broached in the aftermath of the 1967 war, four decades earlier, of land for peace. Since then the situation on the ground had deteriorated, with the accumulated hatreds and suspicions even a cold peace was going to be hard to achieve and then enforce. There were no obvious alternatives. Some Israelis toyed with the idea of a complete return to 1967, with Jordan taking over the West Bank and Gaza into Egypt, but neither country was likely to want to incorporate so many problems into its borders. Unless the old formulas could be made to work, the only real alternative would be a full internationalization, with some sort of trusteeship for the territories.

21

THE MAIN ENEMY?

THE ADMINISTRATION also found no answer to the problem of Iran. While there were times in the late 1980s when Iran appeared to be weakened by extended war, and in the late 1990s when it was flirting with reform and an opening to the West, by the late 2000s it was dominated by hard-liners with a sense of growing regional influence. On August 6, 2005, Mahmoud Ahmadinejad, the former mayor of Tehran, became president of Iran. He ran for office as an austere populist, a true guardian of the principles of the Islamic revolution, catching the pragmatic conservatives by surprise. He soon attracted international attention, and condemnation, because of his demands that Israel be "wiped off the map" and his denial of the Holocaust. His pronouncements were considered particularly alarming because they were combined with the energetic pursuit of a nuclear program, about which he regularly boasted and which seemed geared to military capability, and the equally energetic support of radical Shi'ite forces in the region, particularly in Iraq and Lebanon. Iran's links with Syria and Hamas gave it a potential force that unnerved the more conservative, Sunni states in the Middle East. King Abdullah of Jordan warned of a "Shia Crescent." The Israelis, imagining nuclear weapons directed at them by a leader who, in the grip of almost messianic religious beliefs, became even shriller about the need to prevent a decisive leap forward in Iran's nuclear program. Even while a reformer, Mohammad Khatami, was Iranian president, Bush had labeled Iran as part of the "axis of evil" in 2002. Thereafter, he spoke in threatening tones on the subject, as if creating the case for military action against Iran as the next in the sequence that began with Afghanistan and Iraq.

This was always less likely than assumed. A "surgical" strike against Iran's nuclear capabilities was always going to be problematic, and this was not a route to enforcing regime change. Once the United States got bogged down in Iraq, there was no spare capacity for yet another war, and this was reason enough for Iran to contribute to keeping the Americans bogged down. At the same time, the United States was by no means alone in its concerns, with European countries also alarmed by Iranian bellicosity and a dismissive attitude toward its treaty obligations. There was therefore considerable international support to keep up diplomatic pressure on Iran, with potential for economic sanctions, and Bush was generally content to pursue the issue through the United Nations, hoping perhaps that his reputation for recklessness might induce Tehran to be more forthcoming than it would otherwise have been. This encouraged the belief that Tehran was on the crest of the wave, defying the Americans while the radical groups, which it had long supported, all prospered. In the previous two chapters, we noted the strength of Iranian-backed parties in Iraq and the advance of Hamas in Gaza. In Lebanon Hezbollah was also able to assert its power. Like the other instances, from a U.S. perspective, this was something of a self-inflicted wound.

★   ★   ★

Hezbollah was by far the most important of Iran's creations. Lebanon was a country in which Shi'ites represented some 40 percent of the population, with its share rising. It had followed a careful project of building up popular support through community and welfare activities and, after checking with Tehran, had established itself as a political party with significant representation in the Lebanese Parliament. Even after the Israelis left southern Lebanon in 2000, a move for which Hezbollah justifiably claimed considerable credit, it had not disbanded its substantial military wing, and Tehran had helped to ensure that it remained well equipped. Mutual support for Hezbollah also helped cement Iran's relationship with Syria, which provided the supply routes for arms and ammunition.

Lebanon's civil war concluded with the 1989 Ta'if Accord, which created a complex parliamentary system, with safeguards for the three core groups— Shi'ite, Sunni, and Maronite Christian. The agreement was also followed in 1991 by the Treaty of Brotherhood, Cooperation and Coordination with Syria, ensuring that the overbearing role of Syria was a large issue in Lebanese politics. Elections took place in 1992 (the first for eighteen years), but they were manipulated by Damascus, leading to a Christian boycott. Hezbollah decided to accept the risk of a loss of revolutionary fervor in return for influence over local political developments. It got about 10 percent of the vote, a level sustained in later elections. Rafiq al-Hariri, an extremely rich Sunni businessman, became prime minister, a position he held, except for a brief gap in 1998–2000, until 2004. He worked for reconciliation among the various confessional groups. Although he enjoyed close ties with France, he kept his distance from the Americans and generally maintained good relations with Syria. He did, however, clash with the Shi'ite president Emile Lahoud, effectively Syria's agent in Beirut, who continually undercut him in government. In 2004, he resigned at Syria's determination to keep Lahoud in office after his allotted term. At this point, Hariri in effect became the leader of the anti-Syrian opposition in Lebanon, using his links with France to get a resolution (cosponsored with the United States) through the Security Council, calling for the withdrawal of Syrian forces from Lebanon and the disarming of Hezbollah.[1]

On February 14, 2005, Hariri was assassinated in a car-bomb explosion. The matter is still under UN investigation, but the preliminary findings confirmed what most suspected from the start—that this was Syria's responsibility. Syrian leaders, including President Bashar al-Assad, had issued so many threats about what they would do if their will was opposed that protestations of innocence rang hollow. The UN investigation became, and remains, a major concern for the Syrian leadership, which coped by intimidating all Lebanese daring to point a finger in their direction by trying to have them assassinated as well, an endeavor reaping some success. Hariri's murder produced a wave of anti-Syrian fury within Lebanon, a "Cedar Revolution." Bush was persuaded by President Chirac of France that the best sanction was to work with Lebanon to undermine Syrian influence. For a while the Syrians did appear nonplussed, and even agreed in April 2005 to accede to a UN resolution to withdraw their forces from Lebanon. For Bush, the Lebanon story was clinching evidence that democracy was at last on the move in the Middle East. "Any who doubt the appeal of freedom in the Middle East," he observed in March, "can look to Lebanon, where the Lebanese people are demanding a free and independent nation." He backed it up with a Lebanese quote: "Democracy is knocking at the door of this country and, if it's successful in Lebanon, it is going to ring the doors of every Arab regime."[2]

The setback for Syria made its remaining allies within the country even more important. Hezbollah organized massive demonstrations to thank Syria for all it had done for the country. In a way, this symbolized a new relationship. The elder Assad had been a patron of Hezbollah, but now the relationship was reversed, if anything. Syria was dependent upon Hezbollah as a means of maintaining its position in Lebanon, and as a potential source of pressure on Israel.

Hezbollah never lost its interest in Israel. After 2000, the border area still saw occasional clashes between the militia and Israeli forces, although nothing like the level prior to withdrawal. From Hezbollah's perspective, there were two reasons for this. First, Israel was continuing to occupy an area known as Shebaa Farms, which was claimed by Lebanon, although Israel considered it part of the occupied Syrian Golan Heights. Second, Israel held some Hezbollah fighters. In October 2003, three Israeli soldiers were captured from Shebaa Farms, dying in the process. Eventually, in October 2004 their bodies were returned to Israel with twenty-three Lebanese and 400 Palestinian prisoners freed in return from Israeli jails. Their efforts to capture more Israeli soldiers continued, apparently with the aim of securing the release of other Lebanese prisoners, including one held for the murder of an Israeli family in 1979.

On July 12, 2006, against the backdrop of a barrage of Katyusha rockets fired toward Israeli villages, a Hezbollah unit operating out of a well-prepared and concealed spot on the Israeli side of the border kidnapped two Israeli soldiers, with a view to a prisoner exchange but also as a show of strength for domestic political purposes. In the process, they killed three other soldiers. When an IDF unit pursued the kidnappers into Lebanon, they were ambushed, leading to the deaths of four more soldiers when their advanced Merkava tank was destroyed. A fifth died in a battle to recover the bodies. In the past Israel had found itself haggling for the return of the remains of IDF dead in exchange for live prisoners. Israel did not relish a battle with Hezbollah. It had its hands full with the second intifada and did not need a second front. The Israeli Defense Forces were stretched. Moreover, while Sharon had been in charge, he was aware how a reprise of his 1982 enterprise would be portrayed. But Sharon was now in a coma and the audacity of the raid demanded a response. The timing was also sensitive. Nineteen days earlier, Hamas had mounted a similar raid, and the Israelis had been spending a frustrating time thrashing around in Gaza trying to find the kidnapped and the kidnappers.

In the circumstances, Israel was in a strong international position. There was no excuse for Hezbollah's action, which was roundly condemned. Arab leaders, already alarmed at Iran's growing influence in Iraq, began to acknowledge that if faced with Shi'ite militancy, they might actually have common cause with Israel. Under UNSCR 1559, not only should foreign forces have been removed from Syria but militias also disbanded. Given the existing international focus on Lebanon, there were opportunities for Israel to explore diplomatic options, while building up its forces to move into southern Lebanon if these failed to bear fruit. Instead, it decided, with remarkably little deliberation or consideration of alternative options, on military measures that failed to achieve declared objectives and appeared to depend on imposing collective punishment on the Lebanese people.

Little thought or training had gone into a major operation in southern Lebanon, and intelligence collection had been limited. The head of the IDF, Dan Halutz, was an airman who believed, despite the evidence from recent American campaigns, that airpower could have a strategic effect on its own. He had been influenced by the U.S. Afghan experience and supposed that in many cases Special Forces would be sufficient to provide the necessary targeting information. He wanted to avoid a large-scale commitment of ground forces, because of the risks of high casualties, which he presumed politicians would be reluctant to accept. At the same time, and unusually for Israel, neither Prime Minister Olmert nor Defense Minister Peretz (the Labor Party leader) had any serious military experience.[3] To start with, they had the nation behind them, all-party support, and complete freedom of maneuver. But they began to lose support as soldiers were lost in futile battles in which they failed to achieve their objectives, and the Katyusha barrage was unceasing and apparently unstoppable.

To the extent there was a plan, which had been under development since 2000, it reflected a determination to wound Hezbollah deeply if it took advantage of Israel's withdrawal from southern Lebanon. But this in turn would involve wounding Lebanon, for the plan involved targeting the airport in Beirut, attacking the Daiya neighborhood of Beirut where Hezbollah had its main base, blockading Lebanon from the sea, and cutting transportation links to deprive Hezbollah of new supplies. Here, the hope was that the Lebanese people would turn against Hezbollah for causing these tribulations, although it was always as likely that they would unite against Israel for imposing them. A plan with such focus inevitably made the recovery of the soldiers a secondary priority. The main aim was to undermine Hezbollah's credibility as a fighting force, and if possible get the Lebanese army to take over the south and disarm Hezbollah. The land campaign was tentative, starting with raids geared to targets close to the border, with one of the most dramatic an attack to capture some Hezbollah leaders. It was only toward the end of the campaign that the IDF launched one of the forward drives that used to be their stock-in-trade. This tentativeness possibly flattered Hezbollah, which was able to use to full advantage its networks of bunkers and tunnels, good for surviving air raids, storing arms, and mounting attacks. Little thought had been given to Hezbollah's potential responses, including rocket barrages.

Hezbollah was well prepared for a confrontation with Israel, as it had several thousand fighters, antitank missiles, and rockets with ranges from the five- to twelve-mile Katyushas and others of sixty- to one hundred–mile range. It based itself in populated areas, making it harder for Israel to attack without causing civilian deaths. The basic aim was simply to make life as painful for the IDF and Israelis as possible, and survive whatever attacks came. Over the campaign, 4,000 Katyushas were fired, and in such numbers they were more than a nuisance. Although they were inaccurate and most fell harmlessly, about one-fourth of them landed in urban areas and left much of northern Israel shut down for the four weeks of the conflict, with over 300,000 people moving south and another 1 million spending much of the time in shelters. This included an attack on July 16 on Haifa, Israel's third-largest city, in which eight people died. It took a while before the IDF appreciated the detrimental effect the Katyushas were having on civil society. Although the public was generally resilient, there had been no prior preparation for the barrages. By the time Hezbollah's firing positions had been determined, the launchers had been moved. The IDF directed 180,000 artillery shells into the Katyusha zones without making any evident difference to their rate of fire of as many as 100 to 200 per day.

During the thirty-three days of the war, forty-three Israeli and 1,109 Lebanese civilians were killed. The Israelis lost 118 soldiers, almost a third of them during the last three days of the war when, after some delay and while the UN Security Council was already haggling about a cease-fire resolution, they decided to try a land invasion. The Lebanese army lost twenty-eight, and Hezbollah possibly as many as 500 (though here numbers are disputed).

One explanation for the intensity of the Israeli attack was that this seemed an opportune moment to accomplish something that Israeli—and American—policymakers had been longing to do for some time, which was to shatter Hezbollah as an effective military organization, and in the process send a message to Tehran about the dangers of adopting such a brazen attitude with the United States.[4] Incapacitating Hezbollah would remove one of Iran's retaliatory options in the event of its own military confrontation with the United States. If that was the aim, then the experience would have led to the opposite conclusion. The Israelis, however, denied claims that the attack on Hezbollah was an American idea, and the Americans denied that the Israelis had shared their plans with the Americans.

Regardless, the Israeli response was undoubtedly seen initially by the United States in positive terms, and Bush worked hard to ensure its success. A strong anti-Hezbollah line was taken from the start. Most important, the administration resisted putting pressure on Israel for an immediate cease-fire, because it was more important to deal with "root causes." After meeting with Blair at the Group of Eight meeting of leading industrialized countries in Russia, Bush said that the "recent flare-up . . . helps clarify a root cause of instability in the Middle East—and that's Hezbollah and Hezbollah's relationship with Syria, and Hezbollah's relationship to Iran, and Syria's relationship to Iran."[5] He got the G8 to agree to a statement reflecting this position: "The most urgent priority is to create conditions for a cessation of violence that will be sustainable and lay the foundation for a more permanent solution."[6] According to one report, "Israel's crippling of Hezbollah, officials also hope, would complete the work of building a functioning democracy in Lebanon and send a strong message to the Syrian and Iranian backers of Hezbollah."[7] The conflict was, therefore, viewed by Bush as part of the campaign against terrorist attacks "inspired by nation states, like Syria and Iran."

With the developing refugee crisis in Lebanon, concern about civilian casualties, pleas for help from the Lebanese government, and demonstrations in Muslim and Arab countries decrying Israeli atrocities, pressure for a cease-fire grew. At first the Americans insisted that the conditions were not right, which was taken to mean that Israel needed more time to achieve its objectives. This assumed that the Israelis knew what they were doing, and that the net result of the operation would be to strengthen the hand of the Lebanese government vis-à-vis Hezbollah. This gave Israelis more credit than they deserved. Within two days of the war's start Israeli military intelligence was questioning whether the chosen strategy would meet the declared goals, or indeed offered any obvious way of bringing the fighting to a conclusion. On the evening of July 14, having viewed the report, foreign minister Tzipi Livni, who had been impressed by the early levels of international support, voted against the proposed extension of the campaign into south Beirut. The majority of the cabinet decided to stick with Halutz's plan, and a confident, united face was shown to the rest of the world.[8]

The war was Rice's main preoccupation for its duration, as she first worked to delay moves to a cease-fire, since the inevitable failure to get one would undermine the UN's standing, and then tried to get one as the suffering got out of hand without the realization of any of the early strategic benefits sought by Israel and the United States.[9] In one of the more unfortunate remarks of the crisis, because it appeared to sum up a callous disregard for immediate human suffering in pursuit of a dogmatic and unrealistic political vision, Rice was quoted as saying, "What we're seeing here, in a sense, is the . . . birth pangs of a new Middle East and whatever we do we have to be certain that we're pushing forward to the new Middle East not going back to the old one."[10]

In practice this was looking backward rather than forward. Prime Minister Fouad Siniora of Lebanon was demanding an immediate cease-fire. If the Israelis and the Americans were doing the prime minister a good turn by dealing with Hezbollah, that is not how he saw it. "Are we children of a lesser god?" he asked Western foreign ministers meeting in Rome. "Is an Israeli teardrop worth more than a drop of Lebanese blood?" This from a man considered pro-Western whom the United States had been trying to support. Instead of the destruction turning popular opinion against Hezbollah, at least initially the effect was to increase support for Hezbollah. The Americans urged the Israelis to be "mindful of the Siniora government" and not weaken him, lest this undermine the reformist project for Lebanon. But the damage had been done in the first few days of the bombing, and it could only be eased by the end of hostilities. The situation got worse when, on July 30, as they had done ten years earlier, Israelis managed to hit the wrong target in Qana, this time a residential apartment building. Initial reports were that more than fifty civilians, many children, had been killed. The actual death toll at twenty-eight, including sixteen children, was bad enough. Under American pressure, Olmert agreed to suspend air strikes for forty-eight hours, but attempts to broker a cease-fire had been set back.

As the Israeli operation became more costly and difficult than first imagined, Olmert's views about a cease-fire changed. He ended up supporting the French and American initiative to get a cease-fire resolution, although this meant refraining from further expanding the land offensive after it had just got going. UNSC Resolution 1701 was passed on August 11, 2006, and came into effect three days later. The terms involved using a strengthened international force to monitor the cease-fire and prevent the resupply of Hezbollah. This was not the sort of measure that Israel would have taken seriously in the past, and it soon became evident that the international force would have limited powers, as it would be required to notify the Lebanese army of any suspicions so that it could act upon them. By the end of 2006, most of the militia's stocks had been replenished.

In Israel, this felt like a defeat. Former justice Dr. Eliyahu Winograd was asked to investigate what went wrong. His commission's interim report criticized the lack of a detailed military plan based on an understanding of the complexities of the Lebanon arena, the lack of consideration of alternative political and military options, setting goals that were neither clear nor achievable, and lack of adaptability once this was achieved. Blame was assigned to Olmert, Peretz, and Halutz (who was already on his way out).[11] At the same time, Hezbollah's sense of victory was incomplete. It had received a battering, and many Sunni and Christian Lebanese were furious at its recklessness for provoking the war. Simply stated, Hezbollah had been surprised by the ferocity of the Israeli response. After the war, Hassan Nasrallah, Hezbollah's leader, admitted that he has not thought "even 1 percent, that the capture would lead to a war at this time and of this magnitude." If he had known he would not have done it. "Absolutely not."[12] This was one of the few items in the war's accounting that gave Israel some satisfaction.

Syria stayed quiet during the war, anxious not to give Israel any excuse for its extension. Afterward it held victory celebrations and boasted as if the victory had been its own. There was even some talk, which did not last long, of following Hezbollah's example in developing tactics to liberate the Golan Heights. The main benefit it looked to, with Hezbollah, was to undermine the Lebanese government. Siniora, however, had effectively played a difficult position during the war, and he carefully presented the result as a victory for all of Lebanon and not just Hezbollah. Yet on October 31, Nasrallah told the Siniora government that it must agree to a new arrangement giving Hezbollah a veto over all government business or face demonstrations designed to bring his government down. This led in December 2006 to a massive protest that left Siniora and many of his ministers stuck in their offices. The government refused to be cowed, with key members accusing Hezbollah of caring more about Syria and Iran than about Lebanon. This included Druze leader Walid Jumblatt, a fierce opponent of the Americans in 1983 and until recently still fiercely anti-American ("a country of oil and Jews"). By the end of 2007, the issue had moved to the identity of the next president, as Emile Lahoud's term finally concluded. This was to have been the head of the army, General Michel Suleiman. The deadlock persisted into 2008, with Siniora holding his ground. Hezbollah sustained the pressure but was aware that escalating to a civil war would take the shine off its "victory" over Israel.

In the middle of this crisis, Siniora had strengthened his hand by sending the Lebanese army against a group called Fatah al-Islam, based in a Palestinian refugee camp near Tripoli. This was an offshoot of a Syrian-backed Palestinian group based in Lebanon. In May, Fatah al-Islam took up arms against the Lebanese army, but by September 2007, the army had taken control of the camp. The fighting cost 400 lives. The group's leader,

Shaker al-Abssi, was believed to have been an associate of Abu Musab al-Zarqawi, and therefore connected to al Qaeda.

Syria remained caught in a time warp, the last authentic relic of the old nationalist regimes of the 1960s, but with a leader whose only legitimacy was dynastic and who appeared to have given up trying to be the modernizer he had hinted at when succeeding to power. Syria served as a host to Hezbollah, Hamas, and Islamic Jihad and as a transit route both for arms to these groups and for Arabs seeking to join the insurgency in Iraq. Its close relations with Iran left it unpopular with much of the Arab world, but it had not completely abandoned repairing relations with the West or even Israel. Much to Iranian irritation, for Tehran was boycotting the whole enterprise, Syria was represented at the November 2007 Annapolis conference.

There was also, the previous September, a curious but significant episode, in which it appears that a carefully conducted raid by Israel destroyed a nuclear facility being built by North Korea on Syria's behalf. So complete was Syria's embarrassment that it completely obliterated the site before anyone else could come and take a closer look. The Israelis were pleased that they had nipped another nuclear crisis in the bud and also that they had done so in an inconspicuous way and not provoked a fight with Syria. Some in Israel, particularly in the IDF, still hankered after another attempt to work out a deal with Syria over the Golan Heights, to at least complete the trio of old enemies (along with Egypt and Jordan) with whom it had achieved some sort of coexistence and to further its separation from Iran. Pitted against this was the evident American irritation with Syria's behavior in Lebanon. "My patience ran out on President Assad a long time ago," Bush remarked at a press conference. "The reason why is because he houses Hamas, he facilitates Hezbollah, suiciders go from his country into Iraq, and he destabilizes Lebanon."[13] Even if Israelis were inclined to explore a deal with Syria over the Golan Heights, Bush was making better behavior in Iraq and Lebanon a precondition.

*   *   *

If Bush's language was tough on Syria, it was even tougher with regard to Iran, with little basis for engagement with the regime. For an administration that tended to see diplomatic conversations only as a reward for good behavior, Iran's pursuit of nuclear weapons and support of terrorism precluded dialogue.

The administration found it consistently difficult to get the measure of Tehran. Bush depicted it as a "nation held hostage by a small clerical elite that is repressing and isolating its people," but the reality was far more complex.[14] This was not a straightforward autocratic state, for it had pluralistic features, with competing power centers and regular elections, which were relatively free although permitted candidates were strictly controlled and could only come from a narrow theocratic part of the political spectrum. Although the United States had identified Iran as a troublesome country, there was a dearth of expertise within the government, and even that was fragmented. On her arrival at the State Department, Rice was surprised to find that there was no Iran desk. One problem this created was a tendency to focus on Mahmoud Ahmadinejad as the regime's provocative public face. Real power, however, lay in the office of the supreme leader, Ayatollah Ali Khamenei. He took increasing amounts of power from the president's office when it was under Khatami to prevent the reformers from challenging the country's theocratic power. The 150,000 men of the Islamic Revolutionary Guard, always independent of the regular forces, were also kept close to Khamenei. Because he was operating in the same political space as Khamenei, Ahmadinejad had more power than Khatami, including support among the Revolutionary Guards. He could place people in key positions and manage the budget. Less clear was whether he could challenge the vested interests of the elite, which has done well within the current system. One book spoke of the forces he led as Iran's "neoconservatives," who are "ideologically Islamist, revolutionary in character, and populist in application."[15]

The nuclear issue was always going to be difficult. Like so many nuclear programs, Iran's can be traced back to President Eisenhower's atoms for peace initiative of 1957, when civil nuclear reactors were handed out as an incentive to persuade countries not to follow the military route. The United States was Iran's first source of research reactors. The shah had plans to buy eight American reactors for civilian power purposes, though it seems highly likely that he was after a military option. After the revolution, China stepped in to fill the gap and helped construct a research facility at Isfahan. Then, in 1987, Iran made contact with Pakistan's Abdul Qadeer Khan, "father of Pakistan's bomb" and nuclear black marketer in chief. The Russians also appeared relaxed about the transfer of nuclear technology and supported sensitive aspects of the Iranian program. They refrained from selling a complete uranium enrichment plant under pressure from the Clinton administration, but then had second thoughts and began to renew their cooperation.

Support for nuclear power was not the preserve of the conservatives. There was a widespread view that Iran was entitled to nuclear technology not only for energy purposes but also as a means of demonstrating scientific prowess and gaining some international kudos, raising Iran above the rank of ordinary regional powers. This did not necessarily mean that all agreed this should lead to nuclear weapons. The official position remained that there was no such interest. Iran had, however, seen its army attacked by chemical weapons (with an estimated 34,000 casualties) and its cities by Scud missiles during the war with Iraq in the 1980s. Nobody had been ready to speak up on its behalf or come to its assistance. Pakistan tested its weapon in 1998. While this had been its source for much nuclear technology, at the same time this was a Sunni state, increasingly hostile to its Shi'ite population, and the two had backed opposing sides in Afghanistan.

Iran's international problems lay not with making a case for civil nuclear power or regional deterrence but in the fact that its program had moved forward with subterfuge and deception, disregarding obligations under the nonproliferation treaty. If it did acquire a real nuclear capability, then not only might it be emboldened in its foreign policy but it would also lead rival states in the region to start looking to their own nuclear options, causing the nonproliferation regime to further unravel.[16] Thus in 2006, Egypt announced plans to revive a long-abandoned nuclear program, against the background noise of Muslim Brotherhood demands for an Egyptian nuclear deterrent. Algeria, Morocco, and the GCC states, including Saudi Arabia, made similar announcements that year, and soon all these nations were in conversation with the Russians. The next year Jordan expressed its own interest in a nuclear program.[17]

Other than that, there were reasons to try to get closer to Tehran as a large and important state, with borders touching on a number of strategically important regions. Iranians, more than others in the Middle East, showed real sympathy for the United States after 9/11. When fighting the Taliban, there was close cooperation in support of the Northern Alliance in Afghanistan and then in constructing a new government. Jim Dobbins, American representative at the UN talks in Bonn on reconstructing Afghanistan, reported that he "worked closely with the Iranian delegation," crediting its members with the firm commitment to hold elections in Afghanistan and helping persuade the Northern Alliance to accept this. As Dobbins noted, his meetings with the Iranians were not secret, nor did he need to "justify our behavior to skeptical domestic audiences after every encounter."[18] Despite this positive experience, Bush's hostility to Iran was expressed in the 2002 State of the Union address, though Khatami was still in office. The interception of weapons bound for Fatah in January 2002 does seem to have colored Bush's thinking, as well as the misguided notion that Iran was ripe for revolution if only Washington would give it a nudge.

Although the "axis of evil" speech undermined those Iranians who had argued for better relations with the United States, some discussions do appear to have continued in Geneva over 2002 and into 2003, concerning Afghanistan, Iraq, and the nuclear issue, until just after the invasion of Iraq. The Iranians could not help being impressed by the speed with which Iraq was toppled. The Americans had achieved in a short campaign what they had failed to achieve over eight years. Based on "my enemy's enemy is my friend" reasoning, Iran and the United States would be close buddies. The Iranians had helped with Afghanistan, quietly applauded the overthrow of Iraq, and tackled some, if not all, of the al Qaeda types who had sought sanctuary in their country. On May 4, 2003, Iran proposed broad dialogue with the United States, taking in the nuclear program, termination of support to militants in Palestine, and even recognition of Israel. State Department officials wanted to explore further, arguing that the moment was propitious for a grand bargain with Iran and it should be seized. The idea reached the White House where any suggestion of a positive response was killed by the combined hostility of Cheney and Rumsfeld. So ingrained was the animosity to Iran that the administration was not prepared to think in these terms. Talking to Iran was just not the sort of thing they did. The desultory, limited dialogue that had been under way broke down in May 2003 as the two sides traded accusations on terrorism. The United States accused Iran of harboring al Qaeda leaders who had attacked Saudi Arabia, while the Iranians said that the Americans were not doing enough to disarm an Iranian opposition group based in Iraq. As these talks were already controversial in both Tehran and Washington, public disclosure appears to have stopped them.[19]

*   *   *

During 2003 there was one positive example of what talks could achieve. Since the 1970s, Libya had been interested in nuclear weapons and had even tried to buy one on the open market. Its efforts had not gone very far until the nuclear program was revived in the 1990s. This was as much supply- as demand-led, since the network headed by A. Q. Khan made it possible, a "one-stop shop" for countries wishing "to develop a gas centrifuge uranium enrichment program, to procure weapons information or to gain access to supplier contacts."[20] From the late 1990s to late 2002, Libya was provided with fission weapons and a centrifuge enrichment plant, as well as uranium compounds. It was also getting missiles from North Korea. While this was going on, talks were continuing with the British and Americans about terrorism.

After 9/11, which Qadhafi denounced, the talks resumed and made some progress on the terrorism issue. It was always understood that WMD would be the next item on the agenda, if the economic sanctions were ever to be lifted. In August 2002 the British sent a foreign officer minister to Libya and received some indications that Qadhafi was interested in a grand deal. This was followed up by Tony Blair in a letter to the Libyan leader. Bush agreed that renunciation of WMD would allow for normalization of relations. Inevitably this met resistance from administration hawks, who argued that there should also be progress on human rights and democracy. Undersecretary of State John Bolton, who publicly denounced Libya as a rogue state, tried to get involved until Blair vetoed his participation. By early 2003 the deal on Lockerbie was done. Then, in October 2003, a German ship was found at an Italian port with centrifuge technology purchased for Libya through the Khan network. Aware that the game was now up, the Libyans allowed the British and Americans to come to Tripoli to scrutinize everything it had. This confirmed the work on chemical and nuclear (but not biological) weapons, and also made it possible to unravel the A. Q. Khan network. On December 19, 2003, Qadhafi announced that Libya would eliminate its chemical and nuclear weapons programs, declare its activities to the IAEA, and accede to the Chemical Weapons Convention. It then began to do everything it promised.[21]

*   *   *

In his 2004 vice presidential debate with John Edwards, Cheney claimed that "one of the great by-products, for example, of what we did in Iraq and Afghanistan is that five days after we captured Saddam Hussein, Mu'ammar Qadhafi in Libya came forward and announced that he was going to surrender all of his nuclear materials to the United States, which he has done."[22] As we have seen, one thing had nothing to do with the other. The lesson from Libya was more one of patient diplomacy with disagreeable regimes backed by economic sanctions rather than the exemplary impact of force. The interpretation was relevant for the management of the nuclear issue with Iran, which by now was one of the pressing issues on the foreign policy agenda.

It gained urgency after August 2002 when an opposition group, initially discounted because of its Iraqi links, told of uranium enrichment taking place at Isfahan, south of Tehran. Iran acknowledged that it was indeed developing a capability to produce fissile material. The IAEA, which had never remarked on any Iranian malpractice, visited the Natanz site in March 2003 and was astonished by the array of advanced centrifuges it found. The idea that so much and such elaborate deception was undertaken just for civil purposes seemed far-fetched. So as final preparations were being made to attack Iraq, in part because it might revive its defunct nuclear program, Iran was revealed actually to have one.

Washington appeared bereft of options for putting pressure on Iran. Offering economic concessions or high-level contacts in return for treaty compliance would be seen as rewarding a regime with a special place in American demonology. At the same time, the forms of nonmilitary pressure were unconvincing. The United States had limited economic and no diplomatic relations with Iran to break. Military threats lacked credibility so long as Iraq remained volatile and demanding, and the operational options looked unappealing. The dispute was already partly responsible for pushing the price of oil up, and a war, including the possible closure of the Strait of Hormuz, could send the international economy into a tailspin. As a neighbor of both Afghanistan and Iraq, Iran was well-placed to make trouble for the United States and its allies, especially among the Shi'ite population of Iraq, and it might always reignite Hezbollah in Lebanon.

As the enrichment program was stepped up in 2004, taking advantage of their diplomatic and economic relations with Iran, Britain, France, and Germany, known as the EU-3, tried to see what dialogue could achieve. They acquired promises of good behavior from Iran, including the suspension of its enrichment facilities. Whatever the doubts the Americans had about the credibility of European diplomacy, they did not attempt to block them for want of anything better. At least if frustrated by Tehran, they were more likely to give support in the Security Council, although the problem there was that China and Russia showed little inclination to be helpful. There was a potential breakthrough in 2005, when it was assumed that Hashemi Rafsanjani would return to power in the presidential election. Although hardly a liberal democrat, he was sufficiently cynical and experienced to do business. The EU-3 held back on further concessions until the elections. Then to general consternation Ahmadinejad won. The proposals were made to him and were promptly rejected. He ended the suspension of enrichment and made it clear that any discussions would go back to square one. The Russians showed no inclination to fall in behind the Americans. They had a big stake in Iran and a pivotal role on the Security Council. They offered their own deal, also rejected, promising to enrich uranium for the Iranians.

The Iranian president's inflammatory language and defiant behavior appeared to rule out compromise. The IAEA condemned Iranian conduct and passed the issue to the Security Council, which even moved to nonpunitive sanctions. In Iran, Ahmadinejad used this effectively to shore up support among nationalists, as establishment figures urged prudence and caution. On May 8, 2006, Ahmadinejad wrote a long, rambling letter to Bush, which included a request for direct talks on its nuclear program. This was a sort of opening, especially as the president was given explicit backing by Khamenei. Initially the administration dismissed the letter as a tactical move but was already considering its own offer. The Europeans had been arguing that without some effort to engage Iran in a dialogue, a strong Security Council resolution would be harder to obtain. Rice decided to ask Bush to allow talks with Tehran.

At the end of May, therefore, Rice offered the Iranian regime the choice of either staying on its current path of acquiring nuclear weapons, leading to greater international isolation and a variety of sanctions, or seeking to resolve the nuclear issue by suspending, as it had done before, all enrichment-related and reprocessing activities, and cooperating with the IAEA. Once this was done, she promised, "the United States will come to the table with our EU-3 colleagues and meet with Iran's representatives." This could lead to "a beneficial relationship of increased contacts in education and cultural exchange, in sports, in travel, in trade and in investment." A really improved relationship would require that something be done about Iran's support for terror in Iraq and Lebanon. She also made it clear that "we are not in a position to talk about full diplomatic relations with a state with which we have so many fundamental differences."[23] Within the administration this was clearly a big deal and something of a policy shift. The Europeans were also pleased that the administration was opting for a diplomatic approach.[24] Iran saw no reason why it should give up enrichment for the sake of a conversation, when it was already talking to everybody else, and when recent experience suggested that if it showed patience, a better offer would soon be on the table. Nothing came of the initiative. In the summer of 2006, the Security Council ordered Iran to stop, but it carried on, disregarding subsequent resolutions in December 2006 and March 2007.

Indeed, Ahmadinejad gave every impression of enjoying the crisis far more than Bush. He faced increasing unpopularity at home because of his economic mismanagement, inability to deal with corruption, and eccentric style, and U.S. pressure allowed him to consolidate his political base. He regularly provided updates on the progress of the thousands of centrifuges installed at the Natanz underground enrichment plant. The assumption was that once it was able to run 3,000 centrifuges at sufficiently high speeds for a year, it would have enough fuel for its first bomb.

*   *   *

If there was a time Iran thought it might have the administration on the run, that was at the end of 2006. The administration was clearly rattled by the Democratic victories in Congress and the deteriorating situation in Iraq. Coupled with the events in Lebanon, U.S. allies in the region were anxious about pressures for withdrawal from Iraq, worried that a more general fatigue might hinder responses to other crises and fearful that Iran was getting the upper hand. Iran seemed the only country in the region with any confidence and energy. Egypt, which under Nasser had set itself up as the natural leader of the Middle East, was content to keep clear of trouble—it had, for example, done nothing about the upheavals in its neighbor, Sudan. With the Muslim Brotherhood making a strong showing in domestic politics, but the economy dependent upon American assistance, a bold foreign policy was precluded. King Abdullah in Jordan was well respected in the West, but his country was weak and poor. Iraq lacked any credible central government and Syria was semidetached. The United States decided to demonstrate to Iran that it should take care before throwing its weight around. Two carrier battle groups were stationed in the Middle East, as a reminder of America's military clout and the importance attached to keeping open the Strait of Hormuz. This effort was also said to include "funding sectarian political movements and paramilitary groups in Iraq, Iran, Lebanon, and the Palestinian territories," at a cost of more than $300 million, paid for by Saudi Arabia and other Gulf states.[25]

At the end of February 2007, the United States agreed to talk with Iran and Syria about Iraq. The reversal of policy was made possible because the government of Iraq had issued invitations to its neighbors, including Iran and Syria, as well as to the United States and Britain, to see what could be done to stabilize the country. Instead of this bringing the sides closer together on this issue, at least they started to move further apart, mainly as evidence came in of significant support to the Shi'ite militias, possibly in preparation for a civil war with the Sunnis but also to keep the Americans under pressure. In a speech to the American Legion in late August, Bush sharply criticized Iran for its activities in Iraq as much as for its nuclear program:

> Shia extremists, backed by Iran, are training Iraqis to carry out attacks on our forces and the Iraqi people. Members of the Qods Force of Iran's Islamic Revolutionary Guard Corps are supplying extremist groups with funding and weapons, including sophisticated IEDs. And with the assistance of Hezbollah, they've provided training for these violent forces inside of Iraq.

As evidence, Bush cited the discovery of rockets manufactured in Iran: "I have authorized our military commanders in Iraq to confront Tehran's murderous activities."[26] In his September report to Congress, General Petraeus observed, "None of us, earlier this year, appreciated the extent of Iranian involvement in Iraq, something about which we and Iraq's leaders all now have greater concern." This included not only weaponry, but a faction of the Revolutionary Guards was trying to create a "Hezbollah-like force to serve its interests."[27]

On May 10, just a week after Rice had spoken with the Iranian foreign minister, Cheney, who remained the administration's most senior hawk, stood on one of the U.S. aircraft carriers patrolling the Gulf and sent an uncompromising message to "friends and adversaries alike":

> We'll keep the sea lanes open. We'll stand with our friends in opposing extremism and strategic threats. We'll disrupt attacks on our own forces. We'll continue bringing relief to those who suffer, and delivering justice to the enemies of freedom. And we'll stand with others to prevent Iran from gaining nuclear weapons and dominating this region.[28]

According to Seymour Hersh, the White House, pushed by Cheney, requested that the Joint Chiefs of Staff redraw plans for attacking Iran. Instead of previous plans to attack Iran's known and suspected nuclear facilities as well as other military sites, there was a shift of focus to strikes against Revolutionary Guard Corps facilities in Tehran. Hersh noted, "What had been presented primarily as a counter-proliferation mission has been reconceived as counter-terrorism."[29] Any sort of military action was problematic. Iran was of course well aware of what Israel had done to Iraq in 1981. The relevant facilities were hidden and buried. It would be hard to take out key sites with any confidence except with many sorties over a number of days, and there would still be residual uncertainty. Regular suggestions that Israel would do the job if the U.S. would not played down the limits on the number and range of Israeli aircraft. The administration began with a credibility problem as a result of the stories told about Iraq's WMD program in the buildup to the 2003 war. This would affect any claims about Iranian nuclear programs, especially as the worst-case estimates put an actual weapons capability at some years away. There was also little public or congressional appetite for another war.

But while the military option was unappealing, there were plans to step up the pressure on Iran, and in particular the Revolutionary Guard, by using economic sanctions. These would be directed against Iran's Islamic Revolutionary Guard Corps and Defense Ministry. Essentially, European and Asian banks and companies were being told that if they dealt with Iran, they would be putting at risk their ability to operate in the United States. Iran was vulnerable to economic pressures. Its population was too large to be subsidized by the oil price alone, especially as underinvestment meant that it had to import refined products that were then sold to the population, as with much else, at highly subsidized prices. Investors were wary of dealing with Tehran without any official guidance.

It took until October before the sanctions were ready to be announced. By this time the issue had changed again. The tough stance taken by Bush on the issue, combined with the fact that the governing party in Baghdad was actually close to Iran, got Iran to agree to rein in the militias, and the situation was defused. The focus began to return again to the nuclear issue and the Iranian arming of groups such as Hezbollah and Hamas. But neither Russia nor China was showing any interest in turning the screw on Tehran. If anything, their trade was increasing. Then Ahmadinejad forced the resignation of Ali Larijani as chief negotiator on the nuclear issue, who was considered a relative moderate (with "relative" here the operative term) and one of the president's rivals. As is often the case, this did not mean expulsion from the Iranian power structure but just a requirement to move and find another place within it. At first sight, however, this appeared to be a deliberate signal of declining Iranian interest in any sort of compromise. When European negotiators met with the new Iranian team in late November, they insisted that negotiations had to start all over again, and no past proposals, including those from Larijani, had any standing.[30]

In practice, this meant that if there was going to be any pressure on the issue it was going to have to come from a call by the head of the IAEA, Mohamed ElBaradei, a man who had clashed with the administration in the run-up to the Iraq war and who generally took the view, despite Ahmadinejad's boasting, that it was not particularly proficient in its nuclear endeavors. He did not expect a nuclear military capability until well into the next decade. Iran's strategic aim was to become more of a "virtual nuclear weapons state," with the requisite capabilities to produce a bomb on short notice, but without actually going so far as construction or testing.[31] Notably, when Bush was asked in October if he "definitively" believed that "Iran wants to build a nuclear weapon," he did not reply directly, but spoke of Iran wanting the "capacity, the knowledge, in order to make a nuclear weapon." He then went on to more chilling imagery: "I've told people that if you're interested in avoiding World War III, it seems like you ought to be interested in preventing them from having the knowledge necessary to make a nuclear weapon."[32]

Then, in December 2007, the whole Iran issue was turned on its head by the publication of a new National Intelligence Etimate report on Iran's nuclear intentions and capabilities, which the president knew about when making his earlier remarks. The analysis was complex and nuanced, but the headline was clear enough: "In fall 2003, Tehran halted its nuclear weapons program." Although there was no certainty that this was still the case, there was "moderate confidence" that it was.[33] The last published estimate two years earlier had supported the gloomier view of Iranian intentions. That had been based on attempted weapons design found on a laptop stolen in 2004. The new estimate was based on an Iraqi engineer's notes from the summer of 2007, referring to a late 2003 decision to end a complex engineering effort to design nuclear weapons. This information was considered sufficiently startling for corroborative evidence to be sought and found, including some intercepted communications. They were repeatedly checked to see whether the information was planted or out-of-date.[34] There was a "vivid exchange" when senior members of the government were briefed. As the estimate would have to go to Congress and was therefore bound to be leaked, the administration had better take the initiative.

The new judgment was relevant only to those aspects of the program geared to the actual production of nuclear weapons, and here of course the suggested time for a change of heart was during the previous Iranian government, at a time when the United States seemed likely to strike down any regime guilty of nonproliferation. There was always a risk with pursuing something so at odds with Iran's declared position and which might be discovered. This aspect of the program could also be postponed, until the nuclear fuel cycle had been mastered. The new estimate did not change assessments of the main bone of contention with Iran, which was its efforts at uranium enrichment and represented the most important condition for any military program. The administration could argue that there was no reason for any less concern in this regard. The caveats aside, it was hard to avoid the conclusion that "rarely, if ever, has a single intelligence report so completely, so suddenly, and so surprisingly altered a foreign policy debate."[35]

Allies were astonished. The Israelis were particularly furious because it did not accord with their own assessments that the Iranians were pressing ahead with a military capability. The Europeans were nonplussed, not so much because they disagreed on the headline issue but because that missed the point of the enrichment technology, where neither the U.S. estimate nor theirs gave any encouragement. In the Arab world, the suspicion was that the administration released the estimate precisely to ease the crisis with Iran because of the more positive situation in Iraq. The Arab states were already hedging their bets. Ahmadinejad was asked to speak before the Gulf Cooperation Council, which was originally established to counter Iranian influence, and Saudi king Abdullah invited him to visit Mecca for the haj religious pilgrimage. There was also talk of resuming diplomatic relations with Egypt. A senior official acknowledged that Middle Eastern governments were "confused" by the NIE. "No Arab regime understands why the United States would publish an intelligence estimate."[36]

Bush was reluctant to let the issue pass; when he toured the Middle East in January 2008, he was still urging unity in the face of the Iranian threat. Ironically, if anything, the relaxation of tension was as much a problem for Ahmadinejad as for Bush. It meant that Iranians started to worry more about their domestic problems. For some time the president had been under fire for his eccentric behavior and haphazard management style. Iran suffered from chronic underinvestment, especially in its oil industry, which meant that it actually had to import 40 percent of its gasoline. Oil income was being used to keep gas prices low for ordinary people and subsidize employment, but the net result was to fuel the black economy.[37] Khamenei was becoming more critical, and the president's rivals were gathering. The normal assumption was that Iran was enjoying its strongest position for two decades. The United States had helpfully dealt blows to its regional enemies, supported its local friends, while its own standing and Israel's had been undermined by foolhardy military adventures. This did not mean, however, that it was invulnerable. With a large and growing population and a mismanaged economy, there was a question as to whether it could take advantage of whatever opportunities the new situation offered, before the Americans managed to regain their strength.

* * *

In July 2007, another NIE was published that could be taken as a commentary on a central pillar of the Bush administration's policy, this time the need to prevent another terrorist spectacular in the U.S. homeland. Here the headline was that "the U.S. Homeland will face a persistent and evolving terrorist threat over the next three years." The main risk was Islamist groups, notably al Qaeda, whose urge to attack the United States was "undiminished." The good news was that measures taken since 9/11 had made the United States a much harder target, intended attacks had been disrupted, and barely a handful of individuals with al Qaeda links had been found, so that within the United States the "internal Muslim terrorist threat is not likely to be as severe as it is in Europe." So why an estimate that suggested little security gain since 2001? The bad news was that al Qaeda's leadership had survived in Pakistan's tribal areas, and that this group, already "proficient with conventional small arms and improvised explosive devices," was also still trying "to acquire and employ chemical, biological, radiological, or nuclear material in attacks." There was also now a need to worry about "Lebanese Hizballah, which has conducted anti-U.S. attacks outside the United States in the past, [and] may be more likely to consider attacking the Homeland over the next three years if it perceives the United States as posing a direct threat to the group or Iran."[38]

Much of the caution might be attributed to the natural prudence of people who do not want to be accused of complacency in the postmortems following another major terrorist incident. In addition, outside the United States the trends were adverse. This was the message of yet another NIE of the previous year, which drew attention to the spread of the "global jihadist movement" and its ability to adapt to counterterrorism efforts. Particularly embarrassing was the observation that "the Iraq jihad is shaping a new generation of terrorist leaders and operatives." The Iraq conflict had "become the cause célèbre for jihadists, breeding a deep resentment of U.S. involvement in the Muslim world and cultivating supporters for the global jihadist movement." The underlying factors fueling the spread of the movement outweighed its vulnerabilities. In addition to Iraq, these factors were "entrenched grievances, such as corruption, injustice, and fear of Western domination, leading to anger, humiliation, and a sense of powerlessness; the slow pace of real and sustained economic, social, and political reforms in many Muslim majority nations"; and "pervasive anti-U.S. sentiment among most Muslims, all of which jihadists exploit."[39]

If the measure of the problem was in the support and membership of radical Islamist movements around the world, weakening of "social and religious inhibitions" in the Muslim world on violence, the number of terrorist incidents, and the extent to which "local and global grievances are merging into a pervasive hatred of the United States, its allies, and the international order they uphold," then, according to two prominent American analysts in 2005, "We are losing."[40] A number of surveys of Arab opinion regarding the United States made for grim reading, with massive majorities having an unfavorable view of the United States, for which its foreign policy was largely to blame.[41] In addition, there was no doubt that Islamist groups had gained ground in many countries, including in Western Europe.

Bin Laden's survival and his ability to keep himself in the spotlight, after everything the United States had thrown against his organization, was an achievement. Prior to 9/11 he was largely unknown. After 9/11, instead of being crushed as his comrades were hunted down, he acquired international celebrity status. He became a positive role model for many young Muslims and inspired those ready to emulate his violent form of jihad. What is much harder to judge is whether he thought he was winning his war with the United States.

Bin Laden expected an American onslaught in Afghanistan after 9/11, which would provide a helpful opportunity to demonstrate crusader viciousness toward Muslim people, but he did not expect to lose. The succession of retreats in late 2001 undermined morale, as his men regretted being drawn into an unequal fight. The many Islamists who had never bought into bin Laden's "far enemy" thesis wrote scathingly of how he managed to lose two Muslim states to the Americans, and that his extremism meant that opportunities were missed out for deals with local regimes that might create conditions by which Islamist ideals could advance more peacefully. None would speak up for American foreign policy, but many questioned the wisdom of attacking American civilians, let alone Muslims. Even Hassan al-Turabi, bin Laden's former host in Sudan, writing from his prison cell in Khartoum, observed that "intelligent mujahideen must exercise restraint and refrain from initiating war and must limit operations to military, not civilian, targets."[42] From Egyptian prisons a number of Zawahiri's former associates published works renouncing their previous militancy, questioning the Islamic basis of attacks on civilians, and criticizing those who allowed armed struggle to become an end rather than a means to an end.[43]

It would now be harder to organize spectacular attacks or exercise central control over activities undertaken in al Qaeda's name. The name itself was now a global brand that resonated with angry and disaffected Muslims. The movement could grow and develop almost spontaneously, without any central effort. In addition, because they survived, bin Laden and Zawahiri could continue to offer political direction. They managed to both hide from the Americans and keep themselves in the public eye at the same time. Their regular pronouncements on world events, albeit delivered with some delay, urged action against the crusaders and Zionists and occasionally offered deals to the West to spare it further hurt by leaving Iraq and generally changing its foreign policy.

They became regular features in the new Arab media outlets, particularly Al Jazeera, which ensured a large audience. The Internet was clearly a boon. Bin Laden had always grasped the importance of modern communications and self-projection. Even in antimodernist Afghanistan, which banned television, al Qaeda had used commercial satellite telephones and produced propaganda videos with handheld cameras. After 9/11, the Internet was used to build, indoctrinate, and inspire support, and even to pass on operational knowledge. Instead of the training camps in Afghanistan, militants could learn about how to wage jihad in anonymous cybercafés, following message boards; taking instruction in bomb making, sniping, and how to move across international borders; or even watching snuff videos from Iraq. At the time of the 9/11 attacks, one source had identified twelve jihadist Web sites; four years later, the figure was 4,500. By 2008 it had doubled again. They represented a virtual "community of belief" or "one big *madrassa*."[44]

On the other hand, the actual achievements of al Qaeda over this period were limited. They had done moderately well, if success is measured by regular and deadly bomb blasts at disparate sites around the world. Every explosion in a crowded venue could be proclaimed a great victory, but unless they started to have a tangible political effect, they risked appearing not just cruel but also futile. The occasional big hits, including Madrid in 2004 and London in 2005, were not followed up and turned into sustained campaigns of the sort Israel faced with the intifada or Iraq with the insurgency.

Having set the threshold for a terrorist spectacle so high with 9/11, it was almost anticlimactic that they had managed no equivalent feat in the six years since. The thought that they must be trying for a repeat performance kept counterterrorist agencies around the world anxious and alert, with a special worry that they might just achieve the peak of terrorist achievement by getting hold of a nuclear device, or something almost as nasty, and detonate it in a capital city. At a more routine level, in countries where there was no known threat, the prospect of a small cell of dedicated militants taking advantage of an open society tied down considerable resources. In all countries citizens faced regular and tedious security checks, especially when entering aircraft and public buildings. Challenging debates were generated on the balance between civil liberties and public safety. But this did not result in bringing a single society closer to Sharia law or bringing forward the return of the caliphate (which had died with the Ottoman Empire). As in the 1990s, campaigns caused irritation and alarm among those they were supposed to impress and gave the authorities an excuse to clamp down hard on oppositionists. Bin Laden's attempts to present himself as a figure to be reckoned with in contemporary international affairs, with whom governments would have to deal, were ignored. His continued ability to operate was an evident embarrassment to Bush, who had sought to capture him "dead or alive," and in many parts of the Muslim world his exploits were viewed favorably, but he could not create a political movement of real consequence. Instead, the brand was picked up by new leaders in key arenas of conflict. Their isolation and the loss of so many top lieutenants in Afghanistan and the immediate aftermath, which saw over two-thirds of the leadership captured or killed, meant that their control over these new groupings was limited. For a global movement, it was starting to develop distinctive regional branches.

The most important example of the problems this caused was with Zarqawi in Iraq. He set up al Qaeda in Iraq and claimed, after some negotiations, loyalty to bin Laden, but he showed no inclination to follow his strategic precepts. For their part, bin Laden and Zawahiri dared not disown Zarqawi, the man who was leading the most successful and prominent of all the campaigns against the crusaders. He was also getting the new recruits. Rather than trudge to the Pakistan frontier, young Arab idealists found it much easier to get to Iraq, where there seemed to be many opportunities for an aspiring jihadist. But Zarqawi was in many respects a disaster for al Qaeda. He encouraged the view that it was an organization at war with the Shia and overreached himself, as such leaders so often do, in the people and places he chose to attack. Particularly damning was the November 2005 attack on hotels in Jordan, followed by the compelling television interview of a captured woman wearing traditional garb and a suicide belt confirming the Zarqawi link.[45]

There were similar problems in Saudi Arabia, where Abd al-Aziz al-Muqrin fought under the banner of "al Qaeda of the Arabian Peninsula" (QAP).[46] The Saudi regime was associated with both the development of the ideological climate that nurtured al Qaeda and its alliance with the Americans. Although American forces left Saudi Arabia soon after the Iraq war, the American connection was not broken. As the insurgency took root, more Saudis than any other nationality made their way to Iraq to wage jihad, yet Muqrin saw no point in this, insisting that his task was first to expel the crusaders and Zionists from the peninsula. This went against bin Laden's "far enemy" doctrine, by which the Americans were the first priority, especially now that they had also conveniently placed themselves near at hand in Iraq. This led to an intensive debate, between those who argued that the royal family did not deserve to be spared and others who feared the backlash once attacks led to the deaths of ordinary Muslims.

Until 2003, there was occasional violence in Saudi Arabia directed against Westerners. In March that year, a Saudi blew himself up while engaged in bomb manufacture, and this alerted police to the developing threat. Over the following months and across the country, the police cracked down on cells and uncovered arms caches as car bombs exploded, most notably in May, when three were driven into a residential compound in Riyadh, mainly housing Westerners, killing twenty-six people and nine bombers. In November an attack on another residential compound in Riyadh killed seventeen and wounded more than one hundred. This time the victims were largely Muslim workers. Public opinion, as well as important Islamist sympathizers in the security forces, now turned against QAP. Most importantly, the regime pressured the country's more radical clerics to denounce QAP and keep their distance from extremists. It was one thing to direct hatred and action outside the kingdom, but quite another to be supporting it within. They got the message. After a car bomb struck a police building in April 2004, causing five deaths and many injuries, outraging public opinion even more,

Muqrin stressed the importance of concentrating on "Jews, Americans, and Crusaders in general." That led to an audacious attack at the end of May, when four militants entered the Oasis compound in Khobar and took fifty hostages. They let the Muslims go and kept the others. When Saudi forces stormed the building, three escaped in a car with some hostages. Although forty-one hostages were freed, twenty-two were killed, including nineteen foreigners, and the escape created suspicions of collusion between Islamists and some members of the Saudi forces. Foreigners started to leave the country, and security for those remaining was stepped up. The next month Muqrin and his senior commanders were killed. QAP regrouped and in December attacked first an American site and then the Interior Ministry, bravely but ineptly. Those involved were killed and, with them, QAP as an effective force. The experience of being on the receiving end had encouraged the Saudi elite to look hard at the role of some of the country's more fiery preachers and the financial resources getting to militant Islamists in the guise of charitable donations. It improved cooperation with the Americans on intelligence sharing and training. The Americans publicly praised the Saudis.[47] This was not the result for which bin Laden hoped.

Another group reflecting al Qaeda's struggle to establish itself as a credible political organization was "al Qaeda in the Islamic Maghreb." At its core was the Algerian Salafist Group for Preaching and Combat (GSPC). This emerged out of the wreckage of the old Group Islamique Armé (GIA), which caused such mayhem in Algeria during the 1990s. GSPC disowned GIA's massacres of civilians, but at the same time did not accept the government's 1999 offer of amnesty for former Islamist fighters. Links with al Qaeda were established in late 2001, with the aim of encouraging it away from a purely national focus to a more international perspective. It kept itself going with the ransom it received from kidnapping foreigners, but its isolation from the international Islamist networks limited its activities. At the height of the conflict in the 1990s, there had been as many as 40,000 fighting the government. The numbers were now down to at most just over 1,000, after some 500 had been killed or captured and another 250 had taken up an amnesty offer.[48]

In 2006 Zawahiri brokered a deal to bring together GSPC with other local Salafist groups and establish links with other North African organizations to form the new al Qaeda branch. Zawahiri announced a "blessed union" on September 11, 2006, with the United States and France named as the main enemies. The group also sent some fighters to Iraq to show internationalist spirit. After the past successes of Algerian counterterrorism agencies, the advantage in the broader grouping would be to provide a wider base and space in which to operate. Zawahiri's direct involvement may also have held it to mainstream al Qaeda thinking. It could potentially be the base for attacks into France and the United Kingdom. From late 2006 it began to put car bombs in sensitive areas, including one by the prime minister's office, as well as police stations. In December 2006 a suicide bomb caused carnage around a UN building in Algiers, the sort of target that would appeal to al Qaeda. The occasional and symbolic nature of the attacks indicated that this was a group more geared to making a media impact than mounting a proper insurgency.

For Zawahiri, this new group was still a work in progress and not his main priority. At the end of 2006, he published a long and at times despairing analysis, bemoaning attempts to deal with crusaders and Zionists rather than fight them: "Resistance is a must, and this resistance can be nothing but a popular one at the hands of the Muslim Ummah, because the governments are treasonous and many of the organizations have fallen into the swamp of impotence and going after scraps of the booty." He identified a number of areas of conflict, including Somalia, Algeria, Palestine, and Chechnya, all of which had been on the list for some time as potentially productive areas for Islamists. He still, however, singled out two for special mention: Iraq and Afghanistan. "I repeat what I mentioned previously: the backing of the Jihad in Afghanistan and Iraq today is to back the most important battlefield in which the Crusade against Islam and Muslims is in progress."[49] By this time Zarqawi was dead and al Qaeda in Iraq was in a developing confrontation with local Sunni leaders. The main arena of struggle was returning once again to Afghanistan.

* * *

From the moment the Taliban was defeated in Afghanistan in 2001, difficulties were created by establishing bold designs for the future of the country without the armed forces to make it possible.[50] In addition, the Taliban's defeat involved its members returning to Afghan society rather than being completely eliminated, while the victory of the Northern Alliance allowed for a return to warlordism. One of the major complaints against the launching of the Iraq war was that it left these problems in Afghanistan festering and unattended, until the United States and its allies belatedly recognized their seriousness.

In early May 2003, Donald Rumsfeld suggested that the war in Afghanistan was in a "cleanup" phase, while the army view remained that the basic purposes of the Afghan mission, in terms of destroying "al Qaeda, its Taliban shield and support structure, and the prevention of the territory's use as a sanctuary for continued al Qaeda operations" had been successful.[51] Yet Jim

Dobbins, who had been responsible for the original nation-building exercise in 2001, expressed his concerns: "Low initial input of money and troops yields low output of security, democratization, and economic growth."[52] By this time there were 14,000 U.S. and international troops in Afghanistan, but their command was split between the international stabilization force in Kabul and U.S. forces still searching for remnants of al Qaeda. In October, the international force was authorized to deploy outside of Kabul, and in November it was put under NATO command. But there were still not enough troops to bring stability.

By 2006, there were indications that all was not well in Afghanistan, with American and NATO casualties starting to rise. In the first five months of 2006, there was a 200 percent increase in insurgent attacks, compared to the first five months of 2005. The Taliban was back in the south, while Hamid Karzai's government suffered from corruption and its need to work with local warlords outside of Kabul. Drug trafficking was as bad as ever. In July 2006, Robert Kaplan warned that the "coalition finds itself, like its Soviet predecessors, in control of major cities and towns, very weak in the villages, and besieged by a shadowy insurgency that uses Pakistan as its rear base."[53] It was by now clear that both al Qaeda and the Taliban were working out of Pakistan and that the government of General Musharraf was either unwilling or unable to do much about it.

By the end of the year, NATO forces were facing a serious Taliban challenge in southern Afghanistan, particularly in Helmand Province. People had fled their homes. Tribal leaders dithered about whether to try to make peace with the Taliban, which showed itself to be brutal with opponents, or try to work with a distant government that seemed insensitive to their needs. The alliance asked for more troops in September, getting a lukewarm response except from the British, Canadians, and Dutch, who were taking the brunt of the fighting in Helmand. At the start of 2007, there was a warning that "Afghanistan today is in danger of capsizing into a perfect storm of insurgency, terrorism, narcotics, and warlords. Benign neglect by the United States since spring 2003 has brought Afghanistan back to the brink of state failure. Washington has shortchanged Afghanistan in both personnel and resources."[54] During the course of 2007, the position was stabilized as NATO troops were able to use superior equipment and training to hold back the Taliban and prevent its overrunning Helmand. There were claims that as many as 3,000 alleged Talibs were killed while NATO lost 200 men. The American and British strategy was to concentrate on taking out the Taliban military leadership, on the grounds that there was evidently no shortage of Taliban recruits but experienced commanders were in shorter supply, while also seeking out those among the Taliban who were prepared to be bought off. It was also necessary to show restraint in regard to the opium crop, as its destruction would earn recruits for the Taliban. With a shortfall of 7,500 troops hampering NATO's efforts and Europeans unwilling to provide them, Bush announced in January 2008 a "one-time" deployment of 3,200 marines for the start of the spring fighting season. NATO's military effort remained overstretched and depended on political action to turn the situation around.

*　　*　　*

By the end of the year, there was a further complication with the development of a deep crisis in Pakistan. For the United States this was alarming, given its investment, both political and economic, in President Musharraf. His skill lay in doing enough to keep Washington content without giving the impression at home of capitulating to American demands. The Americans had gone along with this, giving him the benefit of the doubt in order to be able to confirm that all was well with the U.S.-Pakistani alliance. The first major test came with the evidence of the role the A. Q. Khan network played in providing nuclear technology and materials to both Libya and Iran. Musharraf could not deny the evidence or say that illicit nuclear trade was a good thing. Undertaken with the full knowledge and connivance of officials since the 1980s, it was presented as free enterprise by one man. Khan agreed to take the blame but not severe punishment, and he made a public apology in February 2004. As Pakistan was still on the front line in the war on terror and there was no obvious alternative to Musharraf, Western countries accepted the Pakistani story as if true. For the same reasons, they had not made too much fuss in 2002, when he extended his unelected presidency by five years.

They also wanted to believe him when he declared in 2002 that Pakistanis were "weary and tired of the Kalashnikov culture" and that it was time to end religious intolerance. There were reasons to believe him. The country was awash with illegal weapons. The presumption that violence was the preferred form of political discourse was becoming deep-rooted and regularly leading to trouble. In December 2001, a terrorist attack on the Indian Parliament had led to a major crisis, as India demanded a crack down on Kashmiri militants. Then there were a number of assassination attempts against Musharraf, including from radicals within the military, for his treachery in siding with the Americans.

His difficulty lay in deciding just how tough he dared to be with the Islamic groups, fortified by the many al Qaeda and Taliban fighters who had come over the border into the tribal areas from Afghanistan in late 2001. Sections of the military and ISI remained sympathetic to the Islamists. They had trained and worked with them in the past, and they shared much of their ideology. There was a pragmatic element to this as well. Senior officers assumed that eventually the Americans would give up on Afghanistan. It would be foolish to abandon old associates for expedient reasons, when they might well be useful in future struggles.

The tribal areas had never been properly under central control and offered fertile ground for the spread of Taliban philosophy. This became apparent in Waziristan, which was soon being run by Islamists, observed passively by the military. Sharia law was compulsory, with barbers, bands, and DVDs all prohibited and women fully covered. Over 2004–2005, with Islamabad at an apparent loss over what to do, the army signed a variety of agreements that ended up confining soldiers to barracks. A sanctuary was therefore provided for Taliban fighters, as well as al Qaeda, from which operations in Afghanistan could be launched. This explains the upsurge in the fighting from 2005 to 2006. But it also began to spread farther into Pakistan itself, with suicide bombers starting to hit the major cities.

Musharraf claimed to be ready to take the fight to the Islamists. There was a turning point in July 2007, when Pakistani forces stormed the Red Mosque in Islamabad where militants had armed themselves in a large compound close to ISI headquarters.[55] In the short term the biggest problem was that the Islamists were taking the fight to the military, which was not coping well. It was better prepared for fighting the Indians over Kashmir than for a substantial insurgency, with the familiar problems of deploying on too large a scale, relying too much on intense firepower and insensitive cordon-and-search tactics. These led to violent local responses. Even if there was a way of directly intervening in the tribal area without inflaming the situation, the Americans lacked spare capability and the local knowledge to help. Airpower might be provided to support the Pakistani army if it was prepared to venture into the most dangerous areas and if it could identify targets with sufficient accuracy, sufficiently away from civilian areas, to attack.[56] In an attempt to draw lessons from Iraq, ways were sought of working with local tribal leaders—who had seen their power erode and in a number of cases had been killed—to try to empower them to use their local supporters to confront the Islamists.[57] This would be extremely difficult in the heart of the tribal areas where central government and the Americans were viewed as the most serious threats.

In late 2007 Musharraf seemed to be more concerned with protecting his own political future than with taking on the militants. He tried to organize his own transformation from a military imposition into an elected civilian by stepping down as head of the army. The Supreme Court's doubts about the legality of this process led in November to a declaration of a state of emergency, just after Condoleezza Rice had implored him not to do so. This meant that for a few weeks his main enemies appeared to be judges and lawyers.[58] He also tried to limit the political competition by keeping out Nawaz Sharif, the former prime minister he had deposed, until the Saudis insisted that he be allowed back as an alternative to the more secular Benazir Bhutto. Bhutto, secular and anti-Islamist, was the preferred candidate of the United States. The hope was that she would team up with Musharraf to help him achieve greater legitimacy. Until the state of emergency she seemed to be ready to do so. Unfortunately, having survived one assassination attempt when she returned to Pakistan in October, she was caught by a second in December, adding to the turmoil in the local politics. Musharraf, possibly correctly, blamed Baitullah Mehsud, a Taliban warlord and head of a coalition of militias called Tehrik-e-Taliban, for Bhutto's murder. Even if true, Bhutto's supporters were disinclined to believe him. The regime was therefore facing crises of legitimacy and subversion. There was no majority support for the Islamists but growing uncertainty. After presiding over a strong economy and relative stability, balancing the need to respond to international concerns and retain a modicum of domestic consensus, Musharraf put his accomplishments at risk through his efforts to preserve his own position.

The trust American policymakers had placed in Musharraf in 2001 was not unreasonable in the circumstances of the time. Pakistani support was vital to the campaign against al Qaeda and Musharraf was the man in charge. But his readiness to take on Islamists was always qualified. In the event he had done enough to make the Islamists angry with him but not enough to squash them. As a result Pakistan was reaping at home what it had sowed for almost three decades in Afghanistan. Musharraf was now damaged goods, and after a series of political misjudgments, was on the way out. When elections eventually took place in February 2008, his party was defeated heavily. There would be another chance to see if democracy could be allowed to work in Pakistan without a constant risk of a military coup. The new government would need to work out its own approach to the extreme Islamists, including how much to cooperate with the Americans in their pursuit. For the United States, and the West more generally, the stakes were much higher. Pakistan was the base not only of the Taliban but those being instructed on how to mount terrorist attacks in the West. Then there was the nagging anxiety that this was a nuclear weapons state. There were many reassurances that the nuclear program was organized in such a way that neither bombs nor their components could easily be seized, but it was hard to avoid the thought that if the nightmare of a nuclear device in the hands of Islamist extremists ever became a reality, this is where it would start.

22

FRIENDS AND ENEMIES

IN JANUARY 2008 president George W. Bush made a grand tour of the Middle East. As he traveled, he did what many presidents had done before him. He chastised Iran, urged Israel and Palestine to make up their differences, promised Saudi Arabia a vast new arms deal, and asked if it could help hold down oil prices. He spoke as optimistically as he dared about Iraq's future and encouraged more democracy. His official reception in the region varied from warm to courteous, but public opinion seemed skeptical. At this late stage in his presidency, after all that had happened, expectations were low. The headline foreign policy issues passed on by Jimmy Carter to his successor—Afghanistan, Iran, and Palestine—would be handed over by George W. Bush to his.

The issues change in form, with new players in central roles, but they never seem to be truly settled. The United States still has to come to terms with the Iranian revolution and the rise of Hezbollah in Lebanon. It has not found a way to stop Palestinian violence while holding back Israeli settlement construction or to get the Syrians to sound convincing enough on the meaning of peace to persuade Israel to hand back the Golan Heights. The search for reliable levers to influence disorderly Afghan, and now Pakistani, politics remains elusive. The continuity in many of the problems facing the Middle East suggests that they must be managed or endured; they are too rooted in the institutional structures, power balances, and cultures of the region to be solved.

Choosing enemies is an art and not a science, and one that usually takes place in confusing and ambiguous circumstances. The United States chose to respond vigorously to the Soviet intervention in Afghanistan in December 1979, the Iranian push against Iraq in the 1980s, the Iraqi occupation of Kuwait in 1990, the Taliban's protection of al Qaeda, the Palestinian Authority's reluctance to take on Islamist militants, and the Iranian pursuit of nuclear power. On the other hand, it played down the Israeli advance on Beirut and its settlement activity in the occupied territories, the ideology of the mujahideen, the Iraqi use of chemical weapons against the Iranians and the Kurds and its attacks on shipping in the Persian Gulf (though this included a U.S. warship), Saudi Arabian and Pakistani support for Islamists, and Pakistan's boost to nuclear proliferation. The point is not that all these decisions were wrong. As should be clear from this book, I believe that a number of them were fully justified, or at least understandable in the circumstances. But the decisions could have gone another way and in some cases they almost did; in others they were later reversed.

These choices matter. They affect how America pursues its interests, safeguards its own security, and is viewed by the rest of the world. Because many recent choices have not turned out so well, future choices will be watched carefully. Advice is already being offered about how to make better choices in the future: Don't patronize the region and pretend to know its needs better than those who live in it; avoid raising unrealistic expectations; consult widely on new initiatives, work with allies, and take full advantage of multilateral institutions; balance threats with inducements and use force sparingly if at all; don't be afraid to talk to those you dislike; do your best to bring stability to Iraq and Afghanistan, steady Pakistan, crush al Qaeda, engage with Iran, anticipate trouble in Egypt, stop Syria from meddling with Lebanon, and encourage Israel to be sensible and sensitive, Palestinians to make an effort, and Saudi Arabia to loosen up a bit. In practice much of this advice will turn out to be contradictory and irrelevant, as the agenda is dominated by an unexpected crisis, probably in a country hitherto thought to be of marginal concern. The big lesson from past experience is the need to understand the limits to power and the extent to which it is hard for anyone to control events or prevent unfortunate and unhelpful incidents. As the looting began in Iraq, Rumsfeld remarked that "stuff happens," uttering a truth about the region as a whole.[1]

*   *   *

Just as the Americans have to learn to live with the unpredictability of the Middle East, so the Middle East has to live with the unpredictability of the United

States. Washington's political cycle is notoriously short. New presidents often celebrate discontinuity, arriving as agents of change. They have their own agendas and want history to record their distinctive legacies. The rhetorical style also often celebrates discontinuity, promising clean breaks with the past and pointing toward a better future. As a matter of course, presidents will naturally talk up the liberating effects of democracy against the stultification of dictatorship, propose harmony instead of conflict, and promise that no lover of liberty will find a surer friend or an enemy a more implacable foe.

None of this means very much. To translate soaring presidential rhetoric into practical action takes considerable time and energy. Presidents seek to soar on many issues and then find others they had not considered before taking office imposing excessive demands on their waking hours. Because there are so many matters to address and time is so short, they flit in and out, giving different issues bursts of attention, sometimes prolonged but never indefinite, with a risk of disillusioning those who have had their hopes raised. Moreover, even if a president does make a serious commitment, for example, to a peace process, time can run out (and as with Clinton, awareness of this can lead to the setting of deadlines geared to Washington time rather than regional time). Curiously, one of the most effective ways by which presidents have committed their successor to their unfinished business is to commit troops.

The attention span of Congress and the public is even shorter. This means that the case being made for engagement with a particular issue can rarely be made in measured and qualified terms. Justifications for action tend to be stated starkly and urgently. The malign and dangerous features of enemies tend to be talked up, as do the exemplary and deserving qualities of friends. Problem states appear at best as rogues and at worst as evil. They are never presented as merely delinquent or as having strayed from their normal path and being potentially redeemable. Friends whose domestic affairs might not withstand close scrutiny will be presented as brave defenders of freedom. Washington politics is intolerant of nuance and ambiguity, especially when it comes to the large questions of war and peace. Force is justified to right wrongs and defeat evil, not to correct a power balance out of kilter or to protect the vaguely disreputable from the unambiguously awful. This has important consequences for crisis management and diplomacy because it inhibits dialogue with those castigated as unworthy, just as it can encourage excuses for those who are for the moment on the same side.

This produces a major inhibition on American diplomacy. A conversation with the United States is presented as a major prize in itself, something for which the other side should be prepared to pay a heavy political price.

Talking to the unworthy is said to confer legitimacy and create unrealistic hopes of pathbreaking deals. This may be an argument for keeping talks at a low level, informal and away from a media glare, and to recognize that some conversations can be useful without a set agenda. During the cold war many U.S.-Soviet diplomatic encounters had no tangible outcome at all, other than a deeper appreciation of patterns of thinking and the development of lines of communication which sometimes turned out to be useful when a crisis suddenly broke. A conversation with Iran, to take an obvious instance, may end in bad temper but until it is tried it is hard to know. The key point is to reduce the symbolic significance of the fact of conversation and present it as no more than normal diplomacy.

★　★　★

While establishing communications with Iran will have elements reminiscent of cold war contacts with the Soviet Union, one of the challenges with the Middle East is that so many of the key issues revolve around the internal politics of states. During the cold war many states in the region looked to the United States to help meet their security needs in the face of a perceived Soviet threat. By the time the cold war ended, Iran had already taken over as a central feature in regional security calculations. Then in 1990, abruptly and despite a decade of careful cultivation by the West, came a dramatic challenge from Iraq. It pounced on Kuwait before there was time to think about how to deter it. Having broken the rules so brazenly and then failed to recant, Saddam Hussein's regime was kept hemmed in during the 1990s and then in 2003 invaded by the United States, not so much because it had been straining to throw its weight around again but because it might try.

No doubt there will be major events in the future that will be both surprising and transformational, like the Iranian revolution or the Iraqi invasion of Kuwait. As a result the cards will be shuffled and new configurations of power will emerge, probably more as a result of internal upheavals than of external aggression. When the security issues are internal as much as external, it is even harder for an outside power such as the United States to find the right language and measures to respond. It is one thing to back a government against a predatory neighbor, quite another to provide support against an indignant and disenfranchised opposition. In this sort of setting, the classic categories of friend and foe may have little meaning. The most important attributes may be popular support and governance capacity, and a general capacity to contribute to internal order.

This is why it has seemed so important for Americans to encourage reform in the Middle East. Success will create a greater sense of shared values as well as shared interests, and lead to those benefits normally associated with liberal democracy, providing outlets for popular discontent before they reach insurrectionary levels, introducing innovative ideas and fresh faces into political life, encouraging more critical approaches to key issues and policy formation. The people of the Middle East are no less likely to appreciate and welcome the benefits of democracy than others who were once thought incapable of coping with its disciplines and now seem to manage perfectly well. The lack of democracy has been the main feature identified by those seeking to explain the American dissatisfaction with the Middle Eastern status quo, and why such a natural status quo power has found itself inclined to play the part of the radical. President Bush, building on foundations laid by President Clinton, put himself at the head of a third radical wave, offering liberal democracy as the ideology of choice for those who yearn for freedom, security, and prosperity.

This radical wave appeared to falter before it acquired any serious motion, and for reasons that were predictable. Most importantly, the United States is an outside power and not an indigenous political movement. Its motives will always be suspect and its touch will never be completely sure. When a president routinely describes every act of policy as a blow for "freedom," the word gets devalued, just as the word "peace" did when it became a staple of Soviet propaganda. As a major power picking its way among the complexities of regional affairs, the United States will never be able to adhere to strong principles in a wholly consistent way. Even when trying to find ways of making their application more palatable to the local autocracies, suggesting reforms that are modest and precautionary, Americans can expect to be told that they are undermining the foundations of their society and giving succor to their most dangerous foes. In this regard the Bush administration was caught out by the tension between its radical aspirations and those of the second radical wave, which had the benefit of considerable popularity and dynamism. Extreme Salafist Islamists opposed any political forms that presumed to displace the word of God. "We have declared a bitter war against democracy and all those who seek to enact it," said Zarqawi in Iraq, just after President Bush's second inaugural address, in which democracy was a core theme, and just before Iraqi national elections. "Candidates in elections are seeking to become demi-gods, while those who vote for them are infidels," thereby providing justifications for their murder.[2] However, those following the more pragmatic Muslim Brotherhood, such as Hamas, or revolutionary Iran, such as Hezbollah, had no concerns about participating in elections and tended to do rather well in them. If Americans appear to dismiss the outcome of elections that are awkward and maintain diplomatic silence in the face of human rights abuses and wider repression by their favored autocrats, then they will be vulnerable to the charge of a double standard. Such charges will become even sharper when the United States is caught indulging in the very practices, such as torture and detention without trial, it has condemned in others.

In seeking to open up the political and economic life of the Middle East, the Americans have spoken at times as if they have a civilizing mission. Yet it can seem that the influences are in the other direction, that there is something about the region that leads outsiders to act in ways that reflect the region's own established mores and practices. Perhaps that is why Israel's behavior is often found so perplexing: a country that is Western and open in so many respects yet deals with its enemies in a very Middle Eastern manner.

Operating effectively in these arenas requires a keen sense of history and social contexts, of loyalties and patterns of identity that are deep-rooted, of institutional structures that work to a logic that only the most knowledgeable insiders can discern. The players in this sphere relate to foreigners in distinctive ways, careful about not giving too much away. When seeking to exercise influence and open up regional politics, the United States may find it most effective to work with the local grain. It takes time, however, to read the grain effectively. The more deeply the Americans get into the often murky politics of damaged societies, especially when they are helping counter insurgencies, the more they are likely to be making compromises with suspicious warlords and ignoring dubious practices, from prisoner abuse to drug trafficking.

Another reason to avoid describing enemies in overly stark terms is that it encourages viewing them as having an unrealistic homogeneity and missing out on their internal conflicts and potential for implosion. Radical groups in particular are notoriously argumentative with each other, vulnerable to what Sigmund Freud called the "narcissism of small differences," the tendency to reserve our most virulent emotions for those we resemble most. This has always been a useful concept when considering the capacity of radical political movements to fracture and overplay what are often poor hands. A wise policy encourages the splits. For example, it was lack of unity that undermined the ideological credibility of the first radical wave of pan-Arabism in the Middle East and led to its downfall. When looking back over these pages, one becomes regretful about missed opportunities and poor decisions on the American side, but it is also important to recognize that America's opponents have often badly misjudged events and come off poorly. After all, what is left of the first radical wave is a collection of regimes with no obvious purpose but their own survival, and their great cause of Palestine mired in wretchedness and caught in the collision between the first and second waves. The first wave brought with it regular and painful acts of terrorism sponsored by states rather than outlaw groups; in the end they did the perpetrators no good at all and have largely petered out.

Douglas Little has a point when he observes that "from the perspective of a twenty-first century rocked by ethnic wars and terrorized by Islamic extremists, Americans could be forgiven for growing nostalgic about some of the secular nationalists who had given the United States such fits in the Middle East during the last half of the twentieth century." It might have been easier, he notes, to have dealt with Mossadegh if that had avoided Khomeini.[3] It is not clear of course whether that represents a real historic choice, for the nationalists were hardly masters of good governance and, as in Egypt, helped create the conditions for the second wave. Thus far, and Iran remains the main example, Islamists also find good government something of a struggle.

*   *   *

The events of the last decade have taken their toll, and the United States does not enjoy the prestige and influence in the Middle East that it did as recently as the early 1990s. Nonetheless, no other external actor has so much power or applies it so regularly to Middle Eastern affairs. Moreover, although configurations of power will change, there is no reason to suppose that the Middle East will become more coherent and consensual, or that the recent pattern of conflict and instability will just fizzle out. The *Economist* accompanied Bush's trip of January 2008 with a report on Arab gloom. There were many reasons to be dissatisfied: uninspiring leaders, fast population growth racing ahead of failing public education systems and economic performance (although recent higher rates of economic growth were one bright spot), Palestine still far from statehood and divided, chaos in Iraq, slaughter in the Darfur region of Sudan, minimal progress on the human development agenda.[4]

The United States will still find itself invited to choose enemies and stand by friends. We have seen the pitfalls. Designated enemies can find support in unexpected places or learn to play off their opponents against each other. The interests of friends can conflict, creating awkward choices of priorities and challenges of conciliation. The rhetoric of good versus evil, the polarizing demands of "with us or against us," the insistence on one strategic imperative above all others are undermined by the complexity of regional conflict and the interplay of difference. Recent years have demonstrated the challenges facing any attempt to forge a coherent policy toward the Middle

East, but it is not a new problem and was just as evident during the cold war as it has been during the war on terror. For Americans, the challenge is to revive their diplomatic skills, learning how to work with the local political grain without losing a sense of purpose and principle, pushing parties to cooperation, supporting social and economic along with political reform, and encouraging a positive engagement with the rest of the world. If the region is to advance, not only must American presidents make the right choices, but the governments and people of the Middle East must do so as well.

Acknowledgments

This book began with a family conversation and it has been family and friends who have been egging me on to get this finished. It took my agent Catherine Clarke, along with George Lucas, to help me turn a general aspiration into a proper proposal. It has been a pleasure to work with Clive Priddle at PublicAffairs, for both his good advice and remarkable tolerance as the book expanded in length and ambition. Annie Lenth and Michele Wynn have done a remarkable job of getting the book into a fit state for publication so quickly. In this they were ably reinforced by Alan Samson and Bea Hemming at Weidenfeld & Nicholson. Krista Nelson was a great help with the footnotes, bibliography, and dramatis personae. As always my deepest gratitude is to my wife, Judith. At least this time my guilt about the ludicrous hours I was spending on this project was eased by the fact that she was spending ludicrous hours of her own on her writing.

Notes

Preface

1. Michael Oren, *Power, Faith, and Fantasy: America in the Middle East, 1776 to the Present* (New York: W. W. Norton, 2007), p. 603.

2. Edward Luttwak, "The Middle of Nowhere," *Prospect* (May 2007).

3. Richard N. Haass, "The New Middle East," *Foreign Affairs* (November–December 2006).

4. Salin Yaqub, *Containing Arab Nationalism: The Eisenhower Doctrine and the Middle East* (Chapel Hill: University of North Carolina Press, 2004), p. 8.

5. John J. Mearsheimer and Stephen M. Walt, *The Israel Lobby and U.S. Foreign Policy* (New York: Farrar, Straus & Giroux, 2007). For one of many critiques, see Jeffrey Goldberg, "The Usual Suspect," *New Republic*, October 1, 2007.

6. David W. Lesch, *1979: The Year That Shaped the Modern Middle East* (Boulder: Westview, 2001).

Chapter 1: Choosing Enemies

1. "Address to a Joint Session of Congress and to the American People," September 20, 2001, at www.whitehouse.gov/news/releases/2001/09/20010920-8.html.

2. George Tenet, *At the Center of the Storm: My Years at the CIA* (New York: HarperCollins, 2007).

3. See http://archives.cnn.com/2001/US/09/16/inv.binladen.denial/index.html.

4. Interview with *Daily Ummat* of Karachi, September 28, 2001, at www.justresponse.net/Bin_Laden1.html.

5. Lev Grossman, "Why the 9/11 Conspiracy Theories Won't Go Away," *Time,* September 3, 2006. To get the flavor of some of the challenges to the official version of events, see the Web site at www.911truth.org.

6. "Remarks by the President After Two Planes Crash into World Trade Center," Emma Booker Elementary School, Sarasota, Florida, September 11, 2001, at www.whitehouse.gov/news/releases/2001/09/20010911.html.

7. "Statement by the President in His Address to the Nation," September 11, 2001, at www.whitehouse.gov/news/releases/2001/09/20010911-16.html. See Elisabeth Bumiller, *Condoleezza Rice: An American Life* (New York: Random House, 2007), p. xvii.

8. The 9/11 Commission Report, *Final Report of the National Commission on Terrorist Attacks upon the United States* (New York: W. W. Norton, 2004).

9. Grenville Byford, "The Wrong War," *Foreign Affairs* (July–August 2002).

10. Bob Woodward, *Bush at War* (New York: Simon & Schuster, 2002), pp. 33, 43.

11. DOD News Briefing—Deputy Secretary Wolfowitz, Thursday, September 13, 2001, at www.defenselink.mil/news/Sep2001/t09132001_t0913dsd.html.

12. Craig Unger, *House of Bush, House of Saud: The Secret Relationship Between the World's Two Most Powerful Dynasties* (New York: Scribner's, 2004).

13. See the documents gathered by the National Security Archive, "Pakistan: 'The Taliban's Godfather?'" August 14, 2007, at www.gwu.edu/~nsarchiv/NSAEBB/NSAEBB227/index.htm.

14. Adrian Levy and Catherine Scott-Clark, *Deception: Pakistan, the United States, and the Global Nuclear Weapons Conspiracy* (London: Atlantic Books, 2007), p. 293.

15. See http://news.bbc.co.uk/1/hi/world/south_asia/5369198.stm.

16. See www.npr.org/templates/story/story.php?storyId=6126088.

17. 9/11 Commission Report, chap. 10; Karen DeYoung, *Soldier: The Life of Colin Powell* (New York: Vintage, 2006), pp. 349–350.

18. CBSNEWS.com, "Plans for Iraq Attack Began on 9/11," September 4, 2002, at www.cbsnews.com/stories/2002/09/04/september11/main520830.shtml.

19. The book was republished after 9/11 as Laurie Mylroie, *The War Against America: Saddam Hussein and the World Trade Center Attacks: A Study of Revenge* (New York: HarperCollins, 2001). Mylroie developed her arguments further in *Bush vs. the Beltway: How the CIA and the State Department Tried to Stop the War on Terror* (Washington, D.C.: Regan, 2003). Mylroie was prepared to blame Iraq for the October 1991 anthrax incidents, although the evidence here strongly suggested that they originated in the United States. She put her argument to the National Commission on Terrorist Attacks Upon the United States in July 2003, where her claims were challenged directly by Judith S. Yaphe. See their statements in the *Report of the Third Public Hearing of the National Commission on Terrorist Attacks Upon the United States*, July 9, 2003.

20. Richard Clarke, *Against All Enemies: Inside America's War on Terror* (New York: Free Press, 2004), pp. 30, 232. See also Daniel Benjamin and Steve Simon, *The Age of Sacred Terror* (New York: Random House, 2002).

21. Bumiller, *Condoleezza Rice*, p. 165.

22. Bob Woodward, *Bush at War* (New York: Simon & Schuster, 2002), pp. 83–84. See also Woodward, *Plan of Attack* (New York: Simon & Schuster, 2004), p. 25.

23. Woodward, *Bush at War*, p. 49.

24. *9/11 Commission Report*, pp. 334–336.

25. "President Urges Readiness and Patience: Remarks by the President, Secretary of State Colin Powell, and Attorney General John Ashcroft," Camp David,

Thurmont, Maryland, September 15, 2001, at www.whitehouse.gov/news/releases/
2001/09/20010915-4.html.

26. "Remarks by the President in Photo Opportunity with the National Security
Team," September 12, 2001, at www.whitehouse.gov/news/releases/2001/09/
20010912-4.html; "Radio Address of the President to the Nation," September 15,
2001, at www.whitehouse.gov/news/releases/2001/09/20010915.html; "Remarks by
the President upon Arrival, the South Lawn," September 16, 2001, at
www.whitehouse.gov/news/releases/2001/09/20010916-2.html.

27. Robert Draper, *Dead Certain: The Presidency of George W. Bush* (New York:
Free Press, 2007), pp. 153–154.

28. "Address to a Joint Session of Congress and to the American People," September
20, 2001, at www.whitehouse.gov/news/releases/2001/09/20010920-8.html.

29. "Statement by President George W. Bush, the Rose Garden, the White
House," November 26, 2001.

30. "The President's State of the Union Address," June 29, 2002, at
www.whitehouse.gov/news/releases/2002/01/20020129-11.html.

31. See www.britannica.com/presidents/article-9116960.

32. David Frum, *The Right Man: An Inside Account of the Surprise Presidency of
George W. Bush* (London: Weidenfeld & Nicholson, 2003), pp. 231–239.

33. Woodward, *Plan of Attack*, pp. 86–87.

34. Bruce W. Jentleson and Christopher A. Whytock, "Who 'Won' Libya? The
Force-Diplomacy Debate and Its Implications for Theory and Policy," *International
Security*, Winter 2005–2006, pp. 72–73.

35. Bumiller, *Condoleezza Rice*, p. 174.

36. Ibid., p. 88.

37. Frum, *The Right Man*, p. 237.

38. Thomas B. Edsall and Dana Milbank, "White House's Roving Eye for Politics:
President's Most Powerful Adviser May Also Be the Most Connected," *Washington
Post*, March 10, 2003.

39. Michael Ledeen, *The War Against the Terror Masters* (New York: St. Martin's
Press, 2002), p. xxii.

40. Michael Ledeen, "What's the Holdup? It's Time for the Next Battles in the
War Against Terrorism," *National Review Online*, January 7, 2002, at
www.nationalreview.com/contributors/ledeen010702.shtml.

41. Tenet, *At the Center of the Storm*, pp. 311–313.

42. "President Bush Delivers State of the Union Address, Washington, D.C.,"
January 31, 2006, at www.whitehouse.gov/news/releases/2006/01/20060131-10.html.

43. "President Bush Delivers State of the Union Address, Washington, D.C.,"
January 23, 2007, at www.whitehouse.gov/news/releases/2007/01/20070123-2.html.

Chapter 2: The First Wave

1. Ben Fenton, "Macmillan Backed Syria Assassination Plot: Documents Show
White House and No. 10 Conspired over Oil-Fuelled Invasion Plan," *Guardian*,
September 27, 2003.

2. Gilles Kepel, *Jihad: The Trail of Political Islam* (Cambridge: Harvard University Press, 2002), pp. 62–65. The analysis in this section draws heavily on Kepel's book.

3. Ibid.

4. Gershom Gorenberg, *Occupied Territories: The Untold Story of Israel's Settlements* (London: I. B. Tauris, 2007), p. 358.

Chapter 3: Camp David

1. Although the general literature on the Carter administration is not vast, the three top figures wrote detailed memoirs: Jimmy Carter, *Keeping Faith: Memoirs of a President* (New York: Bantam, 1982); Zbigniew Brzezinski, *Power and Principle: Memoirs of a National Security Adviser, 1977–1981* (New York: Farrar, Straus & Giroux, 1983); and Cyrus Vance, *Hard Choices: Four Critical Years in Managing America's Foreign Policy* (New York: Simon & Schuster, 1983).

2. The most important chronicler of Carter's Middle East diplomacy was William B. Quandt. See in particular his *Camp David: Peacemaking and Politics* (Washington, D.C.: Brookings Institution, 1986), which informs much of this narrative, and also *Peace Process: American Diplomacy and the Arab-Israeli Conflict Since 1967* (Washington, D.C.: Brookings Institution, 1993). Also of great value is Kenneth W. Stein, *Heroic Diplomacy: Sadat, Kissinger, Carter, Begin, and the Quest for Arab-Israeli Peace* (New York: Routledge, 1999).

3. *Toward Peace in the Middle East: Report of a Study Group* (Washington, D.C.: Brookings Institution, 1975), pp. 1–3.

4. Vance, *Hard Choices*, p. 174.

5. Quandt, *Peace Process*, p. 61.

6. Carter, *Keeping Faith*, p. 289.

7. Stein, *Heroic Diplomacy*, p. 196.

8. Brzezinski, *Power and Principle*, p. 93.

9. Robert Strong, *Working on the World: Jimmy Carter and the Making of American Foreign Policy* (Baton Rouge: Louisiana State University Press, 2000), p. 203 n. 39.

10. See Stein, *Heroic Diplomacy*, p. 192.

11. Quandt, *Camp David*, p. 46.

12. Stein, *Heroic Diplomacy*, p. 193.

13. Interview, *Time*, October 11, 1982; Strong, *Working on the World*, p. 194.

14. Stein, *Heroic Diplomacy*, p. 209 n. 113.

15. Brzezinski, *Power and Principle*, pp. 91–92, 96–97.

16. Quandt, *Camp David*, p. 131.

17. Ibid., p. 132.

18. Stein, *Heroic Diplomacy*, p. 219 n. 153.

19. Avi Shlaim, *The Iron Wall: Israel and the Arab World* (New York: W. W. Norton, 1999), pp. 372–373.

20. Quandt, *Camp David*, p. 225.

21. Ahron Bregman and Jihan El-Tahri, *The Fifty Years War: Israel and the Arabs* (London: Penguin, 1998), p. 164.

22. Carter, *Keeping Faith*, p. 401.

23. Brzezinski, *Power and Principle*, p. 239.

24. Stein, *Heroic Diplomacy*, p. 256 n. 96.

25. Vance, *Hard Choices*, p. 236.

26. Carter, *Keeping Faith*, p. 425.

27. Quandt, *Camp David*, p. 310.

Chapter 4: Revolution in Iran

1. In addition to the memoirs of Carter, Brzezinski, and Vance, the books I have found most helpful on U.S.-Iranian relations over this period are James A. Bill, *The Eagle and the Lion: The Tragedy of American-Iranian Relations* (New Haven: Yale University Press, 1988); Kenneth M. Pollack, *The Persian Puzzle: The Conflict Between Iran and America* (New York: Random House, 2004); Gary Sick, *All Fall Down: America's Tragic Encounter with Iran* (New York: Random House, 1986); William H. Sullivan, *Mission to Iran* (New York: W. W. Norton, 1981); Ray Takeyh, *Hidden Iran: Paradox and Power in the Islamic Republic* (New York: Henry Holt, 2006).

2. Stephen Kinzer, *All the Shah's Men: An American Coup and the Roots of Middle East Terror* (New York: John Wiley, 2003).

3. Pollack, *Persian Puzzle*, pp. 108–109.

4. Sick, *All Fall Down*, p. 57.

5. David Harris, *The Crisis: The President, the Prophet, and the Shah—1979 and the Coming of Militant Islam* (New York: Little, Brown, 2004), p. 70.

6. "Tehran, Iran Toasts the President and the Shah at a State Dinner, December 31st, 1977," at www.presidency.ucsb.edu/ws/index.php?pid=7080&st=&st1=.

7. Strong, *Working on the World*, p. 66, notes that the shah only admitted to one conversation.

8. On the Iranian revolution, see Ervand Abrahamian, *Khomeinism: Essays on the Islamic Republic* (Berkeley: University of California Press, 1993); Ali M. Ansari, *Modern Iran Since 1921* (London: Longman, 2003); Michael M. J. Fischer, *Iran: From Religious Dispute to Revolution* (Cambridge: Harvard University Press, 1980); Mansoor Moaddel, *Class, Politics, and Ideology in the Iranian Revolution* (New York: Columbia University Press, 1993); Rouholah Ramazani, *Revolutionary Iran: Change and Response in the Middle East* (Baltimore: Johns Hopkins University Press, 1987).

9. Bill, *The Eagle and the Lion*, p. 259.

10. Anthony Parsons, *From Cold War to Hot Peace: UN Interventions from 1947 to 1994* (London: Michael Joseph, 1995), p. 134.

11. Bill, *The Eagle and the Lion*, p. 236.

12. Sick, *All Fall Down*, pp. 42–43.

13. Parsons, *From Cold War to Hot Peace*, p. 98.

14. Hodding Carter II, quoted in Bill, *The Eagle and the Lion*, p. 250.

15. Pollack, *Persian Puzzle*, p. 133.

16. Sick, *All Fall Down*.

17. David Farber, *Taken Hostage: The Iran Hostage Crisis and America's First Encounter with Radical Islam* (Princeton: Princeton University Press, 2005), p. 160.

18. Carter, *Keeping Faith*.

19. Robert M. Gates, *From the Shadows: The Ultimate Insider's Story of Five Presidents and How They Won the Cold War* (New York: Simon & Schuster, 1996), p. 129.

20. Ibid., pp. 294–295.

21. On the hostage crisis, see Mark Bowden, *Guests of the Ayatollah: The Iran Hostage Crisis: The First Battle in America's War with Militant Islam* (New York: Grove Press, 2006); and Farber, *Taken Hostage.*

22. Pollack, *Persian Puzzle,* p. 153.

23. Mark Bowden, *Guests of the Ayatollah: The Iran Hostage Crisis: The First Battle in America's War with Militant Islam* (New York: Grove Press, 2006), pp. 93–94.

24. Farber, *Taken Hostage,* p. 147.

25. Bowden, *Guests of the Ayatollah,* p. 191.

26. Pollack, *Persian Puzzle,* p. 166.

27. Bowden, *Guests of the Ayatollah,* pp. 373–374.

28. This is Brzezinski's recollection. *Power and Principle,* p. 494. Jordan's is that the president responded. Hamilton Jordan, *Crisis: The Last Days of the Carter Presidency* (New York: Putnam, 1982), pp. 253–254.

29. Gary Sick, *October Surprise: America's Hostages in Iran and the Election of Ronald Reagan* (New York: Random House, 1991).

Chapter 5: Uprising in Afghanistan

1. Carter, *Keeping Faith,* p. 474.

2. This account is drawn from Steve Coll, *Ghost Wars: The Secret History of the CIA, Afghanistan, and Bin Laden, from the Soviet Invasion to September 10, 2001* (New York: Penguin Press, 2004), pp. 29–35.

3. On the incident see Lawrence Wright, *The Looming Tower, Al-Qaeda and the Road to 9/11* (New York: Alfred A. Knopf, 2007).

4. Rachel Bronson, *Thicker Than Oil: America's Uneasy Partnership with Saudi Arabia* (New York: Oxford University Press, 2006), p. 148.

5. CIA report cited by Douglas Little, *American Orientalism: The United States and the Middle East Since 1945* (Chapel Hill: University of North Carolina Press, 2004), p. 223.

6. Raymond L. Garthoff, *Détente and Confrontation: American-Soviet Relations from Nixon to Reagan,* rev. ed. (Washington, D.C.: Brookings Institution, 1994), p. 988.

7. Odd Arne Westad, *The Global Cold War* (Cambridge: Cambridge University Press, 2005), pp. 307–308.

8. Ibid., pp. 310–311.

9. See documents on "The Soviet Union and Afghanistan, 1978–1989," *Cold War International History Project Bulletin 8–9* (Washington, D.C.: Woodrow Wilson Center, Winter 1996–1997).

10. "Moscow Said to Urge Shaky Afghan Regime to Broaden Base," *New York Times,* August 2, 1979.

11. Quoted in Coll, *Ghost Wars,* p. 41.

12. Westad, *Global Cold War*, pp. 319–320.

13. Garthoff, *Détente and Confrontation*, pp. 1017–1018.

14. Lester W. Grau and Michael A. Gress, trans. and eds., The Russian General Staff. *The Soviet-Afghan War: How a Superpower Fought and Lost* (Lawrence: University of Kansas Press, 2002), p. 1.

15. Gates, *From the Shadows*, p. 131.

16. This section draws on Douglas MacEachin, *Predicting the Soviet Invasion of Afghanistan: The Intelligence Community's Record* (CIA: Center for the Study of Intelligence, 2002). McEachin was also involved with *The Soviet Invasion of Afghanistan in 1979: Failure of Intelligence or of the Policy Process?* Working Group Report no. 111 (Institute for the Study of Diplomacy, Edmund A. Walsh School of Foreign Service, Georgetown University, September 26, 2005).

17. Brzezinski, *Power and Principle*, p. 429.

18. "Moscow's Geopolitics: A Kissinger Answer to a Global Challenge," *Time*, May 8, 1978.

19. President Jimmy Carter, "Human Rights and Foreign Policy" (commencement speech given at Notre Dame University, June 1977).

20. President Jimmy Carter, Address to U.S. Naval Academy, June 7, 1978.

21. Gates, *From the Shadows*, pp. 74–75.

22. MacEachin and Nolan, *Soviet Invasion of Afghanistan in 1979*, p. 9.

23. "U.S. Indirectly Pressing Russians to Halt Afghanistan Intervention," *New York Times*, August 3, 1979.

24. "How Jimmy Carter and I Started the Mujahideen," interview with Zbigniew Brzezinski, *Le Nouvel Observateur*, January 15–21, 1998. See, for example, Robert Dreyfuss, *Devil's Game: How the United States Helped Unleash Fundamentalist Islam* (New York: Henry Holt, 2005), pp. 264–265.

25. "The Crescent of Crisis," *Time*, January 15, 1979, at www.time.com/time/magazine/article/0,9171,919995,00.html.

26. Zalmay Khalizad, *The Return of the Great Game*, California Seminar on International Security and Foreign Policy, Discussion Paper no. 88 (1980), pp. 70–71; cited by Dreyfuss, *Devil's Game*, p. 255.

27. Both memos are accessible at www.cnn.com/SPECIALS/cold.war/episodes/20/documents/brez.carter.

28. Garthoff, *Détente and Confrontation*, p. 1060 n. 238.

29. "Vienna Summit Meeting Address Delivered Before a Joint Session of the Congress," June 18, 1979, at www.presidency.ucsb.edu/ws/index.php?pid=32498&st=&st1=.

30. For example, on *Meet the Press*, January 20, 1980, at www.presidency.ucsb.edu/ws/index.php?pid=33060&st=&st1=. This database is provided by John T. Woolley and Gerhard Peters, The American Presidency Project [online], University of California–Santa Barbara.

31. "Address to the Nation on Afghanistan, January 4, 1980," at www.presidency.ucsb.edu/ws/index.php?pid=32911&st=&st1=.

32. Carter, *Keeping Faith*, p. 471.

33. Westad, *Global Cold War*, p. 328.

34. Vance, *Hard Choices,* pp. 394–395.

35. Garthoff, *Détente and Confrontation,* p. 1066.

36. President Jimmy Carter, "State of the Union Address," January 23, 1980, www.jimmycarterlibrary.org/documents/speeches/su80jec.phtml.

Chapter 6: The Mujahideen

1. *Wall Street Journal,* June 3, 1980; cited by Westad, *Global Cold War,* p. 334.

2. Ronald Reagan, *An American Life: The Autobiography* (New York: Simon & Schuster, 1990), p. 267.

3. For memoirs of the Reagan administration, see Bud McFarlane and Zofia Smardz, *Special Trust* (New York: Caddel & Davies, 1994); Gates, *From the Shadows;* Alexander Haig, *Caveat* (New York: Macmillan, 1984); George P. Shultz, *Turmoil and Triumph: My Years as Secretary of State* (New York: Scribner's, 1993); Caspar Weinberger, *Fighting for Peace* (London: Michael Joseph, 1990).

4. Jeane Kirkpatrick, "Democracy and Double Standards," *Commentary,* November 1979.

5. Levy and Scott-Clark, *Deception,* pp. 82, 92.

6. Reagan, *American Life,* p. 238.

7. Levy and Scott-Clark, *Deception,* p. 93.

8. Coll, *Ghost Wars,* p. 62.

9. John Prados, *Safe for Democracy: The Secret Wars of the CIA* (Chicago: Ivan R. Dee, 2006), p. 481.

10. Wright, *Looming Tower,* p. 100.

11. I have drawn here on Vali Nasr, *The Shia Revival: How Conflicts Within Islam Will Shape the Future* (New York: W. W. Norton, 2007).

12. Gates, *From the Shadows,* pp. 203–204.

13. Garthoff, *Détente and Confrontation,* p. 1022.

14. Prados, *Safe for Democracy,* p. 486.

15. Westad, *Global Cold War,* p. 375.

16. Garthoff, *Détente and Confrontation,* p. 1022.

17. Joseph E. Persico, *Casey: From the OSS to the CIA* (New York: Viking, 2000), p. 225; Prados, *Safe for Democracy,* p. 483.

18. Coll, *Ghost Wars,* p. 89.

19. Gates, *From the Shadows,* p. 199.

20. George Crile, *Charlie Wilson's War* (New York: Atlantic Monthly Press, 2003).

21. Prados, *Safe for Democracy,* p. 491.

22. Coll, *Ghost Wars,* pp. 51, 180.

Chapter 7: In and Out of Beirut

1. Haig, *Caveat,* p. 167.

2. Carter-Fahd meeting, Washington D.C., May 1977.

3. Rachel Bronson, *Thicker Than Oil: America's Uneasy Partnership with Saudi Arabia* (New York: Oxford University Press, 2006), p. 144.

4. Ronald Reagan, *An American Life,* p. 410.

5. Ibid., 416.

6. Transcript of Reagan press conference, October 2, 1981.

7. Shlaim, *Iron Wall*, pp. 387–388.

8. Ronald Reagan, *The Reagan Diaries*, ed. Douglas Brinkley (New York: HarperCollins, 2007), pp. 24–25. Reagan's first reaction was "I swear I believe Armageddon is near."

9. Shlaim, *Iron Wall*, p. 394.

10. *Reagan Diaries*, p. 57.

11. Sources used for this chapter include Thomas L. Friedman, *From Beirut to Jerusalem* (New York: Farrar, Straus & Giroux, 1989); David K. Hall, *Lebanon Revisited* (United States Naval War College, 1988); Ralph A. Hallenbeck, *Military Force as an Instrument of U.S. Policy: Intervention in Lebanon, August 1982–February 1984* (New York: Praeger, 1991); Agnes G. Korbani, *U.S. Intervention in Lebanon, 1958 and 1982: Presidential Decision Making* (New York: Praeger, 1991); Sandra Mackey, *Lebanon: A House Divided* (New York: W. W. Norton, 2006); Itamar Rabinovich, *The War for Lebanon: 1970–1985* (Ithaca: Cornell University Press, 1985); Ze'ev Schiff and Ehud Ya'ari, *Israel's Lebanon War* (New York: Simon & Schuster, 1984).

12. Speech of August 8, 1982, to Israeli National Defense College.

13. Rabinovich, *War for Lebanon*, p. 132.

14. Friedman, *From Beirut to Jerusalem*, pp. 137–139.

15. Schiff and Ya'ari, *Israel's Lebanon War*, p. 41.

16. Bud McFarlane and Zofia Smardz, *Special Trust* (New York: Caddel & Davies, 1994), p. 206.

17. Haig, *Caveat*, pp. 317–318.

18. Ibid., p. 346.

19. Reagan, *An American Life*, p. 88.

20. Shultz, *Turmoil and Triumph*, pp. 85–86.

21. Stober, *An American Life*, pp. 207–208, 427–429.

22. Weinberger, *Fighting for Peace*, p. 102.

23. Korbani, *U.S. Intervention in Lebanon*, p. 84.

24. Weinberger, *Fighting for Peace*, p. 105.

25. Quandt, *Peace Process*, p. 347.

26. Stober, *An American Life*, p. 445.

27. Weinberger, *Fighting for Peace*, pp. 109–111.

28. Ladan Boroumand and Roya Boroumand, "Terror, Islam, and Democracy," *Journal of Democracy* (April 2002): 19.

29. For an account of Hama, see Friedman, *From Beirut to Jerusalem*, p. 90.

30. Mackey, *Lebanon*, p. 206.

31. *Reagan Diaries*, p. 137.

32. Stober, *An American Life*, pp. 463–464.

33. McFarlane and Smardz, *Special Trust*, pp. 270–271.

34. *Reagan Diaries*, pp. 194, 198.

35. Weinberger, *Fighting for Peace*, p. 116.

36. *Reagan Diaries*, p. 215.

37. Ronald Reagan, "News Conference of February 22, 1984," *U.S. Department of State Bulletin,* April 1984.

38. *Reports on Terrorist Bombings of U.S. Marines in Beirut,* December 19 and 23, 1983 (DOD Commission on Beirut International Airport Terrorist Act of October 23, 1983), at www.ibiblio.org/hyperwar/AMH/XX/MidEast/Lebanon-1982-1984/DOD-Report/index.html.

39. Cited in Jeffrey D. Simon, *The Terrorist Trap,* 2nd ed. (Bloomington: Indiana University Press, 2001), p. 184; Shultz, *Turmoil and Triumph,* p. 231.

40. Shultz, *Turmoil and Triumph,* p. 648. The idea that the United States was engaged in a war against terror is found in a number of publications from the period, including Neil C. Livingstone and Terrell E. Arnold, ed., *Fighting Back: Winning the War Against Terrorism* (Lexington, Mass.: Lexington Books, 1986).

41. Caspar Weinberger, "The Uses of Military Power," Speech to National Press Club, November 28, 1984, at www.pbs.org/wgbh/pages/frontline/shows/military/force/weinberger.html.

Chapter 8: Iraq

1. U.S. Senate, Committee on Foreign Relations, Staff Report, *War in the Persian Gulf: The U.S. Takes Sides* (Washington, D.C., 1987), p. 30.

2. Cited in Efraim Karsh and Inari Rautsi, *Saddam Hussein: A Political Biography* (London: Brassey's, 1991), p. 117.

3. Kenneth R. Timmerman, *The Death Lobby: How the West Armed Iraq* (London: Fourth Estate, 1992), pp. 31–32.

4. *Further Report of the Secretary-General on the Implementation of Security Council Resolution 598 (1987)* (New York: United Nations, 1991).

5. Parsons, *From Cold War to Hot Peace,* pp. 44, 52.

6. Brian Urquhart, *A Life in Peace and War* (London: Weidenfeld & Nicholson, 1987), pp. 324–325.

7. Veliotes and Howe to Eagleburger, *Iran-Iraq War: Analysis of Possible U.S. Shift from Position of Strict Neutrality,* State Department Paper, October 7, 1983. The various documents quoted are found at www.gwu.edu/~nsarchiv/nsa/publications/iraqgate/iraqgate.html and http://nsarchive.chadwyck.com/introx.htm.

8. Shultz, *Turmoil and Triumph,* p. 927.

9. Secretary Shultz's May 10 meeting with Iraqi foreign minister Tariq Aziz, May 12, 1983.

10. State to Interests Section, Baghdad, Message from the Secretary for Fon Min Tariq Aziz: Iraqi Support for Terrorism, May 23, 1983.

11. *Prospects for Iraq,* Defense Estimative Brief, September 25, 1984.

12. Shultz to U.S. Interests Section, Baghdad, March 4, 1984.

13. William Eagleton to State Department, March 7, 1984.

14. J. Pérez de Cuéllar, *Pilgrimage for Peace* (London: Macmillan, 1997), pp. 141–142; Parsons, *From Cold War to Hot Peace,* p. 48.

15. White House, *Measures to Improve U.S. Posture and Readiness to Respond to Developments in the Iran-Iraq War,* National Security Decision Directive 139, April 5, 1984.

16. *Shultz, Turmoil and Triumph,* p. 237.

17. C. Weinberger, *Secretary of Defense Report to the Congress on Security Arrangements in the Persian Gulf* (Washington, D.C.: Department of Defense, 1987).

18. G. Gugliotta, C. Babcock, and B. Weiser, "At War, Iraq Courted U.S. into Economic Embrace," *Washington Post,* September 16, 1990; Bruce Jentleson, *With Friends Like These: Reagan, Bush, and Saddam, 1982–1990* (New York: W. W. Norton, 1994), p. 46; and Elaine Sciolino, *The Outlaw State: Saddam Hussein's Quest for Power and the Gulf Crisis* (New York: John Wiley, 1991), p. 168.

19. Shahram Chubin and Charles Tripp, *Iran and Iraq at War* (London: I. B. Tauris, 1988), p. 194.

20. Memcon: Secretary's Meeting with Iraqi Deprimmin Tarqi Azi, November 26, 1984.

21. Gugliotta, Babcock, and Weiser, "At War."

22. Jentleson, *With Friends Like These*, p. 44.

23. Ibid., pp. 50–51; Timmerman, *Death Lobby,* p. 241.

24. Timmerman, *Death Lobby,* p. 203.

Chapter 9: Iran-Contra

1. President Ronald Reagan, "Remarks Announcing the Review of the National Security Council's Role in the Iran Arms and Contra Aid Controversy," November 25, 1986, at www.reagan.utexas.edu/archives/speeches/1986/112586a.htm.

2. *The Iran-Contra Report,* Congressional Committee Investigating Iran Contra majority report, issued November 18, 1987.

3. Reagan, *American Life,* pp. 494–495.

4. Simon, *Terrorist Trap,* p. 192.

5. Ronald Reagan, "Remarks Announcing the Release of the Hostages from the Trans World Airlines Hijacking Incident," June 30, 1985, at www.reagan.utexas.edu/archives/speeches/1985/63085a.htm.

6. Ronald Reagan, "Remarks and a Question-and-Answer Session with Reporters," October 11, 1985, at www.reagan.utexas.edu/archives/speeches/1985/101185a.htm.

7. Jentleson, *With Friends Like These,* pp. 51–53; Sciolino, *Outlaw State,* p. 164.

8. Jentleson, *With Friends Like These,* pp. 54–55.

9. Wyn Q. Bowen, *Libya and Nuclear Proliferation: Stepping Back from the Brink,* Adelphi Paper no. 380 (London: Routledge/IISS, May 2006), p. 14.

10. President's News Conference, January 7, 1986, at www.reagan.utexas.edu/archives/speeches/1986/10786e.htm.

11. David B. Cohen and Chris J. Dolan, "Revisiting El Dorado Canyon: Terrorism, the Reagan Administration, and the 1986 Bombing of Libya," *White House Studies,* Spring 2005; Brian L. Davis, *Qadhafi, Terrorism, and the Origins of the U.S. Attack on Libya* (New York: Praeger, 1990); Edward Schumacher, "The United States and Libya," *Foreign Affairs,* Winter 1986–1987; Tim Zimmerman, "Coercive Diplomacy and Libya," in Alexander L. George and William E. Simons, eds., *The Limits of Coercive Diplomacy,* 2nd ed. (Boulder: Westview Press, 1994).

12. "Remarks at a White House Meeting with Members of the American Business Conference," April 15, 1986, at www.reagan.utexas.edu/archives/speeches/1986/41586c.htm.

13. Weinberger, *Fighting for Peace*, pp. 199–201.

14. Ibid., p. 249.

15. Prados, *Safe for Democracy*, pp. 499–500.

16. McFarlane and Smardz, *Special Trust*, p. 23.

17. Gates, *From the Shadows*, p. 397.

18. Weinberger, *Fighting for Peace*, p. 250.

19. Sohrab Sobhani, *The Pragmatic Entente: Israeli-Iranian Relations, 1948–1988* (New York: Praeger, 1989), p. xiv.

20. "Minutes of General Toufinian's Meetings with General Ezer Weizman and General Moshe Dayan," July 18, 1977. The transcripts were among the bags of shredded documents seized when the U.S. Embassy in Tehran was taken in November 1979. They were reassembled and then published in a multivolume series, Documents from the U.S. Espionage Den. The Toufanian transcripts appeared in volume 19 of the series. They are also found in the Iran revolution collection of the Digital National Security Archive (items IRO 1199 and 1200).

21. "The Israel-Iran Connection," *Journal of Palestine Studies* (Spring 1987): 210–212.

22. Weinberger, *Fighting for Peace*, p. 255; Theodore Draper, *A Very Thin Line: The Iran-Contra Affairs* (New York: Hill & Wang, 1991), pp. 149–150.

23. Shultz, *Turmoil and Triumph*, p. 793.

24. Draper, *A Very Thin Line*, p. 138.

25. Draper, *A Very Thin Line*, pp. 156–159; Reagan, *American Life*, pp. 504–505.

26. McFarlane, *Special Trust*, p. 38.

27. Draper, *A Very Thin Line*, p. 200.

28. Ibid., pp. 212–215.

29. Reagan, *American Life*, pp. 510–513.

30. McFarlane, *Special Trust*, p. 26.

31. Gates, *From the Shadows*, pp. 398–399.

32. Reagan, *American Life*, pp. 516–517.

33. Draper, *A Very Thin Line*, 330.

34. George Cave, "Why Secret 1986 U.S.-Iran 'Arms for Hostages' Negotiations Failed," *Washington Report on Middle Eastern Affairs*, September/October 1994, at www.wrmea.com/backissues/0994/9409008.htm.

35. Ronald Reagan, *U.S. Initiative to Iran: President's Address to the Nation, November 13, 1986*, Department of State Bulletin (January 1987), pp. 65–66.

36. George Shultz, *Secretary of State's Statement Before the Senate Foreign Relations Committee, January 27, 1987*, Department of State Bulletin (March 1987), pp. 19–20.

37. Ali M. Ansari, *Confronting Iran: The Failure of American Foreign Policy and the Roots of Mistrust* (London: C. Hurst & Co., 2006); Trita Parsi, *Treacherous Alliance: The Secret Dealings of Israel, Iran and the U.S.* (New Haven: Yale University Press, 2007).

38. Bill, *The Eagle and the Lion*, p. 313.

Chapter 10: The Tanker War

1. Shultz, *Statement Before the Senate Foreign Relations Committee*, pp. 19–20.

2. Jentleson, *With Friends Like These*, p. 60.

3. Martin S. Navias and Edward R. Hooton, *Tanker Wars: The Assault on Merchant Shipping During the Iran-Iraq Crisis, 1980–1988* (London: I. B. Tauris, 1996), p. 38. See also Nadia El-Sayed El-Shazly, *The Gulf Tanker War: Iran and Iraq's Maritime Swordplay* (Basingstoke, U.K.: Palgrave Macmillan, 1998); Efraim Karsh, *The Iran-Iraq War: A Military Analysis*, Adelphi Papers no. 220 (London: IISS, 1987); Elizabeth Gamlen, "US Responses to the 'Tanker War' and the Implications of Its Intervention," in Charles Davies, ed., *After the War: Iran, Iraq, and the Arab Gulf* (Chichester, U.K.: Carden, 1990).

4. J. A. Roach, "Missiles on Target: Targeting and Defense Zones in the Tanker War," *Virginia Journal of International Law* 31 (1991): 593–610.

5. Navias and Hooton, *Tanker Wars*, p. 96.

6. R. Leckow, "The Iran-Iraq Conflict in the Gulf: The Law of War Zones," *International and Comparative Law Quarterly* (July 1988): 637.

7. R. Danziger, "The Persian Gulf Tanker War," Proceedings, *Naval Review*, 1985, pp. 160–167.

8. Weinberger, *Fighting for Peace*, pp. 272, 279.

9. Thomas L. McNaugher, "Walking Tightropes in the Gulf," in Efraim Karsh, ed., *The Iran-Iraq War: Impact and Implications* (London: Macmillan, 1989), p. 173.

10. Weinberger, *Fighting for Peace*, p. 273.

11. Shultz, *Turmoil and Triumph*, p. 26.

12. Weinberger, *Fighting for Peace*, p. 278.

13. *New York Times*, July 22, 1987; cited in Janice Stein, "The Wrong Strategy in the Right Place: The United States in the Gulf," *International Security* 13, no. 3 (1988–1989): 149.

14. Richard Murphy, "Assistant Secretary Murphy's Statement, May 19, 1987," *Department of State Bulletin* 87 (1987): 58.

15. Weinberger, *Fighting for Peace*, p. 277.

16. Shultz, *Turmoil and Triumph*, p. 930.

17. J. Muir, "Gulf Shipping," *Middle East Economic Survey*, May 25, 1987.

18. Shultz, *Turmoil and Triumph*, p. 927.

19. Chubin and Tripp, *Iran and Iraq at War*, p. 197.

20. Weinberger, *Report to the Congress*, 1987.

21. Sciolino, *The Outlaw State*, p. 170.

22. House Committee on Armed Services, *Report on the Staff Investigation into the Iraqi Attack on the U.S.S. Stark*, June 14, 1987, reprinted in Andrea de Guttry and Natalino Ronzitti, eds., *The Iran-Iraq War (1980–1988) and the Law of Naval Warfare* (Cambridge: Grotius, 1993), p. 153.

23. Navias and Hooton, *Tanker Wars*, pp. 76–77.

24. "Saddam's Gulf of Threats," *Economist*, July 21, 1990, p. 57. The UAE was the Gulf Arab state with the best relations with Iran.

25. Shultz, *Turmoil and Triumph*, pp. 927–928.

26. United States Senate, Committee on Armed Services, *Senator Nunn's Letter and Response to the Weinberger Report Concerning the Administration's Security Arrangements in the Persian Gulf* (Washington D.C., 1987).

27. Shultz, *Turmoil and Triumph,* p. 926.

28. Ibid., p. 931.

29. Weinberger, *Report to the Congress,* 1987.

30. *Senator Nunn's Letter.*

31. Navias and Hooton, *Tanker Wars,* pp. 157–159.

32. Weinberger, *Fighting for Peace,* p. 251.

33. Gary Sick, "Trial by Error: Reflections on the Iran-Iraq War," *Middle East Journal* 43 (1989).

34. Weinberger, *Report to the Congress,* 1987.

35. Shultz, *Turmoil and Triumph,* p. 34.

36. J. Muir, "The Middle East Situation," *Middle East Economic Survey,* August 31, 1987.

37. Sick, "Trial by Error," p. 241.

38. Weinberger, *Report to the Congress.*

39. Ibid.

40. Stein, *International Security,* p. 150.

41. Patrick Tyler, "Gulf Rules of Engagement a Dilemma for U.S.; American Ship Commanders Operate in Increasingly Dangerous War Zone," *Washington Post,* July 4, 1988; Anthony H. Cordesman and Abraham R. Wagner, *The Lessons of Modern War,* vol. 2, *The Gulf War* (Boulder: Westview, 1996), p. 331; Weinberger, *Fighting for Peace,* p. 295.

42. R. Reagan, "Letter Dated 20 October 1987 from President Reagan to the Speaker of the House of Representatives and the President Pro Tempore of the Senate," *Weekly Compilation of Presidential Documents,* October 26, 1987, pp. 1159–1160.

43. Cordesman and Wagner, *Lessons of Modern War,* 2:330.

44. Molly Moore, U.S. Destroyers Shell Iranian Military Platform in Gulf," *Washington Post,* October 20, 1987.

45. Michael Serrill, "The Gulf Punch, Counterpunch: The U.S. Avenges a Missile Attack, and Iran Replies with a Silkworm," *Time,* November 2, 1987.

46. Ibid.

47. McNaugher, "Walking Tightropes," p. 190.

48. C. J. B. Perkins, "Operation Praying Mantis," Proceedings, *Naval Review,* May 1989, pp. 68, 70.

49. George Wilson and Molly Moore, "U.S. Sinks or Cripples 6 Iranian Ships in Gulf Battles," *Washington Post,* April 19, 1988.

Chapter 11: Iraq Takes Kuwait

1. George Bush and Brent Scowcroft, *A World Transformed* (New York: Vintage, 1998). Much of the material used in the following two chapters can be found in Lawrence Freedman and Efraim Karsh, *The Gulf Conflict 1990–1991* (London: Faber, 1993). Official documents can be found in Elihu Lauterpacht, Christopher

Greenwood, Marc Weller, and Daniel Bethlehem, *The Kuwait Crisis: Basic Documents* (Cambridge: Cambridge University Press, 1991). See also Department of Defense, *Conduct of the Persian Gulf War, Final Report to Congress, Pursuant to Title V of the Persian Gulf Conflict Supplemental Authorization and Personnel Benefits Act of 1991 (Public Law 102-25)* (Washington, D.C., 1992); U.S. Senate, Hearings Before the Committee on Armed Services, *Crisis in the Persian Gulf Region: U.S. Policy Options and Implications* (1990); Christian Alfonsi, *Circle in the Sand: Why We Went Back to Iraq* (New York: Doubleday, 2006); Andrew J. Bacevich and Efraim Inbar, eds., *The Gulf War of 1991 Reconsidered* (London: Frank Cass, 2003); Stephen Biddle and Robert Zirkle, "Technology, Civil-Military Relations, and Warfare in the Developing World," *Journal of Strategic Studies* (June 1996); Norman Cigar, "Iraq's Strategic Mindset and the Gulf War: Blueprint for Defeat," *Journal of Strategic Studies* (March 1992); Anthony H. Cordesman and Abraham R. Wagner, *Lessons of Modern War*, vol. 2; Michael Gordon and Bernard Trainor, *The General's War* (Boston: Little, Brown, 1995); Efraim Karsh, "Reflections on the 1990–91 Gulf Conflict," *Journal of Strategic Studies* (September 1996); Thomas A. Keaney and Eliot A. Cohen, *Revolution in Warfare? Air Power in the Persian Gulf* (Annapolis: Naval Institute Press, 1995); Adrian Lewis, *The American Culture of War: The History of U.S. Military Force from World War II to Operation Iraqi Freedom* (New York: Routledge, 2007); Robert Scales, *Certain Victory: The U.S. Army in the Gulf War* (London: Brassey's, 1994); Micah Sifry and Christopher Cerf, eds., *The Gulf Reader: History, Documents, Opinions* (New York: Random House, 1991); General Khaled bin Sultan with Patrick Seale, *Desert Warrior: A Personal Account of the Gulf War by the Joint Forces Commander* (New York: HarperCollins, 1995); Bob Woodward, *The Commanders* (New York: Simon & Schuster, 1991); Transcripts of interviews conducted for a Public Broadcasting Service documentary are found on www.pbs.org/wgbh/pages/frontline/gulf.

2. Amatzia Baram, "U.S. Input into Iraqi Decisionmaking, 1988–1990," in David W. Lesch, ed., *The Middle East and the United States: A Historical and Political Reassessment*, 3rd ed. (Boulder: Westview, 2003), pp. 331–343.

3. Baghdad Radio, July 18, 1990, cited in Freedman and Karsh, *Gulf Conflict*.

4. See www.pbs.org/wgbh/pages/frontline/gulf/oral/aziz/2.html.

5. Iraqi UN Representative, Mr. Kadrat, to the Security Council. See Lauterpacht et al., *Kuwaiti Crisis*, p. 100.

6. *International Herald Tribune*, August 9, 1990.

7. Patrick Clawson, *How Has Saddam Hussein Survived: Economic Sanctions, 1990–93*, McNair Paper (Washington, D.C.: Institute for National Strategic Studies, National Defense University, 1993), pp. 30, 53.

8. Karsh, "Reflections," pp. 306–307.

9. Shafeeq N. Ghabra, "Kuwait and the United States," in Lesch, *Middle East and the United States*, pp. 314–315.

10. "Excerpts from Iraqi Document on Meeting with U.S. Envoy," *New York Times*, September 23, 1990.

11. Bush and Scowcroft, *World Transformed*, p. 312.

12. Lauterpacht et al., *Kuwaiti Crisis*, p. 293.

13. The transcripts of the PBS interviews can be found at www.pbs.org/wgbh/pages/frontline/gulf.

14. Khaled bin Sultan, *Desert Warrior*, p. 19.

15. Bush and Scowcroft, *World Transformed*, p. 317.

16. Ibid., p. 333.

17. Cigar, "Iraq's Strategic Mindset," p. 3.

18. Bush and Scowcroft, *World Transformed*, p. 337.

19. Ibid., pp. 374–375.

20. Ibid., p. 402.

21. Speech of January 10, 1991; reprinted in Sifry and Cerf, *Gulf Reader*.

22. "US-Soviet Joint Statement," *Financial Times*, August 5, 1991.

23. Speech by President George Bush, *Financial Times*, August 9, 1990.

24. President George Bush, Address to Congress, September 11, 1990, U.S. Information Service.

25. Bush and Scowcroft, *World Transformed*, p. 375.

26. Ibid., p. 415.

27. "This Choice Is Yours to Make," *International Herald Tribune*, January 14, 1991.

28. See Freedman and Karsh, *Gulf Conflict*, p. 257.

Chapter 12: Desert Storm

1. Text of George Bush's statement, "Bush: 'Go the Extra Mile for Peace,'" *International Herald Tribune*, December 1–2, 1990.

2. 101st Congress, Second Session, United States Senate, Hearings Before the Committee on Armed Services, *Crisis in the Persian Gulf Region: U.S. Policy Options and Implications*, September 11, 13, November 27–30, December 3, 1990, pp. 662–664.

3. Cited in Freedman and Karsh, *Gulf Conflict*, p. 315.

4. Ibid., p. 285.

5. Woodward, *Commanders*, pp. 319–320.

6. Stephen Biddle and Robert Zirkle, "Technology, Civil-Military Relations, and Warfare in the Developing World," *Journal of Strategic Studies* (June 1996): 185.

7. Cigar, "Iraq's Strategic Mindset," p. 18.

8. 101st Congress, Second Session, House of Representatives, Hearings before the Committee on Armed Services, *Crisis in the Persian Gulf: Sanctions, Diplomacy and War*, December 4–10, 1990; 101st Congress, Second Session, United States Senate, Hearings Before the Committee on Armed Services, *Crisis in the Persian Gulf Region: U.S. Policy Options and Implications*, September 11, 13, November 27–30, December 3, 1990.

9. House Hearings, p. 894.

10. Ibid., p. 905.

11. Keaney and Cohen, *Revolution in Warfare?* pp. 34–35.

12. Ibid., p. 38.

13. Cordesman and Wagner, *Lessons of Modern War*, p. 418.

14. R. A. Mason, "The Air War in the Gulf," *Survival* (May–June 1991): 211–229.

15. Department of Defense, *Conduct of the Persian Gulf War, Final Report to Congress, Pursuant to Title V of the Persian Gulf Conflict Supplemental Authorization and Personnel Benefits Act of 1991 (Public Law 102-25)*, (Washington, D.C., 1992), p. 128.

16. Keaney and Cohen, *Revolution in Warfare?* p. 54.

17. Department of Defense, *Conduct of the Persian Gulf War*, p. 171.

18. John Barry, "The Nuclear Option: Thinking the Unthinkable," *Newsweek*, January 14, 1991.

19. Avigdor Haselkorn, *The Continuing Storm: Iraq, Poisonous Weapons, and Deterrence* (New Haven: Yale University Press, 1999).

20. William Arkin, Damian Durrant, and Marianne Cherni, *Impact: Modern Warfare and the Environment. A Case Study of the Gulf War* (London, 1991). A Greenpeace study prepared for a conference on a Fifth Geneva Convention on the protection of the environment in time of armed conflict.

21. *New York Times* editorial, reprinted in *International Herald Tribune*, January 26–27, 1991.

22. *New York Times*, February 26, 1991.

23. Bush and Scowcroft, *World Transformed*, pp. 471, 487. The February 20 quote comes from Alfonsi, *Circle in the Sand*, p. 167.

24. *USIA Report*, February 21, 1991.

25. *International Herald Tribune*, October 18, 1990.

26. *International Herald Tribune*, October 26, 1990.

27. Thomas G. Mahnken, "A Squandered Opportunity? The Decision to End the Gulf War," in Bacevich and Inbar, *Gulf War of 1991 Reconsidered*.

28. Powell, *My American Journey*, p. 523.

29. Interview at www.pbs.org/wgbh/pages/frontline/gulf/oral/samarrai/8.html.

30. Freedman and Karsh, *Gulf Conflict*, p. 410.

31. Bush and Scowcroft, *World Transformed*.

32. *U.S. News & World Report* Editors, *Triumph Without Victory: The Unreported History of the Persian Gulf War* (New York: Times Books, 1992).

33. "Unfinished Business: The CIA and Saddam Hussein," *ABC News*, June 26, 1997; cited in Douglas Little, "Mission Impossible: The CIA and the Cult of Covert Action in the Middle East," *Diplomatic History* 28, no. 5 (November 2004): 663–701.

34. *Frontline*, "The Gulf War, Oral History: Richard Cheney," at www.pbs.org/wgbh/pages/frontline/gulf/oral/cheney/2.html. Similar views are found in other memoirs, including Bush and Scowcroft, *World Transformed*.

Chapter 13: Intifada

1. Richard Haass, *Conflicts Unending* (New Haven: Yale University Press, 1990), p. 139.

2. Venice European Council, *Venice Declaration on the Middle East*, June 13, 1980.

3. Interview with Josef Harif, *Ma'ariv*, June 26, 1992; cited in Shlaim, *Iron Wall*.

4. Idith Zertal and Akiva Elder, *Lords of the Land: The War over Israeli Settlements in the Occupied Territories, 1967–2007* (New York: Nation Books, 2007), p. 59.

5. See www.yale.edu/lawweb/avalon/mideast/hamas.htm.

6. Bregman and El-Tahri, *Fifty Years War*, p. 198.

7. Quandt, *Peace Process*, p. 289.

8. Shlaim, *Iron Wall*, p. 470.

9. Bush and Scowcroft, *World Transformed*, pp. 346, 379.

10. Quandt, *Peace Process*, p. 402.

11. James Baker with Thomas DeFrank, *The Politics of Diplomacy: Revolution, War, and Peace, 1989–1992* (New York: Putnam, 1995), p. 450.

12. Shlomo Ben-Ami, *Scars of War, Wounds of Peace: The Israeli-Arab Tragedy* (Oxford: Oxford University Press, 2007), p. 114.

13. Bernard Reich, "The United States and Israel," in Lesch, *The Middle East and the United States*, p. 242.

14. "Excerpts from President Bush's News Session on Israeli Loan Guarantees," *New York Times*, September 13, 1991.

15. Cited in Mark Matthews, *Lost Years: Bush, Sharon, and Failure in the Middle East* (New York: Nation Books, 2007), p. 4.

Chapter 14: Dual Containment

1. The process of putting together Clinton's foreign policy team is well described in David Halberstam, *War in a Time of Peace: Bush, Clinton, and the Generals* (New York: Scribner's, 2001). For memoirs of the administration, see Bill Clinton, *My Life* (New York: Knopf, 2004); Warren Christopher, *Chance of a Lifetime: A Memoir* (New York: Scribner's, 2001); and Madeleine Albright with Bill Woodward, *Madame Secretary* (New York: Miramax Books, 2003).

2. Christopher, *Chance of a Lifetime*.

3. Colin Powell with Joseph E. Persico, *My American Journey* (New York: Random House, 1995), p. 576.

4. Benjamin and Simon, *Age of Sacred Terror*, p. 241.

5. President William Clinton, Acceptance Speech, Democratic National Convention, August 29, 1996; Clinton, Second Inaugural Address, January 20, 1997.

6. Polls cited by Fawz Gerges, *America and Political Islam: Clash of Cultures or Clash of Interests* (New York: Cambridge University Press, 1999), pp. 7–8.

7. An example of the cautionary literature on this topic is John Esposito, *The Islamic Threat: Myth or Reality?* (New York: Oxford University Press, 1992).

8. Cited in ibid., p. 53.

9. Samuel Huntington, "The Clash of Civilizations?" *Foreign Affairs* (Summer 1993): 31.

10. Bernard Lewis, "The Roots of Muslim Rage," *Atlantic*, September 1990.

11. "Interview with James A. Baker III," *Middle East Quarterly* (September 1984): 83. Cited in Gerges, *America and Political Islam*, pp. 76–77.

12. Edward Djerejian, Meridian House Speech, June 1992; cited in Gerges, *America and Political Islam*, pp. 78–80.

13. President William Clinton, "Remarks to the Jordanian Parliament in Amman, Jordan," October 2, 1994, at www.presidency.ucsb.edu.

14. Frank Ahrens, "The Reluctant Warrior," *Washington Post*, February 24, 1998.

15. Thomas Friedman, "Clinton Backs Raid but Muses About a New Start," *New York Times*, January 14, 1993.

16. Frank Anderson interview for PBS, 2000, at www.pbs.org/wgbh/pages/frontline/shows/saddam/interviews/anderson.html.

17. Kenneth Katzman, *Iraq: U.S. Efforts to Change the Regime,* Congressional Research Service, Library of Congress, Report for Congress, March 22, 2002.

18. See www.pbs.org/wgbh/pages/frontline/shows/saddam/interviews/chalabi.html.

19. Prados, *Safe for Democracy,* p. 600.

20. Jane Mayer, "The Manipulator," *New Yorker,* June 7, 2004.

21. Dr. Sami Abdul-Rahman was deputy prime minister and member of the Politburo, Kurdish Democratic Party. See www.pbs.org/wgbh/pages/frontline/shows/saddam/interviews/rahman.html; *The Survival of Saddam,* January 25, 2000.

22. Robert Baer, *See No Evil* (New York: Arrow, 2002), p. 259. For an account based on sources critical of Baer, see Andrew Cockburn and Patrick Cockburn, *Saddam Hussein: An American Obsession* (New York: Verso, 2000).

23. Jim Hoagland, "How CIA's Secret War on Saddam Collapsed," *Washington Post,* June 26, 1997.

24. Prados, *Safe for Democracy,* p. 603.

25. Evan Thomas, Christopher Dickey, and Gregory L. Vistica, "Bay of Pigs Redux," *Newsweek,* March 23, 1998.

26. Independent Inquiry Committee into the United Nations Oil-for-Food Program, *Second Interim Report,* March 29, 2005, at www.iic-offp.org/documents/InterimReportMar2005.pdf.

27. Albright, *Madame Secretary,* pp. 174–175.

28. The humanitarian costs of the sanctions in Iraq have been the subject of numerous studies. Two of the most comprehensive are Richard Garfield, *Morbidity and Mortality Among Iraqi Children from 1990 to 1998: Assessing the Impact of Economic Sanctions,* Occasional Paper Series 16:OP:3, Joan B. Kroc Institute for International Peace Studies; Fourth Freedom Forum, March 6, 2001; and Mohamed M. Ali and Iqbal H. Shah, "Sanctions and Childhood Mortality in Iraq," *Lancet,* May 2000. For a discussion of the issue of responsibility, see David Cortright and George A. Lopez, "Are Sanctions Just? The Problematic Case of Iraq," *Journal of International Affairs* (Spring 1999): 743–745. See also David Cortright, "A Hard Look at Iraq Sanctions," *Nation,* December 3, 2001, at www.thenation.com/doc.mhtml?i=20011203&s=cortright. John Mueller and Karl Mueller, "The Methodology of Mass Destruction: Assessing Threats in the New World Order," *Journal of Strategic Studies* 23, no. 1 (2000): 153–187.

29. Richard Butler, *Saddam Defiant: The Threat of Mass Destruction and the Crisis of Global Security* (London: Weidenfeld & Nicholson, 2000).

30. "Remarks of the President on Iraq," December 19, 1998; "Prime Minister, Mr Tony Blair, Assessment of Operation Desert Fox and Forward Strategy," press conference, December 20, 1998.

31. CNN/USA *Today*/Gallup Poll, November 13–15, 1998 (N = 1,039 adults nationwide). CNN/*Time* Poll, Yankelovich Partners, December 17–18, 1998 (N = 1,031 adults nationwide).

32. Giandomenico Picco, *Man Without a Gun: One Diplomat's Secret Struggle to Free the Hostages, Fight Terrorism, and End a War* (New York: Crown, 1999).

33. Douglas Jehl, "U.S. Seeks Ways to Isolate Iran; Describes Leaders as Dangerous," *New York Times,* May 27, 1993.

34. Martin Indyk, "The Clinton Administration's Approach to the Middle East" (speech given to the Washington Institute for Near East Policy, May 18, 1993).

35. Anthony Lake, "Confronting Backlash States," *Foreign Affairs* (March–April 1994).

36. Pollack, *Persian Puzzle,* p. 263.

37. Warren Christopher, "America's Leadership, America's Opportunity," *Foreign Policy* (Spring 1995): 6–27.

38. Clarke, *Against All Enemies,* p. 118; UPI, "Perry, U.S. Eyed Iran Attack After Bombing," June 6, 2007.

39. Louis Freeh, "Khobar Towers: The Clinton Administration Left Many Stones Unturned," *Wall Street Journal,* June 25, 2006.

40. Secretary of State Madeleine K. Albright, remarks before the American-Iranian Council, Washington, D.C., March 17, 2000.

41. Transcript, Kuwait's Al-Qabas Interviews Indyk, Ricciardone on Iraq, at www.fas.org/news/iraq/1999/01/99020205_nlt.htm.

Chapter 15: Return to Camp David

1. Hussein Agha and Robert Malley, "Camp David: The Tragedy of Errors," *New York Review of Books,* August 19, 2001; Benny Morris, "Camp David and After: An Exchange (1. An Interview with Ehud Barak)"; "Camp David and After: An Exchange Between Hussein Agha and Robert Malley (2. A Reply to Ehud Barak)," June 13, 2002, p. 10. Dennis Ross, the main U.S. negotiator, provides his account in Dennis Ross, *The Missing Peace: The Inside Story of the Fight for Middle East Peace* (New York: Farrar, Straus & Giroux, 2004). For an account more critical of the American stance, particularly Ross's role, see Clayton E. Swisher, *The Truth About Camp David: The Untold Story About the Collapse of the Middle East Peace Process* (New York: Nation Groups, 2004). An insider Israeli perspective comes from Shlomo Ban-Ami, *Scars of Wars, Wounds of Peace: The Israeli-Arab Tragedy* (Oxford: Oxford University Press, 2007). See also Ahron Bregman and Jihan El-Tahri, *The Fifty Years War* (London: Penguin, 1998); Albright, *Madame Secretary*; Ahron Bregman, *The Elusive Peace* (London: Penguin, 2005). For comprehensive accounts of Camp David based on eyewitnesses, see Charles Enderlin, *Shattered Dreams: The Failure of the Peace Process in the Middle East, 1995–2002* (New York: Other Press, 2002); and Jeremy Pressman, "Visions in Collision: What Happened at Camp David and Taba?" *International Security,* (Fall 2003): 5–43.

2. Kenneth W. Stein and Samuel Lewis with Sheryl J. Brown, *Making Peace Among Arabs and Israelis: Lessons from Fifty Years of Negotiating Experience* (Washington, D.C.: United States Institute of Peace, 1991).

3. Bernard Reich, "The United States and Israel"; and JoAnn A. DiGeorgio-Lutz, "The U.S.-PLO Relationship: From Dialogue to the White House Lawn," in Lesch, *The Middle East and the United States.*

4. Ibid.; Albright, *Madame Secretary*; Ross, *Missing Peace*; Bregman, *Elusive Peace.*

5. Cited in Swisher, *Truth About Camp David*, p. 136. The most articulate critique of Oslo from a Palestinian perspective is Edward Said, *From Oslo to Iraq and the Road Map: Essays* (New York: Viking, 2005).

6. Yoram Peri, *Generals in the Cabinet Room: How the Military Shapes Israeli Policy* (Washington, D.C.: United States Institute of Peace Press, 2006).

7. Yezid Sayigh, *Armed Struggle and the Search for State: The Palestinian National Movement, 1949–1993* (New York: Oxford University Press, 1998).

8. Mearsheimer and Walt, *Israel Lobby*, pp. 164–165.

9. Ross, *Missing Peace*, p. 195.

10. Idith Zertal and Akiva Elder, *Lords of the Land: The War over Israel's Settlements in the Occupied Territories, 1967–2007* (New York: Nation Books, 2007), p. 122.

11. Institute for Advanced Strategic and Political Studies, *A Clean Break: A New Strategy for Securing the Realm* (1996), at www.iasps.org/strat1.htm.

12. Ross, *Missing Peace*, p. 337.

13. Ibid., p. 353.

14. "Remarks by the President to the Members of the Palestinian National Council and Other Palestinian Organizations," Shawwa Center, Gaza City, Gaza, December 14, 1998.

15. Clinton, *My Life*, p. 913.

16. On negotiations with Syria, see Jeremy Pressman, "Mediation, Domestic Politics, and the Israeli-Syrian Negotiations, 1991–2000," *Security Studies* (July–September 2007); Jerome Slater, "Lost Opportunities for Peace in the Arab-Israeli Conflict: Israel and Syria, 1948–2001," *International Security* (Summer 2002); Warren Christopher, *Chances of a Lifetime* (New York: Scribner's, 2001); Itamar Rabinovich, *Waging Peace: Israel and the Arabs, 1948–2003* (Princeton: Princeton University Press, 2004); Rabinovich, *The Brink of Peace: The Israeli-Syrian Negotiations* (Princeton: Princeton University Press, 1998); Bruce Reidel, "Camp David: The US-Israel Bargain," July 15, 2002, at www.bitterlemons.org/previous/b1150702ed26extra.html.

17. Rabinovich, *Waging Peace*, p. 132.

18. Cited by Pressman, *Security Studies*, p. 369.

19. Swisher, *Truth About Camp David*, p. 47.

20. Clinton, *My Life*, p. 886; Albright, *Madame Secretary*, p. 478.

21. Raviv Drucker, *Harakiri* (Tel Aviv: Yedioth Ahronoth Books, 2002), p. 87; cited by Pressman, *Security Studies*, p. 370.

22. Clinton, *My Life*, p. 886.

23. Ibid., p. 887.

24. Agha and Malley, "Camp David."

25. Swisher, *Truth About Camp David*, p. 224.

26. Bregman, *Elusive Peace*, p. 83.

27. Enderlin, *Shattered Dreams*, pp. 163–164.

28. Ben-Ami, *Scars of War*, p. 144.

29. Ibid., p. 263.

30. Albright, *Madame Secretary*, pp. 485–486.

31. Clinton, *My Life*, p. 914.

32. Bregman, *Elusive Peace*, p. 109

33. Clinton, *My Life*, p. 916.

34. Gadi Baltiansky, spokesperson for Prime Minister Ehud Barak, "'No One to Talk To': A Critical Look at the Linkage Between Politics and the Media," Herzog Institute for Media, Politics, and Society, Tel Aviv University, January 12, 2005, at www.tau.ac.il/institutes/herzog/talkto-eng.pdf.

35. Peri, *Generals in the Cabinet Room,* p. 102.

36. Gilles Kepel, *The War for Muslim Minds* (Cambridge: Harvard University Press, 2004), p. 14.

37. Ben-Ami, *Scars of War,* 265.

38. Cited in Yoram Meital, *Peace in Tatters: Israel, Palestine, and the Middle East* (Boulder: Lynne Rienner, 2006), p. 74.

39. Yezid Sayigh, "Arafat and the Anatomy of a Revolt," *Survival* 43 (2001): 47–60.

Chapter 16: Choosing America

1. Fawaz A. Gerges, *The Far Enemy: Why Jihad Went Global* (New York: Cambridge University Press, 2005), p. 10.

2. Wright, *Looming Tower*, p. 122.

3. Ibid., p. 95.

4. National Commission on Terrorist Attacks upon the United States, Staff Statement no. 15, *Overview of the Enemy*.

5. Coll, *Ghost Wars*, p. 87 n. 30; Peter Bergen, *Holy War, Inc.: Inside the Secret World of Osama bin Laden* (New York: Free Press, 2001), pp. 64–66. The CIA has issued its own denial: "For the record, you should know that the CIA never employed, paid, or maintained any relationship whatsoever with Bin Laden." At www.cia.gov/news-information/cia-the-war-on-terrorism/terrorism-faqs.html.

6. Levy and Scott-Clark, *Deception*, p. 189.

7. All this is discussed thoroughly in Levy and Scott Clark, *Deception*.

8. "Cracks in the Foundation: Leadership Schisms in al-Qa'ida from 1989–2006," Harmony Project, Combating Terrorism Center, West Point, September 2007, at http://ctc.usma.edu.

9. Douglas Jehl, "Holy War Lured Saudis as Rulers Looked Away," *New York Times,* December 27, 2001.

10. Rachel Bronson, *Thicker Than Oil,* p. 214.

11. Clarke, *Against All Enemies,* p. 142.

12. Alan Cullison, "Inside Al-Qaeda's Hard Drive," *Atlantic Monthly,* September 2004, at www.theatlantic.com/doc/200409/cullison. This article is based on the contents of a hard drive apparently used by Zawahiri, picked up by the author in Kabul in 2001.

13. See www.pbs.org/newshour/terrorism/international/fatwa_1996.html.

14. See www.ishipress.com/osamaint.htm. Magnus Ranstorp, "Interpreting the Broader Context and Meaning of Bin-Laden's *Fatwa,*" *Studies in Conflict and Terrorism* 21 (1998).

15. See www.pbs.org/newshour/terrorism/international/fatwa_1998.html.

16. Gerges, *Far Enemy,* p. 87.

17. Wright, *Looming Tower,* p. 215.

18. Ibid., p. 129.

19. Kepel, *War for Muslim Minds,* p. 32.

20. Theo Farrell, "Sliding into War: The Somalia Imbroglio and U.S. Army Peace Operations Doctrine," *International Peacekeeping* 2, no. 2 (1995).

21. The best account of the battle of Mogadishu is Mark Bowden, *Black Hawk Down: A Story of Modern War* (New York: Atlantic Monthly Press, 1999).

22. Clarke, *Against All Enemies,* p. 87.

23. "Al-Qa'ida's (Mis)adventures in the Horn of Africa," *Harmony Project, Combating Terrorism Project,* West Point, pp. 42–43.

24. Ibid., p. 39.

25. Gerges, *Far Enemy,* p. 55.

26. Ibid., p. 53.

27. Interview with Peter Arnett, 1997, at www.ishipress.com/osamaint.htm.

28. Benjamin and Simon, *Age of Sacred Terror,* p. 152.

29. Cullison, "Inside Al-Qaeda's Hard Drive."

30. Coll, *Ghost Wars,* p. 279.

31. William Clinton, "Remarks on American Security in a Changing World," George Washington University, August 5, 1996, at www.presidency.ucsb.edu.

32. Clinton, *My Life,* p. 798.

33. Clarke, *Against All Enemies,* pp. 184, 211–212.

34. Clinton, *My Life,* p. 799.

35. Clarke, *Against All Enemies,* pp. 200–201.

Chapter 17: The War on Terror

1. Condoleezza Rice, "Promoting the National Interest," *Foreign Affairs* (January–February 2000): 53.

2. Powell, *My American Journey.* See also Charles Stevenson, "The Evolving Clinton Doctrine on the Use of Force," *Armed Forces and Society* (Summer 1996).

3. Lawrence Freedman, *The Transformation of Strategic Affairs* (London: Routledge/ISS, 2006).

4. Department of Defense, *Field Manual 100-5: Operations* (Washington, D.C.: Department of the Army, 1982), pp. 1–2.

5. Cited in Larry Cable, "Reinventing the Round Wheel: Insurgency, Counter-Insurgency, and Peacekeeping Post Cold War," *Small Wars and Insurgencies* (Autumn 1993).

6. Remarks by President George W. Bush at the U.S. Naval Academy Commencement, May 25, 2001, at www.whitehouse.gov/news/releases/2001/05/20010425-1.html.

7. Edward Luttwak, "Towards Post-Heroic Warfare," *Foreign Affairs* (May–June 1995).

8. Cited in Andrew Erdmann, "The U.S. Presumption of Quick, Costless Wars," *Orbis* (Summer 1999).

9. Jeffrey Record, *Making War, Thinking History: Munich, Vietnam, and Presidential Uses of Force from Korea to Kosovo* (Annapolis: Naval Institute Press, 2002).

10. Peter D. Feaver and Christopher Gelpi, *Choosing Your Battles: American Civil-Military Relations and the Use of Force* (Princeton: Princeton University Press, 2003).

11. Such threats are discussed in Gavin Cameron, *Nuclear Terrorism: A Threat Assessment for the 21st Century* (London: Macmillan, 1999); Richard A. Falkenrath, Robert D. Newman, and Bradley Thayer, *America's Achilles' Heel: Nuclear, Biological, and Chemical Terrorism and Covert Attack* (Cambridge: MIT Press, 1998).

12. Brian M. Jenkins, *Will Terrorists Go Nuclear?* (Santa Monica, Calif.: RAND, 1975); see also Ehud Sprinzak, "Rational Fanatics," *Foreign Policy* (September–October 2000).

13. Bruce Hoffman, *Inside Terrorism* (New York: Columbia University Press, 1998).

14. Bruce Hoffman, "America and the New Terrorism: An Exchange," *Survival* (Summer 2000): 163–164; He was responding to Steven Simon and Daniel Benjamin, "America and the New Terrorism," *Survival* (Spring 2000), which offered a much gloomier prospect, with a particular focus on the serious intent and capacity of al Qaeda.

15. The Pew Research Center for the People and the Press, April 11, 1996, at http://people-press.org/reports/print.php3?ReportID=128.

16. U.S. Commission on National Security/21st Century, *New World Coming: American Security in the 21st Century* (Washington, D.C., 1999), p. 48. For a similar emphasis, see also National Commission on Terrorism, *Countering the Changing Threat of International Terrorism* (Washington, D.C.: U.S. Congress, 2000). Pursuant to Public Law 277, 105th Congress.

17. Richard K. Betts, "The New Threat of Weapons of Mass Destruction," *Foreign Affairs* (January–February 1998): 41.

18. Ivo H. Daalder and James M. Lindsay, *America Unbound: The Bush Revolution in Foreign Policy* (Hoboken, N.J.: John Wiley, 2005), p. 73.

19. National Security Archive, Bush Administration's First Memo on al-Qaeda Declassified, September 27, 2006, at www.gwu.edu/~nsarchiv/NSAEBB/NSAEBB147/index.htm.

20. George J. Tenet, "World-Wide Threat 2001: National Security in a Changing World," February 7, 2001, at www.usembassy.org.uk/terror128.html.

21. Bumiller, *Condoleezza Rice*, pp. 154–155.

22. Daalder and Lindsay, *America Unbound*, pp. 75–76.

23. On the history of terrorist methods, see Walter Laqueur, *The Age of Terrorism* (Boston: Little, Brown, 1987).

24. Another individual in custody had been downloading information from the Internet about aerial application of pesticides, or crop dusting. "John Ashcroft Testifies Before House Judiciary Committee," September 24, 2001, at www.usdoj.gov/opa/pr/2001/September/492ag.htm.

25. *Los Angeles Times*, September 30, 2001.

26. Susan Eggen and Bob Woodward, "FBI Issues 2nd Global Attack Alert; Credible Reports Indicate Strikes on U.S. Possible in Next Week, Agency Says," *Washington Post,* October 30, 2001.

27. Michael Howard, "What's in a Name? How to Fight Terrorism," *Foreign Affairs* (January–February 2002).

28. Alan Cullison, "Inside al-Qaeda's Hard-Drive," *Atlantic Monthly,* September 2004.

29. Levy and Scott-Clark, *Deception,* p. 314.

30. Cited in Daalder and Lindsay, *America Unbound,* p. 99.

31. Benjamin S. Lambeth, *Air Power Against Terror: America's Conduct of Operation Enduring Freedom* (Santa Monica: RAND Corporation, 2005), p. 106.

32. Edward Cody, "Taliban's Hide-and-Wait Tactics Tied to U.S. Aversion to Casualties," *International Herald Tribune,* October 22, 2001.

33. Maureen Dowd, "That Yankee Music," *New York Times,* November 4, 2001.

34. R. W. Apple, "A Military Quagmire Remembered: Afghanistan as Vietnam," *New York Times,* October 31, 2001.

35. Nik Gowing, "Outfoxed in the Information War," *Time,* November 12, 2001.

36. Robert Kagan and William Kristol, "A Winning Strategy: How the Bush Administration Changed Course and Won the War in Afghanistan," *Weekly Standard,* November 26, 2001; Gary C. Schroen, *First In: An Insider's Account of How the CIA Spearheaded the War on Terror in Afghanistan* (New York: Ballantine Books, 2005).

37. On Tora Bora, see Philip Smucker, *Al Qaeda's Great Escape: The Military and the Media on Terror's Trail* (Dulles, Va.: Brassey's, 2004). Also on bin Laden's escape and whereabouts, see Peter Bergen, "The Long Hunt for Osama," *Atlantic Monthly,* October 2004.

38. Stephen Biddle, "Afghanistan and the Future of Warfare: Implications for Army and Defense Policy," *Strategic Studies Institute* (November 2002): 36.

39. *New York Times,* November 13, 2001.

40. Remarks by the President at the Citadel, Charleston, South Carolina, December 11, 2001.

41. Alan Sipress and Peter Finn, "U.S. Says 'Not Yet' to Patrol by Allies: In Bonn, Factions Drop Objections to Peacekeepers," *Washington Post,* November 30, 2001.

42. Daalder and Lindsay, *America Unbound,* p. 110.

43. Interview, *Face the Nation,* November 18, 2001; Gary Bernsten, *Jawbreaker: The Attack on bin Laden and al-Qaeda: A Personal Account by the CIA's Key Field Commander* (New York: Crown Publishers, 2005).

44. Woodward, *Bush at War,* p. 195.

45. Dana Priest and R. Jeffrey Smith, "Memo Offered Justification for Use of Torture," *Washington Post,* June 8, 2004; Barton Gellman and Jo Becker, "The Unseen Path to Cruelty," *Washington Post,* June 25, 2007.

46. DeYoung, *Powell,* pp. 369–372; Bumiller, *Condoleezza Rice,* pp. 170–171.

Chapter 18: Regime Change

1. U.S. Agency for International Development, *Iraq's Legacy of Terror: Mass Graves* (Washington, D.C., January 2004), at www.usaid.gov/iraq/pdf/iraq_mass_graves.pdf. These are also the figures used by groups such as Human Rights Watch.

2. For a carefully argued case that these abuses did not turn the 2003 war into a humanitarian intervention, see Ken Roth, "War in Iraq: Not a Humanitarian Intervention," *World Report 2004,* Human Rights Watch, at http://hrw.org/wr2k4/3.htm#_Toc58744952.

3. George Packer, *Assassin's Gate: America in Iraq* (New York: Farrar, Straus & Giroux, 2005).

4. DeYoung, *Powell*, p. 429.

5. John Diamond et al., "Iraq Course Set from Tight White House Circle," *USA Today,* September 11, 2002; Glenn Kessler, "U.S. Decision on Iraq Has Puzzling Past: Opponents of War Wonder When, How Policy Was Set," *Washington Post,* January 12, 2003.

6. See www.newamericancentury.org/iraqclintonletter.htm. On the Project for a New American Century, see Maria Ryan, "Inventing the 'Axis of Evil': The Myth and Reality of U.S. Intelligence and Policy-Making After 9/11," *Intelligence and National Security,* Winter 2002. For a critique of the various proposals for overthrowing Iraq, see Daniel Byman, Kenneth Pollack, and Gideon Rose, "Can Saddam Be Toppled?" *Foreign Affairs* (January–February 1999); Tim Trevan, *Saddam's Secrets: The Hunt for Iraq's Hidden Weapons* (London: HarperCollins, 1999); Scott Ritter, *Endgame: Solving the Iraq Problem Once and for All* (New York: Simon & Schuster, 1999); F. Gregory Gause, "Saddam's Unwatched Arsenal," *Foreign Affairs* (May–June 1999): 54–65. Works on the Iraqi opposition include Daniel Byman, "Proceed with Caution: U.S. Support for the Iraqi Opposition," *Washington Quarterly* (Summer 1999): 23–37; and David Wurmser, *Tyranny's Ally* (Washington, D.C.: AEI Press, 1999). See also Daniel Byman, Kenneth Pollack, and Matthew Waxman, "Coercing Saddam Hussein: Lessons from the Past," *Survival* (Autumn 1998): 127–152.

7. Opening Statement by Secretary of State Madeleine K. Albright Before the Subcommittee on Commerce, Justice, State, and the Judiciary Senate Appropriations Committee, February 26, 1998.

8. Statement by the President, "The Iraq Liberation Act," October 31, 1998.

9. John Burgess and David B. Ottaway, "Iraqi Opposition Unable to Mount Viable Challenge," *Washington Post,* February 12, 1998.

10. Nicholas Lemann, "The Iraq Factor: Will the New Bush Team's Old Memories Shape Its Foreign Policy?" *New Yorker,* January 22, 2001.

11. Daalder and Lindsay, *America Unbound,* pp. 39–40.

12. Rice, *Foreign Affairs.*

13. Ron Suskind, *The Price of Loyalty: George W. Bush, the White House, and the Education of Paul O'Neill* (New York: Simon & Schuster, 2004), p. 74.

14. "Remarks by Deputy Secretary of Defense Paul Wolfowitz, American Jewish Committee, Washington, D.C.," May 4, 2001, at http://usinfo.state.gov/topical/pol/arms/stories/01050711.htm.

15. Meghan O'Sullivan, *Iraq: Time for a Modified Approach* (Washington, D.C.: Brookings Institution, 2001).

16. "Secretary of State Colin Powell, Testimony at Budget Hearing Before the Senate Foreign Relations Committee," March 8, 2001, at www.state.gov/secretary/rm/2001/1164.htm.

17. Woodward, *Plan of Attack*, pp. 20–22.

18. "Remarks by the President and British Prime Minister Tony Blair, White House," January 31, 2003, at www.whitehouse.gov/news/releases/2003/01/20030131-23.html.

19. Statement by President George W. Bush, the Rose Garden, the White House, November 26, 2001.

20. Rob Watson, "'Streamlined' Iraq Sanctions Remain Tight," May 14, 2002, at http://news.bbc.co.uk/1/hi/world/americas/1984526.stm. On the history of the United Nations and Iraq, see David M. Malone, *The International Struggle over Iraq: Politics in the UN Security Council 1980–2005* (London: Oxford University Press, 2006).

21. Woodward, *Plan of Attack*, p. 3.

22. Ibid., pp. 3, 53–55.

23. Patrick E. Tyler and David E. Sanger, "A Nation Challenged: Diplomacy; U.S. to Press Iraq to Let U.N. Search for Banned Arms," *New York Times*, December 1, 2001. On the background to this interview, see Woodward, *Plan of Attack*, p. 39.

24. Stephen Fidler and Roula Khalaf, "Back to Iraq: Washington Is Turning Its Attention to Baghdad. But the Military Success in Afghanistan Would Be Hard to Reproduce Against Saddam Hussein," *Financial Times*, December 1, 2001.

25. "Remarks by President Bush and Prime Minister Tony Blair in Joint Press Availability, Crawford High School, Crawford, Texas," April 6, 2002, at www.whitehouse.gov/news/releases/2002/04/20020406-3.html.

26. Daniel Eisenberg, "We're Taking Him Out," *Time*, May 5, 2002, at hwww.time.com/time/world/article/0,8599,235395,00.html.

27. Richard Leiby, "The Secret Warrior: Gen. Wayne Downing, from West Point to White House," *Washington Post*, November 20, 2001.

28. One of the most influential critiques of the Afghan Model was Stephen Biddle, "Afghanistan and the Future of Warfare," *Foreign Affairs* (March–April 2003): 31–46. For a more positive assessment, see Richard Andres, "The Afghan Model in Northern Iraq," *Journal of Strategic Studies* (June 2006): 395–422.

29. Brent Scowcroft, "Don't Attack Saddam," *Wall Street Journal*, August 15, 2002.

30. Philip H. Gordon and Jeremy Shapiro, *Allies at War: America, Europe, and the Crisis over Iraq* (New York: McGraw Hill, 2004), p. 97.

31. "Remarks by the President at 2002 Graduation Exercise of the United States Military Academy, West Point, New York," June 1, 2002, at http://usinfo.state.gov/topical/pol/terror/02060201.htm.

32. "The National Security Strategy of the United States, Washington, D.C.," September 2002, at www.whitehouse.gov/nsc/nss.html.

33. Gallup poll, August 5–8, 2002.

34. Woodward, *Plan of Attack*, p. 220.

35. Deputy Secretary Wolfowitz, "Interview with Sam Tannenhaus," *Vanity Fair*, May 9, 2003, at www.defenselink.mil/transcripts/2003/tr20030509-depsecdef 0223.html. The Pentagon released the transcript of the interview after the published version had been erroneously taken as confirmation that the real reason for war was oil.

36. Dana Priest, "U.S. Not Claiming Iraqi Link to Terror," *Washington Post*, September 10, 2002.

37. "Iraq: Conditions for Military Action (A Note by Officials)," July 22, 2002, at www.downingstreetmemo.com/cabinetofficetext.html.

38. Woodward, *Plan of Attack*, p. 151

39. Woodward, *Bush at War*, p. 350.

40. Charles Duelfer, Director of Central Intelligence Special Adviser for Strategy Regarding Iraqi Weapons of Mass Destruction (WMD) Programs Testimony to the U.S. Congress, March 30, 2004.

41. Scott Ritter, "The Case for Iraq's Qualitative Disarmament," *Arms Control Today* (June 2000).

42. "Shifting Priorities: UNMOVIC and the Future of Inspections in Iraq, an Interview with Ambassador Rolf Ekeus," *Arms Control Today* (March 2000).

43. An Interview with Ambassador Richard Butler, "The Lessons and Legacy of UNSCOM," *Arms Control Today* (June 1999). See also Richard Butler, *Saddam Defiant: The Threat of Mass Destruction and the Crisis of Global Security* (London: Weidenfeld & Nicholson, 2000).

44. Joseph Cirincione, Jessica Mathews, and George Perkovich, *WMD in Iraq: Evidence and Implications* (Washington, D.C.: Carnegie Endowment for International Peace, 2004).

45. Woodward, *Plan of Attack*, p. 194.

46. CIA, Unclassified Report to Congress on the Acquisition of Technology Relating to Weapons of Mass Destruction and Advanced Conventional Munitions, January 1 through June 30, 2001.

47. Hans Blix, *Disarming Iraq: The Search for Weapons of Mass Destruction* (London: Bloomsbury, 2004), p. 128.

48. IISS Strategic Dossier, *Iraq's Weapons of Mass Destruction: A Net Assessment*, September 9, 2002.

49. For the estimate, see www.ceip.org/files/projects/npp/pdf/Iraq/declassified intellreport.pdf.

50. Bryan Burrough, Evgenia Peretz, David Rose, and David Wise, "The Path to War," *Vanity Fair*, May 2004.

51. Judith Miller, "An Iraqi Defector Tells of Work on at Least 20 Hidden Weapons Sites," *New York Times*, December 20, 2001. For a critique of the links between the INC and Judith Miller and other journalists, see Michael Massing, "Now They Tell Us," *New York Review of Books*, February 26, 2004. The apology from the editors came in "The Times and Iraq," *New York Times*, May, 26, 2004. See also Jane Mayer, "The Manipulator," *New Yorker*, June 7, 2004.

52. Douglas Jehl, "Stung by Exile's Role, CIA Orders a Shift in Procedures," *New York Times,* February 13, 2004.

53. Woodward, *Plan of Attack.*

54. See Seymour Hersh, "Selective Intelligence," *New Yorker,* May 12, 2003. See also Walter Pincus and Dana Priest, "Some Iraq Analysts Felt Pressure from Cheney Visits," *Washington Post,* June 5, 2003; Kenneth M. Pollack, "Spies, Lies, and Weapons: What Went Wrong," *Atlantic Monthly,* January–February 2004; Burrough et al., "Path to War."

55. Jack Davis, "The Challenge of Managing Uncertainty: Paul Wolfowitz on Intelligence Policy-Relations," *Studies in Intelligence* 39, no. 5 (1996).

56. See Briefing by Douglas Feith, USD (Policy), on Policy and Intelligence Matters, June 4, 2003, reproduced in Prados, *Hoodwinked,* pp. 293–305, which has an extensive discussion of these issues.

57. All examples taken from the Carnegie Report.

58. Kenneth Pollack, "Next Stop Baghdad?" *Foreign Affairs* (March–April 2002); Pollack, "Spies, Lies, and Weapons."

59. John J. Mearsheimer and Stephen M. Walt, "Iraq: An Unnecessary War," *Foreign Policy* (December 2002).

60. Zero tolerance of noncompliance provides the least shaky legal basis for the war. For a discussion of the legal aspects of the war, see Adam Roberts, "Law and the Use of Force After Iraq," *Survival* (Summer 2003): 31–56.

61. Cited in Woodward, *Plan of Attack,* p. 232.

62. Blix, *Disarming Iraq,* pp. 141–142.

63. Excerpt from Remarks by President Bush and Polish President Kwasniewski, January 14, 2003.

64. See Philip H. Gordon and Jeremy Shapiro, *Allies at War: America, Europe, and the Crisis over Iraq* (New York: McGraw-Hill, 2004).

65. John Kampfner, *Blair's Wars* (London: Free Press, 2003), p. 207.

66. Woodward, *Plan of Attack,* pp. 247–250. Kampfner suggested some doubts in the prime minister's office as well.

67. Bumiller, *Condoleezza Rice,* pp. 197–198.

68. Most of the controversial allegations about Iraqi capabilities were at last debated within the intelligence community.

69. See Carnegie Report, pp. 23–25. See also Joseph Wilson, "What I Didn't Find in Africa," *New York Times,* July 6, 2003.

70. "Statement by Secretary of State Powell to Security Council," February 5, 2003, at www.whitehouse.gov/news/releases/2003/02/20030205-1.html.

71. The most substantial account is in Woodward, *Plan of Attack,* but see also Burrough et al., "Path to War"; and Prados, *Hoodwinked.*

72. Blix, *Disarming Iraq,* pp. 157, 167. See the site maintained by Dr. Glen Rangwala of Cambridge University, at http://middleeastreference.org.uk/iraqweapons.html.

73. Susan Wright, "The Hijacking of UNSCOM," *Bulletin of the Atomic Scientists,* July–August 1999.

74. Blix in *Disarming Iraq* explains his many misgivings on trying to conduct interviews outside of Iraq.

75. Deputy Secretary Wolfowitz Speech on Iraq Disarmament, Thursday, January 23, 2003 (Policy address on Iraqi disarmament at the Council for Foreign Relations in New York City).

76. Interview with Vice President Dick Cheney, NBC, *Meet the Press*, transcript for March 16, 2003.

77. In *Disarming Iraq*, Blix discusses how this might have worked.

78. Blair's increasingly desperate efforts to get a second resolution are discussed in Kampfner, *Blair's Wars*. Blix's account in *Disarming Iraq* is sympathetic.

79. Thomas Powers, "War and Its Consequences," *New York Review of Books*, March 27, 2003.

Chapter 19: Insurgency

1. David Kay, Testimony Before the U.S. Senate, Committee on Armed Services, January 28, 2004; Charles Duelfer, "Comprehensive Report of the Special Advisor to the DCI on Iraq's WMD with Addendums," September 30, 2004. For the investigation into what went wrong, see U.S. Senate, Select Committee on Intelligence, *Report on the U.S. Intelligence Community's Prewar Intelligence Assessments on Iraq*, 108th Cong., 2nd sess., July 7, 2004. See also Robert Jervis, "Reports, Politics, and Intelligence Failures: The Case of Iraq," *Journal of Strategic Studies* (February 2006).

2. Draper, *Dead Certain*, p. 193.

3. "President Bush Announces Major Combat Operations in Iraq Have Ended," May 1, 2003, at www.whitehouse.gov/news/releases/2003/05/20030501-15.html.

4. Michael R. Gordon and General Bernard E. Trainor, *Cobra II: The Inside Story of the Invasion and Occupation of Iraq* (New York: Random House, 2006), p. 52; Tommy Franks, *American Soldier* (New York: Regan Books, 2004). Additional sources on the war are Williamson Murray and Major General Robert H. Scales Jr., *The Iraq War: A Military History* (Cambridge: Harvard University Press, 2003); and Thomas E. Ricks, *Fiasco: The American Military Adventure in Iraq* (New York: Penguin Press, 2006).

5. David Zucchino, *Thunder Run: The Armored Strike to Capture Baghdad* (New York: Atlantic Monthly Press, 2004).

6. Stephen Biddle, "Speed Kills? Reassessing the Role of Speed, Precision, and Situation Awareness in the Fall of Saddam," *Journal of Strategic Studies* (February 2007): 3–46.

7. Kevin Woods, James Lacey, and Williamson Murray, "Saddam's Delusions: The View from the Inside," *Foreign Affairs* (May–June 2006).

8. Philip H. Gordon and Michael E. O'Hanlon, "Dealing with Iraq," *Washington Post*, December 26, 2001.

9. Ken Adelman, "Cakewalk in Iraq," *Washington Post*, February 13, 2002.

10. Ken Adelman, "'Cakewalk' Revisited," *Washington Post*, April 10, 2003.

11. David Rose, "Neo Culpa: Now They Tell Us," *Vanity Fair*, November 3, 2006.

12. This is a recurrent theme in Bob Woodward, *State of Denial: Bush at War, Part 3* (New York: Simon & Schuster, 2006).

13. Remarks by the Vice President to the Veterans of Foreign Wars, 103rd National Convention, August 26, 2002.

14. Bernard Lewis, "What Went Wrong?" *Atlantic,* January 2002; Lewis, *What Went Wrong?* (New York: Oxford University Press, 2002).

15. Woodward, *State of Denial,* p. 83.

16. Fouad Ajami, "Iraq and the Arabs' Future," *Foreign Affairs* (January–February 2003).

17. See www.undp.org/rbas/ahdr/english2002.html.

18. Thomas L. Friedman, "Arabs at the Crossroads," *New York Times,* July 3, 2002.

19. For the views of Iraqi specialists on the eve of war, see Toby Dodge and Steven Simon, *Iraq at the Crossroads: State and Society in the Shadow of Regime Change,* Adelphi Paper 354 (London: Oxford University Press/IISS, 2003).

20. Peter Slevin and Dana Priest, "Wolfowitz Concedes Iraq Errors," *Washington Post,* July 24, 2003.

21. Hearings, Department of Defense Budget Priorities for Fiscal Year 2004, Committee on the Budget, 108th Cong., 1st sess., February 27, 2003, at www.access.gpo.gov/congress/house/house04.html.

22. James Fallows, "Blind into Baghdad," *Atlantic Monthly,* January–February 2004, at www.theatlantic.com/issues/2004/01/media-preview/fallows.htm.

23. Eisenberg, "We're Taking Him Out."

24. Andrew Cockburn, *Rumsfeld: His Rise, Fall, and Catastrophic Legacy* (New York: Scribner's, 2007), pp. 171–172, 176–177.

25. Draper, *Dead Certain,* p. 191.

26. Nora Bensahel, "Mission Not Accomplished: What Went Wrong with Iraq Reconstruction," *Journal of Strategic Studies* (June 2006).

27. Ibid., p. 461.

28. Eric Schmitt and Joel Brinkley, "The Struggle for Iraq: Planning; State Dept. Study Foresaw Trouble Now Plaguing Iraq," *New York Times,* October 19, 2003.

29. Toby Dodge, "The Causes of U.S. Failure in Iraq," *Survival* (Spring 2007): 94.

30. L. Paul Bremer with Malcolm McConnell, *My Year in Iraq: The Struggle to Build a Future of Hope* (New York: Simon & Schuster, 2006). Other inside accounts of the failure from the perspective of those sent to reconstruct Iraq after the war are David L. Phillips, *Losing Iraq: Inside the Post-War Reconstruction Fiasco* (New York: Basic, 2005); Mark Etherington, *Revolt on the Tigris: The al-Sadr Uprising and the Governing of Iraq* (London: Hurst, 2005); and Larry Diamond, *Squandered Victory: The American Occupation and the Bungled Effort to Bring Democracy to Iraq* (New York: Times Books, 2005). Diamond summarizes his argument in "What Went Wrong in Iraq?" *Foreign Affairs* (September–October 2004).

31. Draper, *Dead Certain.*

32. Edmund L. Andrews, "Envoy's Letter Counters Bush on Dismantling of Iraq Army," *New York Times,* September 4, 2007.

33. Woodward, *State of Denial,* pp. 193–195.

34. Zarqawi, letter, at www.cpa-iraq.org/transcripts/20040212_zarqawi_full.html.

35. "President Bush Names Randall Tobias to Be Global AIDS Coordinator," July 2, 2003, at www.whitehouse.gov/news/releases/2003/07/20030702-3.html.

36. Bumiller, *Condoleezza Rice*, p. 240.

37. Bremer, *My Year in Iraq*, pp. 325–326; Woodward, *State of Denial*, pp. 298–301; Carter Malaksian, "Signaling Resolve, Democratization, and the First Battle of Fallujah," *Journal of Strategic Studies* (June 2006): 423–452.

38. Robert Kaplan, *Imperial Grunts: The American Military on the Ground* (New York: Random House, 2005).

39. Cited in Brigadier Nigel Aylwin-Foster, "Changing the Army for Counterinsurgency Operations," *Military Review* (November–December 2005): 5.

40. Montgomery McFate, "The Military Utility of Understanding Adversary Culture," *Joint Forces Quarterly* (July 2005): 44.

41. George Packer, "Knowing the Enemy," *New Yorker*, December 18, 2006. A Powerpoint briefing by Kilcullen on *Counterinsurgency in Iraq: Theory and Practice*, can be found at www.mcwl.usmc.mil/Counterinsurgency%20in%20Iraq%20theory%20and%20practice2007.ppt.

42. David H. Petraeus, "Learning Counterinsurgency: Observations from Soldiering in Iraq," *Military Review* (January–February 2006).

43. "President Outlines Strategy for Victory in Iraq," November 30, 2005, at www.whitehouse.gov/infocus/iraq/iraq_national_strategy_20051130.pdf.

44. David E. Sanger, Michael R. Gordon, and John F. Burns, "Chaos Overran Iraq Plan in '06, Bush Team Says," *New York Times*, January 2, 2007.

45. Kessler, *Confidante*, p. 174.

46. James Baker III and Lee H. Hamilton, *The Iraq Study Group Report* (New York: Vintage Books, 2006).

47. George W. Bush, "President's Address to the Nation," January 10, 2007, at www.whitehouse.gov/news/releases/2007/01/20070110-7.html.

48. Brian Fishman, "After Zarqawi: The Dilemmas and Future of Al Qaeda in Iraq," *Washington Quarterly* (Autumn 2006): 21.

49. The text of the letter is available in English from the Office of the Director of National Intelligence, at www.dni.gov/press_releases/20051011_release.htm.

50. Text of a document found in Zarqawi's safe house, at www.usatoday.com/news/world/iraq/2006-06-15-zarqawi-text_x.htm.

51. Michael R. Gordon, "Insurgent Leader in Iraq Never Existed, U.S. Says," *International Herald Tribune*, July 19, 2007.

52. *New York Times*, January 1, 2008.

53. A check on casualties is kept at the Web site, at http://icasualties.org/oif/. On the relevance of casualties, see Christopher Gelpi, Peter D. Feaver, and Jason Reifler, "Success Matters: Casualty Sensitivity and the War in Iraq," *International Security* (Winter 2005–2006).

54. See Nick Cumming-Bruce, "Iraq Deaths Examined from Invasion to Mid-'06," *International Herald Tribune*, January 10, 2008. See also www.iraqbodycount.org.

55. Bobby Ghosh, "The Fleeting Success of the Surge," *Time*, December 13, 2007.

Chapter 20: Suicides and Assassinations

1. Ben-Ami, *Scars of War*, p. 286.

2. Peri, *Generals in the Cabinet Room*, p. 112.

3. Cited in Matthews, *Lost Years*, p. 95.

4. David E. Sanger, "Attacks in Israel: The President; Bush, Mirroring Call on Taliban, Demands Arafat Stop Extremists," *New York Times*, December 3, 2001.

5. "President Bush Holds Press Conference," March 13, 2002, at www.whitehouse.gov/news/releases/2002/03/20020313-8.html.

6. Meital, *Peace in Tatters*, p. 153.

7. Thomas L. Friedman, "An Intriguing Signal from the Saudi Crown Prince," *New York Times*, February 17, 2002.

8. Cited in Matthews, *Lost Years*, p. 184.

9. "President Emphasizes Message to Middle East," April 8, 2002, at www.whitehouse.gov/news/releases/2002/04/20020408-1.html.

10. Elisabeth Bumiller, "President Bush and 'Madame Rice': A Personal Bond Helps Align Policy," *New York Times*, November 26, 2007.

11. Matthews, *Lost Years*, p. 191.

12. Ibid., p. 202.

13. DeYoung, *Powell*, p. 383.

14. "President Bush Calls for New Palestinian Leadership," June 24, 2002, at www.whitehouse.gov/news/releases/2002/06/20020624-3.html.

15. Kessler, *Confidante*, p. 125.

16. Meital, *Peace in Tatters*, p. 167.

17. Hillel Frisch, "Motivation or Capabilities: Israeli Counterterrorism Against Palestinian Suicide Bombings and Violence," *Journal of Strategic Studies* (October 2006): 843–870.

18. Daniel Byman, "Do Targeted Killings Work?" *Foreign Affairs* (March–April 2006): 103–104.

19. Peri, *Generals in the Cabinet Room*, p. 207.

20. "President Bush Commends Israeli Prime Minister Sharon's Plan," remarks by the President and Israeli Prime Minister Ariel Sharon, April 14, 2004, at www.whitehouse.gov/news/releases/2004/04/print/20040414-4.html.

21. "President Bush Sworn in to Second Term," January 20, 2005, at www.whitehouse.gov/inaugural/index.html.

22. Fouad Ajami, "Autumn of the Autocrats"; Bernard Lewis, "Freedom and Justice in the Modern Middle East," *Foreign Affairs* (May–June 2005).

23. "Secretary Condoleezza Rice, Remarks at the American University in Cairo," June 20, 2005, at www.state.gov/secretary/rm/2005/48328.htm.

24. Natan Sharansky, *The Case for Democracy: The Power of Freedom to Overcome Tyranny and Terror* (New York: PublicAffairs, 2006).

25. Ben-Ami, *Scars of War*, p. 295.

26. Kessler, *Confidante*, p. 135.

27. Bumiller, *Condoleezza Rice*, p. 280.

28. Kessler, *The Confidante*, p. 142; Barry Rubin, *Pushback or Progress: Arab Regimes Respond to Democracy's Challenge* (Washington D.C.: Washington Institute for Near East Policy, 2007).

29. Jimmy Carter, *Peace, Not Apartheid* (New York: Simon & Schuster, 2006).

30. Walt and Mearsheimer, *Israel Lobby.* Also published in 2006 was James Petras, *The Power of Israel in the United States* (Atlanta, Ga.: Clarity, 2006).

Chapter 21: The Main Enemy

1. On Hezbollah, see Augustus Richard Norton, *Hezbollah* (Princeton: Princeton University Press, 2007). See also Judith Palmer Harik, *Hezbollah: The Changing Face of Terrorism* (London: I. B. Tauris, 2005).

2. "President Discusses War on Terror, National Defense University, Fort Lesley J. McNair," March 8, 2005, at www.whitehouse.gov/news/releases/2005/03/2005 0308-3.html.

3. Efraim Inbar, "How Israel Bungled the Second Lebanon War," *Middle East Quarterly* (Summer 2007); Shlomo Bron and Meir Elran, eds., *The Second Lebanon War: Strategic Perspectives* (Tel Aviv: Institute for National Security Studies, 2007).

4. Seymour Hersh, "Watching Lebanon: Washington's Interests in Israel's War," *New Yorker,* August 21, 2006.

5. "President Bush Meets with British Prime Minister Blair (at G8 Meeting in Russia)," July 16, 2006, at www.whitehouse.gov/news/releases/2006/07/20060716.html.

6. "Statement by Group of Eight Leaders," July 16, 2006.

7. Michael Abramowitz, "In Mideast Strife, Bush Sees a Step to Peace," *Washington Post,* July 21, 2006.

8. Scott Wilson, "Israeli War Plan Had No Exit Strategy," *Washington Post,* October 21, 2006.

9. Her role is discussed fully in Kessler, *Confidante.*

10. Secretary Condoleezza Rice, "Special Briefing on Travel to the Middle East and Europe," July 21, 2006, at www.state.gov/secretary/rm/2006/69331.htm.

11. Israeli Ministry of Foreign Affairs, "Winograd Commission Submits Interim Report," April 30, 2007, at www.mfa.gov.il/MFA/Government/Communiques/ 2007/Winograd+Inquiry+Commission+submits+Interim+Report+30-Apr-2007.htm.

12. *CBS News,* August 27, 2006.

13. "Press Conference by the President," December 20, 2007, at www.whitehouse.gov/ news/releases/2007/12/20071220-1.html.

14. President Bush Delivers State of the Union Address, January 31, 2006, at www.whitehouse.gov/news/releases/2006/01/20060131-10.html.

15. Anoush Ehteshami and Mahjoob Zweeiri, *Iran and the Rise of Its Neoconservatives: The Politics of Tehran's Silent Revolution* (London: I. B. Tauris, 2007), p. 1. See also Ali Ansari, *Confronting Iran: The Failure of American Foreign Policy and the Roots of Mistrust* (London: C. Hurst, 2006); and Takeyh, *Hidden Iran.*

16. On Iran's nuclear program and its implications, see Shahram Chubin, *Iran's Nuclear Ambitions* (Washington, D.C.: Carnegie Endowment for International Peace, 2006); Thérèse Delpech, *Iran and the Bomb: The Abdication of International Responsibility,* trans. Ros Schwartz (New York: Columbia University Press, 2007);

Mark Fitzpatrick, "Can Iran's Nuclear Capability Be Kept Latent?" *Survival* (Spring 2007): 33–57.

17. James A. Russell, *Regional Threats and Security Strategy: The Troubling Case of Today's Middle East* (Carlisle, Pa.: U.S. Army War College Strategic Studies Institute, 2007).

18. James Dobbins, "How to Talk to Iran," *Washington* Post, July 22, 2007.

19. Barbara Slavin, "Mutual Terror Accusations Halt U.S.-Iran Talks," *USA Today*, May 21, 2003. The episode is discussed in Barbara Slavin, *Bitter Friends, Bosom Enemies: Iran, the U.S., and the Twisted Path to Confrontation* (New York: St. Martin's Press, 2007).

20. Commission on the Intelligence Capabilities of the United States Regarding Weapons of Mass Destruction, *Report to the President*, March 31, 2005, p. 257, at www.wmd.gov/report; Bowen, *Libya and Nuclear Proliferation*, pp. 36–37.

21. Bowen, *Libya and Nuclear Proliferation*; Jentleson and Whytock, *International Security*.

22. The Cheney-Edwards Vice Presidential Debate, October 5, 2004, at www.debates.org/pages/trans2004b.html.

23. Secretary Condoleezza Rice, Press Conference on Iran, May 31, 2006, at www.state.gov/secretary/rm/2006/67103.htm.

24. Bumiller, *Condoleezza Rice*, p. 288; Kessler, *Confidante*, p. 203.

25. David Samuels, "Travels with Condi," *Atlantic Monthly,* June 2007, at www.theatlantic.com/doc/200706/condoleezza-rice.

26. "President Bush Addresses the 89th Annual National Convention of the American Legion," August 28, 2007, at www.whitehouse.gov/news/releases/2007/08/20070828-2.html.

27. David H. Petraeus, "Report to Congress on the Situation in Iraq," September 10–11, 2007, at www.defenselink.mil/pubs/pdfs/Petraeus-Testimony20070910.pdf.

28. "Vice President's Remarks at a Rally for the Troops," USS *John C. Stennis*, May 11, 2007, at www.whitehouse.gov/news/releases/2007/05/20070511-5.html.

29. Seymour Hersh, "Shifting Targets: The Administration's Plan for Iran," *New Yorker*, October 8, 2007.

30. "Tehran Defiant on Nuclear Enrichment," *International Herald Tribune*, December 2, 2007.

31. Michael Hirsh, "Another Turn of the Screw," *Newsweek*, October 27, 2007.

32. "Press Conference by the President," October 17, 2007, at www.whitehouse.gov/news/releases/2007/10/20071017.html.

33. Office of the Director of National Intelligence, *National Intelligence Estimate, Iran: Nuclear Intentions and Capabilities*, November 2007, at www.dni.gov/press_releases/20071203_release.pdf.

34. David Sanger and Steven Lee Myers, "Notes from Secret Iran Talks Led to U.S. Reversal," *New York Times*, December 7, 2007.

35. Steven Lee Myers, "An Assessment Jars a Foreign Policy Debate About Iran," *New York Times*, December 4, 2007.

36. Michael Abramowitz and Ellen Knickmeyer, "As Bush Heads to Mideast, Renewed Questions on Iran: Israeli, Arab Leaders Doubt U.S. Resolve," *Washington Post*, January 7, 2008.

37. Ali M. Ansari, *Iran Under Ahmadinejad: The Politics of Confrontation*, Adelphi Paper 393 (London: Routledge/IISS, 2007).

38. Office of the Director of National Intelligence, *National Intelligence Estimate: The Terrorist Threat to the U.S. Homeland*, July 2007.

39. Office of the Director of National Intelligence, *National Intelligence Estimate: Trends in Global Terrorism: Implications for the United States*, April 2006.

40. Daniel Benjamin and Steven Simon, *The Next Attack: The Failure of the War on Terror and a Strategy for Getting It Right* (New York: Times Books, 2005), p. xiii.

41. For example, see Arab American Institute (AAI)/Zogby International poll, December 14, 2006, at http://aai.3cdn.net/96d8eeaec55ef4c217_m9m6b97wo.pdf.

42. Gerges, *Far Enemy*, p. 234.

43. Ibid., pp. 200–210.

44. Steve Coll and Susan B. Glasser, "Terrorists Turn to the Web as Base of Operations," *Washington Post*, August 7, 2005.

45. Frank Scott Douglas, "Waging the Inchoate War: Defining, Fighting, and Second-Guessing the Long War," *Journal of Strategic Studies* (June 2007): 407.

46. Benjamin and Simon, *Next Attack*, pp. 98–102.

47. Bronson, *Thicker Than Oil*, pp. 241–244.

48. Craig Whitlock, "Al-Qaeda's Far-Reaching New Partner," *Washington Post*, October 5, 2001.

49. Shaykh Ayman al-Zawahiri, "Realities of the Conflict—Between Islam and Unbelief," December 2006, at www.ict.org.il/apage/8215.php.

50. Marina Ottaway and Anatol Lieven, *Rebuilding Afghanistan: Fantasy Versus Reality*, Carnegie Endowment for International Peace Policy Brief 12, January 2002.

51. Sean M. Maloney, "Afghanistan: From Here to Eternity?" *Parameters* (Spring 2004): 4–15.

52. James Dobbins, "Nation-Building: The Inescapable Responsibility of the World's Only Superpower," *Rand Review* (Summer 2003): 20.

53. Robert D. Kaplan, "The Taliban's Silent Partner," *New York Times*, July 20, 2006.

54. Thomas Johnson and Chris Mason, "Understanding the Taliban and Insurgency in Afghanistan," *Orbis* (Winter 2007). For a more positive assessment of the counterinsurgency effort up to 2006, see David W. Barno, "Fighting the Other War: Counterinsurgency Strategy in Afghanistan, 2003–2005," *Military Review* (September–October 2007).

55. Carlotta Gall and David Rohde, "Pakistan Losing Control of Militants It Nurtured," *New York Times*, January 15, 2008.

56. Mark Mazzetti and David E. Sanger, "U.S. Finds Few Options as Al Qaeda Fortifies," *International Herald Tribune*, July 23, 2007.

57. Eric Schmitt, Mark Mazzetti, and Carlotta Gall, "U.S. Considers Enlisting Tribes in Pakistan to Fight Al Qaeda," *New York Times*, November 19, 2007; Ashley J.

Tellis, *Pakistan: Conflicted Ally in the War on Terror*, Policy Brief 56 (Washington D.C.: Carnegie Endowment for International Peace, 2007).

58. "Lawyers Against the General," *Economist,* November 10, 2007.

Chapter 22: Friends and Enemies

1. To give the quotes their full context, see *DoD News Briefing: Secretary Rumsfeld and General Myers*, April 11, 2003, at www.defenselink.mil/transcripts/transcript .aspx?transcriptid=2367.

2. "Zarqawi Vows War on Iraq Poll," January 23, 2005, at http://news.bbc.co.uk/ 1/hi/world/middle_east/4199363.stm.

3. Little, *American Orientalism,* p. 317.

4. "Between Fitna, Fawda and the Deep Blue Sea," *Economist*, January 12, 2008.

Bibliography

A Clean Break: A New Strategy for Securing the Realm. Institute for Advanced
Strategic and Political Studies, July 1996. www.iasps.org/strat1.htm.

Abrahamian, Ervand. *Khomeinism: Essays on the Islamic Republic*. Berkeley:
University of California Press, 1993.

Adelman, Ken. "Cakewalk in Iraq." *Washington Post*, February 13, 2002.

_____. "'Cakewalk' Revisited." *Washington Post*, April 10, 2003.

Agha, Hussein, and Robert Malley. "Camp David: The Tragedy of Errors." *New York
Review of Books*, August 19, 2001.

_____. "Camp David and After: An Exchange (2. A Reply to Ehud Barak)," *New
York Review of Books*, June 13, 2002.

Ajami, Fouad. "Iraq and the Arabs' Future." *Foreign Affairs*, January–February 2003.

_____. "The Autumn of the Autocrats." *Foreign Affairs*, May–June 2005.

Albright, Madeleine, and Bill Woodward. *Madam Secretary: A Memoir*. New York:
Miramax Books, 2003.

Alfonsi, Christian. *Circle in the Sand: Why We Went Back to Iraq*. New York:
Doubleday, 2006.

Ali, Mohamed M., and Iqbal H. Shah. "Sanctions and Childhood Mortality in Iraq."
Lancet, May 2000.

Andres, Richard. "The Afghan Model in Northern Iraq." *Journal of Strategic Studies*,
June 2006.

Andrew, Christopher, and Vasili Mitrokhin. *The Sword and the Shield*. New York:
Basic, 1999.

Ansari, Ali M. *Modern Iran Since 1921*. London: Longman, 2003.

_____. *Confronting Iran: The Failure of American Foreign Policy and the Roots of
Mistrust*. London: Hurst, 2006.

_____. *Iran Under Ahmadinejad: The Politics of Confrontation*. Adelphi Paper 393.
London: Routledge/IISS, 2007.

Arkin, William, Damian Durrant, and Marianne Cherni. *Impact: Modern Warfare
and the Environment: A Case Study of the Gulf War*. London, June 1991. A

Greenpeace study prepared for a conference on a "Fifth Geneva Convention" on the Protection of the Environment in Time of Armed Conflict.

Aylwin-Foster, Nigel. "Changing the Army for Counterinsurgency Operations." *Military Review,* November–December 2005.

Baer, Robert. *See No Evil: The True Story of a Ground Soldier in the CIA's War on Terrorism.* New York: Crown, 2002.

Baker, James, III, and Lee H. Hamilton. *The Iraq Study Group Report.* New York: Vintage, 2006.

Baker, James A., III, with Thomas M. DeFrank. *The Politics of Diplomacy: Revolution, War, and Peace, 1989–1992.* New York: Putnam, 1995.

Baltiansky, Gadi. *"No One to Talk To": A Critical Look at the Linkage Between Politics and the Media.* Herzog Institute for Media, Politics, and Society, Tel Aviv University, January 12, 2005. http://www.tau.ac.il/institutes/herzog/talkto-eng.pdf.

Baram, Amatzia. "U.S. Input into Iraqi Decisionmaking, 1988–1990." In David W. Lesch, ed., *The Middle East and the United States: A Historical and Political Reassessment.* 3rd ed. Boulder: Westview, 2003.

Barno, David W. "Fighting 'the Other War': Counterinsurgency Strategy in Afghanistan, 2003–2005." *Military Review,* September–October 2007.

Beilin, Yossi. *Touching Peace: From the Oslo Accord to a Final Agreement.* London: George Weidenfeld, 1999.

Ben-Ami, Shlomo. *Scars of War, Wounds of Peace: The Israeli-Arab Tragedy.* Oxford: Oxford University Press, 2006.

Benjamin, Daniel, and Steven Simon. *The Age of Sacred Terror.* New York: Random House, 2002.

_____. *The Next Attack: The Failure of the War on Terror and a Strategy for Getting It Right.* New York: Times Books, 2005.

Bensahel, Nora. "Mission Not Accomplished: What Went Wrong with Iraq Reconstruction." *Journal of Strategic Studies,* June 2006.

Bergen, Peter. *Holy War, Inc.: Inside the Secret World of Osama bin Laden.* New York: Free Press, 2001.

_____. "The Long Hunt for Osama." *Atlantic Monthly,* October 2004.

Berntsen, Gary. *Jawbreaker: The Attack on bin Laden and al-Qaeda: A Personal Account by the CIA's Key Field Commander.* New York: Crown, 2005.

Betts, Richard K. "The New Threat of Weapons of Mass Destruction." *Foreign Affairs,* January–February 1998.

Biddle, Stephen. *Afghanistan and the Future of Warfare: Implications for Army and Defense Policy.* Carlisle, Pa.: U.S. Army War College Strategic Studies Institute, 2002.

_____. "Afghanistan and the Future of Warfare." *Foreign Affairs,* March–April 2003.

_____. "Seeing Baghdad, Thinking Saigon." *Foreign Affairs,* March–April 2006.

_____. "Speed Kills? Reassessing the Role of Speed, Precision, and Situation Awareness in the Fall of Saddam." *Journal of Strategic Studies,* February 2007.

Biddle, Stephen, and Robert Zirkle. "Technology, Civil-Military Relations, and Warfare in the Developing World." *Journal of Strategic Studies,* June 1996.

Bill, James A. *The Eagle and the Lion: The Tragedy of American-Iranian Relations.* New Haven: Yale University Press, 1988.

Bin Sultan, Khaled, with Patrick Seale. *Desert Warrior: A Personal View of the Gulf War by the Joint Forces Commander.* New York: HarperCollins, 1995.

Blix, Hans. *Disarming Iraq: The Search for Weapons of Mass Destruction.* London: Bloomsbury, 2004.

Boroumand, Ladan, and Roya Boroumand. "Terror, Islam, and Democracy." *Journal of Democracy,* April 2002.

Bowden, Mark. *Black Hawk Down: A Story of Modern War.* Berkeley: Atlantic Monthly Press, 1999.

_____. *Guests of the Ayatollah: The Iran Hostage Crisis, the First Battle in America's War with Militant Islam.* New York: Grove, 2006.

Bowen, Wyn Q. *Libya and Nuclear Proliferation: Stepping Back from the Brink.* Adelphi Paper 380. London: Routledge/IISS, 2006.

Bregman, Ahron. *The Elusive Peace.* London: Penguin, 2005.

Bregman, Ahron, and Jihan El-Tahri. *The Fifty Years War: Israel and the Arabs.* London: Penguin, 1998.

Bremer, L. Paul, III, with Malcolm McConnell. *My Year in Iraq: The Struggle to Build a Future of Hope.* New York: Simon & Schuster, 2006.

Brigham, Robert. *Is Iraq Another Vietnam?* New York: PublicAffairs, 2006.

Brom, Shlomo, and Meir Elran, eds. *The Second Lebanon War: Strategic Perspectives.* Tel Aviv: Institute for National Security Studies, 2007.

Bronson, Rachel. *Thicker Than Oil: America's Uneasy Partnership with Saudi Arabia.* New York: Oxford University Press, 2006.

Brzezinski, Zbigniew. *Power and Principle: Memoirs of the National Security Adviser, 1977–1981.* New York: Farrar, Straus & Giroux, 1983.

Bumiller, Elisabeth. *Condoleezza Rice: An American Life.* New York: Random House, 2007.

Burke, Jason. *Al-Qaeda: The True Story of Radical Islam.* 3rd ed. London: Penguin, 2007.

Burrough, Bryan, Evgenia Peretz, David Rose, and David Wise. "The Path to War." *Vanity Fair,* May 2004.

Bush, George, and Brent Scowcroft. *A World Transformed.* New York: Knopf, 1998.

Butler, Richard. *Saddam Defiant: The Threat of Mass Destruction and the Crisis of Global Security.* London: Weidenfeld & Nicholson, 2000.

Byford, Grenville. "The Wrong War." *Foreign Affairs,* July–August 2002.

Byman, Daniel. "Proceed with Caution: U.S. Support for the Iraqi Opposition." *Washington Quarterly,* Summer 1999.

_____. "Do Targeted Killings Work?" *Foreign Affairs,* March–April 2006.

Byman, Daniel, Kenneth Pollack, and Gideon Rose. "Can Saddam Be Toppled?" *Foreign Affairs,* January–February 1999.

_____. "The Rollback Fantasy." *Foreign Affairs,* January–February 1999.

Byman, Daniel, Kenneth Pollack, and Matthew Waxman. "Coercing Saddam Hussein: Lessons from the Past." *Survival,* Autumn 1998.

Cable, Larry. "Reinventing the Round Wheel: Insurgency, Counter-Insurgency, and Peacekeeping Post Cold War." *Small Wars and Insurgencies,* Autumn 1993.

Cameron, Gavin. *Nuclear Terrorism: A Threat Assessment for the 21st Century.* London: Macmillan, 1999.

Campbell, Kenneth. "Once Burned, Twice Cautious: Explaining the Weinberger-Powell Doctrine." *Armed Forces and Society,* Spring 1998.

Carter, Jimmy. *Keeping Faith: Memoirs of a President.* New York: Bantam, 1982.

_____. *Peace, Not Apartheid.* New York: Simon & Schuster, 2006.

Cave, George. "Why Secret 1986 U.S.-Iran 'Arms for Hostages' Negotiations Failed." *Washington Report on Middle East Affairs,* September–October 1994.

Christopher, Warren. "America's Leadership, America's Opportunity." *Foreign Policy,* Spring 1995.

_____. *Chances of a Lifetime: A Memoir.* New York: Scribner's, 2001.

Chubin, Shahram. *Iran's Nuclear Ambitions.* Washington, D.C.: Carnegie Endowment for International Peace, 2006.

Chubin, Shahram, and Charles Tripp. *Iran and Iraq at War.* London: I. B. Tauris, 1988.

Cigar, Norman. "Iraq's Strategic Mindset and the Gulf War: Blueprint for Defeat." *Journal of Strategic Studies,* March 1992.

Cirincione, Joseph, Jessica Mathews, and George Perkovich. *WMD in Iraq: Evidence and Implications.* Washington, D.C.: Carnegie Endowment for International Peace, 2004.

Clarke, Richard A. *Against All Enemies: Inside America's War on Terror.* New York: Free Press, 2004.

Clawson, Patrick. *How Has Saddam Hussein Survived: Economic Sanctions, 1990–93.* McNair Paper. Washington, D.C.: Institute for National Strategic Studies, National Defense University, 1993.

Clinton, Bill. *My Life.* New York: Knopf, 2004.

Cockburn, Andrew, and Patrick Cockburn. *Saddam Hussein: An American Obsession.* New York: Verso, 2000.

Cohen, David B., and Chris J. Dolan. "Revisiting El Dorado Canyon: Terrorism, the Reagan Administration, and the 1986 Bombing of Libya." *White House Studies,* Spring 2005.

Coll, Steve. *Ghost Wars: The Secret History of the CIA, Afghanistan, and bin Laden, from the Soviet Invasion to September 10, 2001.* New York: Penguin, 2004.

Comprehensive Report of the Special Adviser to the DCI on Iraq's WMD, September 30, 2004 (Duelfer Report). www.cia.gov/cia/reports/iraq_wmd_2004/index.html.

Cordesman, Anthony H. *The Iraq War: Strategy, Tactics, and Military Lessons.* Washington, D.C.: CSIS Press, 2003.

Cordesman, Anthony H., and Abraham R. Wagner. *The Lessons of Modern War.* Vol. 2, *The Iran-Iraq Conflict.* Boulder: Westview, 1990.

_____. *The Lessons of Modern War.* Vol. 4, *The Gulf War.* Boulder: Westview, 1996.

Cordovez, Diego, and Selig S. Harrison. *Out of Afghanistan: The Inside Story of the Soviet Withdrawal.* New York: Oxford University Press, 1995.

Cortright, David, and George A. Lopez. "Are Sanctions Just? The Problematic Case of Iraq." *Journal of International Affairs,* Spring 1999.

Crile, George. *Charlie Wilson's War: The Extraordinary Story of the Largest Covert Operation in History.* New York: Atlantic Monthly Press, 2003.

Crisis in the Persian Gulf Region: U.S. Policy Options and Implications. U.S. Senate, Hearings Before the Committee on Armed Services, 1990.

Cullison, Alan. "Inside Al-Qaeda's Hard Drive." *Atlantic Monthly,* September 2004. www.theatlantic.com/doc/200409/cullison.

Daalder, Ivo H., and James M. Lindsay. *America Unbound: The Bush Revolution in Foreign Policy.* Hoboken, N.J.: John Wiley, 2005.

Danner, Mark. *Torture and Truth: America, Abu Ghraib, and the War on Terror.* New York: New York Review of Books, 2004.

Danziger, Raphael. "The Persian Gulf Tanker War." *United States Naval Institute Proceedings,* May 1985.

Davis, Brian L. *Qadhafi, Terrorism, and the Origins of the U.S. Attack on Libya.* New York: Praeger, 1990.

Davis, Jack. "The Challenge of Managing Uncertainty: Paul Wolfowitz on Intelligence Policy-Relations." *Studies in Intelligence* 39, no. 5 (1996).

Delpech, Thérèse. *Iran and the Bomb: The Abdication of International Responsibility.* Translated by Ros Schwartz. New York: Columbia University Press, 2007.

Department of Defense. *Conduct of the Persian Gulf War, Final Report to Congress, Pursuant to Title V of the Persian Gulf Conflict Supplemental Authorization and Personnel Benefits Act of 1991 (Public Law 102-25).* Washington, D.C., 1992.

Department of Defense. *Field Manual 100-5, Operations.* Washington, D.C.: Department of the Army, 1982.

DeYoung, Karen. *Soldier: The Life of Colin Powell.* New York: Vintage, 2006.

Diamond, Larry. "What Went Wrong in Iraq." *Foreign Affairs,* September–October 2004.

———. *Squandered Victory: The American Occupation and the Bungled Effort to Bring Democracy to Iraq.* New York: Times Books, 2005.

DiGeorgio-Lutz, JoAnn A. "The U.S.-PLO Relationship: From Dialogue to the White House Lawn." In David W. Lesch, ed., *The Middle East and the United States: A Historical and Political Reassessment.* 3rd ed. Boulder: Westview, 2003.

Dobbins, James. "Nation-Building: The Inescapable Responsibility of the World's Only Superpower." *RAND Review,* Summer 2003.

Dodge, Toby. *Iraq's Future: The Aftermath of Regime Change.* Adelphi Paper 372. Abingdon: Routledge/IISS, 2005.

———. "How Iraq Was Lost." *Survival,* Winter 2006–2007.

———. "The Causes of U.S. Failure in Iraq." *Survival,* Spring 2007.

Dodge, Toby, and Steven Simon. *Iraq at the Crossroads: State and Society in the Shadow of Regime Change.* Adelphi Paper 354. London: OUP/IISS, 2003.

Douglas, Frank "Scot." "Waging the Inchoate War: Defining, Fighting, and Second-Guessing the 'Long War.'" *Journal of Strategic Studies,* June 2007.

Draper, Robert. *Dead Certain: The Presidency of George W. Bush.* New York: Free Press, 2007.

Draper, Theodore. *A Very Thin Line: The Iran-Contra Affairs.* New York: Hill & Wang, 1991.

Dreyfuss, Robert. *Devil's Game: How the United States Helped Unleash Fundamentalist Islam.* New York: Henry Holt, 2005.

Editors of *U.S. News and World Report. Triumph Without Victory: The Unreported History of the Persian Gulf War.* New York: Times Books, 1992.

Ehteshami, Anoush, and Mahjoob Zweiri. *Iran and the Rise of Its Neoconservatives: The Politics of Tehran's Silent Revolution.* London: I. B. Tauris, 2007.

Enderlin, Charles. *Shattered Dreams: The Failure of the Peace Process in the Middle East, 1995–2002.* New York: Other Press, 2002.

Erdmann, Andrew. "The U.S. Presumption of Quick, Costless Wars." *Orbis,* Summer 1999.

Esposito, John. *The Islamic Threat: Myth or Reality?* New York: Oxford University Press, 1992.

Etherington, Mark. *Revolt on the Tigris: The al-Sadr Uprising and the Governing of Iraq.* London: Hurst, 2005.

Falkenrath, Richard A., Robert D. Newman, and Bradley Thayer. *America's Achilles' Heel: Nuclear, Biological, and Chemical Terrorism and Covert Attack.* Cambridge: MIT Press, 1998.

Fallows, James. "Blind into Baghdad." *Atlantic Monthly,* January–February 2004.

Farber, David. *Taken Hostage: The Iran Hostage Crisis and America's First Encounter with Radical Islam.* Princeton: Princeton University Press, 2004.

Farrell, Theo. "Sliding into War: The Somalia Imbroglio and U.S. Army Peace Operations Doctrine." *International Peacekeeping* 2, no. 2 (1995).

Feaver, Peter D., and Christopher Gelpi. *Choosing Your Battles: American Civil-Military Relations and the Use of Force.* Princeton: Princeton University Press, 2003.

Fischer, Michael M. J. *Iran: From Religious Dispute to Revolution.* Cambridge: Harvard University Press, 1980.

Fishman, Brian. "After Zarqawi: The Dilemmas and Future of Al Qaeda in Iraq." *Washington Quarterly,* Autumn 2006.

Fitzpatrick, Mark. "Can Iran's Nuclear Capability Be Kept Latent?" *Survival,* Spring 2007.

Franks, Tommy. *American Soldier.* New York: Regan, 2004.

Freedman, Lawrence. "War in Iraq: Selling the Threat." *Survival,* Summer 2004.

_____. *The Transformation of Strategic Affairs.* London: Routledge/IISS, 2006.

_____. "Writing of Wrongs." *Foreign Affairs,* January–February 2006.

Freedman, Lawrence, and Efraim Karsh. *The Gulf Conflict 1990–1991: Diplomacy and War in the New World Order.* London: Faber & Faber, 1993.

Friedman, Norman. *Terrorism, Afghanistan, and America's New Way of War.* Annapolis, Md.: Naval Institute, 2003.

Friedman, Thomas L. *From Beirut to Jerusalem.* New York: Farrar, Straus & Giroux, 1989.

Frisch, Hillel. "Debating Palestinian Strategy in the al-Aqsa Intifada." *Terrorism and Political Violence,* Summer 2003.

_____. "Motivation or Capabilities? Israeli Counterterrorism Against Palestinian Suicide Bombings and Violence." *Journal of Strategic Studies,* October 2006.

Frum, David. *The Right Man: An Inside Account of the Surprise Presidency of George W. Bush.* London: Weidenfeld & Nicholson, 2003.

Gamlen, Elizabeth. "US Responses to the 'Tanker War' and the Implications of Its Intervention." In Charles Davies, ed., *After the War: Iran, Iraq, and the Arab Gulf.* Chichester, U.K.: Carden, 1990.

Garfield, Richard. *Morbidity and Mortality Among Iraqi Children from 1990 to 1998: Assessing the Impact of Economic Sanctions.* Occasional Paper Series 16:OP:3, Joan B. Kroc Institute for International Peace Studies, University of Notre Dame/Fourth Freedom Forum, March 1999.

Garthoff, Raymond L. *Détente and Confrontation: American-Soviet Relations from Nixon to Reagan.* Rev. ed. Washington, D.C.: Brookings Institution, 1994.

Gates, Robert M. *From the Shadows: The Ultimate Insider's Story of Five Presidents and How They Won the Cold War.* New York: Simon & Schuster, 1996.

Gause, F. Gregory. "Saddam's Unwatched Arsenal." *Foreign Affairs,* May–June 1999.

Gelpi, Christopher, Peter D. Feaver, and Jason Reifler. "Success Matters: Casualty Sensitivity and the War in Iraq." *International Security,* Winter 2005–2006.

Gerges, Fawaz A. *America and Political Islam: Clash of Cultures or Clash of Interests?* New York: Cambridge University Press, 1999.

_____. *The Far Enemy: Why Jihad Went Global.* New York: Cambridge University Press, 2005.

Ghabra, Shafeeq N. "Kuwait and the United States: The Reluctant Ally and U.S. Policy Toward the Gulf." In David W. Lesch, ed., *The Middle East and the United States: A Historical and Political Reassessment.* 3rd ed. Boulder: Westview, 2003.

Gioia, A. "Commentary: Iraq." In Andrea de Guttry and Natalino Ronzitti, eds., *The Iran-Iraq War (1980–1988) and the Law of Naval Warfare.* Cambridge: Grotius, 1993.

Goldberg, Jeffrey. "The Usual Suspect." *New Republic,* October 1, 2007.

Gordon, Michael R., and General Bernard E. Trainor. *The Generals' War.* Boston: Little, Brown, 1995.

_____. *Cobra II: The Inside Story of the Invasion and Occupation of Iraq.* New York: Pantheon, 2006.

Gordon, Philip H., and Jeremy Shapiro. *Allies at War: America, Europe, and the Crisis over Iraq.* New York: McGraw-Hill, 2004.

Gordon, Philip H., and Michael E. O'Hanlon. "Dealing with Iraq." *Washington Post,* December 26, 2001.

Gorenberg, Gershom. *Occupied Territories: The Untold Story of Israel's Settlements.* London: I. B. Tauris, 2007.

Gowing, Nik. "Outfoxed in the Information War." *Time,* November 12, 2001.

Grau, Lester W., and Michael A. Gress, trans. and eds. The Russian General Staff, *The Soviet-Afghan War: How a Superpower Fought and Lost.* Lawrence: University Press of Kansas, 2002.

Haass, Richard N. *Conflicts Unending: The United States and Regional Disputes.* New Haven: Yale University Press, 1990.

_____. "The New Middle East." *Foreign Affairs*, November–December 2006.

Haig, Alexander. "Peace and Security in the Middle East." *Current Policy*, May 26, 1982.

Haig, Alexander M., Jr. *Caveat: Realism, Reagan, and Foreign Policy*. New York: Macmillan, 1984.

Halberstam, David. *War in a Time of Peace: Bush, Clinton, and the Generals*. New York: Scribner's, 2001.

Hall, David K. *Lebanon Revisited*. Newport, R.I.: United States Naval War College, 1988.

Hallenbeck, Ralph A. *Military Force as an Instrument of U.S. Policy: Intervention in Lebanon, August 1982–February 1984*. New York: Praeger, 1991.

Harik, Judith Palmer. *Hezbollah: The Changing Face of Terrorism*. London: I. B. Tauris, 2004.

Harmony Project. *Cracks in the Foundation: Leadership Schisms in al-Qa'ida from 1989–2006*. West Point, N.Y.: Combating Terrorism Center, September 2007. http://ctc.usma.edu.

Harris, David. *The Crisis: The President, the Prophet, and the Shah—1979 and the Coming of Militant Islam*. New York: Little, Brown, 2004.

Haselkorn, Avigdor. *The Continuing Storm: Iraq, Poisonous Weapons, and Deterrence*. New Haven: Yale University Press, 1999.

Hendrickson, David C., and Robert W. Tucker. "Revisions in Need of Revising: What Went Wrong with the Iraq War." *Survival*, Summer 2005.

Hersh, Seymour. "Selective Intelligence." *New Yorker*, May 12, 2003.

_____. *Chain of Command: The Road from 9/11 to Abu Ghraib*. New York: HarperCollins, 2004.

Hoffman, Bruce. *Inside Terrorism*. New York: Columbia University Press, 1998.

_____. "America and the New Terrorism: An Exchange." *Survival*, Summer 2000.

Howard, Michael. "What's in a Name? How to Fight Terrorism." *Foreign Affairs*, January–February 2002.

Huntington, Samuel P. "The Clash of Civilizations?" *Foreign Affairs*, Summer 1993.

Inbar, Efraim. "How Israel Bungled the Second Lebanon War." *Middle East Quarterly* 14, no. 3 (Summer 2007).

Iraq's Weapons of Mass Destruction: A Net Assessment. IISS Strategic Dossier. September 9, 2002.

"The Israel-Iran Connection." *Journal of Palestine Studies*, Spring 1987.

Jenkins, Brian M. *Will Terrorists Go Nuclear?* Santa Monica, Calif.: RAND, 1975.

Jentleson, Bruce W. *With Friends Like These: Reagan, Bush, and Saddam, 1982–1990*. New York: W. W. Norton, 1994.

Jentleson, Bruce W., and Christopher A. Whytock. "Who 'Won' Libya? The Force-Diplomacy Debate and Its Implications for Theory and Policy." *International Security*, Winter 2005–2006.

Jervis, Robert. "Reports, Politics, and Intelligence Failures: The Case of Iraq." *Journal of Strategic Studies*, February 2006.

Johnson, Thomas H., and M. Chris Mason. "Understanding the Taliban and Insurgency in Afghanistan." *Orbis*, Winter 2007.

Jordan, Hamilton. *Crisis: The Last Year of the Carter Presidency.* New York: Putnam, 1982.

Kagan, Robert, and William Kristol. "A Winning Strategy: How the Bush Administration Changed Course and Won the War in Afghanistan." *Weekly Standard,* November 26, 2001.

Kampfner, John. *Blair's Wars.* London: Free Press, 2003.

Kaplan, Robert D. *Imperial Grunts: The American Military on the Ground.* New York: Random House, 2005.

Karsh, Efraim. *The Iran-Iraq War: A Military Analysis.* Adelphi Paper 220. London: IISS, 1987.

_____. "Reflections on the 1990–91 Gulf Conflict." *Journal of Strategic Studies,* September 1996.

Karsh, Efraim, and Inari Rautsi. *Saddam Hussein: A Political Biography.* London: Brassey's, 1991.

Katzman, Kenneth. *Iraq: U.S. Efforts to Change the Regime.* Congressional Research Service, Library of Congress, Report for Congress, March 22, 2002.

Kaufmann, Chaim. "Threat Inflation and the Marketplace of Ideas: The Selling of the Iraq War." *International Security,* Summer 2004.

Keaney, Thomas A., and Eliot A. Cohen. *Revolution in Warfare? Air Power in the Persian Gulf.* Annapolis, Md.: Naval Institute Press, 1995.

Keegan, John. *The Iraq War.* New York: Knopf, 2004.

Kepel, Gilles. *Jihad: The Trail of Political Islam.* Cambridge: Harvard University Press, 2002.

_____. *The War for Muslim Minds.* Cambridge: Harvard University Press, 2004.

The KGB in Afghanistan. Cold War International History Project, Special Working Paper no. 40. Washington, D.C.: Woodrow Wilson Center, February 2002.

Khalilzad, Zalmay. *The Return of the Great Game.* California Seminar on International Security and Foreign Policy, Discussion Paper no. 88, 1980.

Kinzer, Stephen. *All the Shah's Men: An American Coup and the Roots of Middle East Terror.* New York: John Wiley, 2003.

Kirkpatrick, Jeane. "Democracy and Double Standards." *Commentary,* November 1979.

Korbani, Agnes G. *U.S. Intervention in Lebanon, 1958 and 1982: Presidential Decision Making.* New York: Praeger, 1991.

Lake, Anthony. "Confronting Backlash States." *Foreign Affairs,* March–April 1994.

Lambeth, Benjamin S. *Air Power Against Terror: America's Conduct of Operation Enduring Freedom.* Santa Monica, Calif.: RAND Corporation, 2005.

Laqueur, Walter. *The Age of Terrorism.* Boston: Little, Brown, 1987.

Lauterpacht, Elihu, Christopher J. Greenwood, Marc Weller, and Daniel Bethlehem, eds. *The Kuwait Crisis: Basic Documents.* Cambridge: Cambridge University Press, 1991.

Leckow, Ross. "The Iran-Iraq Conflict in the Gulf: The Law of War Zones." *International and Comparative Law Quarterly,* July 1988.

Ledeen, Michael. "What's the Holdup? It's Time for the Next Battles in the War Against Terrorism." *National Review Online,* January 7, 2002. www.nationalreview.com/contributors/ledeen010702.shtml.

_____. *The War Against the Terror Masters.* New York: St. Martin's, 2002.

Lesch, David W. *1979: The Year That Shaped the Modern Middle East.* Boulder: Westview, 2001.

Levinson, Sanford, ed. *Torture: A Collection.* New York: Oxford University Press, 2004.

Levitt, Matthew. *Hamas: Politics, Charity, and Terrorism in the Service of Jihad.* New Haven: Yale University Press, 2006.

Levy, Adrian, and Catherine Scott-Clark. *Deception: Pakistan, the United States, and the Global Nuclear Weapons Conspiracy.* London: Atlantic Books, 2007.

Lewis, Adrian. *The American Culture of War: The History of U.S. Military Force from World War II to Operation Iraqi Freedom.* New York: Routledge, 2007.

Lewis, Bernard. "The Roots of Muslim Rage." *Atlantic,* September 1990.

_____. "What Went Wrong?" *Atlantic,* January 2002.

_____. *What Went Wrong: Western Impact and Middle Eastern Response.* New York: Oxford University Press, 2002.

_____. "Freedom and Justice in the Modern Middle East." *Foreign Affairs,* May–June 2005.

Little, Douglas. "Mission Impossible: The CIA and the Cult of Covert Action in the Middle East." *Diplomatic History,* November 2004.

_____. *American Orientalism: The United States and the Middle East Since 1945.* Chapel Hill: University of North Carolina Press, 2004.

Livingstone, Neil C., and Terrell E. Arnold, eds. *Fighting Back: Winning the War Against Terrorism.* Lexington, Mass.: Lexington Books, 1986.

Luttwak, Edward. "Towards Post-Heroic Warfare." *Foreign Affairs,* May–June 1995.

_____. "The Middle of Nowhere." *Prospect,* May 2007.

Mackey, Sandra. *Lebanon: A House Divided.* New York: W. W. Norton, 2006.

Mahnken, Thomas G. "A Squandered Opportunity? The Decision to End the Gulf War." In Andrew J. Bacevich and Efraim Inbar, eds., *The Gulf War of 1991 Reconsidered.* London: Frank Cass, 2003.

Malkasian, Carter. "Signalling Resolve, Democratization, and the First Battle of Fallujah." *Journal of Strategic Studies,* June 2006.

Malone, David M. *The International Struggle over Iraq: Politics in the UN Security Council, 1980–2005.* London: Oxford University Press, 2006.

Maloney, Sean M. "Afghanistan: From Here to Eternity?" *Parameters,* Spring 2004.

Mann, Jim. *Rise of the Vulcans: The History of Bush's War Cabinet.* New York: Viking, 2004.

Mason, R. A. "The Air War in the Gulf." *Survival,* May–June 1991.

Massing, Michael. "Now They Tell Us." *New York Review of Books,* February 26, 2004.

Matthews, Mark. *Lost Years: Bush, Sharon, and Failure in the Middle East.* New York: Nation Books, 2007.

Mayer, Jane. "The Manipulator." *New Yorker,* June 7, 2004.

McFarlane, Robert C., and Zofia Smardz. *Special Trust.* New York: Cadell & Davies, 1994.

McFate, Montgomery. "The Military Utility of Understanding Adversary Culture." *Joint Forces Quarterly,* July 2005.

McNaugher, Thomas. L. "Walking Tightropes in the Gulf." In Efraim Karsh, ed., *The Iran-Iraq War: Impact and Implications.* London: Macmillan, 1989.

Mearsheimer, John J., and Stephen M. Walt. "Iraq: An Unnecessary War." *Foreign Policy,* January–February 2003.

_____. *The Israel Lobby and U.S. Foreign Policy.* New York: Farrar, Straus & Giroux, 2007.

Meital, Yoram. *Peace in Tatters: Israel, Palestine, and the Middle East.* Boulder: Lynne Rienner, 2006.

Moaddel, Mansoor. *Class, Politics, and Ideology in the Iranian Revolution.* New York: Columbia University Press, 1993.

Morris, Benny. "Camp David and After: An Exchange (1. An Interview with Ehud Barak)." *New York Review of Books,* June 13, 2002.

Mueller, John, and Karl Mueller. "Sanctions of Mass Destruction." *Foreign Affairs,* May–June 1999.

_____. "The Methodology of Mass Destruction: Assessing Threats in the New World Order." *Journal of Strategic Studies* 23, no. 1 (2000).

Murray, Williamson, and Robert H. Scales Jr. *The Iraq War: A Military History.* Cambridge: Harvard University Press, 2003.

Mylroie, Laurie. *The War Against America: Saddam Hussein and the World Trade Center Attacks: A Study of Revenge.* New York: HarperCollins, 2001.

_____. *Bush vs. the Beltway: How the CIA and the State Department Tried to Stop the War on Terror.* Washington, D.C.: Regan, 2003.

_____. *Third Public Hearing of the National Commission on Terrorist Attacks Upon the United States,* July 9, 2003. http://govinfo.library.unt.edu/911/hearings/hearing3/witness_mylroie.htm.

Nasr, Vali. *The Shia Revival: How Conflicts Within Islam Will Shape the Future.* New York: W. W. Norton, 2007.

National Commission on Terrorism. *Countering the Changing Threat of International Terrorism.* Pursuant to Public Law 277, 105th Congress. Washington, D.C.: U.S. Congress, 2000.

National Security Council. *National Security Strategy of the United States.* Washington, D.C., September 2002. www.whitehouse.gov/nsc/nss.html.

_____. *National Strategy for Victory in Iraq.* Washington, D.C., November 30, 2005. www.whitehouse.gov/infocus/iraq/iraq_national_strategy_20051130.pdf.

Navias, Martin S., and Edward R. Hooton. *Tanker Wars: The Assault on Merchant Shipping During the Iran-Iraq Crisis, 1980–1988.* London: I. B. Tauris, 1996.

The 9/11 Commission Report: Final Report of the National Commission on Terrorist Attacks Upon the United States. New York: W. W. Norton, 2004.

Norton, Augustus Richard. *Hezbollah: A Short History.* Princeton: Princeton University Press, 2007.

Nunn, Sam. Senator Nunn's Letter and Response to the Weinberger Report Concerning the Administration's Security Arrangements in the Persian Gulf, 1987. Washington, D.C.: United States Senate, Committee on Armed Services.

Oren, Michael B. *Power, Faith, and Fantasy: America in the Middle East 1776 to the Present.* New York: W. W. Norton, 2007.

O'Sullivan, Meghan. *Iraq: Time for a Modified Approach.* Washington, D.C.: Brookings Institution, 2001.

Ottaway, Marina S., and Anatol Lieven. *Rebuilding Afghanistan: Fantasy Versus Reality.* Carnegie Endowment for International Peace, Policy Brief 12, January 2002.

Packer, George. *Assassin's Gate: America in Iraq.* New York: Farrar, Straus & Giroux, 2005.

———. "Knowing the Enemy." *New Yorker,* December 18, 2006.

Parsi, Trita. *Treacherous Alliance: The Secret Dealings of Israel, Iran and the U.S.* New Haven: Yale University Press, 2007.

Parsons, Anthony. *From Cold War to Hot Peace: UN Interventions 1947–1994.* London: Michael Joseph, 1995.

Pearson, Graham S. *The Search for Iraq's Weapons of Mass Destruction: Inspection, Verification, and Non-Proliferation.* New York: Palgrave Macmillan, 2005.

Pérez de Cuéllar, J. *Pilgrimage for Peace.* London: Macmillan, 1997.

Peri, Yoram. *Generals in the Cabinet Room: How the Military Shapes Israeli Policy.* Washington, D.C.: United States Institute of Peace Press, 2006.

Perkins, J. B. "Operation Praying Mantis." *United States Naval Institute Proceedings,* May 1989.

Persico, Joseph E. *Casey: From the OSS to the CIA.* New York: Viking, 1990.

Petraeus, David H. "Learning Counterinsurgency: Observations from Soldiering in Iraq." *Military Review,* January–February 2006.

Petras, James. *The Power of Israel in the United States.* Atlanta, Ga.: Clarity, 2006.

Phillips, David L. *Losing Iraq: Inside the Post-War Reconstruction Fiasco.* New York: Basic, 2005.

Picco, Giandomenico. *Man Without a Gun: One Diplomat's Secret Struggle to Free the Hostages, Fight Terrorism, and End a War.* New York: Crown, 1999.

Pollack, Kenneth. "Containment, Deterrence, Preemption." *Foreign Affairs,* March–April 2002.

———. *The Threatening Storm: The Case for Invading Iraq.* New York: Random House, 2002.

———. *The Persian Puzzle: The Conflict Between Iran and America.* New York: Random House, 2004.

———. "Spies, Lies, and Weapons: What Went Wrong." *Atlantic Monthly,* January–February 2004.

Powell, Colin, with Joseph E. Persico. *My American Journey.* New York: Random House, 1995.

Powers, Thomas. "War and Its Consequences." *New York Review of Books,* March 27, 2003.

Prados, John. *Hoodwinked: The Documents That Reveal How Bush Sold Us a War.* New York: New Press, 2004.

_____. *Safe for Democracy: The Secret Wars of the CIA.* Chicago: Ivan R. Dee, 2006.

Pressman, Jeremy. "Visions in Collision: What Happened at Camp David and Taba?" *International Security,* Fall 2003.

_____. "Mediation, Domestic Politics, and the Israeli-Syrian Negotiations, 1991–2000." *Security Studies,* July–September 2007.

Quandt, William B. *Camp David: Peacemaking and Politics.* Washington, D.C.: Brookings Institution, 1986.

_____. *Peace Process: American Diplomacy and the Arab-Israeli Conflict Since 1967.* Washington, D.C.: Brookings Institution, 1993.

Rabinovich, Itamar. *The War for Lebanon: 1970–1985.* Ithaca, N.Y.: Cornell University Press, 1985.

_____. *The Brink of Peace: The Israeli-Syrian Negotiations.* Princeton: Princeton University Press, 1998.

_____. *Waging Peace: Israel and the Arabs, 1948–2003.* Princeton: Princeton University Press, 2004.

Ramazani, Rouholah. *Revolutionary Iran: Change and Response in the Middle East.* Baltimore: Johns Hopkins University Press, 1987.

Reagan, Ronald. *An American Life: The Autobiography.* New York: Simon & Schuster, 1990.

_____. *The Reagan Diaries.* Edited by Douglas Brinkley. New York: HarperCollins, 2007.

Record, Jeffrey. *Making War, Thinking History: Munich, Vietnam, and Presidential Uses of Force from Korea to Kosovo.* Annapolis, Md.: Naval Institute Press, 2002.

Reich, Bernard. "The United States and Israel." In David W. Lesch, ed., *The Middle East and the United States: A Historical and Political Reassessment.* 3rd ed. Boulder: Westview, 2003.

Reidel, Bruce. "Camp David—the US-Israel Bargain," July 15, 2002. www.bitterlemons .org/previous/bl150702ed26extra.html.

Report of a Committee of Privy Councillors to the House of Commons. *Review of Intelligence on Weapons of Mass Destruction,* July 14, 2004. The Butler Report.

Report of the DoD Commission on Beirut International Airport Terrorist Act, October 23, 1983, and December 20, 1983.

Reports on Terrorist Bombings of U.S. Marines in Beirut, December 19 and 23, 1983 (DOD Commission on Beirut International Airport Terrorist Act of October 23, 1983). www.ibiblio.org/hyperwar/AMH/XX/MidEast/Lebanon-1982-1984/DOD-Report/index.html.

Report to the Secretary General by a United Nations Mission led by Mr. Abdulrahim A. Farah, Former Under-Secretary-General, Assessing the Scope and Nature of Damage Inflicted on Kuwait's Infrastructure During the Iraqi Occupation of the Country from 2 August 1990 to 27 February 1991. New York: United Nations, 1991.

Rice, Condoleezza. "Promoting the National Interest." *Foreign Affairs,* January–February 2000.

Ricks, Thomas E. *Fiasco: The American Military Adventure in Iraq.* New York: Penguin, 2006.

Ritter, Scott. *Endgame: Solving the Iraq Problem Once and for All.* New York: Simon & Schuster, 1999.

———. "The Case for Iraq's Qualitative Disarmament." *Arms Control Today,* June 2000.

Roach, J. Ashley. "Missiles on Target: Targeting and Defense Zones in the Tanker War." *Virginia Journal of International Law* 31, no. 4 (1991).

Roberts, Adam. "Law and the Use of Force After Iraq." *Survival,* Summer 2003.

Rose, David. "Neo Culpa: Now They Tell Us." *Vanity Fair,* November 3, 2006.

Ross, Dennis. *The Missing Peace: The Inside Story of the Fight for Middle East Peace.* New York: Farrar, Straus & Giroux, 2004.

Roth, Ken. *War in Iraq: Not a Humanitarian Intervention.* World Report 2004, Human Rights Watch. http://hrw.org/wr2k4/3.htm#_Toc58744952.

Rubin, Barry. *The Tragedy of the Middle East.* Cambridge: Cambridge University Press, 2002.

———. *Pushback or Progress: Arab Regimes Respond to Democracy's Challenge.* Washington D.C.: Washington Institute for Near East Policy, 2007.

Russell, James A. *Regional Threats and Security Strategy: The Troubling Case of Today's Middle East.* Carlisle, Pa.: U.S. Army War College Strategic Studies Institute, 2007.

Ryan, Maria. "Inventing the 'Axis of Evil': The Myth and Reality of U.S. Intelligence and Policy-Making After 9/11." *Intelligence and National Security,* Winter 2002.

Said, Edward. *From Oslo to Iraq and the Road Map: Essays.* New York: Viking, 2005.

Sayigh, Yezid. *Armed Struggle and the Search for State: The Palestinian National Movement, 1949–1993.* New York: Oxford University Press, 1998.

———. "Arafat and the Anatomy of a Revolt." *Survival* 43 (2001).

Scales, Robert. *Certain Victory: The US Army in the Gulf War.* London: Brassey's, 1994.

Schiff, Ze'ev, and Ehud Ya'ari. *Israel's Lebanon War.* New York: Simon & Schuster, 1984.

Schroen, Gary C. *First In: An Insider's Account of How the CIA Spearheaded the War on Terror in Afghanistan.* New York: Ballantine, 2005.

Schumacher, Edward. "The United States and Libya." *Foreign Affairs,* Winter 1986–1987.

Sciolino, Elaine. *The Outlaw State: Saddam Hussein's Quest for Power and the Gulf Crisis.* New York: John Wiley, 1991.

Scowcroft, Brent. "Don't Attack Saddam." *Wall Street Journal,* August 15, 2002.

Sharansky, Natan. *The Case for Democracy: The Power of Freedom to Overcome Tyranny and Terror.* New York: PublicAffairs, 2006.

Shazly, Nadia El-Sayed, El-. *The Gulf Tanker War: Iran and Iraq's Maritime Swordplay.* Basingstoke, U.K.: Palgrave Macmillan, 1998.

Shlaim, Avi. *The Iron Wall: Israel and the Arab World.* New York: W. W. Norton, 1999.

Shultz, George P. *Turmoil and Triumph: My Years as Secretary of State.* New York: Scribner's, 1993.

Sick, G. "The United States and the Persian Gulf." In H. W. Maull and O. Pick, eds., *The Gulf War: Regional and International Dimensions.* London: Pinter, 1989.

Sick, Gary. *All Fall Down: America's Tragic Encounter with Iran.* New York: Random House, 1986.

———. "Trial by Error: Reflections on the Iran-Iraq War." *Middle East Journal* 43, no. 2 (1989).

———. *October Surprise: America's Hostages in Iran and the Election of Ronald Reagan.* New York: Random House, 1991.

Sifry, Micah L., and Christopher Cerf, eds. *The Gulf Reader: History, Documents, Opinions.* New York: Random House, 1991.

Simon, Jeffrey D. *The Terrorist Trap: America's Experience with Terrorism.* 2nd ed. Bloomington: Indiana University Press, 2001.

Simon, Steven, and Daniel Benjamin. "America and the New Terrorism." *Survival,* Spring 2000.

Slater, Jerome. "Lost Opportunities for Peace in the Arab-Israeli Conflict: Israel and Syria, 1948–2001." *International Security,* Summer 2002.

Slavin, Barbara. "Mutual Terror Accusations Halt U.S.-Iran Talks." *USA Today,* May 21, 2003.

———. *Bitter Friends, Bosom Enemies: Iran, the U.S., and the Twisted Path to Confrontation.* New York: St. Martin's, 2007.

Smucker, Philip. *Al Qaeda's Great Escape: The Military and the Media on Terror's Trail.* Dulles, Va.: Brassey's, 2004.

Sobhani, Sohrab. *The Pragmatic Entente: Israeli-Iranian Relations, 1948–1988.* New York: Praeger, 1989.

The Soviet Invasion of Afghanistan in 1979: Failure of Intelligence or of the Policy Process? Working Group Report no. 111. Washington, D.C.: Institute for the Study of Diplomacy, Edmund A. Walsh School of Foreign Service, Georgetown University, September 26, 2005.

"The Soviet Union and Afghanistan, 1978–1989: Documents from the Soviet and East German Archives" and "Transcripts of CPSU Politburo Discussions on Afghanistan, 17–19 March 1979." Cold War International History Project Bulletin 8-9. Washington, D.C.: Woodrow Wilson Center, Winter 1996–1997.

Sprinzak, Ehud. "Rational Fanatics." *Foreign Policy,* September–October 2000.

Stein, Janice. "The Wrong Strategy in the Right Place: The United States in the Gulf." *International Security* 13, no. 3 (1988–1989).

Stein, Kenneth W. *Heroic Diplomacy: Sadat, Kissinger, Carter, Begin, and the Quest for Arab-Israeli Peace.* New York: Routledge, 1999.

Stein, Kenneth W., and Samuel Lewis, with Sheryl J. Brown. *Making Peace Among Arabs and Israelis: Lessons from Fifty Years of Negotiating Experience.* Washington, D.C.: United States Institute of Peace, 1991.

Stevenson, Charles. "The Evolving Clinton Doctrine on the Use of Force." *Armed Forces and Society,* Summer 1996.

Strober, Deborah Hart, and Gerald S. Strober. *The Reagan Presidency: An Oral History of the Era.* Washington, D.C.: Potomac, 2003.

Strong, Robert A. *Working in the World: Jimmy Carter and the Making of American Foreign Policy.* Baton Rouge: Louisiana State University Press, 2000.

Sullivan, William H. *Mission to Iran.* New York: W. W. Norton, 1981.

Suskind, Ron. *The Price of Loyalty: George W. Bush, the White House, and the Education of Paul O'Neill.* New York: Simon & Schuster, 2004.

Swisher, Clayton E. *The Truth About Camp David: The Untold Story About the Collapse of the Middle East Peace Process.* New York: Nation Books, 2004.

Takeyh, Ray. *Hidden Iran: Paradox and Power in the Islamic Republic.* New York: Henry Holt, 2006.

Tellis, Ashley J. *Pakistan: Conflicted Ally in the War on Terror.* Policy Brief 56. Washington D.C.: Carnegie Endowment for International Peace, December 2007.

Tenet, George. *At the Center of the Storm: My Years at the CIA.* New York: HarperCollins, 2007.

Timmerman, Kenneth R. *The Death Lobby: How the West Armed Iraq.* London: Fourth Estate, 1992.

Toward Peace in the Middle East: Report of a Study Group. Washington, D.C.: Brookings Institution, 1975.

Trevan, Tim. *Saddam's Secrets: The Hunt for Iraq's Hidden Weapons.* London: HarperCollins, 1999.

Tripp, Charles. *A History of Iraq.* 3rd ed. Cambridge: Cambridge University Press, 2007.

Unger, Craig. *House of Bush, House of Saud: The Secret Relationship Between the World's Two Most Powerful Dynasties.* New York: Scribner, 2004.

Urquhart, Brian. *A Life in War and Peace.* London: Weidenfeld & Nicholson, 1987.

U.S. Agency for International Development. *Iraq's Legacy of Terror: Mass Graves.* Washington, D.C., January 2004. www.usaid.gov/iraq/pdf/iraq_mass_graves.pdf.

U.S. Commission on National Security/21st Century. *New World Coming: American Security in the 21st Century.* Washington, D.C., 1999.

U.S. Senate, Select Committee on Intelligence. *Report on the U.S. Intelligence Community's Prewar Intelligence Assessments on Iraq.* 108th Cong., 2nd sess., July 7, 2004.

Vance, Cyrus. *Hard Choices: Four Critical Years in Managing America's Foreign Policy.* New York: Simon & Schuster, 1983.

War in the Persian Gulf: The U.S. Takes Sides. Washington, D.C.: United States Senate, Committee on Foreign Relations, 1987.

Weinberger, Caspar. *Secretary of Defense Report to the Congress on Security Arrangements in the Persian Gulf.* Washington, D.C.: Department of Defense, 1987.

———. *Fighting for Peace: Seven Critical Years in the Pentagon.* London: Michael Joseph, 1990.

Westad, Odd Arne. *The Global Cold War: Third World Interventions and the Making of Our Times.* Cambridge: Cambridge University Press, 2005.

Wilson, Joseph. "What I Didn't Find in Africa." *New York Times,* July 6, 2003.

Woods, Kevin, James Lacey, and Williamson Murray. "Saddam's Delusions: The View from the Inside." *Foreign Affairs,* May–June 2006.

Woodward, Bob. *The Commanders.* New York: Simon & Schuster, 1991.

_____. *Bush at War.* New York: Simon & Schuster, 2002.

_____. *Plan of Attack.* New York: Simon & Schuster, 2004.

_____. *State of Denial: Bush at War, Part III.* New York: Simon & Schuster, 2006.

Wright, Laurence. *The Looming Tower: Al-Qaeda and the Road to 9/11.* New York: Knopf, 2006.

Wright, Susan. "The Hijacking of UNSCOM." *Bulletin of the Atomic Scientists,* July–August 1999.

Wurmser, David. *Tyranny's Ally.* Washington, D.C.: AEI Press, 1999.

Yaphe, Judith S. Statement. *Third Public Hearing of the National Commission on Terrorist Attacks upon the United States,* July 9, 2003. http://govinfo.library.unt.edu/911/hearings/hearing3/witness_yaphe.htm.

Yaqub, Salin. *Containing Arab Nationalism: The Eisenhower Doctrine and the Middle East.* Chapel Hill: University of North Carolina Press, 2004.

Zertal, Idith, and Akiva Elder. *Lords of the Land: The War over Israel's Settlements in the Occupied Territories, 1967–2007.* New York: Nation Books, 2007.

Zimmerman, Tim. "Coercive Diplomacy and Libya." In Alexander L. George and William E. Simons, eds., *The Limits of Coercive Diplomacy.* 2nd ed. Boulder: Westview, 1994.

Zucchino, David. *Thunder Run: The Armored Strike to Capture Baghdad.* New York: Atlantic Monthly Press, 2004.

Index